PENGUIN BOOKS

THE PENGUIN HISTORY OF EUROPE

GENERAL EDITOR: DAVID CANNADINE

THE INHERITANCE OF ROME

'The breadth of reading is astounding, the knowledge displayed is awe-inspiring' Ian Mortimer, *Guardian*

'The wealth of detail he deploys is astonishing' Allan Massie, *Scotsman*

'No one else has combined the same chronological and geographical sweep with Wickham's broad range or source material and unlimited curiosity . . . the result is a convincing picture of an arcane world . . . The author has a broad vision, an easy wit and an engaging style' Jonathan Sumption, *Spectator*

'In a supremely humane and intelligent book Chris Wickham has presented medieval Europe in all its vivid richness and variety' Christopher Kelly, *Literary Review*

'Original and exciting' Charles West, *History Today*

'When I finished *The Inheritance of Rome*, which Wickham dedicates to the students with whom he studied ancient and medieval history at the University of Birmingham from 1976 to 2005, I thought, "Lucky students" and "Lucky us now, too." Tom Palaima, *The Times Higher Education Supplement*

'An accessible account . . . a wealth of scholarship oozes through every page' Matthew Innes, *BBC History*

THE PENGUIN HISTORY OF EUROPE

General Editor: David Cannadine

ABOUT THE AUTHOR

Chris Wickham is Chichele Professor of Medieval History at the University of Oxford and a Fellow of All Souls College. His book *Framing the Middle Ages*, which was published in 2005, won the Wolfson Prize, the Deutscher Memorial Prize and the James Henry Breasted Prize of the American Historical Association. He taught for many years at the University of Birmingham and is a Fellow of the British Academy.

* already published

CHRIS WICKHAM

The Inheritance of Rome

A History of Europe from 400 to 1000

PENGUIN BOOKS

PENGUIN BOOKS

Published by the Penguin Group
Penguin Books Ltd, 80 Strand, London WC2R ORL, England
Penguin Group (USA) Inc., 375 Hudson Street, New York, New York 10014, USA
Penguin Group (Canada), 90 Eglinton Avenue East, Suite 700, Toronto, Ontario, Canada M4P 2Y3
(a division of Pearson Penguin Canada Inc.)
Penguin Ireland, 25 St Stephen's Green, Dublin 2, Ireland
(a division of Penguin Books Ltd)
Penguin Group (Australia), 250 Camberwell Road, Camberwell, Victoria 3124, Australia
(a division of Pearson Australia Group Pty Ltd)
Penguin Books India Pvt Ltd, 11 Community Centre, Panchsheel Park, New Delhi – 110 017, India
Penguin Group (NZ), 67 Apollo Drive, Rosedale, North Shore 0632, New Zealand
(a division of Pearson New Zealand Ltd)
Penguin Books (South Africa) (Pty) Ltd, 24 Sturdee Avenue, Rosebank, Johannesburg 2196, South Africa

Penguin Books Ltd, Registered Offices: 80 Strand, London WC2R ORL, England

www.penguin.com

First published by Allen Lane 2009
Published in Penguin Books 2010
006

Typeset by Rowland Phototypesetting Ltd, Bury St Edmunds, Suffolk
Printed in England by Clays Ltd, St Ives plc

978–0–140–29014–1

www.greenpenguin.co.uk

MIX
Paper from
responsible sources
FSC
www.fsc.org   FSC™ C018179

Penguin Books is committed to a sustainable
future for our business, our readers and our planet.
This book is made from Forest Stewardship
Council™ certified paper.

For the students of AMH, the Ancient and Medieval History degree of the University of Birmingham, 1976–2005, who have heard and discussed much of this before

Contents

CONTENTS

PART III

The Empires of the East, 550–1000

PART IV

The Carolingian and Post-Carolingian West, 750–1000

List of Maps

List of Illustrations

Acknowledgements

Numerous friends read chapters of this book for me; their criticisms and comments saved me from a wide range of errors. In the order of the chapters they read, they were Leslie Brubaker, Conrad Leyser, Kate Cooper, Walter Pohl, Ian Wood, Julia Smith, Paul Magdalino, Hugh Kennedy, Jinty Nelson, Pat Geary, Pauline Stafford and Wendy Davies. Equally essential, for sharing ideas and unpublished work with me, were Teresa Bernheimer, Leslie Brubaker, Leslie Dossey, Caroline Goodson, John Haldon, Guy Halsall, Sarah Halton, Anne-Marie Helvétius, Mayke de Jong, Christina Pössel, Carine van Rhijn, Petra Sijpesteijn and Mark Whittow. Sue Bowen heroically typed the whole text, and Harry Buglass drew the maps; the index is by Alicia Corrêa. I am very grateful to them all. I have not been able to incorporate publications which came out after May 2007; not systematically, at least.

Birmingham
May 2007

Maps

N

W   E

S

ORKNEY

Picts

North Sea

BRITANNIA

Atlantic Ocean

Franks

Rhine

BELGICA II

Alemans

Rugi

NORICUM

PANNON.

RHAETIA

GAUL

AQUITAINE

ARMORICA

NARBONENSIS

ITALY

HISPANIA

CORSICA

Rome ○

CAMPANIA

SARDINIA

BAETICA

M A U R E T A N I A

Mateur ○

SICILY

Hippo ○

Thagaste ○

○ Carthage

NUMIDIA

A F R I C A

TRIPOLITANIA

- - - - -   Approximate borders of the Roman Empire, 400

NUMIDIA   Some Roman provinces and territories

Franks   Some 'barbarian' groups on the Roman frontier

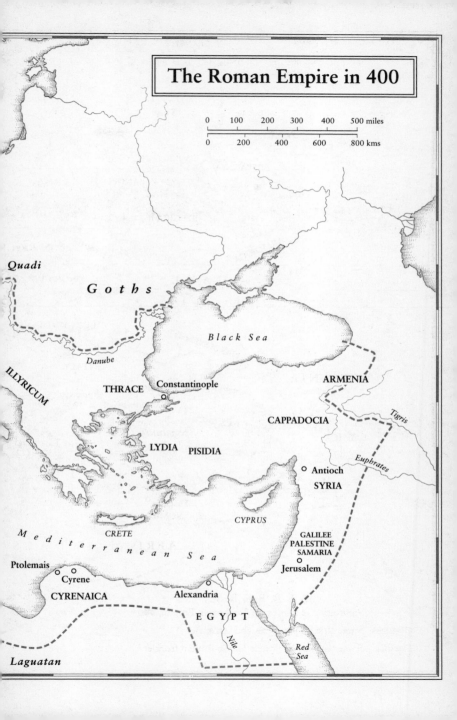

The Roman Empire in 400

Quadi

G o t h s

Black Sea

Danube

ILLYRICUM

THRACE   Constantinople

ARMENIA

CAPPADOCIA

Tigris

LYDIA   PISIDIA

Euphrates

Antioch
SYRIA

CYPRUS

M e d i t e r r a n e a n   S e a   CRETE

GALILEE
PALESTINE
SAMARIA

Jerusalem

Ptolemais
Cyrene

CYRENAICA   Alexandria

E G Y P T

Nile

Red Sea

Laguatan

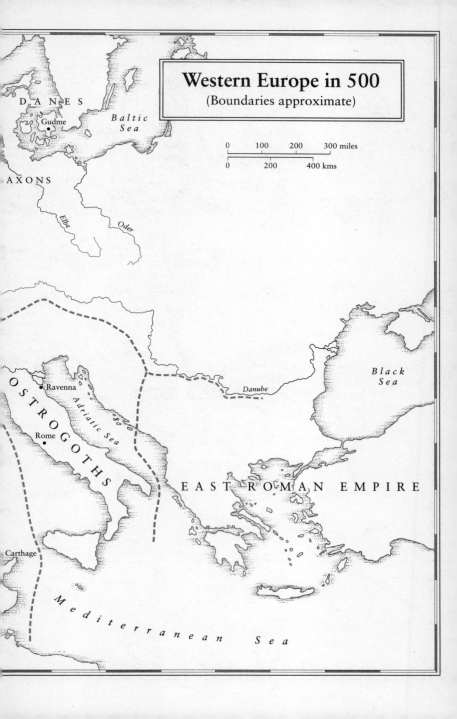

Western Europe in 500
(Boundaries approximate)

```
0        100      200      300 miles
0            200          400 kms
```

DANES

Baltic
Sea

• Gudme

SAXONS

Elbe

Oder

Ravenna •

Adriatic Sea

OSTROGOTHS

Rome •

Black
Sea

Danube

EAST ROMAN EMPIRE

Carthage

Mediterranean   Sea

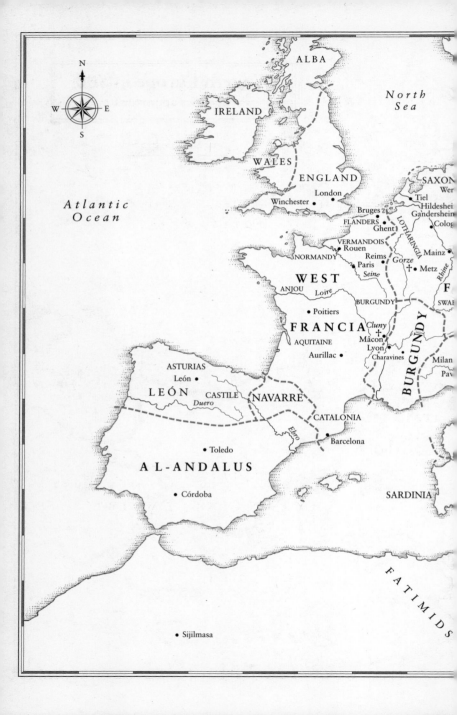

Western Europe in 1000

DENMARK

Baltic Sea

Hamburg

ade

NORTHERN MARCH

Walbeck • Arneburg

LIUTIZI

• Magdeburg

oslar

• Quedlinburg

Merseburg • Meissen

EAST

Elbe

Oder

POLES

BOHEMIA

NCIA

• Augsburg

BAVARIA

CARINTHIA

HUNGARY

Cremona • Venice

Canossa

ITALY

Adriatic Sea

Rome •

Gaeta • Benevento

Naples

Amalfi

Salerno

BYZANTINE EMPIRE

Palermo

SICILY

Tunis

Kairouan

Danube

Black Sea

Mediterranean Sea

0   100   200   300 miles

0   200   400 kms

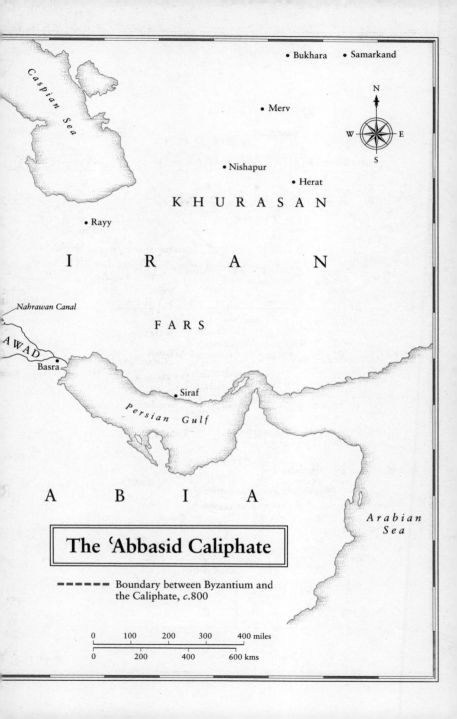

The 'Abbasid Caliphate

- - - - - Boundary between Byzantium and
the Caliphate, c.800

| 0 | 100 | 200 | 300 | 400 miles |

| 0 | 200 | 400 | 600 kms |

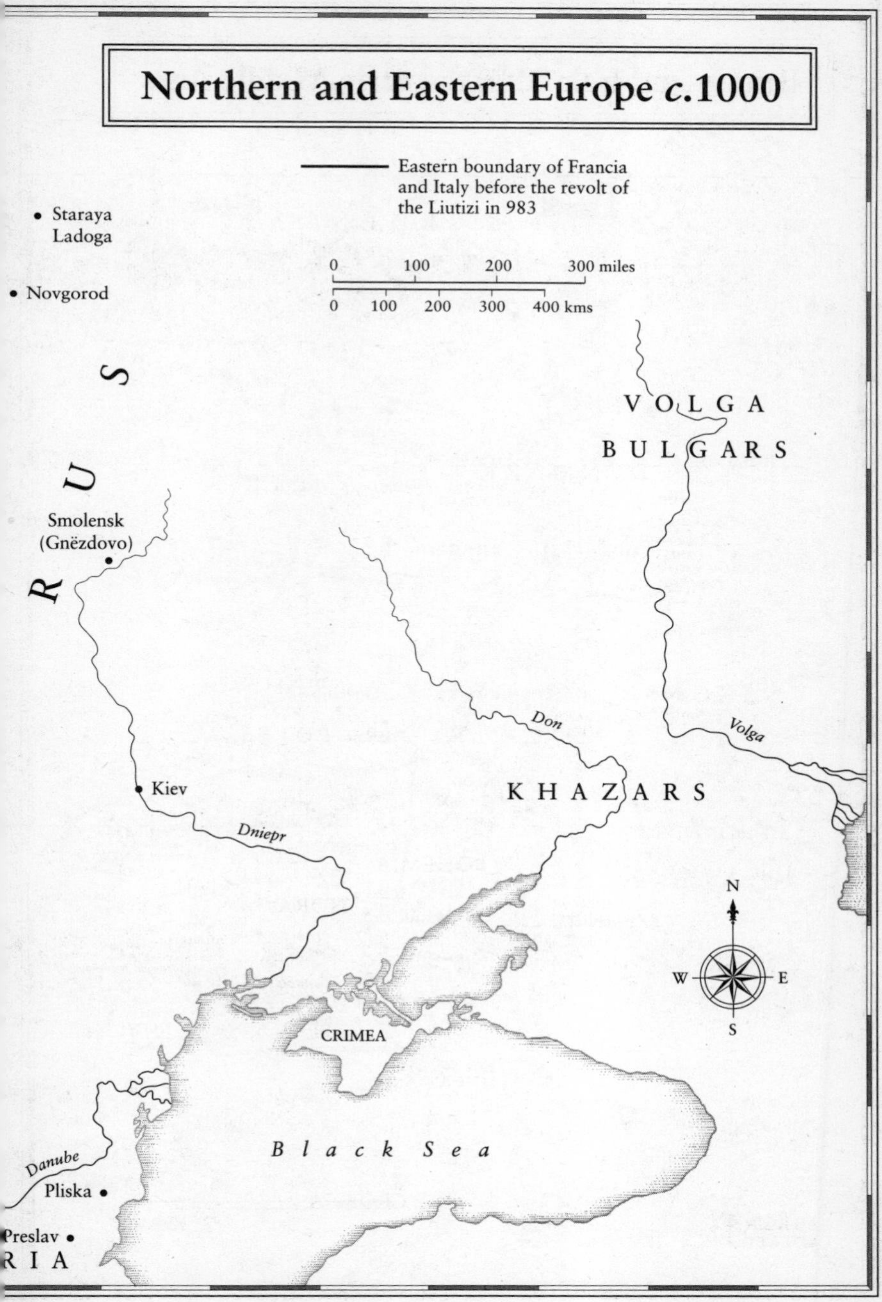

Northern and Eastern Europe *c.*1000

Eastern boundary of Francia
and Italy before the revolt of
the Liutizi in 983

0	100	200		300 miles
0	100	200	300	400 kms

• Staraya
  Ladoga

• Novgorod

R U S S

Smolensk
(Gnëzdovo)
•

VOLGA
BULGARS

• Kiev

Dniepr

Don

Volga

KHAZARS

N

W   E

S

CRIMEA

B l a c k   S e a

Danube

Pliska •

Preslav •
RIA

Britain and Ireland in the early Middle Ages

Orkney

Caithness

*Atlantic
Ocean*

PICTLAND

DÁL RIATA

Iona

Fife • St Andrews
Firth of Forth

Edinburgh • Lothian
STRATH-
CLYDE
GODODDIN

Lindisfarne •
Bamburgh •
Yeavering •

*North
Sea*

BERNICIA

RHEGED

NORTHUMBRIA

Jarrow •
Monkwearmouth •

Hadrian's Wall

Whithorn •

Stainmore •

Catterick •

Whitby •

Ripon •

Catterick •

DEIRA • York

DÁL
RIATA

CENÉL
CONAILL
CENÉL
NÉOGAIN

ULAID

ULSTER
DÁL
FIATACH

Isle of
Man

UÍ BRIÚIN
BRÉIFNE
Armagh •

Lough Neagh

CONNAUGHT

Irish Sea

Lough Ree

BREGA
Durrow • Tara •
Lagore •
MEATH

Clonmacnois •
UÍ DÚNLAINGE
Kildare •

CLANN
CHOLMÁIN

Clontarf
Dublin •

LINDSEY

Humber

Lincoln • Goltho •

Clonfert •

LEINSTER

DÁL CAIS
• Limerick
Cashel •
MUNSTER
ÉOGANACHTA
É.
GLENDAMNACH
Cork •

UÍ
CHENNSELAIG

• Wexford

Waterford •

GWYNEDD

Chester •

POWYS

Shrewsbury •

Wroxeter •

Lichfield •
Tamworth •

Leicester • Stamford
MERCIA
HWICCE
Worcester •

Raunds •
Northampton •

Fens EAST
Peterborough •
Ramsey • Ely • Thetford
ANGLIA

St Neots •
Ipswich •
Sutton Hoo •

CEREDIGION

DYFED

GWRTH-
EYRNION

ERGYNG

GLYWYSING
GWENT

Castelldwyran •

Gower •

Llantwit •

Dinas Powys •

Oxford •
Thames

Chilterns
Verulamium
(St Albans)
London •

ESSEX
Maldon •
Mucking •
Prittlewell •

Severn

Bath •

WESSEX
Hurstborne
Priors •
Winchester •
Hamwic
(Southampton) •

Rochester •
Canterbury •
Cowdery's KENT
Down SUSSEX

Thanet

Dover •

CORNWALL

Isle of
Wight

W N E S

0   50   100   150 miles
0   100   200 kms

MERCIA
RHEGED } Kingdoms

Italy in the early Middle Ages

N
W   E
S

• Chur

NON

Campione   Limonta
Como • Bergamo   • Trento   Cividale •
LOMBARDY   FRIULI •
† Novalesa   Cusago ○ • Milan   Verona   Treviso
Turin • Pavia • Cremona   Mantua   Padua   Venice   ISTRIA
Piacenza • EMILIA   • Nonantola
Bobbio † • Parma   Comacchio
Genoa • Reggio •   Ravenna
Canossa ○   Modena • Bologna
Luni • Lucca
Florence •   • Rimini
Pisa • Fontebona
Montarrenti ○   † Siena   Arezzo •
TUSCANY   Nursia
Monte   (Norcia)
Amiata   Spoleto •
SABINA   Trita
LAZIO   † Farfa   ○ † Casauria
Ostia •   Rome   Vico
Teatino
† S. Vincenzo al Volturno
† Montecassino
Gaeta •   Bari •
Capua •
Benevento •   PUGLIA
Naples •   • Salerno
Amalfi •   Otranto •

Adriatic
Sea

DALMATIA

CROATIA

Tyrrhenian
Sea

CORSICA

SARDINIA

CALABRIA
• Crotone
Squillace •
Palermo •   Reggio •

SICILY

Syracuse •

---- Boundaries in 700
EMILIA Area name
•   City
†   Monastery
○   Settlement

0   50   100   150   200 miles
0   100   200   300 kms

NORTHUMBRIA

North Sea

WELSH KINGDOMS

M E R C I A

EAST ANGLIA

Atlantic Ocean

W E S S E X

KENT

FLANDER

St Bertin † Nivelles
(St Omer)   Tournai
        Annappes •
Quentovic • ARTOIS
St Riquier † Tertry
    Corbie † Quier
        Noyon
    Compiègne La
St Wandrille †
Rouen   Soisso
Pîtres   Meaux
Beauvais Paris †
        Faremoutiers

BRITTANY

Germigny-des-Prés Se
            † Ferriè
Redon † Le Mans • Orléans † *Fleu*
• Vannes   Fontenoy
    Angers Blois *Loire*
    Tours
    ANJOU   B

        Bourges •

Poitiers •

Francia in 843

– – – – Division between West Francia, the
        Middle Kingdom (including Italy),
        and East Francia

†   Monastery

Limoges •   Clermont •
            A U V
            Brioude

        Aurillac •

Bordeaux •

    Cahors •

            Albi •
        Toulouse • *Gellone* †

    P Y R E N E E S   SEPTIMAN

Pass of
Roncesvalles   CATALONIA

            Barcelona •

0   50   100   150 miles
0   100   200 kms

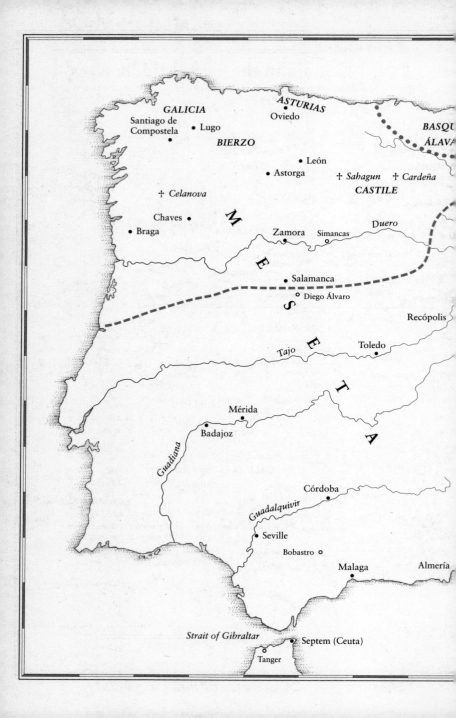

Spain in the early Middle Ages

Toulouse

Narbonne

COUNTRY

P y r e n e e s

Pamplona

URGELL

NAVARRE

Tudela o

Zaragoza

Ebro

CATALONIA

UPPER MARCH

Barcelona

Tarragona

SANTAVER

B a l e a r i c   I s l a n d s

Pla de Nadal o   • Valencia

M e d i t e r r a n e a n   S e a

TUDMIR

Murcia •

Cartagena

GALICIA   Area name
† Monastery
• City
o Other
•••••• Approximate northern boundary of
Visigothic Spain in the seventh century
– – – Approximate northern boundary
of al-Andalus, 1000

0	50	100	150 miles
0	100		200 kms

N
W   E
S

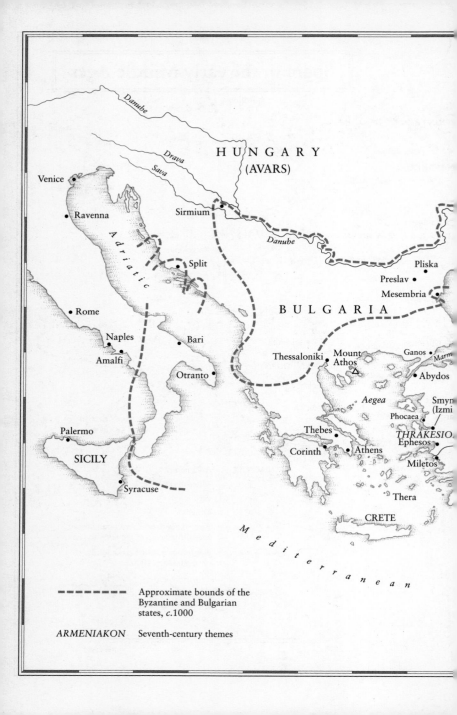

Venice

Ravenna

Adriatic

Rome

Naples

Amalfi

Palermo

SICILY

Syracuse

Danube

Drava

Sava

HUNGARY
(AVARS)

Sirmium

Danube

Split

Bari

Otranto

BULGARIA

Pliska

Preslav

Mesembria

Thessaloniki

Mount
Athos △

Ganos

Marm

Abydos

Aegea

Smyn
(Izmi

Phocaea

THRAKESIO

Thebes

Corinth

Athens

Ephesos

Miletos

Thera

CRETE

M e d i t e r r a n e a n

– – – – – – – – Approximate bounds of the
Byzantine and Bulgarian
states, *c.*1000

ARMENIAKON Seventh-century themes

The Byzantine Empire

Dniepr

CRIMEA

Cherson

Black   Sea

CONSTANTINOPLE

Chalcedon   Klaudioupolis   *Halys*   Euchaita   Trabzon

OPSIKION   A R M E N I A

Ankara   *ARMENIAKON*

Nicaea   Sykeon   Caesarea
(Iznik)

ardis   Nyssa

Maiander   Nakoleia   CAPPADOCIA   Melitene   *Tigris*

Amorion   Samosata

Synnada   Edessa   Mosul

ANATOLIKON   *T a u r u s   M t s.*

Antalya   Tarsus

Myra   ISAURIA   Antioch   Aleppo   *Euphrates*

CYPRUS   S Y R I A

Sea

0	100	200	300	400 miles
0	200	400	600 kms	

The Inheritance of Rome

I

Introduction

Early medieval Europe has, over and over, been misunderstood. It has fallen victim above all to two grand narratives, both highly influential in the history and history-writing of the last two centuries, and both of which have led to a false image of this period: the narrative of nationalism and the narrative of modernity. Before we consider a different sort of approach, we need to look at both of these, briefly but critically, to see what is wrong with each; for most readers of this book who have not already studied the period will have one or both in the front of their minds as a guiding image.

The early Middle Ages stands at the origin, whether authentic or fictional, of so many European nation states that it has taken on mythic significance for historians of all the generations since nationalism became a powerful political image, in the early nineteenth century, and often earlier still. People write books called *The Birth of France*, or, more generally, *The Growth of Europe*, looking as they do so for the germs of a future national or European identity, which can be claimed to exist by 1000 in France, Germany, England, Denmark, Poland, Russia and a host of other nations if one looks hard enough. Early medieval history thus becomes part of a teleology: the reading of history in terms of its (possibly inevitable) consequences, towards whatever is supposed to mark 'why we are best' – we English, or French, or (western) Europeans – or at least, for less self-satisfied communities, 'why we are different'. The whole of early medieval English history can thus be seen in terms of the origins of the nation state; the whole of early medieval Low Countries history in terms of the origins of the commercial dynamism of the future Belgium or Netherlands. The lack of evidence for our period helps make these nationalist readings common, even today. They are false readings all the same; even when they are empirically accurate (the English did indeed have a unitary state in 1000, production and exchange were indeed unusually active in what would become Belgium), they mislead us in our understanding of the past. This is bad history; history does not have teleologies of this kind.

Europe was not born in the early Middle Ages. No common identity in 1000 linked Spain to Russia, Ireland to the Byzantine empire (in what is now the Balkans, Greece and Turkey), except the very weak sense of community that linked Christian polities together. There was no common European culture, and certainly not any Europe-wide economy. There was no sign whatsoever that Europe would, in a still rather distant future, develop economically and militarily, so as to be able to dominate the world. Anyone in 1000 looking for future industrialization would have put bets on the economy of Egypt, not of the Rhineland and Low Countries, and that of Lancashire would have seemed like a joke. In politico-military terms, the far south-east and south-west of Europe, Byzantium and al-Andalus (Muslim Spain), provided the dominant states of the Continent, whereas in western Europe the Carolingian experiment (see below, Chapters 16 and 17) had ended with the break-up of Francia (modern France, Belgium and western Germany), the hegemonic polity for the previous four hundred years. The most coherent western state in 1000, southern England, was tiny. In fact, weak political systems dominated most of the Continent at the end of our period, and the active and aggressive political systems of later on in the Middle Ages were hardly visible.

National identities, too, were not widely prominent in 1000, even if one rejects the association between nationalism and modernity made in much contemporary scholarship. We must recognize that some such identities did exist. One can make a good case for England in this respect (the dismal years of the Danish conquest in the early eleventh century produced a number of texts invoking a version of it). Italians, too, had a sense of common identity, although it hardly reached south of Rome (of course, that is pretty much still true today), and did not lead to a desire for political unity. Geographical separation, such as that provided by the English Channel and the Alps, helped both of these, as it also did the Irish, who were capable of recognizing a version of an Irish community, however fragmented Ireland really was. In the parallel case of Byzantium, what gave its inhabitants identity was simply the coherence of its political system, which was much greater than any other in

INTRODUCTION

Europe at that time; Byzantine 'national identity' has not been much considered by historians, for that empire was the ancestor of no modern nation state, but it is arguable that it was the most developed in Europe at the end of our period. By contrast, France, Germany and Spain (either Christian or Muslim) did not have any such imagery. The Danes may have had it, but in Scandinavia as a whole there is good evidence for it only in Iceland. The Slav lands were still too inchoate to have any version of identity not specifically tied to the fate of ruling dynasties. And, as will be stressed often in this book, a common language had very little to do with any form of cultural or political solidarity at all. The image of the 'birth of Europe', and the 'birth' of the great bulk of the later nations of Europe, is thus in our period not only teleological, but close to fantasy. The fact that there are genealogical links to the future in so many tenth-century polities is an interesting fact, but of no help whatever in understanding the early Middle Ages.

Even more unhelpful are the other, still older, storylines which situate the early Middle Ages inside the grand narrative of modernity itself, in its many variations. This is the narrative which traditionally relegated the whole of medieval history to simply being 'in the middle', between the political and legal solidity of the Roman empire (or else the high summer of classical culture) on the one side, and the supposed rediscovery of the latter in the Renaissance on the other. It was Renaissance scholars themselves who invented this image; since then, the storyline has undergone two major sorts of change. First, later generations – the scientists of the late seventeenth century, the Enlightenment thinkers and revolutionaries of the eighteenth, the industrialists and socialists of the nineteenth and twentieth – have claimed 'true' modernity for themselves, contesting as they did so the claims for the years around 1500 as a cusp. Conversely, in the scientific history of the last century, medievalists have sought to save at least the central and late Middle Ages from the opprobrium of not 'really' being history at all, and beginnings for common long-term European historical processes have been sought in papal reform, the 'twelfth-century Renaissance', the origins of the universities, and in the early state-formation of kings like Henry II of England and Philip II of France, that is, in the period around 1050–1200.

The result of these two developments is that an entire millennium, from the late eleventh century onwards in European history, can be seen as a continuous succession of tides, advancing ever further up the beach of Progress; but, in this imagery, the period before it is still left unreconstructed. The achievements of the ancient world are still seen by many in a shimmering light beyond the dark sea of barbarism which supposedly marks the early Middle Ages; and the fall of 'the' Roman empire in the fifth century (ignoring its long survival in the East) is seen as a primordial failure, the reversal of which was a long and painstaking process, although a necessary foundation for whichever aspect of the modern world the observer most wishes to stress: rationalism, productivity, a global market, knowledge, democracy, equality, world peace or the freedom from exploitation.

I am in favour of most of these final ends myself; but to me as a historian the storyline still seems ridiculous, for every period in history has its own identity and legitimacy, which must be seen without hindsight. The long stretch of time between 400 and 1000 has its own validity as a field of study, which is in no way determined by what went before or came after. To attribute values to it (or to parts of it, as with those who, with the image of the 'Carolingian Renaissance', want to attach the ninth and perhaps tenth centuries to the grand narrative of 'real' history, at the expense, presumably, of the sixth to eighth) is a pointless operation. And to me as a historian of the early Middle Ages, the 'othering' of the period simply seems meaningless. The wealth of recent scholarship on the period gives the lie to this whole approach to seeing history; and this book will have failed if it appears to support it in any way.

This is because it is now possible to write a very different sort of early medieval history. Until the 1970s its lack of evidence put researchers off; and a moralizing historiography dependent on the storyline of failure saw the centuries between 400/500 and 1000 as inferior. Whatever people's explanations for the fall of the western Roman empire in the fifth century (internal weakness, external attack, or a bit of both), it seemed obvious that it was a Bad Thing, and that European and Mediterranean societies took centuries to recover from it; maybe by the time of Charlemagne (768–814), maybe not until the economic expansion and religious reformism of the eleventh century. The eastern empire's survival as Byzantium was hardly stressed at all. The nationalist origin-myths were almost all the period had going for it; they survived longer than the image of the early Middle Ages as a failure, in fact.

Most of this is now, fortunately, changed; the early Middle Ages is not the Cinderella period any more. For a start, researchers into the period have become more numerous. In Britain around 1970 the presence of Peter Brown and Michael Wallace-Hadrill in Oxford, and Walter Ullmann in Cambridge, allowed the formation of a critical mass of graduate students in early medieval (and also late antique) history who then got jobs in the rest of the country (just before recruitment to universities clamped down with the government cuts of 1980); they have had their own graduates everywhere, as research training in history has ceased to be dominated by Oxbridge, and a further generation is coming on stream. Byzantine studies developed rapidly as well. Early medieval archaeology, over the same period, freed itself from a preoccupation with cemeteries and metalwork, and opened itself out to the 'new archaeology' of spatial relationships and economic or material cultural systems, which had much wider implications and allowed for a richer dialectic with documentary history, if, at least, the participants were willing. Outside Britain, similar groups of historians were trying to get rid of past obsessions with political or cultural 'decline' and the history of legal institutions or of the church; only in some countries, notably the United States, has the number of early medievalists increased as much as in Britain (in Germany and Italy there had always been more), but in all countries the sophistication of historical approach has increased dramatically in the last three decades. In much of continental Europe, indeed, early medieval archaeology has also been virtually invented over the same time-span; it hardly existed outside a few countries in 1970 (Britain, East and West Germany, the Netherlands, Denmark, Poland), but now a complex and up-to-date archaeology of this period characterizes nearly every country in the European Union.

Research has also become more internationalized. The project of the European Science Foundation (ESF) on the Transformation of the Roman World in 1993–8 took dozens of researchers from nearly every European country (and beyond) and put them in hotels from Stockholm to Istanbul for a week at a time to brainstorm common approaches. This did not create a 'common European' historiography, for both good and bad reasons (national assumptions and prejudices were often too ingrained; conversely, too international an approach to the subject would risk blandness); but it did mean that participants came to understand each other better, and personal friendships became internationalized. Post-ESF projects have continued to flourish over the subsequent decade, and international work on common themes is now normal, and more organic when it happens. Broadly, the most innovative recent work among historians has often been in cultural history, particularly of high politics and political and social élites; but the more economic approach intrinsic to most archaeology, although not always taken on board by documentary historians, nonetheless allows major developments in socio-economic history too. Early medievalists were also among the first to take seriously some of the implications of the linguistic turn, the realization that all our written accounts from the past are bound by narrative conventions, which have to be understood properly before the accounts can be used by historians at all; as a result, in the last two decades nearly every early medieval source has been critically re-evaluated for its narrative strategies. The landscape of early medieval studies is thus more international, more critical, and much more wide-ranging than it used to be.

This positive picture hides flaws, of course. One is that this newly enlarged community of researchers has as yet been reluctant to offer new paradigms for our understanding of the period. I criticized this in a recent book, *Framing the Early Middle Ages* (Oxford, 2005), in the specific context of socio-economic history, and offered some parameters which might work in that field. In the field of cultural and political history, it is arguable that a new paradigm is emerging, but it remains implicit rather than explicit. That paradigm sees many aspects of late Antiquity (itself substantially revalued: the late Roman empire is now often seen as the Roman high point, not an inferior and totalitarian copy of the second-century *pax romana*) continuing into the early Middle Ages without a break. More specifically: the violence of the barbarian invaders of the empire is a literary trope; there were few if any aspects of post-Roman society and culture that did not have Roman antecedents; the seventh century in the West, although the low point for medieval evidence, produced more surviving writings than any Roman century except the fourth and sixth, showing that a literate culture had by no means vanished in some regions; in short, one can continue to study the early medieval world, east or west, as if it were late Rome. This position is explicit in much recent work on the fifth-century invasions, but it affects the study of later centuries, into the ninth century and beyond, in much more indirect ways. It is rare to find historians actually *writing* that Charlemagne, say, was essentially operating in a late Roman political-cultural framework, even when they are implying it by the ways they present him. This is a problem, however; for, whether or not one believes that Charlemagne was actually operating in such a framework, the issue cannot properly be confronted and argued about until it is brought out into the open. And it can be added that historians have, overall, been much more aware that catastrophe is a literary cliché in the early Middle Ages than that continuity – accommodation – is one as well.

A second problem is that the more attached historians become to continuity (or to 'transformation') rather than to sharp change, the further they diverge from archaeologists. Archaeologists see very substantial simplifications in post-Roman material culture in the fifth to seventh centuries (the exact date varies according to the region), which in some cases – Britain is one example, the Balkans another – is drastic; only a handful of Roman provinces, Syria, Palestine and Egypt, did not experience it. Bryan Ward-Perkins has recently published a short and useful riposte to a continuitist cultural history, *The Fall of Rome and the End of Civilization*, which stresses the force of these archaeological simplifications. This book will, I hope, prompt debate, and also the establishment of common ground between the two traditions; as I write, it is too early to tell. But we do need to develop historical interpretations that can encompass the diversity of our evidence, both literary and archaeological. Both a highly Romanizing literary text – the *Etymologies* of Isidore of Seville (d. 636), for example – and an excavation which shows markedly flimsier buildings and fewer inhabitants than in the Roman period, as with many urban sites excavated in recent decades from Tarragona through Milan to Tours, constitute evidence about the past, and neither of them should be ignored. When the two are put together, indeed, the break-up of the Roman empire, particularly in the West, immediately comes into focus as a major shift. As we shall see in later chapters, however much continuity there was in values or political practices into the early medieval period – which there certainly was – the resources for political players lessened considerably, and the structures in which they acted simplified, often radically. The landscape of politics, society and economics looks very different in the early Middle Ages as a result. Seeing the period in its own terms entails recognizing its differences from the Roman past as much as its continuities.

One result of the implicit nature of recent historical developments is that there are relatively few overviews of the early Middle Ages as a whole. The last survey that covered the entire period up to 1000 in English, by Roger Collins, dates back to 1991, and is largely political in focus. The recent high-quality social histories in French of Régine Le Jan, Jean-Pierre Devroey and Philippe Depreux only go up to 900, and do not include the Byzantine or Arab worlds. Julia Smith's important cultural synthesis, *Europe after Rome*, which gets closer than any other book to offering new paradigms for her field, similarly restricts itself to Latin Europe; so does Matthew Innes's recent *Introduction to Early Medieval Western Europe, 300–900*. (Of all these, this last is perhaps the most similar to the present book in approach, but it only appeared in the summer of 2007, after my own draft was completed, and I have not incorporated its insights.) There are of course many works that deal with shorter time-spans, and some periods, notably the fifth century (especially in the West) and the Carolingian century, are very extensively studied; there are also many regional and national syntheses, some of which cover the whole of the early Middle Ages. But there is space for a new survey which confronts the socio-political, socio-economic, politico-cultural developments of the period 400–1000 as a whole, the period of the end of Roman unity and the formation of a myriad of smaller polities, across the whole space of Europe and the Mediterranean, the ex-Roman lands and the non-Roman lands to the north of Rome alike. That is the intention of this book.

Framing the Early Middle Ages offered some quite sharply characterized interpretations of how social and economic change could be understood comparatively, region by region, England with respect to Denmark or Francia, Francia with respect to Italy or Egypt, Italy with respect to Spain or Syria. Obviously, these interpretations will be reprised in certain chapters of this book, notably Chapters 9 and 15, and they underpin much of the rest. But here the aims are different. First, a political narrative of the period is given, which is informed, as fully as possible, by recent advances in cultural history. The social and cultural (including religious) environment inside which men and women made political choices has been an important focus in each of the chapters of the book. This book intends to be comprehensible to people who know nothing about the period, a period that has few household names for a wider public, and it takes little for granted. I have wanted, however, not only to introduce Charlemagne – or Æthelred II in England, or Chindasuinth in Spain, or Brunhild in Austrasian Francia, or the Byzantine emperor Nikephoros II Phokas, or the caliph al-Ma'mun – but to explain the political-cultural world inside which each of them operated. This interest reflects recent historiography, of course. It also means that there is less about the peasant majority than there might have been, although peasants are far from absent. Conversely, and this is the second aim, these analyses are intended to be understood inside an economic context, derived from both archaeology and the history of documents as well. It is crucial for any understanding of political choices that some rulers were richer than others, and that some aristocracies were richer than others; more complex political systems were made possible as a result. Some traditional political histories put the actions of kings of Ireland, England and Francia, Byzantine emperors, caliphs and Roman emperors on the same level: they were not. This was a hierarchy of wealth, with the last-named at an opposite extreme to the first-named in resources and in the complexity of the state structures in which they operated. These differences lie behind even the most resolutely cultural-political issues, the Visigothic persecution of Jews, the Iconoclast controversy, or the role of intellectuals in ninth-century Francia.

The third aim has been to look at the period 400–1000, and all the sub-periods inside that long stretch of time, in their own terms, without considering too much their relationship with what came before or after, so as to sidestep the grand narratives criticized above. We begin with a still-thriving Roman empire, but only to set out the building-blocks with which post-Roman polities inevitably had to construct their environments: certainly not to lament failure, or to present a model which successor states failed to live up to. Here, as for every other society discussed, I have tried to look at political choices without hindsight. Some political figures did, indeed, make terrible choices (as when Aetius let the Vandals take Carthage in 439, or when al-Mansur's successors in Spain set off the civil war in the 1010s, or perhaps when Louis the Pious fell out with his sons in 830 in Francia: see Chapters 4, 14, 16), which had bad consequences for the political strategies they were trying to further. But in each case they did it in a socio-cultural framework which made sense to them, and it is this that I have sought to recapture, at least fleetingly, in the space at my disposal.

Above all, I have tried to avoid teleology. Any reading of the Roman empire in the fifth century only in terms of the factors which led to its break-up, of Merovingian Francia only in terms of what led to Charlemagne's power and ambitions, of tenth-century papal activity only in terms of what led to 'Gregorian reform', of the economic dynamism of the Arab world only in terms of its (supposed) supersession by Italian and then north European merchants and producers, is a false reading of the past. Only an attempt to look squarely at each past in terms of its own social reality can get us out of this trap.

On the basis of these principles, I look in turn at the Roman empire and its fall in the West (Part I); at the immediately post-Roman polities in Gaul, Spain, Italy, Britain and Ireland (Part II); at the history of Byzantium after the seventh-century crisis of the eastern Roman empire, the Arab caliphate, and the latter's tenth-century successor states, including al-Andalus, Muslim Spain (Part III); and then, returning to the Latin West, at the Carolingian empire, its successor states and its principal imitator, England, and at the array of northern polities, from Russia to Scotland, which crystallized in the last century of our period, including a look at their aristocracies and peasantries (Part IV). Each is analysed comparatively, in the light of what other societies did with the same or similar resources, but above all in terms of its own reality, which must be the starting point of all our work. There is far less evidence for the early Middle Ages than for later, sometimes so little that we can hardly reconstruct a society at all (Scotland is an example); the reasons for this are an interesting issue in themselves, but careful source criticism can all the same allow us to say quite a lot in most cases, of which what follows is only a fairly summary account.

Early medieval history-writing is a permanent struggle with the few sources available, as historians try, often over and over again, to extract nuanced historical accounts from them. For this reason not much (and certainly not much of any interest) is generally accepted without any dispute. More than in some other periods, this period is very visibly the re-creation of its historians; and in the notes at the end of the text I have paid respect to that collective re-creation, as much as space allows. (There are no numbered footnotes in the book, so as not to interrupt the text, but the references at the end are organized page by page.) Editorial policy has meant that these references are mostly in English, however; non-English authorities have only been cited where they are absolutely indispensable. Similarly, all sources are cited in translation, where one exists. English-language historiography is more prominent in this field than it was in 1970, but it is not at all dominant; all the same, authorities in other languages can be found in profusion in the bibliographies to the works listed.

Reading the sources in this period (as in all others) is, however, for the reasons outlined above, not at all a straightforward or automatic process. Each chapter in this book begins with a vignette, as an introduction to the feel of the society or societies to be discussed there, and these will also introduce the reader to some of the issues posed by the sources. But overall it must be recognized from the outset that it is unwise to take any source, of any kind, too literally. This is perhaps easiest to see with narratives of events, in histories, letters, saints' lives or testimony in court cases, which are all the work of single authors with clear agendas, and a host of moralizing prejudices which they tend to make very clear to the reader. The most copious of all early medieval chroniclers, Gregory, bishop of Tours (d. 594), who wrote a long history, mostly of his own century in Frankish Gaul, and also numerous saints' lives, was an active political player in his lifetime with clear likes and dislikes among his royal contemporaries (below, Chapter 5). He was also a high-level aristocrat with huge reserves of snobbery, as well as being – as a bishop – a professional moralist, with the responsibility to encourage, cajole or frighten his contemporaries into avoiding sin. We have to read everything Gregory says with these elements in mind – elements which he does not hide from us – and most historians do indeed do so. Recent work, however, has also stressed Gregory's literary crafting of his writing, which imposes hidden patterns on his superficially artless anecdotes, and in addition this work has analysed the less consciously felt limits that the genres he wrote in imposed on what he was able to write about, or how he was able to describe things. Also, of course, most of what Gregory tells us he did not witness himself, so we have to guess at the narrative strategies and at the reliability of his informants as well. Every 'fact' that we can extract from Gregory has to be seen in this set of contexts.

One might conclude, on the basis of these comments, that one could not believe anything Gregory says at all. And indeed it would be impossible to disprove such a conclusion: not least, in this case, because the absence of evidence from his period means that Gregory is the only source for the huge majority of statements he makes about sixth-century Gaul. All the same, one has to recognize that even if all Gregory's statements were fictions – and crafted fictions, for moralizing purposes, at that – he was still writing in a realist vein. Put another way, the more he sought to moralize about his society, for an audience which had to be persuaded that his moralism spoke to them (even if it was a future audience, for Gregory's main work, his *Histories*, did not circulate in his lifetime), the more he had to anchor it in recognizable experience. So, this king or queen may or may not have executed his or her opponent in this inventive way, this bishop may or may not have bought his office and terrorized his clergy, but this is the kind of thing that people thought rulers or bishops might well have done in his society. Gregory's narratives, and those of all similar sources from Ireland to Iraq, are used here in this way: as guides to the sort of thing that *could* happen – at least in their authors' vision of the world. Often in the chapters that follow, the details of this reasoning will be skipped over; it is impossible, without writing unreadably, to introduce ifs and buts every time a source is used. But it should be understood as underlying every narrative that is cited in this book. It can be added that this also means that openly fictional sources, such as epic poems about heroes, can be used by us as well, for example, the Anglo-Saxon poem *Beowulf*, one of our best sources for aristocratic values in England. The problems of using such sources are not different in type from those involved in using Gregory of Tours, and indeed historians who use them have often found it easier to keep them in mind.

Legislation presents a similar problem. It might seem obvious that a law does not describe how people behave (think of the laws about speeding), but early medievalists have had to face an entrenched historiography which presumes exactly this. Modern history-writing came out of a legal-history tradition, and well into the twentieth century people wrote social history, in particular, under the assumption that if a law enacted something, the population at large followed it. If, however, this is not true in contemporary society, with all the coercive power available to the legal system, how much less could we think it was true in the early Middle Ages, when states were weaker (often very weak indeed), and the populace even knowing what legislation a ruler had enacted was unlikely in most places. Even if a legislator only wanted to describe current custom, which could sometimes be argued to be the case in the

West in the sixth and seventh centuries (though less in later periods, and still less in the Byzantine and Arab worlds), the problem would be that custom was very locally diverse, and a king in Toledo or Pavia, the then capitals of Spain and northern Italy, would not know more than those of the area he lived in, and only a restricted part of them at that. Legislation is in fact best seen as a guide to the minds of legislators, just as the writings of Gregory of Tours tell us first about what Gregory thought. Laws interact with, feed off, reality, just as Gregory's narratives do; it is not that we cannot use them, but that they are not disinterested guides to actual social behaviour.

Most of the other categories of early medieval text can be analysed and criticized in the same way, but we should pause on one important category, legal documents – for gifts or sales or leases of land for the most part, or for the registration of formal disputes, which were normally about land as well. Most or all of these were contracts, with validity in law, on which surviving court cases put considerable weight, if there were any documents available at all. If these documents are accepted as authentic (and not all are; they often only survive in later collections, not as originals, and many were forged), they could be taken, perhaps more than any other source, to be describing real events. This description is not unproblematic; even an authentic document is a highly stylized text, structured by an artificial language, as legal documents still are today, which limits what one can say in it. Even if the principals wanted to describe accurately what they were doing (which not all did; some 'sales' were in reality hidden loans of money, with the land as collateral, for example), they were restricted by the legalese their notary was accustomed to use, and this might bear little relation to the complexities of local social practices. But at least one could assume – later law courts would assume – that this piece of land, situated in village A, with these boundaries, with a tenant cultivator named B who worked it, was sold by C to D for a price of E silver *denarii*.

I would cautiously accept this rare island of certainty. The question is what one does with it. Isolated documents tell us little. We need collections of texts, which, put together, can constitute a guide, to how many people held land in A, to the financial difficulties of C (or of the category of people which C belonged to), to the size and geographical range of the properties of D, and to the differences in social structure or land price between village A and villages F, G and H. These are valuable things to study, if we have enough material to do so (and occasionally, even in the early Middle Ages, we do). All the same, they are only partial shafts of light. We have to engage in careful argument before we can assume that A, or D, are typical of the region and period we are studying. Also, documents in this period (the situation only changes in the thirteenth century) overwhelmingly tell us about land. Except in Egypt, where desert conditions help the survival of all kinds of text, only land documents were regarded as having a sufficiently long-term future importance to be worth keeping, except by accident; social action outside the field of land transactions remains obscure. Furthermore, again except in Egypt, only churches and monasteries have had sufficiently stable histories to keep some of their archives from the early Middle Ages into the modern period (from roughly 1650 onwards), when historians became interested in publishing them. We only know, that is to say, about land which came into church hands, whether at the time of the charters we have, or as a result of later gifts to the church of properties which came together with their deeds, in order to prove title. These are different sorts of limitation from those involving the narrative strategies of writers, but they are limitations all the same, and we have to be aware of them too. What we can do within these particular constraints will be further explored in Chapter 9.

Archaeological and material evidence is at least free from the constraints of narrative. Archaeologists have indeed sometimes been dismissive of written sources (this was a trend of the 1980s in particular), which only preserve attitudes of literate and thus restricted élites, whereas archaeological excavations and surveys uncover real life, often of the peasantry, who are badly served by texts. Excavations are, however, in some respects like land documents: you can say reliable things about how individual people lived, but you need many sites to be sure of typicality, of patterns and generalities. Archaeology also has its own blind spots: you can tell what sorts of houses people lived in, what food they ate, what technologies they had access to, how spatial layouts worked, how far away the goods they possessed came from, but you cannot tell who owned their land, or what rents were paid from it. This at least creates a balance with documentary history, however. Overall, archaeology tells us more about functional relationships, whereas history tells us more about causation; ideally, we need both. And when we use them both we must bear in mind that material culture projects meaning, too. A burial ritual is a public act, and what one buries in the ground makes a point to others; similarly, urban planning, architecture and wall-painting, and the designs on metalwork and ceramics, all convey meaning, often intentionally, which needs to be decoded and appraised with the same care we use for Gregory of Tours. Archaeology (like art history) is free of the constraints of narrative, but not the constraints of communication. We shall look at this issue in Chapter 10.

The kinds of evidence we have for different regions of Europe in different periods act as further constraints on what we can say about each. Seventh-century England is documented above all through church narratives, with a handful of laws and land documents, set against an extensive cemetery archaeology and a more restricted settlement archaeology; we can say a fair amount about ecclesiastical values and the political dynamic, and also about technology and social stratification, but much less about aristocratic values and political structures. After the 730s in England, the narratives and laws virtually cease for over a century, as do the cemeteries, but we have far more documents, and also urban excavations; we can say much more about the state, and about wider economic relationships, but much less about how kings manipulated their political environment to increase their power, or else failed to do so; important historical questions, like the failure of Mercia to maintain its century-long dominance over central and southern England in and after the 820s (see Chapter 19), remain a mystery as a result. Overall, clerics maintained a constant output of texts of locally varying kinds throughout the early Middle Ages, so that we can tell what ecclesiastics (particularly ecclesiastical rigorists) thought; but only in some periods and places did lay aristocrats commit themselves to writing – the late Roman empire, Carolingian Francia, tenth-century Byzantium, ninth- and tenth-century Iraq – so it is only then that we can get direct insights into the mind-set of secular political élites. And even in single political units we can run up against different concentrations of material. The late tenth-century Ottonian emperors had two power-bases, Saxony and northern Italy; the first is documented almost exclusively in narratives, the second almost exclusively in land charters. So we can talk about the nuance of aristocratic intrigue and political ritual in the first, and about the range of aristocratic wealth and its relationship to royal patronage in the second. The Ottonians must have dealt in both ritual and landed patronage in each, but we are blocked from seeing how.

These constraints are permanent in our period, as they also were in the ancient world. New texts are rare; only archaeology will expand in the next decades, moving the balance steadily towards what can be said from the material record. We are always limited as to what we can say, even about élites, who are at least relatively well documented in our crafted sources, never mind the huge peasant majority, whose viewpoint is so seldom visible (for some of what can be said, see Chapters 9 and 22). Hence the fact that a book of this kind covers six centuries, not one or two, as later in the series. But there is enough known, all the same, to have to select, sometimes quite ruthlessly. What follows is only a small part of what we know about the early Middle Ages. It does at least consist, however, of what seems to me essential to know.

PART I

The Roman Empire and its Break-up, 400–550

2

The Weight of Empire

The guilty thief is produced, is interrogated as he deserves; he is tortured, the torturer strikes, his breast is injured, he is hung up . . . he is beaten with sticks, he is flogged, he runs through the sequence of tortures, and he denies. He is to be punished; he is led to the sword. Then another is produced, innocent, who has a large patronage network with him; well-spoken men are present with him. This one has good fortune: he is absolved.

This is an extract from a Greek–Latin primer for children, probably of the early fourth century. It expresses, through its very simplicity, some of the unquestioned assumptions of the late Roman empire. Judicial violence was normal, indeed deserved (in fact, even witnesses were routinely tortured unless they were from the élite); and the rich got off. The Roman world was habituated to violence and injustice. The gladiatorial shows of the early empire continued in the fourth-century western empire, despite being banned by Constantine in 326 under Christian influence. In the 380s Alypius, a future ascetic bishop in Africa, went to the games in Rome, brought by friends against his will; he kept his eyes shut, but the roar of the crowd as a gladiator was wounded made him open his eyes and then he was gripped by the blood, 'just one of the crowd', as his friend the great theologian Augustine of Hippo (d. 430) sympathetically put it. Augustine, an uncompromising but also not a naive man, took it for granted that such a blood lust was, however sinful in Christian eyes, normal. Actually, all the post-Roman societies, pagan, Christian or Muslim, were equally used to violence, particularly by the powerful; but under the Roman empire it had a public legitimacy, an element of weekly spectacle, which surpassed even the culture of public execution in eighteenth-century Europe. There was a visceral element to Roman power; even after gladiatorial shows ended in the early fifth century, the killing of wild beasts in public continued for another hundred years and more.

As for the rich getting off: this was not automatic by any means, as the senatorial victims of show trials for magic in Rome in 368–71 knew. But the powerful did indeed have strong patronage networks, and could very readily misuse them. Synesios, bishop of Ptolemais in Cyrenaica (modern eastern Libya) in 411–13, faced a brutal governor, Andronikos, at his arrival as bishop. Andronikos, Synesios complains in his letters, was particularly violent to local city councillors, causing the death of one of them for alleged tax offences. Synesios got him sacked, which shows that only a determined bishop with good connections in Constantinople could properly confront abuse of power – or else that a local official, whether good or bad, could fail to survive a frontal attack by a determined political opponent with his own ecclesiastical and central-government patronage network. But the patronage was crucial, and most of our late Roman sources (as, indeed, early Roman sources) lay great emphasis on it. One could not be a success without it. The Roman world was seriously corrupt, as well as violent. What looks like corruption to us did not always seem so to the Romans, at least to those who formed the élite: it had its own rules, justifications and etiquette. But corruption and its analogues did privilege the privileged, and it was, at the very least, ambiguous; an entire rhetoric of illegal abuse of power was available to every writer.

I begin with these comments simply to distance us a little from Roman political power. The Roman state was not particularly 'enlightened'. Nevertheless, nor was it, around 400, obviously doomed to collapse. Its violence (whether public or private), corruption and injustice were part of a very stable structure, one which had lasted for centuries, and which had few obvious internal flaws. Half the empire, the West, did collapse in the fifth century, as a result of unforeseen events, handled badly; the empire survived with no difficulty in the East, however, and arguably reached its peak there in the early sixth century. We shall follow how this occurred in Chapter 4, which includes a political narrative of the period 400–550. In this chapter, we shall see how that stable structure worked before the western empire broke up, and, in the next, we shall look at religious and other cultural attitudes in the late Roman world. Fourth-century evidence will be used in both chapters, extending into the early fifth in the West, a period of relative stability still, and into the sixth in the East, for the state did not change radically there until after 600.

The Roman empire was centred on the Mediterranean – 'our sea' as the Romans called it; they are the only power in history ever to rule all its shores. The structure of the empire was indeed dependent on the inland sea, for easy and relatively cheap sea transport tied the provinces together, making it fairly straightforward for Synesios to move from Cyrenaica to Constantinople and back again, or for Alypius to move from Thagaste (modern Souk Ahras in eastern Algeria) to Rome and back. By 300 it was recognized that the empire could not easily be ruled from a single centre, and after 324 there were two permanent capitals, Rome and Constantine's newly founded Constantinople. The empire thereafter had, most of the time, an eastern (mostly Greek-speaking) and a western (mostly Latin-speaking) half, each with its own emperor and administration. But the two halves remained closely connected, and Latin remained the official legal and military language of the East until well into the sixth century.

Rome was a huge city, with a million people at its height in the early empire, and still half a million in 400, when it was no longer the administrative capital of the western empire (which was, in the fourth century, Trier in northern Gaul, and after 402 Ravenna in northern Italy). Constantinople started much smaller, but increased in size rapidly, and may have reached half a million, by now more than Rome, by the late fifth century. Cities of this size in the ancient or medieval world were kept so large by governments, who wanted a great city at their political or symbolic heart for ideological reasons. Rome and Constantinople both had an urban poor who were maintained by regular state handouts of grain and olive oil, from North Africa (modern Tunisia) in the case of Rome, from Egypt and probably Syria in the case of Constantinople, Africa and Egypt being the major export regions of the whole empire. These free food-supplies (*annona* in Latin) were a substantial expense for the imperial tax system, making up a quarter or more of the whole budget. It must have mattered very much to the state that its great cities were kept artificially large, and their populations happy, with 'bread and circuses' as the tag went – though the circuses (including games in the amphitheatres of Rome) were paid for in most cases by the privately wealthy. The symbolic importance of these cities was such that when the Visigoths sacked Rome in 410 the shock waves went all around the empire, as we shall see in Chapter 4.

This concern for the capitals was only the most obvious aspect of the lasting Roman commitment to city life. The whole of the world of culture was bound up in city-ness, *civilitas* in Latin, from which come our words 'civilized' and 'civilization', and which precisely implied city-dwelling to the Romans. The empire was in one sense a union of all its cities (some thousand in number), each of which had its own city council (*curia* in Latin, *boulē* in Greek) that was traditionally autonomous. Each city also had its own kit of impressive urban buildings, remarkably standard from place to place: a forum, civic buildings and temples around it, a theatre, an amphitheatre (only in the West), monumental baths, and from the fourth century a cathedral and other churches replacing the temples; in some parts of the empire, walls. These marked city-ness; one could not claim to be a city without them. And the imagery of the city and its buildings ran through the whole of Roman culture like a silver thread. The Gaulish poet Ausonius (d. *c.* 395) wrote a set of poems in the 350s called the *Order of Noble Cities*, nineteen in number, from Rome at the top to his own home town of Bordeaux at the bottom (he uses the word *patria*, 'fatherland', of both Rome and Bordeaux); he enumerated his cities by their buildings, and, in so doing, he was in effect delineating the empire itself.

Political society focused on the cities. Their traditional autonomy had meant in the early empire that being a city councillor (*curialis* in Latin, *bouleutēs* in Greek) was the height of local ambition. This was less so by the fourth century, however, as the centralization of imperial government meant cities finding that more decisions were taken over their heads; the expansion of the senate and the central administration also meant that the richest and most successful citizens could move beyond their local hierarchies, and the *curia* thus became second best. City councillors became, above all, responsible for raising and also underwriting taxes, a remunerative but risky matter. Slowly, the formal structures of such councils weakened, above all in the fifth century, and by the sixth even tax-raising had been taken over by central government officials. These processes have often been seen in apocalyptic terms, for it is clear from the imperial law codes that *curiales* often complained of their tax burdens, and that some (the poorer ones, doubtless) sought to avoid office; emperors responded by making such avoidance illegal. Put that together with the trickle of literary evidence for local élites in the West preferring rural living to city life, and an archaeology which increasingly shows radical material simplifications after 400 or so on western urban sites, and the tax burden on city councillors starts to look like a cause of urban abandonment, maybe in the context of the fall of the empire itself.

Such an interpretation is over-negative, however. First of all, it does not fit the East. Here, city councillors were indeed marginalized, and are documented less and less after around 450 (except in ever more hectoring imperial laws), but political élites remained firmly based in cities. What happened was that city government became more informal, based on the local rich as a collective group, but without specific institutions. Senators who lived locally, the local bishop, the richest councillors, increasingly made up an ad-hoc élite group, often called *prōteuontes*, 'leading men'. These men patronized city churches, made decisions about building repairs and festivals, and, if necessary, organized local defence, without needing a formal role. Nor did cities lose by this; the fifth and sixth centuries saw the grandest buildings being built in many eastern cities. Once we see this post-curial stability in the East, it is easier to see it in the West too. Sidonius Apollinaris (lived *c.* 430–85), whose collection of poetry and letters survives, was from the richest family of Clermont in Gaul, son and grandson of praetorian prefects, and son-in-law of the emperor Eparchius Avitus (455–6). He did not have to be a *curialis*, and largely pursued a central government career. But he ended up as bishop of Clermont, enthusiastically supporting local loyalties in his letters, including city-dwelling; and his brother-in-law Ecdicius, Avitus' son, defended the city with a private army. So this sort of commitment to urban politics did not depend on the traditional structure of city councils. Essentially, it went on as long as Roman values survived; this varied, but in many parts of the empire it continued a long time after the empire itself fell. The presuppositions of *civilitas* achieved that on their own. In the West, urban élites also had rural villas, lavish country houses where they spent the summer months (in the East, these were rare, or else concentrated in suburbs, like Daphne in the cooler hills above Antioch); but cities remained the foci for business, politics, patronage and culture. Few influential people could risk staying away from them. And where the rich went, others followed: their servants and entourages, but also merchants and artisans who wanted to sell them things, and the poor who hoped for their charity; the basic personnel of urban life.

It is possible to see the network of cities as the major element of Roman society, more important even than imperial central government. By modern standards, indeed, the empire was lightly governed, with at the most some 30,000 civilian central government officials, who were concentrated in imperial and provincial capitals (though this excludes lesser state employees, such as guardsmen, clerks, messengers, ox-drivers of the public post, who could have been ten times as numerous). When we add to this all the evidence we have for the inefficiency and poor record-keeping of Roman government, plus the time needed to reach outlying provinces of the huge empire (to travel from Rome to northern Gaul took a minimum of three weeks; an army would take much longer), we might wonder how the Roman world held together at all. But it did; a complex set of overlapping structures and presumptions created a coherent political system. Let us look at some of its elements in turn: the civil administration, the senate, the legal system, the army, and the tax system which funded all these. The shared values and rituals of the Roman political élite will then be discussed in Chapter 3, along with the growing importance of a new political structure, the church hierarchy.

The administration of each half of the empire was controlled by the emperor, the central political figure of what was, in principle, an uncompromising autocracy. Some emperors, indeed, imposed themselves politically: in the fourth century Constantine (306–37) and Valentinian I (364–75 in the West) are the most obvious examples, to whom we should add Julian (360–63), whose dramatic and failed attempt to reverse the Christianization set in motion by Constantine has fascinated historians ever since; fifth-century emperors were less impressive, but Justinian in the sixth (527–65 in the East) was as dominant as any of his predecessors, as we shall see in Chapter 4. But not all emperors wanted to do much ruling; they could simply live their lives as the embodiment of public ceremonial, as did, for example, the emperors of the first half of the fifth century. Even if they were active, aiming at an interventionist politics and choosing their major subordinates, they could find themselves blocked by poor information and the complex rules of hierarchy from making a real impact (the most active emperors usually had a military background, without direct experience in civil government). Not that most of the major officials of the empire were full-time bureaucrats, either; even the most assiduous politicians were only intermittently in office. The empire, in a sense, was run by amateurs. But the group of amateurs at least had shared values, and family experience in many cases as well, particularly in the West, where there were more old and rich senatorial families, who were often active in politics in the fourth and fifth centuries. And their subordinates were real career officials, who committed themselves to the administration for life. It is that network of office-holders which gave government its coherence. That, and the stability of the offices themselves. The four praetorian prefectures, each with responsibility for a quarter of the empire (and with a hierarchy of provincial governors beneath them), the six major bureaux of central government and the urban prefectures of Rome and Constantinople all had their own traditions and loyalties, going back in some cases for centuries. John Lydos, who wrote an account of government in the 550s, described the praetorian prefecture of the East in which he had served, tracing the office back, impossibly, to Romulus the founder of Rome; he was very loyal to his department, for all its inadequacy and inconsistency, and he saw the whole of imperial history through its ups and downs. One had to put a good deal of effort in to change the entrenched practices and rituals of bureaucracies like these, and not many people did (one was Justinian's right-hand man, the praetorian prefect John the Cappadocian (531–41), who was thus predictably John Lydos' *bête noire*).

One instance of a leading career politician was Petronius Maximus (lived 396–455), from the powerful senatorial family of the Petronii. He seems to have entered the senate of Rome with the ceremonial office of *praetor* in 411, with particularly lavish praetorian games; he was a tribune in 415, and *comes sacrarum largitionum* for the West, one of the main financial officials of the empire, in 416–19, starting that is to say at the age of twenty – young, given the importance of the post. He was urban prefect of Rome in 420–21 and again at some point in the next couple of decades (most of these dates are approximate); in 439–41 he was praetorian prefect for Italy, probably for the second time. He was twice consul, a major honour but without formal duties, and had the coveted title of *patricius* by 445. Unusually, for a career administrator, he was briefly emperor, in 455, for two months before he was killed. In a letter a decade or so later, Sidonius Apollinaris speculates about how much Maximus must have regretted the hourly regulated rituals and responsibilities of imperial office, given the contrast with the 'leisure' (*otium*) of being a senator. This seems surprising at first sight, but 'leisure' is partly just a manner of speaking: Maximus had long been a major political dealer, with a huge clientele (as Sidonius himself says) and imperial ambitions. We must nonetheless recognize that in the four decades of his political career he only seems to have held formal office for around ten years; he had plenty of time for *otium* as well, which indeed contemporary authors, time and again, describe as one of the characteristics of senatorial élites.

The senate had its own identity, partly separate from the imperial bureaucracy; indeed, in the West it was even physically separate, for the government was no longer in Rome. It was the theoretical governing body of the empire, as of the Roman republic four centuries before, and although the senate was by now no longer a reality, it still represented the height of aspiration for any citizen. It brought with it many fiscal and political privileges, although it was expensive to enter and participate in, given the games and other ceremonies senators had to fund. It had no formal governmental function, but high officials became senators as of right; furthermore, by the early fifth century, only the highest of the three grades of senator, the *illustres*, were regarded as full members of the senate, and the title of *illustris* was only available to officials and direct imperial protégés. The senate was thus tightly connected to government, and expanded as the administration expanded in the fourth century; but it was nonetheless separate, with its own rituals and seniority. It represented aristocratic wealth, privilege and superiority, and, although membership of it was not technically heritable, in practice the same families dominated the senate, in Rome at least, throughout the fourth and fifth centuries. All the male heirs of an *illustris* were anyway at least *clarissimi*, the lowest senatorial grade, which involved at least some privileges even after full senatorial eligibility contracted. And all the grades seem to have been regarded as *nobilis*, 'aristocratic', in late Roman parlance. This close but sideways relation to government has some parallels with that of the House of Lords in modern Britain, both before and after the reforms of 1999.

The existence of this effectively hereditary aristocracy was a key feature of the empire. Not because it dominated government; most leading bureaucrats were not of senatorial origin, even if they became senators later (Maximus was in that sense atypical) but rather because it dominated the *tone* of government. The Roman empire was unusual in ancient and medieval history in that its ruling class was dominated by civilian, not (or not only) military, figures. Only China's mandarinate offers any real parallel. Senators regarded themselves very highly, as the 'best part of the human race' in the well-known words of the orator Symmachus (d. 402); their criteria for this self-satisfaction did not rely on military or physical prowess, but on birth, wealth and a shared culture. Birth was important (Sidonius could be contemptuous of a powerful rival, Paeonius, the praetorian prefect for Gaul, because he was 'of municipal origin', that is, from a curial, not a senatorial family), although very long ancestry was less vital; even the Anicii, by far the leading Roman family in the fourth and fifth centuries, only traced their family back to the late second century. Wealth went without saying: no one was politically important in the Roman world (apart from a few high-minded bishops) without being rich. One needed wealth to get anywhere in the civil administration, as both bribes for appointments and the maintenance of a patronage network cost money, but once one was important, the perks of office, both legal and illegal, were huge. In the army, too, although it was more open to merit, all successful generals ended up rich. And the independently wealthy families of the senate of Rome, the Anicii, Petronii, Caeonii and half a dozen others, had estates throughout southern Italy, Sicily, North Africa and elsewhere, 'scattered across almost the whole Roman world', as the historian Ammianus Marcellinus said of the leading politician Petronius Probus in the 370s: these may have been the richest private landowners of all time. When two Roman aristocrats, Melania and Pinianus, got religion around 405 and sold off all their land, which provided 120,000 *solidi* (around 900 pounds of gold) a year in rents, it wrecked the property market, according to Melania's saint's life. The senatorial hyper-rich were only in Rome, however; in Constantinople senators were from the provincial élites of the East, and operated on a smaller scale. Throughout the empire, in fact, there were provincial élites, the leaders of which had senatorial status and were in line for public office; they were locally powerful, but could not match the Anicii. Sidonius was an example, and indeed the élites of Gaul seem to have been a particularly coherent group.

A shared culture perhaps marked the Roman senatorial and provincial aristocracies most, for it was based on a literary education. Every western aristocrat had to know Virgil by heart, and many other classical Latin authors, and be able to write poetry and turn a polished sentence in prose; in the East it was Homer. The two traditions, in Latin and Greek, did not have much influence on each other by now, but they were very dense and highly prized. There was a pecking-order based on the extent of this cultural capital. Ammianus reports scornfully that senators in Rome, the supposed crème de la crème, only really read Juvenal, a racy and satirical poet, so by implication not the difficult texts; whether or not this was true, it was a real insult. Conversely, literary experts, such as Ausonius in the West and Libanios (d. *c.* 393) in the East, could rise fast and gain imperial patronage and office simply because of their writing – in Libanios' case so fast that he was accused of magic – although both were already landowners of at least medium wealth. The emperor Julian in his attempt to reverse Christianization tried to force Christian intellectuals to teach only the Bible, not the pagan classics, thus enclosing them in a ghetto of inferior prose. This failed, but the assumptions behind such an enactment clearly show the close relationship between traditional culture and social status. Some Christian hardliners responded by rejecting Virgil, but this failed too: by the fifth century the aristocracy knew both Virgil (or Homer) and the Bible, and might add to these some of the new Christian theologians too, Augustine in the West or Basil of Caesarea in the East, both of whom were good stylists.

It is this culture which makes the late Roman empire, or at least its élites, unusually accessible to us, for the writings of many of these aristocrats survive: elegant letters or speeches for the most part, but also poetry, theology, or, in the case of the fifth-century senator Palladius, an estate-management manual. Roman literary culture used to be regarded as the high point of civilization; this belief, inherited from the Renaissance, perhaps reached its peak in the late nineteenth- and early twentieth-century English public-school tradition, in which Virgil (and indeed Juvenal, by now seen as a more difficult author) was regarded as a basic training even for the government of India, not to speak of an academic career. This belief is less strong now; few academics know enough Latin to read Virgil (outside Italy), and even fewer politicians. It is thus easier today to see Roman literary culture as an attribute of power, rather than virtue; Roman politicians were at least as cynical and greedy as their successors, and not obviously better at ruling. But it is important to recognize its all-pervasiveness; in all the cities of the empire, even local office was linked to at least some version of this education. The shared knowledge and values that it inculcated was one of the elements that held the empire together, and indeed made the empire remarkably homogeneous, as not only its literature but its surviving architecture and material culture show. It must finally be said that, although the Roman world left a dense legacy of institutions and assumptions to its early medieval successors, a literary education was not part of that, except in the increasingly separate career structure of the church. The culture of post-Roman aristocracies instead became military, based on the use of arms and horses, and as a result we know much less about it from the inside.

Roman law was another intellectual system that was, in principle, the same everywhere, and it acted as a unifying force. It consisted of imperial legislation, which was very extensive in the fourth to sixth centuries, and a network of tracts by earlier Roman jurists, which represented a distillation of case-law precedents and the workings-out of legal principles. To master this properly required a special training, at the law-schools of Rome, Beirut or (after 425) Constantinople, although all education involved an element of rhetoric, essential for court advocacy. Alypius spent time training at the Rome law-school in the early 380s before going with Augustine to work in Milan (where both were converted to a more thoroughgoing Christianity, and switched their career path to the church); Augustine, by contrast, although trained in rhetoric, makes it clear in his writings that he did not feel himself to be a legal expert, for his education was not specific enough. Law was not in fact at all easy to master before Theodosius II had imperial laws collected into the *Theodosian Code* in 429–38. Justinian revised and expanded the code (twice) in 528–34, and had juristic literature of the second and third centuries excerpted and systematized in the *Digest* in 530–33 as well. The *Theodosian Code* remained a point of reference in the post-Roman West, even though the laws of the post-Roman kingdoms were different; Justinian's corpus survived as the law of Byzantium, and was separately revived in the West in the twelfth century. We must, however, be careful about what such a commitment to law means. The complexity of this legal system was such that experts (*iurisconsulti*) were needed in every court, and sometimes just to draw up documents, but they may not always have been available or been fully reliable if they were. Even if legal help was accessible, courts did not necessarily judge justly, and the rich often benefited from judicial corruption and patronage, as we saw at the start of this chapter and as many sources confirm. In Egypt, papyrus documents recording the settlement of civil disputes in the fourth to sixth centuries show a strong tendency to avoid courts altogether, given their huge expense and danger, and to go directly to private arbitration.

It would be tempting to reduce the law to its criminal dimension, with its recourse to torture, and conclude that the legal system was in practice simply an instrument of heavy-handed state coercion, the work of a public power that relied on terror because it did not have the personnel to dominate daily life in any detail. Such a temptation would be largely justified, but all the same the law was important. Egyptian arbitrations may have avoided the courts, but they refer frequently to legislation and legal terminology. Augustine was not expert in the law, but he sought to know it, for example writing to the *iurisconsultus* Eustochius for rulings. An interesting letter survives from Africa of around 400 in which an unnamed landowner chides a neighbour and former friend, Salvius, for tyrannizing the former's tenants: 'Is there one law for advocates, another for ex-lawyers? Or one equity for Rome, another for Mateur?' Salvius, an advocate from (we assume) Mateur, would presumably have thought so, and his illegalities are standard. But his correspondent had been a lawyer too; Salvius had taught him the law of tenancy, and it was this, together with the law of inheritance and possession, which the letter invokes in detail, before offering a deal. Law and its imagery were all-pervading in the empire, and we could indeed suppose that the setpiece denunciations of judicial corruption in our sources at least showed high expectations.

The Roman army was much larger than the civil administration, and was always the empire's major expense: in 400 there were some half a million soldiers, give or take a hundred thousand. These were mostly on the northern Rhine and Danube frontiers, and on the eastern frontier with Persia (the long southern border faced the Sahara, and was less vulnerable), but there were detachments in every province, acting as garrisons and as ad-hoc police. It was of course their existence that made it possible for provincial élites to remain civilian; private armies were very rare before the empire broke up. Conversely, armies were capable of imposing their own candidates for emperor, all the more easily because they held most of the weapons. This had been common in the third century, but was much rarer in the fourth; it revived in the West in the final years of empire in the fifth, but in the East there were no successful coups until 602. Even without coups against the emperor, however, army leaders remained important in politics, and several weak emperors (such as Honorius, western emperor 395–423) had military strongmen ruling for them, who could succeed each other by violence. There was a sense in which the office of emperor was more military than the civilian bureaucracy around him, and emperors were closer to the military than to the civilian hierarchy. Generals were more likely than senior administrators to have risen from nowhere, especially if they came from frontier regions, as was very common; the Rhine frontier and the Balkan frontier in particular were heavily militarized societies, with less and less social distance between the Roman and the 'barbarian' sides of the border, as we shall see later in this chapter. This did not make them so very different from the civilian élites, as long as they were successful, as they could end up with senatorial position, civilian clients and a literary education for their children. But military leaders were less dedicated to expensive prestige buildings or the patronage of games, and senators regularly looked down on them for their lack of culture. Soldiers also moved around more than civilians did. The historian Ammianus (d. c. 395), a Greek-speaker who wrote in Latin, the language of the army, was an ex-soldier who had served on both the Persian and the Rhine frontiers, as well as spending much time in Rome.

The scale of the army and its presence everywhere, and the need to keep it properly provisioned and equipped, made it the major concern of the whole Roman state. The state had a developed system of frontier fortifications and its own food-supply lines: the distribution of oil amphorae along the lower Danube, for example, shows that the army there was supplied from the Aegean into the late sixth century. It also had its own factories for military equipment, of which thirty-five are listed, distributed all across the empire, in the *Notitia Dignitatum*, an account of the imperial military structure dating to the end of the fourth century. Perhaps a half of the entire imperial budget went on feeding and paying the army, and the logistics of army supply were the single most important element that linked all the imperial provinces together, along with the permanent need to feed the imperial capitals.

Underpinning all these structures, and making them possible, was the imperial tax system, which was based above all on a land tax, assessed on acreage, though also buttressed by a much lighter tax on merchants and artisans, by the revenues from imperial lands and by a variety of smaller dues. In recent years some historians have reacted against an earlier image of the 'coercive state' of the late empire, taxing so heavily that land was abandoned and the economy began to break down; this revision is correct, but they seem to me to have gone too far in their arguments. Taxation does seem to have been very heavy overall: in the sixth century a small number of sources, mostly from Egypt, converge in showing that a quarter of the yield of land could go in tax, and it was more in times of extra taxation (*superindictiones*) which was assessed on top of the main tax burden. This is a very high figure for a precapitalist, agrarian society, with a relatively simple technology. But the high taxes were needed to pay the salaries of all those soldiers, bureaucrats and messengers, and to feed the capitals; they were needed to fund the enormous scale of Roman public buildings and state wealth. They also connected the different parts of the empire together physically, as grain moved northwards from Africa, Sicily and Egypt, and olive oil moved out of Africa, the Aegean and Syria, in ships themselves commandeered by the state (shipowners moved goods for the state as part of their tax liability). This movement of goods was essentially Mediterranean-based, as it was far easier and cheaper to transport in bulk by water than by land; Gaul, the Rhineland and Britain formed a smaller and separate network, and inland Spain, far from both sea and frontiers, seems to have been somewhat marginal. The core of the empire remained Mediterranean, and it, at least, or, rather, its two halves, were unified by the fiscal movement of goods.

A land tax cannot work properly, especially when it is high, unless assessment is accurate and collection systematic. This takes work. The state has to have up-to-date records about who owns the land; these are not easy to obtain systematically (and no easier to keep in order for easy reference), and establishing them requires a considerable amount of personnel and intrusive information-gathering. Land sales had to be publicly registered in the late empire for this reason, and such registrations can sometimes be found in the rare collections of private documents from the late empire, usually papyri from Egypt, although a few texts do survive elsewhere. And, most important, from the fourth century onwards the government issued laws to tie the peasantry, who were actually paying the taxes, to their place of origin, so that they would not move around or leave the land, thus making tax-collection more difficult. These laws were part of a general legislative package aimed at ensuring that people essential to the state stayed in their professions, and that their heirs would do so too. *Curiales* were tied to their offices, as we have seen; so were soldiers, and the workers in state factories; so were shipowners and the bakers and butchers of Rome, who were essential for the *annona* of the capital. Even if this network of laws was regularly obeyed, which we can doubt, they make up a large proportion of the imperial codes, and they were generated by the need to stabilize the tax infrastructure of the empire. Add to that the actual collection of taxes, which could be a tense and violent moment, and was certainly undertaken by armed men, and the impact of the imperial fiscal system was continuous, capillary and potentially coercive of nearly everybody in the empire.

This intrusiveness was made worse by illegality. The rich could buy immunity corruptly; assessors and collectors certainly got rich corruptly. The victims were almost always the poor. They responded by fleeing the land (hence the laws tying them down), or by seeking protection from the powerful against having to pay taxes to the state. There are also laws against such patronage, although we have seen that patronage, too, was a stable part of the Roman political system. Most taxes were, it is true, probably paid regularly and even legally; it is striking that the Egyptian papyrus archive of the sixth-century Apion family, then one of the richest families of the Greek East and overwhelmingly dominant in their home town, the city of Oxyrhynchos (modern Bahnasa), shows them paying taxes in a very routine manner. But given the weight of tax, and the endemic injustice that marked the Roman system, it is not surprising that corruption should focus on it. Social critics, more numerous as the empire went Christian and a radical fringe of moralists gained a voice, very frequently stress fiscal oppression in their invective; only judicial corruption and sexual behaviour were as prominent. This would last as long as the empire.

Taxation thus underpinned imperial unity itself, for it was the most evident single element in the state's impact on the population at large, as well as the mainstay of the army, the administration, the legal system and the movement of goods throughout the Mediterranean and else-where, all the elements which linked such a large land area together. If it failed, the empire would simply break up. But in fact the empire broke up for other reasons, as we shall see in Chapter 4. After it did so, taxation was a casualty in the West, but survived in the East. This contrast cannot be underestimated, and it underpins many of the events described in later sections of this book. All the same, fiscal breakdown was not yet predictable in 400, or even 500 in some places. In 400 the stability, and relative homogeneity, of the imperial system was not yet seen by anyone to be at risk.

So far, we have focused on the state, and the imperial political system in general. Local differences have been downplayed, and our vision has been top-down, seen from the viewpoint of administrators and the rich. Let us now look at the rest of the population, and at some of the regional differences which we can pin down in the late Roman empire.

The first thing to be stated is that the population of the empire consisted overwhelmingly of peasants: families of cultivators, who worked the land they owned or rented, and who lived off the food they themselves produced, as well as giving surpluses to landlords (if they had them) in rent, and in tax to the state. Many of them were *servi*, unfree with no legal rights, particularly in parts of the West, but the plantation slavery of early imperial Italy and Greece had almost entirely vanished by the late empire, and free and unfree peasants by now all lived their lives in similar ways. (This book will as a result not use the word 'slaves' for unfree peasants, as it is misleading; the word will be used only for unfree domestic servants, who were fed and maintained by their masters as plantation slaves had been.) In the early Middle Ages, peasants made up 90 per cent or more of the population; the proportion must have been less in the late empire, as more people lived in towns – in Egypt, exceptionally, up to a third of the total population – but could have been as much as 80 per cent, still an extremely high proportion.

Most peasants were probably the tenants of landlords. Legislators certainly assumed so, for their laws tying peasants to the land were directed to *coloni*, the standard Latin word for tenant. The huge estates of the emperor and of Roman senators, and the even greater collective landed wealth of all the provincial and curial élites, also presupposed the existence of millions of dependent tenants who supplied their rents. This was often through middlemen, *conductores*, who leased whole estates from the great landowners; but some of the latter paid considerable attention to managing their own estates for profit, such as the Apions in sixth-century Egypt, and Palladius, the estate-management manualist, in fifth-century Italy. Unfortunately, our evidence is not good enough to tell us how often, and where, peasants owned their own land. Egyptian papyri show that some city territories were dominated by owners of large estates, but others had a substantial landowning peasantry and much more autonomy. A good example is the territory of the large village of Aphrodito (modern Kom Ishqaw), from which many sixth-century documents survive, as we shall see shortly. The still standing late Roman villages of Syria and other parts of the eastern Mediterranean show in the best preserved cases (such as in the Limestone Massif of northern Syria: see below, Chapter 10) an architectural ambition and a homogeneity of house types that is difficult to square with tenurial dependence; there are few visible estate centres, in particular. It is generally thought, therefore, that these villages mostly belonged to independent owners.

Overall, it seems that there were more peasant owners in the East than the West, which also fits the fact that fewer hyper-rich landowners are known of in the East. In the West, by contrast, much of Italy and Africa in particular and parts of Gaul were probably dominated by landowners, and we know of more estates which included large areas; one of Melania and Pinianus' estates in Africa was 'larger than the city itself', that is to say, the city territory of the nearest town, Thagaste. (In Africa, where not all dioceses were based in towns, some estates were so substantial that they had their own bishops.) But in both West and East, even large estates were normally highly fragmented and scattered, and many consisted of hundreds or thousands of separate land parcels; there was plenty of space for peasant owners and village-level élites to exist in between them. Some tenants owned land as well, and the laws on tax-paying distinguish between *coloni* who owned some land, who paid taxes directly to collectors, and *coloni* who owned none (called *adscripticii*), who paid taxes through their landlords. The latter were much more dependent, more similar to unfree tenants (who did not pay tax: their lords paid it directly); Justinian, indeed, in one of his laws, wondered what real difference there was between *servi* and *adscripticii*. The answer probably varied regionally: tenure was certainly more flexible in Egypt, where leases were shorter, more peasants owned land, there was more wage labour and rural unfreedom was very rare; in Italy, by contrast, there were whole estates with only unfree tenants, and rural subjection was probably greater overall.

One real difference between East and West was that peasants lived in villages much more often in the East. Some of the villages still stand, as just noted, at least in marginal areas where the land has since been abandoned to pasture or desert. But documents and archaeology both show that villages (*komai* or *chōria*) were normal in most of the Greek-speaking world, and they could be tightly organized, with their own headmen, as in particular in Egypt. Owners and tenants lived side by side in these villages, and peasant society was, simply for that reason, relatively coherent and autonomous (eastern landed aristocrats, as we have seen, normally lived in towns), as well as potentially more fraught, as village factions fought over pasture and water rights, or over the pecking-order between the successful and the less successful that existed in every village. We know so much about the Egyptian village of Aphrodito because we have the papyrus archive of Dioskoros, son of Apollos (lived *c.* 520–85), who was a fairly well-off village leader there: he was sometimes its headman, as his father had been. Dioskoros had a literary and legal education, probably in Alexandria, and became a local notary when he returned; more unusually, he was also a poet, and wrote praise poems to local dukes and other officials. He is interesting for a variety of reasons. He is the best-documented village-dweller of the whole late empire; but his personal character comes across in the sources as well. Although he was certainly from the local élite, he felt threatened on all sides: by the governor of the nearest city, Antaiopolis, jealous of Aphrodito's autonomy; and by neighbours, tenants, shepherds and creditors in his own village. We have some of his lawsuits; his poems, too, often end with pleas for help; they were transactions in his extensive patron–client network. Aphrodito was not a peaceful village. We even have a double-murder investigation by a senior military official, in which the senatorial aristocrat Sarapammon and his associate, the soldier Menas, defend themselves and accuse the villagers themselves of the crime. It is clear, however, that no single person could control it, and keep down its tensions. Aphrodito was only united when it faced off other villages and threats from Antaiopolis. These fractious societies were typical of the East.

The West was different. Here, villages were rarer, except in some mountain zones; instead, as much archaeology shows, the countryside was scattered with isolated farms and the rural villas or estate-centres of major landowners. Even the concept of the village territory was hardly present in most places; land was simply identified by its owner, and most estates had their own names. We do not have Egyptian levels of documentation here, so it is hard to tell how rural societies worked, but it is likely that they were less coherent than in the East, for there was less to bind them together. Probably the tenants of single estates had something to link them, the common experience of paying rent to a landlord or *conductor*; this did not match the coherence of village life, but it could increase local tensions. The gap between the powerful and the poor was in general wider in much of the West, in fact, and we can sometimes see its results.

One example comes from Augustine's Africa. Augustine, as bishop of Hippo, appointed his monk Antoninus in the 410s to be bishop of a subordinate diocese at Fussala, one of Africa's relatively few villages, in the hills of what is now eastern Algeria. Antoninus turned out to be a bad man – he was young and from a poor family, he was promoted too fast – and he terrorized his village, extorting money, clothing, produce and building materials. He was also accused of sexual assault. Augustine removed him, but did not depose him, and tried to transfer him to the nearby estate of Thogonoetum. Here, the tenants told Augustine and their landowner that they would leave if he came. Antoninus caused no end of trouble, even appealing to the pope in Rome (this being the context in which two surviving letters were written about him by Augustine, in 422–3). Augustine was very embarrassed, as indeed he should have been ('I did not dare look the people of Fussala in the eye'). It is interesting, however, how scared the peasants were: in their angry and bitter witnessing, even after Antoninus' removal, they would not give their names. The people of Fussala included tenants (who were interrogated without their *conductores* being present, to try to get them to relax), but probably not all of them were dependent; it is interesting, conversely, that the *coloni* of Thogonoetum were more prepared to resist Antoninus than were the villagers – illegally, too, for they were of course tied to the land by law. All the same, peasant protagonism here seems largely negative, marked by bitterness, fear and rejection. There was too much separation in this part of Africa between peasants and landlords, and more hostility between them as a result; there was no Dioskoros to mediate between the peasants and the authorities. It is not surprising that Augustine's main fear was that the peasants would revert to the Donatist church (see Chapter 3), abandoning Catholic Christianity altogether.

Another element that was very different from place to place were the patterns of commercial exchange and artisan production. Three decades of archaeology have led to a major revaluation of late Roman commerce, which as late as the 1970s was thought to be marginal to the economy. On archaeological sites, the density of finds of amphorae (which carried wine, oil and fish sauce above all, that is, food products) and fine pottery (a guide to other large-scale artisanal products such as cloth and metalwork) allows us to say which areas of the empire were major exporters, and where their products typically went. North African Red Slip tableware is found all over the late Roman Mediterranean; similar tableware from Phocaea on the Turkish Aegean coast and Cyprus matches it in the eastern Mediterranean as well. It evidently travelled by sea, but can be found quite far inland in Italy and in Syria and Palestine. In northern Gaul and Britain and in inland Spain it was not available in more than tiny quantities, but large-scale local production is found instead; for this reason above all we can say that those areas, although active, were separate from the main Mediterranean economic network. Cloth, always the main artisanal product, is not easy to identify archaeologically, but literary sources (including the detailed lists in the imperial *Price Edict* of 301) show that Italy, Gaul, Egypt and Syria were among the major exporters. Amphorae allow us to add African, Syrian and Aegean oil, and south Italian, Palestinian and Aegean wine. These were large-scale distribution networks, and the commodities concerned were evidently produced on a large scale as well. Indeed, the African (that is to say, above all, Tunisian) and coastal Syrian/Palestinian economies probably depended substantially on exports for their prosperity. Internally, too, the complexity of the economies of southern Italy, the Aegean, Egypt and Palestine in particular, seems to show a dense network of inter-city and city–country exchange.

We have already seen that some parts of the empire sent much of their surplus in tax to other areas: Africa, Egypt and to a lesser extent Syria, Palestine and the Aegean. These provinces were probably in agricultural terms the richest in the empire (the climate was then much as it is today, global warming apart); and they are mostly prominent in these commercial networks as well. It would certainly be wrong to see the archaeological distributions as signs of the tax network only; they extend to too many insignificant places for that to be the case, such as tiny settlements in central Italy or eastern Palestine. But it is likely, all the same, that commercial exchange was underwritten by the tax network. Ships left Africa for Italy every autumn, bringing state grain and oil to Rome as *annona*; doubtless they took commercial goods as well, ceramics and once again oil, the transport costs of which were thus covered by the state, and which could be sold on the other side of the Mediterranean more competitively, whether in Rome or in other ports. Egypt's commercial exports are less well known, but they probably consisted above all of cloth and papyrus, which archaeology does not pick up (Egyptian wine production was enormous in the late empire, but was of low quality, and was for consumption within Egypt only). The tax network made commerce easier, and also contributed to the commercial prominence of certain regions. When the empire began to lose its fiscal homogeneity in the West, which was when the Vandals seized the heartland of North Africa in 439, breaking the Carthage–Rome tax spine, western Mediterranean commerce began two centuries of steady involution; but the East remained politically and fiscally strong, and eastern Mediterranean commerce was as active in 600 as in 400.

The late Roman world always maintained a double face, local and imperial. Latin and Greek were far from its only languages. Proto-Welsh was spoken in Britain, Basque in parts of Spain, Berber in Africa, Coptic in Egypt, Hebrew, Arabic and Aramaic/Syriac in the Levant, Isaurian and Armenian in Anatolia, and there were doubtless other languages too. Coptic, Hebrew, Syriac and Armenian had their own literatures. Local societies were at least as different then as they are now, in the range of realities that stretch from the Welsh mountains to the Egyptian desert, both as a result of their necessary adaptations to the huge differences in local ecology, and as a result of the more human-made contrasts discussed in the last few pages. On the other hand, the Roman world not only held together but increased many aspects of its cohesiveness with time. Christianization swept away many local religious traditions, as we shall see in the next chapter. Cities looked remarkably similar, in their public buildings and their layout, in different parts of the empire. The administration and the army had the same overarching structure everywhere, and the tax system affected everybody. Some cultural differences were lessening: Gaul, for example, lost its local language, Gaulish, perhaps in the fifth century. Egypt, in particular, was much less atypical in its society and culture in the fourth and fifth centuries than it had been in the first and second; it had ceased to use its huge temple complexes and had abandoned their Pharaonic architectural style, and had even deserted its traditional beer-drinking in favour of wine. People felt themselves to be part of a single Roman world, an awareness which extended not only to city élites but even into villages, for Antoninus of Fussala had appealed to the pope in Rome for support against Augustine, and the villagers of Aphrodito appealed to the empress Theodora herself for support against the governor of Antaiopolis.

This awareness of a wider community is linked in our sources, over and over again, with patronage. The patron–client relationship has existed in most societies (the lord–vassal bond of the central Middle Ages is an example), but Roman culture laid immense stress on it. Seeking help from a patron, alongside official channels, was normal. It could be stigmatized as corrupt, but often only by extreme moralists, or else by victims; most people, however, accepted its day-to-day logic. Actually, even the official channels were often expressed in patron–client terms, as with personal or collective appeals to the emperor, which were commonplace, or as with the endless, and legal, personal payments (*sportulae*) which were expected by low- and medium-level bureaucrats who might either facilitate or obstruct tax registration or a court case. The point about a patronage system of this kind is that in the end it involves everybody, and everybody can feel they somehow have a stake in the social system. They will often not get anything out of it, as with the average peasant, but they feel that they can get an element of protection from patrons, if not this time then the next. Everyone except the emperor and his most powerful subordinates needed a patron, and sometimes many. They boasted about it, too, as when John Lydos was fast-tracked as a trainee administrator by the praetorian prefect Zotikos, who was from the same province as him, and did not even have to buy his appointment. Similarly, everyone with even a modicum of local power, from Dioskoros upwards, had clients. Abinnaios, a medium-level soldier stationed in southern Egypt in the 340s, whose archive also survives, preserved requests for special favours from his subordinates, but also from friends and clients who were city councillors, priests, artisans or peasants; he was asked to arbitrate disputes, and to apprehend robbers. Little of this was in his official remit, but it was totally normal. The Antiochene intellectual Libanios was outraged in the 390s when his tenants sought a military patron to protect them against paying him rent; he claimed that their main patron should be their landlord, but anyone in his audience would have known that was specious. A great part of the elegant letters that the educated élite wrote to each other consisted of or included recommendations for clients or requests for help. So did Dioskoros' poetry, as we have seen. Far from 'corruption' being an element of Roman weakness, this vast network of favours was one of the main elements that made the empire work. It was when patronage failed that there was trouble. Peasants in Africa who felt that the Catholic church's patronage was unavailable to them could turn to Donatism. When peasants in Egypt who had used patrons to lift some of their tax burdens in difficult years felt that this did not work, they would flee; and when the new Arab government after 640 excluded traditional rural patrons from political influence, as we shall see later, in Chapter 12, they could revolt. Above all, perhaps, when local élites in the fifth-century West ceased to believe that their traditional patrons in central and provincial government were capable of helping them, they could turn to the new military leaders of 'barbarian' tribes in their localities instead, and a major political shift resulted. We shall look at the causes and consequences of that shift in Chapter 4.

The Roman world was surrounded by 'others', whom Romans regarded with varying degrees of contempt and incomprehension, but who interacted with them in complex ways. To the east, there was always Persia, the great sister empire of west-central Eurasia, ruled between the 220s and the 640s by the Sassanian dynasty. This was a permanent threat, but a stable one: it involved only border wars, at most extending into Syria, for the two hundred and fifty years between Julian's disastrous invasion of what is now Iraq (then Persia's economic and political heartland) in 363 and the temporary Persian conquest of the Roman East in 614–28, which culminated in the siege of Constantinople in 626. The Persian state was almost as large as the Roman empire, extending eastwards into central Asia and what is now Afghanistan; it is much less well documented than the Roman empire, but it, too, was held together by a complex tax system, although it had a powerful military aristocracy as well, unlike Rome. The militarization of Persian culture extended west into Armenia, which Romans and Persians fought over but which remained partly independent and culturally separate. The Armenians converted to Christianity in the fourth century, which separated them further from the Persians, who were Zoroastrian for the most part (although with sizeable Jewish and Christian minorities, and also local traditional religions). Zoroastrianism certainly contributed to Persian 'strangeness' in the eyes of the Romans; for example, its priests, called *magoi* in Greek or *magi* in Latin, gave their name to 'magic' in both languages, even though Zoroastrian religion favoured an abstract theology and public rituals, just as Christianity did. But it was arguably Persia's military culture and enormous respect for ancient dynastic tradition that marked it out as most culturally different from Rome, for the Roman sense of kinship could link far-flung cousins and cousins-in-law in patronage networks, but even 'old' families rarely had more than a century or two of prominence. The dynastic element helped Persian traditions survive better than Roman traditions when both were swept away, from Carthage to Samarkand, by the Arabs in the seventh century.

Rome's other borders were shared with far less organized political groups, all of which the Romans called *barbari*, 'barbarians', a conveniently vague term which I shall adopt (keeping the inverted commas) as well. To the south they faced nomadic and semi-nomadic tribes in the Sahara and its fringes, mostly speaking Berber languages; for a long time these were not taken very seriously as military threats, but such groups were gaining in social and military coherence, largely as a result of Roman influence, and one tribal alliance, the Laguatan, was very aggressive at the start of the fifth century, as Synesios in Cyrenaica, among others, complains; the Vandals in Africa had trouble with Berbers later, too. The Picts and the Irish to the north and west of Britain were also a potential threat, although only to the already militarized British borderlands, especially around Hadrian's Wall (they staged a substantial invasion in 367–8). The long Rhine and Danube frontier faced tribal communities, mostly speaking Germanic languages, which historians since Tacitus in the first century had seen as a whole as *Germani*, although there is no evidence whatsoever that these peoples recognized any common bonds. The main groups along the frontier were by the fourth century the Franks on the lower Rhine, the Alemans on the middle and upper Rhine, and the Goths on the lower Danube and north-eastwards into the steppes of what is now Ukraine. Further back were Frisians in the modern Netherlands, Saxons in modern north

Germany, and Vandals and Longobards or Lombards to their east. These were the main groups, but there were dozens of others. The Quadi in what is now Slovakia and Hungary are perhaps worth mentioning, if only because, after they fought a small war against Valentinian I in 374–5, they met the emperor and argued (correctly, in fact) that their own attacks were a justified and largely defensive response to Roman aggression: this was seen by Valentinian as so insolent that he had an apoplectic fit and died. One might have a soft spot for the Quadi as a result, but they vanish from history soon afterwards: they must have been absorbed into the Hunnic empire in the early fifth century, which was based in the same area, and their probable descendants in the fifth century were called Suevi and perhaps also Rugi.

The transformation of the Quadi is only one example out of many of one crucial feature of all these tribal communities: they were very changeable. For a start, none of them were united ethnic groups; they all consisted of smaller tribes, each with a separate leader (as with the half a dozen Gothic groups, even though the Goths were among the most coherently organized of the Germanic peoples). Historians have indeed sometimes argued that some Germanic tribes had no permanent leadership at all, only generals in times of war. This latter pattern seems less likely (if only because war was pretty common); more plausible is that war encouraged the temporary development of alliances or confederations of separate tiny tribes, each with its own permanent leader, but choosing a temporary leader for that confederation. This at least fits the Alemans of the 350s–370s described by Ammianus, whose seven kings (*reges*) united under Chnodomar and his nephew Serapio to fight Julian in 357, but the latter were also flanked by ten lesser leaders, *regales*, and aristocrats as well, 'from various *nationes*'. Did all of these *nationes* even think of themselves as 'Aleman', or is this, like 'German', just a Roman term for a much more inchoate reality? We cannot be sure, but, if the latter was so, this would at least explain the frequent name changes of the major peoples the Romans described. The problem is, of course, that the Romans wrote our only written sources (the only certainly Gothic source is Ulfilas' Gothic translation of the New Testament, although the *Passion of Saba*, about an early Christian martyr in the Gothic lands who died in 372, may have been written by a Goth too). Roman ethnography was never reliable, and was usually highly moralized, with 'barbarians', naturally inferior but often noble in their savagery, acting as a mirror for the faults of the Romans themselves. It is highly unlikely that even Ammianus, although present on the Rhine in 357, had more than second-hand information about Aleman society and practices, and other observers were further removed still.

Certain things can nevertheless be said about the 'barbarian' groups, partly thanks to written sources, partly thanks to archaeology. The northern and southern neighbours of Rome were all mixed-farming peasant societies (except for the Sahara nomads), living for the most part in villages, with élites generally living side by side with cultivators. They were settled and stable societies; they did not normally move about. They seem, however, in all cases to be better organized by the fourth century than they had been in the early empire. The archaeology shows the slow development of material cultural differences between regions (unfortunately, we have no way of knowing if these mapped onto the ethnic distinctions between Franks, Alemans, Goths, etc., and this is in my view unlikely), and, most important, increasing concentrations of wealth: the rich in the Germanic world, and we can add the Berber world as well, were becoming richer, thus presumably showing that power was slowly becoming more stable too. This was largely the simple result of contact with the Roman empire, which was vastly more wealthy and powerful than any 'barbarian' group. A substantial proportion of the artefacts in rich graves beyond the frontier in the fourth century are of Roman manufacture, as far north as Denmark. The Romans traded beyond the frontiers; they also employed 'barbarians' as paid soldiers, in every century. As the 'barbarians' became better organized, they also became more dangerous, and the Romans had to defend themselves more carefully against them. A long frontier region developed on the northern boundaries of the empire, in which militarization was capillary, affecting much wider strata of society than was the case elsewhere: northern Gaul and the Balkans were the largest such frontier regions, but there were smaller ones elsewhere too. As 'barbarians' were used in the army and often settled in the empire, at the same time as hierarchies developed under Roman influence beyond the frontiers, society on each side of the frontier slowly became more similar: there may not have been so very much difference on one level between Valentinian, himself from the Pannonian frontier in modern Hungary, and the leaders of the neighbouring Quadi whose bold reply killed him.

This type of observation has been used by some recent historians as the basis for an argument that nothing really changed when the 'barbarians' entered the Roman empire in the fifth century and replaced its western half with their own kingdoms. Emperors had long been drawn largely from military families on the frontier; the successor states had kings of a similar type, only from just beyond the frontier. This is a better argument than the traditional one that waves of migrating Germans overbore the weakened (because barbarized) Roman army and state; but it does go too far, all the same. There was a major *political* difference between each side of the frontier: on one side Romans ruled, on the other they did not. Julian and Valentinian could attack Alemans and Quadi precisely because they were not under Roman rule, and the latter saw themselves as structurally different from Romans, something that did not change when they invaded. Conversely, the soldiers of 'barbarian' origin largely deracinated themselves when they joined the army. Take Silvanus, a Frank by origin according to Ammianus, who was a Roman general in the 350s, as his father had been. Silvanus was falsely accused of treason in a piece of palace intrigue in 355, when based at Cologne on the Rhine frontier. He wondered what to do. Should he flee to the neighbouring Franks, his kin? He was dissuaded from this, on the grounds that the Franks would kill or betray him; he claimed the empire instead, as army leaders had often done in the past. This failed, and Ammianus was himself instrumental in having him killed. It would have been easy for Ammianus to depict Silvanus as an untrustworthy and perhaps savage outsider (he does so on other occasions, as with the Romanized Berber aristocrat Firmus, who becomes 'barbaric' when he revolts in 373). But Ammianus was instead sympathetic to Silvanus' plight, and paints him simply as a Roman soldier, and as both politically and culturally separate from the Franks beyond the Rhine; Silvanus' army training had seen to that. The major military politicians of 'barbarian' extraction who were important in late fourth-century politics, such as the Frank Arbogast (d. 394) and the half-Vandal Stilicho (d. 408), both of whom were de-facto heads of state, were similar: they were career soldiers, and operated in an entirely Roman political arena. This was normal in fourth-century politics. It was the politics of the fifth century, when some 'barbarian' military leaders fought for Rome at the head of substantial bodies of troops from their own communities, and who called themselves Goths or Franks rather than Romans, that was often different.

In the 370s the Huns appeared in the East, a nomadic people from central Asia. Ammianus depicts them in very hostile and impossibly schematic terms, as hardly human, eating raw flesh, never entering houses, living on horseback, and without rulers: the classic uncivilized 'others'. They were good fighters, all the same. They may not have been a single political group in the 370s (although they became one, for a generation under Attila, between the 430s and 454). But they destroyed the rule of at least one of the Gothic tribes, Ermenric's Greuthungi, in or before 375, and menaced others. As nomads, they were as alien to the Goths as to the Romans. As a result, the majority of another Gothic tribe, the Tervingi, sought entry to the Roman empire in 376, and so did other sections of the Goths, although others stayed north of the Danube and slowly accepted Hunnic hegemony. 'Barbarian' tribes had invaded the empire often enough in the preceding two centuries; usually they ravaged sections of one of the military zones, the Balkans and northern Gaul, and were then defeated and enslaved, absorbed or driven back. Submissive requests for entry were rarer, and the Romans, including the eastern emperor Valens (364–78), Valentinian's brother, were not sure how to handle this. They accepted the request, and the Goths, immigrating into the eastern Balkans, became in the following decades 'Arian' Christians, the variant Christianity of both their early missionary Ulfilas and, to a lesser extent, Valens himself. But Roman suspicion remained. The Goths were deprived of supplies, and soon revolted under their leader Fritigern; and Valens, underestimating them, was defeated and killed at Adrianople (modern Edirne in European Turkey) in 378. The Goths did not manage to build on this, for they were too few and in a strategically weak position, and they accepted peace in 382. By 394 they were fighting in the east Roman army, against a western usurper put up by Arbogast. But they did not become 'Roman', and remained as a separate ethnic grouping, the first group inside the empire to do so.

This sort of interpenetration became steadily more common, in particular after a larger number of 'barbarian' groups invaded the empire in 405–6, probably as a result of the steady development of Hunnic power. This did not by any means have to be inimical to Roman power structures and in the East was not; but political errors in handling 'barbarians', like those of Valens, continued after his death, and these would be more problematic. We shall see in Chapter 4 how strategic ineptness in the face of a steadily changing political situation in the end helped to sink the western half of the empire. But the stability discussed in this chapter was not illusory, all the same, and many of the political and social patterns described here lasted long into the early medieval world.

3

Culture and Belief in the Christian Roman World

In the late 460s, as Sidonius Apollinaris related to a friend, the bishops of Lyon and Autun had the task of choosing and consecrating a new bishop of Chalon-sur-Saône. There were three candidates, unnamed, one claiming the office because his family was old, one who had built up support in the city by feeding people, and one who promised church lands to supporters. The bishops instead chose the holy cleric John, who had slowly moved up the local church hierarchy, thus confounding local factions. Sidonius himself was not yet bishop of Clermont; when he became so, one of his first tasks was to hold a similar election at Bourges, in 470. Here, although there were again numerous candidates, many of the citizens wanted Simplicius, a local notable from a senatorial family. Sidonius, initially wary of their choice, warmed to him, and preserved his speech to the citizens on the subject, which said, in (considerably shortened) paraphrase: If I choose a monk, you will say he is too other-worldly; if I choose a cleric, many will think I should choose only by seniority [as had happened at Chalon, in effect]; if I choose a lay official, you will say I have chosen someone like myself. But I do have to make a choice; many of you may be *episcopales*, worthy of being bishop, but you cannot all be. So I choose Simplicius, a layman, but one whose family is full of both bishops and prefects – and so is his wife's – and who has defended the city's interests before both Roman and 'barbarian' leaders. So Sidonius did indeed, in this second election, choose someone just like himself, a local secular married aristocrat. The office of bishop in Gaul was becoming a standard part of a secular career progression for city notables, just as the pagan priesthood had been before; the traditional hierarchy of the Roman world had effectively absorbed the new power-structures of Christianity. And yet it was not universally so; Sidonius' own enthusiastic support for the election of

John of Chalon, in the teeth of local notables, shows that it did sometimes remain possible to use different criteria to those of wealth and
birth in the church hierarchy. Christianity was substantially absorbed
into traditional Roman values, but never entirely.

A slightly more combative example of the same point is Synesios of
Cyrene, who was recommended as bishop of neighbouring Ptolemais
in 411 to Theophilos, patriarch of Alexandria. Synesios was another
secular local notable, like both Sidonius and Simplicius; he both represented Cyrenaica in Constantinople, successfully seeking tax relief for
the province, and organized local defence against Berbers; he was the
kind of useful man who would be very valuable as bishop as well, and
he was active in that role in the two years or so before his death, as we
saw in Chapter 2. Synesios, however, was also a skilled Neoplatonist
philosopher, with numerous writings to his credit, so steeped in the
classical philosophical tradition that people have wondered if he was
even Christian (though he surely was), and not only trained by the
renowned pagan mathematician and Neoplatonist Hypatia in Alexandria, but a close personal friend of hers, as his letters show. Theophilos
for his part was a hardliner, who had had Alexandria's most famous
pagan temple, the Sarapaion, destroyed in 391; his successor Cyril's
mob would indeed lynch Hypatia in 415. Synesios nonetheless wrote an
extraordinary open letter before his ordination, stating his philosophical
and moral values. He would not renounce his wife; they would continue
to sleep together, hoping for children. 'As for the Resurrection, an object
of common belief, I consider it a sacred and mysterious concept, about
which I do not at all agree with the views of the majority.' The world
was not due to end, either. Philosophy would remain his private calling
if he was consecrated, whatever untruths he said in public, and Theophilos must know this. We are not here in the sometimes intellectually
provincial world of Gaul, but in the harsh heartland of violent and
uncompromising religious debate. Theophilos consecrated Synesios all
the same. Local status and support counted in Alexandria as much as in
central Gaul, if it was strong enough at any rate.

The Roman empire was by no means fully Christian yet in 400. There
were pagan aristocrats in Rome still, although perhaps not by 450; in
Constantinople there were still some a century later. There were pagan
teachers in Athens and Alexandria until the sixth century (Justinian
closed the Athens school in 529), and some smaller cities, notably

Baalbek and Harran in Syria, probably had pagan majorities. The countryside, that is, most of the population, was largely pagan everywhere except in Syria, Palestine, Egypt and Africa, and there were plenty of pagans in these provinces too. They continued for some time; we have an account by John of Ephesos of his active mission work in Anatolia in the mid-sixth century. There were also substantial Jewish communities in Galilee and Samaria in Palestine, in Syria and the Euphrates valley, in western Anatolia, in north-eastern Spain, in Alexandria, Rome, and in smaller groups in most cities of the empire; these were politically marginal, but less subject to official persecution in this period than later. But all the emperors, except Julian for three years, had been Christian since 324 (Constantine converted in 312, but he did not rule the whole empire for more than a decade). Steadily across the fourth century paganism had become separated from public life, and in 391–2 Theodosius I had banned the mainstays of much traditional paganism, public sacrifice and the private worship of images. This coercive legislation was further reinforced in the fifth century, and Justinian added the finishing touches, banning pagan cults and enforcing baptism on pain of confiscation and sometimes execution. As with laws on Christian heresy (see below), this was never more than partly effective – pagan festivals continued even in major Christian centres like Edessa in the late fifth century – but the exclusion of paganism from the official Roman world was by now complete.

Christian vocabulary, imagery and public practice were thus politically dominant in the empire by 400, a dominance which would only increase thereafter; and in cities, which were the foci for almost all political activity, Christians were for the most part numerically dominant as well. But we must ask what sort of Christianity this was, what effective content it had: how much it absorbed traditional Roman values (and even religious practices), how far it changed them, and what its own fault-lines were, for there were many of these. The first part of this chapter will be concerned with these issues, essentially those of religious belief and practice; the second part will extend the frame more widely, and look at other rituals in the public sphere, and at more deep-seated values, including assumptions about gender roles.

Christianity by 400 was on one level simply defined, as the religion of the New Testament; if one believed in the divine Trinity of the Father, Son and Holy Spirit, and if one believed that Jesus Christ, crucified in around AD 33, was the Son of God, and that no other gods existed, then one was Christian. These beliefs generally went together with an exaltation of poverty – for the good Christian ought to give everything to the poor – and a presumption that this world was only a brief testing ground before the eternal joys of heaven or the eternal tortures of hell, which meant that pleasure was risky, and that asceticism, sometimes self-mortification, was increasingly seen as virtuous. But it has never been the case that most Christians have taken the second of these sentences as seriously as the first; and this presents a problem for us. When looking at the question of what sort of Christianity we are dealing with, whether in this period or later, we immediately run into the question of source material. The huge quantity of Christian writing after 350 or so substantially outweighs in quantity the work of late Roman secular élites (even though this survives quite generously from the fourth to the sixth centuries), but was almost entirely the work of men who were much more rigorist than their neighbours. The degree of rigour varied, from the relative pragmatism of an Augustine, through the more uncompromising denunciations of a Jerome or a Salvian, to the extreme purism, separated from the possibility of normal emulation, implied in the hagiographical accounts of ascetic saints, such as Antony or Simon the Stylite. All of these, nonetheless, were highly critical of the more easygoing but still Christian world around them; and the aim of all such writers was to reform by criticism, rather than to describe accurately. It is therefore not always easy to tell if people ever did the things that were criticized, let alone how common such actions were, or, least of all, what sense these actions made to the people who performed them. Between the comfortable assimilation of traditional hierarchies and values into Christianity by a secular-minded aristocracy, such as that of Sidonius, and the rigorism of a minority of more committed authors – not always a popular or influential minority, either – there was an ocean of different kinds of religious practice carried out by everyone else, whose meaning has to be guessed at through the accounts of hostile observers.

Take festivals. Traditional Graeco-Roman religion had a year studded with major religious festivals, which Christians naturally opposed. An important one was the First of January, a three-day festival marking the changing of the year. The traditional sacrifices associated with this were banned, but did this make the festival religiously neutral, simply marking pleasure and civic solidarity, for Christians as well? It seems clear that people generally thought so, but a stream of Christian writers, including the authors of sermons preached in public, were violently opposed to it – not least because it was competition for Christmas (itself, ironically, the direct replacement of a pagan festival, the Winter Solstice), but also because it was irredeemably tainted with paganism in their minds. The First of January survived as a festival into the eighth century and later, but whether it was perceived by ordinary people as Christian, or secular, or pagan, and when and how much, we do not know. Bishops dealt with festivals of this kind above all by organizing their own, thus creating the Christian religious calendar, with its focus on Christmas, then Lent, then Easter and Pentecost, above all December to May, extended across the rest of the year by local saint's-day celebrations. This did indeed in the end win out over the pagan calendar: Christian time replaced pagan time. A fierce stress on Sunday as an unbreakable day of rest, which by the sixth century was policed by miracles (according to Gregory of Tours (d. 594), Sunday agricultural workers became cripples, and the children of Sunday sexual intercourse were born crippled), also marked the definitive Christianization of time. But people still maintained the 'wrong' attitudes; they treated the new Christian feast-days in the same ways as they had treated the old pagan ones, as opportunities to get drunk and have a good time, as Augustine complained about a local martyrial feast-day. This way of understanding the Christian calendar, through public enjoyment rather than (as Augustine proposed) psalm-singing in church, was pagan in the eyes of most of our sources, but doubtless fully Christian in the eyes of celebrants; and this double vision would long remain.

Much the same can be said about the Christianization of geographical space. Pagan cults had studded the landscape of the Roman empire, a sacred spring here, a hill-top temple there, each perhaps with its own god; indeed, the whole landscape had potential sacred elements. As these were slowly prohibited or destroyed, and new Christian cult-sites built, around the tombs of martyrs or rural saints by preference, there was a risk that the latter would simply give a new religious veneer to older traditions, as with the major rural cult-site of Saint-Julien at Brioude in central Gaul, located at a martyr's tomb to be sure, but also in a place formerly known for an important sanctuary of Mars and Mercury; the changeover seems to have come in the mid-fifth century. People got drunk at martyrs' tombs too, after all; who knows what they were really celebrating, the martyr or the traditional cult-site. Perhaps there were moments when rituals, even festivities, were so significantly inverted that the pilgrims who came to the same cult-site properly took on board that something major had changed, as Pope Gregory the Great intended when in 601 he proposed to the missionaries to Anglo-Saxon England that they should take over pagan temples, but force visiting worshippers to eat the animals they had brought for ritual sacrifice. But perhaps not; a Christian topography could look suspiciously like a pagan one.

But in this case change was possible, all the same. For a start, whereas to pagan eyes an entire landscape could be numinous, to Christian eyes only specific cult-sites were so, points of light in an otherwise secular space. These were always, or soon became, churches, so they were highly visible. Few churches were ever built directly on or in temples, and those few were almost all urban. In cities, indeed, Christian topographies were in general rather more different from those of the pagans. Traditional public religion had been focused on the ceremonial buildings around the forum in the centre of the city, but churches for Christian worship were often on the edges of town, or outside, in cemetery areas. Urban religious activity became much more decentralized as a result, and cities even became spatially fragmented in some parts of the empire (in Gaul in particular), with little settlement nuclei around scattered churches, and in some cases a traditional city centre left in ruins. This was sometimes because city centres seemed just too pagan, or too secular; in Rome, major Christian capital though it became, no church was built in the wide forum area until 526. It was also linked to some real changes in ideas of the sacred, and of what caused spiritual pollution. Traditional Graeco-Roman religion regarded dead people as very dangerous and polluting; no adult could be buried inside city walls or in inhabited areas, and cemeteries were all beyond the edges of settlements. Martyrs and other saints were seen by Christians as different, however: not as sources of pollution, but the opposite, as people to venerate (in some cases, indeed, as not really dead). Relics of saints began to be associated with major churches as early as the fourth century; increasingly, these churches were inside city boundaries. And the positive power associated with these bodies meant that people increasingly wished to be buried beside them. The first burials of non-saints inside cities date from the late fifth or early sixth century in most parts of the empire; first bishops and local aristocrats, later ordinary citizens. By the seventh century urban cemeteries were increasingly common. The dead remained edgy, 'liminal', sometimes powerful – they still are – but the visceral fear of their polluting power had gone.

The unseen world changed, too. To most pagans the air was full of powerful spiritual beings, *daimones* in Greek, who were sometimes beneficent, sometimes not, sometimes controllable by magic, but above all fairly neutral to the human race. To many Christians – including the authors of our sources, certainly, but also the ordinary people who appear in the stories of saints' lives – this unseen world came to be seen as sharply divided into two, good angels and bad demons (the word *daimones* was still used); Christianity inherited this dualism from Judaism, which in turn may have been influenced by parallel beliefs in Zoroastrianism. We get to hear rather more about demons, too: they intervened more in daily life. Christianization thus developed the sense that this unseen world was more fraught with danger than it had previously been (this went for the afterlife, too, for the Christian hell expected to see far more sinners than the pagan Tartarus or the Jewish Gehenna). Demons in Christian eyes caused illness, ill-luck and ill-doing of all kinds, and demonic possession was commonly seen as the cause of mental disturbance. Demons lived among other places in pagan shrines and idols, in uncultivable areas such as deserts, and also in tombs (this latter belief was in part the heir of traditional beliefs about the pollution of the dead). They could be defeated by clerical exorcism, and many Christian ascetics gained a considerable reputation as demon-busters. Theodore of Sykeon (d. 613) was a particularly active example, performing exorcisms throughout central Anatolia, as demons disturbed village harmony or possessed the weak and ill, in some cases as a result of spell-casting, in some cases because the incautious had disturbed tombs, perhaps in a search for treasure. Christianity innovated in religious terms in giving more space to the interventions of human beings in supernatural affairs, if they had church authority or if they were themselves particularly holy. Although all such men and women would have said that they only channelled the heavenly power of God and the saints, they were treated by many less exceptional Christians as if these spiritual powers were wholly theirs, a product of their own charisma.

It has often been implied that pagan and Christian religion operated at different levels, with paganism paying more attention to public ritual (such as sacrifice), Christianity paying more attention to belief. This would be an overstatement if it was put too crudely, for both religious communities practised both, but there is an element of truth in it all the same. Christianity was also concerned with setting spiritual boundaries – between sacred and secular, or between good and bad demons – that were more nuanced (or fuzzier) to most pagans; and it was initially less committed to public and collective activity, too (though this would quickly change). There are some parallels here to the Reformation Protestant challenge to Catholic Christianity in the sixteenth century (parallels which Protestants quite consciously sought to play up). They are there too in the nineteenth-century 'modernist' critique of the public world of the *ancien régime*, as characterized by Michel Foucault. There is, that is to say, a tension between promoting collective ritual which brings social and moral solidarity, and trying to change people's minds; this tension has long existed in human history, and in some societies one side gains ascendancy over the other, for a time. In the late Roman context, it would probably be best to say that this tension existed, not only between pagan and Christian, but inside Christianity itself; for Christian attitudes to the public did quickly change, and the religious enthusiasm involved in festivals and pilgrimages, indeed in churchgoing, was by no means the same as the divine grace or mental discipline, or both, thought by rigorists to be necessary to attain individual salvation. This was something of which Christian writers who were bishops, and therefore had to straddle both, were well aware. This tension in some of our authors indeed provides much of their interest.

Changing people's minds was harder, however, and, at the level of everyday morality and values, Christianization changed much less. For example, apart from the occasional rigorist criticism, for example by Gregory of Nyssa (d. *c.* 395), there is no sign whatsoever that legal unfreedom was regarded as wrong by most Christians, despite Christianity's explicit egalitarianism; anyway, freeing slaves (manumission) as a pious act at death, common in late Antiquity and the early Middle Ages, had impeccable pagan antecedents. Opposition to social hierarchies based on wealth, or to judicial torture, was only developed at any length by heretical movements. Every single Christian writer inveighed against sexual misbehaviour (some against all sexual activity, invoking virginity as superior to marriage, as Jerome (d. 419) did), but it is unclear that this had any effect on daily actions. Christians also campaigned against divorce, however, and this did become increasingly difficult in law, and, in the West at least, eventually impossible later on in the early Middle Ages; practices which legislation could reach were more likely to change, hence also the abolition of amphitheatre games. Family-level assumptions, by contrast, including about gender roles, did not change greatly, as we shall see later in this chapter; nor did the civic values of Roman public life. One important exception was charity to the poor, which had been a mainstay of Christian community activity since its early years as a persecuted minority. It remained a major responsibility for good Christians, more than it had been for pagans, and was also a major role for churches (and for the bishops who ran the principal churches in each city) as they increased in wealth, as well as providing a justification for that wealth, given that the Christian gospels put so much stress on poverty. This emphasis on charity would later be inherited by Islam too.

These shifts in cult practices and religious culture went together with three other important innovations brought by Christianity to the Roman world: the church as an institution; the political importance of correct belief; and new social spaces for religious rigorists and ascetics. Let us look at these in turn.

Pagan religion did not depend on a very elaborate institutional structure, and the cults of each city were all organized locally; rabbinic Judaism, too, was very decentralized (Jews did have a single patriarch until around 425, but it is unclear how wide his powers were). Christianity, however, had a complex hierarchy, partly matching that of the state. By 400 there were four patriarchs, at Rome, Constantinople (since 381), Antioch and Alexandria (a fifth, Jerusalem, was added in 451), who oversaw the bishops of each city. The patriarch of Rome was already called by the honorific title *papa*, 'pope', but it was only after the eighth century that this was restricted to the pope in Rome. Bishops were soon arrayed in two levels, with metropolitan bishops (called in later centuries archbishops) at an intermediate level, overseeing and consecrating the bishops of each secular province. Inside the dioceses of each bishop, which normally covered the secular territory of their city, bishops had authority over the clerics of other public churches (although privately founded churches and monasteries were often autonomous, a situation which produced endless disputes and rivalry for the next millennium). The church in the fourth and fifth centuries became an elaborate structure, with perhaps a hundred thousand clerics of different types, more than the civil administration, and steadily increasing in wealth as a result of pious gifts. It was not part of the state, but its wealth and empire-wide institutional cohesion made it an inevitable partner for emperors and prefects, and a strong and influential informal authority in cities; the cathedral church by 500 was often the largest local landowner (and therefore patron), and, unlike in the case of private family wealth, its stability could be guaranteed – bishops were not allowed to alienate church property. It was ecclesiastical wealth and local status that led the episcopate to become part of élite career structures by the fifth century in Gaul; this process took place later in Italy and some of the eastern provinces, but by 550 or so it was normal everywhere. Even in a church context, bishops generally identified themselves with their diocese first, with wider ecclesiastical institutions only secondarily. But they were linked to the wider church hierarchy all the same: they could be called to order and dismissed by metropolitans and by the councils of bishops that steadily became more frequent, whether empire-wide (the 'ecumenical' councils) or at the regional level, in Spain or Gaul or Africa. The fact that this institutional structure did not depend on the empire, and was above all separately funded, meant that it could survive the political fragmentation of the fifth century, and the church was indeed the Roman institution that continued with least change into the early Middle Ages; the links between regions became weaker, but the rest remained intact. The problem of the relationship between the church as an institution and secular political power has existed ever since in Christian polities, and has often caused considerable conflicts, as it already did in the fifth century, and would again in the eleventh, in the Reformation, and in the post-Enlightenment states of the nineteenth and twentieth centuries.

Pagan political practice valued religious conformity, but did not have sharp divisions over variations in religious belief. Here, Christianity was very different. From early in its history its adherents argued over theology and accused each other of deviant belief, 'heresy', and in the fourth century this became an affair of state. What may well have surprised Constantine most on his conversion to Christianity was the internal conflict in the religion he had chosen, and the importance to its members of winning without any compromise. Constantine took seriously the task of achieving Christian unity, but he did not succeed (this may have surprised him too). To his successors, unity around a single correct view became increasingly important, including for the welfare of the empire as a collectivity; by the end of the fourth century religious deviance was thus politically dangerous and needed to be extirpated by law. The laws against pagans were polished first on Christian heretics, that is, those on the losing side in the great theoretical battles, and they were always far more systematically used against heresy. So heresy was both increasingly dangerous and increasingly common in the late empire. It was regarded as a problem in later centuries, too (particularly in the thirteenth-century West), but only the Reformation matches the intensity of the religious disputes of the period 300–600.

The first dispute Constantine faced was between Donatists and Caecilianists in Africa over whether the bishops who had compromised their faith during the recent persecutions of Christianity could continue to consecrate bishops thereafter. It was a characteristic issue for the pre-Constantinian church, but this African dispute was by far the most serious example. The Donatists held that Bishop Caecilian of Carthage, the local metropolitan, was consecrated by an apostate and could therefore not be a bishop or consecrate others; Constantine judged against them in 313, but they did not concede. This was technically a schism, not a heresy, as it did not involve differences in belief, but it immediately became a structurally serious dispute, for since the Donatists accepted no African bishop consecrated by Caecilian, they created their own rival hierarchy, and there were 270 Donatist bishops by around 335. This schism was restricted to Africa, but it dragged on for a century there, with violence on both sides and also fierce written polemic (Augustine wrote some of it), until a systematic persecution of Donatists, following a formal debate at Carthage in 411 (see Chapter 4), weakened them substantially.

Donatism was the only home-grown division seriously to disturb the late Roman West. It did mark one concern that was more of an issue for the Latin than for the Greek church: the personal purity of the men who consecrated others and who presided over the eucharist, the central ceremony of Christian worship. The next western heresy, 'Pelagianism', declared heretical by the emperor Honorius in 418 and (rather unwillingly) by the western patriarch, Pope Zosimus of Rome, in the same year, as a result of the pressure put on them by Augustine and Alypius, was also related to issues of personal purity. Pelagius argued that a committed Christian could avoid sin through God-given free will, which

Augustine regarded as impossible. Pelagians were never more than a minority, however, and the most lasting effect of this division was Augustine's development of his theory of predestination to salvation through God's grace, which remained controversial (and misunderstood, particularly in Gaul and Italy) but did not result in further declarations of heresy. It may be relevant here to note that the question of the purity of clerics remained important in the West. In the West, but not in the East, all clergy were supposed to avoid sexual activity, according to councils as early as 400 (in the East, this only applied to bishops, and only after 451). Not that western clergy always matched up to theory, and there were legally married clerics in many western regions into the late eleventh century, but the principle that priests should be sacrally distinct from their congregations was established early.

In the East, the most divisive issue was quite different: it was the nature of Christ. Constantine also found that there was dissension between Patriarch Alexander of Alexandria and his priest Arios over whether the Son was identical in substance, or equal, to the Father in the Trinity; Alexander maintained he was so, and Arios maintained he was not. Constantine, who did not think the issue particularly important, called a council of bishops to Nicaea in 325, the first ecumenical council, which, remarkably (it was the only ecumenical council to manage this), got both sides to agree on a formulation, the Nicene creed, essentially supporting Alexander. Some extreme followers of Alexander, however, notably Athanasios (d. 373), Alexander's successor, refused to maintain communion with Arios, even though he had signed up to the Nicene creed, and the dispute broke out again. Versions of Christian belief closer to those whom Athanasios called 'Arians' were popular in many parts of the East, notably at Constantinople, including with the mid-century emperors, Constantius II and Valens; it was not by any means obvious to everyone that the members of the Trinity were all equal. Athanasios was also personally unpopular for his violent style, and had widespread support only in the West. But a new generation of Nicene supporters gained force in the 370s, thanks in particular to Basil, bishop of Caesarea in Anatolia (d. 379), and his associates. At Valens' death at Adrianople in 378, a western ally of Basil became eastern emperor, Theodosius I, and his ecumenical council at Constantinople in 381 finally declared the Nicene creed to be orthodoxy. This paradoxically (but not uniquely among heresies) caused 'Arianism' itself to crystallize as a worked-out religious system, in effect for the first time. All the same, it lost imperial patronage and thus wider support thereafter (although, in the eastern capital, not until Patriarch John Chrysostom's vigorous preaching in 398–404), except among the Goths and, by extension, other 'barbarian' groups in the North.

The Nicene victory meant that Christ, though human and capable of suffering, was seen as fully divine as well; but how were humanity and divinity to be combined? This was the major focus of fifth-century debates, which were in many respects power-struggles between Alexandria and Antioch, with Constantinople generally on Antioch's side. Patriarch Cyril of Alexandria (412–44) argued that the human and divine elements in Christ's nature could not be separated; Antiochenes such as Nestorios, patriarch of Constantinople (428–31), saw them as distinct. The danger in Cyril's position, which we call 'Monophysite', was that Christ would lose his humanity altogether; the danger in Nestorios' position was that he would turn into two people. Neither danger had been realized yet, but opponents of each believed it had been. The third ecumenical council, at Ephesos in 431, a theatre of remarkably cynical management by Cyril, condemned and deposed Nestorios. Ephesos also legitimated the cult of the Virgin Mary as *Theotokos*, 'mother of God', a formulation Nestorios in particular opposed, but one which has dominated most Christian churches since; the great councils as a whole did not only argue about Christology. But the Alexandrian attempt to go after all the Antiochenes, one by one (notably Theodoret, bishop of Cyrrhus, who was briefly deposed in 449), rebounded on them, largely because of western opposition, focused on the actions and writings of Pope Leo I (440–61), and also because the Alexandrians had alienated the empress Pulcheria, their supporter at Ephesos. A fourth council at Chalcedon in 451 rejected the Alexandrian 'Monophysite' position (while maintaining a rejection of Nestorios), and set out a ruling that Christ existed 'in two natures', divine and human, while remaining one person.

This established an orthodoxy that dominated the West and the Byzantine heartland ever after. But it did not end the disputes, for Monophysitism had grass-roots support that previous losing interpretations did not have, in particular in most of Egypt, increasingly in Syria and Palestine, and in Armenia. Emperors, themselves sometimes personally sympathetic to Monophysitism (as with Anastasius, and also the empress Theodora, Justinian's powerful wife), saw the Chalcedonian–Monophysite split as a political rather than a theological issue, and attempted several times to promote intermediate positions between the two: Zeno's Henotikon in 482, Justinian's fifth council at Constantinople in 553, Heraclius' 'Monothelete' pronouncement, the Ekthesis, in 638. These did not work because there was less and less common ground between the two sides (even though the issues at stake became increasingly arcane); by the late sixth century, indeed, the Monophysite provinces were establishing an entire parallel episcopal hierarchy to confront the Chalcedonians. The emperors found themselves anathematized by both sides, and also faced schism with the West, which was uncompromisingly Chalcedonian. (When the popes of Rome were bullied into accepting the council of Constantinople in 554, they too faced opposition from much of the West, the so-called Three Chapters schism, and it took them a hundred and fifty years to end it.) Arianism continued as the Christianity of 'barbarian' groups, notably Goths, Vandals and eventually Lombards, into the seventh century. 'Nestorianism' continued too – in more extreme forms than Nestorios had ever proposed – but mostly outside the empire, in Persia and as far east as China. But it was Monophysitism that divided Roman Christians most radically and completely, and the division was never healed.

It is impossible to characterize these conflicts accurately in a few words, for the theology at issue is amazingly intricate, depending on tight definitions and Platonist philosophical developments of concepts which would take many pages to set out in English (it was, furthermore, a debate which made most sense in Greek even then; Leo I was the last Latin-speaker really to grasp and contribute to it). Such detailed characterizations do not belong here. But it is important to stress that they did matter. Pagan observers found these debates ridiculous, even insane, as well as amazingly badly behaved, but having an accurate and universally agreed definition of God became increasingly important for Christians between 300 and 550, not least because the political power of bishops steadily increased. It is relevant that they mattered more in the East, where technical philosophical debate was longer-rooted in intellectual life, but with the 'barbarian' conquests Christological issues came to the West as well, and Arian–Catholic debates were bitter there, too; anyway, the Augustinian problematic which dominated theology in the West, centred on predestination and divine grace, was no less complex, even though it sidestepped Christological debate. It is of course impossible to say how many people properly understood the issues at stake at, say, Chalcedon: perhaps only a few hundred, although one should not underestimate the theological sophistication of the citizens of the great cities, exposed as they were to the sermons of some high-powered thinkers. But the problem of the real divinity of a human god, who had even died, at the Crucifixion, was at least an issue that would have made sense in the late Roman world, where the cult of the emperors as gods was still remembered (indeed, it was still practised by some) and the divine being was not, in the fifth century at least, as distant from humanity as he (or they) would be in some versions of Christianity.

These divisions also matter because they mobilized large numbers of people. Fifth-century Christianity was a mass religion, reaching more and more of the peasantry. Its participants were very loyal to their bishops and other local religious leaders, and could be mobilized in their support, city versus city or province versus province. Political faction-fighting could be expressed in religious terms too, and local secular leaders could find themselves involved in ecclesiastical disputes for the whole of their political lives. In cities, mobs could fight it out; Cyril in Alexandria, where rioting had a long tradition, was well known for his manipulation of them. The Donatists had an armed wing of Circumcellions, ascetic peasants or seasonal labourers. Monks from the countryside were also used as shock troops, usually on the Monophysite side; Jerusalem was a dangerous place because of the number of monasteries around it, which could quickly be mobilized, as when Juvenal, patriarch of Jerusalem, was expelled by monks in 452 for a year, because he had accepted Chalcedon; the army was needed to restore him. Monks were not normally educated, but they were certainly fervent. The roughness of their political protagonism broke the rules of late Roman élite decorum, and troubled politer observers, as it does some modern historians. These monks look too fundamentalist, too fanatical, and they were; but they were at least a sign that Christianity had penetrated the countryside, and that its divisions involved more people than narrow élites.

This brings us to a final Christian innovation, the development of new spheres for social behaviour. In general, committed Christianity involved a personally pious lifestyle, which indeed mattered more than theological disputes to most of its adherents; but rigorists could and did go well beyond mere piety. From early on in Christianity, self-deprivation of food or comfort, self-harm and the avoidance of human society were regarded by some people as ways in which humans could get closer to God. These forms of ascesis were popularized by Athanasios' hugely influential *Life of Antony*, written at the death of the Egyptian desert hermit Antony in 357 and almost at once translated from Greek into Latin. 'The desert', a physical location for Antony, became an image for all ascesis, and men and women could create their own local deserts by shutting themselves away, or by standing on columns, often for decades, as stylites from Simon the elder (d. 459) onwards did – inaccessible (except by ladder), but clearly visible all the same and of public interest as a result. One influential stylite, Daniel (d. 493), had his column beside one of the major Bosporos ferries, east from Constantinople – he, certainly, was in the public eye (someone even asked him how he defecated: very dryly, like a sheep, he replied); but Simon, too, had his column in the middle of the rich olive-oil hill-country of northern Syria, and crowds would watch him repeatedly touch his toes with his head, counting 1,244 such movements on one occasion, as Theodoret of Cyrrhus recounted. Theodoret wrote a systematic account of the remarkable (and often, to his eyes, foolish) ascetic feats of Syrian holy men, which also stressed how respectful they were to Theodoret himself, their bishop. Ascetics sometimes caused resentment in the standard church hierarchy, for their spiritual powers (accurate advice, particularly effective prayers, sometimes miracles) were the results of their own efforts, rather than being bestowed by bishops. But most had episcopal support and patronage, and some of them (Theodore of Sykeon was one) became bishops themselves.

The influence of these ascetics broke all Roman social rules: few were aristocratic, few were educated, but people sought their advice persistently. We have replies of two elderly hermits living just outside Gaza in the early sixth century, Barsanouphios and John, to some 850 questions of all kinds put to them by laity, clerics and monks, which can pass for the sixth-century equivalent of Dear Abby. If I want to give grain and wine to the poor, should I give them the best quality? (no, you needn't). Since we must not kill, should I lie to allow a murderer to escape the death penalty? (maybe, as long as you tend to lie under other circumstances). Can I buy in the market from pagans? (yes). Can I eat with a pagan? (no). What about when he is important?

(still no, and here is a polite excuse). Do I really have to give my cloak to every beggar, and go naked? (no). And, perhaps the feeblest of all: I can't make up my mind, what should I do? (a perhaps exasperated reply: pray to God, or else ask us again). It is clear in all of this that ascetics were trusted to know; educated or not, they had access to spiritual truth.

Christian ascetic holy men and women have an established niche in modern history-writing by now, and it is important not to be seduced by Theodoret and others into thinking that they were everywhere; as Peter Brown has recently written, they occupied 'little of the public space of late Roman society', even in the East, and they were never as common in the West. But they created an idiom of self-mortification which potential saints would systematically seek to copy in the future, with hair shirts, flesh-eatingly tight belts, chains and the like. Their less extreme acts could be copied by everybody, such as the pious Roman aristocratic women Paula and Melania, whose choice to walk around fourth-century Rome in rags, unwashed and smelly, was eulogized by Jerome in disturbingly lip-smacking terms. And they were regularized and generalized by monasticism. Not that most monks imitated a full-on ascetic extremism, but the development of groups of celibates, living apart (in 'the desert'), was influenced by Antony, and set roots on a large scale in Egypt first; indeed, ascetics themselves eventually found that they had a monastic community forming around them, or they sought one out on purpose. The ascesis of monasticism mostly consisted of absolute obedience to an abbot's rule in a fixed daily routine, and such rules were written down from early on: by or for Pachomios in Egypt and by Basil in Anatolia in the fourth century, by Shenoute in Egypt and John Cassian in Gaul in the fifth, by Benedict of Nursia (modern Norcia) in Italy in the sixth. In the West, Benedict's rule eventually became the gold standard; in the East, it was Basil's. Benedict's rule, more humane than many, is as striking for its insistence on the equal treatment of monks of different social status as it is for its moderate ascesis (only vegetables, except when ill; only light clothes, except in winter): egalitarianism was as difficult in the hierarchical world of late Antiquity as was self-deprivation. Nor were all monasteries remotely egalitarian; many resembled comfortable house-party retreats for aristocratic males and females. But the image of equality (of subjection) was intrinsic to monastic regulation, and in this respect, even if in no other in late Rome, equality was theoretically possible to achieve; a social space had even been created for this.

One simple result of these processes is that Christian writers tell us more about the peasant majority than pagan writers had ever done. Peasants could become saints if they were very exceptional; they also bore witness to the remarkable acts of rural holy men and women, living far from urban élites, so saints' lives give us vignettes of village society that were almost entirely absent in earlier literature. The poor could go to heaven as easily as the rich, after all (in Christian theory, more easily), and even the most aristocratic and snobbish bishops – Gregory of Tours in sixth-century Gaul, for example – regularly preached to them, and sometimes listened to them, too. In recent decades, historians have abandoned their earlier caution about miracle stories, and rightly, given that these tell us so much more about non-aristocratic society and cultural and religious values than we can get elsewhere. They are not a direct window onto peasant society; no text is ever that, and they were seldom written by peasants (though one or two were – the *Life* of Theodore of Sykeon is one). But they are the best guide we have, and, however fully studied they now are, they still have more to tell us.

Part of the reason why ascetics occupied little Roman public space was that that space was huge. Even when we move away from a specifically religious focus, we must recognize that the Romans lived a great part of their political lives in public. The year was studded with public processions in cities; indeed, urban planning itself was affected by it, for the wide and straight streets of Roman cities, in the East garlanded with colonnades as well, were specifically built like that, and kept clear of obstructions, so as to allow processions (when processions ceased in the East after the Arab conquest, streets infilled fairly fast: see below, Chapter 10). Political power was structured around the most formal versions of such processions, as with the rituals for imperial arrival (*adventus*) into cities, which were later matched by the most elaborate ceremonial entries of the Renaissance. One famous case, Constantius II's arrival in Rome in 357, described by Ammianus in detail, shows the emperor in a bejewelled car, with a vast military retinue; Constantius turned neither his head nor his eyes, nor his hands – he did not even spit – during the entire procession to the forum. This was a victory procession (undeserved, Ammianus thought; he loathed Constantius), which had a long tradition behind it, and a long future ahead, at least in the East, for Constantinople's main west–east streets saw regular processions of this kind right to the end of the period of this book and beyond: the tenth-century *Book of Ceremonies*, compiled on the orders of an emperor himself, Constantine VII (913–59), describes them in great detail, stage by stage (see Chapter 13), and it is far from the only source. But major political and religious moments of all kinds were marked by processions in cities. Here, Christianity simply appropriated the practice, and bishops developed formal processions between urban churches as part of the presentation of their local power; these often took on penitential or protective roles, and it became common for bishops to process around city walls with relics or religious symbols, to protect the city during sieges, as during the siege of Clermont in around 525 or at the siege of Constantinople in 626 (according to our hagiographical sources, they were always successful). Pilgrimages to local saints' tombs, themselves commonly orchestrated by bishops, as Gregory of Tours did for St Martin's tomb there, had something of the same public formality, at least at the major festivals of the saint.

The public sphere did not only operate through processions. Constantius after his arrival in 357 hosted games; so did Theoderic the Ostrogoth in his formal visit to Rome in 500. The Circus Maximus, the largest chariot-racing stadium in Rome, was just below the imperial palace on the Palatine hill, from where the ruler could watch; in Constantinople, too, the Hippodrome was beside the palace, with a direct back entrance into the imperial box. This was the location (particularly in Constantinople, for emperors actually lived there) for a structured dialogue between emperor and people. Emperors generally controlled this, but it did at least allow some popular response through the leaders of the main circus 'factions', the Greens and the Blues (the colours of the teams), either through verbal dialogue or through riot. Matters occasionally got out of hand, as with the Nika riots of the Constantinople factions in 532, during which much of the city was sacked and which nearly brought Justinian down, but circus riots in major cities tended more to be a safety valve, a warning of discontent which emperors occasionally heeded, as well as, perhaps most normally, simply being for fun.

Political decision-making had a substantial public element as well. There were public disputations (particularly about religion or philosophy), speech-making was carried out in the forum, and there was a crowd to hear Sidonius choose the bishop of Bourges. The political community meant the élite, of course, and there was nothing even distantly democratic about Roman political procedures, but their results were communicated verbally in public, often quite quickly, at least in cities. Imperial laws were proclaimed as well; Anastasius' abolition of the unpopular merchants' and artisans' tax in 498 was read out at Edessa – a major commercial entrepôt, but a long way from Constantinople – in the same year and occasioned a spontaneous festival.

The emperor had an ambiguous relation to the public world. The late Roman empire was a period in which imperial ceremonial became increasingly elaborate, partly to distance the emperor from other people, 'imprisoned inside the palace boundaries', as Sidonius put it. Inside the palace, etiquette was very elaborate as well. Meals with the emperor, a great honour, were carefully controlled, and Sidonius recounts one with Majorian in 461 at Arles in which the emperor conversed in turn with each of the seven guests, who were expected to shine in their replies, and got applause if they did so. (One aspect of the Persians that seemed very strange in Roman eyes was that their religious rituals forbade them to talk at meals.) But this formality was balanced against a presumption of accessibility. The practice of petitioning the emperor, for help or against injustice, was long-standing in the Roman world, and did not weaken at all in the late empire; indeed, the laws in the imperial codes are often explicitly responses to petitions. Petitioners seldom met the emperor in person, and it was of course the bureaucracy that really dealt with their pleas (or else did not), but the principle of direct response was preserved. Daniel the Stylite briefly left his column in 475 to protest against the usurping emperor Basiliscus' support for Monophysitism, sending critical letters to Basiliscus, and eventually getting the emperor to recant publicly in the cathedral of Constantinople itself; the image of dialogue in his saint's life must have been a plausible one, even if the details were invented. And this sort of imagery worked. Imperial authority remained popular, taken for granted. Roman envoys to Attila's court in 449 greatly offended the Huns when they said that, although Attila was a man, Theodosius II was a god; this was a self-evident statement in Roman eyes, even though the envoys were doubtless overwhelmingly Christian. The gods were gone, but imperial status remained unchanged – *divinus* remained a technical term meaning 'imperial'. The emperor's position was all the more central in that the Roman empire was regarded as, by definition, always victorious, a belief that survived even the disasters of the fifth century. Indeed, Christianization reinforced this: if the empire fell, many believed the world would end. Romans were nothing if not confident.

The Romans drew a clear line between the public and the private. Politics in a formal sense took place outside private housing, which was regarded as in part separate from public activity. Senatorial palaces could be entered by almost anyone, and much political business was transacted there, but they contained carefully calibrated communal and more personalized spaces for the reception of clients and would-be clients; and except for extreme crimes the behaviour of family members inside the walls of a house was the responsibility of the *paterfamilias*, the male head of the household, and beyond the remit of public law. The household was the basic unit, called *domus* in Latin when its physical setting was stressed, and *familia* when referring to its personnel. It was centred on a nuclear family of husband, wife, children; other kin were normally more distant, part of political alliances rather than family structure, although parents, if living, still had a major influence. Slaves were part of the *familia* as well, however, as unfree domestic servants, and they were ubiquitous among families who had any resources to spare at all. The *familia* was very hierarchical; the *paterfamilias* was supposed routinely to beat slaves and children. Augustine's account of his violent father Patricius in his autobiographical *Confessions*, an important source, shows that he considered it commonplace for husbands to beat wives too, although wife-beating seems to have been regarded as normal only in the Latin West, and with greater hostility in the Greek East; in surviving Egyptian divorce petitions, violence is rarely referred to. In law, the authority of the *paterfamilias* did not actually extend to wives, who were still subject to their own fathers (if living), but it is clear that in practice husbands ruled. Augustine, again, depicts his mother Monica (who had no qualms about trying to dominate her son) telling off her female neighbours in Thagaste for moaning about their husbands, saying their marriage contracts 'bound them to serve their husbands'; nor was this just rhetoric: Egyptian marriage contracts systematically enjoin husbands to protect, wives to obey. Augustine criticized a certain Ecdicia for being celibate, wearing widow's clothing and giving her property to the poor during her husband's lifetime and without his permission: this lack of submissiveness nullified the virtue she sought to attain. The state may have stopped at the wall of the house, but Roman values did not, and hierarchy was taken for granted in both. Nor did Christianity change anything significant in this respect.

It would not be hard to argue that late Roman family life was tense and loveless. Marriages were almost always arranged by parents, after all, with an eye to safeguarding and extending property; husbands were routinely a decade older than their wives. Domestic slaves could undermine the stability of their master's family by malicious gossip, and were thought (perhaps rightly) to be deeply hostile to their masters in general: 'It is agreed and totally plain that all masters are bad,' a slave is made to say in the early fifth-century comedy *Querolus*. Children are frequently seen as resenting and rejecting paternal restrictions in late Roman narratives (particularly those where virginally minded daughters are forced into marriage, and then child-bearing, by parents and husbands). Augustine certainly disliked his father, and, while revering his mother, had to resort to deceit to escape her when he left Carthage for Rome at the age of twenty-eight. All the same, in late Rome as elsewhere, happy families give authors less to write about. It may be that the idyllic love and concord celebrated by the pagan Roman aristocrats Praetextatus (d. 384) and Paulina in poems supposedly written to each other and inscribed on a stela after Praetextatus' death, are not totally formulaic or atypical: 'I am happy because I am yours, was yours, and soon – after death – will be yours.' The 'amicable and decorous bonds' of marriage were normally unequal, but they did not necessarily fail because of that.

Women were legally subject to fathers, effectively subject to husbands. They had full inheritance rights over paternal and maternal property, however, equally with their brothers, and legally controlled their own property in marriage. Husbands were expected to front for wives in public affairs such as court cases, but women had full legal rights to act on their own if they chose. Until the late fourth century widows could not be legal guardians of children, and their powers were circumscribed, but in practice they often did so (Monica certainly held the purse strings for the near-adult Augustine after Patricius' death in 372). Women were not regarded as part of the public sphere and could not hold office. But there is at least one example of a female city governor, Patrikia in Antaiopolis in Egypt in 553; and Hypatia in Alexandria, as the city's major intellectual, had a formal role in public ritual, receiving ceremonial visits from officials. Indeed, powerful empresses were common in the late empire (particularly in the fifth- and sixth-century East: see Chapter 4), and not obviously resented for their power, despite the rhetoric of political opponents and some Christian extremists. The sphere of women in the late Roman period was universally regarded as the home: they ran the household economy. But they were not prevented from being economic actors. Egyptian evidence shows widows, at least, buying and selling property without male consent or intervention (women seem to have owned 17–25 per cent of the land of fourth-century Egypt, not a trivial amount), and also renting out property, money-lending, and acting as independent artisans and shop-owners. Women (except prostitutes and dancers) were expected to dress modestly, but they were not veiled in their normal daily lives; they could show or claim status with expensive clothing, and they do not seem to have been secluded. The double standard of sexual behaviour was standard and sanctioned by law (men routinely had concubines, but brides were supposed to be virgins, and female adultery was seen as indefensible); but the empress Theodora may have been an actress, and thus automatically in a legal category akin to prostitution – even if Prokopios' lurid account of her activities is demonstrably rhetorical – without it constraining her later authority. Women were regarded as weak and ignorant, but, even excluding Hypatia, there is plenty of evidence for female literacy and literary engagement, particularly but not only among the aristocracy.

How do we assess this network of contradictions? It is not possible, with the evidence at our disposal, to tell what was typical in practice in each case, female constraint or female autonomy. Doubtless, as in many societies, we could expect autonomy for a few successful women, who nevertheless might find themselves more exposed to greater scrutiny than men, and also to some moral condemnation, particularly if their husbands were alive; the majority were maybe more subject and passive, whether voluntarily (as with Monica) or not. This general picture could well have been the case at every level of the social hierarchy, for the Egyptian material extends to peasants and artisans on occasion. And the space Christianity gave to ascesis allowed small, but visible, numbers of women to escape from family pressures altogether, as long as they maintained celibacy and disciplined behaviour, preferably indoors and in groups. The very quantity of these contradictory rights and constraints, all the same, was greater than in many societies: the early medieval West often assumed rather more uncompromising legal and social constraints on female action, as we shall see in Chapter 8. There was space inside the contradictions for late Roman women to construct their own social personae, if they wished to and if they were lucky. But they did so in a world full of gendered imagery that was negative about women, propagated by the public secular world and the church alike, with maleness and male virtues seen as the norm (*virtus* itself means 'maleness' as well as 'virtue') and femaleness seen as weakness and even danger, particularly to male ascetics, for whom female sexuality was, understandably, one of the greatest threats.

Men, too, faced contradictory signals in the world they lived in. Late Roman society was very hierarchical and social mobility was in many cases constrained by law, as we have seen, although it was also fairly common; the mixture of caste-like assumptions of inequality and the presence of 'new men' always creates tensions. Roman men were very ready to take offence at breaches of etiquette by upstarts and outsiders; they got angry very easily, and could be violent if they did. Faustus, bishop of Riez (d. *c.* 490), remarked sourly in a sermon that a powerful man may do us an injury or angrily abuse us and we suffer in silence, to avoid greater injury, but if an inferior person abuses us we get angry and revenge ourselves. The violence of late Roman political and judicial practice meant that such threats could be dangerous. But educated élites were also trained to decorous and courteous formal behaviour; it was part of élite education, in fact, and it included never losing one's temper and aiming to convince – or humiliate – by rhetorical skill rather than by threat. How could one do both? One could not, of course. Educated men of the late Roman period were appalled by monastic vigilantes, or the mob of Alexandria, or powerful men with a military background like Valentinian I, for their lack of self-control and their violence. On a small scale, Sidonius was delighted when, at his dinner with Majorian, his enemy Paeonius became visibly annoyed at a minor slight *in front of the emperor*, a damning breach of etiquette; the emperor's decorous but amused laugh was enough for Sidonius, who referred to it as 'revenge'. But decorum was all the more important because men were recognized as passionate. And anger could also be used politically, breaking through the barriers of decorum, to make a point, to show that one was serious, all the more effectively because of the formality of 'normal' political behaviour. In the post-Roman West, politics became less formalized, but the political force of anger remained a powerful weapon for kings and princes.

This chapter, and the last, present a stable late Roman world, not unchanging by any means (this was above all a period of notable religious innovation), nor, of course, conflict-free, but all the same not in any sense doomed to dissolution. We shall see in the next chapter how it was that Roman political power did break down in the fifth-century West, despite this internal stability. But it is also worth asking at this stage what, in the political, social and cultural patterns described so far, would survive to form the Roman inheritance for future centuries. This is easiest to answer for the present chapter: most of the patterns described here survived. The structures of the church were the institution which changed least as the Roman West broke up, and they became politically marginal only in the south-eastern and southern Mediterranean, with the Muslim conquests of the seventh century. The importance of correct belief survived in Byzantium and in parts of the West, as we shall see in later chapters. Ascetic religious commitment and religion-based critiques of secular society never lost their force in the next centuries, and we shall see them constantly recur. These were a specific Christian Roman legacy for future ages. The public institutions of the Roman empire survived as a fundamental political template for both Byzantium and the Arab caliphate, too, still based on a continuing system of land tax. Taxation steadily broke down in the post-Roman West, however, and political institutions radically simplified. All the same, the political and institutional framework of the Roman empire was so complex that these new simpler versions could still provide a basic Roman-style governmental system for the 'Romano-Germanic' kingdoms, in particular the Franks in Gaul, the Visigoths in Spain and the Lombards in Italy, the leading polities of the two centuries after 550. And this went with a sense of public power, and of a public space for political practice, which was largely a Roman inheritance. This public politics lasted in the West until past the end of the Carolingian period, up to the tenth century at least, and often later; its breakdown, where it occurred (most notably in France), was momentous. That moment will indeed mark the end of this book, for in the West at least it represents the end of the early Middle Ages.

Many things did change at the start of the early medieval period. Religious and cultural continuities cannot mask the importance of the breakdown of state structures; the exchange economy also became much more localized in both East and West, and less technically complex, too, at least in the West. Aristocratic society became more militarized, and a secular literary education became much less important, particularly in the West; our written sources become far more religious as a result, in both East and West. Aristocratic identity changed everywhere too, with the political changes of the fifth-century West and the seventh-century East; global aristocratic wealth contracted in most places, and the hyper-rich senatorial élite of Rome vanished. One must not overstate this contraction, for aristocrats with Roman ancestors continued to be major players, but, given the cultural changes just referred to, their Roman antecedence becomes much harder to see. Peasants also became more autonomous, as global aristocratic landowning decreased and as state power in the West lessened; by contrast, the constraints on women arguably increased. And, above all, each region of the Roman empire had a separate political, social, economic, cultural development henceforth. Before 550, the East and the West are treated together in this book, but thereafter they must be discussed separately; and the histories of the Frankish lands, Spain, Italy, Britain, Byzantium and the Arab world will all get individual treatment, as will the non-Roman lands of the North. This localization and overall simplification marks the early Middle Ages above all else. But underpinning every political system we look at in the rest of this book, outside the far North at least, was the weight of the Roman past, which, however fragmented, created the building-blocks for political, social and cultural practice in every post-Roman society, for centuries to come.

4

Crisis and Continuity, 400–550

On 25 February 484, Huneric, king of the Vandals and Alans, and ruler of the former Roman provinces of North Africa, issued a decree against the 'Homousian' (we would say Catholic) heresy of the Roman population of his kingdom. The Vandals were Arian Christians, and they regarded the beliefs of the Roman majority as sufficiently incorrect that they needed to be expunged. Huneric, accordingly, adapted the emperor Honorius' law of 412 against the Donatists of Africa, which had been a major Catholic weapon in the days of Augustine, and used it against the Catholics themselves. Huneric was explicit about this:

It is well known that the casting back of evil counsels against those who give them is a feature of triumphant majesty and royal strength . . . It is necessary and very just to twist around against them what is shown to be contained in those very laws which happen to have been promulgated by the emperors of various times who, with them, had been led into error.

Huneric's mode in this decree, and in the persecution it began (which seems to have quietened down after his death in December of the same year), was consistently playful: you did this yourselves; it is therefore right that it should be done back to you. Indeed, his whole preparation for it was a deliberate echoing of the 410s. Honorius in 410 had called for a *conlatio*, a formal disputation, between Donatist and Catholic bishops, which took place in Carthage in June 411; its acts largely survive, and they show a striking mixture of ceremonial power-plays, insult and argument, followed by a judgement against the Donatists – and then repression a year later. The Donatists must have known that they were probably being set up; and when in May 483 Huneric called the Catholic bishops to a similar debate in Carthage for the February of the following year, the latter certainly knew what was coming. Both the Donatists in 411 and the Catholics in 484 tried to pre-empt discussion by presenting a manifesto; but Huneric, if we believe the account of his fervent opponent Victor of Vita, had already prepared his decree, thus cutting short the debate. If this is true, it was Huneric's only deviation from his replay of the Honorian drama. Huneric was enjoying being a Roman emperor in persecuting mode, act by act; and the Catholics knew well what he was doing.

The Vandals in Africa represent a paradox, which is epitomized by this account. The modern use of their name shows the bad reputation they already had, expressed above all in Victor's polemical account of their cruelty and oppression. Most contemporary accounts of the Vandals were indeed negative, from Possidius' eyewitness account of their violent arrival in Africa in 429 to the eastern Roman historian Prokopios' criticisms of their luxurious lifestyle at the moment of the Roman reconquest in 533–4. Under their most successful king, Huneric's father Geiseric (428–77), who brought them from Spain to Numidia and then in 439 to Carthage and the African grain heartland, their ships (ex-grain ships, no doubt) raided Sicily, conquered Sardinia and sacked Rome in 455. Huneric was not the only king to persecute Catholics; Thrasamund (496–523) did the same in the 510s. Conversely, however, there is evidence to show that the Vandals thought they were being very Roman. Those we know about all spoke Latin. Huneric married Honorius' great-niece, and had spent time in Italy. The Vandal administration seems to have been close to identical to the Roman provincial administration of Africa, and to have been staffed by Africans (at most they may have adopted a Vandal dress code); the currency was a creative adaptation of Roman models; the kings taxed as the Romans had; the Vandal élites accumulated great wealth as a result, which they spent in Roman ways, on luxurious town houses and churches, as both literary sources and archaeology tell us. Archaeology, indeed, implies little change in most aspects of African material culture across the Vandal century. And, of course, their religious persecution was entirely Roman. Other conquering Germanic peoples were also Arian, notably the Goths, as we have seen, but they saw their religion for the most part as marking out their own identity vis-à-vis their new Roman subjects, who could stay Catholic. Only the Vandals assumed that their version of Christianity should be the universal one, and that others should be uprooted, as the Romans themselves did: hence also the negative tone of contemporary accounts, which are all written by Catholics.

It is thus possible to turn the Vandals into a version of the Romans themselves. They could be seen as in effect a rogue army that seized power in a Roman province and ran it in a Roman way; although the Vandals had themselves never been imperial federate troops, they were very like them, and one would be hard put to it to identify any element in their political or social practice that had non-Roman roots. But we would be mistaken if we thought nothing changed when Geiseric marched into Carthage. There were two major differences. First, the Vandals ruled Africa as a military landowning aristocracy, who continued to see themselves as ethnically distinct. Roman armies which seized power before the fifth century were content to create their own emperor and retire to barracks with rich gifts; but the Vandals became a political élite, replacing and expropriating the largely absentee senatorial aristocracy (and some Roman landowners who lived in Africa too, though most of these survived). Secondly, the Vandals broke the Mediterranean infrastructure of the late empire; they took over the major grain and oil export province of the West, the source of most of the city of Rome's food. The food had largely been supplied free, in tax; the Vandals were autonomous, however, and kept African produce for themselves – although they were prepared to sell it. The Carthage–Rome tax spine ended. The population of the city of Rome began to lessen precipitously after the mid-fifth century; in the next century it probably dropped more than 80 per cent. And a gaping hole appeared in the carefully balanced fiscal system of the western empire; the Romans faced a fiscal crisis, just when they needed to spend as much on troops as they possibly could. Not to foresee that Geiseric would take Carthage, notwithstanding a treaty agreed in 435, is arguably the main strategic error of the imperial government in the fifth century: the moment when the political break-up of the western empire first became a serious possibility. Hence the belated but intense efforts made to recapture Africa in 441, 460 and especially the large mobilization of 468, which failed disastrously, even though Vandal military strength was not, as far as can be seen, unusually great. Reconquest in 533–4 was easy in the end, but the western empire was gone by then. However Romanized the Vandals were, they were agents of major changes.

This is the key feature of the events of the fifth century, at least in the western empire. Over and over again, 'barbarian' armies occupied Roman provinces, which they ran in Roman ways; so nothing changed;

but everything changed. In 400 the western and eastern Roman empires were twins, run by brothers (Honorius and Arcadius, the two sons of Theodosius I, ruling 395–423 and 395–408 respectively), with little structural difference between them, and, as we saw in Chapter 2, no fundamental internal weaknesses. In 500 the East was hardly changed (indeed, it was experiencing an economic boom), but the West was divided into half a dozen major sections, Vandal Africa, Visigothic Spain and south-west Gaul, Burgundian south-east Gaul, Frankish northern Gaul, Ostrogothic Italy (including the Alpine region), and a host of smaller autonomous units in Britain and in more marginal areas elsewhere. The larger western polities were all ruled in a Roman tradition, but they were more militarized, their fiscal structures were weaker, they had fewer economic interrelationships, and their internal economies were often simpler. A major change had taken place, without anyone particularly intending it. The purpose of this chapter is to investigate how – but not with hindsight. The events of the fifth century were not inevitable, and they were not perceived as such by the people who lived through them. No one saw the western empire as 'falling' in this period; the first writer specifically to date its end (to 476) was a Constantinople-based chronicler, Marcellinus *comes*, writing around 518. We shall look at those events in four chronological tranches, up to 425, up to 455, up to 500, and up to 550, so as to try to pin down what were the principal changes, but also stabilities, at each stage. We shall then deal with the issue of what these changes meant.

Neither Honorius nor Arcadius was any sort of political protagonist, nor in fact were their successors as emperors, and it was not until the 470s that effective rulers occupied supreme political positions again. Others ruled through them. In the West, the strong-man at the start of the fifth century was Stilicho, military commander (*magister militum praesentalis*) of the western armies since 394: a powerful dealer, which he needed to be. For the whole of his ascendancy he faced Alaric, king of the Goths (c. 391–410), in the latter's attempts to establish a stable location for his people. Gothic groups had first come into the empire in 376, as we saw in Chapter 2; after their victory at Adrianople in 378, they were left alone in the 380s in Illyricum and Thrace, the modern Balkans. Alaric was the first Gothic leader to serve with his own followers in a Roman army, for Theodosius in 394. This military arrangement came unstuck by 396, however, and Alaric's Goths (we call them the Visigoths, to avoid confusion with other Gothic groups, though they did not call themselves this) spent two decades trying to regain, by force, a recognized position in the empire. They attacked Greece, then moved north, and entered northern Italy in 401. Stilicho defeated them and drove them back into Illyricum in 402, but they returned in 408. Nor were they the only 'barbarians' in the empire by now; other groups, probably persuaded to take their chances across the border by the development of Hunnic power, came in during the same decade. In 405 an army led by Radagaisus, again largely Gothic, crossed the Alps into Italy from the north; Stilicho defeated and destroyed them near Florence in 406. Stilicho needed a larger army for all this than Italy possessed, especially as he himself also wanted to make Illyricum part of the western, not the eastern empire, and he pulled troops from the Rhine frontier to meet this need. This was probably a mistake, for it was followed by an invasion of central European tribes led by the Vandals, over the Rhine on New Year's Eve 406, an irruption into western Gaul and then (in 409) into Spain which was almost unresisted; and also in 407 another invasion of Gaul, this time by a usurper, Constantine III (406–11), at the head of the army of Roman Britain. Faced with these multiple crises, whispering campaigns against Stilicho began, and after a mutiny he was executed in 408.

Stilicho was brought down by problems that were not entirely of his own making; the western leadership immediately after his death only made errors. Stilicho was half-Vandal in origin, and was regarded by some as too favourably disposed to 'barbarians'; those who were in his Italian army were either massacred or fled to Alaric. Alaric was dominant in Italy in 408–10, but the Romans would not consistently make peace with him, even though he blockaded Rome three times. In the end he sacked Rome in 410, an event which shocked the Roman world much as 11 September 2001 shocked the United States, a huge, upsetting, symbolic blow to its self-confidence; but it was without other repercussions, and was only one step in the long Visigothic road to settlement. The Goths tried to go south to Africa, then went north into Gaul instead, under their new leader Athaulf (410–15); there they found, and contributed to, a still greater confusion, with as many as four rival emperors in 411, most of them the protégés of different 'barbarian' groups. Slowly, the legitimist Roman armies regrouped under a new *magister militum*, Constantius (411–21), who picked off the usurpers one by one and forced the 'barbarian' groups to come to terms. Athaulf's Visigoths were, as Roman armies were, dependent on Mediterranean grain, and the Romans blockaded them into submission in 414–17; they ended up fighting on behalf of the Romans against the Vandals in Spain, who were partially destroyed in 417–18, until, in 418, they were finally settled around Toulouse. Constantius married Honorius' sister Galla Placidia, who had previously been married to Athaulf, and he became co-emperor shortly before his death in 421. Military rivalries continued, but the crisis was quietening down. By 425, after a disputed succession, Honorius' nephew, Constantius and Placidia's young son Valentinian III, was western emperor (425–55), with his mother as regent.

The East faced less trauma in this period. The Balkans was a military district, and was always the most invaded part of the eastern empire; there were also Hunnic attacks on it, both before and after the Goths left. But Constantinople, on the edge of the Balkans, was well defended, and the wealth of the East was in the Levant and Egypt, a long way from the northern frontier. Above all, Sassanian Persia, Rome's traditional enemy to the east, was at peace with the empire for almost the entire fifth century, probably because it faced its own threats elsewhere, which allowed the eastern empire a greater strategic security. Eastern politics were often fraught, sometimes violently so, as with the anti-'barbarian' hysteria in the capital which in 400 destroyed the *magister militum* Gainas, and, soon, his rival Fravitta as well, a foretaste of Stilicho's fate later in the decade. But from then onwards most of the political leaders of the East were not soldiers but civilians, ruling for Arcadius and his equally inactive son Theodosius II (408–50), and indeed empresses were particularly prominent in Constantinople, in this period Arcadius' wife Eudoxia in 400–404 and Theodosius' sister Pulcheria in the 410s–420s. Each of these, among other acts, brought down ambitious and uncompromising patriarchs of Constantinople, respectively John Chrysostom in 404 and Nestorios in 431. This in itself shows that the eastern empire was developing a different political style from the West: the patriarch of Constantinople, only established in 381, was already a protagonist in secular politics in a way that the pope in Rome would not be for another century. The fact that the western empire was run from Ravenna, not Rome, meant that Roman city politics were less central to it; the importance of church councils and doctrinal debate as a focus for unity and dissension was also greater in the East, giving bishops in general more of a political voice than they as yet had in the West. The church–state relationship would remain much more intimate in the East in the future, too, except, much later, during the Carolingian period in the West, as we shall see in Chapter 17.

In 425 the East was stable and had begun the long economic revival that would continue into the late sixth century or early seventh. But the West had achieved, after a decade of turmoil, a substantial stability as well. Most of the frontier was still manned by Roman troops. There were 'barbarian' groups settled in the empire, it is true, separate from the Roman military hierarchy, the Visigoths between Bordeaux and Toulouse and the remnants of the Vandal confederacy in western Spain, Suevi in the north and Hasding Vandals in the south; but all these had been defeated, and the Visigoths at least were in formal federate alliance with Rome. Only in the northern provinces of the West, north of the Loire, was the situation still unstable. The far northern border of Gaul was increasingly settled by Franks from just over the Rhine; in the north-west there were intermittent peasant revolts, of groups called Bagaudae, which began in the confusion of the 410s and continued into the 440s, presumably an exasperated reaction against continued taxation at times of military failure; and Britain had been abandoned by the Roman administration after 410. These areas were even more marginal for the West than the Balkans were for the East, however. Orosius, a Christian apologist writing in Spain in 417, could already use the cliché that 'the barbarians, detesting their swords, turned to their ploughs and now cherish the Romans as comrades and friends', and this did not seem a false vision in the next decade. In that same period, 413–25 to be exact, Augustine wrote his monumental *City of God*, initially in reaction to the Sack of Rome; it was neither a triumphant tract about Christian Roman victory (as was Orosius' text) nor a polemic about the dangers facing Roman ill-doing. Augustine was, indeed, careful not to ascribe too much importance or longevity to the great Roman imperial experiment, for the heavenly city is separate from earthly political forms. But his book nonetheless presumes a considerable confidence in the imperial future. The world itself might end, of course, and, Augustine assumed, would indeed do so soon enough; but there is no hint here that an end to the empire was expected or feared by anybody.

Things shifted in the next generation, up to 455. In the East, politics stayed quiet, except for regular Hunnic attacks in the Balkans. This period was marked by the ambitious compilation of the current laws of the empire, the *Theodosian Code*, completed in 438; these were both western and eastern laws (many of them seem to have been collected in Africa), but they were compiled in Constantinople, and bore the eastern emperor's name. It was also marked by two defining church councils, at Ephesos in 431 and at Chalcedon in 451, as we saw in Chapter 3, although their definitions were achieved at the expense of alienating large sectors of the Christian community of the Levant and Egypt, who found themselves stigmatized as Monophysite heretics. Pulcheria was a prominent operator behind the scenes in each of these councils. She had a relatively small role at court between them, especially in the 440s, but at Theodosius II's death she created his successor Marcian (450–57), by marrying him, and she was again influential until her death in 453. Chalcedon, in particular, was a divisive moment; but the fact that the politics of the East hinged on these great ecclesiastical aggregations, rather than on war, is telling in itself.

The West saw more trouble. Military leaders fought over the young Valentinian, with Aetius, based in Gaul, winning out by 433. Aetius ruled the West as *magister militum* until 454, but his interests remained in Gaul. The responsibility for letting the Vandals move into Carthage essentially lies with him; he reacted, but ineffectively and too late. Aetius' main concern was the Visigoths, whom he at least temporarily pacified in 439. Other 'barbarian' groups in Gaul were also persuaded to accept Roman military hegemony, including the Alans and the Burgundians, whom Aetius himself settled in, respectively, the lower Loire valley and the upper Rhône in 442–3. Gaul remained stable under Roman hegemony as a result of Aetius' attentions, although it is undeniable that there were more autonomous groups settled there by Aetius' death than earlier. Italy, too, the core of the West, was actually less menaced by invasion than in the early years of the century. But Africa had been lost, and Spain, too, after the Vandals left in 429, came largely under Suevic control in the 440s; Spain, though, as we have seen, was much less essential to the imperial infrastructure. It is in the 440s that we get our first indications in western legislation that standard taxation was insufficient to pay imperial troops, which heralded tax rises. The Bagaudae reappeared in northern Gaul, and now in north-east Spain as well, the part of the Iberian peninsula still under Roman control. Salvian of Marseille wrote a long hell-fire sermon called *On the Governance of God* in the 440s which ascribed Roman failures against the (obviously inferior) 'barbarians' to their own sins: notably, unjust and excessive taxation, public entertainment and sexual licence. This is the sort of thing extreme Christian preachers always said (and still say), and its detail cannot be taken too seriously; we could not conclude from this, for example, that the western provinces really were being destroyed by overtaxation, and it would be best to see Salvian's writing as a proof of the continuing effectiveness of the fiscal system. But it is undoubtedly true that Salvian's vision of the West now included the 'barbarians' as stable political players, alternatives to Roman rule, and the same was true of the Bagaudae (though the latter were in reality less stable, and disappear from our sources by 450; Aetius and his 'barbarian' allies had defeated them). Salvian thought that Romans often chose to be ruled by 'barbarians' in order to escape Roman state injustice. This was probably not common in the 440s, but the concept was possible to invoke; the historian Priskos in the East, when discussing the Huns, did so in the same period as well.

Aetius, in his campaigns against the Visigoths and others, relied quite substantially on the military support of the Huns. The latter had, by the 420s at the latest, largely settled just outside the empire in the middle Danube plain, what is now eastern Hungary, a good strategic point for attack both into the Balkans and the West. But they were not a full-scale danger until Attila (*c.* 435–53) and his brother Bleda both unified them and reinforced their military hegemony over other 'barbarian' groups, notably the Gepids and that section of the Goths we call Ostrogoths, around 440. The 440s marked serious Hunnic attacks in all directions, culminating in major invasions of Gaul in 451 and Italy in 452. The Huns were defeated in Gaul, however (Aetius used the Visigoths against them, as he had previously used the Huns against the Goths), and retreated from Italy, for less clear reasons; in 453 Attila died unexpectedly, and in 454/5 conflict among his sons and his subject peoples led to the rapid break-up of the Hunnic hegemony. The Huns were a terrifying because unfamiliar people, but as a direct military threat to the Romans they were a flash in the pan. The same is true for Attila's construction of an alternative political focus to the capitals of the empire, which looked impressive at the time, but did not last much more than fifteen years. It could equally be argued that the Huns helped the Romans, not only by fighting for Aetius but also as a force for stability (and thus fewer population movements) beyond the frontier. But this did not outlast 454 either.

The Hunnic empire collapsed, but Aetius was already dead, assassinated by Valentinian III personally in 454, the latter himself killed as a direct result a year later. Aetius was seen by many later as (to quote Marcellinus *comes*) 'the main salvation of the western empire', largely because he was its last commander to convey an impression of military energy over a long period. His errors, especially in Africa, could be regarded as equally fatal. But the 450s still saw a certain level of stability in the West. It now contained half a dozen 'barbarian' polities, with all of which any Roman leader would have to deal, though still from a position of strength: all those polities operated by Roman rules, and cared enough about the empire to seek to influence its choice of rulers. This was shown in the crisis after Valentinian's death, when Geiseric sacked Rome; Theoderic II of the Visigoths (453–66) persuaded Eparchius Avitus, a senator from the Auvergne in central Gaul and one of Aetius' former generals, at that moment on an embassy to him, to claim the imperial office in 455. Avitus was no cipher, all the same. He did not last long, but there would still have been space for an energetic ruler in the West to maintain at least Aetius' hegemony, and maybe even to regain that of Constantius, if he could get eastern logistical support (sometimes available), and if he was very lucky.

Imperial luck did not hold, however. The next two decades, into the next generation, are the period when the West finally broke into pieces. Avitus, clearly a Gaulish imperial candidate, had been defeated by the Italian army under Majorian and Ricimer, and the former became emperor (457–61). Majorian took the trouble to get both eastern recognition and the support of Avitus' Gaulish clientele; he issued legislation which shows reforming aspirations, too. But, if he was energetic, he was certainly not lucky either, for Ricimer, his *magister militum*, organized a coup against him and had him killed. Ricimer then ruled until his death in 472, through a succession of mostly puppet emperors, although Anthemius (467–72), a military figure from the East, had a certain presence and autonomy until Ricimer fell out with him. It was Anthemius who organized, together with the eastern general Basiliscus (the eastern emperor Leo I's brother-in-law), the great attack on the Vandals of 468, which was not only a failure but an extremely expensive one. After that, Ricimer concentrated on Italy, which he defended effectively, and left the rest of the empire largely to its own devices, although he maintained links with south-eastern Gaul through his son-in-law the Burgundian prince Gundobad, who succeeded Ricimer briefly as the imperial strongman before leaving Italy to become Burgundian king (474–516). Ricimer is hard to assess through sources that are both hostile and sketchy, but there is no sign that he had political interests or ambitions which extended beyond Italy; he is a clear sign that imperial horizons were shrinking. After two more short-lived coups, Odovacer, the next effective military supremo in Italy (476–93), did not bother to appoint any emperor of the West, but instead got the Roman senate to petition the eastern emperor Zeno that only one emperor was by now needed; Odovacer then governed Italy in Zeno's name, as *patricius*, patrician, a title used by both Aetius and Ricimer, although inside Italy Odovacer called himself *rex*, king.

The year 476 is the traditional date for the end of the western empire, at the overthrow in Italy of the last emperor, Romulus Augustulus, although 480 is an alternative, for Romulus' predecessor Julius Nepos held out in Dalmatia until then. But Italy is actually the region of the western empire which lived through least change in the 470s, for Odovacer ruled much as Ricimer had, at the head of a regular army. Italy did not experience an invasion and conquest until 489–93, with the arrival of Theoderic the Amal and his Ostrogoths, and Theoderic (489–526) ruled in as Roman a way as possible, too. The end of the empire was experienced most directly in Gaul. The Visigothic king Euric (466–84) was the first major ruler of a 'barbarian' polity in Gaul – the second in the empire after Geiseric – to have a fully autonomous political practice, uninfluenced by any residual Roman loyalties. Between 471 and 476 he expanded his power east to the Rhône (and beyond, into Provence), north to the Loire, and south into Spain. The Goths had already been fighting in Spain since the late 450s (initially on behalf of the emperor Avitus), but Euric organized a fully fledged conquest there, which is ill-documented, but seems to have been complete (except for a Suevic enclave in the north-west) by the time of his death. By far the best documented of Euric's conquests, though not the most important, was the Auvergne in 471–5, because the bishop of its central city, Clermont, was the Roman senator Sidonius Apollinaris. Sidonius, who was Avitus' son-in-law, and had been a leading lay official for both Majorian and Anthemius, ended his political career besieged inside his home city, and we can see all the political changes of the 450s–470s through his eyes. A supporter of alliance with the Visigoths in the 450s, by the late 460s Sidonius had become increasingly aware of the dangers involved, and hostile to Roman officials who still dealt with them; then in the 470s we see him despairing of any further help for Clermont, and contemptuous of the Italian envoys who sacrificed the Auvergne so as to keep Provence under Roman control. By around 480, as he put it, 'now that the old degrees of official rank are swept away . . . the only token of nobility will henceforth be a knowledge of letters'; the official hierarchy had gone, only traditional Roman culture survived.

As an epitaph for the western empire, this is somewhat muted. It is far from clear that Sidonius saw Rome as having definitively ended; and his claim that the traditional hierarchies had gone was certainly exaggerated. But much was changing in Gaul, for all that. Euric's conquests were soon matched by the Burgundians under Gundobad in the Rhône valley, with Provence a battleground between these two peoples and the Ostrogoths in the decades after 490. In the North, there were still armies which looked to Rome, under Aegidius around Soissons, Arbogast around Trier, and Riothamus, a British warlord, on the Loire; but Aegidius had recognized no emperor since Majorian, and these can be regarded as effectively independent polities, probably using rather fewer Roman traditions than the Goths and Burgundians did. The Frankish kings in the North allied and competed with them, and the most successful of these, Clovis of Tournai (481–511), began to take over rival Frankish kingdoms and the lands of Roman warlords alike.

The north of Gaul had long been the most militarized part of the region, where the army structured exchange, social display and land-owning patterns, and this accentuated across the fifth century. Villa culture had ended here by 450, for example, as also in rapidly de-Romanizing Britain, but unlike anywhere else in the West, where the richest rural residences continued until well into the sixth century; this marks the early end of one of the classic markers of civilian élite culture. Sidonius, who knew all the great civilian aristocrats of Gaul, hardly ever wrote to people north of the Loire (one was Arbogast of Trier, whom he praises for maintaining Roman cultural traditions – Sidonius clearly thought that this was hard in the north). The rest of what we know of the north points at very ad-hoc political procedures, as with the saintly Genovefa's travels to find food for Paris in, perhaps, the 470s, or the bishops who dealt directly with Clovis in the 480s. The south of Gaul was much better organized; Visigothic and Burgundian kings legislated, taxed, shipped grain around, used Roman civilian officials, and created integrated Roman and 'barbarian' armies, including Roman generals. But, everywhere in Gaul, the last two decades of the fifth century were definitively post-imperial, in the sense that half a dozen rulers faced each other with no mediation, no distant Rome/Ravenna-based hegemony to look to. Gaul is the best-documented part of the West in the late fifth century, so we can see this most clearly there, even if it was also arguably the region where change was greatest: more than in Italy, certainly, but more even than in Africa, where Vandal rule, popular or not, was solid and relatively traditional. All of these regions were nonetheless post-Roman too; imperial unity and identity was by 500 the property of the East alone.

It must also be recognized when discussing these post-Roman kingdoms that the shift away from Roman government was often rather less organized, or quick, than narratives of conquest imply. Eugippius' *Life* of Severinus gives us an instance of this. Severinus (d. 482) was a holy man in Noricum (modern Austria) in the 470s, at a time when the Danube frontier was breaking down, but the main 'barbarian' group nearby, the Rugi, had remained firmly beyond the river and restricted themselves to raiding and taking tribute – and also to trading with the Romans. Severinus won the respect of King Feletheus and was able to mediate between Romans and Rugi on several occasions. Life in Noricum was clearly miserable, as well as cold (the imagery of winter is stressed constantly by Eugippius, who was a younger contemporary of Severinus but had left for Italy, and who was writing thirty years later much further south, in Naples). It was a province in which the Romans were concentrated in towns and fortifications, and various 'barbarians' roamed the countryside. The Roman army was still in existence, but there was no political leadership, at least in Eugippius' vision of the province, except for Severinus' mediating role. This sort of no man's land may have characterized other areas, too: parts of northern Gaul, parts of central Spain, much of Britain. The social breakdown involved in these regions would have been much greater than that in any area of quick conquest, no matter how violent. But most of the West was nonetheless under the control of more stable (and more Roman) polities, whether Gothic, Burgundian or Vandal.

The East in the late fifth century was a less tranquil place than under Theodosius and Pulcheria. For a start, it had by now rulers who were much more militarized: Aspar, *magister militum* in 457–71, strong-man for his protégé, Emperor Leo I (457–74), until Leo had him killed, and his successor Zeno, who became emperor in his own right (474–91). Secondly, Zeno had constant trouble with rivals. The main eastern army base had remained the Balkans, but this military region was itself more unstable after the end of Hunnic power, and 'barbarian' groups, mostly Goths, were beginning to enter the empire again: two of their leaders, Theoderic Strabo and Theoderic the Amal, each of them with Roman military experience, tried under Leo and Zeno both to gain power in Constantinople and to settle their respective peoples in a favoured part of the Balkans. Zeno was himself from Isauria, a remote mountain region in what is now southern Turkey, and a traditional source of soldiers (and also bandits) which could be seen to an extent as in competition with the Balkans; Zeno had rivals in Isauria, too; tensions with the army thus increased when he succeeded to the throne. Indeed, for a year (475–6) he was out of office, expelled by the general Basiliscus, and he faced several revolts even after that. It was only in the late 480s, shortly before his death, that he managed to quell rivals, and to persuade the main warlord who survived, Theoderic the Amal, to leave with his Gothic army and occupy Italy in 489. These problems meant that Zeno had no hope of intervening in the West himself, even had the fingers of the East not been burnt by the costly failure of the Vandal war in 468. A substantial stability was, however, restored by Anastasius I (491–518), an elderly but able career bureaucrat who lived to the age of eighty-eight and had time both to quell Isaurian revolts and to put imperial finances firmly in the black. The fact that Anastasius could do this, and without a military base either, must indicate that the eastern political system was essentially solid.

We are now in 500, and the East, despite some trouble under Zeno, was still in a stable state. The West had greatly changed, as we have seen, but there were elements of stability there too. Theoderic ruled Italy from Ravenna, the western Roman capital, with a traditional Roman administration, a mixture of senatorial leaders from the city of Rome and career bureaucrats; he was (as Odovacer had also been) respectful of the Roman senate, and he made a ceremonial visit to the city in 500, with formal visits to St Peter's, to the senate building, and then to the imperial palace on the Palatine, where he presided over games, like any emperor. Theoderic's whole modus operandi was largely imperial, and many commentators saw him as a restorer of imperial traditions. This was certainly the view of Cassiodorus Senator (lived *c.* 485–580), who was an administrator for him after 507 and who wrote an extensive collection of official letters for Theoderic and his immediate successors, which he called the *Variae*; Cassiodorus deliberately wrote up Theoderic as an upholder of Roman values, but it was easy for him to do so. The administrative and fiscal system had changed little; the same traditional landowners dominated politics, beside a new (but partly Romanizing) Gothic or Ostrogothic military élite.

Theoderic looked beyond Italy, too. He ruled Dalmatia and the Danube frontier; and he was well aware of his cultural connections to the second Romano-Germanic power in the West, the Visigothic kingdom of Alaric II (484–507) in southern Gaul and Spain. Orosius had claimed that Athaulf the Visigoth said in 414 that he had considered replacing *Romania* with *Gothia*, but had decided against it, because the Goths were too barbaric, and could not obey laws. Were this story true (which is unlikely), it was reversed by the end of the century. Theoderic in Italy, Euric and Alaric in Gaul all legislated for their subjects, Goth and Roman. The Goths were military figures, it is true, unlike the senatorial stratum (or most of them), and were Arian, not Catholic, Christians, but in other respects they were picking up Roman values fast. In this they were followed by the Vandals and Burgundians, who were both very influenced by the larger Gothic kingdoms by 500 or so. In a sense, *Gothia* really had replaced *Romania*, but had done so in large part by imitating the Romans. In the western Mediterranean, in effect everywhere in the West south of the Loire and the Alps, a common political culture survived.

But the world was changing. The end of political unity was not a trivial shift; the whole structure of politics had to change as a result. The ruling classes of the provinces were all still (mostly) Roman, but they were diverging fast. The East was moving away from the West, too. It was becoming much more Greek in its official culture, for a start. Leo I was the first emperor to legislate in Greek; under a century later, Justinian (527–65) may have been the last emperor to speak Latin as a first language. But it is above all in the West that we find a growing provincialization in the late fifth century, both a consequence and a cause of the breakdown of central government. Augustine thought in terms of the whole empire; Salvian took his moral images at least from the whole of the West (though he only really knew Gaul). But Sidonius was definitely a Gaul. Gaulish élites rarely travelled to Italy by now; although Sidonius was urban prefect in Rome in 468, he was the first Gaul to hold the office since perhaps 414, and also the last. His colleagues were even more clearly focused on Gaulish politics, like his friend Arvandus, praetorian prefect of Gaul in 464-8, and his enemy Seronatus, an administrator in central Gaul in and after 469, both of whom threw in their lot with Euric's political ambitions and were cashiered for it; Euric's Roman generals Victorius and Vincentius were presumably more successful variants of the same type, provincials who saw advancement in the Visigothic court as simply more relevant than the traditional career hierarchy centred on distant Ravenna. These were political shifts which made a lot of sense to local actors, but they were fatal to what remained of the empire. Sidonius himself left the imperial hierarchy when he became a bishop in 469/70, and the growing tendency for aristocrats in Gaul to look to the episcopate for a career (above, Chapter 3) expresses this local focus very clearly. In the next generation, horizons narrowed again; Ruricius of Limoges (d. 510) and Avitus of Vienne (d. 518), bishops in the Visigothic and Burgundian kingdoms respectively, both left collections of letters, written very largely to recipients inside their respective kingdoms (with the main exception of Sidonius' son Apollinaris in Clermont, to whom they were both related).

This provincialization was not restricted to Gaul, either. Hydatius of Chaves (d. c. 470) wrote a chronicle which tells almost entirely of Spain, especially the north-west, where he was based. Victor of Vita in Huneric's Africa saw the Vandals exclusively from the perspective of the Africani; the Roman empire never appears in his text, and even Romani are only referred to when he is being very generic. A common political culture may have survived, but in each former Roman region or province its points of reference were becoming more localized, and its lineaments would soon start to diverge. The easy unity which had taken the biblical scholar Jerome in the late fourth century from Dalmatia to Trier, then Antioch, Constantinople, Rome and finally Palestine, from where he wrote letters to his Mediterranean-wide ascetic clientele for thirty years, had gone. I shall come back to this issue in more general terms later in this chapter.

The high point of the Gothic western Mediterranean was around 500. It was destroyed by two men, Clovis the Frankish king and the eastern emperor Justinian; let us look at them in turn. Clovis reunited northern Gaul, including some non-Roman territories, during his reign; in 507 he attacked the Visigoths, defeating and killing Alaric II at the battle of Vouillé, and virtually drove them out of Gaul (they only kept Languedoc, on the Mediterranean coast). The Burgundians held on for a time, but in the 520s Clovis's sons attacked them too, and took over their kingdom in 534. Theoderic reacted by occupying Visigothic Spain, nominally ruling for Alaric's son Amalaric (511–31), but Spain's political system went into crisis for two generations. It is hard to see that Theoderic's Spanish extension was more than the temporary reinforcement of the Mediterranean coast against the Frankish threat; already by 511 the hegemony of the Goths in the West had largely gone, except in Italy. Clovis's Merovingian dynasty would dominate post-Roman politics in the West for the next two centuries. We shall look at its history in the next chapter. For now, it is enough to stress one important geopolitical consequence of Clovis's success: northern Gaul, long a military border-land, rather marginal to the Roman world except in the mid-fourth century when Trier was the western capital, became a political heartland territory, a focus for great landed wealth and political power. It was initially a focus for Gaul alone, but across later centuries it was one for the whole of western Europe.

Justinian, Anastasius' second successor, took Anastasius' large budgetary surplus and devoted most of his forty-year reign to imperial renewal. There is a bounce about his accession in 527 that had not been visible for any emperor since Julian. As we saw in Chapter 2, starting in 528 he had Theodosius II's law code revised in a year, and by 533 the writings of the Roman jurists were codified as the *Digest*, still today the master text of Roman law. Furthermore, a string of new laws (*Novels*) surveyed and revised the administration of the empire in the 530s, and also tightened laws on sexual deviance and heresy, even Jewish heresy, provoking Samaritan revolts and severe repression in northern Palestine in 529 and 555. Justinian was no liberal, and a growing humourlessness and intolerance of religious difference is visible in the East from this time onwards; he was nonetheless an innovator, and the complaints of traditionalists during his reign about the uncultured radicals in his administration indicate that his organizational changes had some effect. Justinian was also a builder, always an important part of political display in the Roman tradition. He is not the only one in this chapter; Zeno, Anastasius and perhaps also Theoderic the Ostrogoth were particularly active; but the scale of Justinian's building outmatched them all, as with the huge churches he built in Constantinople (such as Hagia Sophia, see below, Chapter 10), Ephesos and Jerusalem. These building campaigns are well documented in a panegyric work, Prokopios' *On Buildings*; as a result, archaeologists have been prone to date almost every major late Roman building in the East to the second quarter of the sixth century, and careful redatings have been necessary to uncover other patrons both before and after him. All the same, the money and the commitment were there to do a lot.

Given the self-confidence of these acts, it is not surprising that Justinian was also interested in war. He faced Persian wars, the first serious conflicts for well over a century, in 527–32 and 540–45, and intermittently thereafter up to 562. Persia was always the major front for the eastern empire (the Balkans were also attacked in his reign, but this was hardly new, and was regarded as less crucial). It was expensive both in resources and in post-war reconstruction, and many emperors would have restricted their attention to Persian defence. But Justinian used the period of eastern peace in 532–40 to attack the West as well. His general Belisarios took Vandal Africa quickly, in 533–4, and moved straight into Ostrogothic Italy; he had almost completely conquered it by 540. Theoderic's last years had shown up tensions with traditionalist figures too, and the aristocratic philosopher Boethius, among others, was executed for treasonous communication with the East in 526; infighting between Theoderic's heirs in 526–36 led to a more serious alienation of some of the aristocratic élite from the Ostrogothic regime, many of whom ended up in Constantinople. But whereas the conquest of Africa was largely a success, Italy was not. Most of the non-Gothic Italians were at best neutral about Justinian's armies, and the Goths regrouped after 540 under Totila (541–52), when the renewal of the Persian war pulled Roman troops away from the peninsula. The 540s saw Italy devastated, as Roman and Gothic armies in turn conquered and reconquered sections of the peninsula, and when war largely stopped in 554 Italy, now Roman again, had a fiscal system in ruins, a fragmented economy and a largely scattered aristocracy. This was not handled well, then. But Justinian had nonetheless absorbed the central Mediterranean back into the empire, and when his armies also occupied part of the Spanish coast in 552, almost the whole of the Mediterranean returned to being a Roman lake.

Justinian was and is a controversial figure. He was hated by many, notably those whom he disagreed with on religious matters and persecuted, who became more numerous as his reign went on. This followed his growing hostility to Monophysites, especially after the death of his influential wife Theodora (herself a Monophysite) in 548, and then his equally controversial attempt to take a doctrinal step in the Monophysite direction at the fifth ecumenical council of Constantinople in 553, which alienated much of the West. Less serious (and far too influential on modern scholars) was Prokopios' set-piece anti-panegyric, the *Secret History*, which depicts Justinian and Theodora as wicked geniuses, in highly coloured and sexualized terms, with Justinian characterized as a demon. Today, Justinian is above all accused of ruining the empire financially, thanks to his anachronistic wars in the West; the eastern empire after his death in 565 is often seen as weakened, both militarily and economically, a state of affairs that would result in the political disasters of the years after 610. We shall look at the seventh-century crisis in Chapter 11, but it does not seem to me to have much to do with Justinian. The western wars were not anachronistic, for the Roman empire was still a meaningful concept even in the West, nor were they particularly expensive; Africa was won on a shoestring, and remained Roman for more than a century longer, and the Italian war would have been less of a mess if Justinian had put more, not less, money into it. Justinian's successors, notably Tiberius II (578–82) and Maurice (582–602), held off the Persians, their main opponents, as effectively as Justinian had done. They also kept out the Avars, the new holders of 'barbarian' hegemony in the middle Danube, who from the 560s turned the most recent invaders of the Balkans, mostly Slavic-speaking (but also Turkic- and Germanic-speaking), into the greatest military threat in the area since the Huns. They abandoned most of Italy to a new people, the Lombards, but given Italy's state this was not necessarily a strategic failure. Furthermore, money was sufficiently loose into the 570s for Tiberius (though not Maurice) to be noted as an extravagant spender. Justinian's reign does not seem to have been a negative turning point for the empire. But the controversy over it does at least mark respect: Justinian put his stamp on a generation, all over the Mediterranean, and, unlike most rulers, the events of his reign seem to have been the result of his own choices. His protagonism gives the lie to the view that the break-up of the fifth-century West in itself marks the failure of the Roman imperial project.

The foregoing pages give a bare summary of the events of a hundred and fifty years; we must now consider what they mean. I shall concentrate more on the West, because it was there that the greatest changes took place, although the stability and prosperity of the East must act as a permanent reminder to us that the Roman empire was by no means bound to break up. In recent decades this view, already discussed in Chapter 2, has indeed become a dominant one among historians. This means that the invasions and occupations of the western provinces must be at the heart of our explanations of the period. But in recent decades we have also moved away from catastrophist views of the 'barbarians', encapsulated in André Piganiol's famous lines at the close of his book on the late empire, written (significantly) just after the Second World War, 'Roman civilization did not die a natural death. It was assassinated.' Recent work has in fact depicted the new ethnic groups in very Roman terms, a view which I fully accept and shall develop further shortly. This does not lessen the simple point that the Roman empire in the West was replaced by a set of independent kingdoms which did not make claims to imperial legitimacy; but it does force us to ask why each of these kingdoms could not have just reproduced the Roman state in miniature, maintaining structural continuities that could, in principle, have been reunited later, by Justinian, for example. For the fact is that most of them did not do so. One thing that archaeology makes very clear, as we shall see, is the dramatic economic simplification of most of the West: this is visible north of the Loire in the early fifth century, and in the northern Mediterranean lands during the sixth. Building became far less ambitious, artisanal production became less professionalized, exchange became more localized. The fiscal system, the judicial system, the density of Roman administrative activity in general, all began to simplify as well. These are real changes which cannot be talked away by arguments that show, however justifiably, that the 'barbarians' merely fitted Roman niches. They are matched by shifts in imagery, values, cultural style, which makes the seventh century in the West noticeably different in feel from the fourth or even the fifth: we are by now out of the late Roman world and into the early Middle Ages. How this could be, given the lack of innovation desired by most of the new ethnic groups, is the issue we need to confront.

To start with, there is an evident continuum between the leadership of the fifth-century western (and indeed eastern) empire and the 'barbarian' kings. The fifth-century emperors were mostly ciphers, controlled by military strong-men, Stilicho, Constantius, Aetius, Ricimer, Aspar, Zeno, Gundobad, Orestes (Romulus Augustulus' father). It is interesting that none of these tried to seize the throne by force, as military figures regularly had in the third century, and only two (Constantius and Zeno) became emperor even by more regular means. One commonly advanced reason for this is that, as ethnic 'barbarians', they were not entitled to imperial office; but, quite apart from the fact that not all of them were of non-Roman descent, there is no contemporary basis whatsoever for an exclusion of this kind. Basiliscus, briefly eastern emperor in 475–6, may indeed have been Odovacer's uncle, and thus a Scirian, from a subject people of Attila's Huns; Silvanus, a failed usurper in 355, was certainly a Frank. More likely they held off from seizing power because of a trend towards a view that imperial legitimacy was allied to genealogy, a view which can be traced back to Constantine's family in the mid-fourth century; it would have seemed safer to control an emperor (or a series of emperors, as Ricimer did) than to usurp the throne. And it probably was; these strong-men had much longer periods of authority than most third-century emperors. An important element in late Roman genealogical legitimacy was marriage, so all the strong-men intermarried with the imperial families, hoping to put their sons on the throne; Constantius and Zeno both managed this. (Zeno became sole emperor himself, of course, but only as heir to his own short-lived son.) But this is equally true of the 'barbarian' royal families, most of whom had, or soon established, links of marriage to the Romans, often doubtless with the same intent. This genealogical network makes a nonsense of cultural difference, at least at the imperial or royal level. So does the fact that nearly every emperor of the East for more than a century after 450 (with only one exception, Zeno) came from the melting pot of the Balkans, where new identities were being refashioned all the time, as also did a high percentage of the imperial strong-men and the 'barbarian' leaders alike. And there were cross-overs in personal terms: both Gundobad the Burgundian and Theoderic the Ostrogoth had careers in and around the imperial court before becoming kings of independent ex-Roman provinces.

The importance of intermarriage as a criterion for succession also put a good deal of stress on imperial women. We have seen that Galla Placidia and particularly Pulcheria were powerful in the early fifth century, and both legitimized their imperial husbands. So did Ariadne, daughter of Leo I and wife successively of Zeno and Anastasius. Verina, Leo's wife, was Basiliscus' sister. Theodora, herself a powerful political operator despite her husband Justinian's dominance, seems to have promoted her kin as well, although she died too long before her husband for any of them still to be in place to succeed him. Sophia, widow of Justin II (565–78), certainly chose his successor, Tiberius II, and perhaps Maurice too. There was a space for female political action here, which was taken up many times. It is thus not surprising that Anicia Juliana (d. 527/8), a rich private citizen in Constantinople but a descendant of Valentinian III and of a whole host of empresses (and also wife of a descendant of Aspar), and bearing the title of *patricia* by 507, should have had an impact on Justinian: her church of Hagios Polyeuktos, in the centre of Constantinople, built around 525, was the largest church in the city until Justinian built Hagia Sophia a decade later, probably in part as a response. This space for female power, however ambivalent (for it was always that), was more of an eastern than a western feature; the military crises of the West favoured a more male military leadership. Women in the West who could dominate a militarized politics would appear later, with the Lombards after 590 and the Merovingian Franks after 575, but their prominence had different reasons.

To return to the 'barbarian' leaders, and to their peoples: what exactly was non-Roman, 'barbarian', Germanic, about them at all? There is at present enormous debate about this, with an endless variety of positions even among those who accept that the new ethnic groups sought to accommodate themselves to Roman rules as much as they could: from the belief that there was a substantial kernel of non-Roman values and traditions, associated with the dominant element in any invading or settling group, which could survive for centuries, to the belief that Germanic ethnic markers were only a renaming of the military identity of Roman soldiers, and that there was nothing traditional about them at all. It does at least need to be recognized, with this second position, that most of the new 'barbarian' groups in the fifth-century empire had a history of employment in the Roman army; the most successful soldiers among them, such as the Visigoths, were effectively indistinguishable from a Roman military detachment. ('Barbarian' armies regularly travelled with their families and dependants, but, although it was theoretically illegal, it would be unwise to presume that Roman armies in practice did not.) We can, however, see a clear distinction in our sources between regular army forces, which, whether of Roman or 'barbarian' origin (as we saw in Chapter 2, there was on the frontiers, whence soldiers usually came, little difference between them), were part of a standard military hierarchy and career structure; and the followers of King X or leader Y, who identified with their leader, generally had a distinct ethnic name, and were accepted into the Roman army as a discrete group. This is the distinction between Odovacer and Theoderic, for example, successive rulers of Italy. Odovacer was the candidate of the Roman army of Italy, which merely happened to consist of ethnic Heruls, Sciri and Torcilingi; Odovacer was himself at least half-Scirian, but he had a Roman military background, and is never called leader of the Sciri, or of any other group in Italy. He became a king, formally autonomous, but he recognized Zeno, and could fairly easily have been refigured as part of the Roman empire. Theoderic, by contrast, was a king *of the Goths*, whose people came with him from the start, no matter how many imperial titles he also had. That people was as mixed as Odovacer's supporters; it certainly contained Rugi (who maintained an identity through intermarriage for fifty years after Theoderic's conquest of Italy), Gepids, Huns and doubtless men of Roman descent as well, and, after Theoderic's conquest, it will have absorbed all or most of Odovacer's following. But it was attached to a leader, and had a name, 'Gothic', Ostrogothic in our terminology; this name characterized the people as a whole, no matter what their origin, and also Theoderic's kingship. It was peoples like this, heterogeneous but – an essential feature – tied together by a single leader, which took over the western provinces, and indeed renamed them, the *regnum Francorum* instead of or alongside Gaul, the *regnum Vandalorum* instead of or alongside Africa. If they stayed in charge of their lands long enough, as the Franks and Visigoths did, though the Vandals and Ostrogoths did not, they tended to forget their disparate origins, and 'become' Frankish or Gothic – and also, crucially, not Roman.

It is this process that has been called 'ethnogenesis' by Herwig Wolf-ram and his school: the recognition that ethnic identities were flexible, malleable, 'situational constructs'; the same 'barbarian' in sixth-century Italy could be Rugian, and Ostrogothic, and (though only after the east Roman reconquest) even Roman. Such people would have picked up different identities successively (or contemporaneously), and these would have brought with them different modes of behaviour and loyal-ties, and even, eventually, different memories. As Walter Pohl has recently put it, the 'kernel of traditions' that made someone Ostrogoth or Visigoth was probably a network of contradictory and changeable beliefs; there does not have to have been a stable set of traditions in each group as it moved from beyond the frontier, to discontinuous service in the Roman army, then to settlement in a Roman province. By 650 every 'barbarian' kingdom had its own traditions, some of them claiming to go back centuries, and those doubtless were by then core elements in the founding myths of many of their inhabitants; all the same, founding myths not only do not have to be true, but also do not have to be old. Each of the 'Romano-Germanic' kingdoms had a bricolage of beliefs and identities with very varying roots, and these, to repeat, could change, and be reconfigured, in each generation to fit new needs. Historians tend to give more attention to the account that Clovis's grandfather was the son of a sea-monster, a quinotaur, than to the account that the Franks were descended from the Trojans, which seems more 'literary', less 'authentic'; but the first record of each of these traditions appears in the same seventh-century source, and it would be hard to say that one was more widely believed – or older – than the other.

From all of this, one has to conclude that post-Roman identities were a complex mixture, and they had a variety of origins: Roman, 'barbarian', biblical; and also both oral and literary. What they had to do was less to locate an ethnic group in the past, than to distinguish it from its contemporary neighbours. This means that to ask what was non-Roman or 'barbarian' about the new ethnic groups is in part the wrong question; Arianism, for example, was a very Roman heresy, but by 500, for most people, it had become an ethnic marker, of Goths or Vandals. The Gothic language itself was by 500 in large part a liturgical tradition, associated precisely with that ex-Roman Arianism, rather than with 'Gothic-ness' in an ethnic sense; many Goths just spoke Latin, without their Gothic-ness being affected either positively or negatively. Indeed, unlike in the twentieth and twenty-first centuries, language was not, as far as we can see, a strong ethnic marker anywhere in our period. Plenty of Franks in 600, say, still spoke Frankish (a version of what we now call Old High German), but very probably not all did, and many were certainly fully bilingual. Gregory of Tours, the most prolific writer of the sixth century in Gaul, who was a monoglot Latin-speaker, never gives the slightest indication that he had trouble communicating with anyone else in the Frankish kingdoms. Neither he nor anyone else in the Frankish world, until the ninth century in fact, makes anything of communication difficulties between primary speakers of Latin and Frankish; it must have happened, but it was not a problem for Frankishness.

This does not mean that the 'barbarian' groups brought nothing of their earlier cultures into the empire, all the same. There is a whole historiography which discusses the German-ness of early medieval social practices, such as large kin-groups, or feud, or personal followings, or meat-eating, or certain concepts of property, or certain types of brooch or belt-buckle. Almost all of this is phoney if seen as a sign of innate identity, as if the Franks of 700 were exactly the same as the Franks of 350. Some of it is inaccurate, too: most early medieval property law had impeccable Roman antecedents, or at least close Roman parallels; similarly, 'Germanic' metalwork sometimes has Roman antecedents, and, even if it does not, does not provide us with any guide to the ethnic identities of the people who wore it. But it would be equally unhelpful to cancel all of this by sleight of hand, and to present the new ethnic groups simply as variants of Roman society itself. A stress on aristocratic meat-eating, for example, genuinely does seem to be an innovation of (among others) the Franks; it was not part of Roman cuisine, where status was conveyed by the complexity and the cost of ingredients, but first appears in a treatise about diet written for the Frankish king Theuderic I (511–33) by a doctor of Greek origin called Anthimus, and it continued throughout the Middle Ages.

A particularly important innovation was the public assembly, the formal meeting of the adult male members of a political community, to deliberate and decide on political action and war, and, increasingly, to make law and judge disputes. The Romans had plenty of large-scale public ceremonials, as we saw in Chapter 3, but in the post-Roman kingdoms assemblies had a wider significance, in that they represented the principle that the king had a direct relationship with all free Franks, or Lombards, or Burgundians; these derived from the values of the tribal communities of the imperial period, but continued in the very different post-Roman world. We can thus trace a continuum of political practice which links the Franks and Lombards, not with Rome in this case, but with the less Romanized or un-Romanized peoples of the early medieval North; the Frankish or Lombard *placitum* assembly, or the Burgundian *conventus*, has parallels with the Anglo-Saxon *gemot*, the Scandinavian *thing*, the Irish *óenach*. These assemblies were not really of all free men, the traditional kingdom-at-arms of Romantic mythology, but they could be wide gatherings for all that, and they derived their power to legitimate political and judicial acts precisely from the fact that many people were there. From 500 to 1000, and sometimes later, public politics in the West was underpinned by the direct participation of wide sections of free, male, society. This went together with an assumption that wide sections of the free had military obligations, which was largely a product of post-Roman conditions, as we shall see in more detail later. But the link between military commitment and assembly politics must have made sense already to the ethnic armies of the fifth century; the generalization of assembly imagery in every Romano-Germanic kingdom (even the heavily Romanized Visigothic state) itself allows us to presume it.

Notwithstanding these new features, 'barbarian' leaders fitted into a Roman world, more and more as the fifth century wore on, and as local Roman élites adjusted to new political situations. It is striking how Roman these élites could make their new rulers in their writings; nearly every new ruling ethnic group had its apologist who was prepared to describe 'barbarian' kings in resonantly Roman terms, as with Sidonius' famous prose panegyric on the Visigothic king Theoderic II, stressing his seriousness, his accessibility to ambassadors and petitioners (and his board-games), and playing down his Arianism. There were not large numbers of 'barbarian' invaders in any province; all raw figures are guesswork, but historians generally propose up to 100,000 for major ruling groups like the Ostrogoths or the Vandals, and around 20,000–25,000 for the adult males who made up their armies, in provinces whose indigenous populations numbered in the millions. Putting together the ethnic flexibility of so many of the actors of the period, the Romanizing images of so many of our texts, and the small demographic impact of the invaders – one in ten? one in twenty? one in fifty? – it is easy to imagine that they had no effect at all on the social practices of each province. But if we argue this line too schematically, we risk ending up with no explanations for change at all. And change, in the fifth century, certainly took place.

This change did not derive mostly from cultural differences, all the same. Regions which experienced the miserable insecurities described earlier for Noricum would have seen substantial social breakdown even if no 'barbarians' ever settled. But in conquered provinces, the majority in the West, change derived most of all from the structural position of each 'barbarian' group. As noted earlier, the 'barbarian' armies that took over provinces had different aims from the Roman armies that seized power for their generals in previous centuries. They wanted to settle back on the land, as their ancestors had done, before the generation or so of intermittent movement and conquest. Their leaders, and probably a good proportion of the middling Goths or Vandals or Franks as well, also wanted to be a ruling class, like the rich Roman aristocrats in each of the provinces they occupied. To fulfil this aim, itself a very Roman one, they needed estates, and, as conquerors, they were in a good position to obtain it. Although the exact details of the land-settlement of each 'barbarian' group are obscure and hotly debated (indeed, they must have been very variable), by 500 or so it is clear that Gothic and other 'barbarian' aristocrats had extensive properties, and were keen to extend them further; Cassiodorus' *Variae* include several instances of Ostrogoths abusing their political and military authority and expropriating the lands of others, for example. Beginning in the fifth century, there was a steady trend away from supporting armies by public taxation and towards supporting them by the rents deriving from private landowning, which was essentially the product of this desire for land of conquering élites. In 476, according to Prokopios, even the Roman army of Italy wanted to be given lands, and got it by supporting Odovacer. Prokopios may well have exaggerated; the Ostrogothic state in Italy certainly still used taxation to pay the army, at least in part, probably more than any other post-Roman polity did by the early sixth century. Overall, however, the shift to land was permanent. After the end of Ostrogothic Italy, there are no references in the West to army pay, except rations for garrisons, until the Arabs reintroduced it into Spain from the mid-eighth century onwards; in the other western kingdoms, only occasional mercenary detachments were paid until well after the end of the period covered by this book. Some of this land may have been fiscal, that is, public property, and distributed by kings; some may have been part of a regular land-settlement, in which fixed proportions of the property of Roman landowners were ceded to the 'barbarians', probably in lieu of tax; some (as in Vandal Africa) may have simply been taken by force. Either way, a move to a landed army, and thus a landed politics, began here; so also did a move to a 'barbarian' ethnic identity on the part of landowners, whatever their origins.

The major post-Roman kingdoms still taxed, into the seventh century. But if the army was landed, the major item of expense in the Roman budget had gone. The city of Rome, another important item, was only supplied from Italy after 439, and lost population fast, as we have seen. The central and local administration of the post-Roman states was perhaps paid for longer, but in most of them the administration quickly became smaller and cheaper. Tax still made kings rich, and their generosity increased the attractive power of royal courts. But this was all it was for, by 550 or so. Tax is always unpopular, and takes work to exact; if it is not essential, this work tends to be neglected. It is thus not surprising that there are increasing signs that it was not assiduously collected. In ex-Vandal Africa after 534, the Roman re-conquerors had to reorganize the tax administration to make it effective again, to great local unpopularity; in Frankish Gaul in the 580s, assessment registers were no longer being systematically updated, and tax rates may only have been around a third of those normal under the empire. Tax was, that is to say, no longer the basis of the state. For kings as well as armies, landowning was the major source of wealth from now on.

This was a crucial change. Tax-raising states are much richer than most land-based ones, for property taxes are generally collected from very many more people than pay rent to a ruler from his public land. Probably only the Frankish kings at the high points of their power, the century after 540 and the century after 770, could match in wealth the states of the eastern Mediterranean, the Byzantine empire and the Arab caliphate, which still maintained Roman traditions of taxation. And tax-raising states have a far greater overall control over their territories, partly because of the constant presence of tax-assessors and collectors, partly because state dependants (both officials and soldiers) are salaried. Rulers can stop paying salaries, and have greater control over their personnel as a result. But if armies are based on landowning, they are harder to control. Generals may be disloyal unless they are given more land, which reduces the amount of land the ruler has; and, if they are disloyal, they keep control of their land unless they are expelled by force, often a difficult task. Land-based states risk breaking up, in fact, for their outlying territories are hard to dominate in depth, and may secede altogether. This would not be common until the late ninth century or later in the West. Many things would have to change before then, as we shall see in later chapters. But it did happen in the end, above all in the wide lands ruled by the Franks.

The shift from taxation to landowning as the basis of the state in the West was the clearest sign that the post-Roman kingdoms would not be able to re-create the Roman empire in miniature, however much their rulers would have liked to. Overall, too, these kingdoms did not match the empire in their economic complexity, either. Archaeology shows a steady simplification of economic structure in most of the West by 550 or so. By then, rich urban and rural dwellings (villas) had often been abandoned, or subdivided into smaller houses; artisan production was generally smaller-scale, and sometimes less skilled (this is particularly clear in the case of pottery production, always our best archaeological indicator of artisanal professionalization); goods were exchanged much less between the provinces of the former empire, and inside those provinces, the new kingdoms, the distribution range of artisanal goods was generally much reduced. The pacing of these changes varied greatly from place to place, and not all of them took place everywhere. In northern Gaul, towns decreased in size and villas were abandoned by 450, but production and distribution patterns dipped much less (northern Gaul's economy had long been separate from that of the Mediterranean), and had stabilized by the sixth century. In Spain, the interior saw a simplification of distribution patterns and a partial abandonment of villas from the later fifth century, whereas the Mediterranean coast saw less change until after 550. In Italy and southern Gaul, the mid-sixth century was the major period of change, but small-scale skilled artisanal production survived, and so did towns. In Africa, the great export region in the late Roman West, little internal change is visible at all until 500 or so, and one can track a survival of the main elements of the Roman economic structure until after 600, even though there is a steady decrease in African exports found in most of the rest of the Mediterranean which begins as early as 450.

These regional differences – which could be multiplied, for our information is getting more detailed all the time, as scientific archaeological excavation becomes commoner in each country – are markers of the different impact the invasions and dislocations of the period 400–550 had on each part of the empire. It was more than one might expect in inland Spain; less than one might expect in Frankish northern Gaul and Vandal Africa. These differences also show that the aristocracies of the newly created kingdoms did not match the wealth of their predecessors or ancestors, partly precisely because it was harder to own far-flung estates now that the empire was divided up (the hyper-rich senatorial élite of Rome ceased to exist, in particular), but this impoverishment was also very variable indeed in regional terms. Seen globally, however, these changes show that the post-Roman kingdoms in the West were unable to match the intensity of circulation and the scale of production of the later Roman empire. The East was very different in this respect; in the early sixth century, towns, industries and the exchange of goods were reaching their height, and continued at that level until the early seventh century. But the empire survived in the East. This correlation is exact: economic complexity depended on imperial unity, in both the eastern and the western empire. The implications that these changes had for local societies in the West will be discussed in Chapter 9.

The existence of 'barbarian' élites in each of the post-Roman kingdoms had an impact on Roman élite culture as well: not because the incomers were culturally distinct – as we have just seen, in most respects they were not – but because they were military. The aristocratic strata of the Roman empire had been mostly civilian, as we saw in Chapter 2. This was already less the case in the world of Aetius; Eparchius Avitus, for example, from a major Gaulish senatorial family, had been one of Aetius' generals before he became emperor, and could be described in very martial terms by his son-in-law Sidonius. But in the post-Roman kingdoms, the secular career structure became steadily more militarized, and more and more ambitious Romans found places in royal armies and entourages alongside the 'barbarian' élites themselves, rather than in the steadily simplifying civilian administration. Sidonius himself never did this, but his son Apollinaris fought for the Visigoths at Vouillé, and

Apollinaris' son Arcadius was a supporter of Childebert I of the Franks. The place where civilian aristocratic values survived longest was Rome itself, because the senatorial hierarchy there was partially separate from state service, but even in Italy senators could make the military choice: Boethius' enemy Cyprian, who had a partly military career, brought up his sons to be soldiers and even to speak Gothic.

These trends persisted; all secular aristocratic hierarchies became military. The only alternative was the church. As we have already noted, aristocrats became bishops in Gaul first, by the mid-fifth century; in Italy this was less common until the Gothic war, but was normal thereafter. This ecclesiastical choice shows the growing wealth of the church, such that it was worthwhile for an élite family to seek to dominate the episcopal office, and thus church land, in a given diocese. It also shows the growing localization of political action, for episcopal power was focused above all inside the diocese, except for the richest and most influential bishops; the church became even more decentralized in the post-imperial West. Being a bishop was sometimes a retirement option (as with both Sidonius and his son Apollinaris in Clermont), but increasingly it became a career choice, with a specifically clerical training: sometimes for younger sons, but sometimes for whole families. The extended family of Gregory of Tours in sixth-century central Gaul included seven bishops in four generations, and only one military figure, the *dux* Gundulf.

The major result of these trends was that the secular élite culture of the Roman empire lost its role as a marker of status. This is probably why rural villas were abandoned: as a sign of ease and luxury, they were out of date in a more militarized society. Meat-eating came in in this context, too. Élite clothing changed as well; early medieval kings and aristocrats dressed like late Roman generals, not like the older toga-clad senatorial tradition. But above all, to know Virgil and the other secular classics by heart, to be able to write poetry and complex prose, which Sidonius still regarded as essential, ceased to be important; swordsmanship, or the Bible, were far more relevant sources of cultural capital. Our written sources change dramatically as a result, becoming much more focused on Christian themes, hagiography, sermons, liturgy (as they would in Byzantium too). It is not that all forms of literary training ended; even in the West, aristocracies were generally able to read until the end of the ninth century. But we should anyway remain neutral about such changes. As stressed in Chapter 2, it is more important to recognize that a complex education had above all existed in order to mark the Roman élites as special, and, now that that élite identity was changing, it was no longer needed.

These changes usually took place slowly: a hundred and fifty years is a long time, after all. (Only in Italy were the changes really rapid, the result of the catastrophe of the Gothic war, in the 540s above all.) People were not usually aware of them; they adjusted easily to each small shift. It is not at all clear how far the majority of western writers saw the Roman world as having ended in the period up to 550, or indeed later. Writers rarely showed much nostalgia for the past, and, although they were certainly capable of complaining about how dreadful present-day morals were, this is a feature of conservatives of every generation. In any case, as writing became more ecclesiastical, it also became more socially critical, more moralizing; but that was a product of genre, not necessarily of social change, whether perceived or real. Traditional Roman aristocracies, the writers of most of our sources, were after all still in place in most parts of the West; they existed alongside newer families, rising in the church or the army, and of course the new 'barbarian' élites, but these latter groups were still copying Roman aristocratic culture. Still, that culture was itself changing. And aristocracies were becoming steadily more localized, drifting apart from each other. In the end – by 650, in every one of the post-Roman kingdoms – they would cease to think of themselves as Roman, but, rather, as Frankish or Visigothic or Lombard. 'Romans' were, by then, restricted to the eastern empire, to the non-Lombard portions of Italy (above all Rome itself), and to Aquitaine, the ex-Visigothic part of Gaul, where the Franks settled least. By then Romans were seen as belonging in the past, too; but it took that long for people to recognize that the empire had really gone in the West.

Why the Roman empire vanished in the West and not in the East is a problem that has perplexed centuries of scholars, and will continue to do so. It does not seem to me to reflect social differences between West and East, or the division of the empire. It probably did derive in part from the greater exposure of heartland areas in the West, Italy and especially central and southern Gaul, to frontier invasion; attacks on the Balkans in the East rarely got past Constantinople into the rest of the empire, but attacks on the western military regions, northern Gaul and the Danube provinces, could get further much more easily. Accepting invading groups into the western empire and settling them as federates was a perfectly sensible response to this, as long as those federate areas did not become so unruly that Roman armies had to be held back to fight them, or so large that they threatened the tax base of the empire, and thus the resources for the regular armies themselves. Unfortunately for the West, however, this did happen. The Visigoths in 418 could be a support for the empire, but fifty years later they were inimical to it. As argued earlier, the conquest of the grain heartland of Africa by the Vandals in 439, which the Romans mistakenly did not anticipate and resist, seems to me the turning point, the moment after which these potential supports might turn into dangers. Army resources lessened too much after that; the balance of power changed. By 476 even the Roman army in Italy may have started to think that landowning was desirable. And, not less important, local élites began to deal with the 'barbarian' powers rather than with the imperial government, which was by now too distant and decreasingly relevant; the provincialization of politics marked the death knell for the western empire. In the East, the control by the empire of that other huge grain resource, the Nile valley in Egypt, was never under threat in this period, and the logistical structure of the empire remained untouched as a result. When the Persians and then the Arabs took Egypt, and also the Levant, from Roman control after 618, the East would however face a huge and rapid crisis as well. The eastern Roman empire (we shall from that point on call it the Byzantine empire) survived, but it was a close-run thing, and the eastern empire changed considerably as a result.

PART II

The Post-Roman West, 550–750

Huneric Africa 429
Vandal admin - currency
Creative adaption of Romans
Administration (vandal) identical
to Roman provincial
kings taxed as Romans had
Rouge army which ran a Roman
style gov.
Vandals autonomous.

5

Merovingian Gaul and Germany, 500–751

In 589 a group of the leading aristocrats of the kingdom of the Frankish king Childebert II (575–96), led by Duke Rauching, plotted Childebert's assassination. They had long been opposed to Childebert's mother Queen Brunhild (d. 613) and her supporters, and, even though Childebert was now an adult (he was probably nineteen), Brunhild was gaining in authority. But they were found out. Rauching, who may have had royal ambitions, was killed at once on Childebert's orders at the king's palace (probably at Reims), and his huge wealth was confiscated. His closest supporters, Ursio and Berthefried, had already mobilized an army, and they fled to a hill-top church in the wooded Woëvre region above Verdun, which overlooked Ursio's estate-centre, and which had been a fortification in pre-Roman times. The king's army besieged the church and Ursio was killed; Berthefried fled to Verdun cathedral, where he sought sanctuary, but he was killed there anyway, to the great distress of the local bishop.

This narrative, like almost all our evidence from sixth-century Gaul, is known to us because of the extensive writings of Gregory, bishop of Tours. Gregory, an active political bishop of Roman senatorial back-ground, had been appointed in 573 by Brunhild and her husband Sigibert I (561–75), and there is no doubt of his support for the queen's party. He detested Rauching for his sadism, and he retells the deaths of the conspirators with verve: Rauching tripped at the door of the king's private room and cut about the head with swords, his naked body then thrown out of the window, Ursio overwhelmed by his enemies outside the church, Berthefried hit by tiles from the partly dismantled cathedral roof. Gregory's partisanship goes with his narrative gifts to make him one of the most interesting and illuminating authors in this book, but we cannot avoid seeing sixth-century Gaul pretty much exclusively through his eyes. It is over-optimistic to take him on trust, and, in the last decade or so, the careful literary structuring of Gregory's work has become widely accepted. But as we saw in Chapter 1, even if we do not believe everything he says, the density of his descriptions allows us to learn from the assumptions he makes. Whatever the accuracy of his account of this conspiracy, we can at least conclude that it was plausible to picture certain things: that a royal court could be riven by factions; that queen-mothers could have considerable political power (note that Gregory ascribes no political protagonism to Childebert's wife Faileuba); that major aristocrats could be very rich, and could have what amounted to private armies, but that their political ambition was concentrated on royal courts; that such men did not base themselves on private fortifications, unlike in the world of castles of the central Middle Ages – for Ursio's last stand was notably makeshift in Gregory's account; and that people might expect sanctuary to be respected, even if this did not always happen. All these conclusions are amply borne out slightly later, by sources from seventh-century Francia; they made up some of the basic parameters of Merovingian political practice. This conspiracy was traditionally read by historians as a deliberate attempt to limit royal power; there is no evidence for that. But the image of the Merovingian political world as one in which kings consistently faced over-mighty subjects who had both character and resources would not be a false one. These points will be developed in this chapter. I shall give a political narrative first, and then set out some of the basic structures and patterns of political action of the Merovingian period as a whole.

The Merovingian dynasty ruled the Franks for two hundred and fifty years until 751; its hegemony was the work of Clovis (481–511). Clovis, son of a late Roman warlord and Frankish king based at Tournai, Childeric I, conquered the rival Frankish kings who had occupied separate sections of northern Gaul, and the surviving non-Frankish warlords of the north; he also established hegemony over the Alemans in the upper Rhine valley, and, as we saw in Chapter 4, in 507 conquered Visigothic Aquitaine as well. Clovis thus reunited three-quarters of Gaul after the confusions of the fifth century. He also converted to Catholicism, the first major 'barbarian' king to do so (perhaps after a brief period as an Arian), and his example, given his military success, would mark future choices in the other Romano-Germanic kingdoms too. By 550 or so, Frankish rule was fully established in the Burgundian kingdom and over the south German tribes who were crystallizing as the Bavarians; a looser Frankish hegemony was recognized in northern Italy, in central Germany, east to Thuringia, in Brittany (the only part of Gaul never fully conquered by the Franks), and maybe even in Kent. The core Frankish lands were always in the north of Gaul, and the major royal centres stretched from Paris and Orléans, through Reims and Metz, to Cologne: these were not exactly capitals in an administrative sense, but they were places where kings could frequently be found, and around which they moved their courts and administrators, from palace to palace, along the Oise valley near Paris or the Moselle near Metz. The kings seldom went to the south of Gaul; from these northern 'royal landscapes', the richer and more Roman south was ruled through networks of dukes, counts and bishops. Frankish hegemony east of the Rhine is less well documented, and was certainly less tight: the dukes of Bavaria and Thuringia usually had considerable freedom of action. But it existed nonetheless, and for a century the kings saw their eastern border as roughly that between modern Germany and the Czech Republic. The Merovingian Franks were thus both the people who created the political centrality of the Paris to Cologne region for the first time, a centrality it has never lost since, and the first people to rule on both sides of the Rhine frontier of the Roman empire. East of the Rhine was a simpler society, and it lacked the basic Roman infrastructure of roads and cities, or Latin as a language, but slowly, between 500 and 800, some of the contrasts between Gaul and Germany receded, and briefly, in the Carolingian period, they would have similar histories.

Clovis put his own family, called by 640 at the latest the Merovingians after his shadowy grandfather Merovech, firmly into the centre of politics: after 530 or so no one is documented claiming the Frankish kingship who did not also claim Merovingian parentage, until the Carolingian coup in 751. It is worth stressing how unusual this was: the Gothic and Lombard kingdoms never had dynasties that lasted more than three or four generations (usually less); only the Anglo-Saxon kingdoms, and, outside the Germanic world, those of the Welsh and Irish, were as committed to the legitimacy of single ruling families, and these were all tiny polities. Early on, the Merovingians associated kingship with wearing uncut hair; this became a family privilege, and hair-cutting was an at least temporary ritual of deposition. The Merovingians also saw ruling as a sufficiently family affair for the Frankish lands at the king's death to be regularly divided between his sons; they did this first at Clovis's death in 511, again at the death of his last surviving son Chlotar I in 561, and again at the death of Dagobert I in 639, whose father Chlotar II had reunited the kingdoms by force in 613. All in all, there were only twenty-two years of Frankish unity between 511 and 679, when the by now weakened family was reduced to a single line. The political history of the period can easily be reduced to rivalries, and perennial wars, between competing Merovingians. This would make for dull reading; what follows focuses on some of the major figures.

The half-century after Clovis was marked by fighting between his sons, but also by external conquests; this was the period in which the Franks gained serious international recognition, particularly from the eastern Roman empire, for the first time, and it must have been the period in which people in Gaul and Germany realized that Merovingian rule was there to stay. The king who best encapsulates that is Theudebert I (533–48), king of the north-eastern Frankish kingdom based on the Rhineland, which held hegemony over central and southern Germany from there. It was probably Theudebert who set up the powerful Franco-Burgundian Agilolfing family as dukes of Bavaria, to act both as the core of a developing Bavarian identity, and as a long-standing sign of Frankish overlordship; and it was certainly Theudebert who took advantage of the Gothic war in Italy and intervened there systematically, for the first time but not the last. The Constantinopolitan historian Agathias in the 560s claimed he was even planning to attack the eastern capital, that is, that he was part of a line of 'barbarian' invaders going back to Alaric and Attila. Theudebert's international pretensions were also expressed by minting gold coins with his name and portrait on: these are the first 'barbarian' coins to claim this imperial prerogative, and the east Romans were greatly offended. It is interesting that, although Theudebert ruled the sector of the Frankish lands where civilian Roman traditions were weakest, the idiom of his rule was so often expressed in Roman terms; the stories Gregory tells about him are frequently expressed in terms of his fiscal policies – a tax remission for Clermont, an unpopular decision to tax the Franks themselves, a large loan to Verdun to kick-start the city's commerce after a time of trouble. But the openness of the Franks to Roman traditions and imagery was there from the start; bishops wrote admonitory letters to kings from the beginning of Clovis's reign onwards, councils of bishops were regularly held in the north of Gaul after 511, and the kings in 566 welcomed the Italian poet Venantius Fortunatus to their courts to write them all impeccably Roman praise-poems, which he did for kings, queens, aristocrats and bishops (including Gregory of Tours) for three decades.

The next generation of Merovingian kings is the best documented, for their rule forms the core of Gregory's work. Chilperic (561-84) and his infant son Chlotar II (584-629) in the north-west, Sigibert I and his son Childebert II in the north-east (Theudebert's former kingdom), and Guntram (561-93) in Burgundy make up an agonistic set, with Chilperic portrayed as the worst of these kings and Guntram as the best (Sigibert and Childebert, even though they were Gregory's most direct patrons, are less clearly characterized). Gregory disliked Chilperic because he saw him as tyrannous, hostile to the church, and the fomenter of civil war; Chilperic had the smallest kingdom with the fewest external boundaries, which partly explains the fact that he fought his brothers, and he also conquered Tours and backed Gregory's local rivals. Guntram's virtues are, conversely, particularly stressed by Gregory after 584; he was then the only adult Merovingian king left alive, and he acted as patron to his two young nephews (the wars between them notably quietened down after a treaty in 587), alongside their queen-regent mothers, Brunhild for Childebert and Fredegund, Gregory's other main enemy, for Chlotar. Gregory knew both kings well; his accounts of his meetings with Guntram are affectionate, but he was very formal and wary with Chilperic, who threatened him (Gregory threatened back). But what is really most striking about the kings is their similarity: they were all prone to violent anger (leading to injustice and cruelty) and equally violent repentance; they constantly sparred, taking city-territories from each other like chess pieces. And they cooperated when they had to, including against a claimant to the throne, Gundovald, who said he was Guntram's brother and who gained quite a lot of support from aristocrats who were on the losing sides in court faction-fighting, in 583-5.

The swirl of war and faction is encapsulated in the Rauching conspiracy of 589 which we started with, and this shows us the importance of the detail of court politics. By now it is clear that the royal courts, and their ruling kings and queens, were the foci for the rivalry of powerful aristocrats, who constantly sought office, at court or as the dukes (army leaders with a regional remit) of each kingdom. Kings when

adult could dominate these factions, and had no scruples about killing
losers, often in unpleasant ways. Queens-regent for younger kings often
had a more difficult time of it, and both Brunhild and Fredegund had
periods of considerable marginality when their sons were small. They
were not respected as much as kings, and when they resorted to violence
to make their point they were often met not so much by fear as by
resentment; every powerful queen had at least one hostile chronicler.
Royal wives during their husbands' lifetimes had less power; for one
thing, Merovingian kings frequently had several wives and concubines
at once, who manoeuvred for the succession of their own sons. But the
importance of Merovingian legitimacy was by now so great that royal
mothers were allowed a substantial political space, even when their
children were grown; nor did their social origins matter (Brunhild was
a princess, but a Visigoth; Fredegund was of non-aristocratic birth).
Brunhild built on this after Gregory's *Histories* end in 591, for she
remained influential throughout Childebert's life, and then was regent
for his two young sons after his death in 596, particularly Theuderic II in
Burgundy, and even, briefly, for her great-grandson in 613. If Guntram
dominated politics in 584–93, Brunhild did in 593–613: on and off,
perhaps, but sometimes in effective control of virtually the whole
Frankish world.

By 613, the seventy-year-old Brunhild had made too many enemies,
particularly in the north-eastern kingdom, now known as Austrasia,
which she had just taken back by force. Chlotar II, who had hitherto been
confined to relatively few city-territories in Neustria, the north-west, got
an aristocratic coalition together and overthrew Brunhild. He had her
torn to pieces by a horse in public, in an act clearly designed to mark a
new beginning, and he and his son Dagobert I (623–39) ruled a more
or less unitary kingdom for a generation. Chlotar maintained the three
courts of the previous period, however, as the foci for aristocratic politics, particularly Neustria and Austrasia (Burgundy tended to go with
Neustria). These courts sometimes had sub-kings (as Dagobert was in
Austrasia in 623–9, before his father's death), but they also now each
had a single aristocratic leader, a *maior domus*, 'leader of the household'
('mayor of the palace' is the traditional English translation). Aristocratic
rivalries began to concentrate on obtaining the position of *maior*, or else
on using that position to overthrow rivals, as with the confrontation
between the *maior* Flaochad of Burgundy and the *patricius* Willibad

in 643, a small war in which they both died; the events were written up dramatically in Gregory's continuator, called by modern historians Fredegar, around 660. These rivalries became sharper after 639, when Dagobert was succeeded by children, Sigibert III (632–56) in Austrasia and Clovis II (639–57) in Neustria; both of the latter were succeeded by children too. It became ever more important to be a *maior* under these circumstances, and there was also often a clash between the *maior* and the queen-regent, who remained a powerful force in this period. The classic example of this is the stand-off between Balthild, regent for her and Clovis II's sons in 657–65, and the Neustrian *maior* Ebroin (659–80, with interruptions); this is well documented above all because Balthild was forced into a monastery at Chelles near Paris in 664–5, and a saint's life was written about her. By now, in fact, saints' lives are our major sources for high politics, for many saints were aristocratic (see below, Chapter 8); this also means that the continuing violence of politics, already stressed by Gregory, was even more emphasized by writers for moralistic purposes.

The seventh century was a turning point for Merovingian royal power: by the early eighth, real authority was in the hands of *maiores*, who were after 687 almost all from a single Austrasian family, the Arnulfings-Pippinids, descended from two of the major Austrasian supporters of Chlotar II, Arnulf bishop of Metz and Pippin (I) of Landen. Historians have therefore devoted considerable attention to determining when it was that the Merovingians began to lose control: was it in 639, with the death of Dagobert? Or was it earlier, or later? An older generation of historians thought that Chlotar II marked the moment of change, arguing that he gave away too much to gain aristocratic support; he does seem, indeed, to have restricted his own taxation powers substantially, as we shall see, even if it is no longer thought that he also conceded local judicial power to the aristocracy. But Chlotar and Dagobert's centrality is by now rarely doubted, and more recent historians have gone the other way, arguing that even late seventh-century kings like Childeric II (662–75) and Childebert III (694–711) had a good deal of power, at least once they gained adulthood, and that the royal courts never lost the importance for aristocratic politics that they had unarguably had a century earlier. This may indeed have been the case, in particular for Childeric II. But royal hegemony was not as automatic as it had been. Fredegar tells us with some gusto of Chlotar II's killing of Godin, son of the Burgundian *maior* Warnachar, around 626, even after Godin had been persuaded to do a pilgrimage around the holy places of Gaul to swear loyalty, and the *Liber Historiae Francorum* is keen to recount the death by torture of the *maior* Grimoald, son of Pippin of Landen, on Clovis II's orders in 657. But when Childeric had an aristocrat called Bodilo bound and beaten in 674, small beer for an earlier king, this was regarded as illegal behaviour, and Bodilo himself apparently had the king and queen killed in 675, precipitating a major crisis.

It seems to me that the late seventh century does indeed mark a considerable diminution of a specifically royal centrality. Perhaps the turning point was less Dagobert's death than those of his sons, for the dominance of *maiores* over the courts became routinized once it was clearly going to last for another generation, and renewed royal protagonism under Childeric II would be more resented. It was, anyway, after the death of Dagobert's sons that *maiores* began for the first time not only to control kings but to choose them. Grimoald, as *maior* of Austrasia (641–57), exiled Sigibert III's son Dagobert to Ireland, and had his own son Childebert made king instead (656–62?); Childebert was Sigibert's adopted son, so Merovingian paternity was theoretically maintained. This odd and ill-documented affair ended badly for Grimoald, who was killed as a direct result, although Childebert somehow seems to have lasted a few years more. Later, at Childeric II's death, Ebroin did the same, temporarily inventing a king in Austrasia to keep his hand in during that political crisis, before switching his support to the new Neustrian king Theuderic III (so says, at least, the saint's life of his bitter enemy and victim, Leudegar bishop of Autun). Seen from this standpoint, Childeric II's politics seem even more atypical by now. Kings still had a role as a rallying point for aristocratic factions, and their courts remained central to aristocratic political aspirations, but *maiores* and political bishops had become the major protagonists. Ebroin dominated his time, but he was always a controversial figure, and he did not establish a stable regime for himself. Pippin II in Austrasia was cannier; he was Grimoald's nephew, and his family was eclipsed for two decades, but it remained very rich and influential around Liège on the Meuse, and by the late 670s he was *maior* in Austrasia again. In 687 the Austrasians defeated the Neustrians at the battle of Tertry, and Pippin became *maior* for all the Frankish lands. Pippin II lived to 714, and the civil disturbances of the thirty years after 656 ended at Tertry, although

Neustria and Austrasia remained separate. That did not change until a briefer civil war, in 715–19, which pitched Pippin's probably illegitimate son Charles (Martel) against his widow Plectrude, with Neustrian anti-Pippinids as a third force contending with them both. Charles defeated them all, and established himself as sole *maior* (717–41), with a firmly Austrasian base. The Neustrian court was abolished; Charles Martel became the only focus of rule, and his heirs, the Carolingians, would remain so for a long time. Charles's victory in 719 thus changed the political scene much more completely than Pippin II did in 687, perhaps even more completely than Chlotar II had done in 613.

Another respect in which the later seventh century saw a real involution of Merovingian authority was its geographical scale. The wide hegemony of the sixth-century kings was still there under Dagobert I, who fought a war in 631–4 against Samo, a king who for a time united the Wends, Sclavenian tribes (see Chapter 20), in or around what is now the Czech Republic. Dagobert called Thuringians, Bavarians and even Lombards from Italy to fight for him there; he also legislated for the peoples east of the Rhine, and appointed bishops there too. But at his death Radulf duke of Thuringia revolted and established autonomy; and across the next generation both Bavaria and Alemannia slipped out of effective Frankish control. More striking still was Aquitaine: this was part of the core Frankish lands, and had in the sixth century been divided between the northern kings, but Dagobert in 629 briefly made his half-brother Charibert II (629–32) king of part of Aquitaine, and by the 650s it had a separate duke. In the political crisis of 675, Duke Lupus seems to have claimed royal status, and in the eighth century Duke Eudo (d. 735) was clearly an autonomous ally of Charles Martel; full-scale war was needed in the 760s to bring this large and rich region fully back into the Frankish fold. War was in fact in general needed to establish Carolingian control over the whole area of traditional Frankish hegemony in the eighth century; the peripheral principalities were keener on Merovingian legitimism than on Charles's new political structure, and Charles found several quasi-autonomous princes even in his core lands whom he had to subdue by force, as well as, further south in Provence, the *patricius* Antenor and then the *dux* Maurontus, whom Charles fought in the 730s. Charles had a large central territory in Neustria, Austrasia and northern Burgundy which still looked to the court, and which he could draw on for the continuous border wars that marked his rule and that of his successors, but it was not until his sons took over Alemannia in 746 and then Aquitaine, and until his grandson Charlemagne took over Bavaria in 788–94, that Dagobert's hegemony was re-established, in rather more solid form by now. This geographical retreat is a marker of the fact that the instability of the post-Dagobert generations did indeed do harm to Frankish authority. The later seventh century also saw a retreat in the internal activities of rulers, as we shall see at the end of this chapter.

The lasting importance of the Merovingian royal courts was in large part due to the huge wealth that every king or *maior* could dispose of. Kings owned very large tracts of land; they had access to commercial tolls and judicial fines. They also for long controlled the surviving elements of the Roman land tax. These are described (and complained about) by Gregory of Tours, and they seem to have been most firmly rooted in the south-west, the Loire valley and Aquitaine. Even in Gregory's time, as noted in Chapter 4, the tax system was not very systematically maintained: registers could go without updating for a generation, tax levels were far lower than under Rome, and royal cessions of tax immunity to whole city territories were beginning. Indeed, an organic fiscal structure of a Roman type could not still have existed if kings moved cities between each other so easily. By the mid-seventh century tax liabilities seem to have become fixed tributes, taken from smaller and smaller areas. In the north, this process may well have started earlier, and Chlotar II formally renounced the right to new taxes in 614; by 626–7 a church council at Clichy near Paris regarded taxpayers as an inferior category, to be excluded from the ranks of the clergy. It is likely that the tax system had already decayed so much that Chlotar could regard it as worth abandoning, for political effect; it only survived regionally after that (it is documented in the Loire valley into the 720s at least). This does not seem to have done Chlotar any harm, all the same; the vast landed resources of the Merovingians continued into the Carolingian period. The major immediate consequence may simply have been the sharp drop in the gold content of Merovingian coins, first visible around 640. The Merovingians could let tax lapse because they did not pay their army, which was by now based on the military obligations of the free: it was above all made up of aristocrats and their entourages, and also of contingents from city territories led by local counts. Their incomings were thus far greater than their structural outgoings, even after Chlotar's reign, never mind before. The *thesaurus*, the treasure, of each king was enormous, and functioned above all as a resource for gifts to courtiers. Courts under powerful kings, queens and *maiores* were where any ambitious aristocrat might want to be in order to gain preferment and land, but, even when rulers were personally weak, the attraction of the *thesaurus* kept courts at the centre of political life. Every account of a coup against a king or an uprising by a rival in the seventh century hangs on the seizing of a *thesaurus*: it was the essential basis for gaining aristocratic support. Charles Martel still did this in the civil war of 715–19; the parameters of politics did not change here at all.

Merovingian government was quite complex; written records of royal orders were regularly made and archived (bishops and cities, and perhaps aristocrats, had archives too), quite apart from the more standard maintenance of tax accounts (until the late seventh century at least) and judicial records. The late seventh-century formulary of Marculf, a collection of templates for documents, preserves forty sample royal documents for copying. Among other matters, they concern the appointment of bishops and counts, the feeding of royal messengers, the confirmation of a marriage agreement, the division of private property, the demand that seized property be returned, a summons to a presumed robber, and the demand that all 'Franks and Romans' should swear fidelity to the king's heir. When documents themselves begin to survive, either as originals or in later cartularies (which is above all from Chlotar II's reign onwards), they show kings doing most of these things as well: besides cessions of land and court records, which are the main currency of all document collections in the early Middle Ages, Chlotar II confirmed the will of a Parisian merchant called John; Dagobert in 626 sent one of his courtiers to divide the land in the Limousin of one of the main aristocratic families of the period; Sigibert III in 644 wrote formally to his southern bishops to cancel a church council because he had not been informed of it; Theuderic III in 677 expelled the bishop of Embrun in the Alps for infidelity, though allowing him to keep his property; and so on. These show a dense set of relationships between kings and their secular and ecclesiastical magnates (even if seldom anyone else), as well as the fact that these relationships were systematically recorded.

Royal courts had, among other officials, *referendarii*, who supervised the production of documents, *domestici*, who were household administrators with a variety of roles, *thesaurarii*, who were financial officials, all of them presumably answering in some way to the *maior domus*. These positions also meant access to the ruler, and their holders were important political mediators as well: for the patronage networks of the Roman empire had their close analogues in the Frankish kingdoms. Being a *conviva regis*, that is to say having the right to eat with the king, was indeed a formal title, with privileges attached. German historians call this access *Königsnähe*, 'closeness to the king', a useful concept, with relevance both in this period and later. We must see royal courts as a permanent bustle: of greater aristocrats seeking *Königsnähe* and office, local élites seeking favours, abbots and bishops, among others, seeking justice in legal disputes, and everyone seeking gifts of land and money. Bishop Praejectus of Clermont had to go to Childeric II's Austrasian court in 675 to defend a land dispute against Hector, *patricius* of Provence. Hector, himself a very powerful magnate, had enlisted the support of Leudegar, bishop of Autun, who was one of the king's main advisers; Praejectus accordingly sought the patronage of Leudegar's opponent, Childeric's mother-in-law Chimnechild, who was also the widow of his uncle Sigibert III. Despite this shrewd move, Praejectus was an apparently unworldly figure; he refused to plead because it was Easter Saturday, and he only won his case because palace politics caused Hector and Leudegar to flee the court. (Hector was killed, Leudegar exiled; Praejectus was killed a year later, in the context of the crisis after Childeric's death, probably by Hector's allies.) But courts welcomed the unworldly as well as the worldly, together with ambassadors from abroad, preachers (such as Columbanus the Irish ascetic and monastic founder, d. 615, who had to flee Theuderic II's court in 609 because he had denounced him for immorality), and beggars. To the average local notable, engaged in city-level politics over who was to be the next bishop, a royal court must have represented the same sort of temptation that Las Vegas represents to poker-players: in this case, almost limitless wealth and power for winners, inventive death for losers.

Kings were more widely visible than this may imply, too. There seems to have been an annual assembly for the king and his armed Frankish people in the spring; Childebert II's laws from the 590s were promulgated on 1 March, for example. It was at this assembly that decisions were made to go to war, which were not entirely under royal control: Chlotar I in 556 was forced against his will by the Rhineland Franks to fight the Saxons, for example, according to Gregory (he lost). Exactly who came to such assemblies is not easy to tell; members of the king's armed entourage, for certain (called *leudes* or *antrustiones*), who were largely from the élite; dukes and counts and their own followings, too. Whether there was a wider participation of free Franks of lesser status cannot easily be said; one has a sense that this was more a feature of the sixth century than the seventh. But the large-scale gathering together in assemblies of the politically active sections of society was a frequent event. It marked the accession of kings; Ebroin did not call an assembly of aristocrats in 673 to mark the accession of Theuderic III in Neustria, which led them to conclude that Ebroin intended to rule without consent, so they recognized Childeric II of Austrasia instead. And legal disputes were resolved in front of assemblies, *placita*, everywhere; they gave legitimacy to all such decisions. These gatherings represented a link between kings and their Frankish people which extended well beyond the habitual visitors to royal palaces and courts, even if it did not include many peasants. It should be repeated that the word 'Frankish' quickly ceased to have an exclusive ethnic connotation. North of the Loire, everyone seems to have been considered a Frank by the mid-seventh century at the latest; *Romani* were essentially the inhabitants of Aquitaine after that.

The Frankish attitude to legislation was more muted. Clovis's basic Salic law, the *Pactus Legis Salicae*, for the 'Salian' (north-western) Franks, is unique among 'barbarian' law codes in that it does not actually mention a king, only a set of four mythical judgement-makers; and the idea of a grass-roots law-making persisted in the *rachineburgii* of local communities who were asked to 'speak the Salic law' at moments of conflict; indeed, it has been noted that the provisions of 'Salic law' that are cited in documents do not in most cases even appear in the *Pactus*. Clovis's successors did legislate, but not often, and the collected laws of the period 511–614 (after which they ceased) only make up twenty-three pages of the standard edition. This aspect of traditional late Roman – and Romano-Germanic – politics was not taken up much in Francia in this period, then. All in all, the Merovingian kings seem to have preferred a relatively low-key ideological presence. Church councils existed (again, more in the sixth than the seventh centuries), but their surviving records mostly deal with internal church affairs, except under Chlotar II and his immediate successors. Royal morality was bound up with doing justice in public, certainly (this image recurs for kings like Dagobert, just as injustice is associated with Chilperic by Gregory of Tours), but not with changing the behaviour of their subjects. We lack the image of the king as a systematic political and moral reformer that is so much a feature of Visigothic Spain and indeed Carolingian-period Francia, as we shall see in later chapters.

Kings were surrounded by aristocrats, who hoped for advantage; but aristocrats were themselves strikingly rich. The private wills we have for the Merovingian period show several people in possession of more than seventy-five estates; no equivalent property collections are known anywhere in the early Middle Ages outside Francia, and such owners, Bishop Bertram of Le Mans (d. after 616), Bishop Desiderius of Cahors (d. 650), *patricius* Abbo of Provence (d. *c.* 750), would only have been outstripped by the richest late Roman senators. The Pippinids, too, must have owned on at least this scale; and so also, above all, must the Agilolfings, the most powerful and wide-ranging aristocratic clan of the early seventh century, who owned land and founded monasteries around Meaux just east of Paris (the powerful Audoin, bishop of Rouen, d. 680, was linked to them), but also owned in the Rhineland, ruled in Bavaria, and even furnished the longest-lasting line of Lombard kings of Italy from 653 to 712. The Paris region, in particular, as we can see from the seventh-century Saint-Denis charters, was full of the properties not only of the Neustrian king, who was based there, but also of his principal aristocrats; the rivalries that ensued may explain some of the tenseness of Neustrian politics, particularly in Ebroin's time, and also maybe back to Chilperic a century earlier. But throughout Francia the simple fact that major aristocrats could be hugely rich meant that politics would be more violent, for all secular aristocratic identity was military by now – even career administrators at court were regarded as having obligations to fight, and dressed in military fashion, with an elaborate belt of office – and what landed wealth could buy above all was an armed entourage, to make one's ambition more clearly marked. It was the existence of such entourages that underpins the faction-fighting of, in particular, the later seventh century, but going back to Rauching and Ursio and earlier still. This aristocratic wealth is clearly visible in Gregory's narratives and in seventh-century documents. In the south of Gaul, it had antecedents going back to the late empire, and some of the great late Roman families can be traced into the seventh century, in one case (the descendants of the emperor Avitus and of Sidonius Apollinaris) up to 700 and beyond. In the north, the evidence is less clear, but the balance of probabilities argues for at least some major families, whether Frankish or Roman (in the north the distinction was never great), surviving right through the confusion of the pre-Clovis period and the killings of rivals which accompanied the creation of Clovis's united kingdom, into the world described by Gregory.

We shall look at aristocratic lifestyles in greater detail in Chapter 8, but the boisterous factional politics visible in Merovingian sources has some other implications. The first is that, early on, political ambition was seen as an aristocratic prerogative. Gregory did, still, confront some counts of low-born origin, like Leudast of Tours (d. 583), a Chilperic supporter and his own opponent; but by the mid-seventh century none can be seen. Even bishops, who did still include some people of relatively modest birth, like Eligius of Noyon (d. 660) or Praejectus of Clermont, were overwhelmingly aristocratic, and indeed increasingly often led a fully military lifestyle, including army leadership in some cases.

A second point is that politico-religious practice, as it affected the aristocracy, changed somewhat in the seventh century. Columbanus was the first important impresario of monasticism in the northern Merovingian heartland, and, after Chlotar's reunification, kings, queens and aristocrats all founded monasteries, usually following the traditions of the main Columbanian monastery in Burgundy, Luxeuil. The shrine of Saint-Denis just outside Paris was also heavily patronized by Dagobert, who was buried there, as were most of his successors; Saint-Denis and the other major cult-centres of Gaul were turned into monasteries by Balthild around 660. Monasteries were closely associated with their founders and their families, and less dependent on the bishops in whose dioceses they lay; they marked a political and religious practice more clearly linked to aristocratic and royal identities and family strategies, which cut across diocesan boundaries. The church in the seventh century thus became more of a resource for factional rivalries, and contributes to our knowledge of them, too, for most of our Merovingian documents and saints' lives are products of monastic archives and religious commemoration. Monastic patronage also contributed to a growing sense that the aristocracy was somehow religiously special; even sanctity took on an aristocratic tinge in many of our surviving lives. This fits with the steady aristocratic takeover of episcopal office, too, although bishops and monasteries were often in conflict.

A final crucial point is that aristocrats were overwhelmingly committed to the Merovingian political system. They had for the most part rural residences, and rural monastic religious centres too, but these were not real power centres in the sense that aristocrats sought to control their local areas as de facto local rulers. Indeed, although the surviving wills tend to show concentrations of estates in most cases, Desiderius of Cahors owning land around Cahors and neighbouring Albi for example, they shared their local territories with others, and most of the greatest owners also had outlying properties, sometimes hundreds of kilometres away. This was very different from the castle-based local aristocracy of the tenth century and onwards (see below, Chapter 21), and indeed, as we saw, Ursio's main centre was not even fortified. Unfortunately, few or no élite residences from this period have been excavated, but the rest of our written documentation confirms that picture. Power was not local, and did not have to be defended by walls; it was seen as royal. That is to say, it came from office or from *Königsnähe*, and preferably both. All great landowners aimed at these, or at their ecclesiastical equivalents; their wealth and armed men were focused on these, not on local autonomy and domination. The most one can say is that some office-holders in the late seventh century were going their own way, in the period of royal involution. The outlying dukes and the *patricius* of Provence were instances, marking a general geographical fragmentation, as already noted; in the central Frankish lands, we might add the dukes of Alsace, for early eighth-century documents for Alsace conspicuously do not mention kings, until the ducal family was removed or died out around 740. Bishops, too, whose political remit was essentially their dioceses, sometimes developed local autonomies ('episcopal republics' in Eugen Ewig's words) which Charles Martel and his sons had to move against, as in the case of Eucherius of Orléans (d. 738). But these were a minority, at least in the core Frankish lands; most aristocrats remained as focused on and as defined by court politics in the age of Ebroin, Pippin II and Charles Martel as they had been before.

It is not that local politics did not matter at all. The cities described by Gregory of Tours and in some of the seventh-century saints' lives, particularly in southern Gaul, seem to have had an active factional politics, focused on obtaining the offices of either bishop or count. That of Clermont is particularly well documented. Counts were royal appointees, but they tended to be local men; they ran the armies and law courts of city territories. Bishops were even more often of local origin, and could face trouble if they were not – as Gregory did in Tours, even though his predecessor was his uncle, for he was brought up in Clermont, and some people saw him as really from there. Episcopal choices were generally made by local élites and neighbouring bishops, as in Sidonius' time, but by Gregory's time and onwards the king had the last word, and could (as in Gregory's own case) select his own candidate: bishops had the task of representing their cities politically, and so it mattered to kings who they were. In a sense, though, counts were most responsive to kings, and bishops were most responsive to their dioceses. Bishops who threw themselves too fully into central-government politics could be unpopular; Arnulf of Metz was nearly removed by his flock for spending too much time at the palace, and when Leudegar of Autun was finally destroyed by Ebroin in 676–8 it is clear that he got little support from Autun itself. These local communities were, nonetheless, connected to court politics by innumerable channels: kinship, marriage, patronage linked them to other communities and to the ambitions of the more powerful, and all bishops and counts had to go to royal courts, and deal with court politics, on a regular basis. 'Episcopal republics' were all the weaker for being isolated from that network.

A particularly good example of this balance between central and local politics is Desiderius of Cahors, for we have not only a saint's life for him but also his letter collection; his experiences sum up much of the foregoing. Desiderius was a member of the remarkable set of administrators educated and trained in the court of Chlotar II and Dagobert I, along with, among others, Audoin of Rouen, who had been Dagobert's *referendarius* before he became a bishop in 641, and Eligius of Noyon, made bishop in the same year, who had been Dagobert's main financial official (we even have some of his coins). Desiderius himself, slightly older, had been *thesaurarius* for Chlotar, and later *patricius* of Provence, before returning to Cahors as bishop in 630. This talented group of men were friends, and, as Desiderius' letters show, stayed so. Audoin and Eligius were bishops of sees close to the royal palaces of Neustria; Desiderius was not, and one gets a sense from the nostalgia of some of the letters that he felt rather cut off from the buzz of politics, for Cahors is more than 600 kilometres south of Paris and Metz. He was not so very isolated, all the same; we have patronage recommendations from the 640s to the *maior* of Austrasia, Grimoald, and to Arnulf of Metz's son, and a letter from Sigibert III agreeing to some of Desiderius' requests. The fact is that all these episcopal appointments, particularly well documented in this period but with plenty of parallels before and after, spread a court consciousness and a court culture across the whole of Frankish Gaul, as Dagobert surely knew. Desiderius got letters from his informants which told him exactly where the king was: he has moved from Verdun to Reims, then he will go to Laon then back to the Rhineland; he is now in Mainz – the bishop needed this constantly changing information, from hundreds of kilometres away, so as to keep abreast of affairs. And he did so even though he was from one of Cahors' major families (he succeeded his brother as bishop), with huge local wealth, and devoted his later life to the city, repairing its water supply, building big stone buildings, defending episcopal lands against other local bishops, and helping along its citizens, not least in the king's court. Desiderius was all the more effective in being a bishop because his heart was still at court, and all the more effective an ambassador for royal centrality because his wealth and office was in the south. Those were Merovingian norms, and they held the kingdoms together.

The troubles of the late seventh century shook this organic pattern, as we have already seen; the Merovingians lost their centrality as political actors between around 655 and 675, and, although their courts remained strong foci for political action, outlying principalities gained practical autonomy, and some other dukes and bishops looked less to Merovingian or Pippinid patronage. The period of instability stopped with Tertry in 687; but it is actually the period of Pippin II that may have seen the lowest level of royal, or, by now, mayoral protagonism. It is striking that the documentation for capillary royal actions of the type listed in Marculf's formulary runs out in the late 670s; later royal or mayoral documents are restricted to the confirmations of rights, and to judicial *placita*. No proceedings survive from any church councils between 675 and 742, either. It seems that Pippin's regime was less organizationally ambitious than those of his predecessors, including Ebroin and Childeric II. This may indeed have contributed to the decisions by some political leaders to deal in local or regional rather than court politics more than they had done before, even in the period of the civil wars. But this localization had not got very far by the time of Charles Martel's reunification. Charles did not reverse the relative inaction of central government just described – that was for the next Carolingian generation – but his overthrow of so many members of an older regime and, above all, the annual aggregation of aristocrats to take part in his wars, the most committed and consistent military mobilization in Francia since the sixth century, reversed any temptation to localization. Nor had it been so very hard; the Frankish political system, even if at times ramshackle, was not yet in poor shape.

6

The West Mediterranean Kingdoms: Spain and Italy, 550–750

In October 680, Wamba, Visigothic king of Spain (672–80), fell seriously ill, and thought he was going to die. Like some other kings, he undertook penance, and was tonsured in the presence of his magnates; he designated his successor Ervig (680–87) in writing and in another document asked for him to be anointed as soon as possible (anointing to the kingship was in fact a novelty, introduced, as far as we can tell, by Wamba himself in 672). Wamba did not die; but he was tonsured now, and the sixth church council of Toledo (638) had prohibited anyone who had been tonsured from being king. Ervig quickly called the twelfth council of Toledo, which met in January 681, less than four months later, in midwinter, and as their first act the bishops of the kingdom ratified his succession and all the associated documentation (this is our only source for it, in fact), and cancelled the oath of allegiance the Spanish had sworn to Wamba. As their second act, they discussed what would happen if someone was given penitence and the tonsure while unconscious and, recovering, wished to reject it and return to a secular career: they enacted that the penitence and tonsuring must hold. Like most commentators, I see this as a response to a protest by Wamba that he had been deposed without his consent; but the careful legal framing of an effective coup is nonetheless striking.

The seventh-century Spanish political community were not always as respectful of the forms of law as this. The rules on legitimate succession laid down by the fourth council of Toledo in 633 were almost never followed, for example. But legal enactments, both secular and ecclesiastical, were part of the currency of Spanish political practice. People were aware of them, if they were aristocrats and bishops, at least; and even kings, if their support was weak enough, as was presumably the case in 680, could be trapped by them. This is a marker of a different style of politics from that of Francia: in Visigothic Spain, as to a lesser extent in Lombard Italy, legal principles were important points of reference, as they had also been in the later Roman empire, to which the Visigoths and Lombards were in some respects closer than were the Franks. In the case of Visigothic Spain in particular, historians have indeed often paid too much attention to law, for there are few narratives and documents for the period, and immense quantities of secular and ecclesiastical legislation. Spanish history often looks fairly arid as a result. But we cannot and should not argue that law away; its very quantity tells us something about the values of the Spanish establishment. I shall begin with Spain, move on to Italy, and then compare them; we shall then see better what sort of range of development from Roman practices was possible in the post-Roman West.

Spain (that is, the Iberian peninsula, including what is now Portugal) was partly conquered by the Vandals after 409, and then, after 439, mostly conquered by the Suevi. In 456 the Visigoths invaded and swiftly destroyed Suevic power, confining it to the far north-west. The obscure process of Visigothic conquest began here, speeded up in the 470s, and was probably complete by 483, when King Euric had the main bridge at Mérida, the Roman capital of Spain, repaired, as an inscription attests. The Visigoths were still based in Gaul, however; even after their great defeat by Clovis in 507 their capital remained in Narbonne, in the tiny strip of Mediterranean Gaul (modern Languedoc) that they kept hold of. After 511 Theoderic the Ostrogoth established a regency for the Visigothic child king Amalaric (511–31), and Spain was effectively ruled from Italy until Theoderic's death in 526. There followed another forty years of relatively weak kings, succeeding each other by coup. Athanagild (551–68), based apparently in Seville in the south, rose up against Agila (549–54) and fought a civil war against him; he asked for Justinian's help to do so, and this gave the east Romans the excuse to establish a bridgehead in Spain, the south-eastern coastal strip, in 552, which they held until around 628. Athanagild died in his bed, unlike any of his sixth-century predecessors; he was succeeded by Liuva I (568–73), who was again based in Narbonne, but who soon divided his kingdom with his brother Leovigild (569–86), giving the latter the whole of Spain and keeping only Visigothic Gaul.

The mark of the whole period 409–569 in Spain is instability. Perhaps in 483–507 there was relative peace, and also probably in 511–26, but in both periods the peninsula was ruled from outside, from Gaul and then Italy. The empire was not so long gone, when the western Mediterranean had been a single unit, but in our rare sources for this period Spain seems an appendage almost in a colonial sense, and largely left to its own devices. As we saw in Chapter 4, the archaeology for the later fifth century, particularly for the inland plateau of Spain, the Meseta, shows a weakening of rural estate centres, villas, and also a sharp contraction of the scale of ceramic production, which became more localized and simpler. The first of these developments, which became accentuated in the sixth century, might simply show cultural changes, as it did in the militarized northern Gaul of the late fourth century, but the second shows a simplification of the economy as a whole, which implies a decrease in aristocratic demand. The insecurity of the fifth and a great part of the sixth centuries, in some parts of the Iberian peninsula, seems to have hit many of the basic economic structures inherited from the Roman world quite hard.

The other effect of this instability was the fragmentation of the society of the peninsula. Spain is mountainous, with poor communications between the great plateaux and the major river valleys, and very great ecological differences between the wet climate of the north-west, which resembles Cornwall, and the desert of parts of the south-east. It would be easy for it to break into pieces with very different experiences, and this is what seems to have happened in this period. In parts of the north, we find references to semi-autonomous communities, either ruled by local strong-men like the *senior* Aspidius (575) in the Ourense area, or, more often, apparently collectively run, like the Sappi of Sabaria, perhaps near Zamora (573), or the hardly Romanized tribal groups of parts of the north coast who were generally called Vascones and many of whom spoke Basque. Such communities could have more Roman trappings, however, as was apparent in Cantabria (574), the Ebro valley upstream from Zaragoza, which was ruled by 'senators' (major local landowners) and a senate. In the south, it was cities that established autonomy, such as Córdoba (550-72). Southern cities could indeed remain very prosperous in an entirely Roman tradition, as is clear in Mérida, not a fully autonomous centre but for a long time hardly looking at all to the kings, whose bishops and aristocrats maintained considerable wealth (attested in the episcopal saints' lives for the city), and where several Visigothic-period urban and rural churches and even some villas survive. There were thus two processes of fragmentation in this period. One was the loss to central authority of numerous sections of Spain, up to a third of the peninsula. The other was the development or revival of political practices that were different from those of Rome, more collective, even tribal, in some parts of the peninsula, notably the north. It must be stressed all the same that much of Spain remained very Roman, whether it obeyed the Visigothic kings or not, especially along the Mediterranean coast and in the rich Guadalquivir valley in the south, a zone which extended inland to Mérida. One of the *Variae* of Cassiodorus from around 524 shows the Ostrogoths taking the land tax, and a document surviving for Barcelona and nearby cities from 594 shows that taxation (in that area it was run by counts and bishops) could, at least locally, be quite high.

It was this doubly fragmented situation that Leovigild faced; he reversed it by military action. The dates in parentheses in the previous paragraph are those of Leovigild's conquests, which were systematic in the 570s, and which culminated in the overthrow of his son Hermenegild's five-year Seville-based revolt in 584 and the annexation of the Suevic kingdom in 585. By Leovigild's death in 586, only the Roman-controlled coastal strip in the south and the Basques in the north remained outside royal authority. As with Charles Martel in Francia in the 720s–730s, the Visigothic power-base cannot have been so reduced, or Leovigild could not have managed this at all, however much more determined he was than his predecessors. It is clear from the Mérida saints' lives that he wanted to make his power felt inside the lands he controlled as well. Leovigild appointed an Arian bishop, Sunna, to oppose the rich and locally influential Catholic bishop of Mérida, Masona (who was himself a Goth), and eventually summoned Masona to his court at Toledo and exiled him for three years. He exiled and expropriated lay aristocrats, too; and, not least important, he issued a major revision of the law code. Leovigild was not simply a soldier; he was a unifier. Toledo had already become the main royal residence under Athanagild, but under Leovigild it became a focus of political and religious activity, a real capital. The choice of Toledo, not previously a major centre, was itself significant, for it was exactly in the middle of the peninsula: it marked royal ambition. Leovigild founded his own new city, too, Recópolis, to the east of Toledo, as a further sign of prestige, although Recópolis was never very large, as excavations show.

Leovigild also faced up to the problem of religious disunity. The Goths in Spain had remained Arian; Leovigild in a church council at Toledo in 580 sought to soften that Arianism doctrinally, to make it more palatable to Catholics, while also persecuting at least some Catholic activists. This has parallels to Vandal procedures in Africa a century earlier, but the attempts to find a doctrinal middle road more resemble the policies towards Monophysitism of eastern emperors such as Justinian, as we have seen. Essentially, however, Arianism was practised by too few people by now; the Goths were only a small proportion of the population of Spain, a few per cent at most, and not all of them were Arian, as Masona shows. Hermenegild, too, adopted Catholicism in the course of his revolt. Once religious unity came to be seen as desirable, it was most likely to be on Catholic terms. Indeed, Leovigild's second son and successor, Reccared (586–601), switched to Catholicism almost immediately after he became king, in 587, and at the third council of Toledo in 589 Arianism was outlawed, far more uncompromisingly than Leovigild had sought to oppose Catholicism. Reccared faced a series of revolts and conspiracies as a result, up to 590 at least and perhaps longer. But Arianism must have been weak by now, for it did not reappear as a rallying call in the renewed instability that followed Reccared's death.

Reccared's son Liuva II (601–3) did not last long, and between 601 and 642 there were nine kings, only one (Suinthila, 621–31) lasting as much as a decade; three were sons of their predecessors, but they were particularly swiftly overthrown. Fredegar in Francia referred to this constant series of coups rather smugly as the 'disease of the Goths' – to a Frank, of course, non-dynastic kingship looked like chaos in itself. But what did not happen in this generation was any reversion to the political fragmentation of the pre-Leovigild period. The kings fought frontier wars, against the Basques, the Franks and the east Romans on their coastal strip, and Suinthila finally conquered the latter region around 628. Internally, the sequence of coups at least shows that the dukes and provincial governors of the kingdom were interested in central kingship, rather than autonomy. The kings themselves, even Suinthila, did not leave much mark; Sisebut (612–21) was an author of poetry, letters and a saint's life, the only western ruler in this book except Alfred of England to gain a reputation as a writer, as well as being the first serious persecutor of the Jewish population of Spain, but he seems otherwise undistinguished. The only major innovation of this period was the inauguration, with the fourth council of Toledo in 633, of a steady series of plenary councils of bishops, called by kings at Toledo – thirteen from 633 to 702 – which became so crucial a part of the political aggregation of the kingdom that periods without regular full councils, notably 656–81, were sharply criticized by the church, even if provincial councils had been called in between. The collective role of bishops in the political aggregation of the seventh-century Visigothic kingdom was a specific feature of Spain; neither Francia nor Lombard Italy put as much weight on church councils. Their legislation was secular as well as ecclesiastical, and the king presided, often reading out an initial statement of intent. They contributed greatly to the ceremonial importance of the capital.

The cycle of coups was broken by Chindasuinth (642–53), who took over the throne at the age of nearly eighty, and who curbed the aristocracy by executing 700 of them (Fredegar claims), depriving others of their civil rights, and enacting a draconian law on treason. Chindasuinth was hated for this even by some of his protégés, such as Bishop Eugenius II of Toledo (d. 657), who wrote an abusive epitaph for him. Feelings remained sufficiently strong that once a king succeeded who was in a weak position, Ervig in 680, the thirteenth council in 683 restored the noble status and civil rights of all those who had lost them since 639: aristocratic (and episcopal) solidarity had kept the issue alive for forty years. But conversely the coups ended, or, perhaps better, remained provincial and no longer succeeded at national level; so Reccesuinth (649–72) defeated Froia in 653, Wamba defeated Paul in 673, Egica (687–702) defeated Sisbert in 693. Royal succession became peaceful, even when controversial: Reccesuinth was Chindasuinth's son; Wamba was elected at Reccesuinth's deathbed; Ervig's succession was at least uncontested; his successor Egica was his son-in-law, and Wittiza (694–710) was Egica's son. Only in 710 was there a contested election, perhaps a coup, with Roderic (710–11) imposed by court officials. This general tendency away from political violence was not lessened by the clear evidence we have that most of these kings were opposed to their predecessors. Ervig with respect to Wamba is one example; Egica with respect to Ervig is even clearer, for at his accession he asked the fifteenth council to let him dispossess Ervig's family (the council refused). Both Ervig and Egica also took some pleasure in reversing their predecessors' laws. Wittiza apparently cancelled his father's expropriations too, and Roderic was later thought to have been opposed by Wittiza's family.

Tensions thus evidently remained, and they could be savage (particularly under Egica), but they were patterned by ceremonies of public solidarity and legislation, not by war.

The last half of the seventh century marks the peak of public activity for the Visigothic kingdom. Reccesuinth and Ervig both revised Leovigild's law code, and legislated substantially themselves; laws survive for all the other kings except Roderic. The church councils were key moments in royal policy-making as well. And the laws that were made were more and more complex, as well as more and more high-flown. They were posed in all the codes as Gothic law, valid for all people in the kingdom, as law had probably in fact been from the fifth century onwards, even when a distinction between the Gothic and Roman population could be drawn, something which had gone by the mid-seventh century. But the antecedents of much of this 'Gothic' law lay in the imperial code of Theodosius II, far more than in other post-Roman kingdoms, and the rising rhetoric of the law looked to Roman models too. It is fairly clear that the late seventh-century Visigoths had the contemporary Byzantine empire as a point of reference as well, at least as a model for ceremonial, and for a close identification between the episcopacy and the king. The importance of religious conformity, implicit since the third council in 589, also became increasingly visible. The major law-givers of the period, Reccesuinth, Ervig and Egica, were fiercely hostile to the main non-Catholic group in Spain, the Jews; they picked up Sisebut's laws and greatly extended them, banning all Jewish religious practices, restricting Jewish civil rights, and in 694 reducing all Jews to slavery. The seventh century in Byzantium, Italy, even the normally tolerant Francia, saw some sporadic Jewish persecution, but these Visigothic laws have no real equivalent in their violence – and violence of expression – against Jews until the late Middle Ages. It is hard to read them today without hostility and alarm. All the same, they are quite parallel with Roman heresy laws, and they are in a line of legislation which in that respect stresses the Romanizing ambition of the kings only too clearly.

It is at this point, however, that questions arise. The complexity of the ceremonial at Toledo is very evident by 650 or so, and the regularity with which bishops and aristocrats went there is equally clear. The elaborate public humiliations which political losers faced in the capital – Argimund in 590 taken through the streets on a donkey with his hand cut off, Paul in 673 brought in barefoot on a camel – look straight back to the victory ceremonies of the Roman empire. Kings were, as in Francia, rich, not least because of Chindasuinth's confiscations (they maintained elements of the land tax, too, into the late seventh century at least), and therefore such a focus on the capital was presumably considered profitable by political players. The administration, the *officium palatinum*, was at least as elaborate as in Francia – although far less than in the Roman world – and hedged about with legal privileges; it included central officials and regional representatives such as dukes, and seems to have had some corporate identity, presumably centred on the king, much as the episcopate did. Indeed, it has been plausibly argued by Dietrich Claude that the aristocracy were, as a whole, more and more involved in palace politics; and the kings could certainly ruin individual aristocrats if they chose. But our sources are so overwhelmingly interested in royal and episcopal aspirations, and tell us so little about what really went on outside Toledo, that it is legitimate – and common – to wonder how much of this legislation was shadow-play. The Jews were so often extirpated, then return to be extirpated again. Wamba's 673 law on army-service was so severe, Ervig claimed when revising it a decade later, that 'almost half the population' had lost their civil rights: do we believe this? Egica in 702 in a law against fugitives said that 'there is barely a city, fortification, village, estate or dwelling-place' in which they were not hiding. This is a law which has been taken literally distressingly often, but it at least shows both the tendency of the kings to get carried away rhetorically and their awareness that it might be very different on the ground.

When we get a sight of local realities, they often seem very variegated as well, just as they had been before Leovigild. The archaeological trends of the fifth and early sixth centuries were not reversed later; if anything, they were accentuated, with the Meseta showing an increasingly localized set of economies, imports dropping in the Guadalquivir valley, and much of the Mediterranean coast showing a sharp economic simplification in the seventh century; the Roman south-east coast was no longer supplied from North Africa after Suinthila's conquest, and it seems to have gone into crisis. Urbanism survived best in some of the southern cities, Mérida, Córdoba, doubtless Seville, and also Toledo in the centre (the latter two have not been excavated, however); much less in most of the north, and only occasionally on the Mediterranean coast

(Barcelona and Valencia are candidates). In economic terms, the seventh-century kings thus presided over a set of separate economic realities, with divergent histories and decreasing interconnection. The seventh-century slate documents that have been found in the central mountains south of Salamanca (it is an area with slate rocks, easily usable for writing; the texts are often quite ephemeral estate texts, lists of cheese-rents and animals) seem to reflect a very localized economy as well: they cite very few place names, except, once, Toledo.

This growing local divergence may also explain some of the inconsistencies we can see in social trends. The aristocracy was clearly as militarized as in Francia, and a pattern of private relationships was developing; the late seventh-century army laws show that the army was largely made up of the personal dependants of lords, and church council legislation shows that the image of personal dependence was coming to structure ecclesiastical hierarchies too. The king, indeed, was seen as everyone's lord; every free man swore a personal oath of fidelity to him, a practice borrowed later by the Franks and Anglo-Saxons. Conversely, we also find institutions and cultural attitudes that were hardly changed from the Roman empire. The obsession with law and with legal delimitation (between aristocrats, *honestiores*, and non-aristocrats, for example) seems likely to be a Roman survival, even if some of the rhetoric of kings like Ervig and Egica could be seen more as revival. And, above all, the dense Roman culture of major political intellectuals like Isidore, bishop of Seville (599–636), author of theology, history, and the *Etymologies*, an influential if very strange encyclopedia, as well as animator of the fourth council of Toledo, must show that a traditional educational structure had survived intact in some of Spain's major cities. The letters of Isidore's disciple Braulio, bishop of Zaragoza (631–51), which are unusually attractive and human, show that this Roman cultural style existed in other parts of Spain as well, and the letters of Count Bulgar, surviving from the 610s, show that it sometimes extended to the secular aristocracy too, as King Sisebut's writings further demonstrate. Isidore and Braulio were in any case heavily involved in secular politics; they were both from aristocratic episcopal families, and were very close to kings. Their 'late late Roman' political practice, which survived in their successors up to 700 at least, must have been recognizable to a substantial part of the political establishment, and was certainly drawn on by legislators; Braulio indeed seems to have personally contributed to Reccesuinth's revised law code.

The seventh-century Visigothic kings thus presided over places and social groups where not very much had changed since the days of Augustine, places and social groups characterized by the same sort of militarized – and ruralized – society as in contemporary northern Francia, as well as some much simpler, more collective, societies, surviving in particular in parts of the north, and some areas of economic disintegration on the Mediterranean coast. They handled this diversity with the ambition of Roman emperors, but with a rather less elaborate administrative structure, which would have made detailed intervention rather more difficult. Small wonder their laws were sometimes rather shrill. It was impossible to encompass this diversity with early medieval western means; the kings knew it, and, unlike in Francia, resented it. But we would be wrong to follow the view of some modern historians and conclude that the late seventh century was a period of general crisis for the kingdom. Far from it; in that period the Visigothic state was the strongest in the West.

One of the reasons why the imagery of crisis has been used is that in 711 the Visigothic kingdom was overthrown by an Arab and Berber army invading from North Africa, and most of Spain remained part of a Muslim political community looking to Damascus, Baghdad and Cairo as a result, for the next five centuries and more (see Chapter 14). When kingdoms collapse quickly, historians have often sought to blame them for their defeat; but the answers can just as easily lie in the chance of a single battle, as with the Anglo-Saxon kingdom of England that ended at Hastings in 1066. It is certainly true that Spain fell to pieces in 711. The Arabs were for long only powerful in the far south. The north-east kept a Visigothic king for a decade; the south-east saw its Visigothic governor, Theodemir (d. 744), cut a separate deal with the Arabs in return for autonomy; the far north returned to communitarian and sometimes tribal traditions, as well as choosing an independent Christian king in the Asturias, Pelagius, around 720, the first of a long series of independent kings in the north (see Chapter 20). These different choices certainly reflect the socio-economic divergences already cited. But it took violent conquest to turn them into political realities; before 711 there is no sign of the sliding away of outlying regions, as in late seventh-century

Francia. Until then, as far as can be seen, the Visigothic kings kept a firm hegemony over all of them.

Italy had even more Roman traditions than Spain to draw on in the sixth century, but handled them differently. The Gothic war of 536–54 did enormous damage to the infrastructure of the peninsula, and Italy had by no means settled down when a federation headed by the Lombards invaded from Pannonia under Alboin (560–72) in 568–9. The Lombard invasion was one of the more disorganized we know of, however. In 574, after the assassination of two kings, the Lombards abandoned kingship altogether for a decade, and operated as a loose federation of dukes. It is likely that they did this as a result of bribes by the east Roman ruler Tiberius II, and Tiberius and his successors were indeed successful in getting many dukes to fight on the Roman side in the wars of the rest of the century. Tiberius also invited the Franks back to Italy to attack the Lombards. The Lombards, facing this, elected kings again, Authari (584–90), and then, in the teeth of the most substantial Frankish invasion, Agilulf (590–616), formerly duke of Turin. Agilulf withstood the major attacks of 590 and counterattacked himself; he established peace with the emperor Phocas in 605, gave tribute to the Franks, and some stability could return. But that peace revealed an alarmingly divided Italy. The Lombards had not managed to conquer more than separate sections of the peninsula: the inland Po valley in northern Italy; Tuscany, connected to the north only by a single mountain pass; and the duchies of Spoleto and Benevento in the central and southern Appennines. The last two were effectively autonomous duchies, with little link to the kingdom of the north until the eighth century. The Romans clung on to the area around Ravenna in the north, extending along the Adriatic coast in both directions, the west coast around Genoa and Pisa, the area round Rome, the area around Naples, and Puglia and the far south, with Sicily and Sardinia. Italy would not be controlled by a single ruler again until 1871. In this patchwork, the old centres of Roman political power, Rome and Ravenna, and all the major ports, stayed out of Lombard hands, and the Lombards were essentially restricted to inland areas, which had already become structurally separate from the Mediterranean world since the Gothic war.

This division could have allowed the Roman parts of Italy – Byzantine Italy as we can now call it – to maintain imperial traditions without further problem, while leaving the Lombard lands in relative isolation. This did not happen, however. The Lombards tended to remain on the offensive, taking Genoa in the 640s and Puglia in the 670s; another peace in 680 stabilized matters a little, but between 726 and 751 the Ravenna area was taken in a series of wars. Lombard isolation from the coast was steadily eroded, and after 751 Byzantine power on the mainland was restricted to Venice, Rome, Naples and the tips of the heel and toe of Italy. This meant that the Byzantines had to remain heavily militarized to defend themselves, and they did so. The ruler of Byzantine Italy, the exarch based in Ravenna, held a military office, and the aristocracy rapidly reshaped itself into a military hierarchy looking to him; even the citizens of the Byzantine cities could be referred to as *milites*, soldiers, or as a *numerus*, an army. They looked more and more like a 'Romano-Germanic' society, in fact, whether Lombard or Frankish. Unlike in the rest of the Byzantine empire, even the tax system eroded in much of the peninsula, much as it did in Francia or Spain. And links with Lombard areas, wars or no wars, slowly developed. The northern Lombards had to cross Byzantine territory if they wanted to reach Spoleto or Benevento, and are sometimes mentioned in sources as visiting Ravenna; the Beneventans and the Neapolitans even shared ownership of public lands in the rich Capua plain on their boundary. In social terms, the various sections of the peninsula developed largely in parallel, and we do not see the divergencies in Italy that are visible in Spain. We shall look shortly at some of the differences that did exist.

The Lombard kings, like the Visigoths, never established a dynasty; even the Agilolfings who ruled from 653 to 712 faced internal coups, and two kings from a rival family in 662–72. But throughout the seventh century they recognized some rough genealogical criteria for succession, if not in the Agilolfing line, then through queens. Authari's widow Theodelinda (d. *c.* 620) married Agilulf in 590, and later tradition said she chose him; she was certainly influential in Agilulf's reign, negotiating with Pope Gregory the Great (590–604) in Rome. Her daughter Gundiperga similarly married two successive kings, Arioald (626–36) and Rothari (636–52); Aripert I (653–61) was her cousin; and Grimoald (662–71), when he overthrew Aripert's son Perctarit (661–2, 672–88), married the latter's sister. This did not, all the same, lead to much female political protagonism; Theodelinda remains an exception here, perhaps because she was a Frank, daughter of the Agilolfing duke of Bavaria, at a time of considerable Frankish influence.

The seventh century is poorly documented in Lombard Italy, in the absence of both documents and detailed narratives, for Paul the Deacon's Lombard history, written in the 790s, is both brief and late; but Agilulf and Rothari stand out. Agilulf stabilized the frontiers, and also established an effective hegemony over the dukes of the cities of the north. The political incoherences of the first thirty years of Lombard Italy ended with him. He used Roman ceremonial imagery, as when he presented his son Adaloald (616–26) as king in 604 in the circus at Milan, and he had Roman administrators and advisers. His wife and son were Catholic, but he was not. All the same, it is significant that we cannot tell from our sources whether he was pagan or Arian; the Lombards included followers of all three religions, and there is no sign from Agilulf onwards that personal religious affiliation had a major political content, unlike in Spain. Rothari, duke of Brescia before his accession, was certainly Arian, but more important than that is that he saw himself as a Lombard legitimist, fighting wars against the Byzantines, and he issued the first Lombard law code, the *Edict*, in 643. This text lists his seventeen predecessors as Lombard kings, well back into myth, and also Rothari's own eleven male-line ancestors, and manuscripts of the law include a brief Lombard history, which may have been there in some form from the start. The Edict of Rothari is the longest early medieval code after those of the Visigoths, but much less influenced by Roman law, although the picture of royal authority contained in it is Roman enough. It was really Rothari who created a specifically Lombard imagery for kingship and society in Italy, and there is little in later Lombard 'ethnic' identity that can be traced back further than 643. Conversely, it is important to recognize that, as in Spain, this identity was erected on the back of a Roman-influenced administration, based from Rothari's time at the latest on a stable capital at Pavia, in imitation of Roman/Byzantine centres such as Ravenna (and maybe also of Toledo), as well as on a network of dukes and gastalds (the equivalent of Frankish counts) ruling over each of the traditional Roman city territories of the north of Italy.

Rothari's successors drew on Lombard imagery, and on Lombard law, but also on the Roman infrastructure that it assumed. They also used the church relatively little; bishops were important in city politics, and are sometimes referred to as royal advisers (under Agilulf in particular), but none of them were major political dealers, unlike in Francia, and councils of bishops had no political or ceremonial role, unlike in Spain, or in the Byzantine empire. After 653 no king was certainly Arian, but the abandonment of Arianism is given little stress in our sources. Slightly more important, perhaps, was the formal abandonment at the synod of Pavia in 698 of the schism of the Three Chapters, which had separated the Catholics of the north of Italy from Rome since the 550s, under the patronage of King Cunipert (679–700), but this did not lead to any increase in the imagery of religious unity in the Lombard kingdom, either.

Liutprand (712–44) was the most powerful Lombard king. Son of the tutor to Cunipert's son, he could claim a link to the family politics of the seventh century, but he was not genealogically associated with his predecessors, and his reign feels like a new beginning. He legislated extensively to fill out and update Rothari's *Edict*, in annual sessions (taking place on 1 March, as in sixth-century Francia); it is clear that he was also regularly acting as a judge, for many of his enactments are the generalizations of specific judgements on quite arcane points of law, such as who is liable if a man is killed when the counterweight from a well falls on his head while water is being drawn, or how much penalty should be paid if a man steals a woman's clothes while she is bathing. One of his first enactments, in 713, made pious gifts to the church legal, and documents for such gifts and for other matters more or less begin then, making the eighth century as a whole much more visible than the seventh in Lombard Italy. And he made war, almost as regularly as his contemporary and ally Charles Martel, against the Byzantines and also against the southern Lombard dukes. By the 740s Spoleto was permanently brought into the political power-structure of the kingdom. Benevento, further away and richer, had always been the more autonomous of the two (except in the 660s, when its duke, Grimoald, had gained the kingdom), and remained so, but at least Liutprand and his successors chose its dukes several times. By Liutprand's death the Lombard king was hegemonic in the entire peninsula, and it became for the first time since 568 conceivable that Italy might become a single political unit again.

Liutprand's successors were the brothers Ratchis (744–9) and Aistulf (749–56), dukes of Friuli in north-east Italy. Both kings legislated, and

Aistulf in particular followed Liutprand's territorial policies. It was Aistulf who finally occupied Ravenna in 751, and in 752 he sought tribute from Rome. But the geopolitical situation had changed by now. It was in 751 that the Carolingian Pippin III claimed the kingship in Francia, and sought ratification by two popes (below, Chapter 16); the debt to the papacy that this represented was quickly called in, as Pope Stephen II appealed for help against Aistulf. Pippin invaded Italy twice in 754-6; he forced Aistulf to leave Rome alone and to hand Ravenna to the pope as well. The next king, Desiderius (757-74), inherited both Aistulf's aspirations and his constraints; he interfered in Roman politics, and also in Benevento, whose duke, Arichis II (758-87), he chose, but the Frankish threat remained. In the end, Desiderius attacked Rome again in 772, and Pippin's son Charlemagne invaded Italy in 773-4; this time he overthrew the Lombard king and took all of Lombard Italy for himself, except Benevento, where Arichis in 774 named himself an independent prince.

The mid-eighth-century kings were trapped between their felt need to absorb Rome, as the key to the south, and the certainty of Frankish retribution, even if it has to be added that Italy's accessibility across the Alpine passes probably means that Charlemagne would have eventually attacked anyway. The Franks were never safe neighbours, and had a history of Italian involvement going back to Theudebert; from the time of Ratchis onward, in particular, the Franks were also keen to welcome Italian exiles, as were the Bavarians. Lombard military activity was probably always on a smaller scale than in Francia, and we have several wills from landowners about to go to war. These hint that actually taking part in fighting was by now not routine, even for large owners, despite all the military imagery that the Lombard aristocracy, just like all their neighbours, now regarded as de rigueur – let alone for the lesser free, who were nonetheless referred to as 'army men' in legislation. But there is no sign of political or structural weakness in the Lombard political system in any other respect. Like the Visigoths in 711, they just lost to superior arms, in this case to the strongest army in western Europe. Lombard political practice, indeed, influenced that of the Franks in the next generations, as we shall see later.

The documentation we have for the eighth century shows a Lombard state that intervened in local society in capillary ways. The kings and the dukes or gastalds of the cities remained regular judges for primary court cases and for appeals, and kings made sure their judgements were followed by sending written instructions; we have a case from Lucca in 771 in which the local bishop re-heard a church dispute because the king had instructed him that his first judgement was improperly made. In difficult cases the king sent *missi*, emissaries of the royal court, to make enquiry on the spot, as in the disputes between Parma and Piacenza over the boundary of their city territories, resolved after an inquest by Perctarit in 674, and the parallel dispute over diocesan boundaries between Siena and Arezzo in 714–15, resolved after two inquests by Liutprand. It was normal for quite ordinary people to go to Pavia to seek justice, or to Spoleto or Benevento, for which we have similar inquests and judgements. The inhabitants of the Lombard lands were also well informed about royal legislation, which gets cited in documents, even in the duchy of Benevento, unlike in Francia. Writing was an important basis for government. There is relatively little evidence in Lombard Italy for the large-scale ceremonial in the capital that is so visible for Spain, however. It seems that the centrality of Pavia was made easier because of two main features of Lombard society. First, the élites of the kingdom were very largely city-dwelling. They lived in one place, they competed over who was to be duke/gastald or bishop, they regularly attended the courts of both; they were loyal to their cities, indeed, as the boundary disputes mentioned above demonstrate. Even monastic foundations, which begin in the eighth century, were with some prominent exceptions urban. Whereas Frankish historians followed the factional politics of major dealers like Leudegar of Autun, Paul the Deacon, when he described the civil war following the coup of Alahis duke of Trento against Cunipert (*c.* 688–90), saw it in terms of the political choices of the citizens of Brescia, Pavia, Vicenza, Treviso. All of this meant that local élites were easily accessible, for all political practice took place inside cities, or nearly all.

The second major feature is that most Lombard aristocrats were fairly restricted in their wealth. Almost none of our documents show any of them with more than between five and ten estates, which is close to a minimum for aristocrats in Francia. The king and the ruling dukes of the south had immense lands, of course, and a small number of powerful ducal families, particularly in the north-east, were rich, but the bulk of the élite owned only a handful of properties, usually only in the city territory they lived in, plus perhaps its immediate neighbours, with, quite often, a house in Pavia. This meant that they could not afford the private armed entourages that were the support for factional politics in Francia; it is not chance that nearly all the usurpers in Italy, successful or unsuccessful, were dukes, who had a right to control local armies. It also meant that they would be satisfied by relatively modest gifts by kings, and indeed as far as we can tell royal generosity was not huge in the Lombard period, although the royal treasury was imposing, in Italy as in Francia. Aristocratic identity was also bound up with office-holding, which was in the king's gift; duchies did not become family patrimonies, except for Spoleto (sometimes) and Benevento. The Lombard kings did not tax, after the first couple of generations of their rule at least. They operated entirely in the framework of a political practice based on land. But inside that framework, their hegemony was very great, and unusually detailed: their capillary power arguably extended to much more modest levels of society than the Frankish or Visigothic kings achieved.

The cities of the Lombard kingdom, despite their social and political importance, were in material terms not particularly striking. They were full of churches by 774, most of them recent foundations by urban notables – Lucca, the best-documented city in Italy, had at least twenty-five – but urban housing was materially nondescript, and commercial exchange for anything except luxuries was local at best. We know less about the duchies of Spoleto and Benevento; the high-mountain core of Spoleto meant that its cities were rather weaker, and its aristocracies more often rural, but Benevento had some rich lowland areas, and the capital there seems to have been a focus for an aristocracy that owned more widely than anywhere else in Italy; Benevento may well have been quite rich and politically coherent. But it was Byzantine cities in Italy, at least major ones like Rome, Ravenna or Naples, that were probably the most economically active. The archaeology for cities like Naples is certainly more impressive – or less unimpressive – than that for Lombard cities, Brescia or Verona or Milan. It was only in the last decades of the Lombard kingdom that even churches, usually the only surviving buildings of the early Middle Ages to show a real monumental aspiration, begin to be architecturally ambitious, as with Desiderius' prestige monastery of S. Salvatore (later S. Giulia) at Brescia. By contrast, Naples and Ravenna, and above all Rome, could sustain that ambition throughout, and in the Byzantine lands it extended even to private housing, as documents show for eighth-century Rimini, and as recent excavations show for Rome.

Byzantine society in Italy had developed parallel to Lombard society, but it did have some particular features. It was broadly richer and more complex, as just implied. In Byzantine Italy the church was also more of a political protagonist: most obviously in the case of the pope in Rome, but also in Ravenna and Naples, where bishops were major figures. Another difference is that the separate Byzantine provinces of Italy moved towards effective independence in the eighth century, just at the moment when the Lombard lands gained some political coherence. The duke of Naples, Stephen II (755–800), became entirely autonomous from Constantinople (interestingly, he ruled Naples first as duke, and then, after 767, as bishop). By the 740s the dukes of the small lagoon islands crystallizing as Venice were effectively autonomous too; and that decade was probably the key moment in the century-long shift towards independence in the Rome of the popes, which was complete by the 770s. Nostalgia for Byzantine rule could remain; it was very much felt in Istria, taken by the Franks from Byzantine/Venetian control in the late eighth century, as a court case from 804 against the Frankish governor shows (see below, Chapter 16). But Italy was spinning away from Byzantine domination. The only major exception to this was Sicily, stably in imperial hands until the 820s.

Rome remained the least typical city in Italy. Although far smaller than it had been under the empire, it remained by a long way the largest city in the West, maybe twice the size of Ravenna or Naples, and five times the size of Brescia or Lucca (these figures are bald guesses, however). Rome's territory, roughly the modern region of Lazio, was also much bigger than that of other city-states like Naples or Venice. The popes had always been major players in religious matters, and remained so – although their political-religious interests for a long time remained focused on the East, and they had almost no influence in Merovingian Francia and Visigothic Spain. But when the senate of the city faded out in the late sixth century, the popes emerged as the authority best equipped to rule Rome, as is already visible in the extensive letter collection of Pope Gregory the Great in the 590s. The eastern emperor could still remove a religiously rebellious Martin I in 653 (see Chapter 11), but could not remove Sergius I in 687 (the imperial envoy supposedly had to hide under the pope's bed to escape the Roman crowd), and in the eighth century the entire imperial infrastructure in Rome steadily became papal. But the wealth of Rome, and of the popes themselves, meant that this infrastructure (and associated ceremonial) remained remarkably elaborate, with dozens of officials in separate hierarchies: far more elaborate than the government in any of the Romano-Germanic kingdoms, and indeed imitating that of Constantinople itself. In the eighth century popes like Gregory II (715–31) and Zacharias (741–52) consolidated papal power inside Lazio; Stephen II (752–7) and Hadrian I (771–95) acted as political protagonists, calling in the Franks against the Lombards, and in Hadrian's case acting as a regional player, whom Charlemagne treated as a (near) equal. The papacy remained fairly marginal to western European politics for some centuries more, but its more strong-minded occupants could achieve quite an effect, as Nicholas I (858–67) would in Frankish and also Bulgarian affairs. In Italian politics, Rome's size ensured that the popes would continue to punch above their weight, too; and popes acted as a legitimating element for Carolingian and post-Carolingian rulers, as we shall see later.

Visigothic Spain and Lombard Italy show two coherent alternatives to the Frankish path away from the Roman empire and into the early Middle Ages. Around 700, indeed, Spain looked more successful than Francia, though Spain's conquest by the Arabs and Charles Martel's reunification of the Frankish lands in the 710s and later have often led modern historians to conclude otherwise. Italy's government, too, was effective enough to be a model for the Franks after 774. These three states show sharp divergencies in their political style, in the force of royal ceremonial (strongest in Spain), in the importance of dynastic legitimacy and in the wealth of local aristocracies (strongest in Francia), in the complexity of the links between central government and provincial society (arguably strongest in Italy). Royal aspirations were different, too: only the Frankish kings sought political hegemony over other peoples; only the Visigothic kings sought to rule like Roman emperors. But there are other aspects in which their developments were similar. They all moved towards social and political hierarchies dominated by military identity; civilian aristocracies vanished. (This happened in the Byzantine empire as well, first in Italy, but eventually even in the Byzantine heartland.) Steadily, at different speeds, they lost control of tax-raising, and became essentially land-based political systems, although all three managed to keep aristocratic political practice and even identity firmly concentrated on royal courts. Indeed, even though all three experienced periods of royal weakness and political fragmentation, successful rulers could in each case re-focus the aristocracy on them, Leovigild after 569, Agilulf after 590, Charles Martel after 719. All three also saw their political identity in ethnic terms, as Franks, Goths and Lombards, but ethnicity rapidly became unimportant in practice: by 700 most 'Franks' had ancestors who had been Roman, and the same is true for Spain and Italy. Indeed, apart from the continuing importance of assemblies (above, Chapter 4), and the assumption that military service was due from all free males, at least in theory (never in practice), there was not so much that was specifically Germanic in the 'Romano-Germanic' kingdoms. Politics, society and culture had moved on from the Roman world, but they can most usefully be understood as products of development from Roman antecedents.

7

Kings without States: Britain and Ireland, 400–800

The seventh-century Breton *Life* of Samson of Dol discusses the saint's early career in Britain in the early sixth century in some detail. Samson was supposedly from an aristocratic family of hereditary royal tutors in Dyfed (modern south-west Wales), but was dedicated to the priesthood and sent to be taught by the learned Illtud, probably at Llantwit in Glamorgan. From there he travelled around south Wales, the Severn valley and Cornwall, looking for monasteries with greater rigour, and ending up as a hermit in a fortification above the Severn. Here, he was recognized and promoted by the local bishop; later, he became an abbot in a monastery founded by his mother, and eventually a bishop himself, before he left for Brittany and Francia. This sort of storyline is a familiar one in hagiographies. Less familiar are his opponents, for he regularly combated and destroyed (or tamed) poisonous serpents, and once he had to face a sorceress with a trident. A particularly significant feature of the text is that, between his high-status origin and his later encounters in Francia (called by the author *Romania*) with King Childebert I (511–58), no kings are mentioned, and hardly any other secular people except his immediate family. In Britain, Samson seems to operate in an almost entirely ecclesiastical world, even though he moves about such a lot and gains preferment so systematically; wider political systems barely impinge there at all, although in his Breton and Frankish travels they are mentioned at once. This is a Breton, not a British, text, but the two culture areas were closely linked, and Breton and Welsh were effectively the same language in this period, thanks to migration from Britain to Brittany. It was at the least unnecessary for a Breton author to imagine that his subject had dealt with kings in Britain, even in order to get land and patronage for his monasteries. This makes Samson close to unique in the world of early medieval hagiography, but it may tell us something about the evanescence of British kingship, whether in the seventh century or the sixth.

Britain faced economic meltdown in the early fifth century, after the withdrawal of Roman armies and the end of the Roman provincial administration around 410. We cannot say if the Romans intended to return after they coped with the civil wars in Gaul in the same period, but anyway they did not do so. Britain effectively fell off the Roman map. In archaeological terms, the consequences were extreme: by 450 at the latest, villas were abandoned, urbanism had virtually ended, the countryside was partly abandoned around the old military focus of Hadrian's Wall (although not elsewhere, probably), and all large-scale artisan production had ceased. In no other part of the empire was this economic simplification so abrupt and total, and it must reflect a sharp social crisis as well. Our early written sources are fragmentary (a few inscriptions, some writing by Patrick, the fifth-century British missionary to Ireland, and a mid-sixth-century hellfire sermon by Gildas), but they seem to show that by 500 western Britain, at least, was divided among a set of small-scale rulers, sometimes called kings (*reges*), sometimes tyrants (*tyranni*: a negative term in Gildas, but maybe related to *tigernos*, 'ruler' in Brittonic). A patchwork of tiny polities had replaced the Roman state. In eastern Britain there was by now a similar set of micro-kingdoms ruled by immigrant Anglo-Saxons; in the late fifth century these had been expanding westwards, but British counterattacks, obscurely led by a warlord called Ambrosius Aurelianus, had held them back at the edge of the Severn river basin. We shall come on to the Anglo-Saxons in a moment, but for now it can be noted that the evidence we have for the small scale of the British kingdoms and of the Anglo-Saxon kingdoms each backs the other up, for otherwise one set would have prevailed more easily against the other.

How the British polities developed has been the subject of endless speculation, as the changes were so great and the evidence so exiguous and contested. (Here I mention Arthur only to set him aside, for the sources that cite him as in some way Ambrosius' successor in the early sixth century in western or northern Britain are all late; by the ninth century, he was a recognized hero figure, but that is all that can be known about him.) Some things can be said, however; first, concerning language. Latin was still the normal literary language of inscriptions, and Roman titles like *civis*, citizen, appear in them, as they also do in

Patrick and Gildas, but most people actually spoke Brittonic, the ancestor of Welsh. The Romano-British élite had doubtless spoken Latin, too (Welsh has a large number of Latin loanwords in it), but the peasantry did not, even in lowland Britain as far as we can tell, and spoken Latin soon ceased to be common, again unlike in most of the West. Secondly, lowland Britain was heavily Romanized in its economy and culture, but northern and western Britain were less so. Roman occupation was more military there (above all around Hadrian's Wall, but in most of Wales as well), there were fewer cities, and traditional social structures were stronger. The kingdoms that seem to have been largest in post-Roman Britain were Dyfed, and Gwynedd in north-west Wales, both in relatively un-Romanized areas. This does not mean that they were simply successors of some pre-Roman political tradition; Gwynedd (Venedotia in Latin) was a new territorial name, and later tradition claimed that its rulers had come in the fifth century from north of the Wall; Dyfed was at least an old name (the Demetae were the earlier British people in the area), but the kingdom was in this period a zone of strong Irish immigration, and its ruler Vortipor, castigated by Gildas, has left us a bilingual inscribed monument in both Latin and Irish at Castelldwyran in Pembrokeshire. But, despite the complex history of both of these kingdoms, they do seem to have crystallized more easily because there were social structures there that did not depend on the Roman state: tight links of kinship and personal dependence, a wide sense of collective loyalty, and a long-standing military style to local authority, that can be called 'tribal'. These tribal communities stretched south into Cornwall and Devon and northwards, past the Wall, into southern Scotland, where the British kingdoms of Rheged, Strathclyde and Gododdin are attested in slightly later sources. They seem to have been stably Christian, as Gildas's denunciations also presume, but this was the only obvious Roman influence on them. One of their leaders may have been the 'proud tyrant', unnamed in Gildas but called Vortigern by the eighth century, who was blamed for inviting the Anglo-Saxons in at some moment in the fifth century; Vortigern (Gwrtheyrn in Welsh) was claimed as an ancestor by kings of Powys and Gwrtheyrnion in eastern Wales by the ninth century.

The post-Roman British in the lowlands probably operated on a smaller scale still. The only lowland powers who can be traced in any detail are the kings of Ergyng, Gwent, the Cardiff region and Gower, all in lowland south-east Wales, some documents for whom, land-grants to churches, survive from the late sixth century onwards: these kings ruled perhaps a third of a modern county each, and sometimes less. This was the Romanized section of Wales, and this sort of scale may well have been normal in the whole of lowland Britain. It probably derived from the first generations after the end of Roman rule, in which local landowners had to look to their own self-defence, and even the Roman city territories, the traditional units of government in lowland Britain as elsewhere, soon fragmented into rather smaller de-facto units. When they did so, they could sometimes call on Roman imagery, such as the *civis* terminology already mentioned, and also the imitative Roman lifestyle implied by the scatters of Mediterranean wine- and oil-amphorae and fine pottery found in several early sixth-century hill-fort sites, probable political centres, especially south and north of the Bristol Channel. Again, they were certainly Christian, as the land-grants show, and as the *Life* of Samson implies: even if they were too small-scale for the latter's author to mention them, that author at least assumed a uniform Christian environment in lowland western Britain. But it is likely that they also drew on the political models of the western British kingdoms, for an imagery of tribal identity, and for the values of small-scale military activity, such as loyalty, bravery and feasting, which were new in the previously civilian lowland areas.

The previous two paragraphs use the words 'seem to have', 'may have', 'likely' and 'probably' in nearly every sentence: this faithfully reflects the surviving documentation. Everything is guesswork. If we follow the British (we can now call them Welsh) into the seventh and eighth centuries, the patterns become slightly clearer, and at least do not contradict what has just been said. By 700 the Anglo-Saxons had taken Somerset, the Severn valley and Lancashire, thus effectively confining the Welsh to three unconnected areas, largely upland, in what is now south-west England, Wales and southern Scotland. In these areas, however, kingdoms had continued to crystallize, and the tiny kingdoms of south-east Wales had merged into a larger one called Glywysing, which joined Gwynedd, Dyfed and Powys to make up the four major polities of Wales in this period. Gwynedd was probably always the strongest; Gildas had thought so already in the mid-sixth century, when he called its king Maelgwn the 'island dragon', and Cadwallon of Gwynedd (d. 634) raided far into the Anglo-Saxon lands, right up to northern

Northumbria, as Bede recounts. In the ninth century its kings would become hegemonic in Wales. Our earliest poetic texts in Welsh date from the seventh century to the ninth, and these contain a number of laments on dead kings, including *Marwnad Cynddylan*, the earliest, for King Cynddylan, based in or near modern Shropshire, who died in the mid-seventh century, and *Y Gododdin*, the longest, for King Mynyddog of Gododdin, who supposedly took his army from his capital at Edinburgh to Catraeth, perhaps modern Catterick, where they all died around 600. These show a homogeneous set of 'heroic' values, which were clearly those of the Welsh aristocracy by 800 at the latest: 'The warrior . . . would take up his spear just as if it were sparkling wine from glass vessels. His mead was contained in silver, but he deserved gold.' Or: 'The men went to Catraeth, swift was their host. Pale mead was their feast, and it was their poison.' It is not unreasonable to suppose that these values were already shared in the sixth century. Whenever they developed, however, they were a world away from those of Rome. This is important as a reflection of the political crisis we began with, for these military élites were lineal descendants of British Romans, unconquered by invaders; all the same, all their points of reference were by now different. They were quite parallel, however, to those of the Anglo-Saxons.

It is not easy to tell what Welsh kings did. They evidently fought a lot, and their military entourage is one of their best-documented features. They were generous and hospitable to their dependants, and (at least in literature) got loyalty to the death in return, although where they got their resources from is not so clear. They took tribute from subject and defeated rulers, and also tribute or rent from their own people, but the little we know of the latter implies that only fairly small quantities were owed by the peasant population to their lords; Mynyddog's gold, silver and glass were a literary image, too. They did justice, along with clerics and aristocrats, that is to say in public, although there is little or no reference to them making law before the tenth century at the earliest. They patronized the church, but that church itself operated fairly informally through families of religious houses, each claiming foundation by charismatic monastic founders of the sixth century, Illtud in Glamorgan, Padarn in the centre-west, and so on. Overall, they acted in the framework of face-to-face, personal lordship, with no institutionalized administration at all. As we shall see in Chapter 20, that would hardly change until well after the period covered by this book.

The institutional simplicity just referred to was one thing that kept British/Welsh kingdoms small; royal power extended to a not always very subject peasantry, to the élites who feasted with (and got gifts from) the king, to the people most recently defeated in battle, and no further. Sometimes wider hegemonies were achieved, but until after 850 they were temporary. If we move northwards, however, we do find one kingdom which sometimes operated on a larger scale, that of the Picts, in what is now central and eastern Scotland: well to the north of any area the Romans influenced, but at least partly parallel in culture to the British/Welsh, and speaking a language descended, like Welsh, from Brittonic. The Picts remain amazingly obscure, even by British standards, including after their gradual conversion to Christianity in the late sixth and seventh centuries. Uniquely among European societies, they were apparently matrilineal, which means that Pictish royal daughters, marrying out, could bring legitimate succession to members of rival families, such as Talorcan (c. 653–7), son of King Eanfrith of Bernicia, but how this really worked is anyone's guess. They were not always united (they had seven provinces by tradition, from Fife to Caithness), but their main king, the king of Fortriu, was often hegemonic over the whole of Pictland, and could fight off enemies with some effectiveness, as when Bridei, son of Beli (c. 672–93), the best-known king of the seventh century, destroyed the over-reaching Northumbrian king Ecgfrith, and with him Northumbrian political hegemony, at Nechtansmere in 685. At the height of Pictish power, in the eighth century, Onuist, son of Urguist (c. 729–61), defeated enemies across the whole of modern Scotland, establishing his own regional hegemony, which lasted on and off until the 830s. How the Picts managed this with no visible infrastructure, in one of the most unpromising terrains in Europe, remains a mystery; but they at least show it was possible.

Given the sharp social and cultural changes in the unconquered parts of Britain, it is hardly surprising that the early Anglo-Saxons were not significantly influenced by Roman traditions. Our written information about them focuses on a later period: Bede's *Ecclesiastical History*, written in the 730s, which really begins with the conversion of the Anglo-Saxons to Christianity from 597 onwards, and the *Anglo-Saxon Chronicle*, a late ninth-century text, which begins to be plausible around the same time. Before the late sixth century, our knowledge has to be constructed essentially from archaeology. But it is at least the case that the Anglo-Saxon settlements were concentrated in the lowland areas of Britain, always the best-documented areas of the island in archaeological terms, and research in these areas has often been dense by European standards, so we can construct a relatively consistent picture of them.

The Anglo-Saxons came to Britain by sea, for the most part from Saxony in modern north Germany, including the small region known as Angeln; they spoke variants of the Germanic languages of Saxony and the Frisian coast. Their raids on Britain had begun as early as the third century (the Romans built coastal fortifications to counter them), but there is no evidence that their permanent settlement began before the second quarter of the fifth. Whether any of it was associated with invitations like that later ascribed to Vortigern cannot be known. Such stories are common after invasions, and there is little sign of post-Roman political units in eastern Britain strong enough to do any inviting, but it would be foolish to be anything other than agnostic about accounts that cannot be disproved (the same is true of the existence of Arthur). What can be said with certainty, however, is that the Anglo-Saxon settlement was very highly fragmented, more even than the pre-Clovis Frankish settlement in northern Gaul, and stayed so. Even in the late sixth century, after a period of political recomposition, we find at least nine documented kingdoms in the eastern half of what we can now call England, from Bernicia in the north to Wessex in the south, and there were probably several more. Most of these were the size of one or two modern counties, equivalent to the size of Roman city-territories, smaller than the smallest ex-Roman units we can ever find Germanic rulers controlling on the Continent. But what has become increasingly clear in recent years is that most of these kingdoms, even though they were so restricted in size, were themselves built out of much smaller building-blocks, sometimes called *regiones* by modern historians (it is a word also found in some eighth-century texts). These often covered around 100 square kilometres, though sometimes more and sometimes even less, 100 square kilometres being just over a quarter the size of the Isle of Wight, and just over a fortieth the size of Kent. Welsh kingdoms like Ergyng were a little larger than this around 600, but the order of magnitude is comparable. The best-attested of these small building-blocks were in the Fenlands and the areas of the Midlands just west and south of them, which even in the late seventh century were not united into a single larger kingdom, unlike their neighbours to the east and west, respectively East Anglia and Mercia. This intervening area, called by Bede a bit weakly the Middle Angles, was listed as a separate set of units in a tribute list, the *Tribal Hidage*, probably dating from the later seventh century: the North and South Gyrwa of the Peterborough area, the Sweord Ora of part of Huntingdonshire, and so on. Units of this kind are also referred to casually in later documents, surviving as identifiable units in many larger kingdoms, and topographical research has identified many more.

This model for the Anglo-Saxon settlements, which I broadly accept, thus has the invaders settling in very small groups, initially covering a handful of local communities for the most part, which could, as in Wales, be called tribal. Political leadership would have been very simple and informal, though of course necessarily military, for a fragmented conquest is still a conquest. This picture further fits with the archaeology of early Anglo-Saxon settlements and cemeteries, which shows a very simple material culture, far simpler in every respect than that found anywhere on the ex-Roman Continent outside the Balkans. Ceramics were all hand-made, without even the use of kilns, before 700; iron-work was small-scale enough to have all been local; glass- and complex jewellery-making was rare before 550 and largely restricted to Kent even then, a kingdom influenced culturally by the Franks and perhaps sometimes ruled by them; even house types were much simpler and village structures more fragmented than in Saxony. These all point to a very modest ruling class and an undeveloped social hierarchy. And, as noted earlier, the eastern British polities that these small units replaced must have been no larger. How the lowland British themselves fitted into such units remains guesswork however. The Anglo-Saxons settled in a still-used Roman landscape as far as we can see, but seldom on former Roman sites; they hardly picked up Romano-British material culture at all (which further attests to the systemic crisis in post-Roman Britain), and adopted almost no loanwords into Old English from Brittonic. The British majority, that must overwhelmingly have been there, evidently adapted to Anglo-Saxon culture, rather than vice versa. This seems even to have been the case for enclaves that stayed under British control up to the years around 600, such as the Chilterns west of London and the region of Leeds.

The end of the sixth century and the start of the seventh seems to have been the moment in which these small units, which had doubtless been expanding in the meantime, began to crystallize into kingdoms the size of one or two counties; the latter emerge in the written record then, but archaeology, too, shows the beginnings of an internal hierarchy in rural settlements, together with some prestige royal centres like Yeavering in Northumberland (which even had a Roman-influenced theatre-like grandstand: below, Chapter 10), and the remarkable wealth of royal graves at Sutton Hoo in Suffolk and Prittlewell in Essex. The kingdoms that arguably crystallized first were Kent, East Anglia, Deira (roughly modern Yorkshire), Bernicia on the Northumberland coast, and Wessex in modern Oxfordshire and Hampshire; of the main Anglo-Saxon kingdoms, Mercia seems to have been the latest to emerge. The late sixth century was also, probably as a result of this crystallization, the period in which the Anglo-Saxons began to expand again at the expense of the Welsh kingdoms after the military stand-off of the early sixth century. Æthelfrith of Bernicia (c. 593–616) is recorded in both English and Welsh sources as a fighter, attacking westwards to Chester and probably also taking over Gododdin, up to Edinburgh; Ceawlin of Wessex (d. c. 593) may have been responsible for conquering the southern part of the Severn valley and the Chilterns, though here the evidence is late. 'Probably' and 'seems to have' recur here too, for our sources are so uncertain. What is clear, however, is that there was a much greater military protagonism among the leaders of these newly coherent kingdoms. They fought each other, indeed, rather more than they fought the Welsh. Some claimed temporary hegemony over neighbouring kingdoms, as Æthelfrith did over Deira, Æthelberht of Kent (d. 616) over his immediate neighbours, and the Deiran king Edwin (616–33) over Bernicia and some of the southern kingdoms as well.

The seventh century was dominated in political terms by two kingdoms, Northumbria and Mercia. Northumbria was the result of the unification of Bernicia and Deira, which became permanent after 651. Edwin, then Æthelfrith's sons Oswald (634–42) and Oswiu (642/51–70), then Oswiu's son Ecgfrith (670–85) all claimed hegemonies in the south at various moments; they also extended either direct rule or overlordship into British and Pictish areas, and Ecgfrith even attacked Ireland once, in 684. These hegemonies remained intermittent, but their frequency presumably resulted from the size of their kingdom, which was the largest in England at that time. Mercia began much smaller, and it is not certain that it even existed as a single kingdom before its first powerful king, Penda (c. 626–55). It was centred in an inland area, around Tamworth and Lichfield in Staffordshire, which was close to the border of early Anglo-Saxon settlement, and as it crystallized it probably came to include smaller British-run units as well. Penda was also allied to Cadwallon of Gwynedd, with whose help he destroyed Edwin in 633; this victory (and Cadwallon's own death a year later) probably gave him the status to absorb or gain hegemony over more of his neighbours, and he killed Oswald, too, in a defensive war this time, in 642. Oswiu destroyed him in return in 655, but Penda's son Wulfhere (658–75) was able to rebuild his regional hegemony. From this point onwards Mercia was usually the political overlord of neighbouring kingdoms like the Hwicce of northern Gloucestershire and Worcestershire, Lindsey in north Lincolnshire, and most of the tiny Fenland polities: it sat squarely in the middle of southern Britain, a good strategic location. Northumbrian influence southwards was blocked as a result, and very soon Ecgfrith's death at Pictish hands lessened its influence in the far north as well. By 700 or so, political power in the Anglo-Saxon lands was shared between four main kingdoms, Northumbria, Mercia, Wessex (which was by now extending its power into the British south-west) and East Anglia, with honourable mention also for Kent, small but unusually wealthy thanks to its Frankish links. Of these, Mercia was clearly the most powerful. Except for Kent, thse kingdoms would survive into the late ninth century.

These four kingdoms were bigger than Welsh kingdoms by now, but had many similarities all the same. The values of small-scale militarism are equally visible in our written sources. *Beowulf*, the longest Old English poetic text, stresses loyalty and heroism, and royal hospitality and gift-giving, much as *Y Gododdin* does. *Beowulf*'s date is contested between the eighth, ninth and tenth centuries, but its imagery fully fits other early texts. One example is Felix's *Life* of Guthlac, a saint's life of the 730s, which depicts its Mercian aristocratic saint as having been the leader of a war-band in his youth in the 690s, 'remembering the valiant deeds of heroes of old', who razed the settlements of his enemies with gay abandon and accumulated immense booty before changing his ways and becoming a monk. As late as the 690s (or 730s), that is to say, it was possible to be a small-scale independent freebooter, and to get credit for it, in that Felix writes it up with some enthusiasm. But kings themselves did not operate on so large a scale yet. The *Anglo-Saxon*

Chronicle, in a passage plausibly drawn from an earlier text, recounts the death of King Cynewulf of Wessex in 786: he was surprised in his mistress's house by his rival Cyneheard, his predecessor's brother, and killed before his entourage reached him; his entourage then fought to the death around him, despite being offered their lives; the following day Cynewulf's army besieged Cyneheard in return, and after a failed negotiation Cyneheard and the eighty-four men with him were themselves killed; again, his men would not desert their lord, and Cynewulf's avengers would 'never serve his slayer'. The text heavily stresses the imagery of loyalty, but it is also important to note that an army of less than a hundred, contained in a single stockade, was determining the fate of a whole kingdom as late as the 780s.

Linked to this is a restricted set of royal resources. Kings had rights to tribute in food from their territory, but the evidence we have for this tribute implies, as in Wales, that it was pretty small, and perhaps only owed when the king or his entourage turned up to eat it. As late as 700, it is hard to say that Anglo-Saxon kings were resource-rich: they had enough gold and jewels to leave impressive burials like Sutton Hoo, but not necessarily enough to reward more than a small entourage or army, except in lucky years when they plundered an enemy. They also controlled land, and Bede makes it clear that by the 730s they used this to reward a military aristocracy, but there were the usual early medieval risks to this; Bede also says that if a king ran out of land his younger aristocrats would leave the kingdom.

These patterns were likely to keep kingship simple, royal administration sketchy, and kingdoms small, as in Wales. But in other respects the Anglo-Saxon kingdoms were beginning to develop. For a start, they occupied the lowland areas of Britain, which are agriculturally richer, can sustain a higher population, and are also closer to the Continent. Archaeology shows us that the late seventh and early eighth century saw a notable increase in exchange between England and the Continent, centred on a series of trading ports which were soon controlled by kings, Hamwic (modern Southampton) in Wessex, London in Mercia (the Mercian kings conquered down to the lower Thames in, probably, the 660s, and quays along the Strand in London have been dated to the 670s), Ipswich in East Anglia, York in Northumbria (see below, Chapter 9). These ports soon developed their own local artisans, and can simply be referred to as towns, the first urban centres of Anglo-Saxon

England; but they remained closely linked to kings, who were privileged recipients of their products, and who took tolls from them. Such tolls were available to kings throughout Europe, but in England, where kings were so small-scale, they were an important addition to royal resources.

Secondly, kings were closely supported by their aristocracies. We perhaps should not put too much weight on the imagery of loyalty in *Beowulf* or the Cyneheard narrative (after all, the men who died with Cyneheard had themselves been disloyal to King Cynewulf), but it is at least arguable that adult aristocrats who did not, or could not, stay loyal to kings had a difficult time, for they often ended up as 'exiles', as texts call them, without evident patronage, rather than simply finding welcome in a rival court. Kings and aristocrats were also linked by a slow development in power over land. Early Anglo-Saxon land-units do not seem to have been landed estates with a single owner and his or her dependent tenants, but, rather, territories from which kings and maybe also their aristocrats could take tribute, which as we have seen could be small, although it is also likely that unfree dependants on these estates paid rather more. Between the late seventh century and the tenth, these territories turned into estates, with rents and services which were much higher, benefiting kings and aristocrats alike, as we shall see in Chapter 19. It may well be that the politics of landed gift that Bede describes was not very old in the 730s, and that it was one of the first signs of this slow change. But the development of landownership would only be steady if political systems were strong and kings powerful. It was thus in the interest of aristocracies to accept increases in royal power, as they developed.

A third change was that the Anglo-Saxon kingdoms converted to Christianity. We know a lot about this because it was the central topic of Bede's history. Bede (lived 673–735) was a monk at the linked monasteries of Wearmouth and Jarrow in northern Northumbria; he was a highly educated intellectual, and not obviously a political dealer (though he knew kings and bishops). He painted the conversion as a heroic narrative. It began with Gregory the Great's Roman mission to Kent in 597, and expanded to several kingdoms including Northumbria in the next generation, but retreated after Edwin's death; it was then revived by an Irish mission from Iona to Northumbria after 634. After the death of the pagan Penda in 655, Christianity was accepted, at least by kings and their immediate entourages, almost everywhere. It was then consolidated by two key events: in 664 the synod of Whitby marked the acceptance in Northumbria and elsewhere of the Roman date for Easter and, more widely, of Roman (rather than Irish) institutional structures for the church; and in 669, after a plague had killed most of the bishops of England, Theodore of Tarsus arrived from Rome as archbishop of Canterbury (668–90), and restructured the episcopacy as a collective hierarchy covering all the Anglo-Saxon kingdoms. Church councils on a Continental model began in 672, and the Anglo-Saxon church was more and more evidently an organized body.

Bede saw these developments as self-evidently good, and divinely ordained. The conversion process was doubtless more political and more ambiguous than that, but his picture of a church victorious by the 670s is convincing, and is backed up by other evidence as well. Both bishops and an ever-growing network of monasteries grew prosperous as a result of royal gifts, documents for which begin to survive from the 670s; one could say that the church was the first beneficiary of the new politics of land, perhaps even before the aristocracy. By the early eighth century, if there was any aspect of Anglo-Saxon society that was by now parallel to that on the Continent, it was the church. This hierarchy was much more solid than that of the Welsh world, or, as we shall see, the Irish world; it was essentially a Continental import, and it looked to Francia and particularly Rome for inspiration. And it linked all the kingdoms for the first time. Bede, indeed, saw the conversion as of a single people, the *Angli*, a word which he tended to understand generically, as the 'English' rather than the 'Angles'. It is not clear that many other people shared his vision of English common identity until Alfred in the late ninth century. But the network of bishops, between one and three per kingdom, covering every Anglo-Saxon polity and no Welsh-ruled areas, and looking systematically to a single archbishop at Canterbury, was at least a potential support to kings who wished to extend their hegemony outside their kingdom. This support was all the more potentially useful in that bishops in England seldom engaged in any political activity independent from their kings; the one exception, the Frankish-trained Wilfrid (d. 709), bishop of Ripon and York at different times, was thrown out of Northumbria by both Ecgfrith and his successor Aldfrith (685–704). They did not bring to the Anglo-Saxon polities any of the secular political ceremonial of Continental kingdoms; royal government remained simple, probably based on assemblies, until late in the eighth century. Anglo-Saxon kings did begin to legislate, however: first in Kent, with the laws of Æthelberht, the first king to be converted, around 602, followed by three successors later in the century, and then in Wessex, with the laws of Ine (688–726) around 690.

The possibilities for an expansion in royal authority that are represented by these developments were first taken up by three Mercian kings, who ruled almost without breaks for over a century, Æthelbald (716–57), Offa (757–96) and Cenwulf (796–821). They were not closely related, and their successions were not straightforward, but they built systematically on each other's power-base. For a start, they conquered; for most of their reigns, all the Anglo-Saxon kingdoms except Northumbria (and after 802 Wessex) recognized their hegemony. Secondly, more systematically than ever before, they took steps to absorb many of these kingdoms into Mercia. The king of the Hwicce is already by 709 called *subregulus*, 'sub-king', in documents, which for two more generations alternates with *regulus* on the one hand and *minister* on the other, and then after 789 becomes stably *minister* or *dux*. The king of Essex had a similar trajectory between 812 and around 835. Kent was absorbed with greater violence, for it threw off Mercian rule in 776, but then after 785 Offa was back in Kent, and acted directly as its king with no intermediary, except between 796 and 798, just after Offa's death, when the local dynasty briefly took back power. Cenwulf put his brother in as king, and Kent was never independent again. Mercia thus steadily expanded; Charlemagne, Offa's contemporary, regarded him as the only real king of the southern English.

This physical expansion was matched by much clearer evidence for some sort of administrative infrastructure. Royal charters to churches from the mid-eighth century begin to exclude from their cessions three 'common burdens', army-service, bridge-building and fortress-building, which were still due to kings; although army-service was doubtless traditional, the other two burdens seem to be new, and had to be organized. In the ninth century, the list of royal officers who no longer had to be entertained by the recipients of these cessions became quite long; the king had a rather larger staff by now. The traditional association of Offa's Dyke, the 100-kilometre earthwork that delimits the borders of Wales, with King Offa seems certain, and the construction of this, crossing relatively remote areas as it often does, would also have required considerable organization. Offa reformed the coinage, and was one of the first Anglo-Saxon kings south of the Humber to put his name on coins. Mercia was by no means the richest part of England; that remained the east coast, where the ports were, and where an exchange economy was developing in the eighth century; but Offa controlled that coast by now, and he could begin to take systematic economic advantage from it. And kings now used church councils, following Frankish example (see below, Chapter 16); a sequence of councils, presided over by kings, is documented from 747 to 836, and many of their decisions were secular. One of them, in 786, hosted a papal legation, and its acts are notably wide-ranging. This network of measures and procedures indicates a structure for royal power which, in Offa and Cenwulf's time, could be called a state.

This build-up of royal power was not inexorable. For a start, although, after Theodore of Tarsus, the church hierarchy linked all the Anglo-Saxon kingdoms, this was modified when Northumbria gained its own archbishopric at York in 735, perhaps to ward off Mercian influence, and when Mercia gained its own at Lichfield in 787. In the latter case, Offa had had trouble with Canterbury, which was too much associated with Kentish autonomism, and he found it safer to create an archdiocese under his own control, at least temporarily (in 803 the south was reunified under Canterbury). Secondly, the eighth century was a period of wars between rival branches of the royal family for kingship in Wessex, Mercia and Northumbria alike. In Mercia, this had no structural impact until 821, but thereafter political infighting undermined Mercian hegemony. The wide stability of the last three generations was lost, and was not picked up by any king until Alfred, in very different circumstances (below, Chapter 19). Charlemagne might recognize Offa as an equal (in diplomatic formality, at least), but Anglo-Saxon kingship was as yet much smaller-scale and less stable. It was also based on profoundly different roots, with no Roman infrastructure to build on, unlike in Francia. Conversely, it was at least moving in the direction of Frankish political structures. The Mercian kings probably did this entirely consciously; Francia was so much more powerful that it would have made complete sense to do so as much as possible. Alfred and his successors would follow Offa's example too.

Ireland, which was never under Roman rule, had certain parallels to Wales and England in the fragmentation of its political structures, but here political decentralization was even more intense. No one knows how many kings Ireland had at any one time, but 100 to 150 is a widely canvassed estimate. Each ruled a *túath* or *plebs*, the Irish and Latin words respectively for the 'people' of each king; *plebs* means a local community in Continental Latin, but here it can equally well be translated as 'kingdom'. These 'kingdoms' or 'peoples' varied very greatly in size and importance, but each was closely linked to a king, and was often named for the king's family, the Cenél Conaill, the kindred of Conall, or the Uí Dúnlainge, the descendants of Dúnlang. Using the characterization already set out in the Welsh context, they can firmly be seen as tribes. Each had a fairly simple social structure, even the large kingdoms (the small ones may only have had a few family groups each): a network of free kin-groups owed clientship dues to a network of lords, who similarly owed dues to the king (himself related to many or most of his lords). These dues were generally in cattle, and were based on temporary patron–client relationships between independent land-owners. Only the unfree were permanent dependants. Irish sources are unusual, for they are in large part law tracts, the private handbooks of lawyers; they are strikingly, often impossibly, detailed about tiny differences in status, obligation and legal category: there were suppos-edly up to fourteen ranks in free society, for example. How these minutely differentiated relationships really worked on the ground usu-ally cannot be said. They were certainly very simply policed; most kings might have a steward to collect dues, a war-band to enforce and an annual assembly of the *túath* to deliberate, and that was all. But lawyers were one of a set of island-wide learned professions, along with poets and pagan priests (after Christianization, the latter were replaced by clerics), with a separate hierarchy and professional education. The elab-oration of lawyers' law could thus run far ahead of its applicability, although, conversely, skilled judicial expertise was rather more widely available than in most societies as simple as these.

Irish kingdoms were themselves arranged in hierarchies, with lesser kings owing tribute and military support to over-kings, and sometimes there were three or four levels of kingship. The lower levels of these hierarchies were probably fairly stable, for the smallest *túatha* had no prospect of going it alone successfully, and a permanent clientship relationship to a larger *túath* was the safest course of action. These 'base-client peoples' (*aithechthúatha* in Irish) were all the same seldom absorbed into larger groupings; this did happen sometimes, for some kingdoms did expand, but most small peoples survived for the whole of our period, as far as we can tell. This stability has sometimes been seen as the product of the archaism of Irish society, for the law tracts are graphic about the rituals and rules governing kingship. *Críth Gablach*, the major eighth-century tract on social status, states: 'There is, too, a weekly order in the duty of a king: Sunday for drinking ale . . . ; Monday for judgement, for the adjustment of *túatha*; Tuesday for playing *fidchell* [a board game]; Wednesday for watching deer-hounds hunting; Thursday for sexual intercourse; Friday for horse-racing; Saturday for judging cases' – an impossible set, of course, but probably a reasonably accurate characterization of the bulk of royal tasks. Kings had taboos, *gessa*, too: an eleventh-century poem lists those of each of Ireland's five provinces, Ulster, Connacht, Meath, Leinster and Munster, and tells us, for instance, that the king of Tara could not break a journey in Mag Breg on a Wednesday or enter north Tethba on a Tuesday. All the same, even if the endlessly fascinating arcana of Irish kingship tell us a lot about the ritual force of tribal communitarian bonds, they do not explain why it was that an ambitious over-king could not sweep them away. Here, the best explanation is that Irish kings did not yet have an infrastructure suitable to rule directly over more than a small area, so that the cellular structure of tiny peoples had to be left to run itself. The patron–client bonds between kings were also less stable at the higher levels; no king could gain a hegemony over the whole of Ulster or Leinster for more than very brief periods, as revolt would soon break out and coalitions would crumble. Kings were fighters (a task curiously omitted from *Críth Gablach*'s list), and not much else.

The two major dynasties of kings in Ireland both contained several separate kingdoms, in rivalry with each other: the Uí Néill, dominant in Meath and western Ulster, the more powerful of the two, and the Éoganachta, dominant in Munster. Each of these dynasties had a main ritual centre, Tara and Cashel respectively, which was not actually lived in (Tara was an ancient and abandoned hill-fort; Cashel was newer, and later had a church built on it); the paramount king of the dynasty at any given moment was king of Tara or of Cashel. The Uí Néill and the Éoganachta seem to have established their dominance in the fifth century, although exactly how is obscure; Níall Noígíallach, the ancestor of the Uí Néill, is a largely legendary figure. Before their appearance, an important centre was Emain Macha (now Navan Fort) near Armagh. This was the focus of the entirely legendary saga-cycle of Cúchulainn, hero-fighter for King Conchobar of the Ulaid, the original core tribe of Ulster, whose kings were pushed east into modern Antrim and Down by the Uí Néill; they made up four kingdoms there by the sixth century. Leinster was largely outside the dominance of the two dynasties, and so even was Connacht, the poorest province, though the Uí Néill seem to have come from there originally and claimed kinship with the major dynasties of kings there. Successful Uí Néill kings could nonetheless claim temporary hegemonies among the kingdoms of any province except Munster (the Éoganachta, by contrast, stayed in Munster until the eighth century).

Amid the hundreds of Irish kings sparely documented in rival sets of annals, a few stand out. Diarmait mac Cerbhaill (d. 565) was arguably the king who moved the Uí Néill from legend into history (though many traditional stories attach themselves to him, too); he was ancestor of the main dynasties of the Uí Néill in Meath, and from his time onwards, at the latest, there was seldom doubt of the family's dominance in the midlands and north of the island. Báetán mac Cairill (d. 581) of the Ulaid kingdom of Dál Fiatach attempted to establish a hegemony over the Isle of Man and Dál Riata in western Scotland as an alternative power-focus to the Uí Néill. He failed, but he shows that the fifth-century political settlement was not immutable. Seventh-century politics was more stable, with kings from the rival branches of the main dynasties succeeding each other regularly in all the provinces. We begin to find wider ambition again in the eighth. One example is Cathal mac Finguine (d. 742) of the Éoganacht Glendamnach in modern northern Cork, who began for the first time to link up with Leinster kings and attack Meath, until Áed Allán (d. 743) of the Cenél nÉogain, the northern Uí Néill of Tyrone, held him back in Munster in 737–8. Another is Donnchad Midi mac Domnaill (d. 797) of the Clann Cholmáin of the Uí Néill of Meath, who from the 770s was paramount in Leinster and keen to fight Munster kings as well. Their successors, Feidlimid mac Crimthainn (d. 841) from the Éoganacht of Cashel, easily the most aggressive Munster king before the end of the tenth century, and his Uí Néill enemies will be looked at in Chapter 20; the ninth century was more clearly a period of political aggregation, when traditional rules were disrupted by Viking attack and increasingly broken by native rulers as well. But there was a continuity from the eighth century all the same; that was when ambitious kingship first broke the old boundary between the Éoganachta and the Uí Néill. Conversely, Donnchad Midi did not obviously have a style of kingship that differed from that of his ancestor Diarmait mac Cerbhaill; the Irish were very slow indeed to consider the sort of political infrastructural change that was developing in England.

Ireland began to convert to Christianity in the fifth century, thanks largely to the mission of the Briton Patrick, whose writings survive but whose own career (and even dating) is largely obscure; by the late sixth, when Irish written sources begin, formal paganism seems only a memory, at least among élites, and the clergy fitted easily into the learned professions after that. But Irish Christianity was different. It had an episcopal network, attached to the kingdoms, but it also had an increasingly wealthy and powerful network of monastic families, whose connections went in different directions from those of political and episcopal hierarchies. Armagh claimed episcopal primacy from the seventh century onwards, on the grounds of a largely spurious association with Patrick. This was contested by Kildare in Leinster, and largely ignored by the churches subject to the monastery of Iona in western Scotland; the latter was the chief cult site of Dál Riata, but was, interestingly, controlled by an Uí Néill dynasty from the time of its foundation by Colum Cille (Columba, d. 597) in 563. The monastery of Clonmacnois in the centre of Ireland had fewer claims to primacy, but achieved considerable wealth by obtaining land and lesser monasteries, in an area of relatively weak kingdoms (its abbots were generally drawn from *aithechthúatha*), and by the mid-eighth century was prosecuting its own secular politics by force of arms. The episcopal and monastic churches had firmer views on accumulating wealth in land (as opposed to cattle) than most kings and aristocrats, and by the eighth century their leaders were probably richer than all but a few kings; this was a future resource for political power (and, by the ninth century, an object of plunder by royal rivals as well). The Irish church had some sense of Ireland-wide identity, just as the legal profession had. Church councils began already in the 560s, education in Latin must have begun around then too, and in the seventh century there was a flowering of ecclesiastical literature – hagiography, penitentials, poetry, grammars – parallel to that of secular law. Irish clerics and intellectuals had some influence in Francia, from Columbanus (d. 615) to John the Scot (d. c. 877), the ninth-century West's greatest theologian. But that identity was not, unlike eventually in England, in itself an underpinning for secular ambition; the Irish church was in its own way as fragmented as secular authority.

The tiny northern Antrim kingdom of Dál Riata seems to have expanded into western Scotland from the late fifth century, occupying what is now Argyll and some of the Hebridean islands. Its king Áedán mac Gabráin (d. c. 609), Columba's patron, had thirty years of military protagonism in northern Britain (he fought and lost to Æthelfrith in 603), and so did some of his successors, at least up to the 640s; after that, Dál Riata power in Scotland fragmented into two or three rival lineages with separate power-bases, a process familiar in Ireland as well. Argyll was nonetheless a solid political focus; it was in size, even though probably not in resources, already larger than any kingdom in Ireland. The colonial bet of sixth-century Dál Riata in this respect paid off. In the eighth century, starting with Onuist son of Urguist, it was subject to Pictish hegemony more often than not, and this continued into the ninth, although by then intermarriage between the two ruling families (made easier by Pictish matrilineal rules, although patrilineal succession was coming in by the ninth century even there) meant that the same king could claim inheritance in both. This was the basis for what seems to have been a double coup by Cinaed (Kenneth) mac Ailpín (d. 858), a Dál Riata prince, first around 840 when he took Dál Riata, and then around 842 in Pictland itself. Kenneth transferred his political seat to the Perthshire heartland of the southern Picts; this reflected the overall dominance of the Pictish lands, but was also, probably, rendered necessary by Viking attacks in Argyll. He seems to have ruled in effect as a Pictish king, but the kingdom of Alba or Scotia which his descendants ruled was after the end of the ninth century ever more clearly one dominated by Dál Riatan, that is, Irish aristocrats, Irish law, Irish ecclesiastical culture and eventually the Irish language. Unification was a slow and intermittent process, but Alba by 900 was nonetheless already much larger and more stable than any Irish kingdom or over-kingdom, and this must reflect the fact that its core area was by now the former Pictish provinces. Dál Riata, so small in Ireland, was thus in purely political terms the most successful Irish kingdom ever. Whatever the Pictish political infrastructure consisted of, it was the foundation for that.

8

Post-Roman Attitudes: Culture, Belief and Political Etiquette, 550–750

Valerius of the Bierzo was an ascetic hermit living in the mountains of north-west Spain at the end of the seventh century; unlike most hermits, he was of aristocratic origin, and wrote accounts of his own life. This life was pretty miserable. Valerius was perpetually tormented by the devil, who got a local aristocrat and a bishop to try to make him a priest, thus regularizing his position (fortunately they both died), and who also turned local priests and monks (of the monastery to which he was loosely attached) against him. Valerius' disciples were rejected by him, or dissuaded by terrible weather, or killed by brigands; one, Saturninus, built a church near Valerius' hermitage, and began to do miracles, but then, also tempted by the devil, he became proud and thought he would get more veneration if he had his own hermitage, so he left, but not before stealing Valerius' books. Only after forty-two years did Valerius get royal patronage without conditions. Sour, self-righteous, ungrateful and paranoid, as well as obstinate in his chosen path, Valerius may give us the most authentic voice of the early medieval hermit. The moral awfulness of the Bierzo in his writings is most likely to be the reflection of his own mind, not of any particular local reality. The solidity of the Christian infrastructure in this relatively cut-off region, notwithstanding the brigands, is equally striking.

One aspect of moral degradation that was apparently absent in the Bierzo was the survival of 'pagan' practices. This may be surprising; Bishop Martin of Braga (d. 579), based slightly further west, had preached against them at length shortly before his death, complaining of people who observed a wide variety of what he considered un-Christian rituals, lighting candles beside rocks and trees, throwing bread into fountains, not travelling on inauspicious days, chanting over herbs. Nor did this end with Martin. A late ninth-century slate text from the Asturias, slightly further north, preserves an incantation against hail, in the name of all the archangels and St Christopher, adjuring Satan not to trouble the village of the monk Auriolus and his family and neighbours; in effect, an entirely traditional magical text, although couched in Christian terms. Maybe north-west Spain was so regionally diverse that practices like these did not occur in the Bierzo; maybe Valerius was so wrapped up in himself that he did not notice them; but maybe he, like Auriolus, did not see them to be as wrong as Martin did. After all, what could be described as weather magic was practised even by saints, as when Caesarius of Arles (d. 542) held off hail with a cross made out of his staff, and when Gregory of Tours did the same by putting a candle from St Martin of Tours's tomb in a tree. We must recognize from the start the diversity of early medieval Christianity in the West, both in beliefs and in practices. And there is another point to note: Gregory also revered Martin of Braga, however different their views about candles. We do not, even among the uncompromising (who were numerous in the early medieval church: Valerius is only an extreme version of a type), often find the ferocity of religious disagreement that was typical in Late Rome. The spiritual challenges and problem-solving sketched out in this paragraph would have been recognizable in the Roman world, but the context had changed. We need to explore how.

The episcopal hierarchy of the late empire in most places survived into the early Middle Ages without a break. As we shall see, the monastic tradition established by John Cassian and Benedict of Nursia did as well, and took on ever greater force in northern Europe. The organizational framework of Roman Christianity, discussed earlier, was still fully in operation. One important difference, however, was that it was less united. This can be explored through looking at the authority of the popes. Nominally the senior bishop of the Latin church, the pope between 550 and 750 was little looked to by people in Francia, Spain, even northern Italy. In religious and political terms, popes themselves were orientated eastward, to the patriarchs in the Byzantine empire and (after the 630s) in the caliphate, their equals, and they sparred over eastern-generated theological issues; as institutional leaders, they were looked to above all by the Byzantine parts of Italy, and even there they had energetic rivals in the archbishops of Ravenna. The register of letters of Gregory the Great (590–604), who was also the most significant theologian to be pope in the early medieval period, has survived; the

850-plus letters in it are overwhelmingly addressed to central and southern Italy, especially Naples and Sicily, and also to Ravenna and Constantinople. Fewer than thirty are to Gaulish recipients, if we exclude Provence, where the pope had lands, and fewer than ten to Spain. Only in England did the popes have real influence, thanks to Gregory's initiative in sending the first mission to Kent in 597 under Augustine of Canterbury. Although the Kentish mission did not convert most of the Anglo-Saxons (the Irish were the most successful mission-aries in England), the Roman connection was made permanent by Theo-dore of Tarsus' reorganization of the English church after 669. Most medieval archbishops of Canterbury from then on received the *pallium*, a linen band representing their office, from Rome, and this, too, gave the papacy considerable leverage in England. Apart from in England, however, the institutional unity of the western church remained nominal for a long time. It recognized a common identity, certainly, but its liturgies became different, and its monastic traditions were extremely various as well. The Carolingians revived the Roman link, and (more importantly) they also centralized church practices along Frankish lines, and monastic practices along Benedictine ones; all the same, a structured western church focused on Rome in any serious way did not develop until after the end of the period covered by this book. The Visigoths and Franks had plenty of church councils, but these were councils of the bishops of a kingdom, and did not look outside the borders of Spain and Francia respectively. Essentially, the political fragmentation of the western empire had fragmented the church as well.

One consequence of all this is that the western church did not have much trouble with heresy in this period. The Arian–Catholic division lasted until 589 in Spain, as we saw in Chapter 6, and was violent while it lasted; well-informed contemporaries like Gregory of Tours and Gregory the Great rejoiced at the Catholic victory in the third council of Toledo. Gregory of Tours had a personal obsession with the evils of Arianism, indeed, which appears many times in his *Histories*. The signs are, however, that his contemporaries in Francia were altogether more neutral on the subject, perhaps considering Gregory's dinner-table speeches about Arianism (at the expense of unfortunate Gothic envoys) somewhat out of place. In Spain, religious orthodoxy remained import-ant, as the late seventh-century persecution of the Jews shows. Indeed, the Spanish bishops even persecuted Priscillianists, a very marginal sect;

vegetarianism itself, a standard ascetic trait, was a little suspect in Spain because Priscillianists refused meat, and the 561 council of Braga required vegetarian clerics at least to cook their greens in meat broth, to show their orthodoxy. But new heresies did not appear even in Spain before the late eighth century, and in Francia, and later in England, religious controversy in this period was hardly ever about doctrine. Only the date of Easter caused difficulties, and then only in the Irish and Welsh churches, where in the seventh and eighth centuries it became apparent that the local rules for calculating Easter diverged from those in Rome. Where controversy lay was in the behaviour of clerics, and whether their sexual activity, mode of dress, or the gifts they may have paid for their office (the sin of simony) undermined their sacrality. There was never a time without rigorists who could wax angry on the failings of bishops and priests in these respects.

As noted in Chapter 3, even under the empire the purity of the clergy may have mattered more in the West than in the East, and their exact beliefs about the Trinity somewhat less. But the lack of intense theological argument in this period probably also betrays a smaller critical mass of highly educated churchmen. The two centuries after 550 were not as low a point for functional literacy, even for the laity, as was once thought. Government was based on writing everywhere on the Continent until after the Carolingian period; kings and the lay aristocracy could normally read, and could sometimes compose quite elaborate Latin, as in the court of Childebert II in the 580s, or that of Sisebut in the 610s. (Writing itself, as a specific technical skill, was probably less widespread, and dictating to copyists was normal.) A more developed literary training was usually restricted to churchmen by now, and it was more orientated towards ecclesiastical works than had been the case two centuries earlier; Gregory of Tours cites more Sidonius and Prudentius than Sallust and Virgil. One could certainly still be well informed in this period; libraries could still be large as was that of Isidore of Seville, and could even be created from scratch, as with the substantial library in Bede's Jarrow, apparently mostly bought by the monastery's founder Benedict Biscop in the 650s–680s during his visits to Rome. Bede was a genuine example of an intellectual who had read widely, at least in Christian literature, as a result. All the same, he was the only one in Northumbria in his age; he had no one really to argue with. He tried; some of Bede's writings (particularly about chronological computation) are quite rude. But this is a long way from the concentration of trained and ambitious theologians in the great eastern cities, Alexandria and Antioch, which had produced Arianism or Nestorianism. This would not reappear in the Romano-Germanic kingdoms until Charlemagne and Louis the Pious established a court ecclesiastical culture, in the three generations after the 780s (see below, Chapter 17). Only Rome would have been large enough to generate such debate in the meantime. That it did not do so may simply show that it was too culturally and spatially fragmented as well. It is also likely that career success in the Roman ecclesiastical hierarchy did not depend much on theological skill; Gregory the Great was the only exception, and there is evidence that he was unpopular.

The political fragmentation of the western church and the absence of heresy were, as has been implied, linked: people simply did not have regular information about what was going on outside their own local and regional circuits. A letter of 613 from the Irish monastic founder Columbanus to Pope Boniface IV survives; it dates to the moment of Columbanus' career in which he had arrived in Lombard Italy, to establish the monastery of Bobbio, after more than two decades in Francia and Alemannia. It expresses great surprise that Boniface (he hears, now he has come to Italy) adheres to the Constantinople line over the Three Chapters schism, and chides him severely for it. Yet the papal position on this had been unchanged since the 550s, and was controversial in northern Italy, at least. Any knowledge of a relatively sharp theological debate seems to have been absent over the Alps, or, at the least, Columbanus could claim it was. If there was that lack of personal contact, then unorthodox belief would not easily expand, and might not even be known about. All kinds of local versions of Christianity could develop under these circumstances, without contestation from elsewhere. It is this localized world that Peter Brown has called one of 'micro-Christendoms', a phrase that has had good fortune in recent years: a world of steady divergence in ritual, rule and tradition, as also in the political structures and socio-cultural practices of secular society.

It is a localization, all the same, that we should not exaggerate. People moved about; Columbanus himself is an example. Above all, pilgrims went to Rome, something which becomes well attested in the late sixth century and developed substantially in the seventh and eighth. The Anglo-Saxons are particularly prominent in our evidence; Benedict Biscop and Wilfrid each went several times. The routes became well known, with the result that, as Boniface of Mainz said in 747, in many cities of Italy and Gaul all the prostitutes were English. And there were Franks as well; several seventh- and eighth-century saints' lives, for Amandus of Maastricht (d. 676), Bonitus of Clermont (d. *c.* 705) or the Bavarian Corbinian of Freising (d. *c.* 725), feature pilgrimages to Rome, some more than once. The Lombards in the 740s instituted a passport system on the Alpine frontier for pilgrims to Rome, giving them a sealed document which they expected back on the return journey. There is an entire literature of guides to Roman churches and tombs which begins in the seventh century, and pilgrim hostels for different ethnic groups, Franks, Frisians, Anglo-Saxons, were built between the Vatican and the Tiber. Outside Rome, there were regional pilgrim centres as well, like St Martin's tomb at Tours, which attracted visitors from all across northern and central Gaul. This might seem less surprising, perhaps, given the extent of élite movement on secular business, and secular communication by letter, across the whole of the Frankish lands, as we saw in Chapter 5 for Desiderius of Cahors; still, pilgrimages involved peasants, too, as is very clear in Gregory of Tours's collection of the miracles experienced by pilgrims to St Martin. The West's local societies were by no means hermetically sealed. But this movement remained ad hoc, and did not as yet lessen the variety of the cultural trends of the post-Roman period. This fits the steady localization of economic exchange, too, which reached its peak in much of the West in the eighth century, as we shall see in the next chapter.

The Christian culture of the early Middle Ages was, however disunited, not under threat. Lowland Britain lost most (though probably not all) of its Christianity after the Anglo-Saxons took over, but apart from that retreat, itself reversed in the seventh century, Christian missionaries steadily pushed northwards: into Ireland in the fifth, Pictland in the sixth, and then Frisia in the early eighth, and Saxony under Charlemagne. It is actually quite hard to reconstruct western Germanic paganism, which would have been highly variable anyway. Unlike Graeco-Roman paganism, it was not literate, and did not survive as a resource for later literary imagery either, as the classical gods did – and as those of Ireland did as well, thanks to the coherence and traditionalism of the Irish learned professions, into which the church was assimilated. We are left with hostile and often stereotyped descriptions of pagan rituals or cult-sites, like the Irminsul, the sacred idol of the Saxons, destroyed by Charlemagne in 772. But there is no reason to think that Christian belief changed much as a result of its exposure to a new frontier of paganism beyond the old bounds of the Roman empire, apart from sometimes in terminology, as with the Anglo-Saxon goddess Eostre, whose spring festival took place in the Easter period and whose name was borrowed by Anglo-Saxon Christians.

What the rigorists of the early medieval church did have to face, all the same, was the fact that traditional rituals of varying origins survived everywhere, routinized into local Christian practice. The churchmen of the late empire had often opposed them, as we have seen, but had by no means uprooted them, and the churchmen of the early Middle Ages, in an era of weaker institutions, were even less likely to do so. This is sometimes expressed in terms of pagan survival or revival by our authors, as in the case of Martin of Braga. This is a rhetorical style that was commonest closer to the old Roman frontier, presumably because real pagans were closer there; so the *Life* of Eligius, bishop of Noyon (d. 660), moves smoothly from Eligius' sermons against pagan practices, themselves by now a fairly formulaic set, to his preaching against 'demonic games and wicked leapings' held on St Peter's day in Noyon. The participants here were much annoyed by this, however, as they held them to be 'legitimate . . . customs', and the implications in the text that this has something to do with paganism are further undermined by the fact that they involved the followers of the major Frankish aristocrat and Neustrian *maior domus* Erchinoald: these were Christians; it is just that they were performing rituals that Eligius (or his biographer) did not like, or could not control. When Anglo-Saxon missionaries spread from now-converted England back to the Continent, with Willibrord (d. 739) and then Boniface (d. 754), they used the imagery of paganism extensively as well. In Willibrord's case he really was in pagan territory, in Frisia; but Boniface worked mostly in central Germany, fully part of the Frankish world even if disorganized ecclesiastically, and the 'pagan' practices he describes there were more likely to be local Christian customs, like those at Noyon. (Boniface, indeed, writing to Pope Zacharias in 742, complained that there were 'pagan' practices even on the streets of Rome, in the First of January celebrations which were still very popular, which Zacharias admitted was true.) As in the late Roman period, simple preaching against such customs was unlikely to get rigorists very far, precisely because they were seen as Christian already. The task of the church would either be to absorb and legitimize them, as perhaps with Eostre, or to set up more 'orthodox' religious rituals in rivalry. Religious processions on major saints' days or to major cult-sites, for example, developed everywhere as part of a Christian ritual aggregation more clearly directed by bishops and other members of the church hierarchy.

This does not mean that 'the church' (which was anyway not a concept anyone used in this period) operated as a coherent unit, however. Far from it; the authors of our sources disagreed, between themselves and with their contemporaries, often quite markedly, about what were legitimate religious practices and what were not, and, more generally, about what correct supernatural power consisted of in an age in which direct divine intervention in human society was considered normal. Let us look at four related aspects of this: the sanctity of the living; cult-sites and the miraculous; good and bad supernatural acts; and the general issue of supernatural causation.

There were not so many isolated ascetics in the West. Valerius of the Bierzo was atypical in this respect. There were some, certainly; Gregory of Tours tells us about several, as for example Hospicius, who in the 570s lived in a tower outside Nice, wrapped in chains, and who could perform miracles, or Vulfolaic, who spent time as a stylite on a column on the edge of the Ardennes, and whom Gregory met in 585 and was much impressed by. But his account of Vulfolaic expresses a significant ambivalence: bishops had come to the stylite and ordered him off his column, saying that the Ardennes hardly had the climate for it, unlike Syria, and instructing him to form a monastery. 'Now, it is considered a sin not to obey bishops,' Vulfolaic said (according to Gregory), so of course he did so, and the bishops smashed the column; Gregory met him in the monastery, where he had remained since then. Gregory's view is clear: the bishops were probably wrong here, but disobeying them would have been worse. Indeed, when ascetics did disobey bishops, Gregory saw them as openly demonic, as with the unauthorized miracle-workers who on two occasions turned up in Tours and attracted crowds around them, and who were rude, not respectful, to Gregory. Gregory of course gives us a bishop's view, and such charismatics could evidently gain a considerable following. But Gregory was not being hypocritical either. Bishops at least had a church organization to legitimize them and train them. The trouble about saintly individuals was that it was hard to know when they were alive if their wonder-working was divine or demonic. Ascetics could come to bad ends, like the Breton Winnoch, dressed only in skins, whom Gregory supported, but who drank too much of the wine offered by his followers and died of alcoholism. What value were his miracles then? The miracles of saints when they were dead were by contrast safer, 'much more worthy of praise', as Gregory says elsewhere, because they came from completed lives, and from people whose sanctity was testable; the bodies of the saintly dead were not corrupted, and smelt of roses, so that it could be seen that they were not ordinary sinners. Dead saints were also easier to control. Bishops could ensure that they were buried in cathedrals, or episcopally controlled churches like Saint-Martin at Tours, and could organize and take benefit from their cult. The cult of relics of the saintly dead became a dominant feature of the medieval church, in both East and West, but in the West it had little rival during the period covered by this book.

Not everyone was as uneasy about living saints as Gregory of Tours. Gregory the Great, who had been a monk before becoming pope and was openly regretful about being forced back into the spiritual dangers of the secular world, was romantic about ascetics; his accounts of them stress the incomprehension of too-worldly bishops more than his namesake in Tours ever did. Saints who were part of the standard church hierarchies, as bishops and abbots, or who accepted the authority of such hierarchies, were also not a problem to most authors, and there are any number of saints' lives about them. And there was clearly a space for isolated charismatic sanctity in the mission situation, as with Patrick's evangelization in Ireland in the fifth century (the savagery of his cursing of the incredulous was enthusiastically described in Muirchu's seventh-century *Life*), or with Cuthbert's miracle-working and companionship with angels in the 650s–680s, in the half-converted lands of what is now Northumberland, written up by two eighth-century authors (one of them being Bede). Patrick was also a bishop, and Cuthbert became one; these were not opponents of hierarchy. But the space for even this sort of charisma steadily decreased, as time went on. Aldebert was a bishop in central or eastern Francia in the 740s, and a rival to Boniface in the latter's reorganization of the Frankish church. He had saintly relics with him, he dedicated churches and crosses, he knew the sins of supplicants before they confessed, his hair and nails were venerated, all standard signs of sanctity: and for this he was formally condemned and defrocked in a church council in Rome by Pope Zacharias in 745. Perhaps he had exaggerated, in that it was seemingly he who distributed his hair; he certainly exaggerated in brandishing a letter written by Jesus which had fallen from heaven in Jerusalem, and was picked up by the archangel Michael (Zacharias concluded he was mad), and in listing an unusual and thus perhaps demonic list of angels to pray to. But in a steadily more ordered church, he was by now out of place, and he had made the mistake of opposing Boniface as well: he had to go.

These accounts show clearly that the miraculous was a normal part of the early medieval world; the contest was over who controlled it. Whatever modern rationalists may think about the possibility of miracles taking place, we must recognize that in the early Middle Ages, as under late Rome, there was little doubt about it. It is not that miracles were natural: the power (whether from God or from the saints) that they represented derived, precisely, from their being *super*natural, a breach of the natural order. Writers did recognize that there was therefore a danger that they might not be believed, and often were more careful than usual to supply chains of sources for miracles, going back to authoritative eyewitnesses; but the incredulous were regularly stigmatized as 'rustic', too boorish to realize how divine providence worked. That is to say, it was incredulity, not (or not only) excessive credulity, that marked peasant inferiority in this period in the eyes of literary élites.

Pilgrimages to saints' tombs were especially marked by miraculous events. This is clearest in the miracle-book about St Martin written by Gregory of Tours, largely based on the records made by his priests at Martin's shrine, which had become a large complex of buildings outside the city, focused on the reception of visitors. There was a network of such major cult-sites all across the West. In Gaul, which is relatively well documented, six of them seem to have been particularly important by the seventh century, the churches of Saint-Denis and Saint-Germain in Paris, Saint-Médard in Soissons, Saint-Pierre in Sens, Saint-Aignan in Orléans and Saint-Martin in Tours, all of which were made into monasteries by Queen Balthild around 660. The cult of St Martin, as we have just seen, was enthusiastically advertised by the bishops of Tours. The first two or three of these six, however, were by contrast very much Merovingian-backed cults, essentially royal foundations. In the most important of these, Saint-Denis, Merovingian kings were regularly buried, from Dagobert in 639 onwards. The kings' support for Saint-Denis (and Saint-Germain, another royal burial place, and probably Saint-Médard as well) shows that a desire to control cult-sites, and to make political capital out of them, was not restricted to bishops. In the Christian topography of the early medieval West, the hot spots, the most powerful points, were all sites with the relics of saints, and it is understandable that people should want to play politics with them. Indeed, this could be very direct: it could involve theft. Rome, which was such a pilgrimage centre largely because of the huge number of saints buried there (thanks to the fact that pre-Constantinian persecution and execution of Christians, martyr-creating, was always most active in the imperial capital), perhaps had more saints than it needed, and certainly many more than it could guard. Stealing saints became particularly common there in the ninth century, as we shall see in Chapter 17. But fighting over saints' bodies was older than that; Gregory of Tours is proud to recount how Martin's body, shortly after he died in 397, was stolen by the men of Tours from Poitiers. All such thefts were justified; if they had not been, the saint would have stopped them, miraculously of course.

Not all supernatural activity was seen as good. Saints' lives and sermons are full of alternative wonder-workers, witches, magicians and soothsayers, who could cast spells, cure, affect the weather and tell the future. These were bad people in the eyes of the writers, but they were clearly numerous. People disagreed over whether they were fraudulent or had real (demoniacal) powers. Among secular legislators, Rothari in Italy in 643 thought that witches should not be killed, for 'it is in no wise to be believed by Christian minds that it is possible that a woman can eat a living man from within', but Liutprand in 727 banned soothsayers both male and female (they were to be enslaved); similarly, the Salic lawgivers in Francia prescribed heavy fines for casting spells to kill someone or to make a woman barren. Among ecclesiastical writers, there is a wider tendency to assume that demons were behind their activity (thus Caesarius of Arles, Gregory of Tours, Isidore of Seville and the Carolingian Hincmar of Reims), although an alternative Carolingian strand (Hraban Maur, Agobard of Lyon), like Rothari, denied that their spells could work at all. Actually, Gregory had it both ways on occasions. He tells a story of two children, servants of his, affected by bubonic plague, one of whom was treated by a soothsayer with amulets and died (that is, the magic did not work), while the other drank dust from St Martin's tomb mixed with water and recovered. This links into the classic hagiographical topos of the magic battle in which the magician/ witch/pagan priest fails and the saint is successful, even if in this case Gregory names himself as an eyewitness. Conversely, plenty of his sooth-sayers really could tell the future, thanks to demons. One notable account from 577 has Prince Merovech and Duke Guntram Boso, both taking sanctuary from King Chilperic in Saint-Martin in Tours, and thus temporary and unwilling (in Merovech's case, unpleasant) tenants of Gregory. Both tried to foresee what would happen to them. Guntram Boso went to a soothsayer, who said that Merovech would become king and Guntram his general, and later a bishop; to Gregory it was obvious that the devil was simply lying to him. Merovech used the *sortes* instead, an entirely Christian divinatory mechanism based on opening the Bible at random and reading sentences (he put the Bible on St Martin's tomb for greater effectiveness) – unfortunately, and more accurately, these said he would die. Gregory used the *sortes* too, backed up by an angelic vision, which said the same. Here we see the degree to which this sort of personalized use of the supernatural could be both complementary and in rivalry. All the parties nevertheless assumed that the supernatural world could be manipulated, whether in a good or a bad way.

This private control over the supernatural, 'magic', persisted, no mat-ter how much it was reviled by rigorists. It would be reasonable to imagine that, throughout our period, most people had access to magic-workers of one kind or another, whether the local wise-woman or even, on occasion, the local priest. The tenth-century manuscripts containing books on medicine from Anglo-Saxon England, such as *Lacnunga* and Bald's *Leechbook*, which are full of healing spells, came from monastic or cathedral copying-schools, after all. And, here as elsewhere, it must be stressed that the village wise-woman, too, would in most cases have seen her powers as operating in an entirely Christian context, and so would her clientele. The supernatural world was all around, and access-ible. The virtue of saints (living or dead) could channel it and make miracles; more edgily, spells and *sortes* could command it. After all, as all our historians repeat, God's justice intervened directly in human affairs, making the bad die young and the good prosper, ensuring that virtuous kings won their battles and wicked kings lost (or else, since this did not always occur, allowing the wicked to prosper in order to punish the sins of others). Anyone who believed this sort of immediate divine causation would have little real trouble with the miraculous, and maybe even the magical; there was so much space in Christianity for the exercise of supernatural power.

It was possible to buy into divine causation so much that people denied there was any other kind. Gregory of Tours largely thought this: kings must know that God's will lay behind everything. As for illness, it derived from demons or God's punishment for sin, and cures came from repentance or the power of St Martin; doctors were not an acceptable alternative to Gregory, but rivals, on a par with magic-workers. (That said, Gregory did have a doctor, Armentarius, with him when he became bishop in 573; Armentarius failed to cure him from dysentery when St Martin's dust succeeded.) But Gregory may have been an extremist in this respect; certainly Caesarius of Arles saw doctors as good, and in themselves rivals to magic-workers. Merovingian kings all trusted doctors enough to have them by them all the time; and a Greek doctor, Paul, even became bishop of Mérida in Spain and a saint in the early sixth century; the abortion he skilfully performed on a dead foetus to save the life of the mother, a fabulously wealthy aristocrat, was said in his saint's life to be the origin of the wealth of the episcopal see thereafter. In medicine as in public life, people were essentially eclectic. One could believe in miraculous cures but, if one was rich enough, still have doctors beside one; and one could believe – everybody believed – that God decided battles, but few generals thought this meant that they did not need trained troops as well, if they could get them. People needed both. And, mostly, people did not see this as a contradiction.

There has been a stress on bishops in this chapter, for they are very prominent in our sources. They really were central, however, if only because the ecclesiastical hierarchy was fairly simple as yet. In the countryside, rural churches were not non-existent, but as yet relatively few. In Italy, a long-Christianized land, there were in the diocese of Lucca sixty rural baptismal churches (*plebes*) by the tenth century, and these had probably for the most part been founded by the sixth; this may seem a substantial number, but each was the main church for many different settlements. Only in the eighth century did other churches begin to be founded, a trend which continued (with some blips) into the twelfth: by then, Lucca had over six hundred rural parishes, a very different pattern. In Francia, too, rural churches with the right to baptize expanded in number only after 700; and in England, where large 'minster parishes' were the norm, this process only really began after 900. So most villages and rural settlements did not yet have their own church; the clergy of the diocese were largely concentrated in the bishop's own entourage (and in urban churches if cities were big enough); as a result, the ritual activity of each diocese focused, far more than would be the case after the tenth century or so, on the bishop. Bishop Daniel of Winchester, an otherwise exemplary bishop, went blind before he died around 744, a circumstance that seems to have prevented him from baptizing; no one took his place, with the result that many children died unbaptized in his diocese in his last years. This was an extreme case, and it could not have happened in Italy, where there were more baptismal churches, but it does show how ritually important the person of the bishop was. He controlled all the diocesan religious rituals, including processions and festivals, that he could, and sought to control more.

The processions organized by bishops could hold off the plague, cause rain to fall, put out fires and confound enemy armies, if we believe the saints' lives about them. In one dramatic case from Ravenna in around 700 (according to Agnellus' episcopal history in the 840s), Archbishop Damian organized a formal penitential procession, divided between men and women, clergy and laity, in order (miraculously) to discover the truth, after one of the urban factions secretly murdered the menfolk of a rival faction. Bishops represented their cities and dioceses politically, but they also did so spiritually. It is remarkable how often episcopal miracles concern the liberation of prisoners held by counts and other secular officials, or the saving of condemned men from death, in many cases quite regardless of their guilt. This matches the more secular ransoming of captives that bishops performed routinely, as well as episcopal pleas for tax relief for their dioceses in front of kings: they were protectors of their flocks in every sense. Bishop Fidelis of Mérida in the mid-sixth century secretly proceeded around the city's urban and suburban churches by night, following a fiery globe, in the middle of a crowd of saints; those who saw him were sworn to secrecy, and if they spoke about it they died. Small wonder that when Bishop Masona of Mérida was exiled by Leovigild in the early 580s, and also when Bishop Desiderius of Vienne was exiled by Brunhild in 603–7, the city experienced famine, plague and storm till its pastor returned.

Bishops thus mattered greatly. Accordingly, it is not surprising that they tended to be of aristocratic origin, something that we have seen for different countries in previous chapters. There were cases in which they were of lesser birth, and rose up the local church hierarchy because they were good administrators or personally virtuous, but this was probably by now relatively rare everywhere. Being an aristocrat meant that one could rely on a secular (and ecclesiastical) political network that would make any bishop's life easier. Praejectus of Clermont (d. 676), who was not of high birth, does not seem to have been an astute politician, as we saw earlier, and was killed by aristocratic rivals. Conversely, his second successor Bonitus, of 'Roman' noble birth according to his saint's life (he was indeed probably a descendant of the emperor Avitus and of Sidonius Apollinaris), was a high official in the court of Sigibert III, and became prefect of Marseille, before succeeding his brother Avitus II as bishop of his home town in 690 thanks to Pippin II's patronage; subsequently he was able to act as a dealer for Pippin, persuading rebels in Lyon to return to loyalty. When he retired a little after 700 and travelled to Rome, it was natural for him to be received by the Lombard king Aripert II, for whom (of course) he did miracles. We have seen similar Frankish bishops operating in the circle of Desiderius of Cahors a generation earlier, too, and the large number of Merovingian saints' lives makes them particularly well attested in Francia, but they had their analogues in Italy, Spain, England and Ireland as well.

Being an aristocrat and, possibly, a former secular official also meant, however, that an aristocratic lifestyle was very familiar to such bishops. They lived well (this is stressed less in saints' lives, but it is quite clear in, for example, Gregory of Tours' *Histories*); increasingly, they took on secular roles even as bishops. They involved themselves in high politics, which sometimes killed them, as with Leudegar of Autun in 678; increasingly, they also led armies in war. In the sixth century this was still rare in Francia, but it was more common in the seventh and eighth, as with Savaric of Auxerre (d. *c.* 721), who invaded five neighbouring bishoprics and died on the way to attack a sixth; his successor Hainmar fought Arab raiders from Spain. The bishops of Trier and Mainz in the early eighth century are well-known examples. Milo of Trier (d. *c.* 757) was the son and great-nephew of former bishops of Trier, an ally of Charles Martel, and a *bête noire* of Boniface; he is depicted in hostile sources as living a classic lay aristocratic lifestyle.

Gewilib of Mainz (d. *c.* 759) succeeded his father Gerold, who had fallen
in battle against the Saxons; Gewilib went back in the next Saxon war
and killed his father's killer. Boniface had him deposed for this in 745,
and succeeded him in his see, although Gewilib lived on, enjoying some
local respect. Boniface achieved no real change of episcopal style, anyway; martial bishops remained common under the Carolingians. All this
must not be seen as a 'secularization' of the church (although Boniface
undoubtedly thought so); Milo and his father Liutwin were keen monastic patrons, and Liutwin indeed became a saint. But they were aristocrats; this is what aristocrats did. In Italy, too, Bishop Walprand of
Lucca, son of Duke Walpert of the same city, another respected church
leader, seems to have died in the war against Pippin III in 754.

The other side to this coin was that aristocratic birth was regarded by
many as intrinsically virtuous. Over and over again, saints' lives stress
noble birth as a positive element in the saint's future holiness; only a
very few writers (Bede, not himself an aristocrat, was one) play it down.
The rapid expansion of monasticism in Francia, England, Ireland in the
seventh century and Italy in the eighth is clearly associated with this sort
of intrinsic aristocratic virtue, more even than the episcopal church. Of
course, aristocrats had the wealth to endow monasteries in the first
place; but they chose abbots and abbesses from their own families, if
indeed they did not become the head of the monastery themselves.
Columba in Iona (d. 597), himself nephew and cousin of kings, was
succeeded by male-line family members, with only one break, in the
next century, as his seventh successor, his biographer Adomnán (d. 704),
proudly relates. Major female monastic founders and abbesses, Hild of
Whitby (d. 680) or Gertrude of Nivelles (d. 653) were also from the
highest ranks, Hild a great-niece of King Edwin, Gertrude the daughter
of Pippin I; they became saints and they, too, were succeeded by relatives.

The foundation of a monastery in fact served two purposes. One was
the honouring of God and the establishment of a group of specialist
devotees to that process of honouring, which was a virtuous act and
would ease one's passage to heaven, reinforced by the prayers of the
monks or nuns, still more if the founder also became a monk or nun,
dedicated to ascesis in the framework of the monastic rule. The other was
to act as an organizing pole for the founder's family: most monasteries
remained under de-facto family control (and, if possible, out of control
of the local bishop), with abbots and abbesses choosing successors who

were either direct kin or family clients; and land given by relatives to the monastery did not really leave the family unless the latter lost control of the foundation. These two purposes were by no means in contradiction; indeed, the more the monastery shone as a spiritual beacon, the more other people would give land to it as well, and the more the founding family would gain status – and the more prayers would be said for them. One had to be careful to do this right. Bede raged against false monasteries in Northumbria in a letter of 734, and Fructuosus of Braga had already said the same for northern Spain around 660: both saw cosy family foundations, with no pretence to religious commitment, as a confidence trick, aimed only at escaping lay obligations. Such monasteries must have been common, in fact, and were probably considered normal by most, indeed virtuous. But the great foundations were more spiritually committed, without, for the most part, abandoning family ties; that would not come until much later, not until after 1000 in most cases.

Linked to these monastic foundations, but not restricted to it, came a huge increase in church land. Kings, bishops, aristocrats and indeed smaller landowners gave land to cathedrals, monasteries and local churches throughout Europe: from the sixth century in Spain, Wales and Byzantine Italy, from the early seventh, probably, in Frankish Gaul and Ireland, from the late seventh in England, from the early eighth in Lombard Italy and Germany east of the Rhine (the dates are those of our earliest references to extensive gift-giving; that for Gaul may be too late). The eighth century seems to have marked a temporary high point for such gifts; they became less frequent in these areas in the early ninth. David Herlihy has estimated, however, that by then almost a third of the land area of Francia and Italy was probably ecclesiastically owned. The motivation for these gifts was of course religious; the imagery of an exchange of gifts, a physical gift to a church in return for prayers, or burial in the church, or even heavenly life, recurs often in surviving documents, for such gifts are the initial basis for most of the documentary archives that survive from this period onwards. But they were part of family strategies, too; the prayers were often for families, and it was common in Italy, for example, for a donor with three sons to give a quarter of his property – an extra son's portion – to the church. The gifts were also often to family foundations, or to the foundations of secular or ecclesiastical patrons whom one might need to impress.

The appearance of landed gifts of this kind often follows on quite closely from the end of the practice, common in the sixth and early seventh century in the Romano-Germanic kingdoms, of burying valuables in the ground as part of the funerary clothing and accoutrements of dead family-members. Getting rid of property in preparedness for death, or as part of the death ritual, was a public act, with resonance for one's social status, for both pagans and Christians. (Not that furnished burials in themselves imply paganism, as was once thought. There were plenty of standard Christian examples, including St Cuthbert himself. But they began in the pagan period, in England for example, and have the same features in both pagan and Christian regions.) It has also been argued that burying goods is a mark of élites still relatively unsure of their local status, and concerned to negotiate it by competitively disposing of property, which became less necessary once aristocracies became stable and wealthy. The argument has particular force in Anglo-Saxon England. Why one might move from the ceremony of burying movable goods to that of the handing over of land (and also movables) to the church remains unclear; but churches themselves vastly preferred the latter, of course, and as they gained in influence this must have had weight. And one result of the shift to landed gifts was that individual churches and monasteries could gain considerable wealth, putting themselves, as institutions, on the level of aristocratic families in terms of resources. This in itself added to the desire of aristocrats to control them; it also made the richest monasteries into powerful political players, as we saw for Clonmacnois in Ireland, and as would soon be the case for Fulda and St. Gallen in Germany, Nonantola, Farfa, S. Vincenzo al Volturno and Montecassino in Italy, Saint-Denis, Saint-Germain and Saint-Bertin in what is now France, to which we should add, for the tenth century, Cluny in France, and Ely and Ramsey in England. Already in the 660s the retired Queen Balthild said to her fellow nuns in her monastery at Chelles that they should play the political game, visiting and giving gifts to kings, queens and aristocrats, 'as was the custom, so that the house of God would not lose the good reputation with which it had begun'; in the ninth century and beyond this would be the mark of a recognizable monastic politics.

The moral king looked after his people, was successful in war, was just and generous and listened to bishops. These were international presumptions in the early Middle Ages, and they were important. In Ireland, indeed, unjust or unsuccessful kingship was explicitly believed to bring climatic disaster, and other peoples thought the same (cf. below, Chapter 17, for the Franks). War was unavoidable; even the most religious of kings had to do it, or their kingdoms were in danger. King Sigeberht of East Anglia retired to a monastery in the 630s, but was called back by his people when Penda of Mercia attacked, to give them courage; this did not work, unfortunately, and he died in battle (Bede, our source for this, tells the story fairly flatly, and he may well have thought Sigeberht's non-military choices were wrong). Doing justice was, together with war, the basic attribute of early medieval government, and all kings were assessed by observers for their fairness in judging and accessibility to plaintiffs; actual law-making was less important before 750, except perhaps in Spain. Generosity was the necessary marker of every king, large or small, who wanted to have or build up a loyal entourage; *hael*, 'generous', was a standard epithet of successful Welsh kings, for example, and we saw in Chapter 5 the political importance of the treasury for Frankish kings; conversely, a vignette in *Beowulf* depicts the Danish king Heremod as mad when he not only killed members of his entourage but 'did not give the Danes treasures in pursuit of high esteem', and his men abandoned him. Listening to bishops is an attribute that is particularly likely to be stressed by our sources, which are nearly all ecclesiastical. Gregory of Tours praised Guntram most out of his contemporaries, perhaps for this reason above all, and Braulio of Zaragoza could in the 640s give unsought advice even to Chindasuinth, controversial and ruthless though the latter was; all the same, bishops were themselves political players, and respect for them was only sensible. Every successful Christian king in our period played church politics, indeed, and some, notably in seventh-century Spain, pursued it very assiduously.

Our sources, even though so very clerical for the most part, nonetheless give secular values a good deal of respect. The effective polygamy of Merovingian kings is only occasionally criticized in our sources; Columbanus was the only ecclesiastic who actually condemned a king for it, Theuderic II, and he was expelled from the kingdom for his pains. (The Franks may have given their kings more licence, though; Visigothic, Lombard and Anglo-Saxon kings were all at least sometimes criticized for sexual excess.) And the violence that was the inevitable consequence of war was hardly ever condemned, at least if it was done to other people. It is crucial to remember that the whole of secular society was by now militarized, throughout the West, and clerics, too, took military virtues for granted. Military obligations at least in theory extended even to the peasantry (see Chapter 9), and characterized all the aristocracy by definition; with this came training in arms and in quasi-military sports such as hunting. Kings put their palaces beside woodland regions that were easy to reach for hunting; the Frankish and Lombard kings began to see some of these regions as 'forest', royal reserves, in which only they could hunt. Aristocrats did not do this yet, but they were certainly as enthusiastic about the sport as kings were; Charlemagne at the turn of the eighth century had to upbraid his counts for cutting short judicial hearings in order to hunt, and Milo of Trier's aristocratic attitude to episcopal office was epitomized by his death, killed by a wild boar. A militarized lifestyle marked kings and aristocrats in every respect, indeed; as we have seen, it was the major change in élite culture that followed the end of the Roman empire. Aristocratic clothing, marked by a large amount of gold and jewellery worn on the person and (for men) a prominent belt, similarly bejewelled, descended from the military costume of the Roman period, and so did the symbolism of the belt itself, which generally represented military or political office (though by now the belt was bigger and flashier than under Rome). Eligius of Noyon, when a secular official for Dagobert I in the 630s, was already saintly enough to give his *ornamenta* to the poor; Dagobert gave him another belt, however; he could not avoid wearing that.

Royal and aristocratic courts also had a different etiquette from those of the Roman world. The *otium* of the Roman civilian aristocracy, literary house-parties in well-upholstered rural villas, and the decorum of at least some imperial dinner parties (above, Chapter 3), was replaced by what sometimes seems a jollier culture. This was focused on eating large quantities of meat and getting drunk on wine, mead or beer, together with one's entourage, usually in a large, long hall. In Italy, drunkenness was possibly less acceptable, but north of the Alps it appears in every society. There is an eighth-century parody of Salic law which turns its enactments into a drinking game, played between the lord Fredonus, his wife and his retainers. In Ireland, drunken competitive boasts between heroes dominate the plot-line of one of the vernacular prose tales, *The Tale of Macc Da Thó's Pig*. And in England and Wales those who drank their lord's alcohol saw their subsequent loyalty in battle as an obligation in return for that hospitality. The etiquette of collective eating did, however, have Roman antecedents as well, even though what one ate and how one ate it had changed; under the empire, as later, eating with someone was a sign of friendship, refusing to do so marked hostility. In 384 it was only under pressure that Martin of Tours ate with the emperor Magnus Maximus, with whom he had religious differences; three hundred and fifty years later, Eucherius of Orléans knew in 732 that Charles Martel had become his enemy when Charles 'left the prepared meal'.

More positively, when kings were in one's own neighbourhood it was a mark of favour, even if an expensive one, if they accepted hospitality. Patronage links with rulers could result from hospitality even to their men, as in the case of Wilfrid in Northumbria, who was presented to the wife of King Oswiu in the 650s on the recommendation of the aristocrats his father had entertained. These patterns of hospitality were carefully calibrated. Retainers 'knew the mode of conduct proper to a noble society', as *Beowulf* puts it. Guests brought gifts to hosts, including kings, as well as expecting them in return. The Irish missionary to Northumbria Aidan of Lindisfarne (d. 651) was notable for not giving money to aristocratic guests, and giving away their gifts to the poor. This was a calculated risk: would it be seen as a sign of charismatic spirituality, or one of meanness or hostility? In Aidan's case the bet paid off, but the risk was still there. Political etiquette did not have fewer rules than in the Roman period, however different they were, and however drunk people got.

Royal and aristocratic women participated in this world of political feasting, as has been seen, and had clear roles on occasion; for example the Danish queen Wealhtheow, 'a lady thoughtful in matters of formal courtesy', was in *Beowulf* the person responsible for passing around the collective mead-cup in the royal hall, at the start of the meal. How many women apart from the host's wife actually attended such gatherings is not clear, however, and the public politico-military world and its values tend to be marked as male. Classic masculine aristocratic virtues included honour, loyalty and bravery. The combination of these three can be seen in the choice of the entourages of both Cynewulf and Cyneheard of Wessex to fight to the death around their lords, and, together or separately, they recur in any number of accounts of military actions from all the societies of the West. The defence of honour could sometimes go well beyond the sensible. Paul the Deacon tells a story from the early eighth century about Argait, a local commander in north-eastern Italy who was pursuing Sclavenian brigands in the area; he lost them, and Duke Ferdulf of Friuli made a joke at his expense referring to the fact that *arga* meant 'coward' in Longobardic. Argait, furious, attacked the full Sclavenian army, in its hill-top camp, by the most difficult route; Ferdulf then thought it dishonourable not to lead the Friulian army as a whole after him, and the Friulians were nearly all killed. Paul tells the story, and doubtless touches it up, as a morality tale about stupidity and disunity, but, as usual, it would only work if its sentiments were recognizable. This sort of imagery of fighting to the death should not be overplayed. Plenty of battles ended with the head-long flight of the losers, usually after a few hours (day-long battles were less common; longer battles very rare). But the close-knit hand-to-hand fighting that was the commonest form of battle in the early medieval period required a basic courage (and a strong physique) to work at all, and it is likely that male aristocrats prone to fear did not last long.

Loyalty cost more than a few cups of wine in a hall. Lords (including kings) in this period, as later in the Middle Ages, might expect to feed and clothe an armed entourage while they were young, but they needed land in order to marry and settle down. It was when aristocrats were young that they moved about, between kings in England for example; once they were settled they would normally only move if they were exiled. But the moment of settling a dependant required sufficient landed resources to set him and his family up. This was a nearly universal requirement in our societies; the only exception was Ireland, where political dependence was expressed through gifts of cattle. Lords needed to have a lot of land (and thus rents, usually in produce) even to feed a large armed entourage, but they needed still more if they were to settle them in the future, and there was a danger that the land they gave to dependants might eventually slip out of their hands altogether. This 'politics of land' remained a basic problem for all early medieval rulers and magnates. It required resources of such size that, on the level of the aristocracy, only Franks could easily afford them; it is not surprising that an aristocratic politics involving autonomous private armies is well documented in this period only in Francia.

The best long-term solution for lords was for families of dependants to be stably located on landed estates, with the sons coming to the lord's court when they were young, to be trained and to become socialized into loyalty, swearing oaths of loyalty, too (an important element in all dependence), before inheriting their father's land, marrying and returning to it. These lands seem usually to have been given outright by lords in this period to their sworn dependants, their *fideles*. There are also signs of experimentation with less permanent cessions of land, to give lords some legally based bargaining powers if their *fideles* were less faithful in the future. In particular, the great ecclesiastical landowners, whose documents we have, can be seen in and after the eighth century to make cessions to their dependants in the lesser aristocracy for three lifetimes (a popular choice in England), or as a lease for rent (a popular choice in Italy), or, in Francia, by precarious tenure (called *precaria* or *beneficium*), which meant that the lord could in principle reclaim it at any time. Church landowners in the eighth century were accumulating land so fast that they could without fear cede quite a lot of land out anyway; it was indeed common for the holders of leases or *precariae* to have been the original donors of the land in question. (Effectively, the donor made a spiritual gift for his soul which often only cost him a very small rent, plus an entry into the church's or monastery's political and military clientele, and this might be a benefit as much as a commitment.) We cannot track the choices of the great lay aristocrats in the same way, but successful magnates tended always to increase their lands, and could thus easily grant them out to military clients too. Essentially, the long-term dangers of the politics of land, in this period as in others, were felt by political losers, who were not increasing (or who were losing) their lands, rather than by political winners. Loyalty to lords was probably both commoner and safer than disloyalty.

Aristocrats, large and small, also had close family connections, with brothers and cousins and, further afield, 'kin' in the widest sense, to whom they felt obligated. These kin-groups were organized in a variety of different ways in western Europe. Sometimes they were restricted to male-line kin, sometimes they respected relationships through females too, although these tended to be less important. Sometimes they were fairly formal, like the three- and four-generation *gelfine* and *derbfine* in Ireland, which had some responsibilities for collective agriculture; more normally, however, there was an element of choice, of which kinsmen one wanted to stay closest to, and which one wanted to avoid. One was expected to support kin in disputes, by swearing oaths in their support or, in extreme cases, fighting for them, and one would also expect to give support in economic or political difficulty. Liutprand in Italy in 717 assumed that if a man was killed and his killer paid compensation for the death (this was the wergild, the honour price for a man, calculated according to social status), the compensation should go to the male heirs of the deceased in the order they would inherit – although not women, for they are 'unable to raise the feud (*faida*)'. Kin loyalty, even if selective, was a universal assumption in our period. An older historiography saw loyalty to kin and loyalty to lords as in contradiction, and tracked the rise of lordship at the expense of kinship. This is a false opposition; most people respected both without difficulty. Where there was conflict (if the different lords of two brothers fought each other, for example) there might be personal tragedy; one example is the Cynewulf–Cyneheard affair, in which kin were on opposite sides. But we cannot track a systematic trend towards one and away from the other; there was usually no need to choose. It is instead likely that, between the Merovingian and the Carolingian period, and still more after the Carolingian period ended, both kin loyalty and lordship became tighter and more articulated, as we shall see in Chapter 21.

Kin-groups feuded. Men (particularly aristocrats) were prone to anger, they drew their weapons (which they often had with them) easily, perhaps especially when they were drunk, they wounded or killed each other, and their kin took revenge. Families could remain in 'enmity' with each other; Liutprand in 731 thought that if this was the case they should not intermarry, and made the voiding of a betrothal easier if enmity had resulted from a kin-killing. We can track some systematic feuding, as with the case in Tournai in 591 in which a man killed his sister's husband for adultery, was killed by the husband's kin in return, and the feud spread steadily outwards to other relatives, never diminishing. (Queen Fredegund solved the difficulty, Gregory of Tours claims, by killing all the survivors.) All the same, most feuds seem to have ended rather more quickly, with the paying of compensation, perhaps after a single act of vengeance. Feuding, like kinship itself, should be seen strategically, not legalistically. 'Enmity' was not likely to persist unless there were more solid conflicts (over political power, say, or land) than those produced by the flaring-up of anger that was so common in our period. One might indeed have felt that kinsmen keen to feud were the ones most to be avoided. The *idea* of feud was important, all the same. It went to the heart of honour and maleness. In the most famous and most-discussed of all early medieval feuds, that involving Sichar of Manthelan (near Tours) in 585–7, terms were established halfway through by Gregory of Tours that involved Sichar compensating his opponent Chramnesind for the death of his relatives. Sichar and Chramnesind became close friends thereafter, until Sichar, when drunk, taunted Chramnesind for doing well out of the settlement. 'Chramnesind was sick at heart. "If I don't avenge my relatives", he said to himself, "they will say I am as weak as a woman, for I no longer have the right to be called a man."' So he killed Sichar then and there. Gregory, whose words these are, clearly applauded Chramnesind, and indeed the latter really had no other choice; Sichar's insult was so serious as to open up the feud again at once. Settlements were like scar-tissue: they could open up again only too easily. And, if they did, refusal of the feud was a denial of masculinity.

Sichar was an aristocrat, a personal dependant of Queen Brunhild; in all our societies feud and honour seem to be seen not only as male but as particularly aristocratic prerogatives. Aristocrats were indeed more 'noble' in the moral sense, at least in their own eyes, and it is unlikely that Gregory would have been as sympathetic to a peasant Chramnesind, if he bothered to record his actions at all. Aristocrats were, as we have seen, more prone to sanctity too, which was by no means seen as in contradiction with their links to honour and violence. Bishop Landibert of Maastricht died around 705, besieged in his house in Liège by his mortal enemy Dodo, *domesticus* of Pippin II, sword in hand until he threw it down to pray just before Dodo's men came in, according to his hagiographer; this did not stop post-mortem miracles and a rapid expansion of his cult in Liège. This sort of image that aristocrats were structurally different from other people did not mean that there were legally defined lines between 'nobles' and the lesser free, particularly not in Francia and Italy; wealth, political patronage, military commitment, or office were all things one could gain separately, if one was lucky, slowly moving up the social ladder. Curiously, the only society with elaborate legal barriers between aristocrats and the lesser free was Ireland, where the wealth differences were probably least important. But training, language and behaviour, including learning how to stand and walk, were important markers that made aristocrats different, probably in all our societies. A Northumbrian aristocrat called Imma was at the battle of Trent in 678, which his side lost; knocked unconscious, he was captured next day, Bede tells us. He pretended to be a peasant who brought food to the army, so he was not killed, but it soon became clear 'by his face, dress and speech' that he was really aristocratic, so he was sold as a slave. English societies were not those with the sharpest social distinctions in Europe, but Imma still stood out. The observations about behaviour and etiquette made in these pages only apply to aristocrats; we shall look at peasants in more detail in the next chapter.

Honour and masculinity were closely tied together, as we have seen. The space for the honour, loyalty and political protagonism of aristocratic women was substantially more restricted. It was not absent, all the same. Women ruling in their own right were not more common in this period than any other; only one is known, and that from a sketchy source two centuries later: Queen Seaxburh of Wessex (672–4), who succeeded her husband for a year. Conversely, we have seen that in Francia queens-regent such as Brunhild, Fredegund, Balthild and Chimnechild could be extremely powerful, and this gives us an insight into the female exercise of authority. The importance of these women was, for a start, very closely associated with the dynastic centrality of the core Merovingian male line. Royal wives and concubines were many in the Frankish world; if they wanted real power, it was as a mother of a king, so they had to ensure that their own son succeeded. Fredegund had to engineer the death of at least two stepsons, for example (at least according to Gregory of Tours, who has, however, to push the evidence somewhat to implicate her in this). When they ruled as regents, their rule was more contested than was Merovingian kingly authority, too. But it was real power they had, all the same; people obeyed them, built careers around them, fought for them. Indeed, Gregory said his patron Brunhild acted *viriliter*, 'in a manly way'. Janet Nelson argues that their authority also derived from the location of so much Merovingian political practice in the royal court, the household whose organization was largely under queenly control. This is likely enough as well, although Merovingian-period queen-mothers were unusually powerful, despite the fact that queens controlled the household everywhere. We see a balance in Merovingian female political authority that is a feature of politically powerful women throughout the Middle Ages: female political action, where it existed, was more fragile and more contested than male action; but there was sometimes space for it all the same. We also could not reasonably doubt that queens like Brunhild had honour.

This role for women was particularly associated with the Merovingian blood-line, in that royal mothers could be powerful whatever their social origins. Among the Frankish aristocracy of the Merovingian period, however, women with a proper aristocratic ancestry could be fairly active as well. The typical aristocratic woman, whether wife or mother, does, it is true, tend to appear in our sources as an appendage to male actors, giving land to churches together with a husband or a son, for example. The few women in the Merovingian period who made surviving wills without the participation of a male relative (because they were widows or consecrated nuns, like Erminethrudis or Ermintrude in Paris around 600 and Burgundofara in Faremoutiers in 634) also possessed much less land than the aristocratic norm; autonomous female actors were, once again, in a relatively fragile situation. Aristocratic women could nonetheless choose to consecrate themselves to virginity and found monasteries, as numerous saints' lives tell. These lives tend to stress the opposition of their fathers to such a choice (as opposed to one of marriage for the advantage of the family), and the support of their mothers. As Régine Le Jan notes, this has to be a *topos*, a narrative cliché: in reality, such female monasteries were very much part of family strategies, and women like Burgundofara of Faremoutiers or Gertrude of Nivelles, and the monasteries they founded, prospered and faltered as their families (respectively the Faronids/Agilolfings and the Pippinids) prospered and faltered. Nevertheless, the monastic option gave such women the chance to be protagonists inside family politics, and Gertrude, like Burgundofara, took that chance and developed it.

Plectrude, widow of Pippin II, illustrates these possibilities further. She was very influential during Pippin's lifetime; we find her at his side as they take over and give land to the monastery of Echternach in 706, for example, a monastery previously patronized by her mother Ermina. This influence was doubtless linked to her own aristocratic background in the Trier area, and the fact that, thanks to her relatives, Pippinid family influence could expand southwards. But Pippin was not just the richest aristocrat of the age; he was also senior *maior domus* for all the Frankish lands, and their effective ruler. At his death in 714, his two sons by Plectrude were dead; with Pippin's deathbed agreement, his young grandson Theodoald succeeded as *maior*, with Plectrude running

the government. Without anything approaching the security of Merovingian dynastic legitimacy, that is to say, the Pippinids were happy to
adopt Merovingian-style queen-regent practice. Plectrude was evidently
tough enough for the job; she imprisoned her only family rival, her
stepson Charles Martel, at once. But a year later there was a Neustrian
revolt against Pippinid rule, and shortly after that Charles escaped and
revolted as well. As we have seen, it was Charles who won the civil war
of 715–19, and Plectrude had to give up Pippin's treasure (and thus all
chance of high political protagonism) to Charles by 717. She failed, and
she did so partly because of her gender: her power was even more fragile
and contested than Brunhild's. But there was at least a political space
for her to make the attempt, and Carolingian-period historians, writing
under the rule of Charles's descendants, treated her with considerable
respect.

The early Anglo-Saxons are much less clearly documented, but their
emphasis on dynastic legitimacy could in principle have had an impact
on royal mothers; loose succession rules meant that there were few child
kings in England before the tenth century, but, when there were, their
mothers would be important (below, Chapter 19). The early prominence
of powerful abbesses in several Anglo-Saxon kingdoms also implies some
parallels to the Merovingian situation. The Visigoths and Lombards put
less stress on female politics, however. This is again partly a problem of
our sources, which include few narratives, and which are also prone to
depict women's political action even more negatively than in the kingdoms further north: the Arian queen of Spain Goiswintha (d. 589), for
example, widow of King Athanagild (and also mother of Brunhild of
Francia), who conspired against Leovigild and Reccared in turn, and
sought to undermine Reccared's conversion to Catholicism, as John of
Biclar recounts; or, in Italy, Queen Rosimunda (d. c. 573), who engin-
eered the assassination of her husband Alboin in 572 but came to a bad
end, according to Paul the Deacon. Paul is indeed consistent in depicting
female political protagonism, by queens or duchesses, in the most negative light, with the exception of his heroine, Theodelinda, wife of two
successive kings, correspondent of Gregory the Great, and probably
queen-regent to her son Adaloald (616–26). Her example at least shows
that given the right circumstances a woman could have considerable
authority in Italy. These circumstances were repeated in the autonomous
duchy of Benevento in 751–5, when Scauniperga, Gisulf II's widow,

ruled with her young son Liutprand, calling herself *dux* together with him, and was listed first in documents. Benevento had a stable ruling family, which must have helped Scauniperga into that role. At other times, adult kings succeeded, often by coup, and the absence of a dynastic principle did not help female protagonism; but attitudes like those of Paul, if widely felt, would have made their space still more limited. The Lombards certainly did not value the sort of independent political action that was sometimes available to aristocratic women in the Byzantine parts of the peninsula, as with the *patricia* Clementina in the Naples of the 590s, who appears in Gregory the Great's letters as a sometimes controversial political figure in Naples, both an ally and an enemy to local clerical leaders (her unfree dependants staged a small peasants' revolt against a papal envoy; she tried to stop the election of Bishop Amandus of Sorrento because she wanted him to stay in her entourage). Indeed, aristocratic female dealers like Clementina, powerful because of their own wealth without any explicit family context, look back to the late empire rather than forward into the early Middle Ages, anywhere in the West, including the Byzantine lands. Later, the bonds of family, whether by birth or by marriage, would be everywhere.

I stress high politics here, not because the exercise of political power is necessarily the most important thing anyone did, but rather because this is where the evidence is located. It was argued in Chapter 3 that gender assumptions, although universally more constraining for women than for men in the later Roman period (and all the constraints listed there applied in the early Middle Ages too), gave more space for a range of female activity than they did later. In general, female protagonism in the early Middle Ages was more clearly tied in to the lifecycle and to family strategies than it had been under the empire. It was also more constrained by legal norms. Even though 'barbarian' laws, even less than those of Rome, did not circumscribe social action much in practice, they at least reflected the mind-sets of legislators; and they universally assume legal disabilities for women. Women were expected to be under male legal protection in most of our societies, that of their father, brothers, husband in turn, until they were widowed. In some early medieval societies they were then legally independent, but they were in a weak position, and the control of the lands they by then had access to (dowry from their father, a 'morning-gift' from their husband – the latter could amount to a lot, a quarter of his property in Lombard Italy, sometimes a third in Francia) was under threat from their children and from male relatives of all sorts. There is plenty of anecdotal evidence of this sort of threat to widows: for example, in Italy, Rottruda of Pisa, whose attempts to found a pilgrim-hostel according to her dead husband's wishes were opposed by his brother in 762, or Taneldis of Clemenziano in the Sabina, who disinherited her son's heirs in 768, for the 'many injuries and bitter trouble and damage' that he did to her. Morning-gifts in land seem also to have been more often sold than any other family property in central Italy, which implies that the land women might inherit was seen as less essential to retain.

Lombard Italy was, indeed, out of all these societies, the one where the legal constraints on women seem to have been greatest; it was probably matched only by Ireland. In Italy, women remained under legal protection, that of their male children, even as widows. Lombard legislation spends a good deal of space setting out the obligations of men to treat women properly, which testifies to a general culture of constraint. In 731 Liutprand listed the mistreatments that would cause a man to forfeit his rights of legal protection over a woman: if he let her go hungry, did not clothe her according to his own wealth, had sex with her or married her to a slave, or struck her (unless 'in honest discipline'). Lombard law also so totally assumed that women did not bear arms that it made no provision for what happened if they committed violent acts, as Liutprand discovered with horror in 734; in future they were to be publicly humiliated, and their husbands, presumed to be the real perpetrators, should pay compensation. This was a law directed at peasants, not aristocrats, but it testifies to a set of gendered assumptions that were particularly Lombard, and are reflected also in the writings of Paul the Deacon. They would have been recognizable north of the Alps, too, but they were most consistently applied in Italy.

The early Middle Ages have traditionally been seen as more 'Germanic' than late Rome, the product of invasion, and also as the location of a cultural 'Romano-Germanic' fusion, which would be developed and perfected under the Carolingians. As I have implied in previous chapters, this does not seem to me an accurate characterization. For a start, early medieval societies in the West had common features whether there had been invasion or not: Byzantine Italy and Wales were in many ways parallel to Lombard Italy and England respectively. Ireland, too, with little contact with the 'Germanic' world, had similarities with it (although, of the societies we have looked at, this was in many respects the most atypical). The real contrast inside the ex-Roman provinces was not between societies that had been invaded or conquered and the others, but between the Continent and Britain: in the former, the basic Roman political and social structures survived (though they were in most places ramshackle and underfunded), and in the latter they did not; tribal societies were a feature of both the Anglo-Saxon and the Welsh parts of post-Roman Britain. Overall, in fact, the major change in political culture was not Germanization but militarization: the age of a dominant military aristocracy began in the fifth and sixth centuries, and continued throughout the West for more than a millennium. As we shall see in Part III, this was a feature of the Byzantine empire, and to a lesser extent the caliphate, as well.

All the same, identities did change. Fewer and fewer people in the West called themselves *Romani*; the others found new ethnic markers: Goths, Lombards, Bavarians, Alemans, Franks, different varieties of Angles and Saxons, Britons – the name the non-Anglo-Saxon inhabitants of Britain had given themselves by 550, the *Romani* having left, and a word itself due soon to be replaced by a Welsh term, *Cymry*, 'fellow countrymen'. Even in a part of the former empire unconquered by invaders, that is to say, the Romans were not the Britons themselves, but other people, earlier invaders, who had come and gone. And although of course the huge majority of the ancestors of all these peoples were men and women who would have called themselves Roman in 400, the Roman world had indeed gone, and Roman-ness with it.

The early Middle Ages was materially a much simpler period than the late empire, and Roman buildings and ruins were all around, generally dwarfing more recent constructions, and generally also more carefully built. Did early medieval peoples feel insecure or nostalgic about the Roman past? There is very little sign of it. Gregory of Tours, although of an aristocratic Roman family, seems hardly aware the empire has gone at all; his founding hero was Clovis, and all his loyalties Frankish. Paul the Deacon wrote up Romans and Lombards alike, and, although he knew well how violent the Lombard invasion was, it seemed to him inevitable, and he was proud of his Lombard antecedents. To those who did not warm to the image of Scandinavia as the 'womb of [Germanic] nations', there was Troy as another non-Roman origin myth, and also the Israel of the Old Testament (the Franks in particular came to use the latter imagery frequently: see Chapter 16). And if writers did not focus their identity exclusively on ethnic origin, they identified with their province instead, as with Isidore of Seville's praise of Spain in the 620s: 'Rightly did golden Rome, the head of nations, desire you long ago. And ... now it is the most flourishing people of the Goths, who in their turn, after many victories all over the world, have easily seized you and loved you: they enjoy you up to the present time amidst royal emblems and great wealth, secure in the good fortune of empire.' For Isidore, the man of the whole early medieval period most imbued with a pre-Constantinian literary culture, that was the past, and the present was equally glorious.

The 'myth of Rome' was indeed, more and more, the new Christian Rome of basilicas and martyrs' tombs. The guidebooks for pilgrims do not put particular stress on the huge pre-Constantinian buildings still standing in the city (as often, thirteen centuries further on, they still are); these were at best a monumental backdrop to the new numinous foci of the Christian world. Tombs were a metonym for Rome: in Ireland, the word *ruaim*, 'Rome', actually came to mean a monastic cemetery. This Rome persisted; the imperial image of Rome and its empire, by contrast, was increasingly abandoned. Carolingian rulers and their entourage would be much more interested in the Roman empire, reviving the title of emperor, using Suetonius on Augustus as a model for a biography of Charlemagne, copying classical texts, recommending Roman histories to each other; but they did so in a framework of a Frankish/Carolingian self-confidence so gigantic that they had to draw on all the models that existed, imperial Rome, Troy and Israel all together, so that they could surpass them. For them, too, however, the Rome they most valued was the Christian one, of basilicas, tombs, and, increasingly, popes.

The final point that needs to be made is that the beliefs and practices discussed here did not change much after 750. For the most part, pre-Carolingian examples have been used here, but instances from any century up to 1000, and indeed beyond, could as easily be given. The Carolingians (Louis the Pious in particular) largely unified monastic regulation, and the scale of their political control brought churchmen from all of the West into more regular contact. They developed a more regular educational system, especially for the élite, which reversed the intellectual isolation of figures like Bede, and which allowed theological debate and even heresy to reappear (see Chapter 17). But the basic presuppositions about religious practices described in this chapter continued to underpin the Carolingian reform programme, and indeed survived its partial eclipse at the end of the ninth century. As for aristocratic attitudes, and concepts of gender difference, these barely shifted at all in the Carolingian period. The political and cultural changes that will be discussed in Part IV of this book rested on a foundation of values that remained stable for a long time.

9

Wealth, Exchange and Peasant Society

In 721 Anstruda of Piacenza in northern Italy made an unusual charter. She sold her own legal independence to the brothers Sigirad and Arochis, because she had married their unfree dependant (*servus*). She and they agreed that her future sons should remain the brothers' dependants in perpetuity, but her daughters could buy their independence at marriage for the same money, 3 *solidi*, that Anstruda herself had received. Although Lombard Italy was a relatively legally aware country (and Piacenza is not far from the capital), this charter breaks at least three laws: the law forbidding free–slave marriages; the law, or at least assumption, that the unfree were not legal persons, so Anstruda's daughters could not be assigned future rights; and the law prohibiting female legal autonomy. Anstruda's father Authari, a *vir honestus* or small landowner, consented to the document, but the money for Anstruda's legal rights went to her directly, and she is the actor throughout. There is an ironic sense in which this account of a young peasant woman, even though she was selling her own freedom, shows how she could make her own rules, create her own social context, even in as restrictive a society for female autonomy as Lombard Italy. This may say something about Anstruda as a person; it also says something about the fluidity of peasant society in Italy.

So also do Sigirad and Arochis, who were some way from home. They were medium landowners and small-scale village leaders in Campione near Lugano in the Alpine foothills, 140 kilometres to the north of Piacenza. They kept charters about their servile dependants; a parallel text for 735 shows them buying control over a second free woman who married one of their dependants, in Campione itself, this time (in more orthodox fashion) from her brother. Their kinsman Toto successfully claimed the ownership of another dependant, Lucius of Campione, in a court case of the 720s, against Lucius' firm opposition; Toto is also found buying a slave from Gaul called Satrelanus from a woman, Ermedruda, in Milan in 725. The members of this family got about, that is to say, and were interested in obtaining or keeping hold of dependants in a variety of different contexts. They were tough to deal with, as Lucius found; perhaps Anstruda's daughters would have found it hard to get out of their control in the future. But this dealing in itself marks a certain fluidity; social relationships in and around Campione seem to have been quite complex.

I begin here with Anstruda and Campione as a way into understanding the complexity of early medieval peasant societies. But it has to be said at once that we do not know much about most of them; peasant social practices were too far from the aristocratic and ecclesiastical interests of the great bulk of our written sources. For the most part, our evidence for peasants in the pre-Carolingian West is archaeological; the relatively small number of western villages which give us enough documents to allow us to discuss real peasant actions tend, with only a few exceptions, to be ninth-century rather than earlier, and this chapter will indeed stray into the ninth century as a result. Otherwise, peasants are seen resolutely from the outside, by legislators and hagiographers, who have very moralistic reasons for mentioning them, and little sympathy for their values. But these hostile external observers were also in all our societies from social groups who were rather more powerful than the peasantry, and who were entirely prepared to coerce them if it was in their interests to do so. If we want to understand peasant society in the round in our period, we have to see it in the framework of an understanding of how much wealth and thus power other social groups had as well. This is why this chapter links general problems of economic structure with peasant society. We have to understand the issue of the distribution of wealth before we can understand how much peasant social action really was constrained, in all the different local realities of the West. But the distribution of wealth also has implications for every sector of the economy, which we shall look at in the second half of the chapter.

We saw in Chapters 5–7 that aristocrats varied substantially in their wealth across western societies. In Merovingian Francia, there were some really rich landowners, with dozens of landed estates each, and a highly militarized factional politics. Bavaria was like Francia, although probably on a smaller scale; only a handful of families (apart from the ruling dukes) seem to have been important owners. In Lombard Italy, however, the wealth of the aristocratic strata was much more modest, and the political dominance of kings was overwhelming. Visigothic Spain was more like Italy in that respect, as it seems from thinner data. And the wealth of aristocrats in Britain and Ireland was, as far as can be seen, markedly less; societies there were on a much smaller scale, and the economic difference between the aristocracy and the peasantry was much less marked. In all these cases, too, except for northern Francia (and Ireland, which the Romans never ruled), levels of aristocratic wealth were far lower in the early Middle Ages than they had been under the Roman empire.

These are important contrasts, and they have several implications. The implications for differences in political practice have already been discussed, and we need not return to them here. There are also implications for peasant societies, as just indicated: the less land an aristocracy owned, the more land was in the hands of the peasantry, and therefore the more space there was for peasant autonomy; if an aristocracy was richer, the opposite was true. So the fluidity of action of some of our Italian village societies was made more feasible by the relatively contained wealth of Italian aristocracies; we might not expect Frankish village communities to be as autonomous. This point is reinforced by the fact that in Italy landowning was usually very fragmented; even an aristocratic estate could be divided into dozens, sometimes hundreds, of separate land plots. Aristocratic-owned lands, and the free or unfree tenants who worked them, were thus not all in a single block, and could well be next door to the lands, and houses, of small peasant landowners, who are quite well documented in Italy. There was space for fairly complicated local social relationships in the interstices of estates as a result, even when Italian aristocrats were locally dominant, which they usually were not.

In some parts of Francia, we find the same degree of fragmentation; the Rhineland is one example. Here, aristocrats were very powerful, and we can indeed identify at least two levels of a Rhineland aristocracy, a lesser level with a few estates each, generally in several different villages, and a greater aristocracy with a vast wealth in land spread over a wide region (this aristocracy by the end of the eighth century included major local monasteries like Lorsch and Wissembourg). Inside that framework, peasants had to be careful, for aristocrats were everywhere, and could do them harm. Peasant landowners attached themselves to aristocratic clienteles in a routine way, to obtain protection. But, as we saw in Chapter 5, in the Merovingian period aristocrats were in general more interested in obtaining wealth and status in royal courts than they were in achieving local domination over peasantries. Peasant society could remain largely autonomous even in Francia at the level of the village, and we can see active groups of small owners running some of the best-documented villages of the Rhineland, such as Dienheim near Mainz and Gœrsdorf in Alsace, in the eighth century.

The major exception to this seems to have been Neustria, particularly the well-documented Paris region, where estates tended to be large blocks of land. Here, peasants less often owned their own land, and village autonomy would have been quite difficult. Most of the villages we know about around Paris are indeed documented as a result of monastic estate surveys, polyptychs, which are a feature of the Carolingian period. The estates of the monastery of Saint-Germain-des-Prés in the Paris suburbs often contained whole villages, such as Palaiseau south of the city, which were thus entirely dependent on their landlord. We know the names of nearly every peasant, including children, who held land from Saint-Germain in the 820s, and what rent they owed, thanks to the monastic polyptych; they are among the completest records of village society we have. The peasants listed in them would have lived their lives largely by landlordly rules, and even the markers for local status would largely have depended on the different relationships each peasant family had with its landlord: the amount of land it held, the amount of rent and services it paid, and the free or unfree status of each of its members.

These Parisian villages were regarded as typical of the whole of western Europe by historians of two generations ago. Now that other sorts of document collection have been looked at in more detail, however, they seem the opposite: they were highly unusual in the early Middle Ages in the degree to which peasants in them were dependent on landlords. In other parts of the Continent, the fragmented landowning of aristocrats meant that very few villages had a single landlord, and most such settlements had a mixture of inhabitants: unfree and free tenants; tenants who owned a little land as well; small peasant proprietors who owned all the land they cultivated, medium owners like Sigirad and

Arochis of Campione, who did not cultivate their own land (and were thus not peasants) but who were not rich enough to operate politically very far outside their own village; and only in a minority of cases anyone richer – only in the villages where aristocrats themselves happened to live, in fact. These mixed villages were dominated by their richest inhabitants, who were not necessarily peasants, but village collectivities could have a considerable practical authority, and peasants could have a voice in that.

Let us look at a couple of examples of villages which have a substantial documentation in the eighth and ninth centuries, to show how this worked in practice. Gœrsdorf in Alsace is one example, documented as it is in nineteen documents from the period 693–797. These texts survive in the charter-collection of the nearby monastery of Wissembourg, which shows in itself that the monastery gained a large amount of land there across the eighth century; nearly all the texts are gifts and sales to Wissembourg, in fact. The dukes of Alsace owned land there too, and so did the Sigibald family, significant aristocratic dealers in the eighth-century Rhineland. But between the lands of these three large owners, other people lived too. Medium owners lived in Gœrsdorf, like Adalgis-Allo, who with his wife and son sold land to Wissembourg in 695 (two tenant houses) and in 712 (four areas of arable land and woodland), and who stood witness for other donors and vendors in 693, 696 and 713. So did small-owning peasants, like Asulf, who stood witness along with Adalgis-Allo in 693 and who sold all his property to the monastery in the 696 document. What he did after that is unclear, though he could well have rented it back and become a free monastic tenant; such processes are documented elsewhere. There were certainly free tenants of the duke of Alsace in Gœrsdorf, for in the 730s they witnessed concerning the rent they had owed him on land now ceded to the monastery; probably the tenants were contesting the level of that rent, but the fact that they could do so in public shows that they had free status. Most tenants in the village were probably unfree, all the same; they are called *mancipia* in the charters, which means 'unfree dependants'. Gœrsdorf was probably most sharply divided between unfree and free. The unfree were all tenants; the free were partly tenants, partly peasant cultivators, partly medium owners. It was the free who stood witness in front of the duke as 'the men who live in Gœrsdorf', as the text says. They also probably ran village affairs: perhaps a small-scale law court (called a *mallus* in Frankish law codes and dispute documents), and almost certainly any collective decisions that had to be made about the economic activities of the *villa* (village) of Gœrsdorf. The village seems to have been a compact settlement surrounded by its *marca*, fields, meadows and woods, all of which would have been exploited for grain- and wine-growing, stock-raising and wood-cutting. Gœrsdorf was near the edge of the great forest of the Vosges, but it was already by 700 in a fully settled landscape, with several other villages close by, and its own woodland would already have been restricted in size and quite fully used for its products. There were expanses of wild land in early medieval western Europe, especially in the woodland zones of central and southern Germany, but mostly people lived in territories that had been created and developed by humans for centuries, even millennia, and Gœrsdorf was certainly one of these.

Gœrsdorf was not directly dependent on Wissembourg (or the duke of Alsace), but it had to exist in a political framework dominated by such figures, and the monastery would have been more powerful than any rival there by the end of the eighth century, leaving less space for autonomous peasant action. Most of the villages we have documents for are like this, but sometimes we can find evidence for more independent communities. One example is the group of villages in eastern Brittany around the monastery of Redon which are documented in Redon's cartulary. These villages, Carentoir, Ruffiac, Bains and others, certainly had tenants, both free and unfree, but it seems that here the majority of local inhabitants were landowning peasants when the Redon charters begin in the 830s (the monastery was founded in 832). Only a minority of these had more than a single peasant holding, or land in more than one village; these were often priests, or else local notables with an official position, called *machtierns*. Every village had a *machtiern* (we know the names of most of the ninth-century *machtierns* of Ruffiac, for example), and they were always among the richest people in the village, sometimes owning well outside it; they had their own special house, often called a *lis* (cf. modern Welsh *llys*, a princely court: the Breton language is closely related to Welsh). One might call them aristocratic, but, by the standards of aristocracies elsewhere in Europe, *machtierns* were not at all rich and powerful; they were no more than medium owners, on the level of Sigirad and Arochis of Campione, and it is not even clear that they were very militarized. In no sense did they dominate their villages, in fact.

1. Hagia Sophia, built by the emperor Justinian as the Great Church of Constantinople in 532–7. The minarets are from the Ottoman period.

2. The interior space of Hagia Sophia. This was the first major church to have a dome on this scale, and was followed by many churches and mosques thereafter. The capitals were specially cut for the church.

3. The Great Mosque at Damascus, built in 705–16. This aerial photograph shows the scale of its great courtyard, inside the walls of a former temple of Jupiter

4. A section of the courtyard mosaics of the Damascus mosque, showing the typical unpeopled buildings of this mosaic cycle, characteristic of Islamic public art from the start.

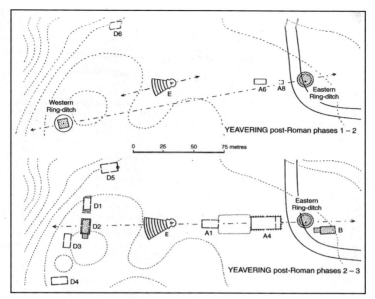

5. Plans of the two main periods of the Northumbrian royal palace of Yeavering in the Cheviots. The first period (*c.* 600) already has a version of a Roman theatre, in wood, as an assembly place; a few years later, the second period sees it linked to a set of royal reception halls, which were doubtless lavish.

6. The empress Ariadne (d. 515), who chose her emperor-husbands, is here depicted with the orb and sceptre of rulership; late Roman tradition did not see female political power as abnormal.

7. The nave of S. Prassede, one of the major prestige churches of the ninth-century papacy
built in 817–24 by Pope Paschal I.

8. The mosaic apse of S. Prassede, with Christ in the River Jordan surrounded by saints, a traditional image for Roman church apses. Paschal is on the far left, with a square halo to indicate that he is alive.

9. The mosaic apse of St-Germigny-des-Prés near Orléans in France, built by Bishop Theodulf of Orléans around 805. It depicts the Ark of the Covenant held up by angels, and shows an iconoclast rejection of human representation.

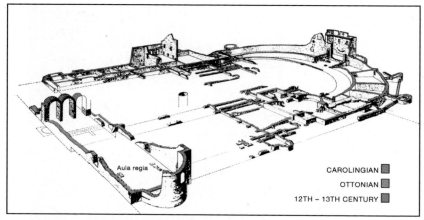

10. A drawing of the still-standing remains of Charlemagne's palace of Ingelheim, near Mainz in Germany. The 'aula' on the left is a ceremonial hall. The palace had a chapel, but it has not been found; the chapel in blue is tenth-century.

CAROLINGIAN
OTTONIAN
12TH – 13TH CENTURY

Aula regia

11. Charlemagne's monumental palace chapel at Aachen, built in the years around 800. The domed central section is the original building.

12. Serjilla, a fifth- and sixth-century village in Syria, one of the best-preserved villages surviving from the Roman world. This is the bath-house (*left*) and the 'andron' or community meeting-centre.

13. Serjilla's best-preserved private house, probably of a peasant family made rich by the olive-oil boom of the later Roman empire in the East.

14. A reconstruction of a tenth-century Danish long-house; this one, excavated at Trelleborg, was part of a royal army camp, and is unusually large, but is characteristic of how Scandinavian dwelling houses could look.

15. Montarrenti, near Siena in Italy, in the ninth century. This imaginative reconstruction follows the findings of the excavation there. The walled upper section is probably an estate-centre.

Only a small minority of landowners in Brittany were large-scale land-owners with a military lifestyle: they made up the entourage of the princes of Brittany (who called themselves kings in the late ninth century, at least briefly). As in the Rhineland, if such people lived or had a lot of land in any given village, then that village would be effectively subject to them. But most villages were not; for them, *machtierns* and priests were the most powerful people around.

The east Breton villages were called *plebes* in the Redon documents: literally, 'peoples' (cf. Chapter 7 for Ireland). They were unusually organized and coherent communities by the standards of the earliest Middle Ages. They ran their own village-level law courts, presided over by *machtierns* or other village officials, where disputes were settled; other public village business was done at such law courts, too. When disputes were dealt with, it was the villagers who reached judgement; they also acted as oath-swearers for the disputing parties, and as sureties to ensure that losers accepted defeat. In one notable case of 858 in the *plebs* of Tréal, Anau had tried to kill Anauhoiarn, a priest of the monas-tery of Redon, and had to give a vineyard to Redon in compensation, as an alternative to losing his right hand; here, six sureties were named, who could kill him if he tried such a thing again. In that case two of the six were *machtierns*, perhaps because the case was so serious, but most judgement-finders and sureties were peasants; the villages around Redon policed themselves.

Once again, we know about these Breton villages because Redon obtained lands (and associated documents) there, steadily from its foun-dation, reaching a peak in the 860s. The monastery was also given political rights in the villages around it, over the head of the peasants, by Caro-lingian kings and Breton princes; by the 860s at the latest, it was at least as locally dominant as Wissembourg was in Gœrsdorf, and perhaps more so. Here as elsewhere, peasant societies are only clearly visible in the early Middle Ages when they are just about to be taken over by powerful out-siders, the people who were likely to have archives that would survive into later periods. But the *plebes* which Redon's land expanded into had, strikingly and unusually, begun as autonomous of landlordly power, and in the 830s their flat social hierarchy still seemed relatively stable. If Redon had not been founded, we would not know anything about them, but, conversely, there is no particular reason to think that their local autonomy could not have continued for a long time.

Document collections in the early Middle Ages generally tell us about the alienation of land, and little else; as noted at the start of this book, these were the kinds of documents which were most normally preserved. They dealt, that is to say, with land which was given or sold (usually to churches and monasteries), or pledged in return for loans, or else leased in return for rent. Reading texts of this kind is sometimes frustrating: surely they give us a very external view of village-level society, documenting as they do the most formal actions villagers could undertake, and, often, the dullest? Court cases, when they survive, generally do so because land was involved too (Anau's vineyard, for example), but at least they can contain detail of more 'human' interaction – hatred, violence, bad faith. They are all the more illuminating because of that. But land transactions are not to be underestimated: they were of crucial importance, for they had to do with the resources available to each peasant family for their very survival. One chooses whom to cede land to; one will alienate or lease to friends or patrons or clients, not to enemies (unless one is forced to by an extreme situation, such as debt, penury or climatic disaster). As a result, if we have a large number of documents for any given village, we can build up pictures of social relationships which are only attested through land deals, but which had wider resonances too. So, for example, it is interesting that the 860s, when Redon got the highest number of gifts from its neighbours, is also a period when we have more court cases between the monastery and its neighbours. In the 830s Redon was a local, still relatively small house, to which one might give land for one's soul without there being any political implications. In the 860s, however, it was the largest local landowner around, and, if one gave it land, one was seeking a patron. Such gifts by then usually involve the cession of the same land back to the donor in *precaria*, for rent; if one feared Redon's power, however, rather than seeking its patronage, one might well oppose it instead, by taking its land, stealing its produce, contesting its property boundaries, or claiming that one's kin had no right to sell to the monastery, hence the court cases. The document collections of the early Middle Ages are still fairly thinly spread, and we seldom have a critical mass sufficient for a dense description of local realities, but when we do, as around Redon, we can get closer to peasant society.

Palaiseau, Gœrsdorf and Ruffiac can stand for three early medieval peasant realities: the village all owned and dominated by a single lord;

the village with powerful external owners but also fragmented property-holding and a significant presence of peasant landowners; and the village where small owners predominated and ran their own lives much more autonomously. How common were each? As already stated, Palaiseau was probably the least typical of the three, at least up to 800; there were village-sized estates in every part of western Europe, but they were only common in a small number of areas, such as the Paris basin. (Royal estates, too, tended to be of the Palaiseau type.) Gœrsdorf was probably a very widespread type indeed; there were, after all, major aristocrats all over Europe, and they had to own land somewhere – indeed, the more scattered their land, the more places they owned it. The Gœrsdorf model can perhaps be seen as typical of most of southern and eastern Francia, Italy (as in Campione), and – though here the evidence is less good – the non-mountainous sections of Spain. Ruffiac can stand for parts of Europe where aristocrats were weaker: Brittany, obviously, but Britain too; other parts of Europe north of the Frankish world; and also more marginal parts of southern Europe, such as the Pyrenees and the Appennines. But there were probably examples of autonomous villages scattered quite widely across Europe, at least in the sixth and seventh centuries. By the ninth and tenth centuries there would be far fewer, as we shall see in Chapter 22. In England, in particular, village-level societies with a relatively high degree of autonomy in 700 or so, at most paying recognitive dues to a king or, increasingly, a church, would have become by 900 or so much more subjected, paying higher rents to a single landlord. England moved, as a whole, from a collection of local societies on a Ruffiac model directly to a collection of societies on a Palaiseau model – a considerable social change, even though a poorly documented one. We shall look at how that process can be characterized in Chapter 19.

Villages were various in many other ways, too: far more ways than can be described in detail here. They varied in their size and spatial coherence, from big nucleated settlements (Palaiseau had 117 holdings, perhaps representing nearly 700 inhabitants), through small hamlets, to sets of isolated farms, and mixtures of all these forms. They varied in the strength of their internal organization; some had structured patterns of decision-making (although this was rare before 1100 in the West, it was not unknown – the Redon villages seem to be examples); some had collectively run pastoral economies (by contrast, collective decisions about agriculture were rare before three-field systems expanded across northern Europe in the central Middle Ages, and before the Arabs expanded irrigation agriculture in Spain and Sicily in the ninth to eleventh centuries). Before 800, overall, villages tended to be smaller and less structured than they would be later, and some historians indeed prefer not to call them 'villages' in this period at all. But the idea of all the people living in a given geographical territory, landowners or tenants, being seen as inhabitants of the same place, the *villa* of Palaiseau or Gœrsdorf or the *plebs* of Ruffiac (*vicus*, *locus* and many other Latin words were also used), is in itself an important element that can be said to be the basis of 'village-ness', and I am happy to use the word here. Some villages were fairly weak or small, some coherent or large, and village coherence would slowly increase between around 600 and around 1000, but in all centuries villages and their territories were important as the basic stage on which the peasant majority, 90 per cent of the population of Europe and maybe more, lived their lives throughout our period.

Villages were not egalitarian communities in any period, even if they did not have lords, and large landowners were marginal or absent. Peasants were divided between owners and tenants, and between richer and poorer owners, in a complex pecking-order. The free–unfree dividing-line was also of crucial importance in most villages, separating people who had legal rights, in public law courts and local decision-making (and also duties such as army-service), from people who had none. This line was violently policed by kings, and marrying across it was illegal everywhere, although we have seen, with Anstruda of Piacenza, that people frequently did so in practice. The practical importance of the free–unfree line was probably very variable regionally, too. It mattered more when all tenants were legally unfree, for example, than when unfree tenure was just one version of dependence beside others (as at Palaiseau, where free and unfree tenants lived side by side, and indeed intermarried on a regular basis). But everywhere it marked an important status difference inside the village, and thus a break in local solidarity: village collectivities would not often be powerful and coherent until unfreedom became less common, which was, once again, a feature of the tenth and eleventh centuries more than the sixth to eighth.

Peasant families were not egalitarian either. Many peasants had unfree servants and farm workers; and gender relations were unequal as well.

Certain tasks were highly gendered: weaving was called 'womanly work'; ploughing was 'manly work'. And the legal subjection of women (already characterized for the aristocratic world in Chapter 8) was at least as complete in the peasant environment, or indeed more so: hence the interest of a woman like Anstruda, who could at least control the terms of her subjection. Few women appear as independent actors in any of our documents, and even fewer of them are peasants. Normally men acted for them, as alienators of land or as plaintiffs in court, or else they appeared alongside brothers or husbands. Their space was in general terms not the public world of law (they appear in it, in fact, hardly more often as independent actors than do the unfree, who at least sometimes appear in law courts to contest their status), but more the world of the household and the house. We do not have any sort of account of internal family relationships at the peasant level, but it is likely that women ran the peasant household commissariat, as we can show that peasant women did in later centuries and that women did at the aristocratic level already in the early Middle Ages. One indicator of this is that in the furnished burials of the sixth and seventh centuries, women are often buried with keys, which seem to represent their control over household money and supplies. We saw in Chapter 3 that the cliché of public roles for men, private roles for women did not fully describe the late Roman world; even in the early Middle Ages it is misleading unless it is properly understood, for many important economic roles were taken by women inside the household, weaving, certainly, and probably other artisanal activities as well (it is a case that has been put for household-level, unprofessional, pottery production, the kind that was normal in early Anglo-Saxon England, for example). But, that said, the public world was not for the most part very accessible to peasant women anywhere in the early Middle Ages. This marked a real change from late Rome.

The kings of early medieval Europe all saw themselves as drawing an element of their legitimacy from their links with the entire free (male) people of their kingdoms, seen in ethnic terms: free Lombards, Franks, West Saxons, men of Dál Ríata and so on. One result is that law codes deal with the whole free population, and often pay a good deal of attention to village-level, peasant society, as we see in the laws of Liutprand in Italy (dating from the years 713–35) or of Ine in Wessex (dating to *c.* 690), or the Frankish *Pactus Legis Salicae* (*c.* 510). These are not descriptions of those societies; as was argued in Chapter 1, royal legislation tells us almost nothing in this period except what was in the mind of the legislator, for, in relatively simple political systems like these, written law was seldom enforced in detail or even known about at the village level. Liutprand, at least, often responded to real cases that were presented to him for judgement, but the *Pactus* might be an entirely imaginative recreation of a peasant society in reality unlived by anybody, a Frankish ideal, as the mythical nature of its legislators indeed hints may be the case. All the same, that ideal reconstruction does at least tell us about expectations of peasant activity. An important law in the *Pactus Legis Salicae* is law 45, 'Concerning migrants', which envisages that any newcomer to a Frankish village (*villa*) could be vetoed by any current (free, male) inhabitant, as long as the latter could obtain the sworn support of ten other free males for an oath-swearing ceremony held three times in as many weeks: a substantial proportion of the village, then, not just a single person, but still a right of veto. Even though we have no account of such a procedure actually being carried out, and no idea how many Frankish villagers even thought that vetoes existed, we can at least conclude that the political culture of the Frankish kingdom assumed that local-level solidarity was coherent enough for such a process to be conceivable. This links back to the identity which is visible in 700 or so for villages like Gœrsdorf; but it also shows that at least some peasant-level protagonism was recognized as legitimate by legislators.

This recognized protagonism was also associated with the duty of free peasant males to attend law courts and to bear arms. The Lombards, Franks, etc. were *armed* peoples; the royal link to the free, associated with the public assemblies referred to in Chapter 4, was above all expressed in terms of justice and military service, always the key elements in any medieval political system. Law courts could be local, as we have seen for the Redon villages; it is unlikely that many peasants went to larger-scale, county-level, hearings, which were more the preserve of élite political communities. Whether many peasants really participated in warfare can also be doubted; armies in this period were generally small, up to 5,000 for the Merovingians and far less than that for the Anglo-Saxons, and could usually have been made up of aristocrats and their entourages, who were also, unlike peasants, trained to fight. We saw in Chapter 8 that the Northumbrian aristocrat Imma in the Mercia of 678 saved his life by claiming to be a peasant, who could therefore be presumed not to have taken part in the battle his army had lost. But it is nonetheless striking how consistently legislation assumes that everybody, including free peasants, was liable for military service – in Visigothic Spain in the 670s–680s, indeed, even some of the unfree were. This was partly a royal image: if you were free, you could and should fight, even if in practice you did not. It was also partly shorthand for wider public obligations. Under Charlemagne, men who had fewer than four tenant houses had to club together and send one of their number to fight, meaning that peasant cultivators would rarely go; conversely, those who did not fight did other public service, building roads or bridges or fortresses. But the existence of these assumptions also meant that if a peasant really did want to serve in the army, and had the money to buy a horse and a sword in order to do so, then such service was possible. Medium owners, in particular, could well have been able to fight as often as there was a war, which in some places (eighth-century Francia is the classic example) was every year.

This network of assumptions about public obligation also presumed that there were no sharp dividing-lines between the various social strata of free society. There was a legal break between unfree and free, but there was as yet no division between a free peasant and an aristocrat. The leaders of village society, if they joined the army, might end up the retainers of a powerful lord; consistent patronage or lucky marriages (or both) over a generation or two might allow them to be lords themselves, for there was no formalized boundary to cross. This must have been rare, but it was possible, and we find low-born bishops and even (but more rarely) counts in our sources on occasion, like Leudast of Tours (d. 583), about whom Gregory of Tours was so disdainful (see Chapter 5). 'Being aristocratic' was as yet a fairly informal affair; being close to kings (*Königsnähe*), holding office, controlling substantial lands, living a military lifestyle, were all necessary to a greater or a lesser degree, according to the time and the place, but people who satisfied local assumptions about aristocratic practice seem to have been more or less acceptable to other aristocrats (except to their enemies, at least, as Gregory was to Leudast) whatever their origin. This would not change until 1000 or so, and, when it did, society itself would change too, as we shall see in Chapter 21.

The early medieval peasantry, even if they were landowners, were circumscribed by their aristocratic neighbours, who were so much more wealthy and powerful than they, but in the last two millennia the period 500–800 was probably when aristocratic power in the West was least totalizing, and local autonomies were greatest – taking into account regional differences, as we have seen. This is one of the main markers of the specificity of the earliest Middle Ages. Another that has often been invoked by historians is a relatively low population, and a relative lack of control of the natural world. An image of the early Middle Ages as one of small groups, huddled together in tiny settlements, surrounded (menaced) by uncultivated woodland and waste, is still widely shared, even among professional historians and archaeologists. This wildness is certainly an exaggeration, however. Woods and pastures were not limitless; the Vosges forest did not extend to Gœrsdorf, and in England there was relatively little woodland at all. Even in what is now Germany, where there were great forests well into the modern period, these were for the most part exploited at least for timber and rough grazing (as well as hunting), already in our period, although it is certainly true to say that using – and clearing – woodland would be more systematic in later centuries, as we shall see in Chapter 22. Early medieval landscapes were less fully controlled than they would be after 1000 or so, but they were by no means wildernesses. Archaeology, too, shows that villages could be ordered. Regular sets of wooden buildings and outbuildings in courtyards are common in north European archaeology from Northumbria and Denmark to Bavaria, particularly from the seventh century onwards, and often before. Vorbasse in Jutland, Kootwijk in the Netherlands, Cowdery's Down in Hampshire, Lauchheim in Alemannia and Kirchheim in Bavaria are particularly well-studied examples (see below, Chapter 10). In southern Europe, village organization was regionally more variable and could be more fragmented, but there are even fewer signs that any part of the land was empty. Indeed, on the rare occasions when we can estimate the size of the population of individual villages in written sources, as in the polyptych of Saint-Germain, or when collective groups of villagers are listed in legal documents, squaring up to expansionist lords (there are examples from the ninth century or early tenth in both the Appennines and the Pyrenees), we can see that in some places early medieval settlement levels could match those of later centuries.

All the same, it would be wrong to leap from a catastrophist reading of the early medieval economy to too much of a continuitist one. It is likely that there was a population drop between the Roman empire and the earliest Middle Ages, not reversed until the tenth century or in some places even later. The density of archaeological sites falls in most places after the Roman period; in both northern France and eastern England, low plateau areas may have been left to pasture, with settlement and fields tending to concentrate in river valleys. Field surveys in other areas have often suffered because identifiable early medieval pottery (the standard marker of settlement in field archaeology) was less widely available or is less well known, but even the most generous interpretation of our Italian or Spanish evidence could not argue for settlement densities matching those of the Roman empire. Any quantification of this would be dangerous, but, overall, it is likely that the landscape was less intensely used in the earliest Middle Ages than either before or after, even if few zones saw any significant land abandonment. Why this population drop took place remains obscure. The early medieval bubonic plague epidemic, which began in the eastern Mediterranean in 541 and is attested in the West on several occasions in the late sixth and seventh centuries, is often invoked as a *deus ex machina* to explain it, along the lines of the Black Death of 1347–9. This argument relies, however, on some very literal readings of narrative texts, which tend to describe plague in apocalyptic terms. The plague existed, certainly, and killed people too, but neither the archaeology of Syria nor the documents of Egypt support a population collapse in the mid-sixth-century East. As for the West, if there was a population decline in northern France and England, it had already begun in the fifth century, far too early for the plague. Demographic drops do seem to coincide with periods of political crisis and a lessening of aristocratic power, however, and it is possible that a decreasing intensity of peasant subjection, together with a lessening concern for systematic estate management (something we shall return to later in this chapter), allowed for slow reductions in local populations. The slow demographic growth of the Carolingian period, conversely, went hand in hand with an increase in aristocratic landowning and in the intensity of exploitation of a tenant population. Rather than being a guide to the very early Middle Ages, in fact, the polyptych of Saint-Germain tells us most about that period of growth. We shall return to the economic system of the polyptychs in Chapter 22.

The early medieval period was also one in which exchange became much more localized. We have already observed that the fifth century saw the weakening of the great Mediterranean routes when the Vandals broke the Carthage–Rome tax spine in 439. These routes by no means vanished overnight, however. African olive oil and Red Slip fine pottery, both of which are easily identifiable archaeologically (the former because it was transported in amphorae), continued to be exported to Italy, southern Gaul and Spain; less went to Italy, but more is attested in Spain, at least at the outset. Nonetheless, across the sixth and seventh centuries African goods are less and less visible in the northern Mediterranean: they vanish first from inland sites, and then from minor coastal centres. By the late seventh century they are found only in major sites, Rome, Naples, Marseille; nor was this compensated for by the late sixth-century revival of exchange with the East, after the east Roman reconquest of Africa in 534. When, around 700, African productions stopped altogether, nothing replaced them in the western Mediterranean on that scale. What we find instead on the steadily increasing number of Mediterranean excavations are local products, of very variable quality and range of distribution. This variability is even more marked if we add the productions of northern Francia and Britain, which had been part of a separate exchange network focused on the Rhine army in the late empire. Let us look at this variability briefly, the simplest productions first, the most complex and wide-ranging last.

Early Anglo-Saxon England is the best-documented example of a really simple exchange system. Its archaeology shows us that all English pottery before around 720 was handmade, and mostly very locally produced, not necessarily by professional potters, and not even in kilns. Nor did the Anglo-Saxons import much wheel-turned pottery from the Continent (most of it is found in Kent). The frequent presence of weaving tools in house-compounds and female graves shows that cloth was made inside individual households, as well. Metalwork was perhaps not so localized – the brooches found in burials could have been transported over wider areas – but this, too, could have been the work of single travelling craftsmen, working to order in local communities. Little else seems to have been exchanged on more than the local level: a little amber, glass beads, the small-scale (and relatively inexpensive) luxuries of a peasant society. Only the relatively rich and powerful had access to more expensive luxuries, in worked and enamelled metal (including gold and silver) for instance, often bought from Francia, but often also made by dependent craftsmen in royal courts; slaves were part of this luxury network too, largely locally produced in the context of the inter-kingdom wars of the early Anglo-Saxon period (Imma was sold as a slave in London to a Frisian). It would be difficult, however, to say that England had much of a market economy before the eighth century; the huge bulk of production of artisanal goods was at the level of the single village. England can here stand for Wales, Scotland and Ireland, where much the same was true. These lands rarely made any pottery at all; they used wood, leather and iron instead, with equally localized production patterns. They imported some pottery from Francia, and, in the years around 500, occasionally even from the Mediterranean, but this was a high-status luxury, and there is, overall, even less evidence of such imports in western Britain and Ireland than there is in eastern England. Outside Britain and Ireland, we can find an equal simplicity in artisan production in northern Germany and Scandinavia, beyond the Roman frontier. Inside the former western empire, only parts of the Spanish Mediterranean coast show similar patterns so far; but more small areas with simple productive patterns are likely to appear, particularly in Spain, as archaeological work becomes denser.

More complex patterns of production and exchange are visible in the western Mediterranean. Here we find more professional types of artisan, almost always made on a wheel, in both fine and coarse (kitchenware) types; these ceramic types were often available across a city territory, and sometimes further afield, in distribution networks which must have been market-driven. We can see patterns of this kind in parts of southern Gaul, Lombard and Byzantine Italy, and at least some of Visigothic Spain. Gaul, Italy and Spain had in fact already in the late empire had productive systems of this type, alongside African imports. In the post-Roman period, these systems became rather more localized, but they survived when African imports dried up. After 700, Africa itself seems to have retained local productive systems of this kind as well. Ceramics are our best guide to the scale of these systems; but there are some signs that iron- and bronze-work was produced professionally at this local level as well – western Andalucía and Rome with its hinterland are two well-studied examples – and metal products of this kind seem to have been available across a wider geographical range than pottery. Italy and Spain contained networks of relatively localized economies in the late sixth to eighth centuries; every zone had a slightly different history, and clearly differentiated products. Some of these economic areas were larger-scale than others, too; Rome, in particular, seems in the eighth century to have been the focus for a much wider region than was normal by now in the western Mediterranean, covering much of the Tyrrhenian Sea: it imported wine from Calabria and Naples, oil-lamps from Sicily, and in the later eighth century developed a new glazed fine ware, now called Forum ware (it was first found by archaeologists in the Roman Forum), which would in the ninth century be available (in small quantities, at least) from Sicily to Provence. Rome was a big city by eighth-century standards, however, and had for long been a transport focus. The eighth century in the rest of the western Mediterranean, except the Adriatic, was pretty quiet, with almost no sign of any interregional trade except for luxuries. Marseille, the traditional entrepôt at the mouth of the Rhône for all traffic going from the Mediterranean north into what was by now the Frankish heartland, went into an eclipse at the beginning of the eighth century, and not even the luxury trade had much effect on it after that for some time. Localized production systems do not need such entrepôts, and it is this localization, even if at a decent quality of product, which marks the seventh and, even more, the eighth century in the western Mediterranean as a whole.

The largest-scale economy in the early medieval West was the Frankish heartland. Here the networks of late Roman ceramic productions, based on supplying the Rhine army but extending across the whole of northern Gaul, in the Argonne forest above Verdun for *terra sigillata* tableware, in the Mayen industrial kiln complex near Trier for coarse-ware containers and tableware, continued after the army vanished, a little reduced in scale but still available over wide areas. Argonne ware had gone by 600, and Merovingian carinated fine wares were generally made on a rather smaller scale, but the Badorf ware of the kiln sites near Cologne, which replaced them after 700, was a new centralized production which could be found throughout the middle and lower Rhine valley, and further afield, and Mayen ware continued to be available over similar areas without a break. We can add to this archaeological material a range of anecdotal documentation of what seems to be fairly large-scale exchange in letters, saints' lives and narratives. Among others, we have a bishop of Reims who writes to the bishop of Verdun in the 540s to ask about the price of pigs; Gregory of Tours who tells us that the merchants of Verdun set themselves up again after a period of trouble in the 530s with a loan of 7,000 *aurei* with interest from King Theudebert – he did not ask for it back, and in the 580s, Gregory says, the merchants were doing pretty well; a king (probably Sigibert III) who tries to stop the citizens of Cahors in the 630s or 640s from going to the fair at Rodez, 110 kilometres away, for fear of plague; the annual fair of Saint-Denis, for wine and other products, set up in the 630s and transferred to Paris as a going concern in the years before 709. Cologne, whose centre has been excavated, was a major metal manufacturing centre throughout the early Middle Ages; Paris was not only a fair but also had shops selling jewellery opposite Notre Dame in the 580s and quite a number of resident merchants who appear in documentary sources of various kinds. Northern Francia even had new towns, such as Maastricht, a seventh-century development with pottery-making, metalwork, bonework, and glass-making. An interlinked network of production extended all across the Seine–Rhine region, some of it very widely available, throughout the pre-Carolingian period. This network was destined to expand even further after 800, but it had active roots.

The core of the evidence presented here is the production and distribution of pottery, always the best evidenced product in archaeological excavations. Metal and also glass seem to have had similar patterns, generally showing distribution networks a little wider than those of ceramics, though they are less clearly visible (one can often tell from petrological analysis of potsherds where they came from; metal and glass are too often melted down for this to be possible, and we are reliant on stylistic analysis, which can be misleading, as there was much local copying of successful styles in our period). Cloth, the most important of all, is the great unknown out of such artisanal productions, for it so seldom survives on sites, but it would be reasonable to argue that the scale of its production often matched that of ceramics, and this seems relatively clear in England at least. These were the major artisanal products of the early Middle Ages, and they are the essential markers of economic complexity, along with more occasional agricultural specializations for sale, like the vineyards of northern Francia and also of parts of the south Italian coast. It is reasonably clear from this evidence that northern Francia had a much more complex and active exchange system than anywhere else in the West before 800, that the Mediterranean lands were more fragmented, with pockets of greater complexity and greater simplicity; and that Britain and the rest of the North was as a whole far simpler in exchange terms than almost anywhere further south. The difference between the two sides of the English Channel was particularly acute, and certainly not overcome by imports into England, which were anyway not so very numerous.

So far, no assumptions have been made here about what sort of exchange these patterns represented. As we saw in Chapter 2, the movement of goods in the Roman period was often the work of the state, taking taxes in food and artisanal products from one province to another, to feed the capitals and to feed and clothe the army. But even in the Roman period this was only one part of exchange, and commerce took other goods further, to cities and rural settlements whose supply was in no sense a fiscal concern. The state was much weaker in the post-Roman world, and one would not expect much of a tax-based movement of goods; an equivalent might be the movement of rents from one estate-centre to another, to feed landowners and kings who were located elsewhere, but the evidence we have for exchange, even in the relatively localized early Middle Ages, seems more capillary than that for the most part. With the exception of the luxuries on high-status sites, which were in some (not all) cases produced by subjected craftsmen, dependent on aristocrats and kings, most of the non-local goods found on archaeological sites were probably bought, and produced for sale. This does not mean, however, that aristocrats and kings were irrelevant to the networks that have been sketched out. Far from it: they were the most reliable buyers, for élites had large entourages who needed to be fed and clothed. The threefold division of the West just sketched out has an exact correlate in the differences in levels of aristocratic (and ecclesiastical, and royal) wealth described in earlier chapters and summarized at the start of this one: for Francia had the richest ruling class by far, and the societies of Britain and Ireland by far the least rich, with the different regions of Spain and Italy somewhere in the middle. A rich aristocracy went with an elaborate exchange system, and vice versa. When looking at the factors which underpinned the geographical range and complexity of exchange, the extent of aristocratic demand was the most important. Globally, we have also seen that aristocracies were less rich in the earliest Middle Ages than they had been under the empire (and, as we shall see in later chapters, than they would be later); globally, too, early medieval exchange was simpler than either before or after.

But the contrasts between the regions of the West were as significant as those global differences.

This account of the trends of early medieval exchange is different from that found in many books of the last seventy years. These took their cue from Henri Pirenne's *Mohammed and Charlemagne*, which first appeared in French in 1937. Pirenne argued for the survival of an essentially late Roman economy, focused on Mediterranean trade, even in Merovingian Francia, until the seventh-century Arab invasions, which broke the unity of the Mediterranean and forced the economies of Europe in on themselves until a commercial revival, this time centred on the North Sea, in the eleventh century. His theory was pre-archaeological, and so the evidence discussed here was simply not available to him; but, beyond that, his model had at least two serious flaws. The first was that it laid far too much stress on long-distance exchange, between the East (sometimes the Far East) and the West, which was always marginal to the main lines of trade; these latter operate above all inside regions or between neighbouring regions, and only very exceptionally extend beyond them (as with the African hegemony over the late Roman Mediterranean, which was, precisely, a product of the needs of an exceptionally powerful state). The second was that most of Pirenne's arguments concerned luxuries: the availability of gold, spices, silk and papyrus in the West (the last of these was certainly not a luxury in Egypt – it was an industrial product – but arguably had become so in the West by the seventh century). This was perhaps forgivable, as luxuries are almost all the examples of traded goods that are mentioned in early medieval written sources. But luxuries, too, are marginal to economic systems; they are defined by their high price and restricted availability, so that only the rich can possess them, and they therefore represent wealth, power and status. (The jewellery shops of Paris presumably sold exclusively to the rich; they certainly sold to Count Leudast, who was arrested and taken for execution while shopping there in 583.) The reason why they tend to be the products which most often appear in written sources is that these tell us about the rich; but they are the surface gloss on economic systems taken as a whole, which depend for their complexity on much more mundane products: clothes, knives, plates. Luxuries also exist in every economy, whether simple or complex – they were present in Ireland and Francia alike – so they are not much use as discriminators. Now, Pirenne was actually wrong to say that the

Arabs closed the Mediterranean; well before the Arabs arrived, the western part of the sea already had dramatically less shipping, as we have seen, and on the luxury level ships continued to link East and West even after the Arab conquests (spices were always accessible in the West, contrary to Pirenne's opinion). But even had he been right, the luxury level he was discussing was still marginal; the real economic changes were inside regions.

It is not easy to say who made profits from large-scale production in the early Middle Ages. The pottery industry of Mayen might have had a single owner (this is not very likely, unless it was the king, but it is not unimaginable); it might also have been a collection of autonomous potters and kiln-owners, turning out similar wares quasi-competitively. This latter pattern seems to be how it worked in contemporary Egypt, judging by sixth-century papyri, which show the rentals of individual workshops to potters and contracts between individual potters and landowners to supply wine amphorae; it seems to me the most plausible hypothesis in the West as well. But we cannot really be sure, for there are no documentary sources for places like Mayen. It is easier to see who made profits out of distribution, for we have quite a lot of references in narrative sources to merchants. They were often quite small operators, like the debt-ridden merchant Cosmas the Syrian whom Gregory the Great helped out in 594, but they could be both important and influential, like Priscus of Paris (d. 582), a Jewish confidant of King Chilperic, or Eusebius the Syrian, who bought the bishopric of Paris with his profits in 591. The most successful merchant of the period by far was Samo, a Frank who actually became king of the Wends in the 620s, and united the neighbouring tribes against King Dagobert I; he apparently reached this status by helping the Wends in war, so even when still a merchant he must have had a certain political visibility (there is no evidence, unfortunately, about what he traded).

These were independent operators, but merchants could also operate in groups. Examples include the eastern merchants who came to Mérida in the mid-sixth century bearing gifts for Bishop Paul, or indeed the mercantile consortium Samo began with before he struck out on his own. They were also often the employees of aristocrats, trading for the latter, presumably with goods from the latter's estates, like Jacob the Jew who sold cloth in Carthage in the 630s on behalf of a Constantinople notable, and who had the option of going on to Gaul; or the traders

acting for the monastery of Saint-Denis, who got a royal privilege from
Carloman II in 769 not to have to pay tolls on the rivers of Francia. But
it is unlikely that most merchants were regularly employees; any of them
could have been sometimes, but the markets and fairs of northern
Francia, in particular, seem to have been the focus of interest of too
wide a range of people for landowners' representatives to have been
more than a small part of their number. Some were 'Syrians', that is,
from the eastern Mediterranean, particularly in the sixth century; some
were Jews (though by no means all Jews were merchants); increasingly
after 600, many, particularly in Francia, were Frisians, from the Rhine
delta and the islands of the modern Netherlands; but merchants could
in reality come from anywhere. Unfortunately, we cannot link either the
origin or the economic scale of merchants to what kind of goods they
carried. Our documentary sources tell us most about luxuries, as already
noted; but it cannot be that most merchants concentrated on luxury
exchange – there was not enough of it for them, and anyway the bulk
goods discussed in earlier pages must have been bought and sold by
someone. A miracle-book by Wandalbert of Prüm, dating to 839,
describes one ship on the Rhine filled with pottery, and another with
wine sent for sale from the monastery of St Gereon in Cologne – the
former was wrecked, the latter saved from wreck, by the miraculous
power of St Goar. Historians have seized on these as examples of a more
normal pattern of trade than most sources give us, and rightly so. But
they remain anecdotal (as well as late, by the standards of this chapter);
our best source for what goods moved around is still archaeology.

We have seen that exchange across the Mediterranean slowly became
less complex in the sixth and seventh centuries, and that African exports
stopped by 700. In the eighth century only one important long-distance
Mediterranean route is documented at all, as Michael McCormick's
work makes clear, the route from Rome, around the south of Italy and
across into the Aegean, up to Constantinople. North-westwards from
Rome, a link still existed to Genoa and Marseille, but it is not well
documented either historically or archaeologically by now; the same is
true of the eastern extension, from the Aegean to Syria and Palestine.
The Anglo-Saxon pilgrim Willibald did get from England to Rome, and
to Jerusalem and back to Rome, in 721–9, but it was a major enterprise,
particularly once he got past the Aegean, and it occupies a large space
in Hugeburc's life of the eventual saint. Other routes did not appear at

all until after 750. Inland in Europe, the main routes were certainly rivers: the Rhine, important all through; the Seine and the Meuse, increasingly; the Rhône decreasingly. In the South, the Spanish rivers are less attested, and even the Po in northern Italy had as yet relatively little documented traffic; a trade treaty between King Liutprand and the men of Comacchio, an active port under Byzantine control in the Po delta, from 715 or 730, stresses salt more often than anything else, from the delta salt-pans. This would change, slowly, from the ninth century onwards. But this restriction of long-distance trade routes was only a marginal aspect of the history of exchange, which was overwhelmingly focused on buying and selling inside regions. The Rhine and the Meuse were important because they linked different zones of northern Francia together, not because they were the start of longer-distance routes out into the North Sea. These did exist, all the same, as we shall see at the end of the chapter.

Two other points need to be made about exchange. The first relates to money. All documented early medieval societies had standards of value, and these were almost all in coins (the exception was Ireland, where valuations were in slave women and cows). The Romans had minted a range of coins, in bronze, silver and gold, to aid tax-collection above all. Given the simpler fiscal systems of the post-Roman world, a complex set of coins might have been no longer seen as necessary, and the successor states certainly minted fewer types and on a smaller scale, after the Vandals and Ostrogoths at least, who followed Roman patterns. The Franks after 550, and the Visigoths and Lombards, minted gold coins above all (with silver coins alongside these in Provence and Lombard Italy). In Francia, where minting was especially decentralized (there were up to a thousand mints in Francia), the percentage of gold in these coins began to drop in the 630s–640s, and by about 675 coins had become entirely silver. Around 760 the Carolingians reformed the coinage, formally establishing the silver *denarius* as their currency, and they extended this single coinage to Lombard Italy in 781, after Charlemagne's conquest. The *denarius* dominated the next several centuries of western European coins. In England, debased gold coins had been minted since the early seventh century, and silver since the 670s; in the 760s these, too, were replaced by silver pennies that were parallel to those of the Carolingian monetary reform. These changes show, first, a narrowing of the range of coins minted; and secondly, a switch from gold to silver, which was complete in Latin Europe (apart from in the independent principality of Benevento, which remained closer to Byzantine traditions) by 800.

These changes are good guides to the simplification of state structures in the West, and also to the gradual lessening of the availability of gold, which was barely mined in Europe in this period. They do not tell us much about exchange, however. Historians traditionally put a great deal of weight on monetary issues, for it seemed to them that commerce was impossible without coins. This is not actually true; any merchant in a traditional society can cope with barter perfectly well as part of a bargaining process, as long as a common standard of value exists, and only an unsuccessful merchant will come away from a market with money rather than with goods to sell at the next market: coins themselves do not have to be involved in the process at all. It must also be noted that once the bronze or copper small change of the Roman empire was unavailable, almost all early medieval issues were fairly high-value: a Carolingian *denarius* was worth around £12 in the money of 2007 judging by the bread prices listed in the acts of the synod of Frankfurt in 794, and a Merovingian or Lombard gold *triens* or *tremissis* was nominally worth four times that, around £50. Only some Northumbrian and Italian issues seem to have been worth substantially less. Coins were thus in this period somewhat clumsy aids to exchange; they were standards of value for bargainers, and they were convenient ways of hoarding wealth, but they were not as yet the metonyms for commercial activity that they would later become. Coins do, on the other hand, if they are found in archaeological excavations, give us reliable guidance as to the geographical scale of economic networks, because where they were minted is normally made clear on the coin, and they can be fairly closely dated. These networks have not been studied as rigorously as one might have expected (the best distribution maps are currently for England), but broadly they seem at present to support the patterns, based on ceramics, already described. There is more work to do in this field, all the same.

The second point relates to gift exchange. Gift exchange is an alternative way of exchanging goods to commerce: it passes goods from person to person, but the purpose of this is to cement social relationships, not simply to allow each party to get what they really need, which they can do from a stranger as easily as they can from a friend. Indeed, gifts do

THE POST-ROMAN WEST, 550–750

not have to be essential items at all, as Christmas-present buying clearly shows. Exchanges of gifts (whether objects or services) were very common in the early Middle Ages. Embassies regularly took gifts with them, and kings could be quite competitive in their generosity to each other, sometimes taking pains to make points to the recipients. A letter of Cassiodorus concerning a water-clock that Theoderic the Ostrogoth gave to the Burgundian king Gundobad around 506 makes it clear that the gift was intended to show the superiority of Italian/Roman technology; so too, we can assume, was the mechanical organ given by the Byzantine emperor Constantine V to Pippin III of Francia in 757, which the Franks wrote up in chronicles. Kings gave gifts to their dependants, too, on a far richer scale than the dependants gave them in return, and part of the quid pro quo was personal loyalty; gifts of land, indeed, had the same assumption underlying them. Donors of land to the church, similarly, expected at least clerical or monastic prayers in return, and often made explicit that they hoped to be rewarded by going to heaven after their death. In England and Wales, giving a lavish feast might mean that the invited guests were expected to fight for their host, as we saw in Chapter 7. All personal relationships were sealed by gifts. They could also be ambiguous, just as personal relationships were, as when Bishop Praetextatus of Rouen, at his trial for treason to King Chilperic in 577, said that he had not bribed men to oppose Chilperic, but had simply given them gifts because they had already given him horses – the gifts (according to Praetextatus, at least) had a different meaning from what outside observers thought.

It was argued by Philip Grierson in 1959 and Georges Duby in 1973 that, in an early medieval economy relatively weak in commerce, much of the movement of goods visible in narrative sources and particularly archaeology could best be described in terms of gift exchange. The large Byzantine silver dish found in the Sutton Hoo burial of around 625, for example, was far more likely to have reached Suffolk as a result of diplomatic gifts, or of a chain of such gifts, than any sort of long-distance commerce. More generally, much luxury exchange could well have been in the form of gifts. But not all of it was – or else the West would not have needed merchants, or the Paris jewel shops; and, above all, none or almost none of the bulk exchange described here could have been restricted to the 'gift economy'. Some of the village-level exchange in places like England could well have been on the level of gift-giving, between people who, inevitably, knew each other very well. (By contrast, merchants were the object of suspicion, and laws survive from both England and Italy which aim to safeguard buyers from the accusation of buying stolen goods from merchants, as long as they bought in public.) But gifts, like luxuries, however central to *social* relationships, were marginal to economic systems taken as a whole, even in the early Middle Ages.

Production of artisanal goods simplified considerably almost everywhere in the post-Roman West, because large-scale demand dropped, as aristocrats became less rich and as states no longer bought goods on a huge scale for armies (or else took them in tax). It would follow that this was likely to be the case for agricultural production, too. The fragmentary signs that we have for the organization of estates in the earliest Middle Ages support that statement. Roman estate-management was very complex and variable, and at least some of it was visibly for profit, like the slave plantations of first-century Italy or the demesnes worked by wage labour in third- to seventh-century Egypt. Post-Roman estates seem, in all the documents we have, to have been worked essentially by tenants who, whether free or unfree, owed stable, customary, rents: the simplest and least flexible way of extracting surplus from cultivators, and the one which left most autonomy to the peasants themselves. This sort of management, which can be found in Francia and Italy, and also in central Spain (in the fragmentary accounts written on slate found in the provinces of Salamanca and Ávila), does not show any particular focus on profit, or sale. The only specializations we see are along the northern edge of wine production, from Paris to the middle Rhine, where in the seventh century there are casual documentary references to vineyards, sometimes run directly by the landowner with an unfree vinedresser: these could well have been for sale, to merchants from further north coming to fairs such as Saint-Denis. The rapid expansion of a more complicated – and exploitative – 'manorial' estate management would come later, in the Carolingian period essentially, in a period in which exchange became more generalized and intense, whether in regions like northern Francia where it was already relatively large-scale, or in northern Italy where it was more localized. We shall look at those forms of management in more detail in Chapter 22.

The earliest sign of that change in the North, at least, was however a little earlier, around 700, and I will end this chapter with it. In the seventh century, at least two Frankish channel ports appeared, Quentovic south of Boulogne and Dorestad in the Rhine delta. Both, particularly Dorestad (which has been excavated), expanded considerably in the eighth century, and they began in the decades around 700 to have equivalents on the other side of the channel, at Hamwic (now Southampton) in Wessex, London in Mercia, Ipswich in East Anglia, York in Northumbria – as well as Ribe in Denmark and Birka in Sweden. These *emporia*, as archaeologists call them (the word is sometimes used in early medieval sources too), were interconnected, and buying and selling across the English Channel and North Sea developed consistently in the eighth century and early ninth, when other such ports came onstream as well, such as Domburg in the Rhine delta and Hedeby on the Baltic coast of Denmark. Actually, in England at least, the greater part of the economic activity of such ports was the work of local artisans, the metalwork and glass of Hamwic or the pottery of Ipswich (the first kiln-fired and wheel-turned pottery of the Anglo-Saxon period); regional and local exchange mattered more than the traffic across the sea even here. But it is nonetheless significant that these *emporia* were on the coast, or on rivers with easy coastal access; whatever their origins (which were diverse), they were developed, almost certainly by kings, in order to funnel whatever maritime exchange there was. We have a letter from Charlemagne to Offa in 796 which makes reference to the size of the cloaks that the Anglo-Saxons were exporting to Francia; there are almost no other diplomatic letters mentioning commerce in this period, and it must have been significant (at least as a political initiative; we cannot say on what scale it was operating). Kings valued maritime trade, and helped it on. And as the Carolingians took power in the eighth century and recentralized Frankish politics, they could give a powerful impulse to trading *emporia*.

The North Sea in the eighth century almost certainly had more shipping than the Mediterranean. Comacchio in the Po delta was a focus of Adriatic-wide exchange in this period, as well as some exchange up the Po, as we have seen; but there are no equivalents to the nodal ports of the North in the Mediterranean between the decline of Marseille around 700 and the rise of Venice after around 780. As we shall see in Chapter 22, Venice was a centre for the slave trade, channelling slaves, created by the Carolingian wars, to the Arabs for domestic service, and getting spices and other eastern luxuries in return. Venice was, that is to say, a gateway port which based its wealth on luxuries directed to Frankish and other buyers, and was probably as yet even more marginal to the economy of northern Italy than Dorestad was for northern Francia and Hamwic was for Wessex. But things were changing here; more ports would appear in Italy in the ninth century, and Venice would eventually, after 950 or so, develop more of a relationship with its hinterland, too. There was, in the end, more scope for the development of commerce in the Mediterranean than in the North Sea after 800 (see Chapter 15). The Mediterranean connected several complex economies, which after the pause of the eighth century would rediscover the advantages of at least limited levels of exchange. The problem of the North Sea was that, even though the Frankish economy was so active, those of its neighbours were not. It was important for the Anglo-Saxons or Danes to get Frankish goods, as luxuries for the most part, but their élites were not yet rich enough to be able to buy all that many of them. Nor were the economies of the North very diversified; Hamwic's artisanal products resemble those of Maastricht and Dorestad in their range, and could not easily have been intended for sale outside Wessex. Economic specialization and diversification would slowly develop in later centuries; but the North Sea trade of the eighth century was more a spin-off of Carolingian wealth and political influence than a sign of the future economic dominance of north-west Europe.

10

The Power of the Visual: Material Culture and Display from Imperial Rome to the Carolingians

Easily the largest single roofed building of the Roman empire, and larger than any subsequent building in Europe until Seville and Cologne cathedrals in the thirteenth century, was Justinian's Great Church in Constantinople, dedicated to the Holy Wisdom (Hagia Sophia). It was built in under six years after a fire damaged the city's earlier cathedral during the Nika riots of 532, and was dedicated in December 537: an unheard-of speed, then or later, for such an ambitious building. It was, all the same, built with considerable care, from the best materials, and has lasted little changed until the present day; the most significant modification was early, for the dome partly collapsed after an earthquake in 557 and was rebuilt, slightly higher, in the next years, allowing a rededication in 562, when Justinian was still alive. Subsequent emperors only tinkered with the building, for example adding a ceremonial door on the south-west porch (the work of Theophilos around 840), or else, later, adding external buttresses (Andronikos II in the 1310s and Sinan in the 1570s for the Ottomans; the Ottomans also added minarets for the Aya Sofya mosque that the church had become). The interior space remained the same, however; the only major Byzantine change here was the addition of figural decoration in the mosaics covering roof and upper walls, from the ninth century onwards, for Justinian's decorative programme had above all been gold mosaic, sometimes interrupted by crosses or floral motifs, and coloured marble.

Hagia Sophia from the outside looks like a giant brooding spider, thanks to the Ottoman minarets. Inside, its central space shows itself at once as the major architectural innovation it was, with its great dome, 100 Roman/Byzantine feet (31 metres) across, balanced on four arches each 120 feet (37 metres) high, creating an unparalleled single volume, unbroken by pillars, which was further extended to the east and west by half-domes and then, to the east, a smaller half-domed apse. The whole is stamped with Justinian's identity, for very many of the capitals have his monogram on, or else that of his wife Theodora. Most of the columns and all the capitals were cut especially for the building, unusually for the late Roman empire, where the reuse of building material was normal even for major monuments. Justinian intended the building to be innovative; he employed academic geometricians, Anthemios of Tralles and Isidore of Miletos, to build it, not, as was normal, master-builders. And people were duly amazed. In the context of the second dedication of the church, Paul the Silentiary wrote a verse description of it, which as a work dedicated to a single construction is unusual in our period, and a decade earlier, Prokopios' *On Buildings*, written to praise all of Justinian's building projects, starts off with an eleven-page eulogy to Hagia Sophia. Both writers stress its size, of course, and the effect of the gold and marble (the green marble was a meadow with flowers to Prokopios, fresh green hills and vines to Paul), particularly given the relationship between the gold of the roof and the light from the windows. 'Whoever lifts his eyes to the beautiful firmament of the roof can scarcely keep them on its rounded expanse, sprinkled with dancing stars . . . whoever puts foot inside the sacred temple would never wish to leave, but would lift up his head and, with his eyes drawn first this way and then that way, would gaze around' (Paul). And Prokopios was also well aware of the building's architectural originality, for he spends two pages describing the dome-work with considerable technical detail, ending up by pre-echoing Paul with the observation – a cliché, but still true today – that it is hard to concentrate on one detail, given the arresting complexity of the whole. These descriptive works had their own literary tradition (artistic and architectural descriptions are called *ekphraseis* in Greek), and they were, furthermore, commissioned by or at least written for Justinian himself, but they at least tell us how the building was intended to be seen, the impact it was intended to have. It was an impact that lasted; Hagia Sophia was almost the first rectangular church focused on a central dome, but almost all later Byzantine churches used this model, in a simpler version at least, and so did Sinan's mosques for sixteenth-century Istanbul.

Hagia Sophia was not just a huge, expensive and innovative building, one of many which Justinian erected, as Prokopios tells us at length. It also sat at the apex of the ceremonial life of the east Roman empire. In

Rome itself, the new churches of the Christian empire were built outside
the walls or on the edge of town for a long time, decentring the old
public focus of the forum complexes, the imperial palace on the Palatine
hill above them, and the great racecourse, the Circus Maximus, to the
latter's south. In Constantinople, Constantine's new foundation, these
public spaces could be and were put together, with the forums leading
in a line along wide colonnaded streets to the Great Church, and the
palace and the Hippodrome just to its south. The people of the city
regularly met in the Hippodrome, and, although access to the church
was often more restricted, many thousands could get into Hagia Sophia.
The ceremonial of imperial life had as its centre movements between the
palace and the church, which were watched by an audience, and public
processions regularly proceeded through the forums to the church–
palace, attended by even more spectators. The church that was there
before 532 was already large for these same reasons, but the size and
ambition of Justinian's church set his own mark on the entire public and
ceremonial space of the largest city in Europe, for close on a millennium.
Justinian's church was remembered by later generations in the same
breath as his legal codifications and his conquests, and if there is one
act which sums up his desire to be recognized as the ideal or archetypal
Roman emperor, Hagia Sophia could be seen as that.

This might seem a lot of weight to put on a single building, but the
Romans intended their constructions to be seen as representative of their
power and wealth, and, judging by the numerous reactions we have in
written texts, they indeed were so. People could build buildings with
quite complex inter-textual references, too; in Hagia Sophia's case, the
rotunda of the Pantheon in Rome, or that of Galerius' palace at Thessaloniki, were models to be surpassed, as also was the private church
of Hagios Polyeuktos, built on a huge scale in Constantinople only a
decade before by the imperial heiress Anicia Juliana, this time in a more
conventional basilica form, which Hagia Sophia could displace simply
by being so different. The force of the politics of building was not
restricted to the Roman empire, either. All the societies described in this
book recognized it and respected it, in fact; and the differences between
the buildings which powerful people erected in those different societies
is one quick way to understand the variation in their aspirations, both
in their scale and in their aesthetics.

This central chapter, accordingly, is intended to be comparative. It sets societies against each other through their different uses of material culture, particularly architecture, for the purpose of display. We seldom have as clear an idea of the intentions of the patrons of a building as we have for Hagia Sophia, thanks to Prokopios and Paul the Silentiary; but we do have many of the buildings themselves, or at least their archaeological vestiges, and we can reconstruct some of these intentions. I cannot do justice to all the societies in this book in a single chapter, of course, but I can at least give a sample of the sort of comparative analysis of display that can be achieved. We shall look in turn at four buildings: Hagia Sophia, already discussed; the Great Mosque of Damascus; the Northumbrian palace complex of Yeavering; and the church of S. Prassede in ninth-century Rome. These buildings are mostly religious, for the survival of secular buildings is much more patchy (Yeavering, indeed, only survives as a set of post-holes), but at the end of the chapter we shall look briefly at the varying structures of royal palaces, and also – outside the restricted world of kings, emperors and bishops – at the changing spatial patterns of villages, for these too are a guide to power, on a smaller scale.

Caliph al-Walid I (705–15) had the Great Mosque built in his capital at Damascus in 705–16, finished after his death. It was not the first mosque in the territory of the caliphate, most of which had been conquered by the Arabs sixty to seventy years before, between 636 and 651; but, together with contemporary constructions in Medina and Jerusalem, it was the first large-scale monumental mosque, and it set a pattern which would be largely repeated in subsequent building projects, in Fustat (Old Cairo), Kairouan, Córdoba and many other cities. Mosque architecture used many elements of Roman (and also, in Iraq and Iran, Sassanian) architectural style, including colonnades; indeed, the columns were for a long time characteristically *spolia*, taken from Roman buildings and reused. The Damascus mosque also had a marble vine-frieze, much praised by medieval writers, which has clear Constantinopolitan antecedents. But the overall effect of an early medieval mosque was quite different from that of any Roman building. It consisted of a walled rectangular courtyard, part of which was open to the sky and part roofed, the latter making up a deep space held up by lines of columns. Sometimes the roofed space was quite small by comparison with the courtyard; sometimes (as at Damascus) it was around the same size, with three lines of columns in that case. (The famous forest of columns in the later Córdoba mosque, with thirty-four lines of eighteen columns in its last phase, is atypical.) The effect was, however, of a relatively unhierarchical space, the open courtyard running into the roofed area without a complete break, with only the mihrab, a niche pointing towards Mecca, operating as a focus. Islam is not a religion with an organized priesthood, and it puts great emphasis on a community of believers. Inside the courtyard, opened and roofed alike, the community could meet in prayer.

The Damascus mosque also had a specific political and spatial symbolism, by no means only directed to Muslims. For a start, al-Walid built it on top of the demolished cathedral of the city, which still had a Christian majority, in a particularly overt assertion of Muslim supremacy. This formed part of the monumental rhetoric he inherited from his father 'Abd al-Malik (685–705), who was, as we shall see in Chapter 12, the first caliph to publicize Islam on a large scale in material form, in coins and monumental buildings; al-Walid simply developed it further, including by bringing it to the capital itself, right at the start of his reign. Like Hagia Sophia, the Great Mosque is very large, with a courtyard 157 by 100 metres in size, and was hugely and visibly expensive. The courtyard used the walls of the precinct of the pagan Roman temple of Jupiter, which the Christians had already left around their cathedral, but that enclosure was now turned into a specific walled-off Muslim religious and political space, reserved for the new Arab ruling class of Damascus. The walled courtyard constituted a typical element of the mosque for ever after. Al-Walid put four minarets at its corners, perhaps to show to all that the old Roman space had a new function; but this was the only important feature of the mosque not to have a later history, for a single tall minaret is characteristic of most later major mosques.

The effect of the Great Mosque was not, however, restricted to its scale and to its appropriation of a former sacred site. Al-Walid had the monumental upper parts of his roofed space, looking out onto the open courtyard, covered in mosaics, probably the work of Byzantine mosaicists; mosaics also covered much of the walls of the roofed space, and the other walls of the courtyard. Sections of these survive; they consist of trees and foliage, interspersed on the courtyard walls with buildings and a river – paradise imagery in all likelihood – of remarkably high quality, but with no representations of humans or animals. This marks out a new style of visual programme. Mosaic decoration was normally figurative in the Roman world, in public buildings and churches alike (Hagia Sophia was atypical in this respect), and vegetation was at best used as a background, or as a divider between scenes. Here, the caliph was making very obvious indeed the fact that the new Islamic religion was beginning to avoid human representation in public spaces (it matched the new coinage developed under 'Abd al-Malik, too, which abruptly abandoned pictures of caliphs in 696). The importance which representation came to have in both the caliphate and the Byzantine empire will be looked at again in the next two chapters; but the Great Mosque is one of its earliest signs.

The other important feature of the Great Mosque was that, as a space, it was closed off to the outside. Roman cities were structured by wide streets leading to central forum areas, to which processions led and where public participation could be considerable, as continued to be the case in Constantinople for centuries. Amphitheatres (in the West), theatres and racetracks were other major venues for public activity, and the Hippodrome of Constantinople carried on this tradition for a long time. In the Islamic world, the mosque courtyard took over from all of these; major political events, like collective oaths of loyalty, took place there, not in any secular location. And the Arab states did not use processions as a major part of their political legitimization; the assembly in the mosque courtyard was sufficient for that. The need for wide boulevards ended; pre-Islamic Syrian and Palestinian colonnades were quite quickly filled in with shops in the eighth century, some of them commissioned as public amenities by caliphs. The narrow streets of Islamic cities resulted directly from this, for there was no public interest involved in keeping them clear from obstructions like vendors' stalls, beyond a certain minimum (enough for two loaded pack animals to pass each other, later jurists said). Public display came to be focused on the mosque, and, secondarily, rulers' palaces and city gates, rather than on the cityscape as a whole. The impact of al-Walid's mosaics would have been all the greater as a result, although that would be a future development, only set in motion in the eighth century. The caliph and his advisers were nonetheless making a set of conscious symbolic and political points by organizing the Great Mosque as they did; and the way the public space in Islamic cities changed, to focus so exclusively on mosques, although less conscious as a process, would have seemed to them auspicious and fitting. In a time when the population of Syria was still mostly Christian, and Greek- or Syriac-speaking, these changes were also probably the most immediate signs they had of the content of the Muslim religion of their new rulers.

At the other end of the former Roman world, in the Cheviot hills of Bernicia (now Northumberland) just south of the modern Scottish border, King Edwin (616–33) of Northumbria had a court (*villa*) called, according to Bede, Ad Gefrin. There is no serious doubt that this *villa* was at Yeavering, where in 1949 air photography allowed the localization of a complex Anglo-Saxon site, which was excavated in the 1950s and published in 1977. This site had lost its topsoil and floor levels, and with them most of the small finds one would normally expect, though it has to be said that the site was, even then, unusually poor in finds for such an important centre, which underlines how limited the resources of early Anglo-Saxon kings were. But in compensation the post-hole foundations of a variety of wooden buildings were identified, which show us a much more elaborate picture of an early Anglo-Saxon palace complex than researchers had previously expected.

Literary images of royal palaces in Old English texts concentrate on a single wooden hall, like Heorot in *Beowulf*, where kings and their retainers met, feasted and slept. Yeavering was both less and more than that. In the late sixth century the Anglo-Saxons had found an earlier stone circle, a Bronze Age barrow, and a large fortified enclosure, some of which seems to have made up a British cult-site. This was further developed by pagan Anglo-Saxons, with small buildings which may have been temples. In the middle of the site, around 600 or so, a building unparalleled in Anglo-Saxon England was set up, consisting of a dais and banked seats looking down on it, 20 metres from front to back, the whole looking in plan (all that survives of it) like the cross-section of an orange segment. This construction most resembles a section of a Roman theatre, imitated in wood, and its parallels are firmly Roman. It is generally and convincingly interpreted as an assembly point for the Bernician, and later Northumbrian, aristocracy when they and the king came to the Yeavering cult-site. A few years later, the site turned into a more typical palace complex as well, with the construction of a line of large halls, some 70 metres long in total, pointing straight at the apex of the 'theatre'. This was the setting for a set piece of Christian conversion and baptism in the 620s by Paulinus, an early missionary to Northumbria, which explains Bede's references to Ad Gefrin. In these halls, which were occupied until around 650, Edwin could easily have lived the sort of life described in *Beowulf* and similar literature; but they were surrounded by a network of earlier architectural representations looking in other directions too.

The pre-Christian Anglo-Saxons settled in a British landscape, but took relatively little from their predecessors and neighbours by way of material culture, even though the British were overwhelmingly dominant numerically. Yeavering was right at the edge of a relatively narrow Anglo-Saxon coastal settlement around the Bernician royal centre of Bamburgh; it may not be so surprising that we find here one of the few documented examples of a British site (and British religious practices, maybe also pagan in this area, north of Hadrian's Wall as it was) having a cultural influence on an Anglo-Saxon one. But, given that, the 'theatre' is all the more striking. We are not so far from the wall here, and Roman material culture was thus at least physically available to the Bernicians; but for Anglo-Saxons living north of the Roman province of *Britannia* deliberately to adopt a Roman-influenced construction for something as emblematically Anglo-Saxon as a public assembly point sheds considerable light on royal aspirations, particularly because it seems to predate Christianization, which would make Roman influences more obviously culturally attractive. Indeed, this may go some way to explaining the readiness of Anglo-Saxon rulers to be converted relatively quickly. And that Roman imagery presumably made sense to an aristocratic and possibly also popular audience too. The early Anglo-Saxons are sometimes depicted as finding the Roman past incomprehensibly grandiose, as in the Old English poem *The Ruin*, plausibly about Bath, which refers to the Roman buildings of a city as 'the work of giants'. However that may be, they could deal with elements of that past with the same sort of creative and expressive bricolage that we find in Arab Syria. Cosy primitivist readings of Anglo-Saxon 'barbarism' are out of place here. The early Anglo-Saxons did not have access to a technologically complex material culture, but despite this the culture they did have could be manipulated in complex ways, with images of legitimacy taken from Anglo-Saxon, Roman and non-Roman British culture all at once.

For our next example, let us move to the Rome of the Carolingian period, by which time the Franks ruled most of western Europe, including a protectorate over the papal city. We shall look here at the building programme of Pope Paschal I (817-24), which was very extensive for what was not a very long reign. Paschal was a controversial pope, who built up an influential set of aristocratic enemies. Although his enemies could draw on Carolingian support, in 823 Paschal had several of them executed, and fiercely defended the executions to Carolingian emissaries. He was not afraid of much, it seems, and his church-building, which includes two of the three largest churches in Rome built between the sixth century and the twelfth, testifies to his confidence. I shall focus here on the earliest and best-surviving of them, S. Prassede, built around 820.

Paschal was not the first builder-pope of the late eighth and ninth centuries. There was probably no break in papal building in the early Middle Ages (and there was certainly no break in reconstruction and repair), but our sources, both written and material, concur that there was more new church construction than before, from S. Silvestro of Paul I (757-67) and SS. Nereo e Achilleo of Hadrian I (772-95) onwards, up to the 850s at least. These churches were all built on a standard basilica plan, looking directly to the great church of St Peter's in the Vatican, originally founded by Constantine; they constituted a self-representation of the unbroken continuity of papal legitimacy and centrality. In three churches, S. Prassede, S. Cecilia and S. Maria in Domnica, Paschal simply did this on a rather larger scale. S. Prassede, some 50 metres long excluding its courtyard, has expensive internal finishings, such as good-quality reused columns and a good deal of marble, some of which is still *in situ*; it also had a remarkable quantity of gold and silver furnishings, as the near-contemporary biography of Paschal in the *Liber Pontificalis* informs us, including a silver canopy weighing 910 pounds, and a silver image of St Praxedis herself on her coffin in the crypt, weighing 99 pounds. The eye is caught today by the dramatic quality of the mosaics in the apse and triumphal arch, and in the side chapel of S. Zenone, a burial chapel for Paschal's mother, Theodora. The apse mosaics, of the risen Christ and associated saints (including Praxedis), with a portrait representation of the pope, copy those of the sixth-century church of SS. Cosma e Damiano in the forum, built by Felix IV (526-30), and are a further sign of Paschal's concern to show himself as part of an unbroken papal tradition. It is worth

THE POWER OF THE VISUAL

remembering, however, that the *Liber Pontificalis*, while mentioning the mosaics, puts rather more stress on Paschal's gold and silver gifts, and also on the pope's clearest innovation in S. Prassede, the moving of a large quantity of saints' bodies from Rome's catacombs to the church, which a contemporary inscription claims to have numbered 2,300 in total.

Paschal had a variety of audiences – one could well say targets – for his activities in S. Prassede. One was the Byzantine emperors, who in 815 had readopted Iconoclasm, a hostility to holy images of God and the saints (on which more in the next chapter) which the pope was in the front line of opposition to. Paschal wrote critical letters to Constantinople about it, and sheltered Iconophile monks in Rome; S. Prassede indeed was endowed with a community of Greek monks, who must have been part of the Iconophile observance. In the context of the material culture of the church, the numerous mosaic figures in S. Prassede's apse were too traditional a set of motifs for their detail to be a specific response to Iconoclasm, but the expense of Praxedis's silver image is quite likely to have been. It must be added that Paschal here could well have had an eye on Frankish Iconoclasts too (see Chapter 17). Only fifteen years before, Theodulf of Orléans (d. *c.* 826) had constructed his intriguing and unique monument to his Iconoclast beliefs, the private chapel at Germigny-des-Prés on the Loire, whose apse mosaics show two angels (not human, so acceptable to represent) and the ark of the covenant. These representations were a polemical response to some of the arguments of Byzantine Iconophiles, and had a complex relationship to Old Testament interpretation, as much of Theodulf's own writings had; they thus show how theological positions could have quite a detailed effect on western visual imagery in this period. Paschal is unlikely to have known about Theodulf's chapel (and his Roman audience is unlikely to have heard of Theodulf at all), but he knew of Frankish Iconoclast sympathizers such as Claudius of Turin, and he opposed them explicitly; S. Prassede could at least serve as a visual reassertion of the centrality of Roman and papal traditions and the superiority of papal positions on the matter of religious belief. Paschal's buildings responded to a network of contestations of papal positions simply by, so to speak, repeating themselves, but louder.

Paschal had two other audiences for his building campaigns. One was the Frankish court itself, to whose power in Rome he was perhaps the firmest opponent in the Carolingian period. There were always Franks in Rome by now, as pilgrims (as we saw in Chapter 8), but also, at the political level, as emissaries and dealers; they were expected to see what the pope was doing, and to report it back northwards. They would have reported that Paschal's churches were not just larger and pricier than those of his predecessors, but were as large as those of the Carolingians themselves; and they challenged monuments like the octagonal royal chapel in the palace at Aachen by, once again, their traditionalism – Rome had no need of Carolingian protagonism, including its moral reform programme; it was simply itself, and could carry on as before.

The other audience was the Romans themselves. Paschal was like Justinian and al-Walid in building big to impress a local audience, the people who would be inside or near S. Prassede most often; the church was indeed on one of the major processional routes of the city, leading out over the Esquiline hill to the basilica of S. Lorenzo fuori le mura. All the major popes of the century after Paul I were builders, indeed, and it is arguable that it was their collective intervention, above all in church-building, that did most to make Rome into the 'papal city' that it remained for the next millennium. But it is Paschal's appropriation of so many relics which marks his position most clearly here. Rome had a highly dispersed array of cult-sites, scattered across the huge field of ruins that the city had become, and based on the burial places of numerous martyrs and other prominent Christians of the pre-Constantinian period; they extended, in particular, way out into the countryside in Rome's extramural cemeteries. These were hard for popes to protect, as Paul I already recognized (he imported several saints into papal churches inside the walls after Lombard attacks); this became all the more pressing in the early ninth century, given a growing Frankish obsession with Roman relics, which by the 820s extended to outright theft (below, Chapter 17). The sites were also hard for popes to control politically; the churches associated with these scattered cults had local communities and aristocratic families as patrons, quite as much as they were under papal patronage. To empty them of 2,300 saints, who were to be transported to a new papal prestige foundation, was thus a notably authoritarian move. It cannot have contributed to Paschal's popularity, which as we have seen led to contestation in 823 by some of the aristocratic officials of the papal hierarchy; but it was certainly an assertion of his

power – and anyway he had defeated his opponents before he unexpectedly died in 824.

Aachen was only the biggest of a long sequence of Merovingian, Carolingian, Ottonian palaces across the centuries in the Frankish world. Most
of the others do not survive, and have not even been excavated (exceptions include the Merovingian Malay and the Ottonian Tilleda, both
fairly small, and some rather grander complexes, such as Carolingian
Ingelheim and Compiègne, and Ottonian Paderborn); but they are
described occasionally in detail, in written texts.

Palaces were long-standing sites of royal or imperial rhetoric, aimed
to impress both royal subjects and ambassadors or other visitors from
outside. Even in societies where kings lived in single wooden halls, these
were seen as remarkable, 'greater than the children of men had ever
heard tell of', as the *Beowulf* poet said of Heorot, and acting as
metonyms for the fate of the kingdom itself, as with Cynddylan's hall,
'dark tonight, without a fire, without a bed', as a ninth-century poet
wrote of an eastern Welsh king after his death in battle. They were
barred by élite guards who would only let in appropriate people, as with
Hrothgar's court-officer Wulfgar in *Beowulf*, or Arthur's door-keeper
Glewlwyd in *Culhwch ac Olwen*, a Welsh text of the eleventh century;
this added to the honour involved in entering them and participating in
the *Königsnähe* ('closeness to the king') inside. These are heroic texts,
in which everything and everyone is larger than life; the east Roman
ambassador Priskos was less amazed at Attila's very similar palace
complex in 449. But he describes it neutrally and with respect, as a
splendid hall made of planed wood, surrounded by other buildings,
including dining halls and colonnades, some carved and well constructed, the whole in a wooden enclosure with towers, 'with an eye not
to security but to elegance'. The furnishings inside, in Attila's case in
linen and wool, and multi-coloured hangings 'like those which the
Greeks and Romans prepare for weddings', were also designed for effect.
Yeavering probably had this sort of impact, too, on a smaller scale,
which would have been all the greater for visitors from smaller centres
than Constantinople.

Frankish royal palaces, or at least the major ones, were more complicated than this. Carolingian Ingelheim consisted of a set of large rooms
(including a royal hall) built in stone, arrayed around a substantial apsed

and colonnaded courtyard, 100 by 70 metres in size, some of which still stands. This was also (apart from the apse form) the case in Aachen, where the scale was larger. This can still be seen from one part of it, the palace chapel, with its internal marbling, nineteenth-century replacements for its rich mosaics and a throne standing in the gallery. The numerous rooms in these palaces, which visitors had to pass through, were doubtless set out for effect. Merovingian sources already make this clear, as when Duke Rauching was shown into King Childebert's private chamber, probably in Metz, in order to be killed in 589 (as described in Chapter 5). But it is Carolingian sources which stress most clearly the intricacy of royal or imperial display. Ingelheim in the 820s was described in a poem as having 'a hundred columns, with many sorts of buildings, a thousand entrances and exits and a thousand inner chambers', as well as having an elaborate painted programme in the church drawn from the Bible, and an even more striking decorative programme in secular areas of the palace, featuring classical heroes and Christian Roman emperors, and leading up to narrative scenes featuring Charles Martel, Pippin III and Charlemagne himself. Notker of St. Gallen, in his *Deeds of Charlemagne* of the 880s, imagines a fantastic story in which Byzantine ambassadors to Charlemagne come into the palace (which palace, Notker does not say), and go through groups of nobles, four times convinced that the central figure must be grand enough to be Charlemagne – one is on a throne, another is in the emperor's private apartments – before they are finally ushered into a separate room, and into the presence of Charlemagne, clad in gold and jewels and glittering like the sun. Notker never went to court, but he had talked at length to senior courtiers, and his image of the spatial complexity of the court rings true, given what we know of the big Carolingian palaces. It may be added that the material culture of display was here focused as much on the dress of human beings as on the walls of the palace (Priskos noted the same of Attila's residence); but if Ingelheim was typical in its decoration, the walls all conveyed meaning too.

Palaces competed in order to impress. The Franks could not match the display of Constantinople, where Liutprand of Cremona, envoy for King Berengar II of Italy in 949, was so struck by the mechanical singing-birds and the mechanical lift under the throne of the Magnaura palace only one of many buildings in the palace complex. But inside the material cultural possibilities of Latin Europe, visiting Carolingian

Aachen and Ingelheim was as complicated and overwhelming an experience as anything available. Notker also claimed that the 'ever-vigilant' Charlemagne could look down from the windows of his chamber at everyone in the palace, including at what was happening in the houses of his aristocrats, so as to see 'everything they were doing, and all their comings and goings'. This precursor of Jeremy Bentham's (and Michel Foucault's) panopticon, even though once again doubtless an imaginative flourish on Notker's part, shows the degree to which such palaces were expected, in all their complexity, to be under the direct control of the king/emperor as well. For that complexity itself made royal power visible, and therefore had to reflect, at least ideally, the concrete operation of that power, that is, knowledge, and, when necessary, coercion based on that knowledge.

Our evidence for village layouts is entirely archaeological, and here I can only discuss a few examples out of a hundred or more. They do not tend to demonstrate any conscious planning, and were built up out of individual farm units, by the peasants themselves. The way this build-up occurred varied from region to region, however, and also across time; it demonstrates changes in sociability, sometimes in village-level competitiveness, and in village hierarchies. In particular, in the last third of our period, the growing internal hierarchies of western European village society began to take material form.

In the western Roman empire, villages were relatively rare. The rural landscape was certainly hierarchical, with the villas of landowners operating as estate-centres for a dependent population, and indeed often acting as highly ambitious monumental complexes, designed to impress aristocratic peers; but the peasant majority in most areas lived in houses scattered across the landscape, without any obvious sociability. One has to move to the East to find nucleated village complexes, and some very striking ones still survive in the landscape, particularly in southern Anatolia, Syria and Palestine. The villages of the north Syrian Limestone Massif, rich from oil export, and lucky in their long-lasting and easy-to-carve stone materials, are the best-surviving of this set, and have been the most systematically studied. The village of Serjilla, for example, is a complex of a church, a community building, a bath-house, and nearly twenty houses, some still with a second storey and a roof, each in its own courtyard, in no obvious spatial order. The houses vary in their scale, most of them having four rooms or less, but some with substantial extensions; they have similar decoration, with regular (if severe) carved surrounds to doors and windows, and quite elaborate roof pediments, but they vary here too; many, for example, have internal colonnades. Building size may indicate family size, but it indicates resources too; architectural elaboration indicates ambition. So also does the village bath complex – a relatively unusual amenity for a village – which was put up in 473 by Julian and Domna, as a mosaic inscription tells us. There is no sign, all the same, that the inhabitants of Serjilla were anything other than peasants (or stone-workers); no house is typologically distinct, as would befit a residence or rent-collection centre for a landlord. But they must have been remarkably prosperous as a group, some of them doubtless with a few tenants of their own (Julian and Domna for example), and also mutually competitive on a substantial scale, above all at the height of Syrian oil production in the fourth to sixth centuries. For once, the density of surviving housing in the Limestone Massif allows us to track that competition through display in some detail. When we have written accounts of eastern village societies, they often appear as very fractious; the buildings of villages like Serjilla allow us to trace that tension on the ground. But the absence of a clearly marked élite housing is all the more striking. It may indeed have made the fractiousness much worse, for society was not formally stratified, and there was more to play for.

Village societies existed in the Germanic world north of the Roman empire; and similar villages also crystallized in the post-Roman kingdoms of the West, sometimes doubtless under the influence of incoming Germanic groups, notably in the case of the Anglo-Saxons in England, though the village-form also emerged in parts of the post-Roman West where there were relatively few incomers, such as southern France or central Italy. When villages did appear, they were in wood, overwhelmingly the dominant medium for rural housing in Europe until after 1200, except for parts of Mediterranean Europe, where stone came in a century or two earlier. We cannot track local relationships with the density possible for Serjilla, partly because houses only survive through their post-holes, and partly because they tended to be even more uniform. In a substantial area from Denmark to the Alps, and west into central France and England, villages were made up of farmstead blocks, centred on a main building (very long in Denmark, up to 40 metres sometimes, where it included living quarters and an animal byre; rather shorter in southern Germany or England), with subsidiary buildings and sunken-floored huts, which seem for the most part to have been outhouses for artisanal activity and storage, the whole set in a yard, usually fenced. The squares of each farmstead often created quite regular patterns for these villages, set on either side of a main road or else in a block around a crossroads, a regularity further enhanced because longhouses and other main buildings tended quite often to be parallel to each other. This regularity enhanced the sense of uniformity created by similar house and farmstead plans.

Farmstead units were not all alike, though. In some villages, they were; but there was often one rather larger house, often on the edge of the settlement. Vorbasse in Denmark is a good example of this, for this settlement, like many in Denmark and the area of northern Germany and the Netherlands, regularly shifted site inside the same agricultural territory, and changes in its patterning can thus be more easily compared from century to century, in this case (unusually) from the first century BC to the twelfth century AD when it settled down on its present site. From the third century to the start of the eighth, there was always one rather larger farmstead in Vorbasse, half again as large as its neighbours, with a bigger main building, and more imported goods found in it. In one of the village's shifts, around 300, the rest of the village shifted but the larger farmstead stayed put, which marks the stability of the social position of its owner even more firmly. Vorbasse evidently had a leader, then; but we would be wrong to see him (or her) as a local lord, still less the village's landlord. His house was larger and richer than those of his neighbours, but, as at Serjilla, it was not otherwise different. And it is interesting that around 700, when Vorbasse reorganized itself more substantially than usual on a new site, the larger farmstead disappeared. Leadership had been stable here for a long time, but was not so structurally solid that it could not be sidestepped, even if we cannot tell precisely how.

Lauchheim in Alemannia, in the upper Danube valley, settled from the sixth century to the twelfth, shows a more hierarchical pattern. Here there were around ten farmsteads along a road, but one was much larger already by the seventh century, and became twice the size by the eleventh. Here, the larger farmstead was indeed typologically distinct, for it had a much larger number of non-residential post-hole buildings, probably for storage, plausibly of grain and other produce collected in rent. It also had its own small cemetery, with rich burials, in the late seventh century, before burials moved to the churchyard of the eighth-century church. It would be fair to call this central farmstead of Lauchheim an estate-centre, and it is quite possible – even if not certain – that its holder was, or became, the landlord of the village as a whole.

Most excavated villages had some sort of identifiable hierarchy, at least of resources, which probably points to village leadership, too; but it was not always stable (different houses could be the largest one in a village in different centuries), and, even in Lauchheim, that hierarchy did not point to a radically different lifestyle for the inhabitants of the largest house. From the Carolingian period onwards, however, we begin to get signs of structural differences. The first innovation was character-istically the village church, often built in stone from the start; village church-building tended to begin after 700, and to gain pace in later centuries (see above, Chapter 8). Once a church was built in a village, the settlement tended to gain a more stable spatial structure (and, in Denmark, to stop moving site); and churches always had aristocratic or local patrons and, generally, resident priests, whose élite status was reinforced by the considerable investment church-building involved. The most striking change came, however, when local leaders or lords began to fortify their residences. This development, which can be summarized succinctly (if simplistically) as 'the rise of the castle', was rare before 900, and not widely generalized until after 1000 (below, Chapter 21), but came in the end to characterize most of Europe. It happened in different ways in different places; in some places, Lauchheim-type estate-centres gained bigger fences, then ditches, then stone walls, then stone residences, perhaps on an artificial hill or motte above the village; in others (as in England) some lords had moved into increasingly fortified residences, which had no necessary connection with still-fragmented peasant settlement, by perhaps 900, a long time before mottes appeared in the wake of the Norman Conquest. In central-southern Italy and other parts of southern Europe, villages were themselves fortified in the tenth to twelfth centuries (and called *castra* or *castella*, castles), with a lord's residence developing as an internal fortification (a *rocca* or *cassero*) inside the village. In each case the relationship between the castle-dwelling lord and the village or villages around was different, the difference being very clear on the ground.

A good example of that Italian development is Montarrenti near Siena in southern Tuscany. Here, a village on the slopes and summit of a hill is documented from the late seventh century onwards; the houses were small and one-roomed, as is typical for Italy; the whole village already probably had a palisade around it, and the hill-top had a separate fence, although the houses there were of much the same size. Already in the early ninth century the hill-top palisade was replaced by a stone wall, surrounding a large wooden building (probably a granary), a grain-drying oven, and a mill-stone: as at Lauchheim, one can see an estate-centre crystallizing here. This burnt down later in the century, but the wall was rebuilt in the tenth. The hill-top still had wooden houses in the tenth century, but in the late eleventh stone towers began to replace them, to create a clearly seigneurial focus. Settlement continued lower down the hill, however (perhaps with breaks), and by the twelfth century the lower hill-slopes were themselves surrounded by a wall which included the whole village, by now mostly built of stone, although the upper *cassero* remained the seigneurial centre. It was this whole village that was called a *castrum* from the end of that century (I would guess by the early eleventh, judging by other Italian examples, but we do not have the documents for Montarrenti), but it had a clear settlement hierarchy in it, one which had begun already in the ninth century, and which was permanently fixed in the towers of the eleventh. This sort of articulated spatial hierarchy has plenty of parallels in the settlement archaeology of Tuscany and Lazio (two well-studied regions of Italy), and has, as we shall see in Chapter 22, clear analogues in our documentation for the increasingly militarized social hierarchies in tenth-century villages, for Italy and elsewhere. The social hierarchy, however, was made increasingly manifest and solid in village architecture. Once village élites moved to stone towers, they were making visual claims to status and lordship, which they could back up by armed force, and which were no longer negotiable, as village leadership had frequently been two or three centuries before. Display here was not intended to compete with neighbours, but to exclude them.

The display involved in building huge prestige constructions like Hagia Sophia and that involved in building a flashier village house was quite different in scale, but it had many of the same aims: to impress, to establish status and power, maybe to elicit fear and submission. (The two types of display were even sometimes linked; the decoration of the emperor Zeno's huge church to honour Simon the Stylite in the 470s at Qa'lat Sim'an in the Limestone Massif was copied by village church builders all over the region in the next generation.) The frames of reference in which display operated varied very greatly from region to region and between different types of building, however; and it is that variability which tells us most about cultural assumptions. Justinian was bouncing his architectural references off earlier pagan buildings and near-contemporary churches, all of which he was aiming to surpass. Al-Walid was aiming to surpass, too, but was also aiming at establishing a fundamental difference from past styles of building-plan and mosaic decoration, to mark out the novelty and superiority of the Muslim religion. Edwin and his predecessors were making claims to links with a Roman past which evidently had local prestige, even though Yeavering was north of the former territory of the later Roman empire. Paschal was reasserting papal centrality through unbroken links with past architectural and decorative styles, inside and against a world with quite different political configurations. Charlemagne was offering his visitors a visual and spatial experience in his palaces which had no recent parallels in northern and western Europe, and which was intended, doubtless successfully, to mark him out as unique, at least to people who had no experience of Constantinople. The lords of Montarrenti were not just showing their local mastery and their defensive capability with their stone towers, but were also drawing on urban models of building, and thus transferring urban power and cultural prestige into the construction of rural lordship; and, in a less top-down and more competitive way, it was also urban prestige that was evoked by Julian and Domna's bath-house.

The intervisuality of architectural style is one of the most powerful conveyors of meaning and visual effect. As remarked at the start of this book, archaeology, and the study of material culture in its widest sense in art history and architectural history, tends to tell us different sorts of things from the study of narrative and documentary texts. Material culture tells us more about the use of space, the function of spatial relationships, as well as, of course, stylistic and technological changes; written culture tells us more about human relationships, choices, conscious representations of the world around us. But the construction of visual meaning, by emperors and peasants alike, links these two worlds:

it is material culture, not words, which tells us about the choices of al-Walid, or Paschal, or Julian and Domna in Serjilla. That is why this chapter is the central one in this book; it offers a way to compare the strategies of every actor in the early Middle Ages, rich or poor, and not – for once – just those who had access to the written word. And the audiences of buildings such as these were also far wider than those of any written text, save of the sections of the Bible and Qur'an most often read out in religious ceremonies, and these latter tended not to change much across time and space. The whole population of Europe was thus involved in the communication discussed in this chapter, and could even, if they chose, participate as communicators, not just as audiences. Indeed, as archaeology makes its inevitable advances in the future, this is a sector of historical knowledge which, for a change, we shall know progressively more about.

PART III

The Empires of the East,
550–1000

11

Byzantine Survival, 550–850

The *Parastaseis Syntomoi Chronikai*, 'Brief Historical Notes', is an anonymous mid-eighth-century text from Constantinople. It consists of comments on the monuments of the city, above all its statues. Some of the text purports to collect notes and letters written by a group of friends, state officials in the 710s, who had a sort of research project exploring who the statues were of and where they had come from. This may well be a literary fiction, for references in the text to other authors are themselves mostly clear inventions, and the text sometimes has an in-jokiness about it which makes the reader mistrustful. But someone did do the work, going around from statue to statue, reading the inscription on the base or asking other people what they thought the figure represented. This was not always easy; the woman seated on a bronze chair in the Hippodrome might be the empress Verina (d. *c.* 484), as the skilled statue-interpreter Herodian thought, but it might also be the goddess Athena, 'as I have myself heard from many people . . . and this I believed'. It was also dangerous work; Himerios the *chartoularios* (a medium-level financial official) and his friend Theodore went to look at the statues in the Kynegion, north of Hagia Sophia, the Great Church of Constantinople; as they were studying one, it fell on Himerios and killed him, and Theodore, who fled, had trouble getting out of a criminal accusation. In the end, the statue was buried on the spot by order of the emperor Philippikos (711–13). 'Take care when you look at old statues, especially pagan ones,' the chapter finishes: pagan statues were maleficent, and one had to be prepared.

Conversely, if an expert knew his statues, and was a skilled enough interpreter, his knowledge was highly useful. Not only could he avoid maleficent ones, but he could tell the future. Herodian knew that one of the Hippodrome statues of women giving birth to wild beasts (Scylla and Charybdis, probably) prefigured the reign of terror of Justinian II in 705–11; the other (the one with the boat) 'has not been fulfilled, but remains'. Asklepiodoros looked at the inscription on the statue of Herakles in the Hippodrome and could at once tell what bad things (unnamed) were going to happen, to his distress ('I would have been better off if I had not read the inscription'). And he could also, of course, reconstruct the past. The authors of the *Parastaseis* did not have access to many books about the past, but they were very interested in it, and sought systematically to locate statue-knowledge in a historical framework. Valentinian III's statue, for example, had not fallen over in an earthquake; this showed that his assassination in 455 was unjust, and not, as people had previously thought, a fair retribution for his murder of Aetius. Constantinople was still a very large city, and, obviously, was full of statues; this text could not conceivably have been written about any other Mediterranean city except Rome – and in Rome, churches and Christian cult-sites were by now the inescapable points of reference, unlike in the eastern capital, as it seems. In the eastern capital, the imperial past still mattered, and the whole history of Constantinople was laid out through its statues. Conversely, this history was above all of the fourth and fifth centuries (often misunderstood), much less of the sixth (there is surprisingly little about Justinian) and less still of the seventh and eighth. This is a key to the text: it represented a genuine antiquarian interest, with statues operating as a memory-theatre in a literal sense, but its author or authors looked at the great days of the Christian Roman empire across a huge divide, and did not by any means know much about what that empire meant. Such is the divide which this chapter explores, for the eighth-century Byzantine empire, lineal heir of the east Roman empire, was a very different society, with most of its points of reference changed.

The reason for this divide was a simple one: it was the catastrophic events which broke Roman control over most of the east Mediterranean between 609 and 642. The drastic downsizing and reorganization of the empire that resulted was the main break in the imperial history of the East in our whole period, and, together with most historians, I call the surviving empire 'Byzantine' from now on. (The Byzantines always called themselves 'Romans', *Romaioi* in Greek; so did their eastern neighbours; westerners called them 'Greeks'. 'Byzantines' in our period only meant the inhabitants of Constantinople, which had once been called Byzantion. But it is a convenient misnomer, all the same.) We left the late sixth-century east Roman empire in reasonable shape in Chapter 4. The emperor Maurice (582–602) was a war leader; he had ended twenty years of Persian frontier war in 591 by intervening in a succession dispute in Persia and helping to set up Khusrau II (590–628) as shah. He also faced out threats to the Balkans. Here, the sixth-century successors to the Germanic invaders of the late fourth and fifth were Sclavenian groups, small-scale tribal communities whose raids are attested from the 540s onwards. (Many or most of these groups spoke Slavic languages, but this is not stressed by our early sources as an identifier for the *Sklavēnoi*, so I shall avoid the word 'Slav' here; see further Chapter 20.) The Avars, a Turkic-speaking nomadic people, came westwards in 558, and by 567–8 had established themselves in Pannonia as the Huns had done over a century earlier; they established a loose hegemony over many of the Sclavenian tribes north of the Danube, and presented a greater military threat, particularly after their capture of the Roman frontier town of Sirmium in 582. After 591, however, Maurice could attend systematically to Balkan defence, and he held these incursions back in the 590s, reinforcing the Danube frontier as he did so. It was Maurice's very success which undid him, for in 602 the Balkan army revolted against his orders to over-winter north of the Danube, and he was killed with his family by one of his generals, Phocas, who succeeded him (602–10).

Phocas' accession was the first successful overthrow of an emperor in the eastern empire since 324; between 602 and 820, however, only five out of twenty-one emperors died naturally in office. There had always been a culture of coups in the East, but from now on they were frequently effective. The army's role in politics changed as a result, as we shall see. There were constant and successful attempts to establish dynasties, which lasted five generations under the Heraclids (610–711), four under the Isaurians (717–802), three under the Amorians (820–67), six under the Macedonians (867–1056: see Chapter 13); the notion of hereditary succession was by no means lost, that is to say. But even this succession was punctuated by coups. Legitimacy was as much linked to military success and to popularity in the capital (coups were hard if the city of Constantinople was opposed) as to family background; the image of the choice of God, which lay behind the decisions of 'the people, the senate and the army', was used even when sons succeeded fathers. The ceremony of imperial accession was much more elaborate as a result, to establish this legitimacy as publicly as possible. The openness of the succession, and its apparent availability to almost anyone who was of sound body (blinding and other mutilation were standard Byzantine methods of neutralizing rivals), marked out the Byzantine world from now on; so did the importance of the image of divine favour for the emperor, which had further consequences, as we shall see.

Phocas is often seen as the turning point in this development, but his reign matches that of Maurice in important particulars. The Balkan frontier remained sound, and, although Khusrau restarted the Persian war in 603, at least nominally to avenge Maurice, it remained a standard frontier war for some years. Phocas was unpopular, however, and could not withstand a north African-based uprising in 608–10 aimed at putting Heraclius, the son of the exarch of Africa, on the throne. It was that civil war which threw the empire sideways, for it was then that the Persian breakthrough began. Heraclius (610–41) already found the Persians raiding in Anatolia in 611; more drastically still, Syria was conquered in 613, Palestine in 614, Egypt in 619; in 616–17 Persian raids reached the Bosporos. Heraclius pulled out all the troops in the Balkans to defend Anatolia, and Sclavenian groups began to settle there permanently; the Avars consolidated a hegemony over them, and by 617 they were raiding up to the Aegean too. In less than a decade, the richest provinces of the empire were all lost, and no part of it was safe from raiding except the Aegean islands and the western provinces of Sicily and Africa. It got worse: in 626, an Avar–Sclavenian army to the west and a Persian army to the east, roughly coordinated, besieged the capital, when Heraclius was 800 kilometres away campaigning in Armenia. Constantinople's huge fortifications stood firm, however, and the Avar siege failed (the Persians, on the other side of the Bosporos, could not get across). The Avar–Sclavenian alliance broke up acrimoniously, and Avar hegemony in the Balkans began to fail from now on. In two years of daring campaigning Heraclius got behind the Persian armies and attacked Khusrau's heartland (what is now Iraq), with the considerable help of an army of Gök Turk nomads from the Caucasus; Khusrau was killed in a coup, and the Persians made peace in 628, surrendering all their conquests. The Sassanian polity went into crisis; seven rulers followed Khusrau in quick succession before Yazdagird III (632–51) established himself in 633–4.

Heraclius in 628 was a hero. He was received in triumph in Constantinople in 629, and in Jerusalem in 630, where he restored the True Cross, taken by the Persians in 614. Heraclius was closely attached to the Cross, Christianity's most resonant relic, which Constantine's mother Helena was said to have found outside Jerusalem in the 320s; as his court poet George of Pisidia put it, '[the Persians] were venerating fire, while you, O sovereign, [venerate] wood'. This was a time for religious renewal, so Jews were massacred and otherwise persecuted, and Heraclius also made the last attempt to reunify the rival Chalcedonian and Monophysite churches (cf. Chapter 3) in 638, when he proclaimed a compromise doctrine, called Monotheletism, which was henceforth to be the only legitimate version of Christianity throughout the empire. But the empire was, of course, devastated, its economy in crisis owing to destruction and political division, and its armies in need of years to recover. It was thus impossible for Heraclius successfully to resist attack from a new quarter, Arabia. Arab armies defeated the Byzantines on the River Yarmuk near the Sea of Galilee in 636, and the disaster of the 610s repeated itself: the Arabs took Syria in 636, Palestine in 638, and Egypt in 639–42. This time the Byzantines did not get them back. Notwithstanding Heraclius' successes in 627–8, the reunification of the empire only lasted for a decade or less. Only after Heraclius' death in 641 would the Byzantines slowly come to see that they would have in future to do without the south-east Mediterranean provinces; but in reality the empire had lost them in the 610s.

How the Arabs were so successful, and what happened in the lands they conquered, we shall see in the next chapter, but the seriousness of these conquests for the Byzantine world cannot be overemphasized. Heraclius has a curiously good press even now, thanks to the events of 627–8, but his reign was, taken as a whole, the most disastrous in a thousand years of Roman history. The empire lost two-thirds of its land and three-quarters of its wealth in the 610s, in Michael Hendy's words, and this loss became permanent in the 630s. The loss of the agrarian and productive wealth of Egypt was particularly serious. Byzantium was reduced to the Anatolian plateau of modern Turkey, the Aegean sea and the lands around it, and, moving westwards, pockets of the Adriatic coast, parts of Italy (including Rome) and Sicily, and North Africa. In the next two centuries, the southern Balkans would be reconquered, but northern and central Italy and Africa would be lost, and then, after the 820s, so would Sicily, although much of mainland southern Italy stayed Byzantine until after 1050.

The Roman empire had always relied on sea traffic to integrate its economy. The Byzantine empire remained a maritime state, too, for only the sea roads connected its far-flung provinces by now, linking the richest but also the furthest province, Sicily, to the capital. The Byzantine navy was far less politically prominent than the army, and we know less about it, but it was a crucial element in the survival of the empire, both strategically and tactically. The fact that the Byzantines held the Bosporos strait was essential to the survival of Constantinople in the great sieges of 626 and 717–18. All the same, the Byzantines had not only lost Egypt, the traditional grain reserve for the capital, but also, at least after the Arab conquests, the Egyptian fleet based at Alexandria. The Arabs held the southern Mediterranean sea roads, restricting the Byzantines to its northern edge, and they used the Alexandrian fleet particularly effectively in the late seventh and early eighth centuries, raiding into the Aegean and, in 717–18, even into the Sea of Marmara. That raiding stopped temporarily in the eighth century, but the Byzantines could never take their sea mastery for granted, particularly beyond their Aegean heartland. Constantinople lost its right to free grain in 618, when Heraclius rapidly drew the correct conclusions from the Persian conquest of Egypt, and the population dropped substantially in size, from some 500,000 to between 40,000 and 70,000: still the largest city in Europe, but a tenth the size of what it had been. This smaller urban community could be supplied from Aegean and Black Sea sources, and would be henceforth, particularly after Sicily was lost.

People knew at once that the Persian-Arab conquests were a catastrophe, of course. The seventh-century crisis in the East was unlike the fifth-century crisis in the West, in that it was so fast. People could not get comfortably used to the new status quo as they did in the West, in the increasingly regionalized politics of the crystallizing Germanic kingdoms; in the East, they knew that they had to adapt quickly, or else be conquered. The atmosphere of crisis is reflected in nearly every seventh-century text. This was a period in which apocalyptic writing was common, both Christian and Jewish. The Christians, of course, could see the conquest of half of their world by Zoroastrians and then by as yet hardly understood Muslims as an immediate presage that the world itself would end. The Jews, although less persecuted in the Persian and Arab empires than in the seventh-century Roman/Byzantine empire, saw the rise of Islam, a rival monotheistic and Abrahamic religion, as a direct cultural threat; but the Persian wars already seemed to them, too, to presage final days. More widely, political disagreements of all kinds gained a religious edge, as we shall see, for divine disfavour seemed so evident.

At a less spiritual level, the first priority had to be the army. The Byzantines needed an army large enough to defend against the Arabs, but had to fund it from an empire with its richest provinces lost. Army supply had to be very streamlined for this to work. Under Heraclius, who spent most of his reign campaigning, there is little sign of army reorganization, but things stabilized a little in the 650s, when a more permanent frontier region, roughly along the Tauros mountains in east-central Anatolia, was established; the late 650s was also a period of Arab civil war. In the period 669–87, we first have references to the four great military districts, or 'themes', of Anatolia, the Opsikion, Thrakesion, Anatolikon and Armeniakon, each of which had its own army, and each of which was supplied locally – each theme had at least one relatively prosperous region at its heart whose produce the army could live off. These themes probably began to take shape in the 640s–650s. They were superimposed on long-standing smaller provinces, which handled civil administration and justice, and also local tax-raising; most of these functions were gradually taken over by the military, but this long process was not complete until the ninth century. Slowly, too, other parts of the empire were organized into themes: Thrace and the Aegean islands later in the century, Greece in the eighth and early ninth century as it was reoccupied, southern Italy in the late ninth with renewed conquests there. Tax was therefore mostly spent locally; the fiscal integration of the empire largely ceased, except that the supply of Constantinople involved longer-distance links, and the capital continued to control the mechanisms of tax-raising and, for a time, provincial administrations. But armies were still paid, with their salaries funded by the land tax, except for relatively untrained militias. Soldiers were locally recruited, and remained local; they were frequently, or became, local landowners too. But they did not, as in the West, come to depend entirely on their landowning to resource them. What did happen was that taxation, and army pay, ceased for the most part to be in money; produce became the major element of the fiscal system until the ninth century. This meant that fewer coins needed to be minted (coin-finds virtually cease for the period between the 650s and the 820s, except in Constantinople and Sicily); it also meant that equipment supply became much more cumbersome, and an entire government department, the *eidikon*, developed to ensure it, with local branches in every theme.

This thematic army system was largely defensive; each army defended its own area. It needed to do so: the hundred years after 650, even though the frontier was by now relatively stable, was one of constant Arab raiding, which meant that no part of Anatolia was secure. Local society became largely militarized as a result; the thematic army, together with a slowly militarizing provincial bureaucracy, became the main political and social hierarchy in each area. When a landowning aristocracy is next documented, in the ninth and (especially) tenth centuries, it was as heavily military as in the West, as we shall see in Chapter 13. It is notable, however, that we can say almost nothing about landowning élites in the Byzantine empire between 650 and 800/850, even given the relatively poor documentation of the period. Landowners probably became poorer in the crisis years, particularly in those parts of Anatolia most exposed to long-term raiding. Cities also became much weaker in the period, and urban society vanished altogether in some parts of the empire (see below, Chapter 15), thus making a traditional Roman local politics, focused on the city as it had been, impossible. But what is above all the case is that social status from now on, in an empire concentrating on military survival, depended on office in the army or administration. We know the names of hundreds of military or civil administrators in this period, for they survive on lead seals, once used to authenticate documents, which have been found on archaeological sites all over the empire. It is just that we cannot say whether they had landed properties as well as offices in the imperial hierarchy, except in a few cases close to the capital, as we shall see in a moment. They probably did; and many of them may well have been both the descendants of sixth-century senatorial and urban élites and the ancestors of tenth-century surnamed aristocrats. But we do not *know* whether they did or not, and this is important. The period 650–800/850 was one in which office in the state overwhelmed landed wealth or local reputation as something to aspire to. Even ancestry became temporarily unimportant, or at any rate it is rarely stressed in our sources. To survive, Byzantine society and politics folded itself around the state.

Constantinople and its immediate hinterland were a partial exception to this. The city remained large, at least by post-Roman standards, and a money economy certainly survived there. A miracle-book of the 660s, rewritten later in the century, recounts the miraculous cures (mostly of genital problems) performed by the body of St Artemios, buried in the church of St John Prodromos. It shows us a bustling urban society full of incomers and artisans (a silver-seller, a bronze-caster, a ship-builder, a bow-maker, and also general workmen who had suffered hernias owing to heavy lifting), sitting in the church hoping for healing; the supplicants had their own associations with a treasurer to hold the money, and played dice to while away the time – as well as stealing from each other on occasion, and, in one case, thoughtlessly urinating in the church itself (the perpetrator was given someone else's hernia by St Artemios for this misjudgement). Constantinople was an active city in the seventh century, evidently. Its élites did own land, especially around the Sea of Marmara; a frequent theme in early ninth-century saints' lives is of public officials retiring to their estates and founding monasteries there. So Platon (d. 814), a middle-ranking bureaucrat from an official family, retired south of the Marmara to found the Sakkoudion monastery on his estates in 783; he became a monastic rigorist, together with his more famous nephew Theodore (d. 826), who was made abbot of the Stoudios monastery in the imperial city around 798. Platon and Theodore's uncompromising political interventions, for example in opposition to the supposedly adulterous second marriage in 796 of the emperor Constantine VI (780–97), were the first known political acts by non-office-holding landed aristocrats since the sixth century. This would only have been possible immediately around the capital.

But Constantinople was very much a creation of the state, all the same. It was dominated, even at its low point around 700, by a highly complex bureaucratic hierarchy, which ran the central government in its six or seven main departments, of which the most important was the *genikon*, which controlled the land tax. The relatively unmilitary culture of the city is explained by the strength of this bureaucracy, just as the wealth of the city was directly derived from its role as the fiscal hub of the empire. The church hierarchy, itself large, was also closely associated with the state; patriarchs were always chosen directly by the emperor, and dismissed if they disagreed with him. And Constantinople was an immense public space, with a complex ceremonial geography, centred on the display of imperial power. The Hippodrome, just in front of the palace, was a major location for public acts, including the proclamation of new emperors, or the humiliation of opponents, including the mock marriage of Iconophile monks and nuns in 765 supposedly commanded by Constantine V (741–75); and also for formal dialogues between emperors and representatives of the city. There were regular processions along the main streets of the city, too, at important moments of the liturgical year and to commemorate major events, which were so carefully crafted that observers could read precise meanings into which gate the procession entered at or how many places it stopped at. This ceremonial aspect of the city looked straight back to late Rome; although Roman traditions had certainly changed, they changed less here than in most other respects discussed in this chapter. It helped maintain a Roman form to the cityscape: wide roads survived longer in Constantinople than in any other post-Roman city, east or west. It helped maintain the statue-laden public spaces discussed at the start of this chapter, too. And it represented the state, public political power, at every stage.

The focus of Constantinopolitan politics and ceremonial, and also of the military hierarchies of the provinces, was the emperor. However unstable his personal position, the imperial office mattered enormously: indeed, the frequency of coups and attempted coups itself showed how much people wanted the imperial title. I have stressed the fiscal and military decentralization of the theme system, but in all other respects the Byzantine empire was more centralized after 650 or so, not less, for social status was so dependent on position in the office-holding hierarchy. The dominance of the imperial city was also far greater after other cities failed; in Byzantium, uniquely in the Christian world, it was commonplace for bishops of sees all over the empire to spend as much time as they could in the capital rather than in their own diocese. It may be added that the empire was by now more culturally homogeneous, too; in 500 only a minority of the population of the eastern empire spoke Greek, and the official language was still, at least nominally, actually Latin, but by 700, after the loss of Syriac- and Coptic-speaking provinces, nearly everyone was a Greek-speaker, and the occasional Sclavenian and not-so-occasional Armenian were exotic. There were no more regional divisions between Christians, as between Chalcedonians and Monophysites, for the Monophysite provinces were almost all lost: religious disagreements were henceforth fought out above all in the capital. The major exceptions to this, the Latin-speakers of the mainland Italian provinces, including the Romans of Rome, slipped away from Byzantine rule in part precisely for this reason. A concentration of religious controversy on the capital also meant its concentration on the choices and actions of emperors; these were watched with considerable attention. Leo III (717–41) was accused, in a polemical text of two generations later (it purported to be a letter written to him by the pope), of saying 'I am emperor and priest'. The claim, however polemical, was not a ridiculous one to make of any emperor. Emperors had a religious importance which even Justinian had not claimed in an earlier century, although earlier emperors, up to Constantine, did do so.

In this form, the pared-down state survived the Arab conquests. And all through, it could continue to defend itself despite a relative shortage of charismatic leaders: in the two centuries and a half after 602, only the Isaurian emperors of the 710s–770s were really on top of events. The Frankish kings could not have survived in this situation, but the infra-structures of the Byzantine empire remained solid enough for it to be possible. Let us look at how this turned out in more detail.

Heraclius died in 641 leaving a succession dispute between his two sons, by different mothers, ruling under the aegis of his widow (and, con-troversially, his niece) Martina. Martina was overthrown a few months later by supporters of his young grandson Constans II (641–68), how-ever; it was Constans who presided over the final loss of Egypt, and over the stabilization of the frontier and the theme system, none of which, probably, had much to do with him. What he is best known for is his religious and Italian policies. Constans was committed to Monothele-tism, and devoted his attention throughout his reign to imposing it on all opponents. The popes in Rome resisted particularly publicly; Con-stans had Pope Martin I (649–53) arrested, tried in Constantinople, and deposed. Constans also faced secular rebellions in the West, by Gregory, exarch of Africa (d. 647) and Olympius, exarch of Ravenna (d. 652), two of the three main western provincial governors, the *strategos* of Sicily being the third. Constans was very interested in his western prov-inces, all the same; they were the part of the empire least affected by the Arab threat. (Gregory was actually killed in an Arab raid on Africa; but the Arabs did not return there until the 670s.) Constans tried to reconquer the Lombard parts of Italy in the 660s, and, most remarkably of all, tried to move the imperial capital to Syracuse. This reflected Sicily's wealth and stability, but it was too extreme a move (it could potentially have led to the abandonment of Constantinople and the East), and Constans was killed in a coup in 668. His son Constantine IV (668–85) returned to Constantinople, and also abandoned Mono-theletism, in the sixth ecumenical council, held in the capital in 680; Christological debate no longer seemed relevant in a rapidly changing political system, and the issues involved hardly resurfaced in the East after the end of the century.

Constantine, like his father, lived on the defensive. The Arabs attacked by sea in his reign, attempting to blockade Constantinople in the mid-670s. The conquest of Africa began in the same period, culminating in the fall of Carthage in 698. In the Balkans, the retreat of the Avars after 626 had left a host of small, effectively independent, Sclavenian groups which could occasionally attack the Byzantine coastal cities (as with Thessaloniki between 675 and 677) though in some way recognizing Byzantine supremacy; but a new Turkic power appeared south of the Danube in 680, the Bulgars, under their khagan Asparuch (d. c. 700), who defeated an imperial army and were recognized as independent rulers of, roughly, the northern half of modern Bulgaria in 681. The Bulgars would henceforth rival the Byzantines for hegemony over the *Sklaviniai* for three centuries. In Constantine's reign, nonetheless, a style of military politics which would have a long future began to crystallize. Constantine dealt with the army as a direct interlocutor. Already under Constans, both supporters and opponents of Monotheletism were accused of causing defeat by wrong belief. The army came to see this as an issue too; the sixth council in 680 was urged on the emperor by the army, as Constantine himself said. In 681, following on from this, the soldiers of the Anatolikon theme demanded (unsuccessfully) that the emperor take back his brothers as co-emperors, supposedly saying 'we believe in the Trinity. Let us crown all three!' – as clear a statement of an imperial office modelled on the divine power as one could imagine. Constantine's son Justinian II (685–95), an intransigent and unpopular ruler, ratified the sixth council in 687, deferring again to the views of the army. Justinian was, however, overthrown in a military coup in 695, and was exiled, with his nose cut off, to the Crimea.

Six emperors followed in the next two decades, each replacing the last by coup. One was Justinian II again (705–11), who had escaped from the Crimea with Bulgar help, and who revenged himself terribly on his enemies. His successor Philippikos re-established Monotheletism; Anastasios II (713–15) abolished it again. The context of all of this was a growing political protagonism of the different themes, in a period of renewed Arab danger. Anastasios was at least competent enough to prepare against the long-planned and widely anticipated Arab siege of Constantinople; he decreed that only people with three years'-worth of provisions could stay in the city. He was however deposed by the Opsikion theme, against whom the Anatolikon and Armeniakon then revolted, and by the time the Arab army and navy arrived, in 717, the *strategos* of the Armeniakon, Leo III, was emperor. Leo survived the great siege of 717–18, the last serious attempt to destroy the Byzantine empire for almost half a millennium. His success broke the cycle of coups, and he and his son Constantine V ruled for nearly sixty years.

The empire could hardly have been in a worse strategic situation in 717, but the Isaurian emperors turned the corner, using the bureaucratic and military structure that had bedded down in the last generation. Leo faced off Arab raids throughout his reign, defeating some of them; partly reorganized the administration; and at the end of his life, in 741, issued the first systematic imperial legislation since Justinian, the *Ekloga*: not a long text, but compiled explicitly because Justinian's laws had become 'unintelligible'. Under Constantine V, for the first time, the Byzantines raided the Arab lands as often as the Arabs raided back. In general, periods of Byzantine military success were made possible by periods of Arab political instability, and Constantine's reign, in particular, coincided with the civil wars that resulted in the overthrow of the Umayyad caliphate in 750. This created an aura of success which on its own made Constantine a figure with a high reputation in military circles, lasting into the 830s at least. Constantine also for the first time moved seriously to re-establish Byzantine power in the Balkans, attacking the Bulgars frequently in the period 759–75 and reimposing imperial hegemony as much as possible on the *Sklaviniai*, particularly those of what is now Greece. Constantine, on the other hand, was less interested in the West. Leo had opposed the papacy, initially over tax-paying issues, and in the 730s he stripped the popes of rights in southern Italy and Sicily. Byzantine control in the south was reasserted here at the expense of the north, however, and Constantine did not resist the Lombard conquest of the exarchate of Ravenna, in 751. The popes began to see themselves as part of a Lombard and Frankish world, not a Byzantine one, from the mid-eighth century onwards. This is when the Latin lands were lost to Byzantium, a fact that Greek sources hardly record. Constantine also intervened, more than any predecessor for a century, in imperial infrastructure, rebuilding the main aqueduct into Constantinople in 767, reforming the tax system, and establishing a non-thematic corps of professional shock troops, the *tagmata*, which would become the élite force in the ninth-century army.

This renewed military and political protagonism is not what Leo and Constantine are best known for, however: for these, famously, are the Iconoclast emperors, the opponents of the developing cult of holy images. In the late Roman empire, east and west, if there was anything that was surely holy it was the relics of saints (and of the Christian divinity, like the True Cross); portraits of Christ and the saints, and paintings of biblical narratives, were simply guides, 'made for the instruction of the ignorant, so that they might understand [scriptural] stories', as Gregory the Great said. This remained the assumption in the West, at least among theorists, but in the East images 'not made by human hand', that is, created miraculously, begin to be referred to in the late sixth century, and one, an image of Christ, was credited (along with the direct action of Mary) with saving Constantinople during the 626 siege. These images can still be seen as pictorial equivalents to relics; but in the last quarter of the seventh century the power of images as a whole was beginning to widen. By 700 it was increasingly common to regard all portraits of saints as windows into the divine; one might pray to a holy portrait (an 'icon' as we would now say, although *eikōn* in Greek just means any image) and believe that, in so doing, one was talking directly to the saint. Anyone could thus have their own saint at hand, and one did not need to go to church to have access to the divine. Already the Quinisext council in 691/2 justified images of Christ as consequences of his human incarnation. Although the council did not go so far as to say that they should be prayed to, the importance of holy images in Byzantine culture was clearly growing. It was this which Iconoclasts reacted against in the eighth century: praying to icons detracted from the honour due only to God, and could be seen as idolatry. Indeed, as Constantine V argued in his *Peuseis* (c. 752), images of Christ only stress the human side of the divinity, and neglect the divine side; Christ is only properly represented in the eucharist, as well as, metaphorically, in the cross. But this is the only point at which the Iconoclast vs. Iconophile controversy referred to the Christological controversies of the past. Otherwise, it was essentially concerned with whether religious images of all kinds could be venerated, and whether praying to (or through) them was a correct, or an idolatrous, form of worship.

Later Iconophile sources saw Iconoclasm as an imperial challenge to image-worship, beginning with Leo III, who supposedly saw the volcanic eruption on the island of Thera in 726 as a sign of God's wrath and began to destroy religious images from then onwards. All the sources that tie Leo to Iconoclast policies are late, however, postdating the first repudiation of Iconoclasm at the second council of Nicaea in 787, some of them being interpolated into earlier texts. (Most descriptions of the spiritual power of images of saints before 700 are similar interpolations.) In Leo's reign, Iconoclast views took root in the empire, all the same, apparently as a grass-roots phenomenon; there were already bishops like Thomas of Klaudioupolis and Constantine of Nakoleia (both sees were in western Anatolia) who opposed images in the 720s–730s, and Thomas was criticized by Patriarch Germanos of Constantinople for actually removing them from public places. In the years around 750, Constantine V took this up and turned Iconoclasm into imperial policy. As we have seen, he even wrote a treatise on the subject (his *Peuseis* survives because it is excerpted and attacked in the *Antirrhēseis* of Patriarch Nikephoros, d. 828); and in 754 he called the council of Hiereia, a palace across the Bosporos from Constantinople, to ban the veneration of images altogether. 'The unlawful art of the painters' was henceforth to be regarded as a secular activity alone. Pictures of the cross were still legitimate, but those of holy humans were not.

Constantine's breaking of icons and persecution of Iconophiles (particularly monks) were much written up by later authors, but they do not seem to have been particularly thorough or consistent. Constantine obviously did not promote icons, and the mosaic cross still surviving in the apse of Hagia Eirene in Constantinople, rebuilt after 753, reflects imperial patronage. But there is little evidence of active destruction. Nor did Constantine systematically target monks, not all of whom were Iconophiles anyway; indeed, he patronized some monasteries. There were some high-profile executions, notably of the monk Stephen the Younger in 765, but they were isolated. It is worth repeating that

Iconoclasm had grass-roots support, including in the episcopate as early as the 720s, and certainly in the army and imperial bureaucracy, and in the capital. It was not just an imperial cult, like Monotheletism, imposed by force on the hostile and indifferent. The *Life* of Stephen the Younger, which is one of the texts most responsible for the image of Iconoclasm as a generalized tyranny, says that Iconophiles had to flee to the Crimea, to Italy (the pope was fiercely anti-Iconoclast), and to the south coast of Anatolia, to escape persecution. This is a text of 809, much later than the events it describes, and heavily tendentious, but the impression one gets is that the core lands of the empire were fairly solidly Iconoclast. In any case, in the last twenty years of his reign, 755–75, Constantine behaved as if the Iconophile issue was mostly solved; his military campaigns were probably rather more to the front of his mind.

Constantine's son Leo IV (775–80) did not live long, and the latter's widow Eirene ruled for her son Constantine VI (780–97) for the next decade. In 785, Eirene, with her newly appointed patriarch Tarasios (d. 806), made her opposition to Iconoclasm clear, and called a council in 786 in Constantinople to deal with it. The army and some bishops broke it up on the first day, and it had to be rescheduled for Nicaea, further from the capital, the year after. The second council of Nicaea condemned Iconoclasm uncompromisingly, refuting (and thus preserving) its theology point by point. It was, in effect, Second Nicaea which invented the theology of images which has remained a structural part of the eastern church. Many of the basic liturgical practices of Orthodox Christianity look back to 787. Images from now on – as never before – not only could be venerated, but had to be. And Nicaea not only invented Orthodoxy, but to a large extent invented Iconoclasm too, turning Constantine V's policies into a totalizing system, which they probably never had been at the time.

It is not fully clear why Eirene did this. She was certainly bothered by the religious break with the pope, who was by now close to the Frankish kings, and she wished to reunify Rome and Constantinople; her first formal announcement of her intentions was in a letter to Pope Hadrian I. (She succeeded, at least on a religious level; the Franks themselves, however, rather favoured Iconoclasm, and formally condemned Nicaea at the synod of Frankfurt in 794; see Chapter 17. But the whole controversy never had the same importance in the West, where religious images were never given the same spiritual attention.) It is also highly likely that Eirene needed an excuse to break with Constantine V's supporters in both church and state, and to put in her own. It may even be that she had been a closet Iconophile all along, just waiting her chance (though if so she had been very quiet about it in the twenty years since her marriage to Leo, carefully orchestrated in imperial ceremonial in 769). But this was not necessarily the case. Eirene was an effective and some-times ruthless dealer. If 787 was not proof of that, 797 would be, for this was when, after several years of partial retirement, Eirene organized a coup against her son, deposed and blinded him, and made herself empress in his stead. If Eirene could make herself empress by force, the only woman in Roman history to do so (or in European history before Elizabeth of Russia in 1741), then she could also orchestrate the inven-tion of Orthodox Christianity to bolster her power. Either way, however, the religious basis of imperial power took a new path from now on.

Eirene was not a very active figure as sole ruler (797–802), however, and she was deposed in her stead by one of her senior financial adminis-trators, Nikephoros I (802–11), with both official and military backing. All the same, she had managed to get together a substantial coalition in 797, inside the imperial bureaucracy and parts of the *tagmata*, and also had the support of the most rigorist clerics and monks around Platon of Sakkoudion and his nephew Theodore, to whom she gave the Stoudios monastery. These people were happy with a female ruler, as not all religious extremists are, and it is worth pausing for a moment to look at why. We saw in Chapter 4 that empresses like Pulcheria, Verina, Theodora, Sophia were influential in the eastern empire from the fifth century; they were part of the imperial hierarchy in their own right, even if subordinate to emperors (usually their husbands). Unlike in the Frankish political system, they not only gained power as regents for their young children, and indeed Pulcheria and Theodora were childless by their husbands (although Theodora was said to have had earlier children); they could have considerable influence over emperors even if the latter were major protagonists, as with Theodora's husband Justinian, and could rule in all but name if they were not, as with Pulcheria's brother Theodosius II. This clearly did not change with the transformations of the seventh century. Martina failed to ride the politics of the capital in 641, but there was still an institutional role and a moral space for a determined empress, and Eirene, who was both regent for her son and already empress in the lifetime of her husband, could make use of that. She had her own household, separate from that of the emperor; she was formally a co-ruler with her son for seventeen years, appearing on coins in the position of senior ruler at times. An element of female power was, if not typical, at least not abnormal in late Rome and Byzantium; and Eirene had a ready-made clientele, who owed their careers to her since 787 and before, when she took sole power in the end. Even after her fall, it was only in the West that people attributed her failure to the fact that she was a woman. And Iconophile religious rigorists were above all won over by Second Nicaea; the chronicler Theophanes (d. 818), who admittedly loathed Nikephoros I, wrote about 802: 'men who lived a pious and reasonable life wondered at God's judgement, namely at how he had permitted a woman who had suffered like a martyr on behalf of the true faith to be ousted by a swineherd.' The image of the pious female being given a chance at power in order to right wrong belief went back to Pulcheria, and was a resonant one.

If Constantine V marks a turning point for military protagonism, Nikephoros I does the same for the administration. He continued Constantine's and also Eirene's campaigns in the Balkans, but for the first time moved to stabilize conquests by creating new themes and thus an administrative infrastructure, including the Peloponnesos in southern Greece, and Thessaloniki in the north. He also revised the census in around 809, a necessary element in any tax-raising state, the first time this is known to have happened since Leo III's reign; Theophanes complains bitterly about this as part of a narrative onslaught on Nikephoros' 'vexations', so its novelty may well be the author's invention, but it is likely that the emperor saw the reorganization of the tax system as a priority. Most of Theophanes' other 'vexations' indeed concerned taxation: remissions were cancelled, some previously exempt church estates were taxed, so was treasure trove, and so on. From now on, references in our sources to fiscal activity increase, and Theophanes' references to taxes in money may also imply that Nikephoros expanded money exactions rather than taxes in kind. The imperial economy could sustain this again by now, and coin finds on archaeological sites increase again from now on too (see Chapter 15).

The Balkans was by now occupied by semi-autonomous *Sklaviniai*, as we have seen, who could be defeated over and over again, but who remained. Exactly how Balkan society worked in the two centuries after

Heraclius is exceptionally obscure, however. The Sclavenians can only have been a small minority of the population originally, and were furthermore always organized in very small-scale tribal groups. It is a measure of the radical disruption of the Byzantine politico-military system in the seventh century that they settled so easily. The Balkans in this respect resembles Anglo-Saxon England more than any other part of the former Roman empire; there, too, quite small-scale groups managed to take over a province more or less completely in the century after 450, and in the end even change its language, even though the descendants of British speakers outnumbered the descendants of settlers by perhaps ten to one. This latter change happened in the northern and central Balkans too. Slavic had become the common tongue for communication there by the mid-tenth century, as Constantine VII Porphyrogennitos records in his *On the Administration of the Empire*; both Greek and Latin were still spoken too (Latin still is in some areas, in forms resembling modern Romanian), and so were more local languages such as the ancestor of modern Albanian, but Slavic would eventually win out, north of present-day Greece and Albania at least. Slavic would indeed take over even in the multi-ethnic khaganate of the Bulgars (below, Chapter 13), whose rulers were Turkic-speaking for a long time. The Bulgars were also, however, always better organized than their Sclavenian neighbours. Constantine V pushed them back to their core areas, around Pliska in northern Bulgaria, their capital, but he did not destroy them, and under Eirene they regrouped – they benefited from Charlemagne's final destruction of the Avars in 796 (below, Chapter 16), and picked up territory and resources north of the Danube. By the time Nikephoros I was extending the themes of Greece northwards, the Bulgar khagan Krum (c. 800–814) had established an effective army, and counterattacked. Nikephoros sacked Pliska in 809 and 811, but Krum cut him off and destroyed him and his army in the latter year. Nikephoros was the first emperor to die in battle since Valens at Adrianople in 378.

The year 811 was a shock to the empire, and Krum's wars of 813–14, in which he defeated Michael I (811–13), captured Adrianople and assaulted Constantinople, made it that much more serious. Constantine V's memory, including his religious policies, suddenly became much more attractive. Conspirators tried to raise Constantine's blinded sons to the throne in 812; a group of soldiers opened the imperial mausoleum in 813 and prayed before Constantine's tomb calling on him: 'Arise and help the state that is perishing!', as Theophanes claims in appalled tones. The new emperor Leo V (813–20) held off Krum, but drew the same conclusions: that it was under Iconoclasm that the state had been victorious. In 815 he re-established it formally, and deposed Patriarch Nikephoros for refusing to assent. Nikephoros wrote sourly in around 819 that if one was going to adopt religious policies just because of military success, one might as well go back to Alexander, Caesar, Herod and Sennacherib; the argument in itself shows how much Second Iconoclasm owed to Constantine V's reputation.

Leo fell in another coup, the fifth since 797; Michael II (820–29) hesitated over maintaining Iconoclasm, but found Theodore of Stoudios, whom Leo had exiled, so uncompromising a spokesman for the Iconophiles that it seemed safer to maintain an Iconoclast position. It is indeed clear from Theodore's own voluminous letters how few people stood out against Iconoclasm in this period, and how much Theodore's attempts to rally the faith fell on stony ground; bishops were almost entirely Iconoclast; and, over all, whatever people's private views, they were happy to accept Iconoclasm as the theology of the regime. Michael's son Theophilos (829–42) was a more convinced religious partisan, and persecuted public Iconophiles with some verve from 833 onwards; most innovatively, by having a condemnatory text tattooed on the faces of two Palestinian monks, Theodore and his brother Theophanes, in 839 (the two, the *graptoi*, 'inscribed' brothers, became Iconophile heroes, and eventually saints). But Iconoclasm had much weaker social roots second time round, and its military justification could not stand up to events. The Bulgars had made peace in 816, but held much wider areas, and did not go away; they marked out their boundary with the Byzantines with the huge earthwork known as the Great Fence of Thrace in this period. The 'Abbasid caliphate was at its height, and Theophilos' attempts to impose himself on the eastern frontier resulted in a massive Arab invasion in 838, led by Caliph al-Mu'tasim himself, which sacked the important city of Amorion. Worse, north African Arabs invaded Sicily in 827 and began a conquest which would remove the whole island from Byzantine control by the early tenth century; and Crete fell to Spanish Arab pirates in 828, thus opening the Aegean to sea raiding again. It was now Iconoclasm, not Orthodoxy, which seemed to bring defeat. At Theophilos' death, his widow Theodora, regent for her infant son Michael III (842–67), and her allies overturned Iconoclasm in a year. In 843 Orthodoxy was restored (Theodora claimed that her husband had repented on his deathbed); Theodora, a second Eirene, had Constantine V's body exhumed and destroyed, and put Eirene's body into the imperial mausoleum instead. Iconoclasm vanished remarkably fast this time; there were no more major military defeats; and Byzantium could from now on continue firmly on its medieval track.

Second Iconoclasm can easily be painted as a superficial deviation, this time – unlike in the eighth century – little more than an imperial cult, tragedy reappearing as farce. It was more interesting than that, however, for two reasons. One was that Second Nicaea, and, later, Theodore of Stoudios and Patriarch Nikephoros, had created an organized Iconoclasm as a negative image, which could simply be reestablished by their opponents. That is to say, precisely because of Iconoclasm's enemies, it could be an entire religious system that Leo V and his advisers invoked, not just the memory of Constantine V, even though the latter lay at the core of their choices. The other was that there were more intellectuals in Constantinople by now to debate about it; we know much more about Second than about First Iconoclasm as a result. The relative prosperity of the eighth century allowed for the development of education in theology, classical literature and philosophy in the capital after 750 or so which is hardly attested in the previous hundred and fifty years. Constantinople had never gone short of the great works of ancient secular and ecclesiastical literature, but from now on they were increasingly accessible to the political élite. Nikephoros used Aristotle to refute Iconoclast ideas in his *Antirrhēseis*; Theodore was steeped in Basil of Caesarea and John Chrysostom. Ignatios the Deacon (d. *c.* 848), whose career we shall come to in a moment, cited many classical authors, above all Homer, but also Hesiod, Euripides and Aristotle, in his writings and invoked the 'Pythagorean doctrine of friendship' in letters. The writings of the major Iconoclast theorist John the Grammarian, who compiled the texts Leo V used in 815 and was patriarch in 837–43, do not survive, but his name speaks for itself. His relative Leo the Mathematician (d. after 869) taught the next generation of the élite, in the schools he ran from the 820s onwards, both before and after 843. These men were capable of serious intellectual debate. The emperor Theophilos, in particular, sought it; remarkably, he freed in 838 the Sicilian Iconophile Methodios (d. 847), who had been in prison most of the time since 821, and kept him in the palace to discuss theology. Methodios was himself to become patriarch at the proclamation of Orthodoxy in 843.

Ignatios the Deacon represents the twists and turns of political culture in this period as well as anyone. Born in the 770s, he was a protégé of Tarasios and a friend of Patriarch Nikephoros in the 800s, which also, even if he does not say so very explicitly, will have made him an opponent of Theodore of Stoudios; even among Iconophiles, Theodore seemed an extremist, until Second Iconoclasm in 815 made them close ranks. Ignatios trimmed much closer to the wind than any of these, however. He may or may not have been the Ignatios who composed Iconoclast poems for the walls of the imperial palace under Leo V, but he was certainly archbishop of Nicaea for a while under either Leo or Michael II, and he wrote public poetry for Michael. Ignatios' collected letters of the 820s–840s show him to be a cultured intellectual, but essentially a regime figure, devoted to patronage relations with bishops and civil officials alike. The collection, made after 843, is expurgated of pro-Iconoclast sentiment, but it contains very little Iconophile sentiment either. In perhaps the 820s he writes to his close friend the archivist Nikephoros, praising him for his stance, which was slightly more critical of Iconoclasm than Ignatios' own, but the letter shows quite clearly that both men were on friendly terms with a leading Iconoclast; relationships of power cut across personal belief in a very obvious way. The year 843 marked a break here; Ignatios was regarded by Methodios as too close to Second Iconoclasm to remain unscathed, and for a while he was exiled (sort of: to a monastery in sight of the capital, not exactly very far away). The letters he writes now are regretful: I am poor now; I 'furiously strayed to the opposite side'. But Ignatios redeemed himself remarkably fast, with heavily Iconophile biographies of his old associates patriarchs Tarasios and Nikephoros, and by his death he was back in the patriarchal entourage – he had successfully trimmed back again to his starting point. In the early ninth century Ignatios was probably the norm, committed Iconophiles or Iconoclasts the exceptions. Byzantium in 843 comes to seem like England in 1660 or East Germany in 1990, full of people trying to show how little they had compromised with a losing political system which in reality they had been largely happy with. Each was the triumph of a better-rooted but also rather more conservative and complacent political regime, which imposed its own orthodoxy, a set of soon-unquestioned assumptions inside which people henceforth would have to operate.

I have spent some time on Iconoclasm, because it is perplexing. One could easily write a history of the period 750–850 stressing quite other things: Constantine V's military protagonism; Nikephoros I's administrative reforms, which were taken further under Michael II and Theophilos (by the mid-ninth century, the army was better paid and equipped, and was reinforced by a strong set of *tagmata* around the capital); or the visible commitment to prestige building in the capital under Theophilos: new palaces with mechanical devices which do not survive, renewed city walls which do. All of these betray a greater confidence, as well as a desire to impress. The empire was in reasonably good shape by 850; it had weathered the worst storms by now. Does it matter, then, that so much imperial and theological rhetoric was taken up with the issue of whether one should venerate pictures? Iconoclasm, the first medieval theological dispute, has seemed to many to be about less 'serious' theoretical issues than the great Christological debates of the past. It is not surprising, then, that much analysis of Iconoclasm has supposed, whether explicitly or implicitly, that it was 'really' about something else. So Peter Brown, in an influential argument, fully recognizes that the Iconoclast debate was about the location of the holy in society, not a small matter, but he goes on to emphasize that the aim of the Iconoclast emperors, in the face of the Arab threat, was to streamline the whole of Byzantine society and culture, and focus it on a few central symbols, the cross, the eucharist, the capital, the emperor himself, rather than face 'a haemorrhage of the holy . . . into a hundred little paintings'.

In a sense, this is quite true; but it is also the case that the Byzantines had become interested in representation and its rules for their own sake. It is already visible in the *Parastaseis*, in an almost entirely secular context: whom statues really represented mattered to people. It was, famously, also an issue important to the Muslim Arabs, who avoided all representations of people in their public art, seeing them as idolatrous (although the Qur'an conveys no such instruction, as we shall see in the next chapter). Caliph al-Walid I (705–15), who probably employed Byzantine mosaicists to erect the complicated foliage patterns on the walls of the Great Mosque of Damascus (see above, Chapter 10), would presumably have been entirely happy that they should take back to

Constantinople accounts of his religious aesthetic. This aesthetic may indeed have impacted on Palestinian Christians, living under Arab rule, who after about 720 began to efface all representations of living beings, even animals and birds, from the floor mosaics of their churches; this obsession has no parallel in Byzantium, and may well show Muslim influence – though it goes beyond Muslim concerns, too. It must be stressed that there is absolutely no sign that the Byzantine Iconoclasts were influenced by the Arabs. But Arabs, Byzantines, Palestinian Christians, were all separately concerned with the *issue* of representation: which elements were holy, which were idolatrous, how and whom images represented and should represent. This was a break with a late Roman Christian tradition, in which images, even of saints, had relatively little special charge; in the East from now on they had, at least potentially, a numinous power, and people had to get them right, in one way or another. And the political system this mattered most in was Byzantium, for emperors were becoming more important foci of religious concern than were either Roman emperors or even, by now, caliphs. Iconoclasm did not begin with the emperors, but once it reached Constantine V and he took a decision on it, it immediately became an imperial initiative, and was tied to him, in a way 'Arianism' never was for Valens, nor Monophysitism for Anastasius I. Representation, and the importance of the visual, thus became tied in with imperial legitimacy. After 843 this became Orthodoxy; the religious centrality of images has been a feature of Orthodox Christianity ever since.

1

The Crystallizatio...
Power, 6...

to Siffin on the Euphra...
some time. 'Ali in th...
part of his army...
group who...
for they...
of th...

In June 656, 'Uthman ibn 'Affan, comn...
al-mu'minīn), deputy of God (*khalīfat A*... ... ...nglish title
'caliph'), was murdered in his house in hi... capital, Medina in western
Arabia. The event convulsed the Arab world, and the First Civil War
(*fitna*) followed, until peace was restored in 661. So much is certain
(it was recorded shortly afterwards, although very sketchily, by the
Armenian chronicler whom we call Sebeos); the rest is, and was, hotly
contested. Was 'Uthman's successor 'Ali (656–61) involved in the murder, as many in the 'Uthmani party thought, hence the civil war? Was
the murder carried out by disaffected pro-'Ali bedouin extremists against
'Ali's will, as one of the earliest Arab historians, Sayf ibn 'Umar (d.
c. 796), claimed? Or was the murder the work of disaffected Egyptian
soldiers, tired of 'Uthman's attempts to direct the Egyptian grain surplus
to Medina and to replace the power of the early Arab conquerors of the
provinces from Egypt to Iraq by more traditional tribal leaders – including members of 'Uthman's own immediate family, the Umayyads – as
other early historians, Ibn Ishaq (d. 767) and especially al-Waqidi
(d. 823), report? And, above all, was the murder a justified response to
'Uthman's illegitimate acts, which meant that he was no longer properly
caliph, or was it illegal, and therefore had to be avenged?

'Ali may have thought the first of these latter two alternatives. Certainly the later Shi'ite tradition did – indeed, that tradition thought that
'Uthman, and maybe his two predecessors, were usurpers, and that 'Ali
had been designated the Prophet's successor by Muhammad himself at
his death in 632. The 'Uthmanis certainly thought the second, not least
Mu'awiya ibn Abi Sufyan, governor of Syria and 'Uthman's second
cousin, thus also an Umayyad. Mu'awiya demanded that 'Uthman's
murder must be punished and led a Syrian army against 'Ali's Iraqi army

s in 657, where the two sides skirmished for
e end agreed to arbitration on the issue, but lost
– and his strategic advantage – as a result; the dissident
eft him, the Kharijites, were outraged at 'Ali's concession,
thought that only God could judge the issue, not humans. One
em assassinated 'Ali in 661, after which Mu'awiya took over as sole
aliph (661–80).

So who did kill 'Uthman, and with what justification? The same
question could be asked of many similar deaths in the early Middle
Ages, as with Childeric II in Francia in 675, or Edward the Martyr in
England in 978. The basic answer is that we do not fully know, and in
these two latter cases historians are relatively relaxed about the fact
that they do not know; it is enough for them to unpick the different
interpretations in the sources so as to identify political alignments. But
in the Islamic tradition it was, and is, not so easy. Religious disagreement
between Muslim communities tends not to be over the nature of God,
as inside early Christianity (a single monotheistic Allah gives less space
for debate than the incomprehensible complexities of the Trinity), but
rather, much more, over political legitimacy. The basic twenty-first-
century division between Sunni and Shi'a Islam goes straight back to
656, even if the two sides did not call themselves that yet. The Kharijites
still exist too, in Sahara oases and Zanzibar, and have not yet forgiven
'Ali for Siffin. It would even now be hard in the Muslim world to discuss
neutrally the behaviour of 'Uthman or his murderers without taking a
position between Sunni and Shi'a/Kharijite interpretations. And this was
even more so around 800, when our first detailed accounts began to be
written down, or around 900, when they were collected in the great
historical compilations of writers like al-Baladhuri (d. 892) or al-Tabari
(d. 923). Even a decision not to be sure who was right in 656 had a
doctrinal implication from the eighth century onwards (it was associated
with the Murji'ites, the 'suspenders of judgement'). Indeed, in the ninth
century this became common ground in much of what was becoming
the majority Sunni tradition, for that tradition held that rulers should
not be deposed, and that communal unity was more important than
sectarian division (by then, Sunnis accepted both 'Uthman and 'Ali as
legitimate caliphs; it was Mu'awiya they had more trouble with). But
the whole issue continued to *matter*, intensely, and all our sources are
structured by partisan positions of this kind.

Writing early Arab history is in many ways a harder task than writing the history of other peoples or states in the same period. One reason is the religious importance of every event, as just discussed; this might seem less surprising, perhaps, when one is discussing Muhammad, who was a prophet above anything else, and maybe even his immediate successors, but Arab history right up to 750 has at least in part to be seen through salvationist perspectives. A second is the late date of most of our narrative sources. This ought not to matter too much to early medievalists – mid-seventh-century Byzantine history is mostly accessible only through early ninth-century writers, too, without Byzantinists being more than regretful about it – but the religious importance of the period, and the irreconcilable sectarian positions of our sources, have bothered Arabists much more and have resulted in the rejection by an influential strand of recent historians of all possibility of knowing anything reliable about Muslim Arab history before the 690s at the earliest. It is also the case that, after an absence of narrative sources for the Arabs in the seventh and early eighth centuries, in the ninth and tenth our source material explodes in quantity. There may be as much writing surviving in Arabic (mostly from Iraq) from those two centuries as from the whole of Europe in our whole period. The huge size of this source material, plus the radical nature of recent critiques of it, has led historians of the early caliphate into ever more enclosed discussions of the criteria for its authenticity, and there are remarkably few recent analyses of the details of the period before 750 (or even after it) in itself. The sources themselves are opaque to the inexpert, too; they are frequently made up of quite bitty stories (*akhbār*), which are given truth-content by chains of informants, maybe going back a couple of centuries, but then often counterposed to other stories that say the exact opposite. One can feel oneself flung into an unfamiliar cultural world, which is further emphasized by the different way in which most historians currently write about it.

And yet the early Arab period is crucial for us to confront. The caliphate did not rule any part of Europe before the Arab-Berber invasion of Spain in 711, but it cannot be excluded from a history of the Continent. For a start, it was the Arabs who broke in half the surviving section of the Roman empire in the seventh century, ending for ever its dream of continued Mediterranean hegemony, and forcing it to reinvent itself as the state we call Byzantium, as we saw in the last chapter. Secondly, the caliphate was itself built on Roman foundations (as also Sassanian Persian foundations). Notwithstanding the difficulty and unfamiliarity of our narrative sources for it, it arguably preserved the parameters of imperial Roman society more completely than any other part of the post-Roman world, at least in the period up to 750; this is a paradox which it is essential to explore. Thirdly, the caliphate was simply richer and more powerful than any other post-Roman polity. By now it was the Arabs that dominated the Mediterranean. After 750, under the 'Abbasids, the centre of the caliphate moved from Mu'awiya's Syria to Iraq, and further from Roman traditions; I shall discuss the 'Abbasids in less detail as a result in Chapter 14. But the 'Abbasids, even more than the pre-750 Umayyads, far surpassed their neighbours in their wealth and in the sophistication of their intellectual culture, and we must pay attention to that, both in Chapter 14 and in 15, when we look at the east Mediterranean economy as a whole. This chapter will discuss the Arab conquests and the Umayyad caliphate of Mu'awiya and his successors. Here, we shall focus on the linked problems of the stabilization of the Arab (or Muslim) political system, and of the issue of social and cultural continuity and change, in the first of the many centuries of Arab dominance of the eastern and southern Mediterranean, and, indeed, of further afield.

Muhammad (c. 570–632) was a merchant in Mecca in western Arabia who around 610 began to get verbal revelations from God; he became a prophet and sought followers. The Arabs were polytheists, although there were substantial Christian and Jewish minorities among them. Muhammad was certainly closest to the Jewish tradition, and was, like the Jews, a very strict monotheist, but the most reliable early Muslim source (the *Constitution of Medina*, dating to the 620s) makes it clear that Muhammad saw the Believers (the commonest early word for his followers) as separate from Jews. Muhammad's revelations were later collected as the Qur'an; Muslim tradition says that the basic recension of the text dates to 'Uthman's reign as caliph (644–56). Some recent western scholars have argued for a much later date, as late as 800 for John Wansbrough, the early eighth century for Patricia Crone, though Fred Donner makes a good defence for the traditional dating on grounds of content and style. However this may be, it is undeniable and important that elements of the Qur'an were already widely circulating in the late

civil wars. But the core reason for the survival of Arab rule as not only a political but also a cultural hegemony was not luck. Rather, it was the result of the decision (traditionally, and plausibly, ascribed to 'Umar I in 640–42) to settle the Arab armies, not as a landowning aristocracy as in the Germanic West, but as paid garrisons in newly founded cities (*amṣār*), Kufa and Basra in Iraq, Mosul on the edge of the Iraq–Syria borderlands known as the Jazira, Fustat (the future Cairo) in Egypt, and others. The tax revenues of the provinces went to these garrisons above all, who thus were well rewarded for their separation from the socio-political life of the conquered population; being on the local *dīwān*, the register of those entitled to army pay, was a coveted privilege, defended against newcomers as much as possible. 'Umar's policy succeeded; relatively little Arab landowning is recorded for any of these core provinces before 750 (although it seems to have been greater in Khurasan, where indeed Arab settlers were eventually Persianized, and also in the later conquest territories of Africa and Spain). This set the template for a structural separation between a paid army and the rest of civil – civilian – society which was greater even than in the Roman empire, and which marked most Muslim political systems ever after.

This decision had several consequences. One was fiscal: the tax system of the Roman – and also Sassanian – empire never broke down, as it did in the West, for it always had an essential political purpose, the payment of a ruling army. Another was, as already implied, that the Arabs were preserved as a separate and superior social stratum. They intermarried with local families, but their children maintained an Arabic language, culture, religion, identity. And they were so separate that anyone from the conquered majority who sought political prominence would have to try to join them, both in culture and in religion. This was less true of the seventh century, when the Arabs discouraged conversion to Islam, and anyway maintained the provincial governments of the conquered provinces, both Roman and Persian, intact. It was possible for two generations after the conquests to be powerful in the civil administration without changing one's culture or identity at all, as with the Mansur family, prominent Greek Christian administrators in the Umayyad capital, Damascus, into the early eighth century, one of whose members was the important Christian theologian John of Damascus (d. *c.* 750). But around 700 the basic language of administration was changed to Arabic; from then on bureaucrats would have to be Arabic-speaking and, increasingly, Muslim. The process of conversion, at least for local élites, was indeed seen as an Arabization process; one had to become the client (*mawlā*, plural *mawālī*) of the tribe of an Arab sponsor, and, usually, to change one's name to an Arab one. Such people 'became' Arabs, with access to political power, and perpetuated Arabic language and culture as they did so. Peasant conversion (which existed from the start; Muslims paid lower taxes, at least in theory) did not ever bring political privilege, but very slowly the links of Muslim clientage extended outwards to the peasantry too, and Islamization/Arabization permeated the countryside as it did so. This process was not a large-scale one until the ninth century at the earliest, but it was steady from then on, and by 1000 the majority of the population from Egypt to Iraq probably spoke Arabic. Of the conquest lands, only Iran maintained its original Persian language, by now however written in Arabic script and full of Arab loanwords.

This early separation between Arab élites and the conquered majority also meant that Roman society and Persian society persisted, remarkably unchanged, into the late eighth century and often later. Egyptian documents show that the cities of the Nile valley remained governed by their traditional élites until past 700; all that the Arabization of the administration meant initially was that Greek was used less and less; most of the population continued to speak and write Coptic. Nor was this process instantaneous; we have some two hundred administrative letters (mostly about taxation) from the governor of Egypt, Qurra ibn Sharik (709–15), to Basilios, pagarch or city governor of the small middle Nile city of Aphrodito, modern Kom Ishqaw, and these are for the most part still either in Greek or bilingual in Greek and Arabic. From this point on, pagarchs would be Muslims, with Arabic names; any local family which wanted to continue to control its city would by 730 or so have to convert. Villages were less affected, all the same; throughout the eighth century Coptic overwhelmingly dominates in our village archives, and Arabic is not prominent except in governmental texts until the ninth. Mosques do not appear in our documents either; rural religion was essentially Christian throughout this period. It is possible as a result to write Egyptian social history up to 800 almost without reference to the Arabs at all, for they were so much shut away in Fustat. This would be a mistake, but it is a tempting one.

Syria and Palestine, the other major ex-Roman provinces, show a more nuanced picture, but a similar one. There were always more Arabs in the Levant, from well before Muhammad's time; some of the most powerful Umayyad-period Arab tribes, notably the Kalb, originated from the Syrian desert fringe. Probably as a result of this long-standing tradition, there were no important *amṣār* in the region; the Arab army of Syria settled in the already existing cities of the Roman empire, less separate from the native population than they were elsewhere. And Damascus became, from Muʿawiya's reign onwards, the capital of the caliphate, replacing Medina; Syria was thus the core province of Umayyad government. One might have expected an early Arabization of the Levant as a result of all these factors. But there are remarkably few signs of it. Damascus probably slowly became Arabized once the administrative language changed to Arabic (evidence for the capital is unfortunately not good), but Edessa, at least, certainly did not; its rich Christian written tradition shows a strong and prosperous Syriac-speaking urban élite until well into the ninth century. In the countryside, Nessana in the Negev desert, which has preserved a papyrus archive into the 680s, has hardly any Arabic documents, even though a substantial proportion of its population were ethnic Arabs, and even though one text in Greek seems actually to be a page of a *dīwān* register. (On the other hand, Khirbat al-Mird, in the desert west of the Dead Sea, was already Arabic-speaking in the late seventh century, as a smaller papyrus collection shows.) And the extensive urban and rural archaeology of both Syria and Palestine shows notable continuities; indeed, the Arab conquest is hardly visible in it at all. There were certainly new Arab administrative and religious buildings put up across the region in the next century, but cityscapes were slow to change; and churches were still being built in cities and the countryside into the late eighth century in what is now northern Jordan and elsewhere. The economic implications of this we shall look at in Chapter 15, but the cultural templates of late Roman urban and rural life were as yet unchanged, even in the Umayyad heartland. The ambitious monuments of the Umayyads themselves, which we shall come to shortly, were only an overlay onto these essential continuities. Here, as in Egypt, wider cultural change only began after 750, and maybe later still.

The trouble with this cultural separation, between Arabs and local populations, was that the age-old patronage links between central and local power were cut, particularly once the administration went Arabic.

Local power-brokers could hope to deal with central government in the seventh century, as it still spoke their language; one of the Nessana papyri from the 680s shows a local notable, Lord (*kyrios*) Samuel, organizing village representatives to go to protest to the governor in Gaza about the provincial tax burden. (The governor was certainly an Arab, but he too wrote in Greek for the most part.) In the eighth century, such power-brokers had to choose: whether to stay Christian with their clients and lose purchase with the administration, or to become Arabized *mawālī*, and thus part of government, but risk losing their local links. In Egypt, the latter choice was rare still, and the eighth century saw tensions rising. Tax revolts began in Egypt in 726, and continued on and off for over a century, with particularly serious uprisings in 750, the year of the Umayyad fall, and 812–32. Arab taxation was not obviously heavier than Roman taxation had been, but Egyptian civil society was too cut off from the Arab military élite, and violent resistance resulted. Arab political power was too entrenched by 750, however, to be structurally threatened by this; and the Arabization of the country-side, which had begun by 832, meant that stronger patronage chains could emerge again.

The Arab/non-Arab cultural separation was nonetheless incomplete, for one crucial reason: Islam itself had emerged from the world of late Roman (largely Jewish) religiosity, and had little difficulty in relating to many aspects of the religious landscape it found in the conquered provinces. This is clearest in the least formalized aspects of religion, those least tied up in political power and legitimacy; several early Muslim accounts claim that Muhammad was recognized and respected by Christian holy men, for example, most notably the Syrian hermit Bahira, who turns up in some Christian sources too. Muslims also respected both Jewish and Christian holy places, Jerusalem most notably (which they sought to appropriate), but also Mount Sinai, location of both Christian and Muslim pilgrimage. Perhaps the best example of this is the Umayyad interest in the cult-site of St Sergios at Sergiopolis, in Arabic Rusafa, in the east Syrian steppe south of the Euphrates. In the decades around 500 this was the location of some highly ambitious imperial church building for the pilgrimage centre Sergiopolis had become; it was also situated in a Christian Arab area, and the Ghassanids linked themselves in the sixth century to St Sergios in general and to Rusafa in particular. It is therefore significant that Rusafa was also the caliph Hisham's favourite country residence in the 730s; he built a mosque there right beside, indeed sharing a courtyard with, one of the major churches of the city, and also a set of shops around the precinct (Hisham was a patron of monumental shop complexes elsewhere, too: see Chapter 15). The caliph was clearly reacting to – indeed, respecting – the religious importance of the place, even though that importance was essentially and traditionally Christian. Rusafa was a Muslim political centre for only two decades at the most, but Sarjis, that is, Sergios, turned into a Muslim holy man in at least some parts of the Arab world in centuries to come. In places like Rusafa, both conquerors and conquered could meet as, in religious terms, some kind of equals.

'Umar I's reign was marked by war, and, apart from the establishment of the *dīwān* system, it was not a period of wider-scale state formation. When the first wave of conquests stopped around 651, 'Uthman found that one danger was that the new provinces risked drifting apart under their new Arab military élites. It is not clear whether under 'Umar the provinces sent any of their tax revenue back to Medina, but all sources agree that 'Uthman laid claim to at least some of them, particularly from the agriculturally rich provinces of Egypt and Iraq. 'Uthman's equally controversial patronage of kinsmen and tribal leaders as governors, instead of the early Muslims, often of no particular tribal status, who dominated the garrison towns, can be interpreted as the caliph trying to ensure chains of loyalty to him that would stabilize the new Arab political system. Both of these policies aimed to centralize power, and it is likely enough that it was indeed these policies that led to his death in 656. But it was his kinsman Mu'awiya who won the First Civil War, and Mu'awiya certainly continued them; he appointed his adopted brother Ziyad (d. 673) to govern Iraq and Iran, for example, and inside Syria linked himself closely to the tribal confederacy dominated by the Kalb, which was the main Arab group in the province. (It is less certain how far he managed to divert provincial revenues to Syria, however; his centralizing practices were above all personal.) Mu'awiya clearly thought dynastically, and ensured that his son (by a Kalbi mother) Yazid I (680–83) would succeed him. This led at his death to a far more serious rerun of 656–61, the Second Civil War of 680–92.

'Ali's son al-Husayn was the first to revolt against Yazid, in 680; he was killed at Karbala' in Iraq in a one-sided conflict that has resonated ever since in Shi'a martyrology. In Medina, 'Abd Allah ibn al-Zubayr, son of another First Civil War leader, also rejected Yazid's authority, and he established himself as caliph there and in Mecca (683–92), with quite a wide authority for some years. Ibn al-Zubayr was not very militarily active himself, but he had substantial support both in Iraq and in parts of Syria. After Yazid's death, Kufa, too, revolted under the 'Alid leader Mukhtar, and was effectively independent in 685–7. And in Syria itself the leading Arab tribes fell out, the Kalb being opposed by the Qays, a coalition of newer settlers from northern Arabia, based in northern Syria and the Jazira, supporters of Ibn al-Zubayr. The Kalb put in a new branch of the Umayyad family as caliphs to confront Ibn al-Zubayr, Marwan I (684–5) and his son 'Abd al-Malik (685–705), the first Marwanids, and Marwan defeated the Qays at the battle of Marj Rahit north of Damascus in 684. Even then, everything risked breaking up, but 'Abd al-Malik held on, carried on fighting, and re-established unity with the reconquest of Mecca and the death of Ibn al-Zubayr in 692. What was clear, however, was that he needed a new and more stable political settlement, to avoid renewed chaos leading to the end of Arab rule.

With 'Abd al-Malik our historical information begins to be rather more reliable and diversified, and we can be more confident in our reconstructions. One thing he did was return to conquest. Westwards from Egypt, Arab armies had rather desultorily moved into the southern parts of Byzantine Africa in the 640s and then the 670s (founding the garrison city of Kairouan in 670); in the late 690s, however, they defeated the powerful Berber tribes of the Algerian plateau, and conquered Africa definitively, taking Carthage in 698. The Berbers took to Arab rule very fast. In 711, under 'Abd al-Malik's son al-Walid I, a Berber and Arab army invaded Spain, and by the end of the 710s it controlled nearly all the Iberian peninsula and was raiding into Francia. To the east, Bukhara and Samarkand fell in 706–12, and the Arabs occupied central Asia, and also parts of north-west India. The scene was set for the greatest conquest of all, Constantinople, with the siege of 717–18 led by Maslama, son of 'Abd al-Malik, although this failed; it turned out that the caliphate had reached its greatest extent under al-Walid, and border wars would be the norm thereafter. These new conquests did not have the economic and political importance of those of 636–51, but they kept the main provincial armies busy and rich, which was better than civil war.

'Abd al-Malik also ruled the provinces as forcefully as he could. Egypt was entrusted to his brother 'Abd al-Aziz (d. 704), and shortly after that to the Qaysi governor Qurra, whose surviving letters show him to be very effective in his exactions and his local control. We still cannot see Egyptian wealth going to Syria, and these governors were probably as rich as the caliphs themselves, but they were certainly loyal. Iraq, the most troublesome province for the early Umayyads, was in 694 assigned to the hyper-loyal al-Hajjaj ibn Yusuf, another Qaysi, who governed it (and, after 697, Khurasan as well) until his death in 714; al-Hajjaj was a very tough, not to say oppressive, ruler who provoked a civil war with the Kufans in 701 and established a Syrian army in the zone after that; Iraqi armies withered, and Iraqi taxes went to Damascus from then on. In Syria, 'Abd al-Malik maintained a balance between Kalbi and Qaysi patronage networks, as these Qaysi governors already imply. The two opposing networks gained in force, all the same; the Kalb joined with immigrants from Yemen who had settled in central Syria, and the alliance is generally from now on called Yamani in our sources; the two networks, which came to include virtually all Arabs, were fierce rivals for patronage from the caliphs, particularly the highly lucrative position of governor. A Yamani or a Qaysi governor could be relied on to appoint only members of his own faction to subordinate posts, but the caliphs themselves were for a long time fairly neutral between the two major groupings.

'Abd al-Malik established a new public prominence both for Arab culture and for Islam. He Arabized the civil administration, as we have seen. That administration gained ever greater coherence, as is visible, for example, in the highly polished state letters of the senior chancery administrator 'Abd al-Hamid (dating 725–50), which prefigure the belles-lettrist *adab* style of the ninth to eleventh centuries, as also the highly literary Byzantine practices of the same period, both discussed later. 'Abd al-Malik furthermore, for the first time, instituted a coinage that reflected caliphal political power. Previously, Arab coins had imitated Byzantine and Persian models, but in 691–2 new standard-weight coins came in, the gold *dīnār* in the ex-Roman lands and in ex-Persian lands the silver *dirham*, which had Arabic and Islamic inscriptions, and which after 696 abandoned images for purely verbal decoration. The caliph also, already during the Second Civil War, inaugurated expensive prestige buildings, beginning with the Dome of the Rock, on the spot to which Muhammad reputedly miraculously travelled for a night from Mecca, on top of the old Jewish cult centre of the Temple Mount in Jerusalem, finished in 691–2; this was followed under al-Walid by the neighbouring al-Aqsa mosque in Jerusalem (709–15), the Great Mosque in Medina (706–10), and the huge Great Mosque of Damascus (705–16), which largely survives in its original form, decorated with mosaics, as we have seen. These and other projects were by far the largest-scale buildings in Eurasia west of China in this period, and they all explicitly celebrated a triumphal and rich Islam. They show, it must be added, that some money at least was by now getting to Syria from the provinces. The Umayyads were also giving a Muslim education to their children; one sign is the religious austerity of 'Umar II ibn 'Abd al-Aziz (717–20), who alone out of the Umayyad caliphs was regarded as a just ruler by later generations. This austerity was not continued by his successors, but by now the stability of the regime was more assured, as the long and relatively peaceful rule of Hisham, the last son of 'Abd al-Malik (724–43), shows.

The Umayyads had a terrible press after their fall in 750. They were seen as dynastic rather than ruling by consensus (though the 'Abbasids would be just as dynastic as they); and as luxurious degenerates, enjoying themselves in their palaces and ignoring the needs of government. They certainly built luxurious palaces; some of them survive, in the Jordan valley and on the Syrian/Jordanian desert fringe, as ambitious in their own way as al-Walid's mosques, and in two cases (the stuccoes of Khirbat al-Mafjar outside Jericho, the frescoes of the Qusayr 'Amra bath-house east of 'Amman) they show a profusion of human forms (often naked and female) that do not look very 'Islamic'. This represents a private decorative tradition that would have a long future in Muslim societies, all the same, rather than indicating that its Umayyad sponsors had not read the Qur'an properly. (Actually, the Qur'an only opposes idol-worship, not all figurative representations of humans; but a caution about public representational art was certainly already accepted by the Umayyad caliphs, as we saw in Chapter 10, for the outsides of these palaces, often heavily carved in high relief, were entirely geometric and non-figurative, just as the mosque of Damascus was.) Several of the Umayyads did indeed have imaginative personal lives, too; but so have rulers throughout history – including, once again, the 'Abbasids – without this impacting very greatly on their conceptions of rule. These accusations are simply a *damnatio memoriae*, like the later Byzantine attacks on Constantine V, rather than an accurate critique of Umayyad government.

The critique of the Umayyads which had the strongest resonance was that they were Arab, not Muslim, rulers. It has lasted ever since, too: even Julius Wellhausen, the great late nineteenth-century historian of the Umayyads, called their realm the 'Arab kingdom'. It is a particularly false claim. For a start, the Umayyad caliphs took their religious responsibilities very seriously, at least from 'Abd al-Malik onwards (Mu'awiya is a rather more shadowy figure). 'Umar II issued highly religious edicts, and was by no means the only caliph to do so. We have one from al-Walid II (743–4), later considered the dynasty's most notorious playboy, which is adamant about the religious duties entrusted to him by God. These include the enforcement of religious obedience, the pursuance of 'that which is most righteous for him in particular and for the Muslims in general', and, overall, 'the completion of Islam'; with a few phrases changed, this could be Charlemagne at his most moralizing. Similarly, his cousin and supplanter Yazid III (744) justified his uprising against al-Walid in exclusively Muslim terms. These caliphs indeed felt their religious role more strongly than did the 'Abbasids, after the fervour of the first 'Abbasid generation at least, for by the end of the eighth century the task of interpreting religious authority had mostly fallen to a new social group, the *'ulamā'* of scholars (see below, Chapter 14).

It has also been proposed that Umayyad Islam was more 'Arabic' than later, universalist, Islam would be. Was Muhammad a prophet only for the Arabs, or for everyone? It has been argued that the early Arab caution about conversion implied the former, and that only the 'Abbasids really opened their religion to all comers. This, too, is largely an overstated reading. The Arabs undoubtedly believed in their own ethnic superiority, and were at best edgy, at worst hostile, to non-Arabs, including converts. Qusayr 'Amra also includes a famous fresco of six kings, of the Roman empire, Sassanian Persia, Ethiopia, Visigothic Spain, and two unidentified countries, apparently gesturing to an adjoining fresco of ethnic Arab victory. But conversion was nonetheless seen as normal, and plenty of *mawālī* reached high positions under the Umayyads, notably Musa ibn Nusayr (d. 716), one of the conquerors of Spain, and several later governors of Africa. Al-Hajjaj, the emblematic

Umayyad devotee, himself appointed a black African, Sa'id ibn Jubayr (d. 713), to the post of *qāḍī* (judge) of Kufa, even if he had to rescind the appointment because the Kufans protested against a *mawlā* holding the role. There was, of course, a contradiction between Arab exclusiveness and Muslim inclusiveness, but it was felt by every Arab, from caliph to foot soldier, until conversion became widespread, for different reasons, in the ninth century; it was also not just a matter of Arab vs. non-Arab, but settled Arab vs. bedouin Arab (each claimed to be the better Muslims), and of course tribe vs. tribe. Arab tribalism had by now little of the desert about it, it can be added; the huge majority of Arabs by 700 lived settled lives and were just competing for military and civilian positions. Their desire to secure such positions for themselves and their families and allies, rather than their rivals, led to tribal- and ethnic-exclusivist actions and rhetoric, but this is true of any society, and would not cease in 750.

An example of this mixture of positions in a single person is the poet al-Farazdaq (d. *c.* 729); he may have had bedouin origins, but he lived most of his long life in Basra. His poetic palette of camels, gazelles, tents and cavalry warfare was more the standard rhetoric of any Arab poet than nostalgia for the desert. So were his attacks on the honour and sexual morality of people (usually poets) from rival tribes, and his complex love poetry. Al-Farazdaq was Arab through and through; he loathed having to go to 'an odious land, the country of the blond-haired Greeks of 'Amman'. But when he wrote eulogies to the caliphs (some fifteen survive, for every caliph from 'Abd al-Malik to Hisham) his imagery turns Muslim: 'Run to Islam, justice has returned to us, the scourge which desolated Iraq is dead, there are no more poor on the earth, Sulayman [caliph 715–17] is the treasure of the universe.' This is not in the least surprising, and indeed precisely recalls the mixed values that any early medieval Christian writer had, western or eastern, as with the glorification of Frankish ethnic and military superiority in Gregory of Tours or Einhard, Christian inclusivism notwithstanding, or indeed the ferocious hostility to Goths of their fellow-Christian Synesios at the start of the fifth century. It is not religious and moral inconsistency that made the Arabs different in our period.

Hisham was the first caliph to face the problems of a no longer expanding frontier. Instead, Khazars and Turks themselves invaded from the north, and were beaten back with some difficulty in the 730s (in the case of the Khazars, by Marwan ibn Muhammad, an able general from the Umayyad family, who became governor of the Jazira). In the far west, too, there was a major Berber revolt in 740–43 which cut off Umayyad access to Spain and even Africa. But these only look like signs of Umayyad collapse in retrospect; they were all dealt with before Hisham's death. More serious was his famous tight-fistedness with money, for this is a sign that the caliphs had not solved the problem of tax money staying in the provinces it had been collected from. Not only Iraqis but also Egyptian Arabs had lost their military role by now, and the late Umayyad army was overwhelmingly Syrian except in the Berber lands of the far west and in Khurasan in the far east, but this did not lead to any further organizational centralization. Yazid III, indeed, promised not to move tax money outside provinces in his 744 rebel manifesto. At Hisham's death, furthermore, serious problems did appear, for the Syrian army broke up into Yamani and Qaysi factions. Al-Walid II was not necessarily pro-Qaysi, but Yazid III's revolt certainly had essentially Yamani support; Marwan in the Jazira, who sought to avenge the murdered al-Walid, ruled the Qaysi province par excellence and recruited a Qaysi army. Yazid died suddenly after a few months, and Marwan replaced him as Marwan II (744–50), but the latter had to spend two years reducing Yamani resistance in Syria, the first time the core caliphal province had ever been under attack.

The years 744–6 are seen as the Third Civil War; this time, unlike the seventh-century *fitna*s, overall Arab rule was too established to be in danger. But Umayyad rule was another matter. There were Shi'ite and even Kharijite revolts, with Yamani support, in Iraq in 744–8 too; these were easy enough to confront, as Iraq no longer had an army of its own, but their appearance is a sign of a loss of confidence in the ruling dynasty. And events in Khurasan, where the main eastern army was situated, were even more serious. It emerged that Shi'ite groups had been quietly preaching revolution there for three decades in favour of the Hashimiyya, the branch of Quraysh that was Muhammad's immediate family. The Hashimiyya included the descendants of 'Ali, of course; but they also included the descendants of 'Abbas, the Prophet's uncle. In 747 one of the sectarians, Abu Muslim, urged open revolt outside Merv in eastern Khurasan, and very quickly this revolt snowballed to include almost the whole of the Khurasani army. Abu Muslim and his associates chose

'Abbasids, not 'Alids, as their religious figureheads, and Abu al-'Abbas was proclaimed caliph as al-Saffah in 749. The Khurasanis moved westward and defeated Marwan in northern Iraq in 750, then took over Syria and Egypt in the same year, where Marwan was killed. The 'Abbasid caliphate began here; and when al-Saffah died in 754, his brother Abu Ja'far, al-Mansur (754–75), soon executed Abu Muslim and took full power for himself. The new regime ended (or at least marginalized) the Qays–Yaman feud, largely because it mattered less in a Khurasani army which was substantially non-Arab; although the 'Abbasids certainly made full use of Yamani support, they made peace with the Qaysis as soon as they could. The fact that they conquered all the provinces and could thus begin from scratch also allowed them to end the fiscal exclusivity of each provincial *dīwān*. They did not base themselves in Khurasan, however, even though it was their main military support. They chose Iraq, which became the new caliphal province. It was central; it was also the archetypal non-Syrian province. Syria, laid waste by Marwan in 744–6 and again by Abu Muslim in 750 – as well as by a severe earthquake, probably in 749 – became a province like any other, and politically suspect as well. Al-Mansur's new capital of Baghdad, founded in 762, soon surpassed anything Damascus had ever been, and the style of the caliphate decisively changed.

The Umayyads largely fell because the dominant Syrian army split, losing them both military superiority and hegemony, the sense that their rule was inevitable. This allowed the sort of millenarian Shi'ism that had fuelled Mukhtar in Kufa in the 680s, and also lesser rebels in subsequent decades, to gain more support than ever before, in the heartland of Islam's second major army, that of Khurasan. (The third army, that of the Berbers, went its own way.) Abu Muslim was himself a *mawlā*, and he had considerable ethnic Persian support in the Khurasani army. As a result, it was then, and has been since, possible to see the Hashimiyya rising as the rejection of particularist Arab rule by a new Muslim community, based on a rate of conversion to Islam that was higher in Khurasan than anywhere else. But the other elements of the rising were entirely Arab, and they drew their support from the opposite source, the resentment of Yamani Arab soldiers, and of Arab settlers in the east who had been subjected to the local rule – and taxation – of Islamized Persian élites. It is at least clear that the breakdown of Umayyad consensus in Khurasan was the result of an interaction, much greater than elsewhere, and highly tense as well, between Arab settlers and the indigenous majority. This might have broken down into local civil war; but the Shi'ites managed to convert this tension into a salvation-based unity that overturned the political system. The salvationism was an illusion, and religious revolts (all by now 'Alid) dotted the 'Abbasid caliphate, as it had that of the Umayyads before them. But the political direction of a caliphate now rooted in Iraq would be quite different all the same.

13

Byzantine Revival, 850–1000

In the *Book of Ceremonies*, traditionally ascribed to the emperor Constantine VII Porphyrogennitos (913–20, 945–59), probably compiled during his second reign and updated later, the emperor is expected to take part in a great number of religious processions in Constantinople: one on every day in the week after Easter, Ascension, Pentecost, 1 May (the date of the dedication of the Nea church in 880 by Basil I, 867–86), feast-days for Elijah, St Demetrios, the Elevation of the Cross, and so on, all across the year. So are a long list of secular officials and religious leaders, tens or often hundreds of people, the wives of officials sometimes, and also the leaders of the circus factions of the city, whose task it is to deliver formal acclamations, as the emperor proceeds through the different halls, chapels and chambers of the Great Palace, out of the Bronze (*Chalkē*) Gate of the Palace (this is where the faction leaders meet him), across the road to Hagia Sophia, the Great Church of the Byzantine empire, and, after a church service, back again. The *Book* lays down rules for which clothing goes with which feast-day, the text of the different acclamations (some are still in Latin, four hundred years after that language was dying out as a spoken tongue in the city), and the locations of the tables for the post-ceremony dinners. The variability in the ritual could be complex. At Pentecost, for example, the description for which is particularly detailed – it goes on for twelve pages of the modern edition – the officials do not prostrate themselves in *proskynēsis* in front of the emperor in the Great Church, because the feast celebrates the Resurrection; it is the Pentecost service which also sees the empress appearing in church with a particularly elaborate set of official wives, twenty-one separate offices entering in seven separate groups.

Can all this really have taken place, for every feast in every year, with all these people? Who could even have kept all its variations in their head? Constantine certainly took it very seriously; he tells us in the *Book*'s preface, which he probably wrote himself, that he wanted to re-establish imperial ceremonial, whose neglect left the Byzantine empire 'without finery and without beauty', and whose celebration would be a 'limpid and perfectly clean mirror' of imperial splendour, allowing 'the reins of power to be held with order and dignity'. It is clear from this that Constantine did think ceremony had been less elaborate before his time, and many of the descriptions commissioned by him were really reconstructions of long-lost activity, some of them successfully revived, some probably not. But Constantine was not unique in his interest in ceremonial. As we have seen, the capital was used to frequent processions of different types, triumphs for example, even in the difficult centuries before 850. Ceremonial was a living and changing process, with new elements invented all the time (as with Basil's Nea church commemoration). Even military emperors might relish triumphal entries, and, when they were in the city, they too respected the regular church processions: one of the most military emperors of all, Nikephoros II Phokas (963–9), interrupted a formal ambassadorial hearing in 968 with the envoy of the western emperor Otto I, Bishop Liutprand of Cremona, to do the Pentecost procession. Liutprand's embassy went badly, so he sought to depict it in his report to Otto as negatively as he could: the dignitaries wore old clothes, only the emperor wore gold and jewels, the city crowd which lined the way from the palace to Hagia Sophia was a barefoot rabble, the acclamations were lies, the food at dinner was horrible. Unwillingly, however, Liutprand confirms the formality of the event, and he adds something to the account in the *Book of Ceremonies*, for the latter had said little about a crowd; this ceremony was not just amazingly elaborate, but was important to at least some of the inhabitants of the city as a whole. They respected the logic of imperial 'order and dignity', too.

The high point of Byzantine success and prosperity was the two hundred years after 850 or so. It was marked in the capital by a very elaborate court culture at all levels. The ninth century saw the generalization of élite education; this was already visible for some people under the Second Iconoclasm (see above, Chapter 11), but by the end of the century no secular official in the capital could easily deal politically without it. The cusp figure here was Photios (d. *c.* 893), who moved up the secular official hierarchy in the 840s and 850s, reaching the post of *prōtasēkrētis*, the senior chancery post, before being abruptly promoted sideways to the office of patriarch of Constantinople (858–67, 877–86). Photios, himself from an élite family (he was a relative of Eirene's patriarch, Tarasios), was a real intellectual, author of several books, a large letter collection, and a set of sermons of a considerable conceptual sophistication. He can be seen as the main creator of the cultural template and intellectual assumptions of the post-Iconoclast Orthodox church. But he also made it normal for major secular and ecclesiastical figures to be educated. Ecclesiastical rigorists saw Photios' great learning as spiritual pride, and criticized him for it, but from now on they would be more politically marginal than under Eirene. And there was much to be learned. Photios' best-known work is the *Bibliothēkē* or *Library*, drafted initially in (perhaps) 845, which discusses 279 separate books in Greek, by both pagan and late Roman Christian authors, in considerable detail, often quoting from them at length (some of these works only survive in Photios' excerpts), and analysing them critically. This was not the whole of Photios' reading – he left out poetry, for example – but, even with omissions, it shows the range of books that were available in Constantinople to a rich, determined, and politically powerful reader. The *Bibliothēkē* was popular already in the tenth century, presumably as an encyclopedia (it was one of several in circulation – the *Book of Ceremonies* is in effect another); Arethas, archbishop of Caesarea, modern Kayseri (d. after 932), in the next generation had a copy, and may have helped to edit it. Arethas was, in a different way, as determined a bibliophile as Photios; we have two dozen of the manuscripts made under his supervision, which collect a notable array of writings from Plato up to his own day, and include annotations which are often Arethas' own work (indeed, they are often in his handwriting). This manuscript collection is certainly very atypical. But the learning Arethas had, and which he displayed in other works in a highly elaborate style, was by 900 or so much more normal.

There are many different signs of the complexity of this élite culture. One is that it included several emperors as authors. Basil I, a hardly literate usurper, made sure his son Leo VI (886–912) was educated, by Photios in fact; Leo wrote a military manual, the *Taktika* (*Tactics*), poems, a monastic advice manual, numerous laws (written in a recognizable personal style), and a set of homilies. Leo's son Constantine VII wrote much of a detailed (if often inaccurate) account of the neighbours of Byzantium, unhelpfully entitled by early modern editors *On the Administration of the Empire*, as well as commissioning the *Book of Ceremonies* and several other works. Even Nikephoros Phokas wrote at least notes on the military tactics he was particularly proud of, which were worked up under his supervision as two books, including *On Skirmishing Warfare*, one of the best of the tenth century's many military manuals. These were not dilettante writers; for these men, writing connected prose was an essential element of statecraft.

Secondly, this learning soon became quite difficult in itself. Constantine VII largely wrote in a fairly direct style; most of his contemporaries, however, wrote in more elaborate ways, rather more like Arethas. Take Leo Choirosphaktes (d. after 920) for example: he was author of several showpiece poems for events in Leo VI's reign, including a lyric panegyric on a palace bath-house rebuilt by the emperor, and also of a long poem called the *Thousand-line Theology*, which sets out an erudite and philosophically complex theology in a verse form itself structured by an acrostic with his own name and titles. Arethas, who was a good hater, and educated enough to know the philosophical allusions, accused Leo of paganism; this was obviously false, but Leo's Neoplatonism led him to argue that only the educated (particularly experts in astrology, as Leo also was) could understand God at all. Leo Choirosphaktes was *mystikos*, or private secretary, to Basil I, and under Leo VI was an ambassador to the Bulgarians in 895–904; we have a set of his letters to and from the Bulgar khagan Symeon (893–927) which show the same literariness. Symeon, who had been educated in the capital, could respond in kind, which was a good thing, for in the 910s and 920s other literary figures acting for the emperors, the patriarch and former *mystikos* Nicholas I (d. 925) and the *prōtasēkrētis* Theodore Daphnopates (d. after 961), also sought to impress the Bulgarian ruler with Platonic or Homeric allusions. Theodore much later wrote a prose panegyric with notably complex symbolism to the emperor Romanos II (959–63); Homer, Heliodoros and Herodotos all find their place here. The letters of Leo, bishop of Synnada (d. *c.* 1005), cite even more classical authors, adding Plutarch, Hesiod, Sophokles; this Leo at least had a sense of humour, and admitted in his will that he read too much lay literature, but he wore his learning as much on his sleeve as any of his predecessors.

This attraction to a past literature recalls the culture of the Carolingian élite in the ninth century, as we shall see, in the density of its allusiveness and the joy in words felt by its authors. (Cf. also Chapter 14, for the ninth-century Arabs.) But there is a difference. The Carolingian kings developed an educated theological culture around them as part of a programme of moral reform; it was possible for people to become politically important solely because of their intellectual ability; Carolingian political crises were all mediated, and moralized about, by intellectuals. In Byzantium, the sense of religious mission was less constant, and, of the figures just mentioned, only Photios could easily be said to have had a political programme based on a worked-out theological or philosophical position. The others were members of an official élite, who saw their education as part of their standing in that élite; they used literary culture as an entry into and justification of political power, not as a guide to how to conduct that power. This is even true for Constantine VII; 'order and dignity' were his touchstones, not Carolingian-style moral reform and salvation. Nor were there, for a long time, any important theological disagreements inside the Byzantine political world after the end of Iconoclasm. Indeed, after Nicholas *mystikos*, even patriarchs were relatively marginal politically for a century or more.

The aim of the tenth-century Byzantine educated élite was different: it was to restore the Roman past, which belonged to them, the true Romans. In the fourth century, membership of the political élite was closely associated with a literary education, as with Libanios, Synesios and Basil of Caesarea (or, in the West, Ausonius and, later, Sidonius Apollinaris). So should it be again, and indeed was. The tenth-century literary language moved away from spoken Greek, sticking closely as it did to late Roman forms. We begin again, as in the late Roman empire, to find snobbish remarks about the lack of literary culture of the military emperors (Constantine VII sneered at Romanos I Lekapenos, 920–44, who had admittedly usurped his own throne, as a 'common, illiterate fellow'). And the search for a Roman renewal led early to the revival of Roman law; begun by Basil I and Photios, and completed by Leo VI, the *Basilika* was the translation and rationalization of Justinian's *Digest*, *Code* and *Novels*. This was henceforth to be (and, as far as we can tell, actually was) the basis of all the legal practice of the empire, as it had not been since the crises of the seventh century. Literary, ceremonial, and legal re-creation went together; with the renewed confidence of the period, the 350-year gap separating Leo and Constantine from Justinian could be conceptually abolished.

Middle Byzantine court culture has often been seen as static and arid; even modern commentators can be found arguing along these lines. Tenth-century writers would be delighted; this was their aim, indeed. But it is not a true account, all the same. For a start, beside all this classical vocabulary there was a dense theological culture in all these writers, as there was not in any of their secular fourth- to sixth-century forebears. Biblical allusions are in fact much commoner in their works than are Plato and Homer, in a way that would have appalled Prokopios, for example. But things were also constantly changing. Ceremonies were always being renewed and developed, even while claiming to be immemorial. They could also be sabotaged, with sometimes sharp political effects. After Leo VI's fourth marriage in 906, which was flatly illegal in canon law, Patriarch Nicholas banned him from Hagia Sophia. This was almost more momentous than excommunication, for it meant that all the court ceremonial we began with in this chapter was thrown into confusion; Leo had to force Nicholas to resign a year later, and he did not regain his office until Leo's death. The patriarch did not win on that occasion, but a weaker emperor would have to have conceded rather more. After the murder of Nikephoros Phokas in 969, which was instigated by his nephew and successor John I Tzimiskes (969–76), with the cooperation of Nikephoros' own wife (and John's lover) Theophano, John too was banned from Hagia Sophia by Patriarch Polyeuktos (d. 970); Polyeuktos demanded that John must give up Theophano and expel her from the city, and repent his crime, before he could even get into the church to be crowned, and this time the emperor gave in. The denser a ceremonial system, the more easily it can be used to make points, major ones as here, more subtle ones elsewhere. Byzantine politicians played with their system, and it changed, steadily, under their hands, as a direct result.

The Byzantine court, with all its processions, had in fact become a hugely elaborate stage, on which an equally complex politics could be fought out between rival players. The network of offices and titles were ever more crucial parts of a hierarchy which was focused directly on the emperor, and which underpinned the system of imperial power. This could itself be subverted, in the sense that emperors could be removed or marginalized, but the power of the system was nonetheless maintained. It was more solid than any other political system in Europe after the sixth century, and indeed more solid even than the parallel structures of the caliphate, except in the first century of 'Abbasid power, as we shall see in the next chapter. This was not, however, a 'theatre state', a political system only consisting of ceremonial, as on Bali in the nineteenth century, as described by Clifford Geertz. Ceremonial cost money (so did it on Bali, of course), and so did official status. The other aspects of imperial self-presentation, like the bronze tree full of mechanical singing birds which so impressed Liutprand of Cremona on his earlier, happier, embassy to Constantine VII in 949 (as they were intended to – impressing envoys was a major aim of Byzantine ceremonial), cost money too. The Byzantines could be very direct about this, as with the salary-paying ceremony in the week before Palm Sunday also witnessed by Liutprand in 949: the emperor distributed bags of gold coins which were put on the shoulders of each senior court and military official in turn, across a three-day period – for there were so many officials to pay – with lesser officials paid the following week by the chamberlain. (Liutprand told Constantine that he would like it better if he could take part, and got a pound of gold coins for his spirit.) This procedure unveils the underlying motivation of the whole official class: they needed paid office, not only to wield power (which few of them would ever really manage to do), but to sustain their prosperity and lifestyle. As in the time of Theodosius or Justinian, the solidity of the state depended on an effective tax system. Since the early ninth century, this had become more and more organized again, and only this could permit the ceremonial world of Constantine VII to exist at all. Liutprand in 949 certainly did not miss the point, and even in 968, however grudgingly, he had not forgotten it. Byzantine rulers, by now, were simply richer than anyone else in Christian Europe; by 949, indeed, most Muslim rulers did not match them either. It was this that their extreme formality was designed above all else to emphasize, and indeed did so.

The stage we have been looking at was set, in this format at least, by Theodora and her advisers in 843, with the end of Iconoclasm and the proclamation of Orthodoxy (on 11 March, a day commemorated thereafter on the first Sunday of Lent by another formal procession, all across the city, as the *Book of Ceremonies* tells us). Theodora's son Michael III (842–67) was dominated by others, herself, then her brother Bardas, then, after Bardas' murder in 866, by the former groom, now chamberlain, Basil. Basil capped his rapid rise – unusual even in Byzantium, where ancestry was less crucial than in the West, as we shall see shortly – by murdering Michael in 867 as well, and becoming emperor as Basil I. Michael had to be subjected after his death to a campaign of vilification as an inept drunkard to justify this, but Basil established a stable regime, and a family succession for his 'Macedonian' dynasty that lasted nearly two centuries, up to 1056, longer than any family had managed before in the history of the empire.

The politico-military situation facing Basil was in most respects a favourable one. Above all, the 'Abbasid caliphate had dissolved into political crisis after 861, thus neutralizing the strongest power in Eurasia and Byzantium's most immediate threat; it never recovered, except for a generation roughly coinciding with Leo VI's reign. This freed up the Byzantines, as Arab civil war had under Constantine V, to be real military protagonists if they could manage it. Already in 863 the emir of Melitene (modern Malatya), one of the main border warlords, was defeated and killed on a raid to the Ankara region; in the 870s Basil went onto the offensive, leading raids over the Tauros mountains into Cilicia and the Euphrates valley. This protagonism remained. Even in the generation of 'Abbasid revival, the Byzantines at least managed to hold the frontier, and they gained an increasingly concrete hegemony over the lawless borderlands; Basil destroyed the autonomous (apparently heretical) Christian Paulicians of the Tauros in the 870s, and he and his successors had steadily more influence over the newly unified Armenians and their Bagratuni kings as well. Basil in the 880s then looked westwards. He was no more successful than his predecessors in holding back the long-drawn-out Arab conquest of Sicily (its capital Syracuse fell in 878), but he took advantage of the confusion produced by Arab raids in mainland southern Italy, and conquered most of it himself (not in person, this time) in 880–88, turning the Lombard principalities, much of whose territory he had taken, into client states. This meant that, even though Sicily had gone, Byzantium maintained a strong western presence for another two centuries.

The most obvious target for Byzantine aggression was the Bulgar khaganate, which had dominated the central and northern Balkans for fifty years, since the time of Krum; we need to focus on the latter, and its relations with Constantinople, for a moment as a result. Exactly how the Bulgar political system worked is not at all clear. Archaeological excavation in its successive capitals, Pliska and (from the 890s) Preslav, show considerable wealth and, in the latter, architectural ambition; so does the Great Fence which bounded Bulgar rule to the south. But what sort of fiscal infrastructure the khagans had is hard to see; they took tribute from their subjects, but it is not certain how systematically they did so. They could be very effective militarily, but they relied on perhaps semi-autonomous aristocrats (*boilades* or *bolyary*) to supply their armies. If they were to withstand the Byzantines, freed from eastern defensive needs by the 860s, they needed to borrow techniques of government from them fairly fast. The first of these was Christianity and the Christian church. The Byzantines attacked Bulgaria in 864, and Khagan Boris I (852–89) immediately agreed to be baptized in 865, and to allow missionaries in. It was such a prompt concession that it must have been on the cards for some time, although it was far from popular – Boris faced rebellion almost at once. The Bulgar mission nonetheless continued, and became a political football between the rival missionary projects of Constantinople and Rome, both of whom Boris invited in. Relations between the two churches were already bad, for the Moravian ruler Rastislav, who ruled a powerful Sclavenian polity in the Frankish borderlands (see below, Chapter 20), had in 863 invited Byzantine missionaries, Constantine-Cyril and Methodios, to proselytize, rather than the Latin missions which Pope Nicholas I (858–67) considered proper. Nicholas protested about this missionary rivalry, but without effect. More successfully, he pressed the usurping and still politically insecure Basil I to remove Photios as patriarch in 867, on the grounds that his election was uncanonical, although Photios soon made peace with Basil: he was Leo VI's tutor by the early 870s, and became patriarch again in 877. Competition between Rome and Constantinople for the conversion of two Christianizing polities, the restored Photios' under-standable resentment at papal interference, and growing differences over Christological details, sent relations between the two churches into the worst crisis since Iconoclasm.

The Moravians and Bulgars eventually accepted geopolitical logic, and the former went Latin, the latter Greek; once this finally happened in the 880s the tension between the churches quietened down again. But Boris, in particular, had got substantial concessions in return for his Greek choice: in 870, the Bulgar church was recognized as autonomous outside of Constantinople, with its own archbishop. After 885, Boris welcomed Methodios' missionaries, now expelled from Moravia, into his kingdom, and adopted the Slavonic liturgy that Constantine-Cyril had created for the Moravians as his own – it still exists as the core of Slav Orthodoxy. The Cyrillic alphabet was developed in Preslav in the late ninth century, too, and a Slavic religious literature followed quickly. Slavic also slowly became the dominant language in the Bulgar khaganate, largely as a result of these developments. The Bulgars were creating an increasingly Byzantinizing style of rule, but were giving it an identity separate from Constantinopolitan influence. This stood it in good stead when Bulgar–Byzantine relations became cool again under Symeon, with wars in 894–7 and 913–24, in both of which the Bulgars were notably successful, raiding the suburbs of Constantinople itself in 913, and again in 920–24, in an echo of Krum. Symeon took the title *basileus*, emperor (*tsar*, from 'Caesar', in Slavic) in 913 or shortly after, and was feared to be aiming for the throne of Byzantium too – he called himself 'emperor of the Bulgars and Romans' by 924 (why don't you call yourself caliph as well, Theodore Daphnopates retorted). But Constantinople's walls held, and Symeon died; under his successor Peter (927–68) peace returned. This was the apex of Bulgar power and status; under Peter we begin to find more and more lead seals, signs of a literate Byzantinizing administration, particularly in Preslav; the Bulgar archbishop had been upgraded to a patriarch, too. The Bulgar state even developed its own popular heresy, Bogomilism, during Peter's reign. The Bogomils were dualists, and believed that the world had been created by the devil; this enabled them to generate a social critique of the growing differentiations inside Bulgar society, as is made clear in an attack on them in Slavic by Cosmas the Priest in the 960s. The Bogomils directly influenced the Cathar heresy which was so influential in western Europe in the twelfth and thirteenth centuries; their beliefs were second only to the Slavonic liturgy as the most lasting cultural exports of Symeon's and Peter's Bulgaria. The Bulgar state fell fairly rapidly in the end, as we shall see, but it left these legacies, at least.

Leo VI, hemmed in by resurgent Bulgars on one side and more briefly reviving 'Abbasids on the other, was less of a military figure than Basil had been, but he held his ground, and his *Taktika* revived the genre of military handbooks to considerable effect; a dozen similar handbooks, some as we have seen drafted by other emperors, follow in Byzantium in the next century. Leo focused on law and on administrative reform. He was also concerned with the centrality and survival of his and

Basil's dynasty, and the church crisis over his fourth marriage, to Zoe Karbonopsina, was caused by his iron determination to safeguard the legitimacy of his only son, Constantine VII, who was born to Zoe when she was still Leo's mistress. Constantine was only eight when he succeeded as sole emperor in 913, however, and rivals fought over who was to be regent, or perhaps emperor, for the next seven years: the re-enthroned Patriarch Nicholas, the *domestikos tōn scholōn* (in practice, the head of the eastern army) Constantine Doukas, who attempted a coup in 913, Tsar Symeon, whose second war began in the same year, Zoe Karbonopsina herself, who took over the regency council in 914 and ruled the empire until 919, and finally the head of the navy, Romanos Lekapenos, who staged a successful coup in 919, married his daughter Helena to Constantine, and became senior emperor in 920. The Macedonian dynasty had already achieved too much status to be easily overthrown, and Romanos (through Theodore Daphnopates) indignantly protested his loyalty to Constantine when writing to Symeon in 924. But Constantine, though still at court, was marginalized, and, when he finally overthrew the Lekapenoi in 945 and ruled directly, saw himself as in his second reign, with a quarter of a century's break between the two.

Romanos I had an exceptionally loyal and able *domestikos tōn scholōn*, John Kourkouas, who held the post from 922 to 944, when Romanos was overthrown by his sons, a month before Constantine's own coup. After the Bulgar peace in 927, John raided systematically and boldly on the eastern frontier for fifteen years, achieving military dominance in the borderlands as the 'Abbasids folded into crisis again. He turned this into conquest in 934 when he took Melitene; he had considerable influence in Armenia; and in 944 he forced the emir of Edessa not only to make peace but also to hand over one of the great Christian relics, the Mandylion with Christ's miraculous image, to be held henceforth in the palace in Constantinople. Constantine VII as sole ruler in 945 appointed Bardas Phokas as *domestikos tōn scholōn*, returning as he did to a family which had held this position for most of the reigns of Leo VI and Zoe, as we shall see later. Bardas and then his son Nikephoros, who succeeded him as *domestikos* in 955, followed John Kourkouas in pushing eastwards; Nikephoros in particular sought to conquer. In 958 he took Samosata on the Euphrates, and by 962, under Constantine's son Romanos II, he was in control of the whole upper Euphrates valley; in 962-5 he took Cilicia, in 965 Cyprus, in 969 Antioch, the old Roman capital of the East. As important was his conquest of Crete in 961, the strategic key to the southern Aegean, which the Byzantines had unsuccessfully tried to take back several times since 827.

Nikephoros Phokas, the most successful general for centuries, was thus in a good position to repeat Romanos Lekapenos' coup when Romanos II died with young heirs in 963. He moved swiftly to the capital, married Romanos' widow Theophano, and, as in 920, reduced the children Basil II and Constantine VIII to the status of marginal co-emperors. He then returned to war, the first emperor to command his own troops since Basil I. So after 969 did his nephew and murderer John Tzimiskes, who was John Kourkouas' great-nephew as well; John attacked on the eastern frontier as far south as Beirut, and by the end of his reign in 976 all the Arab rulers of the rest of Syria paid him tribute. John was also, for the first time in this period, successful in the Balkans. Svyatoslav, prince of the Rus of Kiev (see below, Chapter 20), attacked Bulgaria in 967, probably at Nikephoros' instigation, and took Preslav; he returned in 969 and overran the Bulgar state, threatening Byzantine territory as well. John in 971 pushed the Rus out of Bulgaria in a quick campaign, the reverse of the long-drawn-out and inconclusive Bulgar wars of the last two centuries. He drew the logical conclusion to his military supremacy and deposed Tsar Boris II (968-71) as well, in a formal ceremony in the forum of Constantine in Constantinople. Bulgar power, fearsome for so long, thus suddenly collapsed, and John ruled from the Danube to the Euphrates, over a third as much again as Romanos I had ruled at his accession.

These conquests were not, on one level, enormous. The Byzantines were more experienced in defensive than in offensive war, and they were too cautious to go for the big sweep, down to Jerusalem or Baghdad – and perhaps they were right, for the one example of it in the 960s-970s, the conquest of Bulgaria, did not hold, at least initially. They were most concerned with solidity, and this they obtained. The Arabs did not get the eastern lands back; it was only the Seljuk Turk conquest of the Arab world and eastern Byzantium alike in the 1060s-1070s that would reverse the work of Nikephoros Phokas and John Tzimiskes.

A recurrent historiography of eleventh-century Byzantium sees a civilian faction and a military faction at loggerheads, each rising or falling with each successive reign. This is an over-simple view of the eleventh century, and it is even less true of the tenth. It might seem that there was a civilian, not to say bookish, legitimist Macedonian tradition, which was marginalized by soldier-emperors, Romanos I, Nikephoros II, John I. We know that Nikephoros felt himself constrained by ceremonial, even though he appears to have carried it out when he was in the capital; and there were certainly cultural differences between all these figures and a Leo VI or Constantine VII. But Romanos, who started in the navy, spent most of his reign in the capital, just as Leo and Constantine did. Military officials were as important in court ceremonies as civilian ones, unless they were on campaign. A single career could include both military and civilian offices, as with Nikephoros Ouranos (d. after 1007), who was keeper of the imperial inkstand, with a responsibility for producing documents, in the 980s, but then became a notably successful general, against Bulgaria in 997-9, and as ruler of Antioch after 999 (he too wrote a military manual, but also poetry and hagiography). A civilian official could have a military son or brother, too, as with the Argyroi family, mostly a military one, which produced Romanos Argyros (he would become Emperor Romanos III, 1028-34), a highly literary eparch (governor) of Constantinople and economic manager of Hagia Sophia, as well as his brothers Basil and Leo, who were generals in Italy and on the eastern frontier. There was no structural political opposition between the two traditions. A good indication of this is the career of Basil Lekapenos (d. after 985), bastard son of Romanos I, who was made a eunuch by his father. He rose in the civil administration, as eunuchs generally did (though even he fought in at least one campaign, in 958), and in 945 supported the coup of Constantine VII, who was after all his brother-in-law; he gained the title of *parakoimōmenos*, guardian of the imperial bedchamber, and was effectively head of the civilian government for the whole period 945-85, except for Romanos II's four-year reign. He actively supported the rule in turn of Constantine VII, Nikephoros Phokas, John Tzimiskes, and then Basil II (976-1025) in the difficult first decade of the latter's sole reign after John's death. He changed sides when he had to, notably from Nikephoros to John (he too was complicit in Nikephoros' murder), and gained great wealth from his office; he was not necessarily a lovable man. But he represented a continuity which successive emperors could not easily reject. The civil government of the capital and the heads of the armies needed each other, the first to produce the funds to pay the second, the second to defend the first, and they both knew it.

Basil II was anyway the heir of both political strands: the legitimate Macedonian heir, he was also an ascetic military figure in the Nikephoros Phokas mould (he never married or had children), and uninterested in learning. Michael Psellos in the 1060s stressed his dislike of ostentation, within the framework of a ceremonial practice which Basil, too, respected: 'Basil took part in his processions and gave audience to his governors clad merely in a robe of purple, not the very bright purple, but simply purple of a dark hue, with a handful of gems as a mark of distinction.' He spent most of his life campaigning; in 991–5, for example, he was not in the capital at all, with the result that there was a four-year vacancy in the patriarchate, for any patriarchal election needed imperial participation. But he was also highly attentive to taxation, and rumour grew at the end of his extremely long reign of a financial surplus so huge that tunnels had to be built under the palace to hold it.

Basil did not establish his position easily. In his early years he faced revolts from generals who aspired to repeat the careers of Nikephoros II and John I. First was Bardas Skleros, *doux* of Mesopotamia on the far frontier (976–9); in 978 Basil sent Nikephoros' nephew Bardas Phokas the younger, back in the family office of *domestikos tōn scholōn*, to push the rebels over the frontier. Basil was himself more concerned with Bulgaria, where revolts on the western edge of the former Bulgarian state (in the area of modern Serbia and Macedonia) were beginning by the late 970s to turn into an attempt to reverse the Byzantine conquest. Their leader was by the mid-980s Samuel, who defeated Basil himself in 986 in what is now western Bulgaria, and who already by then controlled all Symeon and Peter's former realm except the old heartland around Preslav. After the 986 defeat, eastern revolts broke out again. Bardas Skleros returned in 987; Bardas Phokas was sent against him once more, but this time he declared himself emperor as well, allied himself with Skleros, and then imprisoned him. A rebel Phokas, given Nikephoros II's heroic reputation, was much more dangerous for Basil. Bardas Phokas had controlled all the eastern armies anyway, and they remained loyal to him. Basil to confront him had to seek help from the Rus, and in 989 he defeated and killed Bardas Phokas at Abydos on the Dardanelles. Skleros surrendered a year later, and was quite well treated by Basil.

This was unusual; Basil normally treated opponents savagely (including even prisoners of war). But Skleros' revolt, at least second time around, was that much less threatening.

Basil II ruled without trouble after 989, and remained fully in control both of the armies and the palace (he had removed Basil Lekapenos in 985). He did not continue the 960s–970s focus on the Arab frontier, partly because Arab power in Syria, in the form of the Fatimids, was becoming stronger again, as we shall see in the next chapter; most of his wars were with Samuel. They took a long time. Samuel was by no means on the defensive, and attacked far into Greece from his Macedonian base, where he declared himself tsar in 997. It was not until 1014 that Basil destroyed Samuel's army, and only in 1018 did he mop up resistance. Basil did fight in the East as well, all the same; here, he was mostly interested in gaining hegemony over Armenian and Georgian princes. His successes here pushed the frontier as far as the modern Turkey–Iran border, further east than even the Romans had reached, though independent Armenian kings still remained in the capital at Ani. Basil's control here was not fully stable; Armenians were hard to rule. But the very quantity of his campaigns, over so many decades, created a certain stability, even in the Armenian lands – and certainly in Bulgaria. Armenians and Bulgars were easily absorbed into his own armies. The war economy, across fifty years (seventy, if one starts with Nikephoros Phokas' campaigns), became structural to the state. Basil may have had a reputation for heavy taxation, but his wars must have paid for themselves if he died with money reserves. And this was so even though he relied almost entirely on a professional, and well-paid and equipped, army, the *tagmata*, the expanded heir of the eighth- and ninth-century specialist regiments, as well as mercenaries from wherever he could get them. In the early eleventh century Byzantium looked in good shape. None of Basil's successors for fifty years had his (rather grim) charisma, but the state did not falter until the Turkish onslaught in the 1070s.

By the mid-tenth century, most of the political players in Byzantium had surnames. This was a new development; it is far less true of the ninth, when nicknames were less often inherited. Even in the tenth, surnames were not always stable, as with John Tzimiskes ('the Short') who was a male-line Kourkouas descendant, or else not always used, as with the Lekapenoi, who are called that in eleventh-century, not tenth-century texts. Although we can track a few aristocratic families back into the eighth century, most of the greatest families of the tenth were themselves fairly new: the Phokades began with Phokas, apparently an ordinary soldier promoted by Basil I to several provincial governorships from the 870s onwards; the first Kourkouas and first Lekapenos were also contemporaries of Basil; the Argyroi and Doukai are first documented in the 840s; the Skleroi went further back, but only to Nikephoros I in the early ninth. If these families had aristocratic ancestors further back in the past, there was no need to recall them; family identity could begin here. Leo VI could happily use the (borrowed) opinion in the *Taktika* that generals should not be of distinguished origin, for those of obscure origin would have much more to prove; this view would certainly have been shared by his Phokas contemporaries, and may not have been controversial to many around 900. But even Basil II a century later, when complaining in a law of 996 about the misdeeds of 'the powerful' (*dynatoi*), explicitly envisaged that a *dynatos* could be 'originally a poor man, [who] was afterwards granted titles and raised to the height of glory and good fortune'; his idea of an old family was a *domestikos tōn scholōn* whose descendants were 'likewise *dynatoi* with success extending over seventy or a hundred years'. Although we should not take the phrase too literally, this image, too, only takes us back to Leo. The tenth century certainly saw a crystallizing aristocracy with a visible family consciousness, and elements of that consciousness can be traced back to the ninth century at least, but the concept of the special nature of high-status ancestry was not dominant as yet.

Official titles certainly did figure in aristocratic identity, on the other hand. And so did land. All these families had lands that were above all on the Anatolian plateau and the eastern frontier: the Phokades and Argyroi in Cappadocia, the Skleroi close to Melitene. It is hardly surprising that they rose in the army under these circumstances, although the quasi-chivalric values of the great nostalgic border epic of the twelfth century, *Digenēs Akritēs*, cannot yet be seen in our sources. The Phokades were the most consistently ambitious of these families in our period, but are also the best documented, and they can serve as an example. Phokas' son Nikephoros Phokas the elder was the first of them to become politically prominent; he was, like his father, a personal favourite of Basil I, and became *domestikos tōn scholōn* at the start of Leo VI's reign, a post he held for nearly a decade. His son Leo held the same post under Zoe, and was seriously defeated by the Bulgars in 917; Romanos I had him sacked in 919, and he was blinded after a revolt. Leo's brother Bardas was excluded from power under Romanos, who clearly (and unsurprisingly) saw the Phokades as rivals, but was, as we have seen, recalled by Constantine VII, and he and his son Nikephoros the younger ran the armies of the empire for twenty-five years, first as *domestikoi*, then as emperor. Nikephoros' brother Leo was a general too, though a less popular one, including in the capital, where he became a civil official during Nikephoros' reign; that, plus a lack of speed in reaction, meant that he could not reverse John Tzimiskes' coup. After a revolt in 971, however, he too was blinded. Bardas the younger, first *domestikos* then rebel, was his son; it is hardly surprising that Basil II did not promote the family much after 989. But Bardas' son Nikephoros could still stage a revolt from his Cappadocian base in 1022, and his son or nephew Bardas tried again in 1026. These two were respectively killed and blinded, and the family is not heard of again.

The Phokades ended their family history as rebels, and were remembered for that thereafter, but until the outrage of Nikephoros II's death – and, in fact, until Bardas the younger's revolt in 987–9 – they were quite different: they were one of the most established families of military leaders in the empire, holding the supreme command of the East for forty-five out of the hundred years before that revolt, not to speak of a string of provincial commands in the Anatolikon and in Cappadocia, and the occasional civil office as well. Out of power under Romanos I, they were by no means forgotten, and this must have been true even under Basil II if the last Nikephoros Phokas could reappear in 1022 (apparently persuaded by the governor of the Anatolikon, Nikephoros Xiphias, who needed him as the popular figurehead for a bid for power on his own behalf). The point is that, although they had a landed base they could retire to – and plenty of land elsewhere, including in the capital – they only really existed as major players when they held office. Without it, as an Armenian chronicler put it, they 'ranted like caged lions'. The Phokades had a family identity, to be sure, but it could only really be expressed through office-holding. Wealth, land, and three or four generations by now of ancestry were by no means enough on their own. This was even truer of the other families, who hardly appear in the sources at all when out of office.

Aristocratic landowning was nonetheless increasing. An early example, the first really wealthy private owner we have clear documentation for since the sixth century, was Danelis (d. *c.* 890), who was one of Basil I's first patrons before he came to imperial attention; she reputedly owned over eighty estates in southern Greece. The figure may well be exaggerated, but the order of magnitude might be a guide to aristocratic wealth in the East, where most of the powerful families were based. Certainly emperors thought that *dynatoi* were gaining too much power in the localities. Every emperor from Romanos I in 928 to Basil II in 996 (except John Tzimiskes) issued laws against the oppressions of 'the powerful', laws which survive as a group, and which refer to each other. The emperors sought to make it difficult for *dynatoi* to buy land from peasants, who were sometimes forced to sell because of misfortune (as in the great famine of 927–8), or else simply because they were intimidated by local aristocrats. Neighbours and village communities were to have the right to buy such land back; if the peasants were soldiers (that is, in the thematic armies, an element of the Byzantine military rather marginalized by the *tagmata* in this period) they could not sell land at all, unless to poorer soldiers. Romanos I in 934 said this was because land accumulation by *dynatoi* threatened tax collection; Constantine VII in 947/8 was worried that peasant soldiers might enter the private armies of 'the powerful'; Basil II in 996 provided anecdotes of state officials expropriating whole villages, and also envisaged that *dynatoi* might force merchants to move markets (and thus market tolls) onto their lands. Who the *dynatoi* actually were was rather vaguely and inconsistently defined in this legislation, but certainly included state officials, and there is no doubt that the Skleroi, Phokades, etc. formed part of them. It has been easy to see 'the powerful' as threatening everyone in the empire, free peasant owners, the organization of the army, the fiscal system, and, thanks to private armies and regular revolts, the whole state.

It is a mistake to try and talk this legislation away, as some historians do, in an understandable reaction against the apocalyptic readings of some earlier writers. What we call aristocrats were certainly more politically prominent than before, and therefore presumably richer, across the tenth century, and indeed later; this sort of local oppression is what aristocrats demonstrably do in other times and places; it is therefore unreasonable to deny it for tenth-century Byzantium, given that we actually have an unusually explicit set of texts. Nor would it be surprising that emperors feared that it would be harder to collect taxes from 'the powerful' than from 'the poor' (that is, everyone who did not have political clout); it always is, and similar problems are well attested in the late Roman period. But there are plenty of reasons why we might not want to rely on the intensity of imperial rhetoric too much when looking at such texts. First, the tax system was not under threat, as Basil II's accumulation of reserves, despite constant war, shows. Secondly, local oppression, precisely because 'the powerful' always do it, was less threatening to the state than the emperors claimed. Village communities were certainly well entrenched, including in law and in tax-paying, especially in Anatolia; it would be logical for emperors to seek to support them. (They did so in quite late Roman terms as well, as befits a century as Roman-revivalist as the tenth; when Nikephoros II in 966/7 said, 'it is our wish that *dynatoi* purchase from *dynatoi* only, the soldiers and the poor from persons who have attained the same status as they have', he was echoing the laws against social mobility of the fourth century.) But this does not mean that peasants were universally under threat.

It is also not at all obvious that great landowners really did dominate the countryside by the late tenth century. They did in parts of southern Greece, as Danelis already implies, and as is further confirmed by the Thebes Cadaster, a brief local tax survey from the later eleventh century, which shows a preponderance of relatively large owners in an area north of Athens (although a few peasant proprietors as well). We could hardly doubt that the situation was the same in some core aristocratic areas in central and eastern Anatolia. But aristocrats do not dominate in the earliest, tenth-century, Athos documents from northern Greece, which show monasteries (themselves expanding landowners, as Nikephoros II and Basil II complained) opposing, but also being opposed by, local communities such as Hierissos, the closest large settlement to Mount Athos. Although large landowning steadily gained ground after 1000 in northern Greece, this was not the case everywhere even then; and peasant landowning still continued on the Aegean coast of Turkey for centuries. So did it in Byzantine southern Italy, although this was a more marginal area for aristocratic interest. Anyway, even if some of the great families were as rich as Danelis, they were not so very numerous. It is far from clear that the Byzantine aristocracy had achieved the dominance over the landscape that was normal in the West (see below, Chapter 21), even in the eleventh century, never mind the tenth, whatever emperors claimed in their laws.

The great families of Byzantium thus seem to me for the most part less locally preponderant than they were in the West; and also more reliant on office-holding for real political protagonism than they were in the West. There were also, probably, more areas of Byzantium than in the West by the tenth century that were not dominated by 'the powerful'; this seems a reasonable conclusion to draw, even though Byzantine evidence tells us so little about peasant society. Even in the West, as we shall see in Part IV, aristocratic élites were closely connected to the state in Carolingian Francia, Ottonian East Francia (the future Germany), late Anglo-Saxon England; they owed their identity and status to royal patronage, and they did not seek to establish autonomous local power, or to undermine royal power, unless the crisis of a kingdom forced them to go it alone, as in tenth-century West Francia (the future France). In tenth-century Byzantium, where the state – based on taxation as it was – was far stronger, where office-holding commanded huge salaries, where public position was tied up with army commands and regular presence in the capital, autonomous local power did not stand a chance. The fragmentary evidence we have for provincial judicial procedures, too – mostly court cases from Athos, where the monasteries spent a strikingly large amount of time squabbling with each other – shows effective and systematic official interventions, with judges regularly sent from the capital and interacting with a network of local officials as well; this network of public power, again without parallel in the early medieval West, would not easily give way to private autonomies. In any case, Basil II, who is often held to have been particularly hostile to the dangers of the great families, did not fear them so much as to make any provision for the survival of his own dynasty. Not only did he never marry, but he never even tried to persuade his colourless brother Constantine VIII (who succeeded him, 1025–8) to marry off his two daughters while they could still bear children, and perpetuate the line that way. Basil knew that other families would soon take over the imperial office, and this clearly did not bother him. Nor, given the continuing power and stability of the Byzantine empire for another half century, can he be said to have been wrong.

14
From 'Abbasid Baghdad to Umayyad Córdoba, 750–1000

The Arab geographer Ibn Hawqal (d. *c.* 990) hated Palermo and the Sicilians. Palermo itself, conquered by the Arabs from the Byzantines in 831, was rich and impressive, and Ibn Hawqal spends many pages on its amenities: the large mosque (the ex-cathedral) which could contain 7,000 people; more than 300 other mosques, in an unparalleled density, sometimes actually adjoining each other; the very numerous and varied markets; the specialized papyrus production, the only one existing outside Egypt; the richly irrigated gardens surrounding. But the Palermitans wasted this latter fertility on cultivating onions, which they ate raw; the consequence was that 'one does not find in this town any intelligent person, or skilful, or really competent in any scientific discipline, or animated by noble or religious feeling'. No one was qualified to be *qāḍī* (judge) there; they were all too unreliable. Schoolmasters were very numerous, but all idiots: they did the job in order to avoid military service; nevertheless, the Sicilians as a whole considered them to be brilliant. They pronounced Arabic wrong; they could not hold down a logical argument (Ibn Hawqal provides examples); they had no idea of what Iraqi legal and theological schools really believed, 'even though their doctrinal position is very well known'. Nor did the Sicilians know Islamic law properly, particularly in the countryside. Ibn Hawqal was so incensed about all this that he actually wrote a whole book about Sicilian idiocy, unfortunately lost; but he tells us quite enough in his huge geographical survey, *The Book of the Depiction of the Earth*. He ends amazed that the Sicilians could be so poor, at least these days (in the 970s), when their land was so rich. The only thing they made really well was linen.

What the Sicilians had done to make Ibn Hawqal so cross (geographers often criticized the inhabitants of regions, but this is extreme) is not easy to see. But it is fair to say that he knew what he was talking about. He was born in Nisibis in the upper Tigris valley and was brought up in Baghdad; he left the latter city in 943 for thirty years of travel, to North Africa, Spain, Armenia, Fars and Khurasan in what is now Iran, back to Mesopotamia and Syria, Egypt, and finally to Sicily. He may by now simply have been tired and grumpy, but he had traversed the whole Islamic world. He saw it as a whole, and constantly compared its parts; the great city of Fustat in Egypt, for example, had a third of the surface area of Baghdad, whereas Córdoba in Spain had almost half; the nougat of Manbij in northern Syria was the best he knew except for that of Bukhara in central Asia; the merchants of Sijilmasa in the Moroccan desert were so rich that people in Iraq or Khurasan hardly believed Ibn Hawqal when he told them how much they were worth. Ibn Hawqal made these journeys, however, when the Islamic world was divided into between ten and fifteen separate polities. This hardly poses him a problem; rulers appear casually in his account, some good, most bad, some sufficiently threatening that he had to leave quickly, but all of them simply controlling sections of a single Muslim community. Ibn Hawqal's geography transcended politics; he, and other geographers like him, saw the Islamic world as essentially a whole.

This cultural and religious unity was first established by the military conquests of the Umayyads. It was made permanent, however, in the century and a half of the 'Abbasid caliphate, which was politically hegemonic as a centralized state between 750 and 861, and still powerful until around 920; the disunity of Ibn Hawqal's time (and ever after) was hardly a generation old when he set out from Baghdad. In this chapter, we shall look at the 'Abbasid achievement, in the decades of their most effective political centralization, and in the creation of a dense religious and scientific written culture in Baghdad, which was strong enough to survive tenth-century fragmentation. We shall then follow the history of two of the successor states, those closest to the European focus of this book, the Fatimids of North Africa and Egypt, and, in particular, the Umayyads of Spain. The Spanish Umayyads were autonomous under 'Abbasid power already in the 750s, but they too looked to Baghdad for a long time. Baghdad, although by no means part of a history of Europe, or even of the former Roman world, had an economic and cultural importance in the last third of our period that outclassed anywhere in the world, and that certainly impacted on Europe: on Spain, on Constantinople, and even on far-off Aachen, where Charlemagne's court paid attention to that of Harun al-Rashid, even if the reverse was probably not the case.

In Chapter 12, we left al-Mansur, the second 'Abbasid caliph (754–75), in control of the whole of the Muslim lands from North Africa to what is now Pakistan. This control was not simply the result of the 'Abbasid 'revolution' of 747–50; the political system was not yet stable in 754, and al-Mansur, in order to feel secure, had to defeat rivals from inside his immediate family and also a serious 'Alid revolt in 762–3, as well as establishing a balance of power between the Khurasani army which had brought the 'Abbasids victory and the Iraqi and Syrian factions they displaced. This political settlement was a success, however, the product of al-Mansur's brilliance as an operator, buttressed by his famed religious austerity and financial caution. It was crystallized in the foundation of a new capital at Baghdad in 762, focused on a monumental round city (no longer surviving), which was the political and ceremonial centre of the caliphate: Baghdad was to be the home of the Khurasani army, the *abnā'* or 'sons', and also of the administrative élite, who came from everywhere in the caliphate, but particularly from Iraq, the 'Abbasid heartland.

Baghdad seems to have expanded enormously fast; 500,000 inhabitants or upwards seems to me a plausible guess for the ninth century. This was made possible by the water-supply of the Tigris, which runs through it (Damascus has much less water, and had never been anything like so large), as well as by the great agricultural resources of the Jazira between Iraq and Syria and (above all) southern Iraq, the 'black land' or Sawad, which were further developed through irrigation projects by the early 'Abbasids to outstrip the productive wealth even of Egypt. But it was also made possible by 'Abbasid control, mostly by conquest, of every part of the Islamic world except Spain: al-Mansur had a clean slate, and, after his execution of his great Khurasani general Abu Muslim in 755, owed nothing to anyone. In particular, he could begin the reorganization of the fiscal system that the Umayyads had never managed. The Arabs living in the provinces steadily lost their rights to live off provincial taxation, and it began to flow more consistently to the military and political focus that was Baghdad, a secure resource for the city's population, whether the soldiers and administrators who were paid by it, or else the mass of shopkeepers, merchants and artisans, and public and private servants, who supplied and depended on them.

That process of fiscal centralization could not be established overnight, of course, given the size and complexity of the caliphate. As we shall see, the 780s–790s and the 830s saw further developments in that direction. But it started with al-Mansur, who already had more resources at his disposal than any previous caliph, or than any Roman emperor since, probably, the fourth century. Al-Mansur can as a result also be seen developing an administrative network that might become capable of organizing and distributing these resources. The Umayyads already had secretaries (*kuttāb*) who had a considerable administrative importance, but it is under the early 'Abbasids that we begin to find them more clearly responsible for separate branches of government or *dīwān*s and it is in particular under al-Mansur that we see an executive head of the whole central administrative system appear, the *wazīr* or vizir; the first seems to have been Abu Ayyub (d. 771), who ran al-Mansur's government for around fifteen years (*c.* 755–70). The powers of the vizir continued to expand across the 'Abbasid period, although they were never complete; vizirs did not normally control provincial governors, for that was a caliphal responsibility (although they did control provincial tax officials), and there were always autonomous offices inside Baghdad itself, not least the chamberlain (*ḥājib*), who ran the caliph's large household and often had the caliph's ear, and who could thus be a serious rival to any vizir. But for the first time we see a clear structure of government in the Arab world, one with its own complex internal politics, as we shall see, made all the more cut-throat by the huge amount of money it had to direct.

Al-Mansur had no doubt as to the dynastic nature of his rule, and, thanks to his removal of rivals, a continuous line of caliphs, all descended from him, held office up to 1517. His son al-Mahdi (775–85) and grandson al-Rashid (786–809) continued his political practices, in a period of general peace and prosperity which aided the trend to centralization. 'Peace' is perhaps too bland a term; there were always frontier wars with the Byzantines, and provincial rebellion was far from unknown, particularly in Egypt and in eastern Khurasan, and including a peasant revolt in the Jazira, west of Mosul, in the 770s. But none of them threatened the structure of the state, which continued to develop. Al-Rashid, also known by his birth name of Harun (all 'Abbasid caliphs had both a birth name and a ruling name, though historians otherwise tend to use only the latter), is by far the best-known 'Abbasid, and perhaps the best-known medieval Muslim ruler in absolute along with Saladin, thanks to his starring role in the *Thousand and One Nights*, in its present form a mostly late medieval collection of stories. In his lifetime, however, although an active general, he was a relatively retiring figure in internal politics, devoted largely to ceremonial. Between 786 and 803 the state was dominated by his vizir Yahya ibn Khalid ibn Barmak (d. 805), son of one of al-Mansur's leading officials, and Harun's old tutor. Yahya ran the government together with his sons Ja'far (Harun's closest friend and associate, both in life and in the *Thousand and One Nights*) and al-Fadl, who distributed most of the offices of state between them and also a succession of provincial governorships; together they are known as the Barmakids. The Barmakids ever after had a high reputation for being skilled and honest administrators, and they seem indeed to have been so; they were the principal architects of the mature 'Abbasid fiscal system, bypassing provincial governors (except when they themselves held such offices), and directing ever higher proportions of tax revenue to Baghdad. Their memory was also enhanced by their abrupt fall, when in 803, almost out of the blue, al-Rashid had Ja'far beheaded and his relatives imprisoned, for no obvious reason except, presumably, his growing resentment of the family's power. Arab writers pondered for centuries the tragedy of the ideal administrator, Yahya, brought down by an almost-as-ideal caliph – especially as it was only a few years before al-Rashid's own death ushered in a serious civil war.

It was standard 'Abbasid practice for rulers to seek to control the succession by naming first and then second heirs; this frequently did not work out, as political alignments changed, but it at least helped to ensure that the initial heir would succeed without opposition from his presumed successor. Al-Rashid went one further: he designated one of his sons, al-Amin, as the next caliph (809–13), and another, al-Ma'mun, as his successor, but he also assigned al-Ma'mun an apanage, Khurasan, in which he was to be effectively autonomous during his brother's reign. This was probably because Khurasan had become a tense province again, with local aristocracies unwilling to accept the right of Baghdad to take their tax (ironically, to pay the ex-Khurasani *abnā'* army, in the capital and on the Byzantine frontier); that would cease, at least temporarily, once al-Rashid died, and Khurasanis could feel that they had a future caliph who would safeguard their interests. The tensions did not stop with the division of 809, however, and now each side had an 'Abbasid at its head. Al-Amin at once tried to undermine his brother's rule, and the Khurasanis persuaded al-Ma'mun to declare independence in 810. Unexpectedly, his general Tahir ibn al-Husayn defeated al-Amin's large invading *abnā'* army in 811, and al-Ma'mun, now claiming the caliphate (811–33), sent Tahir against Baghdad.

Tahir besieged the capital for a year, until he managed to break down local resistance in 813; al-Amin was caught and killed. Al-Ma'mun however stayed in Khurasan, making Merv (now in Turkmenistan) his capital; furthermore, he showed in this period a Shi'ite commitment, above all through his unique decision to make an 'Alid his heir in 817, 'Ali ibn Musa, whose ruling name was to be al-Rida, 'the chosen one'. This secured the loyalty of parts of Khurasan and Iraq, but alienated the rest of the caliphate. Baghdad revolted again, choosing a brother of al-Rashid, Ibrahim, as the caliph al-Mubarak; Egypt, too, which had had its own civil war between supporters of the rival brothers since 812, fell into chaos in 819 with the most serious tax revolt of the Christian population since 750. Al-Ma'mun had to backtrack, and moved to Baghdad, and definitively away from 'Alid imagery, in 819. Iraq fell into line straight away and Ibrahim fled (he survived this debacle and was reconciled in 825; he died at court in 839). Egypt, however, took much longer to subdue; al-Ma'mun had to lead an army there himself in 832 to subjugate it properly. Only then, just before the caliph's death, did he have full control over his father's domains, with the exception of North Africa, an always rather marginal province, which never returned to 'Abbasid rule.

The civil war of 811–13 thus unleashed trouble. The resentment of the provinces over taxation was perennial; the more the 'Abbasids ensured taxes were sent to Iraq, the more acute local resistance would be. In the Umayyad period, this resistance could be posed in terms of loyalty to the person of the caliph (it was just that local Arab armies should have the right to keep provincial taxation); but, if that right was no longer recognized, the risk was that the province would throw off caliphal authority altogether, as first with al-Ma'mun himself in Khurasan. This would indeed eventually lead to the break-up of caliphal power. But it is necessary to stress that it did not do so yet. Al-Ma'mun kept the loyalty and cooperation – and the taxation – of Khurasan, largely thanks to the family of his general Tahir, who provided four generations of Tahirid governors there from 821 to 873, but who were simultaneously rulers of the city of Baghdad, which depended on provincial revenue. Egypt, at the other end of the caliphate, was finally quiet after 832. Al-Ma'mun's army, no longer based on the early 'Abbasid *abnā*', was initially a rather uncertain collection of east Iranian aristocratic levies, who had trouble taking Baghdad against informal gangs of civilians (*'ayyārūn*) even though the defending regular army disintegrated; but he, and especially his military-minded brother and successor al-Mu'tasim (833–42), built up an army of mercenaries, particularly from Turkic central Asia, many of whom were former slaves, whom our sources generically refer to as Turks. This was an effective fighting force, not sufficiently Islamized to have its own political programme, not associated with any particular province of the caliphate, and very loyal, at least to al-Mu'tasim. They provided the muscle behind the last really big 'Abbasid attack on the Byzantine empire, which took Amorion in 838, and Turkish leaders were increasingly used as provincial governors. With the provinces quiescent, a model army, and an increasingly elaborate and extensive fiscal and administrative machine, the 830s and 840s under al-Mu'tasim and his more colourless son al-Wathiq (842–7) represented a new high point for the centralized 'Abbasid state, one that could have real staying power: or so one might have thought.

Ninth-century Baghdad, huge, wealthy and politically central as it was, became a real cultural focus. The startlingly large number of surviving works in Arabic from the ninth and tenth centuries, mostly (particularly before the 930s or so) written in or near the capital, themselves attest to it. They are only a portion of what was actually written, too, as is shown by the *Fihrist* or *Index* of al-Nadim (d. *c.* 990), which lists over 6,000 book titles, nearly all written in the last 250 years (this far outweighs the 279 Greek books in Photios' *Bibliothēkē*, though Photios had at least read them all), or by an anecdote in the *Fihrist* itself about the 600 cases of books allegedly possessed by the historian al-Waqidi (d. 823) – an impossible figure for such an early date, but significant as a tenth-century image. Theology, philosophy, law, poetry, administration, history, medicine, science and geography all had their experts in this hyperactive cultural world.

These branches of knowledge increasingly developed their own micro-cultures, with lawyers above all reading other lawyers, historians reading other historians, poets reading other poets. They were tied together, all the same, by two main networks, one cultural-religious, one literary. The intellectual strata as a whole were seen as a community of scholars, the *'ulamā'* (from *'ilm*, 'religious knowledge'). The community was defined initially and principally in terms of religious expertise, but came soon to extend out to the more specialized disciplines; its identity is most visible in biographical dictionaries of scholars, which were already being written in the early ninth century. It was this community, led by Qur'anic scholars and jurists, which was increasingly seen, in a religion with no formal priesthood or ecclesiastical hierarchy, as the determinators of what Islam was and how it should be understood, and indeed, in the twenty-first century, it still is.

The community did not, of course, always agree. We have already encountered the fault-line between Sunni and Shi'a, which crystallized as alternative political-religious systems in the ninth century. Each of these systems, however, also had their own sub-systems, rival schools of thought about how religion, political practice and law ought to be conducted. Inside what would be called the Sunni tradition, for instance, there was from early in the eighth century considerable debate about the degree to which Islamic legal practice (*sharī'a*) should be based on legislation (presumably by caliphs), or else reasoning from basic ethical principles derived from the Qur'an, or else on the increasingly elaborate sets of 'tradition' (*ḥadīth*), obiter dicta attributed to Muhammad the Prophet on almost every legal or moral issue imaginable. (These pronouncements in reality gave a religious legitimacy to local custom, although custom on its own was never regarded as a legitimate fount of law.) The 'traditionists' essentially won out, but the four main law schools of medieval Sunni Islam, looking respectively to Abu Hanifa (d. 767), Malik (d. 795), al-Shafi'i (d. 820) – the most intellectually influential – and Ibn Hanbal (d. 855), varied considerably in their commitment to *ḥadīth*, with Hanafis most receptive to legal reasoning and Hanbalis most rigidly attached to literal readings of *ḥadīth*. These schools, and other less long-lasting ones, achieved a mutual toleration all the same, as each constitutive of Sunni *'ulamā'* opinion, and by 900 or so they had developed what has been called the 'closing of the gate of independent reasoning': no new law or legal opinion, including by a caliph or other political leader, would, in theory, any longer be acceptable. Islamic law thus became increasingly fixed (even if legal practice did not). This served further to define the *'ulamā'* as a cultural grouping, although other disciplines continued to develop for centuries, much as the doctrinal rules of eastern and western Christendom bounded the developing thought-worlds of Europe throughout the Middle Ages as well.

The other way in which the realms of written culture were linked was through *adab*, roughly translatable as 'polite education', or 'literary etiquette'. This became the foundation of Arab written culture by around 800, and remained so throughout our period and beyond. It linked learning with stylistic elegance, and required of its practitioners a general knowledge of most of the intellectual disciplines of the period, but particularly language, poetry, stories, administrative practice and *ḥadīth*. The administrative practice is the give-away: *adab* was above all a qualification for careers in government. It was the exact equivalent of the senatorial literary education of the Roman empire and of the classical and theological training necessary for administrators in Byzantium after 900, except that the knowledge it required was mostly of a much more recent vintage. And indeed the scope of intellectual activity in Baghdad and other centres showed the range of skills that were acceptable in government; intellectuals from the geographer Ibn Khurradadhbih (d. *c.* 885) to the seriously influential and original philosopher-physician Ibn Sina (Avicenna, d. 1037) held governmental and administrative offices. This range marks one of the particularities of *adab*. So also, however, does storytelling. Literary culture gave considerable space to narratives; 'Abbasid histories are composed of thousands of short exemplary accounts, with plenty of direct quotations, supposedly taken from the lips of caliphs and their advisers. Rhetorical skill required remarkably recondite knowledge as part of such storytelling; hence the existence of several encyclopedias of 'curiosities', such as that of al-Tha'alibi (d. 1038), which contains such information as the name of the first Arab to wear dark silks, the first caliph to build a hospital, the vizir with the longest unbroken chain of ancestors who were also vizirs, the most generous female pilgrim, the two caliphs who each killed three political rivals whose names began with the same letter, and the alarming (but untrue) fact that every sixth caliph was 'inevitably' deposed. This knowledge, these days restricted to adolescent boys, was in this period a requirement for statecraft, along with knowing how to write a letter properly and memorizing the Qur'an.

The strata of professional administrators, from viziers and other senior secretaries down to the clerks in provincial tax offices, were complex, and generated their own cultural traditions. There are collections of administrative exemplary stories, just as there are political ones in histories; accounts of how and why individuals got promoted and demoted, and of the clever things they said to heads of *dīwān*s and viziers. *Nishwār al-muhādara, Desultory Conversations*, another *adab* text, by the Basra judge al-Tanukhi (d. 994), shows how dense this specifically administrative historical memory could be, and how it extended, even in the late tenth century, without a break back to the caliphates of the mid-ninth, and even of al-Rashid and al-Mahdi. Among other things, one is struck by how accidental promotions could be in this world, as ordinary officials came to the eye of the powerful. Al-Fadl ibn Marwan (d. *c.* 845), a kitchen steward to an aristocrat and then a minor clerk in al-Rashid's time, made enough money to buy land and live in the country during the siege of Baghdad, where he reputedly gave hospitality unknowingly to the future caliph al-Mu'tasim; thanks to this chance, he rose steadily in the administration, and became vizier at his patron's accession in 833 – though, conversely, he was soon dismissed (in 836), and had to pay huge sums in fines, because he tried to prevent the caliph from spending public money. The chance of fate was linked to a good deal of administrative competence; al-Fadl was an able administrator who brought in considerable revenues to at least two caliphs. It is also clear that plenty of these revenues stuck to his own fingers, given his wealth in the 830s. Much paperwork was indeed expended to try to cut down peculation, but al-Tanukhi's stories show that this could easily be subverted, with misleading papers put in the records, until or unless rivals uncovered the fraud.

One gains a picture of a tight but very jealous administrative community, in which a common profession counted as a tie of kinship (as al-Fadl said, quoting a retired clerk whom he met as a youth), but in which promotion often depended on the destruction of others. At least al-Fadl kept his life in 836; plenty of others, including in particular many viziers, did not. To say that administrative and court politics was cut-throat is indeed an understatement; unlucky 'Abbasid politicians could die by tortures as inventive as those of the Merovingians, or indeed more so, as 'Abbasid science was more developed – al-Fadl's successor as vizir, Ibn al-Zayyat (836–47), died in a torture machine of his own devising. But Ibn al-Zayyat had also supposedly kept his position as vizir at the accession of al-Wathiq in 842, even though the new caliph loathed him and had sworn to kill him, because he was the only senior official who could compose a formal letter to the satisfaction of the ruler. This mixture of ambition, greed, violence and genuine professionalism marked the administrative class as a whole, or at least its upper echelons.

The complex and dangerous world of the administration was mirrored in the other two arenas of caliphal politics, the army and the caliphal household. The civil administration and the army are often seen as rivals in 'Abbasid historiography, much as in middle Byzantine historiography, and probably as wrongly; as in Byzantium, the same person could do both, as with the Barmakid al-Fadl and the Tahirid 'Abd Allah ibn Tahir (d. 845), and even the occasional Turkish general, such as Utamish (d. 863), who held the vizirate for a year before his death. Factions in reality crossed both areas of government without difficulty, even when the Turks, disliked and distinct, came to dominate the army. The numerous large palaces of the 'Abbasids also had their own staff, not least the even more numerous slave mistresses of the caliphs, whose head was either a queen, or, if the caliph did not formally marry – which was the norm after the early ninth century – a queen-mother; the factions crossed into this arena too.

As with the Merovingians, equally dynastically minded and polygamous, political influence for women in the 'Abbasid period tended to be restricted to the mothers of caliphs or designated future caliphs. The most famous examples of this were Khayzuran (d. 789), the mother of Harun al-Rashid, and Zubayda (d. 831), al-Rashid's wife and mother of al-Amin. Zubayda even kept some of her influence after al-Ma'mun overthrew al-Amin – she brokered, for example, the reconciliation of the anti-caliph Ibrahim in 825. But it has to be said that 'Abbasid political practice gave less scope to female protagonism than either the Frankish or the Byzantine tradition. The complicated and ever-developing ceremonial of the 'Abbasid caliphate, which must have matched that of the tenth-century Byzantines, had rather less space for women as public players; but it is above all the case that succession rules focused on choosing appropriate candidates for caliph meant that child caliphs, for whom mothers could act as regents, were less common than royal minors were in Byzantium or Francia. The first was not until al-Muqtadir (908–32), whose reign was indeed dominated by his formidable mother, a Byzantine ex-slave called Shaghab ('troublesome'), or, simply, al-Sayyida ('the lady'). Shaghab (d. 933) is not handled in a consistently hostile way by the sources, despite their general suspicion of female power, magnified by the disasters of her son's reign; she followed Zubayda in making public displays of charity on a large scale, a recognizable 'Abbasid gendered female role, thanks to her vast wealth, and this allowed at least some chroniclers to depict her neutrally. Shaghab established a parallel bureaucratic hierarchy of male secretaries and female stewardesses which exercised direct power in these decades. It is important, however, to recognize that such offices were already normal in the female areas of the palaces. Queens, chief mistresses and caliphal mothers had long been wealthy, and needed administrators to run their affairs; if, on rare occasions, such as under Shaghab, these took over caliphal politics too, they had all the qualifications to do so.

Caliphs are portrayed in the sources in conventional ways, al-Mansur as eloquent and ascetic, al-Mahdi as generous and poetry-loving, al-Mu'tasim as martial, and so on. Al-Ma'mun (who conventionally had a sense of humour and a gift for poetry) is perhaps the one who most established his own identity through his actions. His attraction to Shi'ism is one such, which did not end when he backed down over his 'Alid heir in 818–19. So is his patronage of scientists, who engaged in a programme of translations of Greek scientific works, Ptolemy, Galen, Euclid and so on, and the determination (among other things) of an accurate calculation of the circumference of the earth: this came to be carried out from a library and scientific research centre known as the Bayt al-Hikma, 'House of Wisdom', founded by the caliph in Baghdad in 830. Al-Ma'mun was also a doctrinal protagonist, sympathetic to a rationalist school of Islam known as Mu'tazilism. The role of the caliph as a religious authority, which was seen as normal in the Umayyad period, and which was urged on al-Mansur by his Persian secretary and adviser Ibn al-Muqaffa' (d. c. 757) at the start of the 'Abbasid caliphate, was being undermined by the growth of the authority of the 'ulamā', but al-Ma'mun had a sufficient confidence in his mission to put doctrine into the heart of politics. In 833 he decided that one element of Mu'tazilist thought, the doctrine of the createdness of the Qur'an (that is, that God had created the book within time; it had not pre-existed the world), was sufficiently important that all judges and 'ulamā' should be forced to subscribe to it, particularly the 'traditionists', who were bitterly opposed to it. Almost alone, Ibn Hanbal defied him, and went to prison. The created Qur'an remained a tenet of the next two caliphs as well, and was only abandoned in 847, at the accession of al-Wathiq's brother al-Mutawakkil (847–61). This period, of the so-called *miḥna* or 'inquisition', is the only one in which a doctrinal issue mattered politically in medieval Islam, as opposed to the permanent debates about the legitimacy of early caliphs. The apparent obscurity of the religious issue at stake is one element that reminds us of the Christological schisms of the later Roman empire. The sense one has of a political regime using such an issue to kick religious extremists into line is also a reminder of the near-contemporary Second Iconoclasm in Byzantium, and indeed al-Ma'mun recalls his younger contemporary Theophilos in his interest in religious-philosophical debate as well. Why al-Ma'mun chose the created Qur'an as the issue to make a stand on is, however, even less clear than the reasons for the Iconoclast controversy. It may be that any issue would have done, to re-establish caliphal religious authority, especially in the face of the 'traditionists'. But the *miḥna* failed; Ibn Hanbal returned; after 849 doctrine was fully in the hands of the 'ulamā', and caliphs – and, still more, their tenth-century supplanters in Iraq and Iran, who did not have their formal religious role as 'commanders of the believers' – became essentially secular powers. They would be patrons of intellectuals, jurists, 'ulamā', but not intellectuals themselves.

Al-Mu'tasim's Turkish army got on particularly badly with the Baghdadis, who were after all the heirs of the previous paid army, the *abnā'*, so the caliph built a new capital at Samarra, further up the Tigris, and moved both himself and his army there in 836. The establishment of new capitals was a standard part of early 'Abbasid political affirmation; Baghdad itself was the key exemplar, and al-Rashid's period in Raqqa (796–808) and al-Ma'mun's in Merv (811–18) were others. Samarra was the most serious foundation after Baghdad, and was, as usual with the 'Abbasids, built on a huge scale: its ruins extend along the Tigris for 40 kilometres. All the same, like Raqqa earlier, it was not intended to rival Baghdad as a population centre, and it remained largely a military and administrative centre during its period as the capital, 836–92. The problem was that the caliph was thus isolated together with his army.

Both the Umayyads and the early 'Abbasids used armies paid out of general taxation, which were separated from their areas of origin, the early Arab settlers in their *amṣār*, the Khurasani *abnā'* in Baghdad. In this respect, the Turks were not unusual, except that they came from beyond the frontiers, and they would have plenty of successors in the more fragmented tenth century too. There was always a tension between the paid military and the rest of tax-paying society in the medieval Arab world as a result of this pattern. Furthermore, because provincial élites converted to Islam, above all in the ninth century, and were matched by Arab settler families acquiring land – in the early eighth century in Khurasan, the late eighth in the boom-town hinterland of Baghdad, the late ninth in Egypt – there therefore came to be Muslim provincial aristocracies who could be very resentful of the political power and the financial weight of the army. This was particularly so in Khurasan, where the pre-Islamic Persian ruling class largely remained, with highly aristocratic and military values, however Islamized by now. Some of this Persian ruling class did indeed join al-Ma'mun's and al-Mu'tasim's army, like al-Afshin of Ushrusana (d. 841), a hardly Muslim prince from central Asia, although he, significantly, perished because he was thought to have plotted against the Turks.

The caliphs could not, however, simply leave military affairs to local aristocracies; they would have instantly lost their tax revenues, and the caliphate would have broken up very fast. Given that, they might as well pay men from outside the caliphate, who had no aristocratic pretensions and were at least good at their job. But there were dangers too. In an anecdote laden with hindsight, the historian al-Tabari has the Tahirid Ishaq ibn Ibrahim tell al-Mu'tasim: 'your brother considered the roots and made use of them, and their branches flourished exceedingly; whereas the commander of the believers has utilized only branches, which have not flourished because they lacked roots.' Which is to say: al-Ma'mun used Tahirids like myself, and other people rooted in the community, and that worked; but you use the Turks, who do not have such roots, and this is a real problem. Al-Mu'tasim is supposed to have sadly recognized the truth of this. However this may be, the deracination of the Turks ceased to be an advantage when al-Mutawakkil turned against them in the 850s and sought to bring down their leaders, for they had nowhere to go. In the end, they responded by assassinating him in 861. This unleashed a decade of crisis in Samarra, 861–70, in which Turkish factions set up five caliphs in turn and killed three of them; the crisis extended back to Baghdad when one of them, al-Musta'in (862–6), fled to the old capital and its Tahirid governor, with a section of the Turks, and Baghdad was besieged and captured again in 865–6. Stability only returned in 870 when the 'Abbasid family developed its own military strongman, Abu Ahmad al-Muwaffaq (d. 891), who had in fact led the siege of Baghdad and was very close to the surviving Turkish leadership; he was put in charge of the army by his brother al-Mu'tamid, who was caliph by now (870–92), and left the latter in Samarra while he gradually transferred himself to Baghdad. When al-Muwaffaq's son and heir al-Mu'tadid became caliph (892–902), he formally re-established Baghdad as the capital, and the Samarra interlude ended.

The years 861–70 were not so very long, but, like the civil war of the 810s, they opened up fault-lines in the 'Abbasid polity which were hard to close. The revived 'Abbasid protagonism of 870–908 (it extended to al-Mu'tadid's son al-Muktafi, 902–8) faced widespread difficulties. Iranian rebels, the Saffarids (they did not have aristocratic roots, and they were close to fringe Muslim sects), had defeated the Tahirids in Khurasan between 867 and 873, and marched on Iraq; they were defeated there in 876, but they continued to control much of Iran, paying taxes only intermittently. The Turkish governor of Egypt, Ahmad ibn Tulun (868–84) was not directly opposed to the 'Abbasids, but he too did not pay much tax to Iraq, and he extended his power into Syria and Palestine, which thus did not pay much either; only after his son Khumarawayh (884–96) succeeded him did an 'Abbasid army manage to re-establish a greater measure of tax-paying from the Tulunid provinces, and not until 905 did the 'Abbasids regain direct rule in Egypt. Only in Iraq did the 'Abbasids exercise fiscal control in the 870s and 880s, and here, around Basra in the south, they faced a huge slave revolt, of the Zanj, African slaves used to maintain the irrigation system: this revolt, lasting from 869 to 883, was the most successful slave uprising in history before the Haitian revolt of 1791, resulting in an independent Shi'ite state which was only destroyed by four years of war under al-Muwaffaq in 879–83. The 'Abbasids were seriously short of money until the mid-880s, and even after that had to fight without a break, with their still-Turkish armies, to keep on top of events. They succeeded in their core lands, with the exception of Iran, which increasingly slid away under local dynasties. But they could not afford to relax their pressure. After 908, al-Muqtadir was a very inattentive ruler, and his mother Shaghab did not have control of the army. By the 920s, with infighting inside the bureaucracy, rival generals in Iraq, bedouin raids from the Arabian desert, and Syrian and Egyptian governors who had begun to stop paying taxes again, the gains of recent decades were all lost; in the 930s caliphs began to be deposed once more, and after 936 the caliph lost all power to a military governor, the *amīr al-umarā'*, 'amir of amirs'. In 945 Ahmad ibn Buya (d. 967), from the most successful of the rising dynasties of Iran, the Buyids, took Baghdad, and became *amīr al-umarā'* with the ruling name of Mu'izz al-Dawla, 'fortifier of the [still nominally 'Abbasid] state'. Iraq was controlled from western Iran from then on for a century.

The break-up of the 'Abbasid caliphate, for a hundred years the strongest state in the world (Tang China had run into trouble in and after the 750s), would ideally need as detailed an account and set of explanations as did that of the Roman empire. If I dispose of the sequence of events in a couple of pages, it is only because by now, after the 860s, its history hardly extended beyond Iraq except for brief periods, and is too far from the history of Europe. The tenth century in the Islamic world was, as already observed, even more fragmented, with the Samanids and then the Ghaznavids in eastern Iran, two or three Buyid polities in western Iran and Iraq, two Hamdanid polities in Aleppo and (more briefly) Mosul, a set of Kurdish dynasties in the mountains to their north and east, the Qaramita in the Arabian desert, the Ikhshidids and then the Fatimids in Egypt, and other smaller polities too – as well as those of the Maghreb, which had not been under 'Abbasid control since the early ninth century or even before, the Aghlabids and then the Fatimids in what is now Tunisia and Sicily, the Idrisids in what is now Morocco, and the Umayyads in Spain. We cannot follow all their histories here. But before we look at two of them, we do need to take stock of the century of 'Abbasid unity and of its failure.

One simple reason why the 'Abbasid caliphate broke up was that it was too large. Local societies were too different; communications were always slow; the caliphate was larger than the Roman empire, and did not have a sea, with its relatively easy bulk transport, at its heart. Conquests and reconquests, with new ruling armies and a clean slate, helped periodic reunifications: in 636–51, 747–50, 811–13, as subsequently with the

Buyids, and the Seljuk Turks in the 1040s and later, but tensions would always rise again. This was particularly the case in Khurasan and in Iran as a whole, whose pre-Islamic ruling class, with some military protagonism, survived better than elsewhere (and whose pre-Islamic past was still celebrated by Muslims in oral and written literature, unlike anywhere further west except Spain); and which, being mountainous, was much harder to control in depth; significantly, the most successful and long-lasting later Islamic empire, the Ottomans, never held Iran. Trouble for the 'Abbasids generally began in Iran; Iraq and Egypt were much easier to rule, and Syria was not any sort of power-centre for two centuries after the fall of the Umayyads.

This straightforward geopolitical argument is largely backed up by one basic point about the tenth-century Muslim successor states: they were almost all tax-raising states with a central paid army and bureau-cracy, just as the caliphate had been. Only some of the Kurdish states of southern Anatolia and the Iranian mountains, followed by bedouin dynasties in Syria and the Jazira in the eleventh century, had a simpler structure, based on block gifts of tribute to armed transhumant groups. Unlike at the end of the western Roman empire, there was no structural breakdown inside the majority of these smaller polities. Unlike in the Romano-Germanic kingdoms, the new ruling groups were not con-cerned to make themselves into a landowning aristocracy. Land indeed did not bring political power in most medieval Muslim societies, only state position did that: or so it seemed to medieval political actors. Wealth, too, was most reliably obtained through positions in the state; and old families, whose longevity was ensured by private wealth – inevitably in land, in the Muslim as in the Christian world – were not especially privileged in any Islamic state structure, even in Iran. The political model established by 'Umar I and two centuries of Umayyad and 'Abbasid caliphs thus continued to hold. Indeed, it intensified, as the idea of ex-slaves holding military power, with no links to local communities and no family background, first experimented with al-Mu'tasim's Turks, became an increasingly common model in later cen-turies. Independence from the caliphate just meant that taxation stayed in the province concerned and paid a local army: a basic aim of provincial élites from the Umayyad period onwards, and only fully overridden by the strongest 'Abbasid rulers, with reversions whenever 'Abbasid control slipped, as in the 810s and 860s. From this standpoint, the break-up of the caliphate could even be seen as unproblematic, as simply consisting of the reversion of politics to its optimum size, the province.

Broadly, I think this interpretation is a fair one. But it does concentrate attention too much on the state; provincial societies get left out of the equation. Local social leaders were hugely diverse, extending from the old families of parts of Iran to the rapidly changing Iraqi élites, who tended simply to be the heirs of the most recent wave of administrators, who had made money from taxation and settled down; all the same, they existed everywhere. They certainly did have land by now, and also sometimes commercial wealth, which they turned into land as well. The great local political centres, almost all urban – major cities like Aleppo, Mosul, Rayy (modern Teheran), Merv and Nishapur in Khurasan – were full of local élite families, of 'ulamā' and others, who sought the post of qāḍī, an important focus of local power, and who squabbled over local and provincial position, rather than seeking it from the state; here, land, private wealth and birth did matter (being an 'Alid was increasingly chic, especially in Iran), just as it did in the West. 'Abbasid governors always had to come to terms with local power-broking families, or else they would fail: they would be unable to collect tax (a process itself controlled by local figures), or face revolt, or both. So did the smaller-scale rulers of the tenth century. And indeed this in itself shows that there was a relationship between local societies and the 'state class'. Even the most deracinated army family could put down local roots, at least as rulers, as the Tulunids did in Egypt; and all rulers, bureaucrats and local military men had to negotiate with their subjects, or at least the richest of them. Some sections of the 'state class', particularly the civil administration, had origins in local societies, too; they, at least, had tight local obligations.

All the same, a separation between the 'state class' and local and provincial societies did exist, and was a problem. By and large, making a career in the local city and making a career in the state were different, not only in the geographically large-scale 'Abbasid caliphate but in the provincial polities of the tenth century as well. This meant that local societies could view the changing fates of their rulers with a certain equanimity: the latter were largely external figures, whether benevolent or violent, generous or fiscally harsh, cultured or martial, without a structural connection to the strata of the governed. As government became more secular, now that the fate of Islam had devolved to the 'ulamā', the salvationist imagery of right rule so effectively invoked by Abu Muslim and the early 'Abbasids was also no longer part of most political programmes. Only the Fatimids tried it in the tenth century, as we shall see in a moment. When a local ruler faced military failure, then, because a blockage in the tax supply made it hard to pay troops, or simply because of defeat in battle, he could be replaced without local society really being involved, as long as the new ruler did not take over too violently. There were certainly some examples of a loyalist protagonism by local élites, as when the citizens of Mosul in 989 expelled the Buyids and temporarily restored their earlier rulers, the Hamdanids, but they were not so very many. On one level, indeed, the very ease with which the 'Abbasids lost control in the 910s to 940s, to be replaced by regimes which for the most part resembled them, was a real structural failure: however dismal the period was, it ought to have been possible for someone to make more of a stand, a heroic loser committed to an older legitimacy. The 'Abbasids did not leave stories of that kind, and nor did the Buyids later. The stories that continued to hold attention were still Sassanian – or else of the timeless fantasy Baghdad of Harun al-Rashid and the *Thousand and One Nights*.

The Fatimids were the most successful, richest and most stable of the tenth-century Muslim states. They outlived their major rivals, the Buyids, by over a century, and indeed ruled over all, first in Kairouan in Ifriqiya, modern Tunisia, and then (after 973) in newly conquered Egypt, for more than two hundred and fifty years, 909–1171. They also represent, as just observed, the only serious attempt at a salvationist revival after the early 'Abbasids, and are thus a special case in the tenth-century Islamic world. Their salvationism was, however, Shi'ite, not Sunni. The first Fatimid, 'Ubayd Allah al-Mahdi, was an Isma'ili Shi'a living in Syria, who belonged to one of the sects of Shi'ism which held that a hidden *imām* or supreme spiritual leader, descended from the caliph 'Ali, would return to redeem the world. In around 899 he declared – controversially inside the Isma'ili movement, which he split in two – that he was himself the imam. He had to flee Syria, and ended up among the Kutama Berbers of modern Algeria, a sensible move, for the Berbers often had 'Alid sympathies – an earlier 'Alid exile, Idris ibn 'Abd Allah (d. 795), had founded the Idrisid kingdom in central Morocco in 789. The Berbers were also good fighters, and were the core of the Fatimid army until well after our period ends. The Kutama adopted al-Mahdi as a charismatic leader, and keenly took to the role he offered them as the equivalent to the Khurasanis in the 'Abbasid 'revolution'. Their general, an Iraqi named Abu 'Abd Allah, the Fatimid version of Abu Muslim, took Ifriqiya from the faltering Aghlabid dynasty in 909, and al-Mahdi proclaimed himself caliph (910–34) outside Kairouan a year later. Like Abu Muslim, Abu 'Abd Allah was also killed by his patron-protégé inside a year, and al-Mahdi was not troubled by rivals thereafter.

Like both the 'Abbasids and the Aghlabids, al-Mahdi set up his own capital in 920, at Mahdiyya on the Tunisian coast. He used the same governmental structures as the Aghlabids, although his Isma'ili messianism set himself, and his Kutama army, apart from his Sunni subjects. That messianism, however, meant that al-Mahdi would not be content with Ifriqiya; from the start, the Fatimids looked eastwards, with raids on Egypt. This strategy was deflected by another salvationist Berber revolt, by Kharijites this time, in 944–7, but it was defeated, and by 960 al-Mahdi's great-grandson al-Mu'izz (953–75) ruled all North Africa, unified for the first time since the 730s. This stability allowed a renewed attack on Egypt, which was rudderless after the recent death of Abu'l Misk Kafur, a black ex-slave, a eunuch of fabled ugliness, who had ruled Egypt with skill and vision for twenty-two years (946–68). The Fatimid general Jawhar (d. 976), another ex-slave, a Slav this time, took the country with little violence in 969, and al-Mu'izz moved there four years later. Jawhar and later generals pursued Fatimid ambitions on into Palestine and Syria, but they ran aground around Damascus, and when the frontier stabilized in the 990s it did so between Damascus and Aleppo. Fatimid expansionism stopped, and a modus vivendi emerged in Syria between the main regional powers, the Fatimids, the Buyids, and, since the 950s, the Byzantines, as we saw in the last chapter. Perhaps surprisingly, by the 990s the caliphs, now situated stably in wealthy Egypt, were prepared to let control over Ifriqiya slip, to a family of hereditary governors; from now on the Fatimids would be an Egyptian and Levantine power, which they remained for nearly two centuries more.

It is easy to see 909–10 as a rerun of 749–50, and at one level one whose religious fervour had greater staying power, for the Fatimids began a long way from the old power-centres of the Islamic world, which they would have to fight for longer to reach – indeed, they never reached Baghdad. As Shi'ite imams, too, the Fatimid caliphs did not have to pay attention to the *'ulamā'* in any of their domains, for that was by definition Sunni, and anyway an imam drew his authority direct from God. But, even more than in Ifriqiya, Fatimid rule in Egypt was simply a continuation of the – already effective – rule of their predecessors. The Kutama in Egypt and Syria were another paid army, far from home, like the *abnā'* and the Turks. Al-Mu'izz and his successors recentralized the fiscal administration of Egypt, as had the early 'Abbasids, but in Egypt it had never been very decentralized. A strong state aided commercial development, but in any case Egypt had by now outstripped Iraq again as a productive region. In large part, the Fatimids allowed it to develop simply by creating stability; Egypt remained one of the major Islamic powers until the very end of the Middle Ages as a result, with a political protagonism unmatched since Cleopatra. Their administrative capital, al-Qahira, that is, Cairo, was founded in 969 just outside the previous provincial capital Fustat, which remained the commercial focus of Egypt; Fustat–Cairo was for a long time the major economic powerhouse of the whole eastern Mediterranean, surpassing even Baghdad, as we shall see in more detail in the next chapter.

So the Fatimids can be construed simply as normal rulers of the tenth century and onwards, just successful at it, and lucky with the region they ruled. All the same, this did not make the Fatimids exactly the same as their peers elsewhere in the Islamic world. Isma'ilism, a secretive sect with esoteric and abstract Neoplatonist elements, including a complex letter and number symbolism, continued to mark out the court and the army, isolated among an ocean of Sunnis, Coptic Christians and Jews, and caliphs could continue to have messianic dreams: not least al-Hakim (996–1021), who erected anti-Sunni slogans on Sunni mosques, who demolished the church of the Holy Sepulchre in Jerusalem, and who was, and still is, venerated as divine by the Druzes of Lebanon. Al-Hakim was also a capricious and violent autocrat in a rather more familiar mould, but his religious imagery marks out the originality of the Fatimids nonetheless.

Tariq ibn Ziyad, the Berber leader of a largely Berber army, invaded Visigothic Spain for the Umayyad caliphs of Damascus and defeated and killed King Roderic in 711. The Berbers and Arabs had taken nearly all the peninsula by around 718. Muslim armies raided into Francia for another decade and a half, but without much commitment to conquest; Spain – al-Andalus in Arabic – was already on the very edge of their world, and it is likely that, if it had not fallen so easily, they would have stopped at the Straits of Gibraltar. Be that as it may, the occupation of the peninsula was quick. With the Visigothic army defeated, the Muslims made separate treaties with several local lords, in particular Theodemir in south-east Spain in 713. They did not base themselves in the old Visigothic capital of Toledo, but in Córdoba, in the rich south; Toledo was rather more of a frontier area, with an extensive uncontrolled land further north in the Duero valley between Muslim al-Andalus and the Christian polities of the northern fringe of the peninsula. At Córdoba, a succession of governors ruled, chosen by the caliphs. Al-Andalus looked like a normal, if outlying, province of the caliphate. It was as affected as was North Africa by the great Berber revolt of 740, but Caliph Hisham sent Syrian armies into Spain in 742, who won back the peninsula in 742–3 and settled there, thus increasing the Arab element of the Muslim settlement. The Syrians in Spain replicated the Qays– Yaman faction-fighting of the fertile crescent, however, and for a decade from 745 there was civil war between them. When the Umayyads were overthrown in Syria in 750 and largely wiped out as a family, one of Hisham's grandsons, 'Abd al-Rahman ibn Mu'awiya, fled to the Berber kin of his mother, first in Africa and then, in 755, in Spain. Here he found support, both from Berber lineages and from the Yamani Arab opponents of the Qaysi governor, Yusuf al-Fihri. (The Yamanis in Spain were thus pro-Umayyad, not anti, as they had come to be by 749 in the East.) Inside a year he had defeated Yusuf and had taken Córdoba. 'Abd al-Rahman I then ruled as *amīr* for more than thirty years, 756–88, wholly independent of his 'Abbasid enemies in Baghdad. So did his descendants, until 1031.

Spain was not like most of the other caliphal provinces, however. It was far more decentralized, and also, for a century at least, had a rather simpler economy than many, more like the economies of the rest of western Europe, with relatively unskilled and far more localized artisanal production, than like the economically complex and heavily urbanized provinces of the caliphate, Egypt or Syria or Iraq. Even its major cities, which under the Arabs as under the Visigoths were Córdoba, Seville, Mérida, Toledo, Zaragoza and a few others, were for a long time relatively small by comparison with those of the eastern Mediterranean.

Spain was also, crucially, one of the only provinces conquered by the Arabs which did not have more than a fragmentary tax system. The standard procedures for Arab occupation, based on a paid military élite in a (perhaps new) garrison city, were thus impractical. The Berbers, newly Islamized (when converted at all) in the 710s, anyway doubtless wanted simply to settle on conquered land, and did so. But even the Syrians, who were sent in in the 740s as a normal paid army, soon settled on the land too – initially as tax-farmers, soon as landowners – and just did military service (for which they were paid by the campaign); they intermarried with the Visigothic aristocracy, and into the tenth century, as we shall see, there were families who were proud of both their Arab and their Gothic ancestry.

The amirs took what tax they could from the start, and were heavily criticized by chroniclers for it from the start (as witnessed by a mid-century Christian source, still in Latin, the *Chronicle of 754*). All the same, they had none of the fiscal control of governors elsewhere. Unlike anywhere else in the caliphate, they had to face a Muslim landed aristocracy from (nearly) the start as well, who might be able to resist tax-paying more successfully than their still-Christian neighbours. Nor was there much of a paid 'state class', either civilian or military, for some time. The existence of the frontier with the Christians in the north also led to a military-political fragmentation, with half of al-Andalus separated off into marches (*thugūr*), based on central-northern centres like Toledo and Zaragoza, or Tudela, power-base of the ex-Visigothic Banu Qasi family, over which the Umayyad amirs, based in the south, had little control for a century and more. Spain is very regionally diverse, with bad communications, and the Muslim conquest had caused its local societies to move sharply in different directions; these contrasts were also further exacerbated by the diversities of Arab and Berber settlement. The Berbers, for example, seem to have settled in tight tribal groups in more marginal areas, but to have become ordinary (and Arabized) landowners when living in or near cities. Given this local diversity, this political fragmentation, and the need for the Umayyad amirs from the start to recognize the relevance of the politics of land, Muslim Spain was indeed as much part of western Europe as it was part of the Arab political environment.

Faced with this reality, the Umayyads were eventually rather success-ful for a time, but it was a long process and it was far from straightforward. 'Abd al-Rahman I essentially established the centrality of his own family, which was a task not yet completed in 756 – the Banu Fihri, a powerful family in both Africa and Spain, who had supplied four governors in al-Andalus alone, were still revolting into the 780s. Father–son succession then followed into the 880s without a break, and, although there were certainly succession disputes between sons, and killings of potential rivals, there was actually no protracted disagreement about which Umayyad should rule until after 1000, a remarkable record, and one which both aided stability and was made possible by it. The state was still fairly skeletal until the 820s, however. 'Abd al-Rahman I did employ a small paid army, but it is unlikely that his tax-base extended far outside the Córdoba–Seville region, linked by the lowlands of the Guadalquivir valley, and attempts by his grandson al-Hakam I (796–822) to stabilize that taxation led to revolt in 818, not only in marcher centres like Toledo, where uprising was fairly frequent, but among the urban population of Córdoba itself. It was not until 'Abd al-Rahman II (822–52), a subtler ruler, that an administrative system resembling that of the caliphs of the East took shape, with higher taxation, a bureaucratic class (headed here by the $ḥājib$, the chamberlain, not by the vizir – the latter was a lesser office in Spain, and there were usually several of them) and a wider political control. 'Abd al-Rahman II in 825 built a new city, Murcia, in the previously marginal south-east, and settled it with Arab loyalists; he confronted the rebellious tendencies of Mérida by building a large internal fortress there in 835, and another in Toledo in 837; and he developed a formal court in Córdoba, now fast expanding as a city, whose growth in power, wealth and buying-power meant that it would not henceforth be disadvantageous to the capital for the amir to be strong there.

Al-Andalus under 'Abd al-Rahman II and his son Muhammad (852–86), seen from the standpoint of the state, thus came more and more to match the 'Abbasid heartland. The former patronized poets and scholars from the East, not least the important Iraqi musician and poet Ziryab (d. 857), who was rewarded for coming west by a huge salary. 'Abd al-Rahman's reign was also marked by the crystallization of an 'ulamā' on an entirely eastern model, dominated by the Maliki law school, and soon present in every major city and plenty of minor ones. Al-Andalus, with its Umayyad legitimist tradition, was almost devoid of the disputes about right rule that were so important elsewhere, and even its law was

not up for discussion. This in part marks its provinciality by comparison with the East, but the cultural continuum that linked them was
unbroken; that would remain true in Ibn Hawqal's time, as we have
already seen. Indeed, Spanish historians, once history-writing began in
the peninsula (with 'Abd al-Malik ibn Habib, d. 853, a wide-ranging
intellectual), were capable of writing in detail about eastern events on
occasion; Andalusis were consistently informed about what went on in
the 'Abbasid world. The population was also, even if slowly, converting
to Islam; a majority of al-Andalus was probably not Muslim until well
into the tenth century, and Christians and Jews never ceased to be
influential in Andalusi culture, but political leaders and major political
centres were in general mostly Muslim now. A sign of this is the strange
minority movement known as the 'martyrs of Córdoba', Christian
extremists led by Eulogius (d. 859) and Alvar, who deliberately provoked their death in the capital by insulting Islam in public in the 850s.
There were less than fifty of them, and they were clearly unrepresentative
of the still-large Córdoba Christian community, despite the fascination
their writings (conveniently in Latin) have had for recent scholars; but
the desperation of their stand implies that they saw only extreme
measures as adequate against the steady advance of Muslim hegemony.

This process of increasing amiral power on eastern political models
was falling apart, however, by Muhammad's death, and the 880s–920s
were a long period of generalized disturbance or *fitna*. Muhammad
already had trouble with Toledo and Mérida; he made peace with the
former in 873, and sacked the latter in 868, but then nearby Badajoz,
which became an alternative political centre to Mérida in the 870s,
turned to revolt too under the former Méridan leader 'Abd al-Rahman
ibn Marwan al-Jilliqi (d. 892). In the 880s 'Umar ibn Hafsun (d. 917)
also revolted from his base at Bobastro in the far south, above Málaga.
Under Muhammad's son 'Abd Allah (888–912), more and more local
lords established effective independence, both in the marches and in the
Andalusian heartland of the Guadalquivir valley. 'Abd Allah was an
ineffective and reclusive ruler, but the problem was a wider one. The
Muslim landed aristocracy, many of whom (including Ibn al-Jilliqi and
Ibn Hafsun) had at least partial Visigothic ancestry, had effective local
bases and local loyalties. They could be happy with an expanding state,
from which they could benefit, even though the growing fiscal demands
of that state were opposed to their immediate interests, but if the state

faltered they would look to their localities, rather than to the person of the amir. Beneath the 'Abbasid-style political system in Córdoba, that is to say, the more western-style local political practice, already discussed, continued to exist. Iran, with its surviving Sassanian aristocratic families, offers the closest parallel, including the survival of pre-Arabic political imagery in local social memory; the Zoroastrian legitimists that can be found in Iran as late as the tenth century have their parallel in 'Umar ibn Hafsun, who actually converted to Christianity in 898. But Iran also had other regions with strong paid armies and depoliticized local societies, which tended to dominate politically. In Spain, the permanent paid army was still not substantial, and military service was largely controlled, as in other parts of the West, by the very aristocrats whose loyalty was now in doubt. When even Seville in 899 established effective autonomy under a member of one of its local élite families, Ibrahim ibn al-Hajjaj (d. 911), called 'king' (*malik*) in the sources, the state risked breaking up.

'Abd Allah's grandson and successor, 'Abd al-Rahman III (912–61), was the ruler who reversed this trend, and by doing so he inaugurated three generations of strong central power, the strongest known in Spain between the Romans and the thirteenth century. 'Abd al-Rahman III understood that the only way to cope with this decentralization was to fight, systematically and without a break. In only two years he re-established control over the Guadalquivir valley; thereafter he pushed outwards, expanding his army as he did so, not just in the old amiral heartland but in the marches as well. Bobastro fell in 928, Badajoz in 930, Toledo in 932. 'Abd al-Rahman for the most part incorporated the lords he uprooted into his army or else into the civilian state class in Córdoba, but they were, crucially, separated from their local power-bases and incorporated into a tax-based political system that was less superficial in its similarity with the East than in the previous century. This was underlined further by a great increase in slave and ex-slave soldiers, who were mostly *Saqāliba*, 'Slavs' (though the word extended to include other northern Europeans). From as early as 916 this enlarged army was also sent north against the Christians, which further allowed 'Abd al-Rahman (who, unusually, often led his own troops) to impose himself in the marches. In the end, he came fully to control all of al-Andalus except the Upper March in the far north-east, whose lords gave him military service and tax but remained autonomous. Even there, the main old ex-Visigothic family, the Banu Qasi, had lost its power by 907, and was replaced as a regional focus by the Tujibis, a family close to the Umayyads, which had been given Zaragoza in 890 in one of Amir 'Abd Allah's rare effective interventions. This hegemony was not weakened, except partially in the Upper March, by 'Abd al-Rahman's only serious military defeat, against the Christians of León in 939 (see Chapter 20). This overall success, plus the collapse of 'Abbasid power in the same period and the Fatimid establishment of a rival Shi'a caliphate in 910, led 'Abd al-Rahman III to proclaim himself caliph, as al-Nasir, in 929.

The tenth century was the period when the ceremonial of the ruler developed most fully. Córdoba gained a series of new suburbs, and, with its monumental mosque in the centre, greatly enlarged by 'Abd al-Rahman's son al-Hakam II (961–76), moved into the league of Constantinople and Cairo as a metropolis. 'Abd al-Rahman also founded around 940 an impressive new court and administrative centre at Madinat al-Zahra', just north-west of the city. Here, caliphal ritual is recorded in a number of texts, from the *Life* of John of Gorze, ambassador for Otto I in around 953–6, intransigent in its (and its subject's) hostility to Islam but unwillingly impressed by the complexity of the court, to the 971–5 section of the history by 'Isa al-Razi (d. 989), preserved a century later in the *Muqtabis* of Ibn Hayyan (d. 1076), which provides us with several detailed accounts of particular ceremonial moments at the high points of the Muslim religious year. In the caliph's main reception hall at Madinat al-Zahra', all major officials had their allotted positions, in two lines, with the caliph at the end; the majesty of caliphal power was intended to be, and was, made very clear.

The tenth century was also a period of larger-scale economic activity. We shall see in the next chapter that al-Andalus participated in Mediterranean exchange, through the port of Almería, founded (or, rather, walled and expanded) by 'Abd al-Rahman III in 955. Internally, too, we can see in recent archaeology the development of centralized and professional artisanal production of ceramics and glass, including glazed pottery in east Mediterranean styles, not least a 'green and manganese' decorated ware, which appears extensively on Spanish sites of the period, and which seems to have been made largely in Córdoba and other major centres. That latter ware has explicit caliphal associations, as can be seen in the frequent inscription *al-mulk* ('power') along the edges of plates and bowls, especially but not only in Madinat al-Zahra'. But this sort of artisanal activity cannot be in itself ascribed to 'Abd al-Rahman or his political success. Tenth-century artisanal work built on that of the ninth, which was notably more professional than that of the eighth; it testifies to the steady development of hierarchies of wealth and élite demand in most of the Muslim parts of the peninsula. (Not the Christian parts; but Arab-made artisanal goods, especially carpets, cloth and leather, were nonetheless prized there as luxuries.) One thing this growing economic complexity shows is that the rich aristocracies of the ninth century had by no means gone away; they had simply been absorbed into the caliphal political hierarchy, or else into the local *'ulamā'* hierarchies of the cities of al-Andalus – or else both, for Spain was not that large, and the deracinated Slav (and, later, Berber) armies were only part of the 'state class'. Their identity and assumptions are well expressed by the historian and grammarian Ibn al-Qutiya (d. 977), son of a judge in Seville, who wrote a chatty history full of stories about the huge landed wealth of his ancestors, who supposedly included Sara 'the Goth' (*al-Qūṭiya*), granddaughter of King Wittiza; Ibn al-Qutiya was nonetheless as focused on the doings of the Umayyads as any other historian, and clearly bought into the values of the court. All that 'Abd al-Rahman did here – not a small thing, however – was to create the political foundation for the linkage of the local economies and societies of the ninth century in a single network, covering the whole of the Spanish caliphate.

Al-Hakam continued his father's political practices; he was well known as a literary patron, too. His military expansion, especially in 972–5, was southwards, into Morocco, which had been largely left to its own devices after the Fatimid move into Egypt. At his death, however, his son al-Hisham II (976–1009, 1010–13) was only fifteen; power was seized by one of al-Hakam's military leaders in Morocco, Muhammad ibn Abi 'Amir, who had a loyal detachment of Berbers to help him win a coup against their Slav rivals. Ibn Abi 'Amir steadily eliminated all other powerful figures in the court, and in 981 assumed supreme power as ruling *ḥājib* for a figurehead caliph, even giving himself the ruling title of al-Mansur (in Spanish Almanzor, 981–1002). Al-Mansur greatly developed the Berber component of his army to counterbalance the Slavs. He fought in Morocco, too; but he principally sent his armies to the north, against the Christian kingdoms and principalities, whom he defeated time and again, notably but not only in the devastating sack of Barcelona in 984 and of Santiago de Compostela in the far north-west in 997; his son al-Muzaffar (1002–8) continued this as well. In this military dominance, coupled with a substantial internal stability, and a continuation of the central ceremonial role of Córdoba – where al-Mansur built yet another suburban administrative centre, Madinat al-Zahira – the Umayyad caliphate appeared to reach its height.

As with the 'Abbasid high point under al-Mu'tasim and al-Wathiq, however, this hegemony would not last. Indeed, almost as soon as al-Muzaffar died, al-Andalus disintegrated into a twenty-year civil war (1009–31). The detailed reasons for this lie outside our period; they essentially lie with the political ineptness of al-Muzaffar's successors, and power-struggles between Berber and Slav leaders. But this *fitna* was far more serious than its predecessor a century earlier; it included a violent sack of Córdoba itself in 1013, and the abandonment of the nomination of caliphs altogether, by now all of them figureheads, in 1031. By that date al-Andalus was divided between thirty or so kingdoms, known as the Taifas (from *ṭā'ifa*, 'faction'), and it never recovered 'Abd al-Rahman's political unity or al-Mansur's military protagonism. This collapse was so fast and so complete – far faster than that of the 'Abbasids, and resulting in independent polities that were in many cases single city territories, far smaller than the successor states in the East – that it needs some comment.

Some of the Taifa kingdoms were ruled by regional army commanders, Slav or Berber, who simply turned their commands into autonomous, and then independent, units as central authority collapsed in the 1010s, as in the East. Some, especially in the north-east, were ruled by long-standing families whose local power had been recognized even by 'Abd al-Rahman III, the Tujibis in Zaragoza or the Dhi'l-Nunids of the upland Santaver area, who in 1018 occupied Toledo. But some, including perhaps the richest, Seville, were taken over by local landowners who had civic, not state, office: not necessarily from the same families who had dominated around 900, but at least from the same social stratum. We have to conclude that 'Abd al-Rahman III had not definitively ended the presumption, which had always been stronger in al-Andalus than elsewhere in the Muslim world, that landownership brought potential rights to political authority. And, even more important: notwithstanding the substantial territorial reorganizations of the caliphal period – with governorships both large and small tightly controlled by central government, and many of the local fortifications of the first *fitna* simply taken over by the state – 'Abd al-Rahman and his successors had not succeeded fully in undermining that other core Spanish presupposition, that practical politics was local. In both these respects, the Visigothic inheritance of al-Andalus comes out in the Taifa period. The amirs and caliphs succeeded in establishing a tax-based state, such as had not existed in Spain since the Roman empire, and this indeed continued under the Taifas; but they did not manage to move their Andalusi population to the assumptions that prevailed in Egypt or Iraq, even in the fragmented tenth century, that only the control of the state mattered, and that a land-based local politics was marginal. When the state faltered, in the 1010s as in the 880s and, earlier, in the 710s, Spain's localities at once moved centre stage. When a degree of reunification belatedly came this time, with the Almoravids at the end of the eleventh century, the Christians had taken Toledo and the whole balance of power had shifted.

15

The State and the Economy: Eastern Mediterranean Exchange Networks, 600–1000

Being a tradesman in Constantinople around 900 was by no means a straightforward process. According to the *Book of the Eparch* (or *the Prefect*), a set of official regulations from this period, merchants, shopkeepers and many artisans had to be members of a guild (*systēma*) to operate, and had to sell their wares in specific places, the gold- and silver-dealers in the Mese, the merchants of Arab silk in the Embole, the perfumers in the Milion beside Hagia Sophia, the pork butchers in the Tauros. Ambulant sellers were banned; they would be flogged, stripped of guild membership, and expelled from the city. Sellers of silk could not make up clothes as well; leather sellers could not be tanners. Some guilds, such as the merchants of Arab silk or the linen merchants, had to do their buying collectively, with the goods then distributed among guild members according to how much money they had put in, to keep down competitive buying. Sheep butchers had to go a long way into Anatolia to buy their sheep, to keep prices down; pork butchers, by contrast, had to buy pigs in the city, and were prohibited from going out to meet the vendors; so also were fishmongers, who had to buy on shore, not on the sea. The eparch, the city governor, had to be informed if silk merchants (divided into five separate guilds) sold to foreigners, who were prohibited from buying certain grades of silk. He determined all bread prices, by which bakers had to sell, and the price of wine the innkeepers sold; and he also determined the profits that many vendors made – grocers were allowed a 16 per cent profit, but bakers only 4 per cent (with another 16 per cent for the pay of their workmen), over and above the price they paid in the state grain warehouse.

Later medieval western towns often had quite elaborate guild regulations like these, aimed at maintaining monopolies and internal hierarchies in trades. The *Book of the Eparch* stands out, however (apart from in its early date), in the degree of state control it assumes. The regulation of profit was particularly important here, and also the regulation of the ways sellers were allowed to buy their goods. Silk was controlled because its production and distribution reflected directly on imperial prestige (the regulations for linen merchants were looser). Above all, however, it was vital that the food market was controlled, for Constantinople had to be fed reliably, at prices the inhabitants could afford. Bread was no longer free, as in the late Roman empire; that had stopped abruptly by imperial decree when the Persians took Egypt in 618 (above, Chapter 11). Constantinople was much smaller now; it did not need Egyptian grain any more, and could provision itself from its Aegean and southern Black Sea hinterland. All the same, as we have seen, it was still very substantial in size; it was the largest city in Europe even at its low point in the seventh and eighth centuries, and was now growing again, reaching maybe 100,000 inhabitants in 900. (Córdoba may well have surpassed it in size in the tenth century, but it shrank in the eleventh, leaving the top spot to the Byzantine capital again.) Emperors and eparchs could not afford the trouble from its inhabitants that would inevitably appear if there were food shortages – and these, indeed, were seen by the urban population as the fault of public authorities. Trade was independent in Constantinople, but the terms of trade were closely linked to the state. We can of course doubt how effective all the rules in the *Book of the Eparch* were, but they are very striking as an aspiration, and it is at least true that narrative sources regularly ascribe this sort of power to officials. Liutprand of Cremona did buy prohibited silk in 968, but it was discovered and confiscated, to his fury. The Byzantine government had the infrastructure to make its laws obeyed, at least sometimes.

This introduces us to a standard feature of both Byzantine and Arab exchange, its close link to the state. This varied, certainly. It was probably greater in Constantinople than in the Byzantine provinces; it seems to have been greater in Egypt than in al-Andalus; and state control was always more likely to be enforced in the arena of urban provisioning than in that of the international luxury trade (silks and other state-interest goods apart), for that trade relied so much on private mercantile risk-taking. Arab port authorities in the tenth and early eleventh centuries even then regularly assigned official prices to imported goods, but these were only guides to market prices, which varied by supply and demand. But grain in Constantinople was only one out of several commodities which were bought from government warehouses; in Egypt, too, flax (for linen), one of that region's principal productions, was also sold to merchants (whether for internal sale or for export) by state offices, and some of the major linen-weaving centres, such as Tinnis and Damietta, were largely publicly owned. Egypt, as already implied, had in every period a rather more dominant state sector than existed in some other regions, but the existence of operations on this scale is striking. Commerce itself might be in the hands of independent merchants, but they operated in a framework in which the public power had a considerable say. And, above all, states were huge sources of demand. Egyptian documents from the decades around 1000 show merchants regularly (and sometimes unwillingly) selling to the government itself; and, even when this did not take place, the focusing by merchants and artisans on great political centres such as Constantinople, Baghdad, Fustat–Cairo and Córdoba was because these cities had so many rich buyers who were paid by the state, bureaucrats or soldiers and their own dependants.

As we have seen, and as we shall see again, after the end of the Roman empire in the West, which was a strong and centralized state and which moved large quantities of goods around on its own behalf, exchange in the post-Roman kingdoms depended for its intensity on the wealth of landowners – aristocrats, churches and kings. The richer landowners were, the more exchange there was, and the more complex its patterns. This was broadly true in the eastern Mediterranean as well; but state power, based on tax-raising, continued here, and state buying-power was normally on a somewhat larger scale than that of private landowners. Furthermore, private wealth allowed people access to state office, and thus access to the greater emoluments made possible by taxation. This was so even in the Islamic world, where private landowners were usually less automatically linked to political power, and so could be seen as a rival source of demand to that of officials and soldiers. Taken as a whole, it is the changing wealth of the state sector that is the best guide to the changing scale of demand, and thus exchange, in the Byzantine and Arab East. Where private landed wealth had a different trajectory to the wealth of the state, it must have affected demand as well, and its local variation adds a further level of complexity to our analyses. But broadly the two moved in tandem in most of the East, and the state system is also rather better documented. I shall be saying more about the latter in this chapter as a result.

The gap in our evidence for the landed aristocracy matches the very serious gap in our seventh- to tenth-century evidence for the peasant majority in the East. The millions of documents regularly produced for governments and private individuals in Byzantium and the caliphate have almost all been lost. Only for Egypt do we have the sort of local land documentation that we can find in Francia and Italy, thus allowing in a few cases the reconstruction of peasant societies, as in the case of the eighth-century Coptic village of Jeme, in western Thebes in Upper Egypt; and the uneven publication of Egyptian documents in Arabic means that we cannot as yet easily do this for the period after 800. Rural archaeology is currently poorer for the period after 650 or so than for before, too, in nearly every region. We looked at Byzantine and Andalusi aristocracies in Chapters 13 and 14, and I shall of course be referring to some aspects of peasant economy and society in this chapter, for they will inevitably impinge on issues of wealth-creation, taken as a whole: put simply, the richer élites were (whether from tax or rents), and the higher aggregate demand was, the more the peasantry was exploited – an equation which must be understood to underlie this whole chapter. But we shall have to wait for future research before we can confront the detail of most eastern peasant social realities after 600–650, so as to compare them with those of the West. Urban society is better attested, as we have also seen in the last four chapters. One urban society is particularly clearly documented, the Jewish sector of the city of Fustat in Egypt, whose *geniza* or storehouse of waste paper (kept because Jews would not destroy the word of God, and thus any paper with writing on), founded in 1025, preserves thousands of texts, which begin to be numerous around 980. Most of these are eleventh-century or later, rather than from the tenth, but I shall use some early eleventh-century *geniza* texts here as well, as they transform our understanding of how urban societies could function at the very end of our period. Despite the wealth of the eastern Mediterranean, then, our surviving information about the socio-economic history of the period 600–1000 is even bittier than it is for the West. I shall focus here, necessarily briefly, on three regions in turn: Byzantium, with its seventh-century crisis and ninth-century revival; Syria and Iraq, rivals throughout, where economic protagonism moved decisively from the first to the second in 750; and

Egypt, the region with the most continuity. We shall then look at the international commerce which linked them.

As we saw in Chapter 11, the military disasters of the 610s and 640s caused the Byzantine state to change markedly. It adopted a localized and mostly demonetized tax structure, matching a localized military structure, focused on defence. Never again would the state transport its own goods long distances on any scale, even if Constantinople maintained itself as a fiscally supported focus for commercial demand. It is also likely that the landed aristocracy, never as rich as in the West, lost some ground, given its invisibility in the sources before 850 or so, and given the constant raiding that will have reduced agricultural productivity in much of Anatolia until the frontier stabilized in the eighth century; as noted in Chapter 13, even in the tenth century, when our sources all agree that a process of local affirmation of aristocratic power was firmly under way, it is hard to argue that they were as dominant across the whole empire as was normal in the West. The tiny amount we know about peasant society at least shows that there were indeed some areas of the empire where aristocrats did not have full control in the seventh and eighth centuries. The lands west of Ankara described in the early seventh-century *Life* of the ascetic Theodore of Sykeon had largely independent peasant communities already in the years leading up to the Persian invasions, indicating that aristocrats never had been wholly hegemonic in parts of the Anatolian plateau. If the *Farmer's Law*, a private handbook of agrarian law from the period 650–850, can also be located in Anatolia (as the absence of reference to olive-cultivation in it may imply), then such peasant communities continued to exist there after the invasion period as well. In both texts, the state remains present, unquestioned, as a tax-raising and judicial power. There were also considerable wealth differences in each, with richer peasants dominating the community and leasing land to poorer peasants. But external landowners are relatively unimportant in the earlier text, and absent in the later. This is not a guide to the empire as a whole, or even to the whole of Anatolia (aristocrats were rather strong in Cappadocia, further east, in both the fourth to sixth centuries and the ninth to eleventh, so plausibly in between as well); but the patchiness of local aristocratic dominance is made clear by these texts, and this almost certainly increased in the crisis centuries.

Corresponding to the difficulties experienced by the Byzantine state and aristocracy, the seventh and eighth centuries show, particularly clearly in fact, a crisis in urbanism. Archaeologists and historians argue about whether there was already a dip in urban vitality in the Byzantine lands after 550; but no one any longer seriously argues that there was not a systemic crisis in the early seventh century. Urban archaeology makes this too clear. Building cannot be shown to have continued after 650 in most of the dozen or more cities with decent excavation; most show areas of systematic abandonment in the same period, as with the particularly well-excavated street of shops in Sardis, in the Anatolian lowlands close to the Aegean, which were abruptly deserted in the 610s, or the gymnasion in Ankara whose burning can be precisely dated to the Persian sack of 622, for a Persian ring-stone was excavated in the burnt level. I am normally cautious about drawing too catastrophist conclusions from anecdotal examples like these (prosperous cities have abandoned areas too, and can also recover from being sacked), but the accumulation of evidence in the Byzantine lands is too great to be gainsaid. It is significant that the best counter-example, Gortyn on Crete, was on an island, and thus safer from Persian/Arab or Avar/Sclavenian raids: here Heraclius (610–41) reconstructed the city after an earthquake, and a late seventh-century artisanal quarter, probably extending later as well, has recently been excavated. Elsewhere, all we get is new walls, sometimes enclosing only portions of the ancient city, and sometimes on hills above the old town.

The Byzantine state continued, as we have seen. Even small hill-top cities (now often called *kastra*) could still have a political-military role, and also still had bishops (although these, as we have also seen, often preferred to live in the capital). There is some evidence, furthermore, that some hill-top fortifications were citadels for islands of surviving settlement in the ancient cities below, as at Euchaita and Amorion, both on the Anatolian plateau, or at Corinth in central Greece, or at Myra on the south coast of modern Turkey. Whether this scattered occupation was sufficiently dense and economically diversified to be called 'urban' cannot yet be said: of these, Amorion and Corinth are perhaps the most likely. Overall, however, we have to recognize a new urban typology. Some ancient cities were wholly abandoned or reduced to small strongholds. Some developed this scattered pattern, with greater or lesser levels of organization or urbanization. A few continued to be active as urban centres, though on a considerably reduced scale, like Ephesos, Miletos and Athens on the Aegean coast – Ephesos's new walls left much of the old city centre outside them, but still enclosed a square kilometre of land; the city is recorded by Theophanes as having a major fair, yielding a large sum in taxes, in 795–6. And a handful of cities may well have seen rather less change, though excavation is less good in them precisely because of the urban continuities there: Thessaloniki, Iznik (ancient Nicaea), Izmir (ancient Smyrna), Trabzon, major political centres in each case. This is not total urban collapse, but even on an optimistic reading of the evidence we might propose that four-fifths of Byzantine cities lost all or most of their urban characteristics.

The significant feature in common to most 'successful' early Byzantine towns is that they were thematic centres. (Ephesos, long a commercial entrepôt, is the main exception.) It looks as if the state focused on its main local military and administrative centres; if landed aristocrats joined the army and civil bureaucracy, they may well have gone to such towns too. These towns thus remained sufficiently potent centres of demand to retain their urban characteristics: markets, perhaps some artisanal specialization. But there were far fewer of them than in 600. When Byzantium achieved greater military and political stability again, slowly after 750, more visibly after 850, the number of active cities did not greatly expand, either. They increased their own sizes again, although it is as yet hard to be sure exactly when from the archaeology; the eleventh century shows it better than the tenth, although in Sardis, and also in Hierapolis on the western edge of the Anatolian plateau, it is already visible before 1000. But the Byzantine empire never again re-created the density of late Roman urbanism in its territory.

Our evidence for commerce outside the capital, also largely archaeological, both mirrors this picture and nuances it. The seventh century saw the abrupt end of the Aegean's main industrial tableware production, Phocaean Red Slip ware, and its more local imitations; painted wares of reasonable quality sometimes replaced it (for example in Crete), but their distribution was very localized, and in some places (notably in inland Greece) all we find is handmade pottery, indicating the end of professional production. Amphora production, for oil and wine, also localized and simplified; the standardized Aegean globular amphora, LRA 2, was replaced by a variety of related but more local types. These developments, into the eighth century, imply a breakdown in demand for goods, and thus the weakening of concentrations of wealth, whether public or private. But this is not the whole picture. Constantinople itself had an industrial ceramic production, of Glazed White ware (GWW), which began around 600 and continued for many centuries. In the next two centuries there are sporadic finds of this pottery type in a wide range of places across the Aegean, down to Crete, and even Cyprus (which had its own productions). These show that the Aegean did not lose a certain level of medium-distance exchange. This is supported by the (probably) eighth-century *Rhodian Sea Law*, another private legal manual, which discusses the relationship between ships' captains and merchants on ships, and which presumes as standard cargoes an array of goods that are hard for archaeologists to find: slaves, linen, silk, grain, as well as wine and oil in (presumably) post-LRA 2 amphorae. Seventh- to ninth-century saints' lives also regularly feature shipping, often but not only for grain. The Aegean was by now, as we have seen, Constantinople's agrarian hinterland; the demand of the capital, even if nothing else, kept ships on the sea. GWW tableware was probably one of the things the capital sold in return.

The Byzantine empire at its low point thus never entirely lost a network of exchange that covered its heartland, the Aegean and Marmara seas and the coasts around them. This was so even if most local production had simplified, sometimes radically. This seems to reflect what else we know about the empire: that the state had localized its own structures, but that it was still dominated by a powerful capital. Arguably, the local differences in productive professionalism around 700 reflect areas of greater or lesser aristocratic power on the ground, although the evidence is not yet good enough for this to be developed further. The Aegean-wide exchange we do see was not run by the state; our written sources stress independent merchants in the period before 800, just as the *Book of the Eparch*, for all its regulatory interest, does in 900. But state-fuelled demand was the most solid agent of buying power all the same; and this commerce focused on the capital first, although secondarily, in other surviving centres as well, Thessaloniki, Ephesos or Smyrna.

As we move into the ninth century, one visible change is an increase in the numbers of coins found on sites. It is normal in excavations to find coins up to Constans II in around 660, and then nothing, or almost nothing, for a hundred and fifty years; even though every emperor still minted coins, they vanished from circulation, and we could not conclude that they were at all commonly available outside the capital. This changed from the 820s onwards. At Corinth, nearly four times as many coins are known for Theophilos (829–42) as for all his predecessors put together after Constans; those for Leo VI (886–912) are six times as numerous as for Theophilos, those for Leo's son Constantine VII double again, and the figures go on up from there. This can most plausibly be linked to a revival in taxation and army pay in money, which is most often ascribed to Nikephoros I (802–11: above, Chapter 11); such a shift depended on a more reliable supply of metals, but also presumed (and furthered) market exchange, sufficient to move the coins around. In the ninth century, too, we come upon larger-scale finds of GWW outside the capital, for example at Mesembria, a Byzantine port in modern Bulgaria, and even in field survey, in the countryside outside Sparta; in the tenth, this extends to Thebes. Local imitations of Constantinople pottery begin to be found at Athens, and, significantly, at Preslav in independent Bulgaria. Large-scale ceramic production at Corinth also began by the tenth century, and so did the amphorae of the Ganos area, in the Sea of Marmara, destined for the newly systematic export of local wine. The wine trade could already extend far afield, indeed, if the large consignment of wine-amphorae, marked with their shippers' names, found in a wreck off south-west Turkey dating to around 880, really was from the Crimea, as the excavators think. Linen was exported from Bulgaria and the southern Black Sea (as also from Egypt) to the capital as well, and both Constantinople and Thessaloniki made glass. We are beginning to move into the complex Byzantine productions of the central Middle Ages.

In the ninth century, and still more in the tenth, the state was getting stronger and richer in Byzantium. In the tenth, so was the aristocracy, in some areas – often away from the Aegean focus of the archaeology, but including in southern Greece, where already in the 880s the wealthy Danelis (see Chapter 13) had access to elaborate linens and silks, and the textile workers themselves, whom she gave to Basil I and Leo VI. A century later, Basil II, in his complaints about 'the powerful', was worried that they would monopolize rural markets, too. What we see in this whole list of examples is an increasingly elaborate and diversified set of agrarian and artisanal productions, with an increasingly wide and complex distribution, to and from the capital, certainly, but between provinces as well: Thessaloniki was a particularly important entrepôt. This was made possible by élite demand, which was clearly increasing again, and was also furthered by direct élite involvement in artisanal production and exchange. If there was ever a natural location for medium-distance exchange, of course, it was the Aegean, largely land-locked and protected, and studded with islands, as it is. The years around 900 merely saw a return to normality in this respect; they point up the abnormality, the crisis, of the two centuries after the Persian and Arab invasions. But the growing power of the Byzantine state would push that exchange still further in the two centuries to come. After 1000, a demographic expansion, which is quite likely to have already started in our period, begins to be more visible in our documentation, as does a trend to reclaim uncultivated land; the agrarian base of the empire was clearly expanding. The eleventh century shows some agricultural specializations as well, not least in mulberry trees for silk in various parts of the empire: these too must have existed already before 1000, for Byzantium was certainly producing its own silk in our period. The old view that the empire saw economic stagnation in the eleventh and twelfth centuries is now decisively rejected; the roots of the generalized economic expansion of that period lay in ours, even though we can as yet only see occasional signs of it. And that expansion affected areas outside the empire as well: by the early eleventh century the Byzantines were exporting silk to Egypt. This is a point we shall come back to.

Syria did not for the most part see the seventh-century crisis of the Byzantine empire. After 661 it was the political centre of the Umayyad caliphate, and that period saw major monumental building in the capital, Damascus, as also in the regional religious centre, Jerusalem. Damascus was never a huge city, which partly reflects problems of water supply, but is partly also due to the fact that the Umayyads had difficulties getting taxes from the provinces of the caliphate. But enough came into Syria to ensure the wealth of the caliphs themselves, and their urban and rural palaces still survive in the landscape of Syria and Palestine. The Arab conquest was anyway quick enough for Syria not to suffer in its basic infrastructures. Most of the numerous excavations in both Syria and Palestine, both urban and rural, show continuities that extend to 750 at least, particularly in inland areas. In and around the city of Madaba, for example, in what is now northern Jordan, Christian churches were founded into the late eighth century, with impressively decorated mosaic floors which show both wealthy patrons and skilled artisans: in the city, in rural monasteries, and in villages around.

Cities changed in structure. Their Roman monumental centres tended to fall out of use, as the Arabs had a different ceremonial style, with fewer religious or political processions and a focus on the enclosed public space of mosque courtyards. But they continued to be active demographic and productive centres; Roman public buildings were replaced by artisan workshops, colonnaded streets were replaced by rows of shops, often monumentally built (particularly, as we saw in Chapter 12, by Caliph Hisham, 724–43). So at Gerasa (modern Jerash) north of Madaba kiln complexes were built in a Roman theatre and a temple, part of a network which made Gerasa ceramics a major feature of the economy of the Galilee area until 800 or so; at nearby Scythopolis (modern Bet She'an) there were by 700 or so kilns in the theatre and amphitheatre, linen workshops in a bath complex (Scythopolis linen was well known already in the Roman empire), and one of Hisham's shop complexes on the site of a sixth-century hall. These patterns are repeated, in greater and lesser detail, in twenty other cities; the production of glass, dyeing (and thus textiles), iron, copper are all attested in recent archaeological work. Substantial élite town houses have been found in some cities, too; and of course the Arab period had its own monumental buildings, mosques and governors' palaces.

This picture was clearly very different from that in the Byzantine heartland, although the sources – almost all archaeological – are the same. There are almost no usable written sources on these issues for Syria and Palestine, in fact, although the Syriac chronicles for Edessa also paint a glowing picture of the commercial activity of that city and of the wealth of its Christian élites: Athanasios bar Gumoye, a great landowner and a tax official for 'Abd al-Malik in Egypt around 700, reputedly owned 300 shops and nine inns in Edessa. Two changes nuance this picture of continuing élite and rural prosperity, however. The first is that the coast of Syria and Palestine, a major oil and wine export area under the Roman empire, saw stagnation under the Umayyads, the weakening of major coastal cities such as Antioch, and the abandonment of marginal lands. Umayyad Syria was not closely linked to the Mediterranean; it hardly even had any economic links with Egypt, although some Egyptian products still came in through the major surviving coastal entrepôt, Caesarea in what is now Israel. But actually – this is the second change – Syria and Palestine were no longer a single economic unit. The productions that can be best traced by archaeologists, once again mostly ceramics, remain of very high quality in the Umayyad period, and show industries that were large-scale and many-levelled, aimed at élites and non-élites alike; but they were much more localized than in the Roman period. Gerasa pottery rarely reached the Mediterranean coast, or 'Aqaba on the Red Sea, or northern Syria, for example; even Jerusalem, only 100 kilometres away, largely had its own – again, high-quality – ceramic tradition. So the Syro-Palestinian economy remained prosperous and complex under the Umayyads, but it was much more internally fragmented, and cut off from its neighbours. It was, in fact, even more internally fragmented than the crisis-bound Byzantine empire, as it seems on the basis of the archaeology of the moment.

This economic fragmentation further underscores the difficulty the Umayyads had in centralizing the fiscal system of the state, even in their own political heartland, although they were certainly more successful here than elsewhere. But the complexity of (almost all) the different sections of Syria and Palestine also points at the continuing force of *local* demand, and thus of the continuing wealth of urban élites, that is to say the local landed aristocracy. It is often said that the Arabs gave more respect to merchants than the Romans had, which is true; Muhammad had been a merchant, and there was never in the Islamic world any stigma attached to wealth 'from trade', unlike in much of the West, or even Byzantium. It is often also said that this ideological shift is already visible in the changing forms of cities, with more artisanal and commercial activity in old public centres; this seems less likely, however. These changes are better explained as the normal result of shifts in the focus of monumental building, from colonnaded streets and theatres, etc., to mosques (above, Chapter 10); if a city remains economically active, unused buildings will get taken over for private uses, and so it was here. But we should also not overstate the mercantile element in élite activity. Athanasios bar Gumoye, notwithstanding all his shops, was a great landowner first and foremost; it is likely indeed that most urban patricians in this period (who were anyway mostly still Christians) were above all landowners, and at most used landed capital to get into commerce, if they wanted. This would be so later, too, in 'Abbasid Iraq, where such élites would usually be Muslims, and in post-'Abbasid Iran, where '*ulamā*' biographies show land as much as mercantile activity as the basis for élite wealth. Even the Jewish mercantile élites of Fustat in Egypt, who may well have gained their initial wealth entirely in the commercial sector, bought land or tax-farming concessions with their profits, for land remained overwhelmingly the chief source of wealth overall. Exchange was, and remained, only a spin-off of agricultural wealth, even around the great cities of the second half of our period, and still more in Umayyad Syria.

The year 750 marks a change in the economy of Syria and Palestine. The 'Abbasid takeover marginalized the region politically, and, with the fiscal centralization of the caliphate from the 780s onwards, Syrian taxes were firmly directed to Iraq. Cities which stayed as prosperous as before into the ninth and tenth centuries were rather fewer, Ramla near Jerusalem, Tiberias on Lake Galilee, Caesarea, 'Aqaba, Aleppo, Damascus, entrepôts or major local governmental centres. The devastating earthquake which hit the Galilee area in 749 left cities in ruins, which, significantly, were often not rebuilt and can thus be excavated; Bet She'an is a particularly impressive sight, with white limestone columns (including those of Hisham's shops) even now lying across black basalt roads. Syria would henceforth be mostly governed from elsewhere, from Baghdad, Cairo, or (for the North in the late tenth century) Constantinople; only Aleppo was sometimes independent at the end of our period. This, plus the wars fought over it in the tenth century, sapped its prosperity. But it was by no means in economic crisis even then, and 'Abbasid centralization brought with it a widening of economic horizons, with more evidence of exchange with Iraq: new polychrome glazed ware spread from Iraq into Syria/Palestine from 800 onwards, the beginning of a new international taste in fine pottery which would by 1100 dominate the whole Mediterranean, Muslim and Christian regions alike. It is for this reason that entrepôts flourished under the 'Abbasids; interregional networks were beginning to develop again, west to Egypt (via Caesarea), south down the Red Sea (via 'Aqaba), east to Iraq (via Aleppo). This network would continue even after the 'Abbasid caliphate collapsed, as we shall see in a moment.

The 'Abbasids, of course, invested in Iraq. Iraq had been a major political and economic centre for millennia; the Tigris and Euphrates created a fertile and irrigable basin matched only by the Nile for its agricultural wealth. The Sassanians were only the most recent rulers to develop its irrigation, with the great Nahrawan canal, probably built in the sixth century, which brought Tigris water to a network of smaller canals north and east of the capital, Ctesiphon, situated just south of what would become Baghdad. An early and influential 1950s field survey of the Nahrawan area by Robert Adams indeed saw the Sassanian period as the economic height for Iraq, with the pre-tenth-century caliphate, however prosperous, failing to match Sassanian levels after the political crises of the 620s–630s, in which canal dykes were not maintained. The dating of sites in Adams's work, and thus his assumptions about the number of settlements that were actually occupied in each period, were however more influenced by his over-literal readings of narrative sources than a field survey would be today (if one were possible in Iraq in 2007). The land north of Raqqa in modern eastern Syria, a more short-lived 'Abbasid capital on the Euphrates, showed a clear 'Abbasid-period settlement peak in a more recent field survey. The Umayyads, anyway, and even more the 'Abbasids, were committed canal-builders and land reclaimers, and the 'Abbasids were particularly active in southern Iraq, as we saw in Chapter 14; it was to build dykes and to desalinate land in the marsh areas of the south that they imported the large-scale African slave gangs of the Zanj. The 'Abbasid construction of the huge metropolis of Baghdad after 762 required systematic provisioning, and it was in the interests of every public official who bought Iraqi land with his tax profits to develop that land with an eye to the urban market. Samarra, at the northern end of the Nahrawan canal, only added to that market in the mid-ninth century. The sharecropping contracts discussed in legal sources from 'Abbasid Baghdad, which presumably best reflect the Iraq the legists lived in, show landlordly investment; state investment in the irrigation network is assumed as well, largely through wage-labour; the legists say less about the Zanj. Wage-labourers were also used in agriculture, which shows that some landowners were cultivating estates directly, a sure sign of a market-orientated approach. One result was the expansion of Iraqi rice cultivation, which was a ninth-century phenomenon.

Tax revenues only went to the capitals, but their resultant vast size itself created a stimulus to Iraqi agriculture, and the Iraqi commercial economy as a whole. Baghdad (and to a lesser degree other Iraqi cities) was also an artisanal hub which was for a century unmatched anywhere in the world. Silk, cottons, glass, paper (the Baghdad paper-mills were founded in 795, using technology brought from Samarkand and, before that, from China) were all made in the city. Baghdad was a focus for internal Iraqi exchange, and also an entrepôt for interregional commerce between the provinces of the caliphate, which was by now moving ceramics or cloth across the whole terrain from Iran to Egypt. Indeed, this commerce went further; the 1960s–1970s excavations of the Iranian port of Siraf (as yet only partly published) show that the caliphate had opened up to Indian Ocean and Chinese trade on a large scale by the late eighth century. *The Seven Voyages of Sinbad* in the *Thousand and One Nights* symbolizes this for most of us, but that is perhaps matched by the remarkable collection of plausible and implausible stories (some of them first-person experiences) made by the Iranian ship captain Buzurg ibn Shahriyar in the 950s, who discusses wonders, strange customs, storms and remarkable animals right across to the South China Sea. The trade thus established continued for the rest of the Middle Ages.

Baghdad's wealth, and also Iraq's, faltered in the tenth century. The region had lost its political and fiscal dominance by now. The cutting of the Nahrawan canal in 937 for short-term military reasons was soon reversed, but the precedent was a bad one; the city and the canals were refurbished several times (most committedly by the Buyid 'Adud al-Dawla in 981–3), but Iraq's prosperity did not again match that of the ninth century. All the same, that prosperity had been so great that Baghdad remained one of the principal cities of Eurasia, larger than any western city, and a major entrepôt into the twelfth century at least.

None of these regions matched the stability of Egypt. Egypt was the Roman empire's richest province by far, with the most complex economy, and it remained so in the post-Roman world into the fourteenth century. In the caliphate, too, if it was surpassed by Iraq, that was only in the 'Abbasid century, and it had regained its primacy by 950 or so. The power-house of the tenth- to fourteenth-century Mediterranean exchange system, which was not driven by fiscal factors as was that of Rome or the caliphs, was Egypt. The basic reason for this was the relative reliability of the Nile flood, which allowed continuous cropping of agricultural land and produced wheat yields of around ten to one (three or four to one, with fallow periods, being the best that dry farming could produce in the Middle Ages). Egypt's canal system has also almost always been regularly maintained; the country has almost always been governed by a single political authority, which helps, and it certainly was so throughout our period and beyond. The large yields of Egypt's agricultural land, not only in wheat, but also wine and flax, allowed a whole hierarchy of non-cultivators to be fed from the labour of the peasantry, including landowners, tax officials and soldiers, of course, but also complex networks of artisans, shopkeepers and merchants. It can be plausibly argued that in the later Roman empire a third of the population of Egypt lived in cities, a figure that is unparalleled in the ancient or early medieval world, and there is not much reason to think that it dropped later; if it had, the drop had certainly been reversed by 1000. Certainly the rather restricted archaeology in Arab-period cities shows dense private housing, in apartment buildings, from the seventh to the tenth century: in Alexandria, Fustat, nearby Saqqara, and Akhmim in Middle Egypt.

Egyptian agriculture was carried out through a hierarchy of substantial villages, whose head-men also handled tax-raising, subordinate in this respect to provincial capitals. The records of taxation, which are good for Arab Egypt, show its systematic nature, inherited from the Roman period, and not relaxed later (as eighth- and ninth-century tax revolts show). Landowning was fragmented in Egypt, however; there were always peasant landowners, and the élites which ran villages were usually rich peasants, and little more. Post-conquest documents imply that great landowners were notably fewer and less rich in the early Arab period than under the later Roman empire, and this did not change until the late ninth century. After 850 three developments led to larger landholdings again: more Christians converted to Islam, thus gaining access to state patronage, which was by now sometimes expressed in terms of grants or leases of state land; more Arabs began to acquire land as well (for a long time Arab immigrants had stayed in Fustat and lived off state salaries, as we saw in Chapter 12); and, from 800 or so, the financial administration began to farm out the rights to collect local taxes, rights which could under certain circumstances be turned into effective landholding over wider areas. Tax-farming turned into full ownership less often in Egypt than it did elsewhere in the Islamic world, for the state never relaxed its grip on the mechanisms of taxation, but it certainly helped the establishment of local control. For the first time in many centuries in Egypt, a late ninth-century estate (*ḍayʿa*) could consist of a whole village (indeed, by the eleventh century *ḍayʿa* could simply mean 'village'). This was not universal, and fragmented ownership survived past 1000 in Egypt, as did direct tax-paying, but a clear change is visible here at the end of our period.

This weakening and renewed strengthening of a landowning aristocracy, which is paralleled elsewhere (for example, in Byzantium) as we have seen, had less effect on the rest of the Egyptian economy, however, than it did in other regions, precisely because of the continuing strength of the tax system, which independently brought wealth into the cities, and, above all, Fustat. This was the basis for an active exchange network which, throughout our period, unified Egypt into a single economic whole. The Nile helped here, as an easy and cheap routeway which ran by or close to nearly all the population of the region. As a result, we can trace artisanal productions which were available from north to south. The fine pottery of Aswan in the far south can be found up to the Mediterranean, 1,000 kilometres away, throughout the early Middle Ages, a unique achievement in scale and continuity in our period. The Aswan kilns continued to produce Red Slip ware in a Roman style until the end of our period and beyond, too, centuries after tastes had changed elsewhere, although increasingly alongside other ceramic types, white-slipped and painted wares, and, after 800, polychrome glaze, following Iraqi fashion. And, although archaeology cannot track it, we can tentatively say the same for cloth; linen and wool production had always been substantial in Egypt since Roman times, and there is never a period in which its sale is not attested in documents. A cache of late ninth-century papyri from the Fayyum, a large agricultural basin to the west of the Nile 150 kilometres south of Fustat, shows a set of Arabic-speaking cloth merchants and related officials buying and selling up and down the Nile from Qus in the south to Alexandria in the far north. The main figure of this papyrus set, Abu Hurayra, lived in Madinat al-Fayyum, the main city of the basin, in the 860s–870s, although others were based in Fustat, which was clearly a major node in the whole exchange process.

These wide exchange networks were not all that Egypt had, either. We can see an exchange hierarchy in ceramics, with local productions (based on local clays) fitting into the Aswan hegemony, and cloth production was certainly associated with many local centres too (based on local flax and sheep), as well as well-known major artisanal cities like Tinnis and Qus for linen, and Bahnasa in Middle Egypt for wool. There were differences here in status, price, taste and convenience, as in all elaborate commercial systems. And the Egyptian system, in the whole period 650–1000, was by far the most elaborate anywhere in Europe and the Mediterranean. Continuous urban demand saw to that. The demand was also, of course, for food, and also certainly for more diversified artisanal goods than cloth and pottery, too; we can say little about them between the sixth century and the late tenth, for our documents are about other matters, but, given the rest, there is no reason to doubt it. One of these goods was still papyrus, an industrial production based in the Delta; it was only in the late ninth and tenth centuries that it was supplanted by paper, a linen by-product.

The *genīza* documents of the late tenth century and onwards thus illuminate a world that had been economically complex for centuries, not to say millennia. But there were also changes at the end of our period. Already in the late ninth century, we can see signs of a larger-scale investment in artisanal production that seems to be new. The governor Ahmad ibn Tulun (868–84), who ruled Egypt more or less autonomously, invested privately in linen according to early tenth-century narratives, and so did lesser officials. The largely state-run Tinnis linen industry appears in these narratives, as it also did in the Fayyum letters, as a major textile centre. It is hard to trace it earlier than 850 with any certainty, but Ibn Tulun upgraded its infrastructure with public money, and dated Tinnis textiles survive from the 880s. These are luxury items, and the state factories were substantially devoted to the production of court fabrics; but the Delta linen towns also sold on the open market, and by the tenth century exported cloth too, to the Mediterranean (Tinnis is on an island, and is also a port) and to Iraq. The word 'export' is the main novelty here. Since the Arab conquests, Egyptian production and consumption had mostly been internal. Even with 'Abbasid fiscal centralization, it is hard to find very much reference to exports and imports in our evidence. Demand inside the region was evidently steady enough to make interregional exchange less necessary, except for the luxury trade, which always existed. But in the tenth century our evidence for it increases, and by the end of the century Alexandria and other ports were full of ships, moving goods from Egypt to Palestine, Tunisia and Sicily; from the latter two, other ships went westwards to al-Andalus. Egypt exported not only made linen cloth but also flax, to be made up in Tunisia and Sicily; sugar, another industrial product, was also an Egyptian speciality. But the range of goods exported from Egypt, and also imported, was by the end of our period very substantial indeed. The Fatimid conquest in 969 meant that Egypt, Tunisia and Sicily were for a while under the same government, which facilitated this; but Egypt was the major motor of this commerce thanks to the continuing strength of its internal market, as the Fatimids recognized and promoted.

Joseph (Yusuf, or in Hebrew, Yosef) ibn Ya'qub ibn 'Awkal (*fl. c.* 970–1040) is the first really large-scale merchant in the *genīza* documents. His family may have come from Iran initially, but were settled in Fustat by his father's time; he spent his life at Fustat and in the new Fatimid capital of Cairo just outside it. He and his sons ran an import-export business, employing numerous secretaries in their headquarters, and agents in both Egypt and abroad, above all in Tunisia and Sicily. They exported flax from Egypt, buying it from small towns in the hinterland of Bahnasa and in the Fayyum and sending it down the Nile from Fustat to Alexandria (thus bypassing the linen factories on the other side of the Delta) and then to the west. They also exported dyestuffs, madder (Egyptian-made), indigo and brazil-wood (both imported); imported pepper and spices, and Egyptian-made sugar; and more expensive luxuries, in particular pearls; 83 different commodities in all. The imports were largely from the Indian Ocean trade; Fustat–Cairo was becoming the principal commercial node between the Indian Ocean and the Mediterranean, which it remained for centuries, although that latter trade was not Ibn 'Awkal's speciality. The business bought in return, from its Mediterranean partners, gold (North Africa was the contact point for the Sahara gold trade), copper, lead, olive oil (still an important Tunisian product), its by-product soap, wax, animal-hides, and silk. This sounds solid enough, but Ibn 'Awkal's business was in reality rather more delicate than that. The *genīza* letters are full of descriptions of the difficulty agents had in selling at exactly the right moment to get a decent profit; and Ibn 'Awkal, like every other merchant, had to make informal deals with friends, clients and even rivals, who were on the spot, trusting them to act in his interests. This did not always work. We have a long indignant letter from Samhun ibn Da'ud ibn al-Siqilli ('son of the Sicilian') from around 1000 in which a by now probably ex-friend, or client, complains among other things that he had made a loss on Ibn 'Awkal's brazil-wood; that he has had to sell Ibn 'Awkal's pearls without taking any profit; worst of all, that the latter had not paid Samhun's creditors despite promises, and despite all that Samhun was doing for him to the detriment of the latter's reputation; and overall, that Ibn 'Awkal had been critical with no reason and high-handed into the bargain. There is no reason to think that the Fustat merchant was an especially sympathetic character, in fact. But most letters to him were highly courteous, and explained how the sender had protected his interests, often in adverse situations (war, water damage, low prices), but usually with success.

Ibn 'Awkal did not trade with Iraq or further east, or with Byzantium, and little even with Syria/Palestine, but he can in other respects stand for an entire network of (usually smaller) Fustat merchants, above all in the diversification of his activities. He was also, it may be added, a pillar of the Fustat Jewish community, and a local representative of the important yeshivas (religious academies) of Baghdad and Jerusalem; had he been Muslim, he would have been a leading member of the *'ulamā'*. He was socially central, that is to say, not just economically representative. The only misleading aspect of the entire Ibn 'Awkal dossier is that it deals with external trade at all. Most Egyptian commerce remained internal to the country. However active the Mediterranean network was, or any other external exchange network, it was Nile traffic, between the major cities and towns, that dominated Egyptian exchange, in 1000 as much as in 700. The real-life feel of the world of the *genīza* letters leaves such an effect on the reader that one can forget this basic economic fact; but it was important, all the same, and would remain so.

The economic history of each of these regions was different between the seventh and the tenth centuries, but it had structural elements in common for all that. The continuing strength of the state in both Byzantium and Egypt compensated, as a motor of exchange, for the temporary weakening of local aristocratic wealth, though this compensation was rather less pronounced in Byzantium, where the state had its own difficulties in the seventh and eighth centuries. In Syria, aristocracies stayed prosperous until 750, but were less integrated into a single regional market by the Umayyad state than Umayyad governors managed in Egypt; after 750, the reverse occurred, with local foci of prosperity slipping, but a fiscal-led integration of regional commerce developing. In Iraq, finally, both aristocracies and (overwhelmingly) the state increased their force in the late eighth century, and set the region up as a major agrarian, artisanal and commercial focus for a century and a half, after which the region slipped back again. We could add al-Andalus, over in the West, to this gallery of examples too, where a set of localized aristocracies of varying wealth existed throughout, but the state became notably stronger in the tenth century (above, Chapter 14), allowing the integration of the economy of the whole peninsula and the creation of some export specializations, silk, saffron and qirmis (crimson dye) among them. Much the same could be said of the Tunisian heartland of Ifriqiya, though there we can see an effective state already in the ninth. The ninth century in many places (except perhaps Syria) saw more internal exchange than the eighth, the tenth century everywhere (except Iraq) saw more than the ninth.

These broadly drawn trends occurred in the internal economies of these regions; but they had an effect on interregional exchange, too, especially in the Mediterranean. The first great Mediterranean trade network was that of the Roman empire. As the empire fragmented, Mediterranean exchange lessened: slowly in the West from 450 onwards, reaching low levels by 600, and snuffing out by 700, as we saw in detail in Chapter 9; rapidly in the East in the seventh century, in the context of the great wars of the 610s–640s, and the fiscal decentralization of both Byzantium and the caliphate thereafter. In the eighth century there was less Mediterranean-wide trade than there had been for over a millennium. Not none; there was always a small-scale network of boats nosing from port to port. The Aegean, as we have seen, maintained a certain enclosed identity as the focus for one level of Byzantine exchange. So did the Tyrrhenian Sea, in the triangle between Rome, Calabria and Sicily, fortified by the continuing force of the city of Rome as a market, as we saw in Chapter 9. As we saw in that chapter too, Michael McCormick has pinpointed the route from Rome to Constantinople as the most important sea route still open in the eighth century. It is not chance that it is the route which linked these two more localized maritime networks; it must have been further reinforced by the fact that Sicily was still a Byzantine province in that century, and probably one of the richest ones. We must recognize, too, that a luxury trade always existed in the Mediterranean, as also in the Indian Ocean, bringing silk and spices to Italy and Francia in return for timber and slaves. But, as we have also seen, luxuries are marginal items to the economy as a whole. In the eighth century, outside restricted areas, the bulk trade in food and artisanal goods had gone, even in the Arab-ruled provinces of the southern Mediterranean, which were always in our period the richest. The seas must have been relatively quiet.

In the ninth century this was slowly reversed. The rise of Venice and the Adriatic route after 750 or so is one small sign of it: small, because Venice focused on the luxury trade mentioned earlier, although this must have been expanding for Venetian wealth to increase as fast as it did in the ninth century (below, Chapter 22); Venice traded with Byzantium and also with Alexandria, from where it stole the body of St Mark, henceforth the city's patron saint, in the 820s. The ninth-century Tunisian conquest of Sicily allowed for more movement, for Sicily was a great deal closer to Tunis than it was to Constantinople, and there was much exchange between the two regions henceforth; we have seen them operate as a pair in their links with Egypt two centuries later, and that pairing began here, at the latest. South Italian ports like Amalfi and Naples benefited from Arab connections which were now nearer (they indeed colluded in Arab attacks on the Italian mainland), and Amalfitans were regularly to be found in Egypt and the Aegean a century later too. Inside the Arab world, we find more casual references to movement along the African coast, using Tunisia and Sicily as halfway points in the route from Egypt to Spain; and 'Abbasid centralization, even if focused on Iraq, helped to link Egypt closer to Syria, a link which remained, for autonomous Egyptian rulers after the 860s tended to control Syria as well. All this movement was doubtless still largely in the luxury trade, but there was more of it, in ever more complex patterns; and not all of it was luxury, as with the Arab merchant ships carrying large quantities of olive oil, captured off Sicily by a Byzantine fleet in the 880s, oil that probably came from Tunisia.

In the tenth century there were two further developments. One was that sections of the Mediterranean which had hitherto been relatively cut out of these developing systems, like southern France, were brought in as well; several Arab wrecks from the mid-tenth century have been found off the French coast, apparently from Spain, containing amphorae (for oil?), tableware, copper or bronze, and glass. Byzantium, too, less of a protagonist as yet in the ninth century, is much more visibly so in the tenth, selling quality silks and timber in the Egyptian market, and, later, cheese, a major source of protein for Egyptians; on the south

Turkish coast, Antalya became an important entrepôt for trade with Syria and Palestine, and south to Alexandria. The development of the port of Almería in 955 by the Andalusi caliph 'Abd al-Rahman III was intended to focus and expand the Spanish contribution to this exchange network, and as far as we can see it did just that; Almería makes frequent appearance in the *genīza* documents around 1000 and later. Though certain routes (such as from Alexandria to Tunis) were doubtless more prominent than others, one gains the impression that by the late tenth century one could sail from almost anywhere in the Mediterranean to almost anywhere else – not always directly, but without very much difficulty.

The second development, already indicated by these references to oil-amphorae and cheese, is that it became more normal to transport bulk goods again, for a relatively large-scale market. Tunisian olive oil reached both Egypt and Italy by 1000, just as it had done in 400, although grain was never again a major item of international exchange; that had depended on the fiscal needs of the Roman empire rather than any natural interchange, since it was produced everywhere. Probably on the back of oil, we also, as in 400, find Tunisian glazed pottery in Italy by the end of the tenth century. And, above all, the astonishing choice by a sector of Egyptian merchants, by 1000 at the latest, to send flax to be made into linen cloth in Tunisia and Sicily rather than in the great Egyptian linen factory towns, testifies to a set of commercial relationships that had become large-scale and symbiotic, as well as complex and competitive. Bulk trade did not dominate everywhere yet, or ever; all the same, it is here that we can speak of real interregional/international exchange *systems*, rather than the thin luxury-based links of two centuries earlier. By the tenth century, the second great Mediterranean trade cycle had properly begun, and would continue to the late Middle Ages. In the eleventh century, newly active Italian ports, Genoa and Pisa, would begin to take over the western part of these Mediterranean networks by force and direct them northwards; the Crusades had similar results in the East; but the trade cycle remained, and even expanded, thereafter.

The tenth century thus saw Mediterranean trade reach the complexity that North Sea trade already had in the eighth and ninth (see Chapter 9), and indeed surpass it. Egypt's agricultural wealth and productive complexity lay at the heart of it. Even after Italian fleets had partially taken over the role of middlemen, including for the Arab world, by 1100, Egypt was still the hub of this exchange, as well as being the nodal point for luxury goods coming in from the Indian Ocean; it was arguably the motor that ran the entire medieval trade cycle. What happened in the tenth century was that the economies of other Mediterranean regions began to be, in some sectors at least, as complex as that of Egypt, so that relations of mutual economic dependence became more reliable, less risky, solid enough to be built on. This was the basis of the exchange of bulk goods in every period of history.

All the same, we must end this account by repeating a point already made earlier: in every part of the Mediterranean, the most important exchange systems were inside, not between, regions. City–country exchange, and micro-regional agricultural and artisanal specializations, lay at the heart of this, not the wharves of Venice or Almería, Tunis or Antalya, Palermo or Alexandria. Nor are we looking at self-sustaining exchange processes here; however active the merchants of Fustat and Venice were, these would not develop for many centuries. Internal economic development essentially depended on the force of internal demand, and thus on the wealth of élites, and thus on the extraction of surplus from the peasantry. These increased in the ninth and tenth centuries, in the Mediterranean as in northern Europe, creating a more complex and colourful environment, and some artisanal products (like cloth) that could be cheap enough to be bought in villages; but they are nonetheless signs of exploitation as well as dynamism. We shall come back to this issue in the north European context in Chapter 22, where there is more evidence for its effect on the peasant majority.

PART IV

The Carolingian and Post-Carolingian West, 750–1000

16

The Carolingian Century, 751–887

In one of the few non-diplomatic letters of Charlemagne (768–814) that has survived, the king wrote to his wife Queen Fastrada in 791. Charles relates that his son, Fastrada's stepson Pippin king of Italy (781–810), has told him of a victory against the Avars of what is now Hungary, and lists the bishops, dukes, counts and vassals who performed particularly well in the war. (The letter omits their names, unfortunately; it only survives as a model for future writers.) The text then lists the religious litanies that Charlemagne and his court performed for three days, probably immediately after the news of the victory, including a prohibition on eating meat or drinking wine, which however people could buy out of with a graduated payment according to wealth. Charles asks Fastrada to take advice about performing similar litanies, and ends with an injunction to send him more regular communications.

The tone of most of this text is hardly intimate; it reads like a ruler communicating with a high-ranking subordinate, which a queen indeed was. There is no reason to think that it tells us much about the personal relationship between the couple. But in its mixture of military action and religious ritual it reflects what else we know of the tone of early Carolingian politics. It also shows that Charlemagne, even when not actively campaigning (he was probably forty-three in 791, fairly old for campaigns, though he did lead armies for another decade and more), received and expected up-to-date and detailed information from his generals: this information-exchange was a regular part of the political structures of the Carolingian century. The Merovingians had such information, but, as far as we can see, less systematically; it is also significant that this letter has survived when equivalent Merovingian letters have not. It has survived by chance, but in the context of a vast increase in surviving information about the political process in Francia, which reaches its height in the 830s–840s. It is also unlikely that the Merovingians articulated politics through as much penitential ritual as this. Charlemagne was not unusually pious (he was rather earthy, and loved jokes, songs, sex, hunting and swimming, and roast meat – less so drinking, it is claimed), but he introduced an ecclesiastical and moralizing edge to political practice which lasted throughout the Carolingian century and beyond, and which had many ramifications, as we shall see in this chapter and the next.

When Charles Martel (717–41) took over the office of *maior* of the Frankish kingdoms by force in the civil war of 715–19 (see above, Chapter 5), he re-established the practice of annual summer campaigning that had been intermittent at best for over seventy years. Between 720 and 804 there were only, probably, eight years without a campaign, and in some years there were two or three. Charles fought on all his borders, reabsorbing Provence and blocking Arab advances from Spain as he did so, taking over Frisia, and re-establishing Frankish hegemony in Alsace and Aquitaine. Most important, however, was the total authority he established in the Frankish heartland, thanks to this military aggregation, and to its success – Charles never lost a war. The Merovingian kings were only puppets by now, and the lay aristocracy and the episcopate both followed Charles; he overthrew any potential rivals without qualms or (apparently) difficulties. This continued under his sons Pippin III (741–68) and Carloman I (741–7) – they divided the mayorship just as the Merovingians had divided the kingship, until Carloman resigned his office, apparently willingly, and went to Rome, becoming a monk at the monastery of Monte Cassino. So did the annual campaigns, which included the subjection of Alemannia in the bloody battle of Canstatt in 746, extended to Italy in 754–6, and continued with the full reconquest of Aquitaine in a sequence of invasions in 759–69.

In his last years, after 737, Charles Martel ruled without a king. Facing revolts, Pippin and Carloman re-established one, Childeric III, in 743. Nonetheless, after Carloman retired, in the context of disturbances caused by family rivals, Pippin wrote to Pope Zacharias (741–52), to ask (in the words of the official *Royal Frankish Annals*, written some forty years later) 'whether it was good or not that the kings in Francia at that time had no royal power'. Zacharias correctly replied 'that it was better to call him king who had the royal power than the one who did not', and Pippin took the throne in 751, the first Carolingian king.

Childeric was tonsured – that is, had his Merovingian royal hair removed – and imprisoned in a monastery. (The Carolingians henceforth wore short hair and moustaches.) Later Carolingian sources of course depict this as a straightforward succession, buttressed by concord and ceremonial, including the agreement of the Frankish magnates and a formal anointing by Boniface archbishop of Mainz. Pippin was indeed the first Frankish king to be anointed; although this followed Visigothic practice in the late seventh century (and also the traditions of the Old Testament), the innovation clearly shows the need to make the Carolingians special, through a new set of ecclesiastical rituals. But in reality this was a coup, and it presented immediate problems of royal legitimacy. Pippin was able to reinforce the rituals of 751 when the new pope Stephen II (752–7) came north to the Seine valley in 753–4, the first time a pope had ever travelled north of the Alps, to ask for help against the Lombards; Stephen re-anointed him king, and Pippin duly invaded Italy, twice. The fact is that king and pope needed each other, the pope to gain protection against attack, the king to gain legitimate authority; for the Carolingians, although the strongest aristocratic family in Francia by far since the 680s, were not royal until two successive popes – importantly, an external, non-Frankish, moral power – said they were. The two processes went together. Pippin and Carloman were already more concerned than Charles Martel had been with church reform, and called at least four church councils in 742–7, the first since the 670s; this intensified after 751, under the aegis of Chrodegang bishop of Metz (d. 766), a leading adviser of Pippin. In 765 Pippin also introduced compulsory tithes to the church, which dramatically increased the wealth of the episcopal hierarchy everywhere in Francia. The help the church gave Pippin in 751 was already paying off, on a substantial scale.

This was the pattern Charlemagne inherited in 768, together with his brother Carloman II (768–71): the two got on badly, and Carloman's early death was perhaps not unplanned. Charles *Magnus*, 'the Great', was initially called this to distinguish him from his own son Charles, but already in the ninth century the adjective began to be used to mark his especial charisma, and he is one of the few people in history to find their epithet absorbed into their own name, 'Charlemagne' in modern French and English. One of the early signs of this charisma was the fact that two exceptionally forceful rulers, Charles Martel and Pippin III, became reduced to predecessors, and are hard to see clearly in our later eighth-century sources. Charlemagne followed Pippin's political path, but across his long reign transformed it, transforming the parameters of European politics as he did so, for a longer period – three centuries at least, arguably – than any other single early medieval ruler.

The first element in this was simply war, which certainly continued the practice of the previous two generations, but greatly extended it. Four areas stand out in Charlemagne's wars. The first is Saxony, Francia's northern neighbour, and location of border wars for over two centuries. Saxony was pagan; it was also not a single polity, but rather a collection of small tribal territories which met in a single annual assembly and fought in larger or smaller groupings according to choice and need. Charlemagne from 772 onwards set out to conquer it. He started, programmatically, by sacking the major Saxon cult-site, the Irminsul, and taking home a rich booty, but it took him over thirty years to complete his task (in 804; there was also a period of peace, when Charlemagne thought he had won, in 785–93). Saxony was hard to conquer precisely because it was disunited, and it was the theatre of considerable violence, not least for the 4,500 Saxon prisoners massacred in 782 after a Frankish defeat. The conquest was by 780 associated with a conscious process of Christianization; this was one of the few conversion processes openly brought about by force in our period. More important perhaps, Frankish conquest resulted in a social revolution, in which members of the Saxon aristocracy were given for the first time landowning rights over their free neighbours, alongside Frankish incomers and a newly endowed Saxon church system. Saxony remained marginal to Carolingian politics, but the wealth of that aristocracy developed further, and it would be the basis for tenth-century kingship itself in East Francia, as we shall see in Chapter 18.

The second area was Lombard Italy, and it was an easier task. In 773 Charlemagne was asked for his help by Pope Hadrian I (772–95), just as Pippin had been; this time he went the whole way, and annexed the Lombard kingdom in 773–4 in an unusual summer and winter war. Conquering Italy was a controversial decision (several of Charlemagne's advisers, including his mother Bertrada and his cousin Adalard, were against it), but it turned out to be straightforward once the Lombard capital, Pavia, fell, for the kingdom was sufficiently centralized for resistance to cease almost completely. Again, wealth flowed north to Charlemagne's treasury. Italy was, however, not absorbed into the

Frankish lands in the way Saxony would be (and Alemannia and Aquitaine had already been). Charlemagne took the title of 'king of the
Franks and Lombards', reflecting the fact that Italy remained conceptually separate, and Pavia remained a separate political centre, the only
one in the Carolingian kingdom; after 781 a subordinate king returned
to Italy, Charlemagne's son Pippin. Lombard Italy would nevertheless
be a source, not only of wealth, but also of governmental expertise, for
Francia. As noted in Chapter 6, only the duchy of Benevento remained
independent; in the face of Frankish power its duke, Arichis II, took the
title of prince in 774.

Of the old areas of Merovingian rule, the last one still to remain
autonomous was Bavaria. Duke Tassilo III (748–88) had begun as a
protégé of Pippin III, his mother's brother, to whom he swore an oath
of fidelity in 757 at adulthood; but he stopped participating in Pippin's
wars in 763, and ran an independent politics for two decades; he was
particularly close to the last Lombard king, Desiderius. After 781 Charlemagne sought to rein him in, and he threatened invasion in 787. Tassilo's
aristocracy persuaded him to capitulate, and he became Charlemagne's
vassal, or sworn follower. This was not enough, however, and in 788
he was victim of a show trial for disloyalty. A tribunal of Franks,
Bavarians, Lombards and Saxons, a rarely invoked image of multi-ethnic
cooperation, condemned him to death. Charlemagne then commuted
this sentence to forced penance and he was, like Childeric in 751,
tonsured and confined in a monastery. The trial of Tassilo in itself marks
the Carolingians as different from their predecessors. It has been noticed
by historians that, whereas the Merovingians killed those who lost royal
favour, the Carolingians often simply imprisoned them, and confiscated their land. This is an exaggeration; the Carolingians often did
kill opponents, or else blinded them (following both Visigothic and
Byzantine practice: cf. above, Chapter 11). But the ritual of a legal
condemnation to death, followed by the 'milder' sentence of blinding or
imprisonment, did become rather more common, and the deaths by
slow torture of the sixth and seventh centuries virtually disappeared.
Imprisonment did not always work (people escaped), and death might
well then follow, but these changes do show a growing belief that a
show of legal process and an elaborate ritual of political exclusion were
good ways to marginalize opponents, and that killing was not always
necessary. They fit in with other Carolingian changes, as we shall see.

In the meantime, Bavaria and the Bavarian aristocracy (who survived almost without exception, apart from the ruling Agilolfings) were absorbed directly into the Frankish political system.

The absorption of Bavaria brought Carolingian borders eastward to the lands of the Avars, and Avar wars began in 791. Avar power was by now far less great than it had been in the early seventh century, but the wealth of the Avar khagan remained enormous. In 795–6 three armies were sent eastwards to the Avar royal residence, the Ring, located somewhere on the Hungarian plain. The sack of the Ring produced booty on such an immense scale that it enriched the Carolingians and their magnates (including the pope) for a generation – Einhard said in his *Life of Charlemagne* that 'no one can recall any war ... that left them richer or better stocked with resources'. The Avars were not conquered, but they soon disappeared, their place taken by newer Sclavenian polities, who remained on the Frankish/Bavarian borderlands (see Chapter 20 for the term Sclavenian).

By 804 the lands ruled by Charlemagne were half again as large as in 768, and over twice the size of those ruled by Charles Martel at his death. Nearly all borders were further away than in 768, even that of Spain, where northern Catalonia had been taken from the Arabs in 785 and 801. This was a fairly thin strip, however, and Charlemagne's bolder attack on Zaragoza in 778 led to one of the few military setbacks of the reign, the attack on the retreating Frankish rearguard by the Basques at Roncesvalles in the western Pyrenees. The Carolingians had new neighbours now, the Danes, the Arabs, the Beneventans, and half a continent of Sclavenian tribes from the Baltic to the Adriatic. Few of these gave rich pickings, and they were mostly fairly far away. Expansion stopped as a result. Carolingian military activity largely became one of policing, and extracting tribute from, their still independent neighbours, for a generation. It has been plausibly argued that this had bad consequences for the Franks, for their aristocracies now had to aggrandize inside, not outside, the Frankish kingdoms; kings themselves had greater difficulties as a result. But this too was a generation away in 804, and had other roots as well. Charlemagne's last decade was one of relative peace, and unheard-of prosperity for the ruling élite of Francia by early medieval standards.

It is worth insisting a little more on the roots of this prosperity. Charlemagne had conquered new territories, and seized, not only extensive booty, but the royal treasure of two peoples, the Lombards and the Avars: essential resources for royal generosity in gift-giving, to aristocrats and to foreign rulers, which the Carolingians needed as much as their predecessors. He also now controlled the royal land of Italy and the ducal land of Aquitaine and Bavaria, and the confiscated land of rebels across the whole of Saxony and (to a lesser extent) elsewhere; and also a network of new offices, counties, abbacies and bishoprics, to add to those in the Frankish heartland. (Over all Charlemagne's lands, there were some 600 counties and 180 dioceses.) All of these could be given out to his supporters as *honores*, 'honours', as both royal land and offices were called. So could the extensive lands of churches and monasteries, which all the Carolingians disposed of without many qualms when they needed. Royal wealth was thus the wealth of aristocrats as well, as long as such men were in the king's favour. The lands and offices were revocable; Charlemagne gave few permanent landed gifts, preferring to distribute royal and church land as temporary cessions, *beneficia* or 'benefices'. Aristocrats hoped to keep these and pass them to their sons, but had to remain committed to the king, faithfully attending court, in order to do so. And there was so much wealth around in these decades that Charlemagne could attract whom he liked to his court, including poets and intellectuals from outside Francia, and endow them as he chose. The self-confidence of the Frankish élite became sufficiently great that it was by the 790s possible for writers to describe them as in effect the new chosen people in succession to the Jews; Old Testament imagery was standard in Carolingian political programmes, and Charlemagne was commonly called David by court intellectuals. Hence or otherwise, it may be added that the Carolingians were notably tolerant of Jews, and Charlemagne's son Louis the Pious (814–40) in particular protected them, to the great distress of writers like Agobard archbishop of Lyon (d. 840), who came from ex-Visigothic Spain, and had inherited the anti-Semitism of late Visigothic political culture. In less religious imagery, Einhard preserves for us with some smugness a Byzantine proverb, '[if] you have a Frank as your friend, [then] he is not your neighbour', which he actually cites in Greek; the Franks were proud of their greed and aggrandisement, and regarded it as a proof of their virtue.

The court crystallized in two further ways in the 790s. The first is that in the years 794–6 Charlemagne founded his own capital, at Aachen in the heart of Pippinid northern Austrasia, and across the next decades he and his son Louis endowed it with ambitious buildings, one of which, the cathedral-scale palace chapel, still survives. As Charlemagne grew older, he spent more and more time here (it was close to the Ardennes forest, one of the best royal hunting reserves), and it became a stable political and administrative focus for the first time in Frankish history. Kings still moved around, taking their court with them, but two generations of courtiers came to see Aachen as a natural backdrop for politics. The second is that in 800 Charlemagne obtained a new title, emperor, in a ceremony in Rome, in which he was anointed (again) by the pope. The importance of this title should not be exaggerated; it was only honorific. But Charlemagne was proud of it, and was keen to get recognition of it by the Byzantine (as one might say, the 'real') emperors, which he achieved in 812 after menacing the still-Byzantine enclave of Venice. Imperial imagery began to infuse Carolingian legislation after 800 as well. The truth is, though, that already by the late 780s, thanks to his military successes, Charlemagne had achieved a western European-wide dominance, and a near unanimity of support from his subjects, a political centrality, that is to say, that no one had matched in those lands since the Roman emperor Valentinian I. Even the strongest Merovingians, Clovis or Dagobert, did not rule as widely or enjoy such long-lasting success. Charles Martel's military machine, and the luck of four almost unbroken generations of single rulers (for Charlemagne's sons, between whom he fully intended to divide his lands, all predeceased him except Louis), were the basis of this success, but Charlemagne's charisma capped it. The question would then be what he would do with it.

It cannot be denied that Charlemagne – and his advisers, but animated beyond doubt by the king himself – had a conscious and ambitious political project. In the widest sense, it was one of 'reform' (*renovatio*), or, a much commoner word, 'correction' (*correctio*), of the inner life as well as the external acts of lay and ecclesiastical subjects alike. It is very clear in one of Charles's relatively early legislative acts, the *General Admonition* of 789. In this widely circulated text, the king re-enacted canons from church councils to provide a template for the proper activity of clerics, but also instructed the laity in the necessity of concord, justice, the avoidance of perjury, the avoidance of hatred, and, overall, the necessity of the preaching of the Christian faith. These were keynotes of the moral reform programme of the Carolingian period. They were matched by a systematic education programme, which was (as was the *General Admonition*) largely the work of the most influential intellectual of the first generation of the Carolingian reform project, the Northumbrian Alcuin (d. 804). Alcuin was at Charlemagne's court for most of the period 786 to 796, and then continued teaching in one of the several monasteries Charlemagne gave him, Saint-Martin in Tours. As the king said in an open letter of the 780s or 790s, also written by Alcuin, good behaviour and spiritual understanding were impossible without a literary education, for 'knowing comes before doing', and even the Bible was full of figures of speech which had to be decoded. The Carolingians promoted basic literacy, but expected more, especially from leading clerics and aristocrats: a proper understanding of the Bible and of theology, without which a path in the Carolingian political world could not properly be walked.

The successes and failures of this project have been very intensively discussed; but that there were successes is not at issue. The whole of the Carolingian élite cared about theology, or had to pretend they did. Already in 794 an assembly of bishops and magnates at Frankfurt could devote much of its time to discussing heresies, Adoptionism and the Byzantine rejection of Iconoclasm (the Franks had greater sympathy with the Iconoclasts), for the first time in the West in two centuries. By the 830s and 840s, the whole political process, including coups and civil wars, could be seen in theological terms. By then, there were two dozen or more political actors who were also active writers, participating in what were often pamphlet wars about the theology of political practice. Some of them were lay aristocrats, including Dhuoda (d. *c.* 843), wife of the sometime royal chamberlain Bernard of Septimania (d. 844), who wrote a handbook on correct behaviour for her son, suffused with biblical imagery and citing an array of church fathers, which were evidently available to her in Uzès, far in the south of the Frankish lands. This will all be discussed in the next chapter, but it marks the Carolingian period out.

Exactly why this project developed is rather harder to understand. Many of its roots are obvious. The Carolingians had to identify with the church, for it was the church that gave them legitimacy as a ruling family; the coup of 751 was still in living memory at the time of the *General Admonition*. The church councils, which had become commoner again after the 740s, and which continued without a break thereafter, were a natural source of moralizing enactments, many of them absorbed into royal legislation already under Pippin III. Frankish self-confidence led to Old Testament parallels, as we have seen, and also to Roman parallels, thus encouraging people to look back to the fourth to sixth centuries, when correct belief was a burning political issue (see above, Chapter 3). Although the Merovingian period was not an age of explicit ideological programmes in Francia, seventh-century Visigothic Spain had been, showing that an overtly moralized politics already had potential roots in early medieval western soil; and Theodulf bishop of Orléans (d. *c.* 826), the major theologian of Charlemagne's reign, was of Visigothic origins. (It must be said, however, that the Franks, if they borrowed from the Visigoths, did not borrow the Gothic zeal for religious exclusion, as we have already seen.) Once Alcuin, Theodulf, Paul the Deacon from Lombard Italy, the Franks Angilbert of Saint-Riquier and Einhard, and others, combined in Charlemagne's court in the 780s and 790s, a critical mass of intellectual debate and competitive writing ensued, enough to expand and continue for another three generations. But it is hard not to see a plan at the back of this. It was Charlemagne who invited these intellectuals, and gave them such big gifts that they stayed in or near the court for decades. Programmatic legislation, too, although not, of course, composed by him, went out in his name, and was new. The successes of the 770s (particularly in Italy) seem already to have persuaded the king that he was special, and that he had a mission, not just to rule the Franks and their neighbours, but to save their souls. He may have been educated to this in the already more ecclesiastical political environment of Pippin's reign – however incompletely; Charlemagne could appreciate poetry and theology, but he never fully learned to write. All the same, it seems to have been his own choice. Charlemagne thus matches Justinian as an innovator in moral-political practice (although he had a better sense of humour than Justinian; his son Louis, famous for not smiling, was a better parallel there). The fascination with him that has resulted in such a dense historiography, unbroken across the centuries but if possible even more elaborate now, is not entirely unjustified.

All kinds of legislation were commoner under Charlemagne. Royal assemblies produced *capitularia*, 'chapter-collections' or 'capitularies'. These varied in their formality (some were official written texts; some seem to have survived only because participants took private notes of their content); they also varied in their aim, for some were guidelines for local representatives, some were one-off enactments, but others were systematic additions to existing law, Frankish or Lombard. But there were many of them; the standard capitulary edition has eighty-five from the reign of Charlemagne alone, plus some enactments that survive in more fragmentary form. Some of the impetus for this must have come from Italy, for they start in the late 770s, and are matched in frequency earlier than that only by the Lombard laws of Liutprand; church council legislation, which partly overlaps with capitulary legislation (as with the *General Admonition*, and the 794 synod of Frankfurt), was another model. Charlemagne also reissued the *Lex Salica* in a new edition, which was widely copied in the ninth century, and made laws for newly conquered peoples such as the Saxons. Not all capitularies were widely copied, it is worth stressing; many survive in only a single manuscript. When Ansegis, abbot of Saint-Wandrille on the Seine, went looking for capitularies to turn into a rearranged collection to present to Louis the Pious in 827, he only found (or used) twenty-nine of them, and only one (the *General Admonition*) from before 803. As in the Roman empire before the *Theodosian Code*, it was hard to be sure what laws had been passed, even though the Carolingians, Roman-style, regarded ignorance of the law as no excuse. But some were very carefully circulated, such as the capitulary adding to Salic law of 803, which survives in fifty-three manuscripts (Ansegis used it, too), one of which states that Stephen count of Paris had his copy of it read in a public assembly there, and local political leaders signed their names on it. Such a mixture of oral publication and formal subscription was probably common for the major enactments. The capitulary 'habit' continued under Louis the Pious, at least up to 830, and then in West Francia and Italy until the late ninth century; in East Francia, too, the acts of church councils continued to be recorded. In the ninth century, informal capitulary collections begin to be commoner as well, particularly but not only in Italy; they seem to have been intended for use in court. None of them were 'complete' sets (capitularies tended, after all, to be repetitive), but they do attest to a recognition that a wide range of new law now existed, and that it was useful to be informed about it.

These laws, and the other sources for Charlemagne's reign such as annals and letter collections, show that the government of the Carolingian lands was essentially based on old foundations, but that these were fairly carefully reshaped as required. The network of public assemblies that were crucial for the Merovingians and the Lombards remained crucial in the Carolingian period. Royal assemblies were held just before the campaigning season every year and were the points of reference for army muster as well; kings could call smaller or larger assemblies later in the year, too, to prepare policy for the next year or if there was urgent business. Major political figures, lay and ecclesiastical, attended regularly. These were venues for genuine discussion, not just royal instructions; Hincmar archbishop of Reims (d. 882) in his 882 treatise *On the Organization of the Palace* (which itself drew on Adalard of Corbie's lost text of *c.* 812 with the same title) indeed tells us that kings did not attend all assembly discussions, but instead stood outside glad-handing – and Hincmar was one of the major advisers of King Charles the Bald (840–77), as Adalard had been for his cousin Charlemagne, so whichever wrote this would have known. Early in Charles the Bald's reign, during the preparation for the civil war of 841–2, Charles's follower and cousin Nithard (d. 845) records in his contemporary history how Charles's May 841 assembly argued about which way the king and his army should march; Charles went with the minority, not the majority, view – wrongly, in fact, Nithard said – but, either way, he had the benefit of hearing real argument. Even without that argument, participation in assemblies, and in the rituals normal in all of them, powerfully reinforced a sense of collective participation in public affairs.

These national assemblies were matched in every county by local assemblies, *placita*, meeting two or three times a year under the count's presidency, in which local élites were brought into the same public network; these heard reports of national deliberation (Count Stephen's Paris gathering of 803 was one such), and decided on court cases. The Carolingians regularized these assemblies, too, for example determining that local judicial experts should be called *scabini* everywhere, which by the early ninth century they were indeed coming to be, from the English Channel to Italy. It was also county assemblies that administered the taking of oaths to the king, another older tradition systematized in this period. Charlemagne instituted these in 789 after regional revolts in Hesse and Thuringia in 785–6; in 793 he had them repeated after a second revolt, by his disinherited eldest son Pippin in 792, since some of the rebels said they had not sworn in 789, perhaps because they were too young (not that this did them much good; Charlemagne had them killed). These were the only revolts in Francia in his reign, and they seem to have been fairly small-scale, but the king's response was to make formal oaths more systematic. Every free man over the age of twelve had to swear, and their names had to be recorded by counts and *missi*; in 802 these obligations were further extended, as oath-swearers had to swear a much more detailed oath to the emperor. Oaths mattered in this world; oath-breakers were perjurors, and risked damnation, not just secular penalties – dispossession, mutilation and sometimes death. They could be dangerous: Charlemagne banned oaths of association made to anyone except the king and one lord, and in 806 enacted that men who did so should beat each other and cut off each other's hair (or, in extreme cases, slit their noses). Oaths to the king further added to the intensity of ritual at even the most remote assembly, and to the local presence of royal authority.

The Carolingian empire was huge, larger than any subsequent state in Europe has ever been except for brief years at the height of the power of Napoleon and Hitler, and also extremely diverse, stretching as it did from the half-converted and roadless lands of Saxony to the old urban societies of Provence and Italy. How it could all be controlled, without the elaborate fiscal and administrative system of the Roman empire or the caliphate, was an almost impossible challenge. Assembly politics was one part of it; so was army muster; and the palace, the court of the king or emperor, whether at Aachen or elsewhere, was furthermore a magnet for the ambitious in every period, as they came to seek justice, gifts or preferment. Kings did not just give gifts; they received them too, the 'annual gifts' of horses and the like presented at each general assembly. These gifts seem to have had a military edge to them, and were probably associated with the fact that soldiers on campaign had to bring their equipment and three months' provisions with them, not a small investment. Rather than a proto-tax system, which cannot be identified in the Carolingian period (kings were not short of resources even without taxation, until late in the ninth century), this was another element in the gift-exchange of political participation. Palaces were also the focus of a particularly large amount of collective and increasingly moralized ritual, as we shall see further in the next chapter; the other elements of Carolingian political aggregation had clear roots in the Merovingian period, but this was largely new. But kings did not move around the whole of the empire, except when on campaign; Charlemagne, Louis and Louis's sons seldom strayed out of the three great 'royal landscapes', of the Seine valley, the Middle Rhine valley, and between them the core block of royal and ex-Pippinid estates around Aachen. Not every local leader ever went there; the kings had to reach them too.

One way they did so was by strategically placing their most trusted aristocrats. Counts tended to be from long-standing local élites, except after conquests, as in Alemannia after Canstatt, or in Italy in the early ninth century; so did bishops. But beside these local élites, and inter-locking – and intermarrying – with them, there were also greater families, those of the *Reichsaristokratie*, the 'imperial aristocracy', as Gerd Tellen-bach called them in 1939. He and his successors identified between forty and fifty such families, who could be found in any part of the empire, and whose members could move around (or be moved around) with some facility. Most of them were from the old Pippinid heartlands of Austrasia, extending southwards into the Middle Rhine and northern Burgundy, though they could come from anywhere except Italy. Very few if any of these families were newly created; but the Carolingians could make favoured members of them rich and powerful beyond any previous imagining, even though Merovingian aristocrats could already be pretty rich, as we saw in Chapter 5. A well-known example of these is the 'Widonid' family (as we call them – surnames did not yet exist), originating in the Middle Rhine and Moselle valleys; they seem in the eighth century to be linked to Milo of Trier (see Chapter 8) and to an important church in Mainz. Under Louis the Pious and his sons, they are found simultaneously in the far west of modern France and in the duchy of Spoleto in the central Appennines of Italy, running the frontier marches facing Brittany and Benevento respectively, while keeping their Rhineland links, where they controlled the major monastery of Hornbach. They did not follow a simple family political line (in the crisis of 833–4, which set Louis the Pious against his sons, Guy count of Vannes fought a battle for Louis against his brother Lambert marquis of the Breton march, fighting for Louis's son Lothar, and was killed), and they could be unscrupulous about establishing themselves locally, as in distant Spoleto, where they ran a largely autonomous politics. All the same, they were loyal to Carolingian ideals, including Carolingian unity – Guy III of Spoleto (d. 895), after Carolingian power ended in 887, tried to make himself king in both West Francia and Italy, and was actually crowned emperor in 891. Without that unity, the geographical range of their power would have ceased to exist, and, indeed, did cease, for the family is not attested after the 890s outside the Rhineland (though there it remained important: the Salian dynasty of German kings was probably descended from it). Kings relied on families such as this a great deal, but the reverse is true too; in many respects the Carolingian empire was an immense oligarchy, and, given the rooted local power of aristocracies both large and small, it had to be. The point will be explored further later.

Not all royal dependants in the provinces were from great families like this. The Carolingians made considerable use of royal vassals, not all of whom were rich, but all of whom had particularly close ceremonial ties to the kings, in rituals of personalized oath-swearing and homage. These could be local men, called to the palace and the army, or else aristocrats, both rich and middling, brought in from outside; either way, they are invoked in legislation as the sort of men kings could particularly rely on. (Aristocrats had, and relied on, their own vassals as well.) Vassalage was the lineal successor of the personal fidelity of the Merovingian world and of Lombard Italy; what was new about it was once again that vassals might be moved around. It is this movement of men, of families, which marks the early Carolingians out from their predecessors.

The kings also, systematically, sent representatives to the provinces. These representatives, *missi*, were the king's eyes and ears. They had Merovingian and especially Lombard antecedents too, but Charlemagne regularized them, and the Frankish heartland was in 802 divided into *missatica*, territories in which pairs of *missi*, a count and a bishop, regularly toured, to hear appeals against local counts and others. Italy and most of the other conquered lands had *missi* of their own. *Missi* were not often outsiders to their territory – local archbishops were popular *missi*, for example – but they again owed loyalty and responsibility directly to the king, to whom they were expected regularly to report, in writing if necessary. We have some of the court cases in which they held local officials to account, such as the 804 case at Rižana in Istria in which three *missi* heard the complaints of 172 local leaders against Duke John of Istria's trampling of local customs; John apologized, and the customs seem to have been restored. It would be wrong to see *missi* and their territories as fully institutionalized, but kings certainly regarded them as normal until late in the ninth century, except, it seems, in East Francia. And we certainly have chance-surviving evidence of regular written communication, to the provinces and back again, whether through people called *missi* or other officials, such as the instruction from Hetti archbishop of Trier (as *missus*) to the bishop of Toul in 817 telling him to mobilize against the revolt of King Bernard of Italy, that very day; or the letters Louis the Pious sent in 832 to tell two vassals to stand by as messengers in case his *missus* or his count needed to send a message to the emperor; or the demand made by Charles the Bald to his churchmen in 845 for systematic information about his monasteries, which Abbot Lupus of Ferrières sought actively to fulfil; or the lists of men who swore fidelity to Charles the Bald at Reims in 854, attached to a copy of a capitulary by Archbishop Hincmar, who was probably himself the local *missus*. Men must have been moving around the entire time, looking for the king/emperor, or sometimes, the queen (this was not straightforward, for they moved about too), and informing them; Hincmar indeed supposes in *On the Organization of the Palace* that receiving them was a major royal task. (Aristocrats and bishops had their own communications networks, to keep abreast of politics, which presumably filled the roads still more.) Without this presumption of regular and detailed communication, again not new but greatly extended, running the empire would not have been possible.

Did this complex network of instructions and accountability actually work? There are two views. One is that the complexity and flexibility of the Carolingian administration was self-supporting. The kings and their advisers were constantly innovating and retouching, and could move quickly; Louis the Pious's muster against Bernard in 817, for example, was so fast that it caught the rebel entirely by surprise. The 'system' of the capitulary legislation or of Hincmar's *On the Organization of the Palace* was more flexible in reality, and that was a strength, for it could be moulded to fit the diversity of the provinces. And the centrality of the royal court (or, after 840, courts) remained undiminished, as all political leaders or would-be leaders continued to circle around kings into the 880s, imbibing as they did the elaborately moralized programme of Carolingian *correctio*; there is good evidence for aristocratic literacy and even book-buying, which backs this argument up. This was further extended into the provinces thanks to the network of rich royal monasteries, from Corbie in modern northern

France to St. Gallen and Reichenau in modern southern Germany and on into Italy, and the even denser network of cathedral communities, many of which had extensive libraries, and trained intellectuals who could and did debate about theology and politics until the end of the ninth century, with effects on political practice in some cases.

The other view is that this was all a sham. The aristocracy, secular and ecclesiastical alike, were corrupt and out for themselves, from top to bottom. Theodulf of Orléans wrote a poem around 800 against (among other things) judicial corruption, which would have been incomprehensible to the people of his south French *missaticum*, given the degree to which litigants apparently pressed gifts on him; many of the abuses *missi* are recorded as correcting were in fact the oppressive acts of other *missi*; Adalard of Corbie's younger brother Wala (d. 836), when a *missus* for Italy in the 820s, uncovered an elaborate cover-up of the expropriation and later murder of a widow which stretched from top to bottom in the Italian kingdom; Matfrid count of Orléans, one of the major court figures of the 820s, was criticized in about 827 by Agobard of Lyon for providing 'a wall' between the emperor and criminals, 'to protect them from *correctio*'; there are plenty of other examples of aristocratic bad behaviour from the period, which was in fact also marked by a notable oppression of the poor, as capitularies themselves tell us. As for the imperial project, it was already disintegrating in the 830s and was only fully maintained after that by Charles the Bald and his adviser Hincmar; most other Carolingians soon moved towards the rougher realpolitik of the tenth century. In any case, the ambition of Carolingian reform legislation betrayed its hopeless naivety, and its constant repetition betrayed its failure. (Maybe this was a good thing, Michael Wallace-Hadrill thought, writing in an otherwise sympathetic account: 'had [Hincmar's programme] worked out, Carolingian society would have been a police-state.') The Carolingians were unusual only in their rhetoric, and in their military success, which petered out in the ninth century, leaving the empire open to civil war and demoralizing (because unremunerative) defence against external attack.

The interest of the Carolingian period lies in the fact that both of these views are largely accurate. Aristocrats are always violent, corrupt and greedy, but they were at least aware of the ideology of public responsibility in this period, and presumably – sometimes, as with Dhuoda, demonstrably – linked it to their desire for personal salvation after death, which they certainly always also possessed. The state was ramshackle and far too large for the governmental technologies of the period, but it is, all the same, constantly striking how often it makes its presence felt even in resolutely local document collections. Throughout the ninth century, we have examples of peasants appealing to public courts against their lords, in Italy, Francia, Septimania (modern Languedoc), over personal status, rent levels or seized lands; they almost always lost, but the fact that they bothered to do so at all, in a political system so obviously run by the aristocracy, implies that they knew the system could at least sometimes work as it was supposed to, and such cases are much rarer later. There was a constant dialectic between the state, with its immense patronage powers, and local societies, throughout almost the whole empire (royal power fell back only at the edges, like eastern Bavaria, Spoleto or Catalonia). Local powers had to pay attention to kings, and accept their political guidelines, including whatever ideological programmes they had, not least because kings were also dangerous, and by no means did all the things their own programmes enjoined. We shall explore these contradictions, and their ironies, further in this chapter and the next.

Charlemagne died in 814, and Louis the Pious, who had been crowned emperor by his father the year before, immediately marched north to Aachen from his sub-kingdom in Aquitaine to take over. He represented himself as a new broom, and summarily expelled his sisters, led by Bertha, from the palace, where they had been acting as a sort of collective queen for their father since his last wife died in 800. The imagery of Louis's early years stresses his moralism, as opposed to the sexual licence of his father's reign; Charlemagne had had a string of mistresses up to his death, and his daughters, whom he would not allow to marry, had lovers too – Bertha's was the court scholar Angilbert, by whom she was the mother of the historian Nithard. Louis's own sex life, once he became an adult, was in fact as far as we know restricted to the marriage bed, unlike most male Carolingians, but his criticism of the sexual immorality of the palace (the ideal moral centre of the polity, thus very vulnerable to such criticism, as we shall see in the next chapter) was a standard part of ninth-century political rhetoric, and would be applied back to Louis's own court in the 830s. Louis was committed to monastic reform, and his first substantial political initiative was two reform councils at

Aachen in 816–17, which revised the *Rule* of Benedict of Nursia and extended it to all the monasteries of the empire. In 817 he also set out how the empire would be divided at his death between his three sons, which excluded from the succession Bernard, son of his brother Pippin, who was already king of Italy (812–17); Bernard unsurprisingly revolted, with the support of not a few Frankish magnates (including Theodulf of Orléans), but, as we have seen, failed. He was tried in 818 and condemned to death, but, following the common Carolingian pattern, this sentence was commuted to blinding, from which however he died anyway.

After 818, Louis understandably had little opposition for some time, and the next decade can be seen as the apogee of Carolingian self-confidence. Wars were small-scale by now, and the emperor's attention was focused on an elaborate and complex court politics in Aachen, marked by regular embassies from different neighbours, another dense set of capitularies (many of them collected by Ansegis in 827), and an administrative reordering under the arch-chancellor Helisachar (814–30), who had come with Louis from Aquitaine, and the arch-chaplain Hilduin, abbot of Saint-Denis and four other monasteries (819–30). The emperor's control of court ritual was marked above all by his decision in the 822 general assembly at Attigny to perform a public penance for the death of Bernard, imitating Theodosius I's penance of 390, according to one of his biographers. At the same time, he called back the (male) relatives he had exiled from court, notably his cousins and possible rivals Adalard and Wala; Carolingian family reconciliation was to be complete.

The calm of the 820s was, however, broken abruptly in 829–30. Court factions were crystallizing around, on the one side, Louis's oldest son Lothar (817–55), already emperor (since 824) but with a political remit confined to Italy, and, on the other, Louis's second wife Judith and her family. In 828 Lothar's father-in-law Hugh count of Tours and his associate Matfrid of Orléans had lost their offices. In 829 Bernard of Septimania, count of Barcelona, was brought in as chamberlain, an office traditionally very close to the queen, and was for a few months regarded as 'second to the king'; he was (for unclear reasons) a highly controversial figure, however, and by 830 was accused of adultery with Judith. Lothar gained the support of his brothers Pippin king of Aquitaine (817–38) and Louis king of Bavaria (817–76) to set in motion in

April 830 a quiet coup, significantly also supported by the old guard of the court, Helisachar, Hilduin and Wala. Bernard fled and Judith was temporarily exiled, until Louis the Pious regained control in October and brought Judith (but not Bernard) back. In 833 tensions rose again, and much the same occurred; this time, the emperor Louis marched with an army to meet Lothar and his brothers, who were joined by Pope Gregory IV, in Alsace. At the meeting-point, later called the 'Field of Lies', Louis's army melted away, joining Lothar, and Louis was deposed in favour of Lothar. This time his public penance was not voluntary; the best he could do was refuse to take monastic vows when he was confined in Saint-Denis. But, as in 830, Lothar and his brothers fell out – Lothar, like his father, was too clearly committed to being the dominant Carolingian – and Louis was restored in 834. He was ceremonially re-crowned at Metz in 835, and re-established himself, confining Lothar to Italy again, though Louis did not take violent revenge on any of Lothar's supporters (they merely lost their lands and offices north of the Alps, and some of them, such as Hilduin, soon got them back). Louis then remained in control until his death in 840.

The events of 830–34 certainly greatly disrupted the balances of imperial government and the patronage networks of the Carolingian lands. They have also been typically seen until very recently as a sign of imminent Carolingian breakdown, perhaps fuelled by aristocratic hostility, and also as a sign of the weakness of Louis 'the Pious' himself. Louis was not, however, either pliable or accommodating, any more than his sons were – hence, indeed, the fact that the uprising occurred twice; and aristocratic reactions to the crisis show alarm rather than any sense of a new opportunity. Einhard (d. 840), by now in retirement in his monastery of Seligenstadt near Frankfurt, although a supporter of Louis (he preserved in his letter collection a very rude letter to Lothar, written in 830), prudently fell ill during both crisis moments, but then was worried that this might be taken the wrong way by the kings, and wrote to friends at court to ask them to ensure that his loyalty was recognized, by Louis the Pious, but also by Louis of Bavaria (whose power-base was close to Seligenstadt), and even by Lothar; one letter to a dependant in 833 asks him to give the 'customary gifts' to the temporarily victorious Lothar, and to report back on how Lothar received them. Einhard was, thanks to his long-standing palace connections, a major local patron and political intermediary, and it is clear in his letters of these years how much mediation would need to be done in a period of sharp political swings, for the kings could and did remove the benefices of the less than fully loyal. So Einhard in late 833 wrote to a friend asking him to intercede with Lothar for a certain Frumold, who had been given a benefice near Geneva by Charlemagne but was too ill to travel to court and commend himself to the new ruler (Geneva was a long way from Seligenstadt; Einhard's patronage stretched widely); or again, around the same time, to another courtier who might, he hoped, persuade Lothar to let an aristocrat and his brother hold benefices jointly in the kingdoms of both Lothar and Louis of Bavaria. That Einhard kept these letters indicates that they were normal, and also, perhaps, successful: his younger contemporary the poet Walahfrid Strabo (d. 849) wrote a prologue to Einhard's *Life* of Charlemagne noting rather wryly how well the author had kept 'a certain remarkable and divinely inspired distance' from the crises of Louis's reign. This was unlike Walahfrid himself, in fact, who was exiled from his monastery of Reichenau by Louis of Bavaria in 839–42; Walahfrid is thus doubly a witness to how hard it was to avoid trouble in the 830s. This was not a crisis period which magnates would easily seek to exploit.

It is probably best to see the crises of the 830s as a product of two underlying problems, a struggle between court factions, and the normal tensions any ruling Carolingian had with adult sons itching to succeed. This confluence was only exacerbated by arguments over theology and political ethics, and the more mundane fact that Judith gave Louis a fourth son, Charles, in 823, who would have to be fitted somewhere into the partitioned empire (he was given Alemannia in 829, a politically tangential area, but in a significant year – Nithard later thought that this was the excuse for Lothar's first rebellion). It has at least to be said that Louis's father Charlemagne managed his sons better, and so did Louis's own sons: Lothar, Louis and Charles each weathered the rivalries of their adult sons without ever losing the initiative. Misjudgements in the crucial years around 830 seem to have marred Louis the Pious's standard toughness. After Louis's death in 840, however, it is not hard to see how his heirs fell into civil war. Pippin of Aquitaine had died in 838, allowing Louis to substitute Charles as his heir in the western part of the empire (at the expense of Pippin's son Pippin the Younger), which ought to have made things easier; but Charles 'the Bald' and Louis 'the German', as historians from now on call them, were not at all inclined to let Lothar have the leading role which he regarded as his right. It was because of this that civil war ensued in 841–2. A bloody but inconclusive battle at Fontenoy in 841 scared the Frankish magnates, however – another sign that they were by no means ready to exploit crisis – and Lothar, driven out of Aachen in 842, agreed peace; the empire was divided again, rather carefully, at the Treaty of Verdun in 843. Charles took West Francia (including Aquitaine), Louis East Francia (including Bavaria, Alemannia and Saxony), Lothar the lands around Aachen, Burgundy, Provence and Italy. The Frankish heartland, where royal estates were thickest, was divided neatly into three; each brother got one of the 'royal landscapes', and was in addition assigned the outlying kingdom in which he was strongest. The fact that the division looks idiotic on a map, much as Merovingian divisions often had, underlines the extent to which all three brothers still saw the empire as a common project; it perhaps also shows that none of the parties really thought it would be permanent. It was permanent, however. The only major exception was the lands around Aachen, named Lotharingia after Lothar's son Lothar II (855–69) who inherited them, which were divided between Charles and Louis at Lothar II's death. (Aachen became marginalized after that, as a borderland; in the tenth century Lotharingia was absorbed into East Francia.) Verdun should not be overstated as a dividing point all the same. We know that West Francia eventually became 'France', East Francia became 'Germany', but contemporaries did not, and the imagery of a single Francia under several rulers survived until after 1000, as we shall see in Chapter 18.

The division of the empire was a return to the norms of the sixth and seventh centuries, and was regarded as inevitable and indeed appropriate by nearly everyone; after all, Charles Martel and Pippin III had both divided their lands temporarily, and Charlemagne would have done so. It was also a return to the bickering and occasional warring of the decades around 600. Lothar's northern heartland around Aachen looks the quietest, though this may be because the two major continuators of the *Royal Frankish Annals*, the *Annals of Saint-Bertin* and the *Annals of Fulda*, were written in Charles's and Louis's kingdoms respectively. Louis the German, too, seems to have been in full control of East Francia, at least after his bloody quelling of a peasants' revolt, the Stellinga, in Saxony in 842. Louis spent his long reign (he died in 876) fighting on the eastern frontier, particularly against the Bohemians, and the increasingly powerful Moravian rulers Rastislav (846–70), who was captured and blinded by the Franks, and his successor Sviatopluk or Zwentibald (870–94): these princes had expanded their power into the political vacuum that followed the collapse of the Avars. Zwentibald, in particular, fought the Franks as an equal, and had considerable influence over eastern Bavarian aristocrats by the mid-880s. But the importance of the eastern frontier, and the traditional nature of the campaigns there, allowed Louis to sustain a military effectiveness focused on offensive war that had not been known since Charlemagne's time. Hence, doubtless, the ease with which he faced down successive revolts by his three sons in 857–73. East Francia was harder to rule, on one level, for very little of it had been part of the Roman empire, so it lacked good communications or cities except in the far south and far west; Louis probably had little direct control in still-peripheral Saxony, and rarely went there. All the same, he ran *placita* there and did justice, like any Carolingian king, when he did go there, most notably in 852; and, although he did not issue capitularies, and seems to have had a simpler administration than his brothers, his bishops, headed by the influential archbishops of Mainz on the Rhine – a Roman city, and in a Carolingian royal heartland – behaved just like other Carolingian ecclesiastical communities, holding councils and making law. (Louis's first appointment to Mainz was indeed the influential theologian and biblical commentator Hraban Maur, 847–56.) This, plus Louis's armies, made the East Frankish kingdom a still-functioning heir of that of Charlemagne and Louis the Pious.

In Italy, too, Lothar's son Louis II (840–75), who was in sole control of the kingdom (with the imperial title) by 850, operated without recorded difficulty, and seems to have been an effective ruler. He was certainly a practitioner of Carolingian reform, and as early as 850 enacted capitularies and conciliar legislation to combat abuses, the first of an Italian sequence that would only end in 898. He and his wife Angilberga (d. 891), an unusually influential queen, had a more hands-on control over government than most Carolingians; Louis was secure enough to promote Lombard aristocrats for the first time in half a century, alongside three or four major families of the *Reichsaristokratie* (including his wife's kin, the 'Supponids'). He was clearly the heir of kings like Liutprand, while also taking seriously his imperial title; in a letter to the Byzantine emperor, he claimed to represent the whole

Carolingian dynasty. Louis II, uniquely among Carolingian rulers, could take the risk of a long unbroken period (866–72) campaigning abroad, against the Arabs who had taken Bari in southern Italy; he took Bari back but was then imprisoned by Prince Adelchis of Benevento (853–78) in 871, who had no reason to welcome Carolingian power stretching so far south. This was a humiliation for Louis, and he had to be re-crowned to counteract it – but he was still unopposed in the north of Italy. Here, too, then, the norms of Carolingian power were not yet under threat.

Charles the Bald faced by far the greatest problems out of the Carolingians of this period. This, plus the extensive documentation for his reign, has meant that he is the best-studied later Carolingian, although he was also the least typical. For a start, his was the only kingdom in 843 with another claimant, Pippin the Younger, who contested Aquitaine rather effectively until 848 and then intermittently until his death in about 864. Secondly, he had to face the most systematic external attack, from Viking raiders. The Vikings in Francia and England were mainly from Denmark (Norwegian Vikings went mostly to Scotland and Ireland). They were standard war-bands of an early medieval type, on the scale of early Anglo-Saxon armies, although they were never as large as Frankish ones, even when they got bigger later in the century. They were private enterprises, in that they were not under the control of the kings of Denmark (at least, this is what the latter said when the Franks upbraided them, and it was plausible enough, given the limits on Danish royal strength: see Chapter 20). They were pagan, so were less inhibited than Christians about sacking churches, major wealth depositories, to the particular horror of ecclesiastical writers. And they were based on ships: this was the big difference from local Frankish border raiding, which was otherwise very similar, for it allowed the Vikings to hit and run, far up rivers into Francia, before any defence army arrived.

Major Viking raids began in 834, with an attack on the Rhine port of Dorestad; ship-owners were also merchants, and knew Dorestad well – as well as also knowing that the Frankish political system was busy in 834. They attacked Dorestad and, more widely, Frisia after that as well, and as early as 841 Dorestad was given in benefice by Lothar to Harald, a Danish royal family-member, and then to his younger brother Rorik. Rorik controlled much of Frisia, and defended it for the Franks more faithfully than not, for most of the period 845–75. Almost certainly as a result, Vikings seldom came further up the Rhine to bother Lothar's and Louis the German's heartlands, except for big raids in 881–3. Charles the Bald, however, had to face regular attacks on his long coastline, and up the Seine, Loire and Garonne, without a break from 841. Charles could never get rid of them; they were a permanent wound in his side. Vikings soon over-wintered at river-mouths as well. Charles alternately fought them off and bought them off with tribute (the least popular but most effective response); twice at the end of his reign he actually organized a general tax to pay them. Most effectively of all, perhaps, he fortified bridges over the Seine in 862 and the Loire in 873, to block their path. The major Viking push for fifteen years after 865 was into England, which eased the pressure on Francia a little in Charles's last years. But the Vikings never really went away.

The aura of military failure, or at least crisis, thus hung over Charles the Bald, and this must be one of the main reasons why he had greater difficulties with his aristocracy than did his brothers and nephews. Charles's anti-Lothar alliance with his brother Louis broke down in the 850s, and in 854 Louis the German's son Louis the Younger went to Aquitaine to test out the seriousness of invitations to his father by Aquitanian aristocrats. It turned out to be weak then, but by 858 disaffection was much stronger (it was a bad period in terms of Vikings, and Pippin the Younger had reappeared in Aquitaine), and numerous magnates, lay and ecclesiastical, were prepared to invite Louis the German in. Charles still had support, not least from Hincmar of Reims and most of his other bishops, and Louis retreated; but the episode showed the uncertainties Charles had to face. The pro-Louis group, which included the powerful Robert 'the Strong', count of Anjou (d. 866), who was from a major Rhineland imperial aristocratic family, the 'Rupertines' or 'Robertines', gave in, and retained their *honores*. Charles did not have to face a revolt like this again, but he had to negotiate with critical aristocrats on other occasions too, such as when, at the end of his reign, he occupied Italy (and took the imperial title) after the death of the son-less Louis II in 875, while simultaneously attacking in 876 – and losing – against Louis the Younger (876–82), who had succeeded his father in most of East Francia. Charles was trying to assert himself as the dominant Carolingian, without securing his base. Hincmar was furious, and several of Charles's magnates thought he was over-stretching himself. But Charles died in 877, and normal politics resumed.

Charles did remain hegemonic over his aristocracy. He built up the power-bases of his most useful *fideles*, such as Robert of Anjou, at least before 858, or Bernard marquis of Gothia, a new name for Septimania, who was his mainstay of support in the far south after 865. In particular, he patronized Boso (d. 887), brother of Charles's second wife Richildis, who was made chamberlain of his son Louis 'the Stammerer' in his new sub-kingdom of Aquitaine in 872, as well as count of Bourges and Vienne, and in 876 Charles's viceroy in Italy and husband of Louis II's only daughter, Ermingard. But he also removed *honores* from magnates at will, and moved them around; when Robert died in battle against the Vikings, his son Odo did not inherit Anjou, and lost others of Robert's counties in 868 – he did not return to royal favour until 882, when he became count of Paris. Similarly, Bernard of Gothia, who rebelled in 878 against Louis the Stammerer (king of West Francia 877–9), was summarily stripped of his lands and offices, and never got them back. Charles was generous with land; he gave out far more estates in full property than did other Carolingians, not just benefices; but he took them back as well with some ease.

Charles also threw himself into the complexities of Carolingian *correctio* and Carolingian ritual. He developed his palace of Compiègne as another Aachen, including its buildings; he created some original ceremonial, as when he hosted a month-long synod at Ponthion in June–July 876, after his imperial coronation, wearing Frankish costume at the start but Byzantine costume plus a crown at the end. Imperial echoes were already visible in the most substantial of his many capitularies, the 864 Edict of Pîtres, which draws substantially on the *Theodosian Code* (as well as, explicitly, on Ansegis). Charles was as concerned for administrative refinement as was his father; Pîtres, for example, also involved a coinage reform, which coin-hoards show to have been effectively implemented. His *missi* still ran as in Charlemagne's day. And Charles had a court almost as full of intellectuals as Charlemagne's, including Hincmar of Reims, who wrote much of his legislation and was always at hand for advice, wanted or not, as well as writing some of the longest political tracts of his generation, and twenty years of the *Annals of Saint-Bertin*. The core of Charles's ruling was not undermined, for all his military difficulties; and his ambition as a reformer was more elaborate than any other Carolingian after 840. Even Charles the Bald, then, despite many problems, remained on top of his kingdom in most respects, in different ways from Louis the German and Louis II of Italy, but with a similar result. The Carolingian project was still in operation into the late 870s.

But it did not last a decade more. In 887–8 the empire broke up into five kingdoms, with six or seven claimants, only one of whom was a male-line Carolingian. This was seen as an end even by contemporaries, as a takeover by *reguli*, 'kinglets', as the *Annals of Fulda* put it. Historians have understandably sought long-term explanations for it, mostly in the 'rise' and growing autonomy of major aristocratic families, for it was these who provided the new kings of 888, the 'Robertine' Odo of Paris in West Francia, the 'Widonid' Guy of Spoleto in West Francia and then Italy, Boso's son Louis in Provence, the 'Unruoching' Berengar of Friuli in Italy, and the 'Welf' Rudolf, from Queen Judith's family, in Burgundy. All these were however families very close to the Carolingians, linked by marriage in the last three cases (Louis and Berengar had Carolingian mothers). Only one of them, too, had any serious track record of disloyalty: Boso, who broke with the whole Carolingian tradition in 879 and declared himself king in the Rhône valley (he only lasted until 882 as king, for all the Carolingians combined against him). The others show no signs of seeking power on their own account until the 887–8 crisis itself, which forced them onto the centre stage.

What destroyed Carolingian power was simply genealogy. There had always been too many Carolingians, given the presumption of political division the family had inherited from the Merovingian past. Rulers had developed methods of excluding minor branches from succession, either by force (as with Carloman I's son Drogo, or Pippin of Italy's son Bernard) or by agreement (as with Adalard and Wala, who were content to be major players in their cousin's court, or Bernard of Italy's son Pippin, count of Beauvais, who effectively turned into a regional aristocrat; his heirs were the central medieval counts of Champagne), or through a growing concern to exclude illegitimate children. Even then, there were still a large number of them; as late as 870 there were eight legitimate adult male Carolingians, all kings or ambitious to become kings. In 885, however, there was only one. None of Lothar's sons had legitimate male heirs; nor did Louis the German's; Charles the Bald's son Louis had three, but two were dead by 884 and the third, Charles 'the Simple', born posthumously, was only eight in 887. One by one, as the Carolingians died in the 880s, Louis the German's last surviving son Charles 'the Fat', king of Alemannia (876–87, emperor 881) inherited their kingdoms, until he reunited the whole empire in 884 for the first time since 840.

Charles the Fat has had a bad press. This is and was linked to some over-pragmatic showings against the Vikings, as when Odo of Paris fought off a big siege in 885–6, but Charles paid them to go away; and is coloured above all by hindsight, for he was overthrown by his illegitimate nephew Arnulf in 887, a few weeks before his death in 888. Charles was more able than this implies. But everybody must have known that the world was likely to change, for Charles was ill, and himself had only an illegitimate son, Bernard. (Boso indeed must have seen it coming in 879: most of these genealogical problems were by then predictable.) Lothar II had spent most of his reign trying to legitimate his illegitimate son Hugh, and failing, as we shall see in the next chapter; Charles the Fat had no rivals, but even he could not make Bernard his legal heir. Hugh, who had visible royal ambitions, was caught by Charles and blinded in 885; this, and also Arnulf's succession, means that Bernard could well have tried to succeed anyway (he did rebel against Arnulf, and was killed, in 891), but Charles did not change the rules fast enough to make illegitimate sons normal royal heirs. Instead, he tried in 887 to divorce his wife Richgard, as Lothar II had also tried, so that he could remarry and aim for legitimate sons; it was then that Arnulf, who had previously been kept away from central power on the Carinthian borderlands of eastern Bavaria, staged his coup and took the East Frankish throne. This coup made the decisions of the most powerful aristocrats of the other sections of the empire easier; Arnulf had some standing in West Francia, Burgundy and Italy, but his genealogical claims did not seem so strong to most political actors outside the eastern kingdom, and someone had to rule. When they did, they varied in their effectiveness; but they did not use most of the Carolingian political practices discussed in this chapter.

More important than the 'rise' of an aristocracy was its growing regionalization. This, paradoxically, was a reflection of royal power. Kings could confiscate benefices and offices, *honores*, and aristocrats feared this. We saw this in Einhard's letters in the 830s; Nithard in the 840s is still clearer, for the whole of 840–41 was a phoney war in which Lothar and Charles prowled around each other trying to tempt followers from each other by promises, threats and an appearance of future success, which would be convincing enough to persuade worried aristocrats to tolerate losing *honores* temporarily in order to gain more later. Louis the German's failed move into Charles's kingdom in 858 was similarly structured. Each king who did this hoped for a catalytic change that would bring all a rival's followers running in, as at the Field of Lies in 833; this seldom happened (887 is the only parallel), so what happened instead was usually that the followers of one king lost *honores* in the lands of the other. They were more likely to keep the land they held in full property, as Matfrid of Orléans did in the case of his family land in northern Francia when he followed Lothar to Italy in 834, or as a group of aristocrats in East Francia did in 861 when Louis the German abruptly expelled them from power. This land could remain very widely spread, as in the case of the 'Unruoching' Everard marquis of Friuli in Italy (the father of Berengar, future king of Italy, 888–924), whose will of 863–4, made with his wife Gisela, disposes between his sons and daughters of a book collection and rich treasures, but also estates stretching from Italy up through Alemannia to what is now Belgium. Such wide spreads favoured support for a single political system, as has already been noted for the 'Widonids'. But Everard and Gisela gave at least their younger sons more geographically restricted territories; they also included explicit provisions for what might happen if political tension made it necessary to divide this land up further. The family regionalized itself as a result; Berengar's brother Rudolf (d. 892) spent his career, not in Italy, but in Artois and on the English Channel. Similarly, the 'Welfs', whose lands lay both in Alemannia and in Burgundy, had to choose between Charles and Louis in 858; it may possibly be that those who chose Charles kept some of their properties in East Francia, but henceforth their careers would be entirely restricted to Burgundy, and their history became totally separate from that of their brothers and cousins who stayed with Louis. The tensions between the Carolingians, that is to say, persuaded prudent imperial aristocrats that it was sensible to have both their *honores* and their properties in one kingdom, not widely scattered as they had been since Charlemagne's time. As kingdoms became smaller, this would become still truer.

Aristocrats always wanted to leave all their power-bases – fully owned properties, benefices, rights over monasteries, counties – to their sons. This was only assured for their properties, but already in Charlemagne's time a loyal aristocrat could assume that his son might well inherit his county. The county of Paris, for example, was probably held by a single family between the 750s and the 850s; kings restricted themselves to choosing which heir took it over. The sons of Louis the Pious actually moved counts around more than their father and grandfather had, but all the Carolingians recognized that the sons of counts should normally get a county *somewhere*, and as the geography of practical politics contracted it might well be that this might be in or near their father's county or counties. The sons of counts sometimes actually feuded against men who were given their father's counties, as happened on the Bavarian eastern frontier in 882–4, admittedly a marginal and somewhat wild area. The memory of former power lingered too; Odo of Paris got some of his father's Loire counties back in 886, a full twenty years after his father's death – and very usefully timed, given his takeover of the West Frankish throne in 888. This further aided the process of regionalization. Odo's father Robert had moved without difficulty from the Rhineland to the Loire in the 840s, when long-distance career moves were still normal, but the 'Welf' move to Burgundy in 858 was more controversial, and after that such shifts were rare, or else resented as the irruptions of outsiders. (Perhaps only Boso, who moved from Lotharingia to the Rhône valley and Italy, is a counter-example, but he was a queen's brother, and anyway a mould-breaker in other ways too.) When Charles the Fat inherited seven separate kingdoms, separate political power networks visibly continued to operate in most or all of them; by now, it would have taken a Charles Martel-style war to unify them, and Charles the Fat did not have time for that. They went their separate ways again in 888. These were, genuinely, long-term causes for the break-up of the empire. They did not make that break-up more likely, but they made it possible, once the Carolingians died off. By then, a sense of empire-wide identity was attached only to the Carolingian family (and, not to be underrated, its army-muster). But aristocratic networks were prepared for a new regionalized politics; which was fortunate, for it was this which faced them now.

17
Intellectuals and Politics

Early in the morning in late January 828, Einhard met Hilduin of Saint-Denis sitting outside Louis the Pious's bedchamber in Aachen, waiting for the emperor to get up. This was Hilduin's job; as imperial arch-chaplain, he formally controlled access to Louis. But Einhard had come to see Hilduin. They chatted while looking out of the high window into the rest of the palace, perhaps the window which Notker in the 880s would claim that Charlemagne had built so that he could see what was going on everywhere (see above, Chapter 10). Einhard had a bone to pick with Hilduin, however.

Hilduin had in 826 initiated a fashion for buying relics from Rome, acquiring the body of St Sebastian for one of his monasteries, Saint-Médard at Soissons. In 827 Einhard had imitated him, with the help of a professional thief and dealer, the Roman deacon Deusdona, and had sent his own notary Ratleig to steal the bodies of Sts Marcellinus and Peter from their tomb on the Via Labicana outside Rome and bring them north. After Ratleig crossed the Alps, he no longer had to hide them, and in a public procession, in front of crowds of bystanders, he brought them to central Germany, where most of Einhard's properties were. He took them to their destined church in Einhard's planned retirement home of Michelstadt in the Odenwald forest; but the saints did not like it there, and demanded in dreams that they be transferred to Einhard's other church at Seligenstadt near Frankfurt, which Einhard duly arranged. Healing miracles began when he did, and had continued without a break, often in great numbers, up to when Einhard wrote his account of these events in late 830. But Hilduin's servant Hunus, who had gone to Rome with Ratleig, had stolen from him some of St Marcellinus; and when Einhard met Hilduin the rumour had already spread that Hilduin had both bodies at Saint-Médard. The rumour was almost worse than the fact, for Einhard's reputation and that of his own relics; Einhard had to get them back. Hilduin admitted he had Marcellinus, rather grudgingly (one must note that Einhard was writing this account after Hilduin's fall from power in October 830). The relics were brought from Soissons to Aachen, and Einhard received them in April 828. There, they certainly reversed the rumours, for, in a sense thanks to Hilduin, Einhard's relics were now in the centre of the empire; they were (Einhard says) met by crowds, and Louis and Queen Judith themselves visited them and gave them gifts. Miracles began again, and continued after Einhard rejoined both sets of relics at Seligenstadt at the end of the year. Einhard made the most of it; Marcellinus took a long route home to his fellow saint. Soon after Easter, as Einhard happily records, his friend the palace librarian Gerward was staying outside town, and was told the palace news: 'At present the courtiers are mostly talking about the signs and miracles happening in Einhard's house by means of the saints . . .' It must have been one of the high points of his life.

This account foregrounds the importance of the palace, the import-ance of public ritual, and the importance of intellectuals, in the Carolin-gian political world, for Einhard was the biographer of Charlemagne and had been a mainstay of court society for three decades by now, and Hilduin was no minor scholar: in 828 he had just painstakingly trans-lated a Greek text, the works of St Dionysios (that is, St Denis), sent by the Byzantine emperor Michael II to Louis, into Latin. In this chapter we shall look at these three issues in turn, and then at some of their implications.

The royal or imperial palace, whether at Aachen or elsewhere, was the core political centre of the Carolingian lands, a whirl of activity – and noise, as Paschasius Radbert's *Life* of Adalard of Corbie complains. Every political actor had to go there when called, which in Einhard's case was often, just as every victim seeking royal justice had to come there, to be interrogated by the arch-chaplain or the count of the palace to see if the king needed to get involved. As usual with the Carolingians, this was a Merovingian tradition writ large, and also systematized. Hincmar's (or Adalard's) *On the Organization of the Palace* can list the palace officials, headed by the arch-chaplain (in charge of church affairs) and the arch-chancellor (in charge of the writing office), in order, down to the hunters and the falconer, and there are consistent indications that this was a real hierarchy – although it could always be modified, as when Bernard of Septimania, as chamberlain in 829–30 (in charge of the palace commissariat under the queen, and fourth-ranking official, according to Hincmar/Adalard) was seen as 'second to the king' after Louis. Notker, although he never went to court, could imagine that the palace hierarchy was preserved in dining etiquette, with Charlemagne served by dukes, dukes served by counts and aristocrats, and so on down through court scholars, and greater and lesser palace officials. The court certainly had an ever-changing etiquette of behaviour, which no aspiring politician could risk not knowing. And it had an organized, explicit, patronage network. Hincmar/Adalard even supposed – certainly over-schematically – that officials were deliberately appointed from different regions, so that everyone could use a kinsman or at least someone from their locality to facilitate access to the palace. Notker imagined that, at the death of a bishop, all aspiring applicants put their names forward through those closest to the emperor. Einhard, although never (it seems) a palace official in a formal sense, routinely acted as a patron, and he is seen in his letters requesting the kings, either directly or through current office-holders, to approve the appointment of an archbishop or an abbot, or the renewal of a benefice, or simply to hear an appeal. This was a competitive and often unscrupulous world of favours, structured by court procedures.

The palace was thus a worldly (and corrupt, and vicious) political hub. But it was also the moral centre of the empire, particularly once, after 780 or so, Charlemagne embraced the task of moral *correctio*. It was not chance that the senior Carolingian palace official handled church affairs: these were the court's special concern. Louis the Pious was a priest even more than he was a king, at least in that he promoted religious learning, according to one of his biographers. Charlemagne instituted penitential fasting at court, as we saw at the start of the last chapter, which he extended to the entire empire in 805 to combat a famine; Louis did the same in 823 in the face of dangerous portents. The seventh-century Irish tract *On the Twelve Abuses of the World* circulated very widely in Carolingian Europe, and Abuse 9, 'the unjust king', argues that if kings were oppressive and unjust, and if they did not defend the church, then famine, invasion and ruin would follow. A succession of ninth-century writers composed treatises for kings on just rule, culminating in Hincmar's *On the Person and Ministry of the King*, and most of them quoted Abuse 9, alongside, at great length, the Old Testament. They held that the king should start with controlling himself and his own behaviour, before he could properly govern others, through law and its enforcement. The whole empire was at risk if he did not. The king/emperor could appoint his bishops (this right was never contested in the Carolingian period), but they, conversely, were responsible for policing the moral world, and that included royal actions, both private and public. Bishops often took this role very seriously, particularly in the crisis years of 829–34 and the civil war period of 840–43, when the public good was obviously threatened.

The political and the moral roles of the palace did not have to be in contradiction. The secular and the spiritual could be seen to work in much the same way. Einhard regarded Sts Marcellinus and Peter as his spiritual patrons in just the same way as the emperors were his secular patrons, and his heartbreak over the death of his wife Imma in 836 was only worsened by the realization that his spiritual patrons had failed him, in not answering his prayers. Thus at moments of crisis the Carolingian world could lay itself open to moral panics. Given the high political profile of queens, the permanent ambiguity of female power and the new emphasis on personal morality, it is not surprising that many of these panics centred on queenly sexuality. Charlemagne's daughters, who ran his palace in his last years, were accused of fornication in 814 (as was Charlemagne himself). Judith was accused of adultery with Bernard in 830, an accusation which recurs in every account of the period, favourable or hostile – it must have been a very high-profile charge – and which was theorized by Paschasius Radbert in the 850s as marking a total reversal of the right order of the world, a sign above all that Louis the Pious, who could not control his palace, was not fit to govern. Lothar II accused his wife Theutberga of sodomy and incest (see below); Charles the Fat his wife Richgard of adultery with, again, his principal counsellor, Bishop Liutward of Vercelli; Arnulf's wife Uota was accused of adultery too. It would be wrong to see these accusations, doubtless all false except the first, as signs that the political role of queens was under threat: it was their high profile, not their weakness, that exposed them to criticism. The Merovingian tradition of powerful queen-mothers was less in evidence in the Carolingian period, for few rulers were children at their accession (there would be more of them in the late tenth century); but Carolingian queens were more prominent during their husbands' lives than their Merovingian predecessors had been. Conversely, except when rulers themselves sought (perhaps unwisely) to use queenly impurity as an excuse for divorce, all these accusations had as their primary target, not the queen but the king/ emperor, whose capacities as a corrector of his people were thus cruelly exposed. Control, or the appearance of control, was necessary at all times.

Both harmony and tension were mediated by elaborate rituals, whether regular (as with the ceremonial associated with assemblies or Easter celebrations), or specific to the occasion. Einhard when he first brought his saints to Seligenstadt prepared 'those things that ritual stipulates for the reception of saints' bodies', and then performed two masses. When he got St Marcellinus back from Hilduin, the latter organized a choir to chant an antiphon; Einhard's party then proceeded, chanting, to his own chapel, which attracted a large crowd; when he joined the bodies again in Seligenstadt, he again prepared the process carefully. According to his own account, that is, and this is important: for ritual was always a means of self-presentation (Einhard wanted to make sure that no one could doubt the saints were his and that they were properly treated), and different observers could read different things into it. One of the most elaborate secular rituals that expressed kingliness and royal order was regular hunting; it recurs with almost obsessive frequency in the annals of Louis the Pious's reign, for example, especially after major events, and it is significant that Louis is said by Einhard to have gone hunting just after he had seen the latter's relics in 828. It is interesting, then, that the *Annals of Saint-Bertin* do not mention hunts in 830–34; it is not that Louis did not hunt then (one of his biographers explicitly says he did in 831 and 834), but rather that a ritual of order did not seem appropriate to the annalist in a period of crisis, even though Louis was presumably himself trying to present 831, for example, as business as usual. Louis's two penances, in 822 and 833, were particularly prone to be read in different ways. In 822 at Attigny he performed a voluntary penance whose orchestration he controlled, to cauterize the wound caused by the death of Bernard of Italy; but did this really end the matter? In 833 Bernard's death was as fresh as ever in the indictment proposed by Lothar's bishops; it is as if Attigny had not occurred. Paschasius Radbert, for his part, in his *Life* of Adalard, could not ignore Attigny, for it had brought Adalard back to court, but he contested how in control of the ritual Louis really was: 'all contemplated his willingness and perceived his unwillingness.' Louis had gone out on a limb in 822, probably with success at the time, but hindsight and hostility could see it as failure, and as leading directly to Louis's deposition penance in 833. The latter, in an interesting reversal, was written up as voluntary by Louis's enemies, but as forced and therefore invalid by his friends.

Every major event in the Carolingian period, whether involving ritual or not, was written up by writers to make political points of this type; they either upheld or subverted the correct order of the empire. This means that it is, often enough, impossible to enter in detail into what 'really' happened. But what is abundantly clear is that the ninth century was a period in which the ceremonial terrain – the public sphere, one could say (the Carolingians used the word *publicus* extensively) – was particularly wide and important. It was terrain which had to be claimed by every political actor, even though he (or she) could not fully control the perceptions of the audience of each ritual act, given that it was the audience who would ultimately determine whether the act worked properly or not. There always had to be a process of negotiation. This is why, for example, Charles the Bald at the 876 Ponthion synod, which was largely devoted to ecclesiastical court cases, ended the proceedings with an elaborate procedure intended to make real to the Franks the fact that he was now the emperor: he wore Byzantine costume and a crown, as we saw in the previous chapter, then papal legates went to fetch Queen Richildis with her own crown, and then the same legates performed the closing liturgy. Did this work? Hincmar, who wrote this up for the *Annals of Saint-Bertin*, was greatly hostile to most of the decisions of the synod, but he was clearly impressed by the ritual: he was himself the writer of elaborate coronation rituals, and he could understand the internal structure and the roots of this one. The Fulda annalist, anyway opposed to Charles, and also writing in East Francia, where much less was known about the Byzantine empire, dismissed Charles's 'Greek customs' in two lines; but it was men like Hincmar who were Charles's intended audience, not the Frankish East, and for them this ritual had a considerable success.

This large and moralized political arena was also populated by intellectuals, at least three generations of them after Charlemagne began to patronize them in the 780s. It is this group of (in nearly every case) men which really characterizes the Carolingian period as different from its predecessors; in other respects, the politico-cultural world of the sixth to early eighth centuries was still fully operative. The importance of intellectuals for the political practice of the ninth-century West was as great as or greater than it would ever be again in the Middle Ages, and the ninth century matched the French Revolution as a focus for collective intellectual political activity. This did not make political actors behave better, of course, but it greatly increased the range of the excuses and self-justifications for bad behaviour, which also mark out the period. To have had an education was, simply, enough for prominence. It is not that aristocrats did not sneer at the low-born, as with Louis the Pious's biographer Thegan's highly coloured hostility to Archbishop Ebbo of Reims for his servile birth (Thegan claims), or with Liutward of Vercelli, who was compared to the biblical villain Haman by one of the Fulda annalists; both ended their political careers in disgrace, too – Ebbo was one of the few people to face punishment for having supported Lothar in 833–4. Neither of these, all the same, was a major writer. Education and intelligence, however, linked Einhard and the poet and liturgist Walahfrid Strabo, whose backgrounds were relatively undistinguished, with genuine aristocrats such as Hraban Maur, Hincmar, or the theologian Gottschalk (d. c. 869: Walahfrid's friend, but Hraban's and Hincmar's enemy), as well as, of course, incomers from England, Ireland or Spain, with no roots in the Frankish lands, from Alcuin and Theodulf at the start of the Carolingian period to the theologian John the Scot (d. c. 877) at the end.

Part of this sense of collectivity derived from being educated together, at Aachen itself or Tours or Corbie or St. Gallen or Fulda (where Einhard, Hraban, Walahfrid and Gottschalk had all been trained) or any of two dozen other active centres. Much of it, however, was because such writers had a communality of knowledge, of the Bible, canon law, Virgil, Augustine, Gregory the Great, Isidore, Bede, and the rest of the Latin church fathers: they knew what they were each talking about. And they could assume that their peers did too; as we have seen, aristocrats had to be literate to be able to operate politically in this period. Hincmar could write highly erudite texts for Charles the Bald and expect him to pick up the allusions; Charles sought books on his own behalf as well, as when Lupus abbot of Ferrières (d. 862), one of his most loyal scholars, sent him a sermon of Augustine against perjury. Aristocrats had libraries;

Marquis Everard of Friuli's 863–4 will had bibles, biblical commentaries, several law books (including, probably, one Lupus had collected for him), works by Vegetius, Augustine and Isidore, several saints' lives, two or three histories, and more. Most of these books were not ninth-century texts, but they attest to the same interests that our ninth-century writers demonstrably had. There was a common intellectual community, which extended a long way beyond the writers of the period.

This community could sustain some quite elaborate theoretical interventions. Late in 828 Louis the Pious called four church councils for the following year, in Mainz, Paris, Lyon and Toulouse, to discuss the 'anger of God' – some unspecified natural disaster – and how he could be placated. According to Paschasius Radbert's *Epitaph of Arsenius* (an often obscure biography, in dialogue form, of Wala), this involved specific requests for advice. Wala duly responded with a *schedula*, which he formally presented in one of the 829 councils: this seems to have criticized uncanonical episcopal elections and the lay control of church lands. Interestingly, Einhard presented a pamphlet of *capitula* to Louis at almost the same moment, and it is very likely to have been in response to the same generalized request for opinions. We do not have these, but we do have the summary of a similar pamphlet composed in Einhard's circle around the same time, which denounces oppression and the full range of standard sins, in particular hatred and mistrust, a generic enough set of misdeeds it is true, and maybe less useful to Louis, but certainly heartfelt on Einhard's part. In a bizarre framing, he attributes the second critique to the demon Wiggo, speaking through the mouth of a possessed girl, and the *capitula* to none other than the archangel Gabriel, appearing in a dream (in the guise of St Marcellinus) to a blind man, recently cured at Seligenstadt. Louis's decision to open up debate allowed criticism to come from some unusual sources.

We must not overstate the success of this sort of discursive initiative. Einhard remarks sorrowfully that 'of the things that [Louis] was ordered or urged to do by this small book he took the trouble to fulfil very few'. The 829 council of Paris listed many things that the Frankish people and king could and should do as well, but what Louis actually did was appoint Bernard of Septimania as chamberlain, a cure worse than the disease to most observers. Wala (though not Einhard) went over to the other side, and, together with Paschasius, was in Lothar's camp at the Field of Lies; but Louis's temporary overthrow was not reassuring

to Wala at all. Paschasius' account portrays himself and Wala dumb-
struck at the ease with which Louis's army melted away: 'they had flown
completely around, like chickens under wing . . . without serious counsel
and careful arrangement . . .' and, worst of all, without listening to
Wala's advice! Aristocrats were not taking it seriously enough, that is
to say; they were simply engaging in politics, without considering its
moral implications. It would be a common moan of intellectuals at later
times of political change as well. All the same, scholars elaborated both
sides of the key ceremonies of 833–4: Agobard of Lyon drafted part of
the core accusations against Louis in his forced penance of 833; after
Louis's restoration the emperor had his own version of the 833–4 crisis
written down by his bishops and abbots, and formally read out at
the Thionville assembly in 835; meanwhile, Hraban Maur in 834 had
written a tract on the duties of sons, which Louis reprised in instructions
sent to Lothar in Italy in 836. Whether or not magnates were governed
above all by realpolitik, they felt a strong need to express their political
choices in moralized terms, and writers sought to argue about them as
a result. Nithard, Lupus and then Hincmar would do the same for
Charles the Bald later as well.

Did the increasingly elaborate education of Carolingian élites aim to be
inclusive, or exclusive? It is not wholly clear. The more complex the
Latin used by the educated strata, the further it departed from the
Romance spoken by the huge majority of the population of the western
and southern parts of the empire; the earliest form of French came to be
seen as a separate language for the first time by authors precisely in the
Carolingian period. And a high percentage of the Carolingian élite spoke
German; ninth-century texts for the first time regularly describe people
as bilingual, including Charlemagne, Louis the Pious and Wala, which
implies that plenty of people were not. (Einhard was most struck by the
fact that the demon Wiggo spoke Latin, for the girl he possessed only
spoke German.) It might be that the complex Latin of our texts was only
a court and clerical language, a 'mandarin' language, pronounced in an
increasingly un-French way because of the influence of the Anglo-Saxon
Alcuin, and therefore deliberately closed to most people, including even
most aristocrats. But at least among the aristocracy there is good evidence of a wider awareness of Latin than that. Lupus of Ferrières could
be trained for several years at Fulda in the 830s without ever having to

learn German; Latin was totally hegemonic in this large monastic school in the middle of Germany, which had lay students too. Everard's books show what an aristocrat might read or at least listen to (many would read less today), and it is notable that he expected his daughters, who inherited some of them, to do so as well: Judith was given some Augustine, some Alcuin, and the Lombard law code. And Dhuoda, down in Uzès, clearly shows in her *Handbook* someone who has bought the whole Carolingian package: not only had she read the Bible, some church fathers and some Christian Latin literature, but she could manipulate it with sophistication. It may have been wasted on her son William (see below, Chapter 21), but its very survival implies that he kept her text by him. Dhuoda is seen as being from the high *Reichsaristokratie* because she was married in 824 to Bernard of Septimania, in Aachen, too; but, given the striking absence of her own kin among the lists of relatives she thought William should pray for, one might wonder about that. Either way, a dense literary education was available to a lay woman by 810 or so, only twenty-five years after Carolingian schooling started, which, given the patriarchal values of the period, must surely mean that it was normal for aristocratic men, and not necessarily just the top families either.

Conversely, this was, overall, overwhelmingly an élite affair. The Carolingians did sometimes contemplate general schooling, but they did not seriously develop it. Similarly, there were some efforts to translate the Bible into German (though certainly not into proto-French), but they did not get past Genesis and the Gospels, for the most part in poetic versions. Indeed, the wide peasant world was hardly in the field of vision of any Carolingian king or intellectual except for preaching (a genuine commitment, but one which only reached a minority), or else as a source of wonder at ignorance, as in Agobard of Lyon's exasperated attack on local beliefs in weather magic. Too great a separation would be an exaggeration; Agobard also inveighed against the idiocy of widespread beliefs that a cattle plague had been caused by malign dust sent by Prince Grimoald IV of Benevento, but a chance remark of Paschasius Radbert shows that Corbie intellectuals had been panicked by that too. Similarly, Einhard's descriptions of the miracles and visions of Sts Marcellinus and Peter and their popular reception show no break at all between his sensibilities and those of the peasants around Seligenstadt. Education did not separate people from the religious culture around them, which did not fundamentally change from the sixth century to the tenth (above, Chapter 8). But the imagery of *correctio* and the need for education was confined to the aristocracy and to clerics, the political actors. Local priests, growing in number in this period as more rural churches were founded, were the lowest down the social scale it even theoretically reached. There are some signs (for example, in the signatures to Italian documents) that these priests could at least write, and bishops certainly expected them to be basically educated, often in a cathedral school. But even the common assumption in church statutes that priests would know the Psalter was not necessarily true of the majority, and little detailed control of their daily activities and culture was in practice possible; most priests came from local élites, and their social networks were linked to their localities, not to the bishops who sought to command them. The Carolingian project reached local societies through the structures of public justice, not through those of moral reform.

The educated, political world was nonetheless dense and many lev-elled, even if it only included élites. The court of Charlemagne, at the start of the process, saw legislation, theology, biblical commentary and poetry written; under Louis and his sons, the genres of educated writing increased further, with works on liturgy, history and political theory as well. These were sought after. Hraban Maur, the great biblical commen-tator of the 820s–850s, dedicated his (rather daunting) books to queens and kings, including a commentary on the *Book of Judith* sent to Queen Judith in the key year of 834. The Carolingian world also copied enor-mous quantities of texts, usually patristic writings but also including pre-Christian Latin works (these were only a small proportion of Carolingian copying, but it is because of that proportion that most classical Latin literature survives). Scholars wrote to each other begging for texts to copy; a dozen of Lupus of Ferrières's letters in the 830s–850s are requests for books, some very specific, like the letter to Pope Benedict III (855–8) asking for the commentary of Jerome on Jeremiah 'starting with the seventh book and continuing to the end' – for many texts were defective or corrupt, and intellectuals sought both to complete them and to find the best versions. They were helped by a technical advance, the fast and easy-to-read Caroline minuscule script, which won out over older cursive hands in the late eighth century and had become uniform across most of the empire by the early ninth. Libraries of laymen could reach fifty books, as was the case with Everard of Friuli, but the larger monastic libraries could have hundreds, many of them containing more than one work. This added to the sense of the communality of culture, for writers in the different parts of the empire could increasingly assume that they had the same texts to hand.

This was the essential context for the growing importance of theological debate. This is already visible in the 790s, for Carolingian political circles were then flustered by the discovery of Adoptionism, the first new western heresy for nearly four centuries, associated with two Spanish bishops, Elipand of Toledo and Felix of Urgell (it used the image of adoption of the Son by the Father to explain Christ's humanity). They also reacted very negatively to the Byzantine repudiation of Iconoclasm at Nicaea in 787 (above, Chapter 11). Carolingian theologians did not have full access to the Byzantine debate, and did not understand its principles (Greek was relatively little known in Carolingian Francia), but the continuing status of Byzantine theology ensured attention to the issue, and Theodulf of Orléans, in the *Libri Carolini*, wrote a detailed condemnation of the veneration of religious images in 790–93. The synod of Frankfurt in 794 formally rejected both doctrines, and Alcuin wrote at length against Adoptionism in 800, to match the work of his rival Theodulf. These were, emphatically, not widespread disagreements; it would be surprising if there were more than a dozen Adoptionists in the Carolingian lands (outside the ex-Visigothic far south), or hardline Iconoclasts for that matter. But they mattered to the state, and also to theorists. Theodulf took the trouble to create an Iconoclast pictorial programme for the apse of his private chapel at Germigny-des-Prés near Orléans, which still survives (see Chapter 10), and Iconoclast theorists (mostly from Spain) argued into the 820s, with Bishop Claudius of Turin going so far as to attack pilgrimages, and the veneration of the cross and of relics, as idolatrous – this went too far, however, and seems to have brought him condemnation in his turn.

Carolingian thought never claimed to be novel; in fact, like most late Roman, Byzantine and central medieval thought, it was explicitly the opposite, the return to older authority, often cited at great length. But Charlemagne and Alcuin made it possible for a critical mass of intellectuals to accumulate in Aachen and argue, and this took theology and political thought off in new directions whether writers liked (or realized) it or not. The 'virtual' community of the great monastic and cathedral schools of the ninth century, all in communication with each other,

16. The crypt at Jouarre near Paris; the sarcophagi are for a Frankish aristocratic family of the seventh century. The crypt was rebuilt later, but the capitals are seventh-century too.

17. Offa's Dyke, a late eighth-century defensive earthwork separating central England from Wales, built under the orders of King Offa of Mercia.

18. The city walls of Barcelona; the large stones in the centre are a Roman section of the walls, surviving in the later medieval walling.

19. The ninth-century house recently excavated in the Forum of Nerva in the forum area of Rome (the classical forum is behind). Note the colonnaded courtyard at the right, and a window-sill, indicating a second storey, above the colonnade arch to the left.

20. The seventh-century walls of the citadel of Ankara, Turkey. The line of circles to the right of the gate are reused classical columns, for decorative effect.

21. A street in the city of Scythopolis (Bet Shean, Israel), showing the columns of the colonnade which collapsed on the street in the earthquake of 749.

22. The Byzantine emperor Basil II (d. 1025) in a contemporary manuscript. Basil, under God and crowned by archangels, dominates his subjects, prostrate before him.

23. The Frankish emperor Louis the Pious (d. 840) in a contemporary manuscript. He wears a Roman military costume, and a dedicatory poem by Hraban Maur is written across the image. Several contemporary copies survive.

24. Brixworth church (Northamptonshire), the largest surviving Anglo-Saxon church, dated to the early ninth century. The spire is later.

25. The Jelling runestone, set up by King Harald Bluetooth of Denmark for his father Gorm in the mid-tenth century. Harald was Christian, but the imagery of the stone is not.

26. St Sophia in Kiev, built by Byzantine craftsmen for the newly Christian princes of Kiev in the early eleventh century. It is the best-preserved Byzantine church surviving for the period, although situated in Ukraine.

27. The castle of Canossa in the Emilian Appennines, Italy. It was a major centre of the Canossa family, one of Italy's leading aristocratic families around and after 1000.

28. The palace of Ramiro I of Asturias (d. 850), at Oviedo in northern Spain. Soon a church, it seems to have been built as a secular hall, probably separate from the palace proper.

29. A peasant ploughing and a man (doubtless a lord) being served food at a table, in the early ninth-century Utrecht Psalter. The picture illustrates Psalm 103, which celebrates the world in its right order.

continued that critical mass. And the importance of theory to the political élite kept debate in the public eye, doubtless encouraging it further. People made very individual choices sometimes, like the deacon Bodo, a court scholar, who in 839 converted to Judaism and fled to Spain, to the horror of Louis the Pious and his courtiers. And every so often writers went outside the bounds of debate, and were condemned at church councils, as Amalarius of Metz was at Quierzy in 839 for his views on the liturgy, or as Gottschalk was at Mainz in 848 and Quierzy in 849 for his views on predestination (a condemnation which, significantly, was referred to in the *Annals* both of Fulda and of Saint-Bertin). These deserve some attention.

Amalarius of Metz (d. 850), successively archbishop of Trier and Lyon, was the main liturgical expert of the early ninth century, and was intermittently patronized by both Charlemagne and Louis. Out of office in the 820s, he wrote the *Liber Officialis*, a detailed exegesis of the allegorical significance of every act of the liturgy, which he circulated widely and revised in response to queries, criticisms and new information from Rome, three times in the next decade or so. This brought him back to royal and episcopal attention, and when Agobard was expelled from Lyon in 835 for supporting Lothar, Amalarius was appointed to replace him. This good luck was also bad luck, for Lyon seems to have been solidly behind Agobard, and Florus of Lyon, the major scholar left in the city, already thought that Amalarius' allegories were ridiculous insults to the intelligence. Allegory was only supposed to be applied to the Bible, the word of God, which liturgical practices were not; and some of Amalarius' attempts at symbolic meanings were simply bizarre – indeed, maybe heretical. Both Agobard and Florus wrote tracts against Amalarius, savagely pointing out his errors. This was why he was called to Quierzy in 838, to answer this criticism and to justify his arguments by authority. Amalarius replied that 'whatever I have written I have read deep within my own spirit' – in other words, he had no authority. This was fatal; he was condemned for heresy and was himself expelled from Lyon, although his works continued to circulate widely (the liturgy did, after all, still need explication).

Gottschalk was a more serious scholar; he was trying to make sense of Augustine's theology of predestination, which he certainly did through appeal to authority, but which he interpreted in a novel way: that humans could separately be predestined to salvation and damnation, and that Christ's crucifixion only affected the former, not the latter. Even after his condemnations in 848–9, this split the intellectual world of the 840s and 850s. Florus, Ratramn of Corbie, Prudentius of Troyes and Lupus of Ferrières supported Gottschalk, at least to some extent; Hincmar and Hraban vehemently opposed him. So did John the Scot, though his tract on the subject was itself controversial. The debate spun out of control in the 850s, and at least five church councils came to different views on it, until Charles the Bald and Lothar II together put a stop to it in 860, with a rejection of some of Gottschalk's key positions at the synod of Tusey. As with Amalarius, an apparently arcane disagreement became the stuff of high politics; Francia briefly became the eastern Roman empire of Nicaea and Chalcedon, when correct doctrine was crucial for the stability of the state.

The political resonance of Amalarius' condemnation was a simple one: he was both beneficiary and victim of the aftershocks of 833–4. When he was dismissed from Lyon, indeed, Agobard was called back, and it is hard not to feel that Amalarius might have had a different experience at Quierzy if Louis the Pious had not wanted to reintegrate old opponents. But it is still significant that the public debate was entirely a theoretical one; Florus undoubtedly held his views sincerely (he had protested to the Thionville assembly against Amalarius' initial appointment), and Amalarius' chosen defence, once he was forced to give it, would have sunk him, no matter what the political context. 'Practical' politics and abstract theological debate could run along parallel lines, reinforcing each other, thanks to the intensity of the moral imperatives of *correctio*. The Gottschalk dispute is a different case, for it did not map straightforwardly onto other political rivalries. Here, however, the issue of predestination bit into the whole intellectual underpinning of the Carolingian reform project. Authority was not an issue here (both sides rooted their arguments in Augustine); but if Gottschalk's hardline predestination was to prevail, which (unlike that of many of his supporters) ignored the need for faith and good works, that is, human action, to get into heaven, then much of the Carolingian project was pointless. This was one of Hincmar's core concerns, and, although his extensive arguments were not always coherent, it was this, plus doubtless his personal influence with Charles the Bald, that won the day for him. The Carolingian project could not, he was in effect arguing, be allowed to be ruined by an intellectual argument devoid of social context. Of course, many disagreed with him; but all of them, including Gottschalk himself, would have seen the project as sacrosanct. Its moral purpose was at the root of their theological interests themselves, whatever the theological conclusions they each reached.

One essential element in the Carolingian politico-cultural world was Rome. Rome did not contribute much to the intellectual elaborations just discussed, but it had an authority that went back to the start of Carolingian kingship, and the king/emperors treated it with great care: most emperors were crowned in Rome, after all. For a start, the territory of Rome, the Patrimony of St Peter, was not formally incorporated into the empire. The Carolingians, and also local powers like the marquis of Spoleto, leant on Rome, but they never fully controlled it, and (despite attempts) seldom had much say in papal elections. Rome was, with 20,000–25,000 people, a huge and rich city by western standards, with its own political procedures, a set of rituals as elaborate as those of Aachen, an equally complex network of official hierarchies, and a dense factional politics which the Carolingians openly admitted they did not understand. They constantly sent representatives to try to work it out, but only too often, as the *Royal Frankish Annals* put it in 823, they 'could not determine exactly what had happened'. The ever-changing succession of popes (there were twenty-one in the ninth century) meant that the factions had to be understood anew at each election. And tough popes, like Hadrian I (772–95), Paschal I (817–24), Leo IV (847–55), Nicholas I (858–67), John VIII (872–82), had unpredictable political positions, at least to Frankish eyes. Hadrian and his successor Leo III (795–816) were very close to Charlemagne, and keen to do what he asked in return for a free hand (and armed support when needed) in Rome and central Italy. This was a position shared by many of their successors; the presence of Gregory IV (827–44) at the Field of Lies may well have been his own choice, but he was part of Lothar's entourage. By contrast, Paschal I seems to have executed two officials in 823 (the year of the *Annals* quote cited earlier) because they were supporters of Lothar; Paschal, a major church-builder, was locally controversial, but he was probably less controversial in seeking to undermine a Carolingian power that seemed, in those years at least, too close (above, Chapter 10). Lothar reasserted that power after Paschal's death, but from then on, in practice, the Carolingians usually restricted themselves to intervening when factional struggles seemed too out of control.

The detail of papal authority vis-à-vis the Franks fluctuated. Over-all, the Carolingians did not care what the popes thought, any more than the Merovingians had done, as long as they maintained their legitimization of Carolingian power, which was not in doubt. Papal hostility to Iconoclasm, for example, had no effect whatsoever over the Alps. And the Franks could easily look down on Roman intrigue, given that they did not understand its complexity. (Admittedly, sometimes they were right, as in the gothic events of Christmas 896, when the corpse of Pope Formosus (891–6) was dug up by his enemy and successor Stephen VI and put on trial; but that horrified the Romans, too – Stephen did not survive another year. Normally, Roman violence to losers had its own stately logic.) But the intensity of the Carolingian theoretical debates of the second quarter of the ninth century, and the perpetual pacing of church politics through appeals to episcopal councils, gave the popes a new prominence as the final court of appeal in the Latin church. Nicholas I in particular found that his judgement was sought, for example over epis-copal depositions, or in marriage cases (as we shall see in a moment), and also over theological issues – Gottschalk appealed to him after Tusey for example, though Nicholas died before he heard the case. In return, Nicholas, in his conflicts with the Byzantines over the legitimacy of Patriarch Photios and the conversion of Bulgaria (above, Chapter 13), which were international problems specific to Rome, given its continuing links with the eastern patriarchates, sought and obtained the support of Hincmar and other Frankish bishops, who even wrote treatises for him. Nicholas used the legal superiority of the papal office to considerable effect, in a Carolingian world attuned to such issues. His successors did not, however, at least not so effectively. John VIII sought to make emperors after the death of Louis II in 875 (he would have liked to persuade them to fight Arabs in the south of Italy), but choosing them, as opposed to crowning them, was out of his control. When the Carolingian project receded at the end of the century, the international standing of the papacy lost force again, even if the pope's legal powers remained.

All these different trends converged in the great *querelle* over Lothar II's divorce from Theutberga, in 857–69. This ought to have been simple. Lothar had married Theutberga, from the prominent aristocratic family of the 'Bosonids', in 855 but soon turned against her and sought in 857 to return to his former partner Waldrada, with whom he had had a son, Hugh. Marriage law was tightening up in the ninth century, however;

Charlemagne could put away a wife, but Lothar had to have reasons. He came up with the claim that Theutberga had had anal sex with her brother Hubert, had become pregnant as a result (impossibly, of course; his supporters invoked witchcraft), and had aborted the foetus: incest, sodomy and infanticide all at once. Theutberga proved her innocence in an ordeal in 858, but Lothar staged a show trial at a council in Aachen in 860, where she was forced to confess her guilt and retire to a monastery. This was carefully ratified at a synod in 862, in which Waldrada was proclaimed queen; papal legates agreed at Metz the following year, where Theutberga confessed again; Lothar's two senior archbishops, Gunther of Cologne and Theutgaud of Trier, then took the case to Rome for final ratification in 863. But Nicholas I refused to support them; in a *coup de théâtre*, he annulled the synod of Metz, demanded that Lothar take Theutberga back, and deposed the two archbishops themselves. Lothar never got his marriage dissolved, and died of fever in 869 in Italy, where he and his brother Louis II of Italy were trying to 'persuade' Nicholas's perhaps more pliable successor Hadrian II (867–72) to change the judgement.

The malignly inventive humiliation Lothar and his advisers devised for Theutberga was so extreme that it is hard not to be pleased at its failure. That apart, however, the case had important implications. First, it involved realpolitik: if Lothar had no legitimate male heir, other Carolingians would take over Lotharingia, and indeed in 869–70 his uncles Charles the Bald and Louis the German did just that. Unsurprisingly, the latter supported Theutberga; Charles took her and her brother in, and Hincmar, as his major theorist, wrote a long tract in her favour, whereas Lotharingian bishops wrote tracts against her. But, once again, there were issues of principle: of the inviolability of marriage; of the finality of a successful ordeal (Hincmar and Nicholas thought the case should have stopped in 858); of the disaster for the body politic if a queen confessed such misdeeds (Lothar's supporter Adventius bishop of Metz argued that Theutberga's confession alone was enough to disbar her as queen); of the disaster for the body politic if a king was weak enough to get into this kind of marriage difficulty in the first place; and of the rights of the pope as supreme judge in the West. Except the last, these were all issues that had been explicit or implicit in Carolingian theorizing in recent decades, and, as in the 830s crisis, or as with Amalarius, it was the theoretical issues which were at the front of the debate. And this time, it was theory which won; Nicholas I had no axe to grind over who should succeed in Lotharingia, but his violent condemnation of Lothar (who, he correctly said, had misused two women, not one), his synod and his archbishops, could not, in the political environment of the 860s, be got around. No one in Francia had expected this; Nicholas was genuinely trying to exert a real authority over at least the sectors of Frankish politics which came into an ecclesiastical remit, and this, as we have seen, was a lot. Gunther of Cologne was outraged, and we have the text of his rejection of Nicholas's 'abusive sentence . . . delivered against us without justice or reason and against the canonical laws'. Hincmar had no sympathy with Gunther, but when Nicholas followed this up in 865 with disrespectful letters to Charles and Louis and also, in a separate case, reversed the deposition of a bishop of Soissons by senior Frankish prelates including Hincmar, the tone of his account changes substantially too. But the Frankish élite were too committed to correct legal procedure by now, so, when an obstinate pope stuck to legal decisions which the Franks themselves had asked for, they were stuck too. At least until the pope died, for Nicholas was unique in this period; Hadrian II totally failed to prevent Charles and Louis from taking over Lotharingia, and retreated over the appeal of another deposed bishop, Hincmar of Laon, in 871–2. But in the meantime a theoretical debate had caused the eclipse of a kingdom.

The three major political systems of the ninth century, Francia, Byzantium and the caliphate, all had an intellectualized politics in one form or another, and it is worth looking at them comparatively for a moment. The fact that they were roughly simultaneous seems to me to be chance; nothing links together the military success and sense of ecclesiastical mission of Charlemagne, the stabilization of the reduced Byzantine empire in the eighth century which allowed for the revival of writing in the capital by 800 or so, and the fiscal centralization which funded Baghdad and the enormous intellectual activity of the 'Abbasid period. All the same, their contemporaneity at least makes it harder to see each of them as unique, as historians often do. Medieval governments characteristically saw themselves as legitimized by their superior religious moralism (governments still do); and strong governments, as all three of these were, could develop a considerable density of moral and intellectual initiatives. But they were by no means identical, for all that; their differences are, indeed, more interesting than their similarities.

In Byzantium, an educated ruling class steadily developed across the ninth and tenth centuries. This class was very largely a secular élite; Byzantine education, and some ninth-century institutional reform as well (notably in the field of law), were aimed at reviving Graeco-Roman traditions, which included the assumption that the men who ran the state should have a developed literary culture. But that culture had a strong religious element by now; and this in turn was linked to the religious importance of the emperor as the focus of Orthodoxy and as the centre-point of elaborate political rituals. We saw in Chapter 13 that the Byzantines did not have the political and moral urgency that can be seen in Carolingian *correctio*. That urgency perhaps in part came from the relatively recent roots of the Carolingian project. The Byzantines knew that they had a millennium of imperial power behind them, over half of it Christian, and that its revival ought to be enough, given Roman success in the past; but Frankish religious self-esteem was new in the late eighth century, and very much bound up with Charlemagne's belief in his own uniqueness and Louis the Pious's sense of his personal moral task. The Byzantine state was also, of course, more solid than the Frankish one, and education and literary culture could build up slowly over several centuries, unlike the three-generation history of the Carolingian experiment. If the Byzantines felt less need of urgency, given that they were, in their own minds, simply rediscovering their Roman past, they were not necessarily wrong in that.

The 'Abbasids were, in a general way, as convinced of their central role in human religious salvation as either of the other two; but the way it worked in the caliphate was different. The religious centrality of the caliph himself was slipping after 750 (above, Chapter 14); only the *miḥna* of 833–47, introduced by al-Ma'mun, sought to reinstate it, without success. The absence of a specialized priesthood in Islam meant that the interpreters of the Muslim religion, who effectively became its sole guardians by 850, were much more loosely defined as an educated class, the *'ulamā'*. Education trained one for statecraft, in the ninth-century caliphate as in ninth-century Byzantium, in the increasingly elaborate traditions of *adab*, but it also, often simultaneously, trained one for religious authority. On the other hand, no formal hierarchy personified that authority in Islam; it was religious knowledge and philosophical rhetorical skill that established one as a religious leader, not one's appointment as emperor, patriarch/pope, bishop or abbot. The result was a plurality of voices, which at its best was highly stimulating, but which seldom moved the state in any particular direction after 847. Indeed, the caliphs and other political leaders were largely cut out of moralized politics from then on, except in the Fatimid caliphate; as a result, although education, including religious education, was a core training both for a political career and for religious prominence, it did not produce the equivalent of the political intellectuals of the Carolingian court, simply because attendance on rulers, and involvement in their policies, was not so essential for moralists. There were certainly some politically powerful intellectuals in the Islamic world; one thinks of Nizam al-Mulk (d. 1092), vizir to the Seljuk Turks and an important theorist of government; men like him match Photios in Byzantium, and, of course, Alcuin and Hincmar in Francia. But political power was not part and parcel of being a Muslim intellectual; it was simply the most remunerative career path. Moral reform did not proceed through the state, as it did in Byzantium, given the emperor's religious centrality, and as it did in the West. Arab political ceremonial – as elaborate as that of Constantinople – had less of a religious charge, and was less systematically written up than either in Byzantium or in Francia.

The solidity of the Byzantine and Arab political systems (in each case derived from a complex tax structure, absent in the West), reinforced in the Arab case by a steady separation between the caliphal and post-caliphal political system and the question of religious salvation, thus gave plenty of space to the idea that education was a passport to political prominence; but it did not produce the conclusion that a specifically religious education for the élite was essential for the survival of the state, or that the task of the state was in large part the salvation of the community of the realm. This marks the originality of the Carolingian project. The Carolingian state was, for over a hundred years, very successful indeed, and so confident of itself that the task of salvation seemed actually possible. The network of intellectuals that surrounded three generations of Carolingian rulers existed precisely for this purpose. So did the public space of political ritual, which, although simpler than in the East, was at least as charged with meaning, watched and analysed as in Byzantium, and at key moments (as in 833–4, to name only one obvious case) was perhaps even more so. All major political moments were theorized, moralized, in ninth-century Francia, often with competing interpretations. There was space in Francia for the pure political intellectual, men who were important in the state, heard in its councils just because of their knowledge and intelligence, even though they never had an administrative role in it, like Einhard or Lupus of Ferrières, in a way that was rare if not unknown in Byzantium or the Arab world; and there were, for a time, many more Hilduins or Hincmars, men who held official positions but who also had a political or moral programme, than there were Photioses or Nizam al-Mulks.

If one looks at the Carolingian reform programme from the standpoint of the early medieval West, it can sometimes seem stately: as the product of the most successful political régime in Latin Europe between 400 and 1200 (at the earliest), it does not seem surprising that it had as much self-confidence and as dense a cultural activity as it did. If one looks at that same programme from the standpoint of contemporary Constantinople or Baghdad, then it seems over-anxious, hyperactive, shallow in its roots, and – of course – temporary. Essentially, given the underlying structural weakness of all western medieval polities, this latter is true. (The over-anxiousness is also forgivable; it must have been hard to have God as attentive an audience to one's every action as the Carolingians believed.) But it is still interesting, indeed striking, that the Carolingians achieved so much. In the moralization of Frankish politics, in the education of at least two generations of lay aristocrats, as also in the increasing systematization of government, the Carolingians had an effect: different from the Byzantines or the Arabs, but an effect all the same.

The Carolingian project receded in the 880s, even before the fall of Charles the Fat in 887. Hincmar, who died in 882, was the last political leader really to be committed to theory, just as Charles the Bald was probably the last king who really wanted to read it. The latter may be the crucial point. Tenth-century Frankish bishops presided over reform councils, but they were mostly local, and less connected to royal politics, except occasionally in late tenth-century Germany; education (and manuscript copying) continued in monasteries and cathedral schools, but it did not have an effect on political decisions after the 870s. The ecclesiastical world did not change so much, that is to say; but the political context changed substantially. The optimism and confidence of the Carolingian century, the sense that what Frankish politicians decided mattered to God, was what kept the reform project going; and the failure of the dynasty in the years 877–87, followed by a much less ideologized politics in the non-Carolingian successor states, pushed reform onto the local stage of episcopal pastoral activity.

Successful political systems could nonetheless return to parts of the Carolingian programme. The early eleventh century in Germany, and also the late tenth century in England, both saw partial revivals of moral reform imagery as part of high politics. The programme, that is to say, was there waiting to be used, even if the smaller polities of the future could not re-establish the critical mass of competitive writing which marks the middle decades of the ninth century; that would need a new environment, the towns and the money economy of the twelfth century, in order to return. And the political presupposition that kings and bishops were in partnership, with kings choosing bishops but bishops having the right to 'correct' kings, all in the aid of both effective and moral rule, and prosperity in both this world and the next, continued to be axiomatic in western politics, at least as an aspiration, until the late eleventh century at the earliest, and in many respects for a long time later. This presupposition was pushed centre stage by the Carolingians, and it had a long legacy.

18
The Tenth-century Successor States

Gerbert of Aurillac, arguably the leading intellectual of the tenth-century West, had a remarkable career. He was born around 940 to, as it seems, a non-noble family, and educated in his home-town monastery of Saint-Géraud at Aurillac, a regional pilgrimage centre but isolated in the mountains of south-central France. Around 967 he was talent-spotted by Count Borrell of Barcelona, and trained in Catalonia for some years; he accompanied Borrell to Rome around 970 and moved on to the entourage of Pope John XIII and the emperor Otto I (936–73) as a teacher, of mathematics, astronomy, logic and rhetoric – basic elements in the central medieval curriculum. In this role he moved to Reims in 972, and was for two decades both a renowned teacher and the private secretary to Archbishop Adalbero. The only break here was in 982–4, when he impressed the emperor Otto II (973–83) with his philosophical and debating skills, according to his pupil the historian Richer, our source for most of this, and was made abbot of Bobbio in Italy; at Bobbio, however, Gerbert offended vested interests, and he had to flee back to Reims at Otto II's death. From then on, as his letters, surviving as a collection for the years 983–97, show, he was an active political dealer, both on behalf of his patron Adalbero and independently. He operated in support of the infant Otto III (983–1002) and his mother the queen-regent Theophanu in East Francia and Italy, and also Duke Hugh Capet of West Francia, the main rival to the West Frankish king Lothar (954–86). Adalbero and, secondarily, Gerbert facilitated Hugh Capet's non-hereditary succession as king of West Francia (987–96). After Adalbero's death in 989, Gerbert might have expected the archbishopric, but Hugh chose Arnulf, King Lothar's illegitimate son, largely to undermine support for Lothar's brother Charles, duke of Lower Lotharingia (d. 991), who was fighting for the throne. This was a miscalculation; Arnulf almost at once handed Reims to Charles. When he captured Charles and Arnulf in 990, Hugh deposed the latter for treachery in a synod at Saint-Basle-de-Verzy, organized by Gerbert, who now succeeded him as archbishop (991–7). But Hugh had not consulted Pope John XV, who objected to the deposition. The West Frankish bishops argued that it was canonical, but pressure built up on Gerbert, and after Hugh's death he left Reims for Saxony and the court of Otto III. Here he became the still-young emperor's tutor in 997, and was promoted away from Reims: to the archbishopric of Ravenna, and then, in 999, to the papacy itself. He died in 1003 as Pope Silvester II.

Gerbert's career had serious setbacks, but the favour of the great always set him right again. If one reads his letters, they show an assured dealer, playing a complex political game for himself and Adalbero, and, later, for himself alone. It is true that he was consistent, in his support of the Ottonian king/emperors (even though he was in West Francia at the time) and also, increasingly, of Hugh Capet. All the same, he sailed so close to the wind in his dealings that one constantly might expect, if one did not know how his career would end, that he would come unstuck: a man with no social background, entirely reliant on patronage, playing high politics in a period of switchback political shifts, and made an archbishop in dubious circumstances – such a situation destroyed Ebbo of Reims in the 830s, as we saw in Chapter 17, and Gerbert was incredibly lucky not to fall too. What saved him was his scholarship: Gerbert was always welcome as a court intellectual. He wrote letters asking for manuscripts (particularly of mathematical works, and of Cicero) as systematically as Lupus of Ferrières had done a hundred and fifty years before. His skills ensured that he could and did travel with ease across every part of the old Carolingian empire. Gerbert is an illustration that many aspects of the ninth-century political and intellectual practice described in the last chapter had by no means gone away a century later.

But there are differences. One was in the fate of the Carolingian programme. Even second-level intellectuals like Lupus had been able to lecture kings on their moral duties in the ninth century; but, when Otto III wrote to invite Gerbert to be his tutor, Gerbert replied, not with moral advice, but with an enthusiastic evocation of the mathematics he could teach him. (The Saxon historian Thietmar bishop of Merseburg, d. 1018, remembered him for the astronomical clock he built for Otto at Magdeburg.) None of his letters admonish the great; they give information, make practical suggestions, ask for favours. The Ottonians, although in many ways as ambitious as the Carolingians (Thietmar compared Otto to Charlemagne), did not inherit their moralized politics, except to an extent with Henry II after 1002; they barely even issued any laws. The rhetorical frame of ruling had changed. And so had its scale. Among non-royal political operators, Adalbero and Gerbert were by now rare in their interest in more than one kingdom (Reims was near a boundary, and Adalbero had close kin in Lotharingia). Historians certainly were not interested; Flodoard and Richer, the tenth-century West Frankish historians, recount almost nothing of East Francia or Italy, and in the East the Saxon historians Widukind and Thietmar similarly only chronicle East Frankish affairs, adding Italy, somewhat perfunctorily, when Otto I conquered it in 962. The only exception was Liutprand of Cremona (d. 972), the historian of Italy, who paid attention to East (but not West) Frankish politics because he was writing for Otto I, in exile in Frankfurt.

The future countries of Italy, France and Germany were diverging, then. This was not complete, as Gerbert shows. Otto I, too, as we shall see, not only took over Italy, but was a player in West Frankish politics as well, without it seeming inappropriate. And the separate concepts 'France' and 'Germany' did not yet exist; nor even, except occasionally, did 'West' and 'East' Francia, the terminology historians currently use; both were normally just *Francia*, or *Francia et Saxonia* in the case of the eastern kingdom, to reflect the Saxon origins and political base of the Ottonians. ('France' is of course simply the French for *Francia*; by contrast in the German lands, the Frankish heartland was only one region among the old ethnic territories of Saxony, Alemannia, Bavaria, and so a new inclusive name eventually appeared, the *regnum Teutonicum*, though not until the eleventh century.) But the lack of interest of the historians reflects a slow cultural separation. For Flodoard and Richer, *Francia* was 'really' (northern) France; the East Franks were *Transrhenenses*, from over the Rhine, or else the inhabitants of *Germania*, the old Roman geographical term. For Widukind, similarly, West Francia was *Gallia*, proto-French the *Gallica lingua*, and *Francia* was seen as 'really' being in the East. When Thietmar says that 'rule by foreigners is the greatest punishment', he certainly would have included the West Franks. The political history of these three regions will have to

be discussed separately as a result. But the procedures of political practice had not diverged very greatly, all the same, and in the last section
of the chapter I shall discuss these for all the post-Carolingian regions,
seen as a whole.

East Francia was easily the most powerful of the successor states. This
was not because of its infrastructure. It was heavily forested, particularly
in the centre and south, and its communications were dependent on
rivers: for centuries, the only practicable north–south route, except for
single and expert travellers, was the Rhine corridor in the far west of
the kingdom, which was also the main ex-Roman region, with roads
and East Francia's major cities, Cologne and Mainz. Saxony and Bavaria
were a month's travel apart, and had little to do with each other; rulers
based in one tended to leave the other alone. But the regional political
system created by Louis the German largely survived the troubles of the
decades around 900, and could still be used by the Ottonians, and
indeed for another century or more on from them.

Arnulf of Carinthia (887–99), who seized power from his uncle
Charles the Fat, ruled from Bavaria. He was clearly the senior ruler of
his time in all the Carolingian lands; he was the lord of Rudolf I king of
Burgundy (888–912) and Berengar I of Italy (888–924), and had perhaps even been offered the throne of West Francia in 888. In 894–6 he
took Italy briefly and made himself emperor. But he had a stroke in 896
and soon died; and his young son and successor Louis the Child
(900–911), the last eastern Carolingian, never made much impression.
The years 896–911 saw a power-vacuum in the eastern kingdom. It was
filled by new regional rulers, called dukes: of Bavaria (in particular the
'Liutpolding' Arnulf, duke 907–37), of Alemannia (now increasingly
called Swabia: in particular Burchard I, d. 911), of Saxony (in particular
the 'Liudolfing' Otto, d. 912), of Lotharingia (at least after 903, under
the 'Conradine' Gebhard, d. 910), and even of the East Frankish heartland, which seems to have crystallized as a duchy under Gebhard's
nephew Conrad around 906. Bavaria and Swabia had been Carolingian
kingdoms with their own local political structures (and an autonomous
political past), and it is relatively easy to see, particularly in Bavaria,
how it was possible for a local ruler to move from being a duke *in*
Bavaria to being duke *of* the region; Arnulf ran Bavarian-wide assemblies
and armies, appointed his own bishops, and even briefly called himself

king, in 918. Saxony was harder, for it had never been a unified autonomous region, and Duke Otto's father and brother Liudolf (d. 866) and Brun (d. 880) had, although each were called *dux*, only a frontier command; but that command involved successful wars against Sclavenians or Slavs and a military machine, and Otto by his death had come to be more or less in full control of Saxony, which he passed on to his son Henry. Lotharingia and the Frankish heartland took longer still, for these were core Carolingian territories and still contained the largest concentrations of royal lands, around Aachen and Mainz respectively; but it is a sign of the power of the duchy as a political concept that they too had more or less hegemonic dukes by Louis the Child's death. The Frank Conrad, ruler of the most 'royal' duchy, was a natural successor to Louis, as Conrad I (911–18), but he failed to gain the respect from his ducal ex-peers that he hoped for, in particular Henry of Saxony and Arnulf of Bavaria; he also lost Lotharingia to the West Frankish king Charles the Simple (898–923). When he died, the magnates of *Francia et Saxonia* chose Henry of Saxony as the new king (Henry I, 919–36), possibly even at Conrad's suggestion, and certainly with the agreement of Conrad's brother and heir, Eberhard duke of the Franks (d. 939). The Swabians and Bavarians were, however, absent.

East Francia at this point could have been easily divided into (at least) three, as it had been in 876; the two southern duchies had their own traditions, after all, and a Saxon king was far away – and was also not Frankish, so not obviously more 'royal' than a Swabian or a Bavarian. Henry proceeded with care; he was probably not anointed king, so as not to claim too much authority, and he established pacts of 'friendship', implicitly of quasi-equality, with the other dukes. They were prepared to make them, however, and Henry also established momentum by retaking Lotharingia in the 920s. Saxon armies were, furthermore, active against Slavs, and above all against the Magyars or Hungarians, a semi-nomadic people who had overthrown Moravian power in the decade after 894 and established themselves in what is now Hungary. The latter were very effective raiders across much of central Europe and Italy in the early tenth century, and Henry achieved considerable status (not least in Bavaria, on the front line of their attacks) by defeating them in 933 and quietening them for two decades. Henry's supremacy was also, like Arnulf's, recognized in Burgundy (though not Italy). When he was succeeded by his son Otto I in 936, Otto could choreograph an election and coronation in Aachen itself, with a very formal anointing by the archbishop of Mainz, and a banquet in which all four dukes, plus the king's deputy (*a rege secundus*) in his home duchy of Saxony, served him dinner, the clearest sign of subjection.

Otto when he inherited the throne had brothers, for the first time in the eastern kingdom since the 870s (and the last until 1190); Henry had excluded them from succession, in a deliberate departure from Carolingian norms. In 939–41 two of them, Thankmar and Henry, revolted, fortunately (for Otto) not at the same time, and found considerable support both from other dukes and from inside Saxony itself; only Hermann of Swabia (926–48), a Conradine put in by Henry I, was consistently loyal to the king. But Otto won the wars, and was able to remove dukes everywhere; in the Frankish heartland, he abolished the title after Eberhard's death in battle against him and Hermann, and ruled it directly himself. Otto consistently chose his dukes from now on. They were almost all from the ducal families that had already emerged, which did not give him a wide range of choice; the Ottonians, unlike the Carolingians, could not create a new *Reichsaristokratie* on any scale. But often Otto chose his own relatives, his now-reconciled brother Henry in Bavaria (947–55), his son Liudolf in Swabia (948–53), his youngest brother Brun, archbishop of Cologne, in Lotharingia (954–65), before going back to more local families.

Liudolf revolted in 953–4 as well. But his revolt, although widely supported, was subverted by the last great Hungarian invasion, which Otto destroyed on the Lechfeld outside Augsburg, on the Swabian border, in 955. After that, Otto's hegemony was unquestioned. It extended to West Francia, as already shown by the synod of Ingelheim in 948, in which King Louis IV (936–54) brought his grievances against Duke Hugh the Great (d. 956) to Otto's own assembly, to be judged by the East Frankish king and the papal legate. Otto was also able to extend himself to Italy, first in 951–2, when his overlordship was recognized by Berengar II (950–62), then in 961–2, when he annexed the Italian kingdom and was crowned emperor. Otto was strong enough to spend most of the rest of his reign in Italy, and was, in the last two decades of his life, by far the most powerful ruler of the tenth century – Thietmar was not wrong to make the Charlemagne comparison. Otto's political structure was strong enough to survive the relatively lacklustre reign of his son Otto II (973–83), who was unsuccessful in his wider forays, outside Paris in 978, and, most disastrously, when he was defeated by the Arabs in 982 in the far south of Italy, near Crotone; and the long royal minority of the three-year-old Otto III (983–1002). The younger Ottos, however, had Otto II's mother Adelaide (d. 999) and wife Theophanu (d. 991) to look after them: tough queens-regent in the Merovingian mould, and themselves proof of the now-established centrality of the Liudolfing/Ottonian family as East Frankish kings. At Otto III's death without children the magnates of the eastern kingdom hesitated between Hermann II of Swabia and Ekkehard, marquis of the Saxon march of Meissen, but without much difficulty in the end they plumped for Henry IV of Bavaria (Henry II, 1002–24), who was Otto I's brother's grandson and Otto III's male-line heir. There was no doubt at any of these royal accessions that East Francia was a single political system, which by now included Italy as well.

How this system actually worked is more of a problem. The Merovingian and Carolingian assumption that assemblies were the key moments of political aggregation was certainly maintained, and indeed heavily stressed: the new Saxon royal centres of Magdeburg and Quedlinburg attracted aristocrats and bishops from all over the kingdom at the big Easter feasts. Royal diplomas show that the legitimacy of royal grants of land and rights were important throughout the kingdom, too. But Ottonian local control was more mediated than it had been under their predecessors. The king/emperors chose the dukes, but the dukes of the two southern duchies controlled all the ex-royal land of Swabia and Bavaria; indeed, Otto I's son Liudolf when he succeeded Hermann in Swabia had to be married to Hermann's daughter Ida, in order to succeed, 'with the duchy, to all his property', as Widukind put it, implying that if Hermann had had sons, Liudolf might have been a duke with little land. Inside duchies, assemblies, army-muster and justice were all under ducal control; there had never been many royal *missi* in Carolingian East Francia, and the court chaplains the Ottonians sometimes sent out were very ad-hoc representatives. Kings chose bishops too, often from the court chaplains; an episcopal presence in the royal entourage was important, and they could also carry royal interest back into their duchies. But they, too, tended to be from local families, except for the key archbishops of Cologne and Mainz. The best the kings could do was to undermine ducal power, sometimes by dividing duchies (Carinthia was carved off from Bavaria in 976, Lotharingia was split into Upper and Lower from the late 950s) and, often, by encouraging the autonomous interests of both bishops and other local magnates, especially through grants of judicial immunity. In the end, the default Ottonian political practice in the outlying duchies, and also in Italy, was simply to divide and rule. This, plus assembly ceremonial and frequent royal presence – for the Ottonians moved around a lot, far more than the Carolingians had, and could be found in most places except Bavaria – was a large part of Ottonian government, outside Saxony at least.

All the same, the Ottonians had major strengths, too: in their royal land, in the still-surviving Carolingian heartland regions around Aachen and Mainz–Frankfurt, to which they added their own family heartland in the south of Saxony, between Hildesheim and Merseburg; in their powers of patronage, to benefices, duchies, bishoprics, which, as with the Carolingians, kept their courts essential locations for the distribution of political power; in the silver-mines providentially discovered in their Saxon heartland around Goslar about 970, which funded the kings for two centuries; and, above all, in their large army. The core of the latter was Saxon, and it was honed on the eastern marches, which under Henry I and Otto I had become tightly organized military territories aimed at eastward aggression. The Slavs of the Elbe–Oder lands (roughly the East Germany of 1945–90) were largely subjected, and they and their eastern neighbours paid tribute; the Saxon aristocracy gained massively from this, which helped the loyalty of most of them, but the king/emperor kept control of the whole process. (Dukes of Saxony developed again in the tenth century, once the Liudolfings/Ottonians had become kings, but they were essentially based in the eastern marches, and did not yet displace direct royal power.) The core Saxon army was supplemented by units from everywhere else in the East Frankish kingdom when the Ottonians fought elsewhere, drawn largely from church lands, as is seen in the *Indiculus Loricatorum*, a rare administrative document from the tenth century, an army-list for the reinforcements called for by Otto II in southern Italy in 981. The Ottonians never lost control of army-service from the whole kingdom. Even the great Slav revolt of 983, after Otto's Italian defeat, which drove the Saxons out of much of the land beyond the Elbe and held off their advance for a century, did not break the Ottonian grip on the army and on the Saxon frontier. All this made possible Ottonian supremacy, despite the relative simplicity of the political structures in much of their realm, and it showed no sign of slipping in 1000.

The kingdom of Italy, the Italian peninsula stretching down to Rome, was the opposite to East Francia, an institutionally coherent polity whose kings were weak. It still had its capital at Pavia, the location of the royal court and an increasingly active centre of judicial expertise. Italian court-case records are elaborate and relatively homogeneous until late in the eleventh century, and appeals to Pavia were normal. Most such court records are of county-based judicial assemblies, which were thrice-yearly public meetings headed by counts or royal *missi* (who continued to exist in Italy, though the office was by now a local one), usually held inside Italy's strong network of cities: this had parallels with the assembly politics of East Francia, but was much more localized, much more regular, and also explicitly judicial; such assemblies were full of semi-expert lay *iudices*, judges, who were generally literate, as well as lay notaries. Italian revenues from tolls and royal lands were also more systematic and larger-scale than in Germany, away from the Saxon frontier at least, particularly in the royal heartlands of what are now called Lombardy and Emilia, around the capital. Italy was worth conquering in 962, in the same way as it had been in 773–4.

This institutional coherence coincided with a much more regionalized politics. The aristocracy of the eighth-century Lombard kingdom had been local, and modest in its wealth. The Carolingians introduced Franks from the great northern aristocratic families, who owned more widely, such as the 'Widonids' in the southern duchy of Spoleto and the 'Suppon-ids' (kin to Louis II's queen Angilberga), as we saw in Chapter 16. But these families failed in the early tenth century, or else localized them-selves, or else both, as with the 'Bonifacian' counts of Lucca, a family from Bavaria first documented in Italy in 812, who became entirely regionally focused, as marquises of Tuscany for the period 846 to 931, after which they were overthrown and died out. After an early Carolin-gian period in which incomers monopolized almost all secular offices, Lombard families re-emerged in the later ninth century and onwards, who might gain lands and offices on a substantial scale, as with the Aldobrandeschi in southern Tuscany, protégés of Lothar I and Louis II, or the Canossa in eastern Emilia, protégés of Hugh and Otto I (see Chapter 21); but these, too, usually had major interests only in three or four contiguous counties, and most of the aristocratic players of the tenth century had interests in only one. Italy outside the royal heartland was divided into duchies or marches as was East Francia: Friuli in the north-east, Spoleto in the south, Tuscany in the centre, Ivrea and then Turin in the north-west (the first two of these had Lombard antecedents, the others were Carolingian or post-Carolingian). These had semi-autonomous political structures and armies, as did their analogues north of the Alps. But the particular point about Italy was that the solidity of the majority of counties, usually coterminous with the local bishopric and centred on a city where most local political players lived, meant that secular and ecclesiastical aristocracies could very easily focus on single city-territories as their major points of reference, bypassing even the marches. In the tenth century, not only Friuli and Tuscany, but their constituent elements, such as Verona, Padua, or Pisa – and, in the royal heartland, Parma, Bergamo, Milan – began to have their separate histories. They were institutionally connected to Pavia, but city-focused identities and political rivalries mattered rather more. These localized territories were more coherent than in most of East Francia, and were for the most part less dominated by single families than in West Francia. They therefore absorbed more of the political interests of local powers, and kings and even marquises intervened in them very largely from the outside. Beyond the city network, only Tuscany survived as a fully coherent regional territory into the eleventh century.

This was the backdrop for the political shifts of the tenth century. Berengar marquis of Friuli was the first to make himself king after Charles the Fat was overthrown; he faced no less than five rivals in his thirty-five-year reign, Guy and Lambert of Spoleto (889–95; 891–8), Arnulf from the north, as we have seen, and later Louis III king of Provence (900–905), and Rudolf II king of Burgundy (922–6). Berengar I survived the early deaths of the first three and blinded the fourth; between 905 and 922 he enjoyed the widest and most uncontested power of any king of his time. But he was not actually very popular outside his own power-base in north-east Italy (all his rivals except Arnulf were actively supported in the north-west; Tuscany usually remained neutral); nor was he a great military leader (he lost battles to the Hungarians, and, later, to Rudolf of Burgundy). He initiated in the 900s a trend to local structures of defence, concentrated on cities, or else on privately owned fortifications, to which he often gave judicial immunities. Guy and Louis III, and then Berengar, also granted comital rights inside the walls of cities to bishops, thus breaking up comital jurisdiction further. This should be seen as Berengar exercising a well-structured and largely successful political protagonism, to reward support both inside and outside his heartland; but it also strengthened the trends to localization already referred to. There is little sign under Berengar I of either a Carolingian programmatic politics or the ceremonial royal assemblies of the Carolingian and Ottonian systems north of the Alps. Even the verse panegyric on Berengar from around 915 (an atypical but not unique text; both Charlemagne and Otto I had them) makes no reference to such initiatives. Berengar ended badly, when his Hungarian mercenaries stirred up a new revolt and Rudolf's invasion, the Hungarians then sacked Pavia, and in 924 Berengar was, unusually for the period, murdered.

The Italian magnates were still looking for an effective ruler, and in 925 they tried Hugh, count of Arles, who ruled energetically for two decades, 926–47. Hugh, who had no local power-base, operated from the royal heartland around Pavia, and sought systematically to control the marches by choosing their rulers. In this respect he operated in almost exactly the same way as his younger contemporary Otto I: he moved established families around (more than Otto did, in fact), and appointed his own kin, as with his brother Boso and illegitimate son Hubert, successive marquises of Tuscany (931–69). He also relied greatly on a network of bishops, whether his relatives or from more local families, who had considerable powers (as with his son Boso, bishop of Piacenza, who was also arch-chancellor in Pavia). Again, we lack much evidence for a more public, assembly-based politics (except in the field of law), although this might be expected to have been normal at least in Pavia. Our main narrative source for Hugh, Liutprand of Cremona, systematically disregarded the standard markers of royal legitimacy when he discussed the Italian kings, faithful protégé as he was of Otto I, but clear signs of royal ceremony, or political aggregation around Hugh, are absent in our other evidence as well. We gain the sense that Hugh remained an outsider to the local political preoccupations of the Italians, and he fell too, in the end, when the exiled Berengar marquis of Ivrea invaded with an East Frankish army in 945 and Hugh found himself with no supporters. Berengar II ruled under the hegemony of Otto I after 951, and was easily removed in 962.

A political system which has both wealth and institutional coherence, but whose rulers are relatively marginal politically and have little military support, is both attractive and easy to conquer, as Rudolf, Hugh, Berengar II and Otto I found in turn. It is arguable, though, that Ottonian rule by now suited Italy best. Otto I and Otto III spent some time in Italy, nine and five years respectively, but kings were present in the kingdom itself for less than a third of the period 962–1000, and in the eleventh century the figure dropped precipitously. The Ottonians promoted episcopal immunities where counts were strong, and appointed and endowed counts where bishops were strong: an ad-hoc procedure aimed at reducing local power-bases, as beyond the Alps. They did not do much else; they imported no new families. The strength of their armies, when they were present in the country, made explicit opposition rare, although Otto III had considerable trouble in Rome, which he tried to make his political base in 998–1001, in a romantic and largely rhetorical attempt at a *renovatio* of the Roman empire. But most of the time they were absent, and the local politics of the Italian bishops and urban aristocracies could continue with little external interference, linked together essentially by the Pavia-focused network of judicial assemblies and also by the regular seeking of diplomas granting lands and rights from the king/emperors beyond the Alps. This was a pattern which would persist until the civil wars of the 1080s–1090s forced Italian city communities to think about ruling themselves; on the other hand, the coherence of city territories was, after 1000, itself eroded by the crystallization of even smaller lordships with autonomous political rights (see below, Chapter 21).

Otto I and III intervened directly in Roman politics, and all three Ottos also sought to intervene south of Rome. The independent principality of Benevento had held Charlemagne off, but in 849, after a ten-year civil war, it divided into two, Benevento and Salerno, and Capua split off from Salerno by the 860s. These three principalities then variously combined, fought each other, and fought the small ex-Byzantine city-states in the same area, Naples, Amalfi and Gaeta, for two centuries. They were not very internally coherent as polities, and already in the mid-tenth century they were dividing into smaller lordships, with the exception of Salerno. They were also militarily weak: Louis II had already sought to dominate them in the 860s–870s, though he failed; the Byzantines had also, more definitively, annexed the southern portions of

Salerno and, in particular, of Benevento in the 880s–890s. The southern principalities thus looked like possible new conquests to the Ottonians, and, if they did not become so, it was only because they were so far away from the main Ottonian power-bases, and because Otto II's 982 defeat was so traumatic.

Conversely, however, inside southern Italy, the independent principality under its own ruling dynasty was the unchallenged political model. This is doubtless why Rome, under four generations of the Theophylact family (c. 904–63), moved in the direction of the dynastic pattern as well. It was one strong enough even to tolerate an independent female ruler, Marozia *senatrix et patricia* (c. 925–32), one of a small handful in the tenth century (the others, discussed later, were in Mercia and Rus); her son Alberic (932–54), who overthrew her, called himself *princeps*, prince, in clear imitation of the princes just to the south. These rulers chose their bishops – that is, the popes – just as the princes of Capua–Benevento and Salerno did, and also just as the Ottonians did in the north. Alberic drew back from the pattern, however, when he was not only succeeded by his son Octavian (954–63/4), but persuaded the Roman aristocracy to elect the latter pope, which they did, as John XII, in 956. Rome's traditions and papal-orientated bureaucracy made an episcopal leader more appropriate in the long term than a princely leader. But this brought renewed instability, after John's overthrow by Otto I, as rival families supported rival pontiffs across the rest of the century. Otto I and III only exacerbated this in their own high-handed, violent and temporary interventions. But although the king/emperors could and did give up on the south of Italy, they could not give up on Rome, where they needed to be crowned emperor. Otto III tried to solve Roman faction-fighting by choosing non-Italian popes (including Gerbert), for the first time since the mid-eighth century. This failed, but it would be imitated by Henry III in the 1040s, with unpredictable future effects.

West Francia was easily the least successful of the post-Carolingian kingdoms. Even the shadowy kingdom of Burgundy in the Rhône valley managed an essential durability (except in the south, ravaged by Arabs) and also dynastic continuity, between 888 and its absorption into the East Frankish kingdom/empire in 1032. West Francia, however, combined the personalized kingship of the Ottonian East with the political instability of early tenth-century Italy – a fatal mixture. Already by the 940s the kings of the West had hardly any authority, and for the next hundred and fifty years they hardly gained any more.

In 888 the 'Robertine' Odo of Paris took the throne of West Francia (888–98). The only surviving western Carolingian, Charles the Simple, was a child, and an adult was needed to confront the Vikings. In 889 Odo held substantial assemblies, and counts and bishops from as far south as Barcelona and Nîmes came to them; but his non-Carolingian blood did not help his authority south of the Loire, in Aquitaine and elsewhere, and by 893 lack of success against the Vikings allowed Archbishop Fulk of Reims (d. 900) to get away with setting Charles as king against him. Civil war followed; Odo and Charles made peace in 897, and Charles was recognized as Odo's heir, in return for Odo's brother Robert being recognized as in sole control of the family counties and monasteries between the Seine and the Loire and around Paris. When Charles succeeded as king (898–923), he was thus cut out of a large section of the traditional royal lands in the Paris region. The counts of Vermandois, Heribert I (d. c. 905) and his son Heribert II (d. 943) – themselves distant Carolingians, for the former was grandson of Bernard of Italy – had occupied most of the royal properties in the Oise valley north of Paris, too; Charles was left with Laon to the north-east as a political base, extending to Reims whenever he could. It is not surprising that he spent the 910s trying to make good his control of Lotharingia, for the royal properties around Aachen would have increased his wealth and political influence dramatically. But he did not have the full support of the West Frankish aristocracy for this enterprise, and they also seem to have resented his Lotharingian advisers. In 920 'almost all the counts of [West] Francia' revolted, as Flodoard of Reims put it, and in 922 they made Robert king against him. Robert was killed in battle the next year, but the Franks would not take Charles back, and chose instead Rudolf duke of Burgundy, Robert's brother-in-law (923–36). Charles was captured by Heribert II of Vermandois, and died in prison in 929.

Charles was not an entirely useless king. His Lotharingian adventure was at least a sensible strategy, even if a desperate one. He also had the vision to deal with the Vikings of the Seine by recognizing them and settling their leader Rollo as count of Rouen in 911. The Vikings (*Nortmanni* in Latin) of the Seine more or less respected their side of the deal, and held off future attacks; they settled down and soon began to behave in ways analogous to other Frankish magnates, and 'Normandy', though prone to civil war, remained fairly firmly in the hands of its count/duke. But Charles had several insurmountable problems. One was that he had very little land in West Francia as a whole; in the two decades preceding 898 the counts and dukes of both the north and the south had occupied most of it for their own purposes, except in the Paris heartland region, which Robert and Heribert divided with him. The second was that he and his successors had no power to choose counts and dukes, unlike the kings of East Francia and Italy; no tenth-century West Frankish king had any significant effect on the succession of a major county or duchy, unless its ruler died without heirs. This power had been lost only recently, for Charles the Fat exercised it in the 880s, but it had now gone, with the consequence that the territorial chequerboard of West Frankish politics was strategically uncontrollable except by war; only some of the bishops and abbots of the north, notably the major regional power of Reims, could usually be chosen by the king. The third was that the magnates of West Francia were themselves regionalized; already in 898 Robert, Heribert I, Baldwin II count of Flanders, Fulk of Reims, Richard the Justiciar duke of Burgundy, William the Pious duke of eastern Aquitaine and Odo count of Toulouse had interests that were restricted to the counties they controlled and their immediate neighbours, and not to the kingdom as a whole. This was quite like the East Frankish or Italian situation, and it was Charles the Simple's task to establish the political centrality of his assemblies, as Henry of Saxony would do. But he had not the landed resources to do it, and his attempts to create them were unsupported.

King Rudolf in 923 at least had a new landed base, in the duchy of Burgundy, and was strong there. But he also largely remained there; Flodoard's *Annals* describe him as having to be 'summoned' to the West Frankish heartland, not that far away, by Heribert of Vermandois or Robert's son Hugh the Great (d. 956), when he was needed to fight wars. At his death in 936, Hugh recalled Charles's son Louis IV from exile in England to rule. Louis had effectively no land or power at all, and strove constantly, but without success, to establish himself independently of Hugh, who had become 'duke of the [West] Franks' in 936. Hugh even imprisoned him in 945–6, an action which brought Otto I more firmly onto the scene, and resulted in Louis's appearance at Ingelheim in 948 to seek Otto's judgement against Hugh. (Hugh was excommunicated for it later in the year, but paid no notice, although he did make peace with Louis in 950.) Louis died in 954, leaving a thirteen-year-old son, Lothar (954–86), as king; Lothar's mother Gerberga was regent for several years. But Hugh's death in 956 gave the king respite, as his own eldest son Hugh Capet was only eleven. Gerberga and Hugh Capet's mother Hadwig were sisters; they were also sisters of Otto I, whose authority in the West was at its height in these years; it was exercised through their brother Brun of Cologne, who is often found in West Francia in the next decade, and who orchestrated the confirmation of the title of duke on Hugh Capet in 960. Lothar as he grew up fell out not only with Hugh Capet but with Otto I and Otto II, fighting a war with the latter in 978–80, like that of sixty years earlier, in an attempt to regain Lotharingia. But his greater protagonism was based on no greater strength on the ground. When his son Louis V died young in 987, Archbishop Adalbero of Reims argued successfully for Hugh Capet's succession, as we have seen. The running sore of Carolingian–Robertine rivalry was ended when Charles of Lotharingia was captured in 990, and male-line 'Capetians' then ruled West Francia/ France without any significant break until 1792, a record unsurpassed, as far as I know, in all history, except in Japan.

This was not the end of royal trouble, all the same. Adalbero (or Gerbert) could already in 985 write a brief 'secret and anonymous letter', probably to the archbishop's Lotharingian kin, saying that 'Lothar is king of Francia in name only; Hugh not in name, it is true, but in deed and fact'; this was 751 all over again, on the surface. But time had not stopped for the Robertines either. Hugh the Great's power-base was in a block of around twenty counties stretching from Paris to Orléans and west to Angers: a substantial area of land by tenth-century West Frankish standards. But during Hugh Capet's minority the formerly subordinate counts of the western half of this block, notably those of Angers and Blois, gained effective independence, and began to operate their own local and regional politics; Fulk Nerra of Anjou (that is, the territory of Angers; 987–1040) was famously insubordinate to Hugh Capet's son Robert II (996–1031), and Odo II of Blois (995–1037) also took over Champagne around 1021, thus hemming the Robertine/Capetian heartland in from both sides at once. The already small geographical scale of the political and military operations described in Flodoard's *Annals* in the 920s became, if possible, smaller still in the eleventh century. Royal traditions such as assembly and army-muster had even less force after 1000 than before. West Francia north of the Loire, an area much the size of Saxony, was by 1025 the terrain of six or seven effectively independent 'principalities', Brittany, Anjou, Normandy, Blois–Champagne, Flanders, with the kings in the middle and the archbishops of Reims on the edge. South of the Loire there were more again.

The Merovingian-Carolingian system of counties was stronger in West Francia than in the East, and there were no strong traditions of ethnic difference, except in Brittany, which was finally absorbed into Frankish politics in the fragmented tenth century, and, by now, Normandy. The eastern model of the ethnic duchy had less force here. Each political unit that was larger than a single county, as all the small principalities north of the Loire were, was thus created, painstakingly, territory by territory, and could risk falling back into its constituent parts again, as the Robertine lands were doing by 987. In the south, too, the 'Guilhelmid' counts of the Auvergne (see Chapter 21) had accumulated a string of counties in eastern Aquitaine and called themselves 'dukes of the Aquitainians' by 900, but the west of Aquitaine, notably the counts of Poitiers, did not recognize their authority, and there was no real reason why they should; when in 927 the Auvergne dukes died out, the counts of Poitiers took the title, but could only exercise power in the Auvergne if they took it militarily, and so on. Actually, the Poitiers dukes were quite successful in this, and William IV (963–93) and William V (993–1030) exercised, at times, wider authority than anyone north of the Loire by now. The regional church councils which preached against aristocratic violence and in favour of the 'Peace of God' in the last half of the century in Aquitaine were partly taken over by William V after 994 and turned, in effect, back into Carolingian-style large-scale assemblies, the only ones still in existence in West Francia by the end of the tenth century. But the core of William's power and land was still Poitou, and elsewhere he had to gain the fidelity of counts and other local lords, by force or persuasion or ceremony. This was a fidelity that had constantly to be reinforced, as we can see in a surviving agreement of around 1025 between William and Hugh of Lusignan (a powerful lord in Poitou itself) which discusses in great detail the tense, prickly, and armed stand-offs between the two sides before settlement was reached. This was so everywhere. The counts of Flanders, the count/dukes of Normandy, the counts of Anjou, the counts of Toulouse, the counts of Barcelona, all ruling collections of counties, some of them quite large, did manage to establish real and lasting hegemonies over the different powers in their principalities. Others, however, were at best intermittent overlords. And after 1000 or so there was a further involution in much of West Francia, when counties themselves began to break up into smaller lordships, each with their own localized political, military and judicial powers: all the political system of Charlemagne's huge empire reduced to the scale of a few villages. This process, the so-called 'feudal revolution', will be looked at again later.

The late twentieth-century hegemony of French history-writing over the central Middle Ages, which begin for these purposes around 1000 or a little before, has made the West Frankish experience seem the typical post-Carolingian development. As should be clear to readers of this chapter, it was not. Still less, as we shall see, was the 'feudal revolution' typical, for it only affected parts of West Francia itself. Everywhere, it is true, power was highly local, built up of lands, rights, armies and oaths of fidelity; and in Italy, too, and even in some of East Francia, it was more local in 1000 than 900. But in most places aristocratic status and identity was still tied up with being close to kings, or at least major regional powers such as the duke of Bavaria, the marquis of Tuscany or the count of Flanders. Even in Italy, although identities could be closely tied to city-territories, the institutional force of the kingdom remained, as an inheritance from the Lombard and Carolingian periods. And elements of a common political practice, also inherited from the Caro-lingians and only partly modified after 900, existed throughout the post-Carolingian lands, even in the West. Let us end this chapter by looking at how some of them worked.

The tenth century gave less space to Carolingian-style political theology. There was some: Abbo of Fleury (d. 1004), in particular, could praise Carolingian legislation to Hugh Capet and Robert II; but he seems fairly isolated in his commitment. (The West Frankish kings around 1000 were also not the most suitable recipients of such ideas; but Abbo was also patronized in England, which was different, as we shall see in the next chapter.) Conversely, it would be wrong to conclude from this absence that the tenth century had moved away from the world of writing. The educational traditions of the ninth century had continued in Carolingian centres such as St. Gallen, Corvey and Reims, and indeed extended geographically, to remoter locations such as Gerbert's Aurillac, and to the new south-east Saxon royal heartland, in Quedlinburg, Gandersheim, Magdeburg. Some of the literary results were striking: the rhymed prose of the Lotharingian Rather, bishop of Verona (d. 974), the heavy use of Sallust in the Saxon historian Widukind of Corvey (d. after 973), the knowledge (and pretentious use) of Greek in the Italian Liutprand bishop of Cremona (d. 972), and the Virgilian poetry and – most unusual of all – Terence-influenced play-writing of the Saxon Hrotsvitha of Gandersheim (d. 975). Hrotsvitha and her patron (Otto I's niece) Abbess Gerberga show that the women of the Saxon aristocracy could be formidably educated. And all the people named in this paragraph, although undoubtedly trained in ecclesiastical milieux, had close court connections, usually but not only with the Ottonians.

Translators are certainly more commonly referred to in tenth- than in ninth-century sources, even for kings and dukes. Otto I is sometimes thought not to have known Latin, for example, because Liutprand had to translate for him in Rome in 963. But it is more likely that Otto was simply avoiding giving away that he did not have full control of public rhetoric in Latin, as well as making the political point that he, the new ruler of Rome, was a Saxon-speaker. Hrotsvitha thought it worthwhile dedicating her verse *Gesta Ottonis* to him (and to his son Otto II, who was certainly educated), and it would be odd if he had patronized so many literary figures he could not understand at all. Furthermore, writing (in Latin) was as regular a means of political communication in the tenth century, alongside spoken messages, as it had been in the ninth and earlier, even outside Italy with its widespread lay literacy. Gerbert's letter collection (probably a working collection, even if he subsequently edited it for publication) shows how dense a political correspondence could be in the 980s. Gerbert and the people he wrote for, Adalbero, Hugh Capet, Lothar's wife Queen Emma, sent terse and practical messages to each other and to other significant political players, very frequently – as when Hugh, now king, writes in December 988 to the empress Theophanu about her health, promises peace, and proposes a diplomatic meeting in the next month, all in eight lines. It is likely enough that most aristocrats were no longer fully literate, and they certainly did not match the literary commitment common in the ninth century. All the same, this was not an 'oral' culture, as some more romantic historians have described it, except in so far as all cultures, including our own, are essentially oral. And, whether with writing or without it, some aspects of tenth-century government could be (by early medieval western standards) tightly organized and monitored. Berengar of Ivrea's poll tax to pay off the Hungarians in 947 is one example. Another, perhaps more striking, is Otto III's decision in 997 to defend an important Saxon border castle, the Arneburg, with four-week garrisons headed by important local aristocrats, who had to hand over to each other in relays; when a handover slipped up and the Slavs sacked the castle, the emperor demanded an accounting. Meissen was similarly garrisoned in the next decade. This represents systematic government, at least in Saxony, and it was experienced by the lay aristocracy too, not just their ecclesiastical brothers and sisters.

Side by side with this daily communication, tenth-century polities maintained the large-scale public arena of political action of the Carolingian world. Assemblies were probably smaller in West Francia, whether for political or judicial purposes; indeed, judicial assemblies died out in much of the western kingdom by 1000 or so. The 987 assembly of magnates who elected Hugh Capet was called a *curia* by Richer, a 'court', a rather more restricted word than *placitum*, the large judicial assembly surviving in Italy, or than the *universalis populi conventus*, the 'meeting of the whole people', referred to often by Widukind for the East Frankish lands. Even in West Francia, though, the peace councils of William V of Aquitaine and others could sometimes revive the image of wider public participation; and elsewhere all the members of local or kingdom-wide political communities could meet together and become the audience for political acts, which had power simply because of the size of the audience.

These acts could be very elaborate. Otto I's coronation, already referred to, was one, potent with images of Carolingian legitimacy and supremacy. There was a stateliness about many of them, a rule-boundedness, which has been influentially characterized by Gerd Althoff in his phrase *Spielregeln*, 'the rules of the game', rules which everyone in the community knew, and which held off open disagreement in public. This was all the more necessary because the single court hierarchy of the Carolingian world had, in reality, gone; there were by now far more players, whose relative position could no longer be established from above. Equality between kings was carefully choreographed, as when Otto I and Louis IV in 948 sat down at the synod of Ingelheim at the same moment, or as when kings met at the boundaries of kingdoms: Charles the Simple, for example, met Henry I in 921, each watched by their *fideles*, in a boat on the Rhine, to which they had each come in their own separate boats. In a parallel case, Rudolf of West Francia met Duke William II of Aquitaine at the River Loire in 924, when Rudolf was threatening war to get William's submission to him as king. Messengers crossed by day to negotiate, then William crossed at night, got off his horse, and met the still-mounted king on foot, from whom he received the kiss of peace; this was the crucial element that began the submission process, involving a symbolic river-crossing and a posture of inferiority, but taking place in the dark, so less publicly visible (the negotiations must have largely been about that). Subjects regularly greeted their lords kneeling, or even prostrate on the ground (as also did kings, when kneeling or prostrating themselves before altars): particularly when asking for favours, but even in normal greeting, as with the story by Rodulf Glaber (d. 1047) of the unfaithful Heribert II of Vermandois receiving Charles the Simple's kiss of peace while prostrate in 923. And when kings (or even, later, counts) came to cities there were regular *adventus* rituals of greeting, in a tradition surviving from the Roman empire and continuing to the modern period. Rome had by far the most elaborate ones, which signalled Rome's own status, but all cities had their own, as when the *cives fortiores*, leading citizens, of Pavia came out to greet King Hugh 'by custom' in about 930, according to Liutprand, or when Louis IV was formally received at his accession in 936 at Laon and nearby cities, according to Richer. All of these latter accounts are literary reconstructions, but the imagery was a recognizable and a strong one. Rituals could also be used to humiliate. Prostration was particularly commonly used by people confessing crimes and seeking pardon; and kings could demand very specific public humiliations, like the dogs which the leading supporters of Duke Eberhard of the Franks had to carry publicly into Magdeburg in 937 after a minor revolt. This had Carolingian antecedents (under Louis II of Italy it would have been saddles), but as a sign of royal right, and of the subjection and penitence of the guilty, it must have had quite an effect.

The point about elaborate systems of rules, conversely, is that they can be subverted to make points. Sometimes this is the work of the writer, as when Dudo of Saint-Quentin (d. *c.* 1020), the Norman chronicler, supposes that in 911 Rollo of Normandy's follower, when kissing

Charles the Simple's foot to represent the formal submission of Rollo's Vikings, pulled the foot up into the air to kiss it: Dudo here simply wants to convey Viking/Norman egalitarianism and disrespect. More complex was Duke Hermann Billung of Saxony's decision in 968 to call an assembly in Otto I's city of Magdeburg, where he was received by the archbishop, dined in the emperor's place, and slept in his bed; or when Marquis Ekkehard of Meissen in 1002, who was seeking the throne after Otto III's death, came to the electoral assembly at Werla, and, when he realized he had lost, commandeered a feast that had been laid on in the palace for Otto III's sisters, and ate it himself with his allies. We rely on Thietmar of Merseburg for these stories, and he had his own agendas, inevitably, but his close relatives were anxious witnesses in each case. Hermann and Ekkehard were certainly making points: about the fact that the Ottonians were potentially replaceable (in Ekkehard's case, certainly), and also (in Hermann's case, more ambiguously) the critical comment that Otto I had been too long away in Italy, and the claim that the duke of Saxony himself had, or should have, considerable formal power. Watchers knew that these sorts of points were being made; Ekkehard was killed for it, and the archbishop of Magdeburg (though not, interestingly, Hermann) was heavily fined by an angry Otto I. As with the Carolingians, once again, public acts always had audiences, who needed to be persuaded of arguments, and who could be convinced by creative reworkings of the rituals they were familiar with. This in turn generated new rituals and public procedures, like the Peace of God councils: I have described these in terms of Carolingian antecedents, but they were also seen as collective religious responses and counters to aristocratic violence, organized locally (as was the violence), rather than necessarily as the product of traditional political hierarchies. As the tenth century moved into the eleventh, the readings of public acts by local political actors could change quite a lot, at least in the West Frankish lands.

Rome was still one element of legitimization. It was still a pilgrimage centre and the location for imperial coronation, and most major political players found themselves there at one time or another. Popes, too, maintained some of their late Carolingian authority, at least in the field of law. Both John XV and Gregory V demanded the reversal of Arnulf of Reims's deposition in 991, and got their way in the end (his enemy Gerbert himself, as Pope Silvester II, reconfirmed him in office in 999).

Earlier, Agapitus II had at least initially demanded the same when Arnulf's predecessor Hugh was deposed in 947; although he was persuaded to reverse his position in 949, his opinions mattered, and his agreement needed to be obtained. Not many bishops were actually deposed in this period, but they were politically important in every kingdom, and they answered to Rome in certain limited respects. Tenth-century popes were not usually protagonists; they were mostly in rather weak positions inside the city of Rome, and, rather than act, they reacted to requests, usually along the lines the powerful wanted. But if they were to make decisions on their own, against the interests of the powerful – as over Arnulf of Reims, who had no significant support among the laity – it was hard to force them to change their minds, and the powerful might have to back down. The Latin church thus maintained the skeleton 'international' values and procedures that had begun in the Carolingian period.

One respect in which political practice changed was that it became more dynastic. This was a recognizable Carolingian inheritance, too; the Carolingians themselves had a strong dynastic consciousness, and the families of the *Reichsaristokratie* were also conscious of their rights of inheritance to land, which included an expectation that sons would succeed fathers in office at least somewhere, as we saw in Chapter 16. In the tenth century, however, nine of the great Carolingian aristocratic families gained the royal title, at least for a time, and others doubtless thought they might join them; and many others gained practical autonomy in a duchy, march, or accumulation of counties, which they could expect to pass to their heirs in a regular way. They appropriated some of the public rituals described above; they also appropriated a much more direct sense of hereditary entitlement than aristocrats had had in the ninth century. The West Frankish kings could not intervene in ducal or comital succession at all, as noted earlier, and even the Ottonians did so only with some care, or in response to revolt – or else when magnates died without sons, when they could manipulate marriage alliances. As a result, it was possible for the first time to suppose that dukes or counts might inherit as children; and this was also true of kings (Otto III in the East, Lothar in the West), as it had not been in the ninth century. Queen-mothers reappeared as important and recognized political forces, as we have seen, and a less contested force than were some of the powerful queens of the century before. Women were sometimes powerful even when kings were adults: Otto III used his aunt Matilda of Quedlinburg (d. 999) as a regent in the north when he went to Italy in 998. And, interestingly, we begin to find quite a few active duchess-mothers and marquise-mothers as well: powerful dealers for their deceased husband's families, like Bertha (d. 926), regent of Tuscany for her son Guy after 915, or Hadwig, widow of Hugh the Great, politically active in 956–60, or her daughter Beatrice, who ran Upper Lotharingia for a decade after her husband's death in 978. It is interesting how little hostility is expressed towards these ruling women in most of our sources, even though our writers are full of patriarchal clichés about female fragility. The one exception is Liutprand of Cremona, a selective misogynist, who frequently explained female power as the result of sexual licence; but his targets were essentially Italian, and this can be linked to his desire to delegitimize all aspects of Italian independence. It may be that the weakening of the heavily moralized politics of the Carolingian period left female power less exposed to suspicion and censure, outside the work of Liutprand.

A more dynastic set of political assumptions also meant a politics more rooted in the control of specific lands. Aristocrats still needed *Königsnähe*, 'closeness to kings', to keep their power and wealth and to gain more, except, increasingly, in West Francia, but they looked to the royal court from a clearly defined regional base by now, which would not shift geographically except in very rare cases, and which would, if it grew, result only in a greater domination of their own region. The effects this would have on aristocratic identity, and on the structures of local domination itself, we shall look at in more detail in Chapter 21, which deals with the aristocracy. It had an effect on wider-scale politics as well, however. Regional interests had led to the eclipse of the relevance of the West Frankish kings, as we have seen. They also contributed to the readiness of Italian magnates to cope with absentee kingship, and to focus instead on much more localized rivalries. Even in East Francia, the Ottonians had to deal with five separate political networks, Bavarian, Swabian, Frankish, Saxon and (crystallizing more slowly) Lotharingian, with their own identities and loyalties and (relative) lack of interest in their neighbours. Thietmar tells us little about Italy or West Francia, but actually not much about Bavaria and Swabia either, much less than about the most immediate Saxon rivals to the east, such as the Poles. If Otto I had been in Bavaria in the 960s and not Italy, Hermann Billung might well still have staged his critical ceremony in Magdeburg. One long-term result of this localization of identity was that, everywhere, it was not quite as entirely essential as in the past to go to kings, or to dukes or marquises or counts, to gain social status and legitimacy as an aristocrat. At a pinch, one might claim it oneself. In East Francia there was still no contest: significant players needed offices and *Königsnähe* or its ducal equivalent, and so would they for another century and more. But it would be just possible to imagine the choice by now, even in East Francia. In the West there were already some people in the tenth century who were beginning to go it alone, and there were many more in the eleventh. The parameters of political power itself would change when they did.

The tenth century has had a problem of double vision in the eyes of historians: should it be seen as a post-Carolingian century, prolonging ninth-century political structures and values (although, in the eyes of some, not so effectively), or as a prelude to the often quite different politics and polemics of the centuries after 1000 or 1050? A book which stops in 1000, as this does, is probably inevitably going to pay more attention to the first of these, and I have done so here. But the tenth century does indeed seem to me more 'Carolingian' than does the eleventh, including in the fragmented world of West Francia: even a small western principality like Anjou or Catalonia was still using many Carolingian public procedures in the late tenth century, and Tuscany or Saxony, or the Ottonian kingdom/empire as a whole, was using nearly all of them. I do not want to argue here for a simple and unchanging stability, and indeed the last couple of pages have argued the opposite. But the political parameters of the tenth-century world, including its violence, and a fair measure of cynicism and opportunism, seem to me – if one has to choose – to look backwards rather than forwards. Above all, the tenth-century emphasis on the public world of assemblies and large-scale collective rituals would lessen in the future. It was already beginning to disappear in the last decades of the tenth century in West Francia; in Italy it would continue for another century, but disappear quite fast around 1100; in East Francia it would persist for rather longer at the level of the kingdom, but would fade much faster in some of the localities. Assembly politics slowly turned into the politics of royal and princely courts, groups selected by rulers rather than being representatives (however much in practice aristocratic ones) of political communities. A sense of belonging, of loyalty, and of hierarchy would become more personalized as these changes took place, and the lord–dependant relationship would come into the foreground more, gaining as it did a more elaborate ceremonial and etiquette. These are markers of the central Middle Ages, not the early Middle Ages; and they were hardly more than at their beginning in 1000.

One result of that change is that the eleventh century, at least in West Francia but to an extent also in Italy, seldom looked back much to the tenth. History-writing in Italy after 1000 is very localized, and pays little attention to the politics of the kingdom at all; the tenth century only gets remembered in tiny vignettes, such as Hugh's lustfulness, or Otto I's saving of his second wife Adelaide from Berengar II. Rodulf Glaber in West Francia, writing only a generation after Richer, is at least interested in the kings of his own time, but before the 990s has almost no information, and it is again expressed in isolated stories, Heribert II's capture of Charles the Simple, or Lothar's war against Otto II, or the Arab capture of Abbot Maiolus of Cluny in 972; his highly detailed account of his own times needs no back history to explain matters, and maybe it would not have explained them, to his eyes. This reordering of historical consciousness marks the failure, in the west and the south of the Frankish lands, of the Carolingian political world and its traditional methods of legitimization: too much of the past did not mean anything any more. Only Charlemagne survived, as an increasingly mythic and dehistoricized figure, flanked in some areas of West Francia by Pippin III and Clovis: safe symbols of the distant past, legitimizing the present but not explaining it. The tenth century was thus eclipsed; some of its major players still cannot easily be understood. But this would not have been in anyone's mind in 1000, when, to a Gerbert or a Thietmar, the world, even if dangerous and unpredictable, was carrying on just fine.

19

'Carolingian' England, 800–1000

In 990 or 991, a landowner named Wynflæd made a plea against Leofwine (possibly her stepson) before the English king Æthelred II, about the ownership of two estates in Berkshire. She had a heavyweight set of witnesses, the king's powerful mother Ælfthryth (see below), the archbishop of Canterbury Sigeric, and a bishop and an ealdorman, the Anglo-Saxon equivalent of a Continental duke or count. Leofwine insisted that the matter be first heard at a shire assembly (*scirgemot*), the Anglo-Saxon equivalent of the county-level *placitum* in the Frankish lands; this was correct in law, but was also important to Leofwine, presumably, because the twenty-five-year-old king might not easily judge against his mother, even in the period before 993 when she was temporarily not part of his court. The move of venue did not help Leofwine much, however, for after Æthelred formally committed the case to the Berkshire assembly, with his seal and (apparently verbal) instructions, the queen-mother and twenty-four named men and women appeared and swore in favour of Wynflæd's ownership of the land. It was pointed out to Leofwine that, if the case reached the oath-swearing moment, he would risk a huge fine, and also the end of 'friendship' between the parties (though that had, one feels, long gone). He therefore conceded, handing over the land, in return for the gold and silver of his father, which Wynflæd still had. She was very reluctant to return it; it was this which had probably sparked off Leofwine's occupation of the land. But the document relating the case (an original text) ends here, and we cannot follow the parties further.

English court cases often ended in deals; Leofwine had done quite well to get this rather half-hearted one, given the odds against him (perhaps he was even in the right over the money, hence the court being prepared to broker an arbitration). But it is equally important that the deal took place in public, in the Berkshire judicial assembly. By the later tenth century, England, like the Carolingian lands, had a network of public assemblies whose main purpose was to hear disputes in front of a large number of locally powerful people. By law, these should include the local bishop and ealdorman, as usually in Francia; in the event two bishops and an abbot presided over this one, and the king's reeve Ælfgar was there too (probably he was the shire reeve, the 'sheriff', by now the king's direct representative in the locality, more directly responsible to the king than was the ealdorman). And it is clear just from Wynflæd's witnesses that the assembly was substantial in size. It will have consisted of all the local notables of Berkshire who could get there, the 'good men' as the text called them, including the aristocracy, the thegns of the county. This assembly heard local disputes, and also did royal business. The case was royal in origin, and was decided as the king would undoubtedly have wished, but his will was carried out by the whole county community. This balance between royal power and collective validation is very Carolingian in style; so is the large penalty for losing an oath. As we shall see, it is likely that there is direct Carolingian influence at work here. But we are also in 990. By now, this sort of regular royal-controlled public politics had vanished in most of the Carolingian lands, either because kings were themselves weak, as in West Francia, or because (as in Italy in particular, but also parts of East Francia) local assemblies and courts by now had a rather intermittent relationship to kings. Charlemagne's image of how the local judicial assembly should work had come to be perpetuated only in England, even though no part of England was ever under Carolingian rule. This is the paradox which we shall explore in this chapter: first, through a narrative of ninth- and tenth-century English politics; then, through a discussion of political structures and Carolingian influences on them; and finally through an analysis of English difference. For, however influential Continental practices had become, the structures of English society remained distinct too.

We left Anglo-Saxon England in Chapter 7 with Offa (d. 796) and Cenwulf (d. 821) of Mercia dominant south of the Humber. After Cenwulf's death, however, Mercian hegemony quickly broke down under a series of short-lived kings, from rival families. Ecgbert of Wessex (802–39) defeated the fourth of these, Wiglaf (827–40), in 829 and ruled Mercia directly for a year. Wiglaf recovered his throne in 830, and in 836 could call all the bishops of the southern English to his court, as had the eighth-century Mercian kings, but from now on there were two major powers in the south, Mercia and Wessex. By 840 Anglo-Saxon England was more or less back to the situation it was in in 700, in fact, with four roughly balanced kingdoms, for we must add to these two East Anglia, ill-documented but by far the most economically complex kingdom, and Northumbria, which in the early ninth century under Eardwulf (796–c. 810) and his son Eanred (c. 810–40) had a period of relative internal peace. The Mercian supremacy had firmly developed the structures of royal power, and linked the episcopal network more closely to government; it had also contributed to the definitive eclipse of the smaller kingdoms, with the Hwicce now finally attached to Mercia, and Essex, Sussex and Kent first attached to Mercia, and then, after 825, ruled stably by Wessex. (Only Kent maintained a certain autonomy, ruled as it was by Cenwulf's brother Cuthred, d. 807, then informally controlled by Archbishop Wulfred of Canterbury, d. 832, and then after 825 governed by three West Saxon sons of kings in turn.) All the same, eighth-century Mercian power had not changed the geopolitics of England, which could easily revert to the older four-kingdom framework. In the mid-century Northumbria fell back into civil war, and Mercia and Wessex were increasingly clearly the major kingdoms, cooperating quite closely on occasion, under Berhtwulf (840–52) and his probable son Burgred (852–74) of Mercia, and Æthel-wulf (839–58) of Wessex, who married his daughter to Burgred and helped him fight the Welsh. Æthelwulf had a wider prestige too, for late in life he married Charles the Bald's daughter Judith; but he was happy to concentrate on controlling southern England. At most he nibbled at Mercia's boundaries, taking over Berkshire in the 840s, although he retreated from London, leaving it and its wealth as an isolated outlier of Mercian rule.

What changed this political pattern was the Vikings. They raided the English coasts from the mid-830s, just as they did in West Francia and elsewhere; they were particularly active in Kent and East Anglia, and they stepped up their attacks in the 850s, by when they were over-wintering in some places. But, whereas in Francia they always had to leave temporarily when a royal army finally appeared, the scale of insular politics – and armies – was far smaller, and Anglo-Saxon armies could lose to Viking ones, as Berhtwulf of Mercia found in 851 and a Kentish army found in 853. The Vikings had eventually realized that this gave them the chance for more permanent gain, for it was in England that leading Danish Vikings grouped together in a 'Great Army', *micel here* in the Old English of the *Anglo-Saxon Chronicle*, in 865. The Great Army numbered in the thousands, rather than the hundreds of earlier raiding parties, and was larger than any Anglo-Saxon army; it had a collective leadership, but it acted as an effective conquering force. In 866–7 it conquered Northumbria, killing its two warring kings; in 869 it took East Anglia, again killing its king, Edmund, who was afterwards venerated as a martyr; in 870–71 the West Saxons under Æthelwulf's sons Æthelred I (865–71) and Alfred (871–99) only just, somehow, managed to hold the Army off for a time; in 873–7 it took half of Mercia, leaving Ceolwulf II (c. 874–8) with only the north-west and the south. In 876–8 it attacked Wessex again and cornered Alfred in the Somerset marshes (the location of the famous, but sadly only eleventh-century, 'Alfred and the cakes' story), before the latter managed to call an army together in 878 and defeat the Vikings at Edington in Wiltshire. This was a key battle for Wessex. The Viking leader Guthrum was forced to make peace, and even accepted baptism, retreating to East Anglia, which he turned into a stable Viking kingdom. Thereafter, the wars stopped for over a decade.

Alfred was left in control of all his father's lands, to which he added London in 886. His kingdom was thus the only one fully to survive the Viking onslaught. And he was probably also, by his death, the only Anglo-Saxon king. Ceolwulf's successor Æthelred II of Mercia (c. 879–911), Alfred's son-in-law, was called king on occasion, but is usually entitled *dux* or ealdorman in our sources; Mercia was slipping into the status of a sub-kingdom of Wessex, certainly as a result of Alfred's political choice. The only other autonomous Anglo-Saxon ruler was Eadwulf (d. 912) in Bernicia in northern Northumbria, where the Vikings did not reach; his family's rule survived off and on up to the Norman Conquest, but they may not have used the royal title. There were Danish kings, of course, in East Anglia and in York (and also apparently collective leaderships in the Five Boroughs of Danish Mercia). We do not know much about their political infrastructures. Kings were certainly less powerful in Denmark than anywhere in England, so they would not have brought strong ruling traditions with them; only the kings of York leave much impression in our (largely West Saxon) evidence, and even then not until after 919, with Røgnvald (d. *c.* 920) and Sigtryg (d. 927), both from a Dublin-based family. Once the Great Army had moved from conquering to ruling, in fact, it became strategically weaker. It had had to divide up; this fact in itself probably explains Alfred's survival, for Guthrum did not have with him the Vikings who were establishing themselves in Northumbria; and the Vikings in England not only never united again, but also seem to have ruled less stable polities than the increasingly coherent West Saxon (plus Mercian) kingdom in southern and western England. Alfred may have owed his success in 878 to luck, but he built on this systematically in the next two decades, above all – necessarily – in military preparedness: he seems to have developed a large-scale military levy from the population, and he certainly established a dense network of public fortifications, *burh*s, throughout southern England, defended by public obligation, which was sufficiently effective to hold off a second large-scale Viking assault in 892–6. Alfred died 'king of the Anglo-Saxons', or, in the *Chronicle*'s words, 'of the whole English people except that part which was under Danish rule'; he may have been the first king to see himself in 'English', not West Saxon or Mercian, terms, as his neat footwork with respect to Æthelred of Mercia's autonomy also shows. But it was the Vikings who made that choice possible for him.

Alfred's son Edward 'the Elder' (899–924) began to counterattack, at first in border wars, and then, after Æthelred of Mercia's death, systematically. In 911 Edward and his sister Æthelflæd, Lady of the Mercians (911–18) in succession to her husband Æthelred, moved eastwards, and had taken East Anglia and the Five Boroughs by Æthelflæd's death. In this period Wessex and Mercia were still operating as an alliance of near-equals; but in 919 Edward also fully annexed English Mercia, sweeping aside Æthelflæd's daughter Ælfwyn. In the 910s, the core of the English kingdom thus took shape, with finality, for across the next century Alfred's dynasty never lost control of Mercia and eastern England again, except for a brief conquest of the east Midlands in 940 by Olaf Guthfrithson, king of Dublin and York, reversed in 942. Northumbria was a different matter; the English kings and two Norwegian families fought over it for nearly thirty years, 927–54, before the last Scandinavian king of York, Eirík 'Bloodaxe', was killed on Stainmore in the latter year. But most of Northumbria was always a peripheral, only half-controlled, part of England across the next two centuries, and indeed for a long time after, and it is arguable that these wars were only really fought for the increasingly rich trading entrepôt of York itself. Edward's son Æthelstan (924–39) and his successors indeed seem to have regarded successful war against, and hegemony over, kings in Wales and of Scotland as being as important as their rule in Northumbria, as is represented by the increasingly grandiloquent claims in their documents. Æthelstan was 'king of all Britain' from 931, '*basileus* of the English and all surrounding peoples' in 938, and *imperator* became increasingly common from now on too. Overall, apart from York, one could regard the major shift of the tenth century, the invention of the kingdom of England, as being complete in military-political terms by 919.

Edward and Æthelflæd's conquest of midland and eastern England was above all a West Saxon conquest. It involved the West Saxon aristocracy, quite as much as the kings, and in the next generation the families of ealdormen of East Anglia and also, significantly, Mercia were predominantly of West Saxon origin. A surviving Mercian-focused affinity seems to be both visible and quite effective when successions were tense or disputed between brothers, as in 924 or 957–9, in each of which the Mercian-supported brother ended up as king, but the West Saxons had the strategic edge, and their aristocratic placements under-lined it further. The Wessex dynasty thus created a *Reichsaristokratie*, as the Carolingians had done, and as their Ottonian contemporaries did not manage. None of Æthelstan's successors – his brothers Edmund and Eadred (939–46, 946–55), Edmund's sons Eadwig and Edgar (955–9, 957–75), Edgar's sons Edward 'the Martyr' and Æthelred II (975–8, 978–1016) – were over eighteen at their accessions except Eadred, but, almost uniquely in history, this did not result in a weakened political system. The influence of queen-mothers, notably Edmund and Eadred's mother Eadgifu (d. after 966) and Æthelred's mother Ælfthryth (d. *c.* 1000) was very considerable, which helped the continuity of royal power, as often in Francia. But the loyalty of the leading ealdormen was as important. Under Eadgifu (that is, Edmund, Eadred, Edgar) the family of Æthelstan 'Half-king' (d. after 956), ealdorman of East Anglia from 932, came to dominate in Mercia and East Anglia; Eadwig's brief reign saw the emergence of a rival family, that of Ælfhere, ealdorman of Mercia (d. 983). These two families, both West Saxon, thereafter shared power, along with a handful of other inter-related ealdormen. We can see them as an oligarchy, ruling through a succession of young kings with, apparently, considerable coherence. And they needed to be coherent. If the English political system broke down, they could not hope to remain as powerful, given the geographical range of their landholding and office-holding, extending as it did in each case across much of southern, central and eastern England, thanks to Edward the Elder's conquests and to royal generosity thereafter.

Not that this coherence necessarily meant amity. Eadwig in particular seems to have tried to shift alignments; his reign was marked by extraordinarily large-scale royal gift-giving, and new families appeared as a result. Eadgifu and Æthelstan 'Half-king' responded by setting up Edgar in Mercia against him, apparently without violent conflict however, unlike in contemporary succession disputes in Francia; the two brothers reigned together for two years until Eadwig died, and his protégé Ælfhere actually joined Edgar, presumably in order not to lose his own Mercian clientele. Edgar and his supporters then patronized a large-scale monastic reform movement, which after 964 converted even cathedral churches into monasteries, under Dunstan of Canterbury (d. 988), Æthelwold of Winchester (d. 984) and Oswald of Worcester and York (d. 992), all of them monk-bishops; free-standing monasteries were also founded and patronized by kings and aristocrats, including the rival Fenland houses of Ramsey (968) and Ely (970). The landed politics of these increasingly rich houses was itself controversial, and the reign of Edward the Martyr in particular saw trouble, with aristocrats taking, or taking back, monastic lands. Edward was actually murdered in 978, in obscure circumstances, a bad start to the reign of Æthelred II and his (but not Edward's) mother Ælfthryth. But none of these tensions resulted in more than sporadic violence, and the ealdormanic oligarchy survived into the 990s. Æthelred II was by then strong enough to end it. Ælfhere's probable brother-in-law and heir in Mercia, Ælfric, was expelled for treason in 985; when Æthelwine, the powerful son of Æthelstan 'Half-king', died in 992, his sons did not succeed him in East Anglia; by 1006, all the old families were gone, most of them permanently. It was Æthelred II, then, who decisively broke with the 930s–940s political system of Æthelstan and Eadgifu; his later protégés were all new. Unfortunately, they also seem to have been less effective. Æthelred's reign also saw the return of Viking raiding, sporadic from 980 and serious after 990; from 1009 the invading armies were ever more successful, and

English defences ever more feeble. In 1013 King Svein of Denmark (d. 1014), who had led some of the earlier raids, engaged in a full-scale conquest of England, which was completed in 1016 by his son Cnut (1016–35).

The wars and instability which the southern English had managed to avoid for a century returned a hundredfold in the 1010s. The sense of political collapse that is so visible in the bitter pages of the *Anglo-Saxon Chronicle* for these years has few parallels in the whole of English history since. But Cnut nonetheless managed to inherit a rich and stable kingdom from Æthelred. We must not underestimate the stresses and factions in that kingdom, and maybe the difficulties in making an English identity stick in the face of more local loyalties. All the same, it had achieved, in the generations since Edward the Elder, a structural coherence that could outlast the destruction of its ruling élites by Æthelred and the military ineptness of their successors. The rest of this chapter will look at how and why this occurred.

The structures of government did not change much in the early ninth century, except that royal entourages seem to have become more complex in that period, with increasing numbers of officials travelling the country and having to be fed. Major shifts seem to have begun with Alfred. Exactly how this worked will never be fully known. Anglo-Saxon sources are never generous, including by early medieval standards; even those for Alfred, although more numerous than for the reigns of his father and his son, are very much the mouthpiece for Alfred himself, who was not only the patron of writers but an author in his own right, well aware of the possibilities of political spin, and visibly skilled in covering cynical political calculation with a moralistic veneer. What is clear, however, is that Alfred was very influenced by the political values of the Carolingian court. He sought intellectuals from Francia; we have a letter from Archbishop Fulk of Reims rather reluctantly granting Alfred's request for Grimbald of Saint-Bertin in 886. Einhard's *Life* of Charlemagne was available in England, and was one of the models used by Alfred's Welsh protégé Asser in his own *Life* of Alfred. That text, written in Alfred's lifetime, creates an image of Alfred heavily influenced by hagiography, including an illness (piles) which protected his youthful chastity, and another debilitating disease which undermined him in later years (the illnesses may well have been real, but their role in Asser's text parallels hagiographical writing), as well as a heavy emphasis on Alfred's learning and spiritual commitment. Alfred was indeed unusually well educated, even by Carolingian standards; he thought it essential to sponsor translations into Old English of some of the fundamental Latin Christian works of the early Middle Ages, such as Gregory the Great's *Pastoral Care*, to make them accessible to the Anglo-Saxon élites, and three of these translations are his own work. Alfred's often fairly free translation of Boethius' *Consolation of Philosophy* shows a king fully familiar with a biblical and theological conception of kingship, pragmatic (kings need resources) but also self-aware (when the rich and powerful go abroad and meet people who do not know them, they realize how much their position is owed 'to the praise of foolish people'). Alfred looked systematically to the Bible; his law code goes further even than those of Charlemagne in its insertion, as a preface, of a set of extracts from the laws of Moses in Exodus, which were evidently intended to have at least meta-legal force. This sort of literary royal ideology was unparalleled in England before Alfred's generation, but it has direct roots in the thought-world of Louis the Pious and Charles the Bald.

The Carolingian reform programme thus took root in England during just the decades in which it was running out of steam in Francia. But Alfred also borrowed political practices from the Frankish world. One of the clearest is the collective oath of loyalty sworn to the king, which is the first law in Alfred's code, and which looks straight back to Carolingian legislation (Alfred states just before that law that he 'dared not presume to set down in writing at all many of my own [laws]' but this is typical Alfredian disinformation); one of the tenth-century developments of this law, Edmund's code of about 943, quotes directly from a capitulary of 802. In England, indeed, that law was interpreted rather more harshly than in Francia, for the next century is scattered with cases of aristocrats who lost all their land for breaking their oath, something that rarely happened in either the Carolingian or the Ottonian world. The great emphasis on the oath in the Wynflæd–Leofwine case seems related to this too. The detail of Alfred's own government, including his army reforms, looks back to the Anglo-Saxon past rather than over the Channel, as far as we can see. But the precedent he set allowed his tenth-century successors, as they developed the increasingly coherent and self-confident southern English state, to draw from Frankish

example wherever necessary, alongside extensions of indigenous practice. Edward the Elder and his successors spread the pattern of West
Saxon shires across Mercia, obliterating the old Mercian regional divisions (in a particularly overt act, perhaps dating to the 920s, the old
Mercian royal centre of Tamworth was actually bisected by the boundaries of Warwickshire and Staffordshire, thus marginalizing it for ever
after); the *burh* network of Wessex was extended to Mercia already in
the 910s, although it seems increasingly likely that the Mercians had
had a similar system of fortified centres before as well. Conversely, the
new subdivision of the shire, the hundred, seems to have been a Frankish
import, not a West Saxon one, and it too was established in the tenth
century. Tenth-century assembly politics (the king's own large consulta-
tive assembly, the shire assembly, the hundredal assembly) similarly had
Anglo-Saxon – indeed, common Germanic – roots; but the increasingly
visible judicial activity of these bodies, and their association with royal
direction, the king's seal and attached instructions, betrays Frankish
influence. So does royal legislation, as already implied; Alfred's revival
of it in itself probably shows his awareness of Carolingian law-making,
and the numerous codes of the 920s–1020s resemble Frankish capitularies, sometimes quite closely. As with Edmund in 943, when Æthelred II
in 1009 decreed a three-day fast in great detail in his seventh code, as a
response to the great Viking invasion of that year, he was directly
echoing Charlemagne.

These Frankish influences are not surprising. (More surprising is how
seldom they were noticed before the 1970s.) Carolingian Francia was
so much more powerful than any English kingdom, and its governmental
technologies were so much more sophisticated, that, once the idea of
borrowing developed, it could continue for a long time. We must add to
this the increasing integration of the tenth-century West Saxon dynasty
into Continental politics. Edward the Elder was the first Anglo-Saxon
king to engage systematically in marriage alliances abroad, and his
daughters ended up married to Charles the Simple, Hugh the Great and
Otto I; Æthelstan intervened in West Frankish politics, sheltering his
nephew Louis IV in his years of exile, and sending armies twice to the
Continent. The English kings were increasingly regarded by the Franks
as political players, and mutual interest increased: Asser and the *Anglo-
Saxon Chronicle* include an account of the 887–8 Frankish succession
crisis; Flodoard and Thietmar both include (a few) English events in

their chronicles. Cultural relationships developed as well. English clerics sometimes spent time in Continental monasteries, as Oswald did in Fleury and Dunstan in Ghent (Æthelwold, too, sent a monk to Fleury to learn local practices); Continental intellectuals came to England in their turn, from Grimbald in the 880s to Abbo of Fleury in 985–7. Archbishop Wulfstan of York (d. 1023), who wrote several law codes for both Æthelred II and Cnut and some compilations of his own, was also a rousing social and political critic in the Hincmar mould, and his work is clearly influenced by the idiom of Carolingian *correctio*. The later tenth-century monastic reform in England was sister to that of Gorze, or that favoured by the abbots of Cluny (see below, Chapter 21), and the new English national monastic rule, the *Regularis Concordia*, drawn up by Æthelwold in the late 960s, both explicitly drew from contemporary example in Ghent and Fleury and owed its wider ambition to the unification of monastic practices set in motion by Louis the Pious after 816.

This international dimension, so visible in tenth-century England, does bring a paradox all the same. For tenth-century Francia, as noted at the start of the chapter, was by no means still Carolingian in its aspiration. In Alfred's time the values of Charles the Bald and Hincmar were still alive, but they were far weaker on the Continent by the time of Æthelstan or Edgar. Carolingian institutions, rituals, values came to England not (or not only) through the observation and emulation of practice, but through books. Wulfstan owned a copy of Ansegis's capitulary collection, and it is likely enough that one had existed in England since Alfred's time. Alcuin (himself Anglo-Saxon, of course) was certainly well known, Theodulf and Amalarius were available, and Hincmar may have been as well, at least second-hand. But it is still striking that the English took this literature so seriously. This may in part have been the legacy of Alfred's highly moralized kingship; it must also have been a spin-off of the self-confidence of the tenth-century political community, whose members, however fractious, were the creators and maintainers of the largest, strongest, and most internally stable polity in Britain since the Romans left, and proud of it too.

Tenth-century English government was both more and less coherent than that of the Carolingians. Although Old English, not Latin, was the main language of legislation and much theology, implying a desire for wider dissemination in the country, the English court seems to have used writing less; royal orders seem to have been largely (although not always) verbal across the century, and writs, written orders, only clearly survive from Æthelred II's reign. For all the elaboration of tenth-century law-making, it is never explicitly referred to in our surviving court cases, and one has to look hard even to find implicit echoes; it often matches the political theology of Charlemagne's reign, rather than his practical institutional changes, although Æthelstan and some of his successors did consciously innovate in their laws. The sophistication of English government, often written up in recent years, has to be set against the relative roughness of some 'administrative' practices: when the inhabitants of Thanet robbed some York merchants in 969, Edgar simply ravaged the island; Æthelred II similarly sacked the diocese of Rochester in 986, and, later on, Harthacnut (1040–42) sacked Worcestershire in 1041 because two tax collectors had been killed in Worcester cathedral.

Conversely, there is clear evidence of royal strength. The importance of oaths to the king enormously widened the scope of 'treason' in the period, and it seems to have been easier in England than elsewhere for people to lose their lands and lives because of the king's displeasure. Monastic reform was very heavily dependent on royal authority, and enhanced that authority in its turn. And in the 990s Æthelred II, in order to pay off the Vikings, instituted a tax system that in a few years was capable of generating considerable sums; this went way beyond anything the Carolingians ever attempted (Charles the Bald had begun the same process, but only tried it twice). How the Anglo-Saxon state managed such a task, given the detailed assessment which was necessary for it to run at all, without a very developed writing-based administrative infrastructure (as it seems), and in a period of continuous military defeat and demoralization, cannot be explained at present. But it was successful; eleventh-century English taxation was more elaborate than any other post-Roman state managed in the West until after 1200, and it generated, among other things, the most systematic governmental survey before the late Middle Ages, *Domesday Book* of 1086. Taxation was organized harshly; people who could not pay it lost their lands to people who could pay in their stead, and collective rejection of taxation brought reprisals, as at Worcester in 1041. The late Anglo-Saxon state, here as elsewhere, was heavy-handed and not notably benign. But taxation continued. It further increased royal wealth, and thus power, by the time that Cnut's conquest allowed the money raised to stay in England, and it made possible the enduring solidity of the English state that was conquered, first by Svein and Cnut in 1013–16, and then by William I in 1066.

The tenth-century English kingdom had a rich aristocracy, as we have seen, one that saw its identity and political future as very much tied up with the success of the West Saxon dynasty. In Wessex, and also in English Mercia, it had deeper roots, but in much of the country it was entirely new, for its wealth in Danish Mercia and East Anglia derived from Edward the Elder's conquest in 911–18 and partial expropriation of the political élites there, whose power in turn had presumably in most cases been new as well, a product of the Viking conquest of 869–78. It is interesting to realize, however, that despite the great importance of that conquest as a catalyst for the creation of a southern English state, the effect of the Vikings themselves on the country is very difficult to see. It is not clear that either Danish or (in north-west England) Norwegian settlement was very extensive; Scandinavian place names are dense in many areas, particularly Danish Mercia and Yorkshire, but this seems mostly to indicate the renaming of estates by new owners, not a mass peasant immigration. A distinctively Scandinavian material culture is also hard to find in the archaeology; the settlers seem to have become Christian fairly quickly; even Danish law, whose existence is implied by the later use of the term 'Danelaw' for northern and eastern England, seems, in the rare compilations that mention it, to have been much like Anglo-Saxon law elsewhere. There must have been some clusters of people with a Danish culture and identity in later tenth-century England, and there were certainly plenty of aristocrats with Danish ancestors (Oswald was one), but, overall, the eastern 'Danelaw' was probably less different from Wessex and English Mercia than Northumbria was from either. What the Vikings left for the West Saxon incomers was a more complicated and fragmented estate structure, with more space for a landowning peasantry (although even this may predate the Great Army's conquests); and, in the southernmost part of Northumbria, the notable cosmopolitanism and openness to long-distance links of tenth-century York. For the rest, it is the West Saxon aristocratic stratum, overlaying the Viking period, that remains the most visible, at least south of the Humber.

The coherence of the English kingdom is perhaps best expressed in one of the witnesses to its late tenth-century defeat, the poem known as *The Battle of Maldon*. This text celebrates the fight to the death by Ealdorman Byrhtnoth of Essex and his entourage against the newly invading Vikings at Maldon in 991. Byrhtnoth, an ally of the family of Æthelstan 'Half-king', had been one of the major figures of the kingdom since the start of Edgar's reign and an important patron of Ely abbey; his death came as a considerable shock. The poem is written up in the best heroic style by an anonymous poet, probably (though this is debated) shortly after the battle. Byrhtnoth's troops have the same personal attachment to him that heroic warbands had in earlier poetry, but there are differences. One is that he has with him a county levy from Essex, heir to the collective defensive levies set up by Alfred, as well as a core group of personally loyal dependants. Another is that the men who fight on, with proud speeches, around their dead leader are from different parts of England (a Mercian aristocrat, a Northumbrian hostage, as well as men of Essex) and also from different social classes (a simple peasant, an old retainer): they are intended to represent a cross-section of English, not just Essex-based, identity and loyalty, and they explicitly fight not just for Byrhtnoth but for 'the kingdom of Æthelred, my lord's people and his country'. This kingdom-wide identity (at least in the vision of the Maldon poet) briefly unravelled in the chaos of the early 1010s, when, as the *Anglo-Saxon Chronicle* grimly claims, 'in the end no shire would even help the next', but it revived after that. There was no permanent regional breakdown in at least southern England, no equivalent to the increasingly separate marches, duchies, counties of the Continent. Nor did private lordships develop; the shire and hundred assemblies controlled nearly all justice right up to the Norman Conquest. By 1066 even Northumbria was beginning (although with difficulty) to be incorporated into the political system. Of course, there were local differences, and also local loyalties and rivalries. But, as *Domesday Book* shows, the wide geographical spread of the land-owning of the tenth-century ealdormanic élite continued throughout the eleventh century as well, and in 1066 that spread is equally visible for the next level down, the thegns, the basic aristocratic stratum of the country. That landowning, fully matched by the spread of lands of cathedrals and monasteries, held the country together. The newly minted tax system simply added to this pre-existing coherence.

England may have been Carolingian in its aspirations; but the long-lasting solidity of the political settlement of Edward the Elder's reign has so little parallel on the Continent that we cannot ascribe it all to the Carolingian lesson so systematically learned. What its roots really were must remain speculative: we do not have enough evidence for late Anglo-Saxon England to be sure of any argument of this kind. I would myself, however, associate it with a ninth-century development entirely separate from Viking conquest and Alfredian ideology: the formation of exclusive rights to property. We saw in Chapter 7 that early Anglo-Saxon land-units can best be seen as territories from which kings and some aristocrats, and, thanks to royal gift, churches and monasteries, took tribute, which could be quite light. In such territories, which were often substantial, covering the territories of a dozen later villages or more in some cases, a variety of people could live, from aristocrats to peasants, with, it seems, a variety of rights of possession; only the unfree seem to have paid heavy rents and services to lords or masters. That was the situation in the late seventh century, when our documents (all of them initially gifts by kings to churches) start. By 900, though, a list of rents surviving from Hurstborne Priors in Hampshire shows a village with much more serious obligations: here, the *ceorlas*, free peasants, had to pay money and produce in rent, and also do labour service, ploughing and sheep-shearing. These detailed requirements show tight control, and they are the first signs of what would become the standard landlord–tenant relationship in England: for the *ceorlas* of Hurstborne are best seen as tenants of the bishop of Winchester, the holder – we can now say owner – of the land. By the late tenth to early eleventh century, this sort of relationship seems quite generalized in the west Midlands and Somerset, too, for this is the broad area of origin of a text, called the *Rectitudines Singularum Personarum*, describing the standard dues owed by several strata of dependants on an unnamed estate, apparently as a guide to good estate-management. By *Domesday Book* in 1086, such an estate pattern characterized the entire country, in the former Viking-ruled lands no less than in the west and south. The global wealth deriving from rents and services was by now both great and capable of being described in detail.

These changes represent a revolution in land tenure, in which not just unfree, but also free, peasants ended up paying not just tribute to lords and rulers, but rents to landowners; these rents, importantly, were much heavier as well. The absence of any documented resistance to this process indicates that it was slow, certainly starting with the unfree (who were numerous), but then probably extending steadily to different groups of the free, first at the centre of land-units, and then coming to include their fringes and outliers, whose inhabitants paid lower rents and services well into the central Middle Ages. The more influential inhabitants of early Anglo-Saxon territories for the most part, by contrast, ended up not as tenants but as lords. Territories split up as time went on; a land-unit covering a dozen later villages might turn into twelve smaller units, which we can now call estates, each covering a single village territory. When held privately, these estates were characteristically in the hands of thegns, whether they held the land outright (in gift from the king, their former territorial lord, perhaps), or in lease from a church; the latter relationship is particularly well documented on the lands of Worcester cathedral, which kept its leases and recorded them in two eleventh-century cartularies. We cannot easily date the main period of the shift from land-units to estates, for the terminology of our documents remains much the same; but the break-up of larger units into village-sized blocks seems, from documentary evidence, to be a feature of the ninth and tenth centuries. This is also the period of a generalized concentration of settlement in the Midlands and central-southern England, into the villages at the centre of each of these blocks; this was a slower process, but probably a related one. The Hurstborne document, however isolated, would thus mark a change that was by then widespread, even, maybe, already nearing completion: the creation of a landscape of estates, one which had for long been typical of Continental western Europe, but which had not existed in England since the departure of the Romans.

This shift is as ill-documented as it was fundamental; my characterization of it in the last two paragraphs has to be seen as hypothetical. But its consequences are more visible, and several of them are important. One is that disposable wealth was sharply concentrated, and in fewer hands: those of kings, greater and lesser aristocrats and churches. As a result, an exchange economy, and more elaborate patterns of production, are notably more visible in the tenth century than in the eighth. In the eighth, exchange was still focused on a handful of ports, Southampton, London, Ipswich, York. In the tenth, York expanded dramatically, in part thanks to the international links of the Viking world (as we shall see in the next chapter), but so also did a network of inland centres, Lincoln, Thetford, Stamford, Chester, Winchester, and, to a lesser extent, a wide set of the *burh*s or boroughs of Alfred, Edward the Elder, and their Danish opponents, in particular the network of county towns, Leicester, Worcester, Shrewsbury, Oxford. This can be seen as a capillary urban network, at least one per shire and often more. And, in productive terms, wheel-thrown pottery with relatively wide distribution patterns begins to appear in the decades around 900, first in the east Midlands, at Stamford, Thetford, St Neots, and then elsewhere; references to wool, England's central medieval export strength, begin to appear by the end of the century too. The tenth-century kings greatly increased the money supply, and exchange was sufficiently widespread for the tax system of the 990s to assume that taxes could be paid in silver coin. That wealth may have been creamed off to Denmark, at least initially, but it was still wealth. The infrastructure for its extraction from the peasantry evidently existed fully by then. Rare excavations of thegnly residences, at Raunds in Northamptonshire and Goltho in Lincolnshire, also show concentrations of wealth that were invisible in the eighth century; so do late Anglo-Saxon private churches, which were for the first time becoming numerous, and which after 1000 were increasingly built in stone.

This concentration of wealth was all the greater because of its geographical completeness, the second consequence of the estate-formation process. Most of England split into village-sized estates, or perhaps half- or quarter-villages; any space for a free landowning peasantry virtually vanished. This pattern was less regular in parts of the Danelaw, in particular the east Midlands, where some more independent peasant groups persisted (many were called *sochemanni*, 'sokemen', in *Domesday Book*, indicating that they had rights to seek justice with, it seems, some autonomy from lords, even when they were tenants); the Danelaw, from Yorkshire to East Anglia, also had more fragmented estates, which in itself gave more space for peasant landowning, and which allowed for reduced subjection on estate outliers. But even there, the process of estate formation seems to have had the same sort of timescale; and even there, the percentage of landowning peasants was lower than on most of the Continent. England had thus moved from being the post-Roman province with least peasant subjection, in 700, to the land where peasant subjection was the completest and most totalizing in the whole of Europe, by as early as 900 in much of the country, and by the eleventh century at the latest elsewhere. The lordships of France based on private justice did not develop in England, but they hardly needed to; peasants were already entirely subject to lords tenurially, and many were unfree (unlike in France: see Chapter 22) and thus had no rights to public justice either.

A third consequence is that this crystallization of landed power, with the substantial increase in dues from peasants that came with it, greatly favoured kings. Kings had had rights of small-scale tribute from most of the land-area of their kingdoms – all the land which they had not already conceded to churches. When this turned into rent, churches and indeed lay aristocrats all found their local power (and their own wealth) more certain, in the village blocks they controlled, but kings were still the main beneficiaries. By the tenth century, kings ended up with a high proportion of the land under their direct control. Although that proportion was higher in some areas than in others, the tenth-century kings of southern England controlled, overall, a far higher percentage of the land-area of their kingdom than did Charlemagne; the Frankish king/emperor was certainly much richer than they, but only as a result of his rule over ten times the land-area of the realm of Æthelstan. English kings thus had a uniquely favourable position in Europe: they could be enormously generous, creating a new aristocracy or giving it hitherto unknown wealth, whether on a large scale (Æthelstan 'Half-king', Ælfhere of Mercia) or a small, while still maintaining overall dominance, as a result of the extensive lands they still owned. They thus kept the strategic upper hand, which was further safeguarded when taxation came in. Royal courts and royal power, as we have seen, remained central even in the mid- and late tenth century, characterized as it was by royal minorities and the oligarchy of the queen and her leading aristocrats; this centrality was greatly aided by royal dominance over land. No one in early medieval Europe was ever as generous as Eadwig in his documented land grants of 956–9, but his successors were not weakened, and Æthelred II rolled back the tide of generosity when he took offices and often private property off the ealdormanic élite again; Cnut's conquest displaced more aristocratic families, and William I's did even more completely. Kings could thus remain crucial to all political calculation in England, simply because of their undiminished powers of patronage. It is this, above all, that marks England as different, and marks out its trajectory as separate from that in any of the Carolingian successor states. The 'politics of land' here definitely favoured royal power, and, eventually, central government.

This was further reinforced by another special characteristic of England, already referred to: the tenth-century kings' continuing relationship to free society. One consequence of the exclusion of the peasantry from landowning might have been that they were also excluded from any relationship to the public world, as indeed happened in West Francia, and often elsewhere in the Carolingian world too. In England, as we have just seen, more of them were tenants of the king than was the case elsewhere; royal dependants seem to have had more rights than other tenants (this was still so later in the Middle Ages), and they were at least not subjected to private lords. But the traditional public obligations of all free men persisted as well. The national emergency of Alfred's reign required a wider military participation than was by now necessary on the Continent, and *burh* defence was added to it; these public commitments continued without a break, alongside the more skilled military strike forces of the aristocracy, whenever national defence required. Similarly, even shire judicial assemblies had space for the free peasantry, and the basic law for the hundredal assembly indeed presumed that their attendance was normal; this public role for the free continued without a break thereafter, as it did not in most regions of the Carolingian world.

England's development thus remains paradoxical. It became the European country where aristocratic dominance, based on property rights, was most complete, while also being the post-Carolingian country where kings maintained most fully their control over political structures, both traditional (assemblies, armies) and new (oaths, taxation). But the paradox seems to me expicable, nonetheless: it is the consequence of both the oligarchical compact that allowed the West Saxon conquest of the rest of southern England in the 910s, and the crystallization of property rights that took place in the ninth century and into the tenth. England's history as the longest-lasting state of medieval Europe began there.

20

Outer Europe

Anskar was a missionary sent by Louis the Pious to evangelize the Danes and Swedes, which he attempted off and on between 826 and his death in 865. His saint's life, written by a well-informed younger contemporary, Rimbert, is a rare account of an unsuccessful conversion process. In Denmark, Anskar might have got somewhere, thanks to the patronage of kings Horic I (827–54) and Horic II (854–c. 870), not Christians but not unsympathetic either. But the mission only had patrons (both royal and aristocratic), not any powerful and committed converts, except among some of the merchants of Hedeby, and in the confusion after Horic II's death it folded. In Sweden, Anskar's main attempt, probably in the 840s, involved a meeting with King Olaf at the trading town of Birka, in which Olaf said he could not accept the mission without asking his own gods through drawing lots, and without asking the assembly (*placitum* in Rimbert's Latin) 'for it is the custom for [the Swedes] that any public business is more in the will of the unanimous people [*populus*] than in [that of] royal power'. The lots were negative, but an elder in the assembly argued that the Christian god might help in the face of dangers at sea, and the *populus* agreed to accept the mission. Olaf agreed to ask another assembly in his kingdom to accept it as well. This assembly politics seems to have been more powerful in Sweden than in Denmark (though there were certainly assemblies there too), but we must note that in both kingdoms the discussion was only about whether to accept a Christian mission, not about whether actually to convert en masse, which did not happen in either. Even if kings were personally Christian, as Håkon I (c. 934–61) was in Norway, they could not easily demand conversion from their countrymen, and Håkon is praised for not trying to do so in a probably contemporary poem. The wider conversion process only began in the late tenth century in Denmark, and later still

in Sweden and Norway: it was, in part, a consequence of stronger
kingship, although, by Continental European standards, only a little
stronger.

When trying to understand European societies outside the ex-Roman
and Carolingian kingdoms of the West and South (and, eventually, their
Anglo-Saxon offshoot), we need to recognize the weakness of political
structures straight away. Royal politics did not delineate the history of
the Scandinavians or Slavs with any consistency until the late tenth
century. Indeed, it is not clear, despite the certainties of external texts
like the *Life* of Anskar, that rulers had any consistent 'kingly' titles;
jarlar, jarls or earls, were independent powers in the northerly Trondheim district of Norway until after 1000, for example, and the Slavs
seem to have had a very eclectic set of titles for rulers. It may be
that there was as yet no clear distinction between 'kings' and leading
'aristocrats' in either, that is, between independent rulers, nominally
dependent but autonomous rulers, and more subject political leaders;
aristocrats, too, were probably leaders of followers rather than landlords
of tenants for a long time. In Wales, Scotland, and Ireland before 800,
as we saw in Chapter 7, rulers were regularly called 'kings', but the
reges of our sources ruled tiny kingdoms (except in Scotland), and their
power was more easily assimilated to that of the small-scale rulers and
leading aristocrats of Scandinavia than even to Anglo-Saxon kings, never
mind Frankish ones. Some of these regions were beginning to move
towards more centralized political systems with stronger rulers by the
very end of our period, 950–1000: Poland, Bohemia, the core lands of
what is now Russia, and Denmark. Conversely, this process of 'state-
building' was still highly incomplete in Norway, Scotland, Wales and
Ireland; and in Sweden (as in some of the smaller Slav communities) it
had hardly started.

These were slow developments, and by no means consistent; kings
were stronger in Denmark, for example, in 800 than in 900. But they
do act as a guide to comparison, in these non-Carolingian regions. They
also give a justification for my decision to consider such heterogeneous
cultures together. I do this partly to avoid a set of fragmented chapters,
each of them short because the evidence for each region is so very much
thinner in the pre-1000 period than it is for Francia, Italy, or England.
But the 'outer European' lands do have features in common, as we
shall see. So also does post-Visigothic northern Spain, which had very

different antecedents, but some parallels all the same, and this region is considered here too. One of these common features was the Vikings, who had a major effect in Russia and in Scotland, Ireland and Wales (as also in England, as we have seen). Scandinavia's internal history cannot be reduced to the Viking label, but it is undeniable that the Vikings at least came from there. We shall start with Scandinavia, therefore; we will then move to the Sclavenian or Slav lands, before moving westwards to Britain, Ireland and Spain.

Denmark is in agricultural terms by far the richest part of Scandinavia – it is an extension of the North European Plain, and is not heavily forested, as are Sweden and Norway – and it was both economically and politically the most complex northern region until well past 1000. Already in the fifth and early sixth centuries it had some very rich centres, as archaeology shows, particularly Gudme on the central island of Fyn, where several dozen houses and a large hall have been excavated, and also a wealth of gold finds, in cemeteries and elsewhere, so far unparalleled in northern Europe. Some of these were locally made; others were imported from the Roman empire. It is most likely that Gudme was a royal or princely centre: not the only one in Denmark, but one which well shows the wealth that Danish rulers could already lay their hands on, at least in the period of west Roman crisis.

This concentration of wealth fell back after 550, and in the next hundred and fifty years Denmark shows more muted, and probably more fragmented, power structures, focused on isolated 'magnate farms' and villages. Around 700, however, we can see signs of a larger political system in the south of the Jutland peninsula, in western Denmark; a central power of some sort created Ribe, a trading town parallel to the king-centred *emporia* of eighth-century England, in 705–10, and in 737 the Danevirke, a defensive wall across the south of the peninsula, was substantially rebuilt. (These unusually exact dates by archaeological standards are based on tree-ring dating.) Southern Jutland was the political zone of the *reges Danorum*, which Frankish sources begin to name from the 770s; by the time of Godofrid (c. 800–810), the kings seem to have had a hegemony extending throughout the territory of medieval Denmark (which also included modern southern Sweden), and also north into Vestfold around Oslo in southern Norway and south into the territory of the Sclavenian Abodrites. Godofrid even faced off

Charlemagne, attacking Frankish Frisia; he founded his own trading town at Hedeby, too. Horic I was his son; it took fifteen years of instability and infighting for him to establish himself, but his opponents all seem from their names to be relatives, indicating a relatively solid hegemony for the family. After the 870s, however, the Danish kingdom broke down, and we hardly even know the names of rival kings for over half a century. It is entirely likely that the unity of the previous century dissolved. Gorm (d. 958) and his son Harald Bluetooth (958–c. 987) had to start again; they were also based in southern Jutland (at Jelling, where Harald set up a large and boastful runic grave-monument for his father), but were probably not from Godofrid and Horic's family. Harald managed to recreate the Denmark-wide power of the latter, all the same; and his polity was by now notably more organized; nearly identical circular military camps survive in four or five sites in the kingdom, datable to around 980, which show a regularity of military and naval obligation almost certainly invented by Harald himself. Harald claimed hegemony in Norway too; and it was he who was both baptized a Christian (in c. 965) and also began to impose Christianity on his whole kingdom. His son Svein (987–1014) was the conqueror of England, in 1013, as we saw in the last chapter, a clear sign that the military reorganization of his father was more than wishful thinking; and his son Cnut, ruler from England to Norway, was in the 1020s–1030s second only to the German emperors as a western European power.

Norway and Sweden did not match this development, Sweden least of all. The Swedish kings we know of were based in the old ceremonial and cult centre of Uppsala (not far from the rich trading town of Birka, which they also controlled), but they cannot be said to have ruled much outside this area. We do not know the names of most of them up to 1000, and it is likely that even in their core area, not to speak of the rest of the (future) Swedish lands, rulers of different types coexisted with the assembly-based politics which Anskar found. This was also the case in Norway. Norway is very mountainous, and communications between its few fertile areas (Vestfold, the south-west fjords, the Trondheim area) were generally by sea. These areas seem to have had very different histories for a long time, with independent rulers and assemblies; some of these polities must indeed have been very small, as both local ecology and archaeological finds imply. The Danes, who were also seaborne (Denmark being composed largely of islands) could all the more easily establish local hegemonies in parts of Norway, which can be documented more on than off from Godofrid to Cnut. Only in the period of Danish weakness did a Norwegian king, Harald 'Finehair' (d. *c.* 932), try to do the same, extending his hegemony from the south-west to the whole of Norway up to Trondheim, and demanding tribute. It is highly unlikely that Harald had all that much power, and his sons and grandson were locally contested or expelled: Eirík Bloodaxe (*c.* 932–4) finished his career as king of York (948–9, 952–4), and his brother Håkon I was killed by his nephew, who was himself killed around 970. Later Norwegian kings were adventurers, Olaf Tryggvason (995–1000 – he died in battle against Svein of Denmark) and his cousin Olaf Haraldsson (1015–30 – he died in battle against Norwegian opponents of his centralizing ambitions, who were supported by Cnut). These kings also coexisted with powerful jarls, notably the already-mentioned jarls of Hlaðir in the Trondheim district, dominant in the later tenth century, who were happier with the loose Danish hegemony which was the alternative to local kingship. The Olafs did bring Christianity to Norway, but a stable and uncontested Norwegian kingship did not exist until the mid-eleventh century, or even later.

It is interesting how much opposition these kings in Norway generated. Indeed, later Icelandic traditions consistently ascribe the Norse settlement of Iceland itself to men fleeing Harald Finehair's tyranny. This is chronologically impossible, for that settlement began around 870, when Harald cannot yet have begun his career, quite apart from the unlikelihood that he was so very powerful. But it is at least true that the Icelanders, who were largely from western Norway (or from its offshoots in Scotland, bringing Irish slaves with them too), set up a political system in their newly settled island in the early tenth century which clearly sought to make difficult any permanent accumulation of power. This system consisted of a hierarchy of legal assemblies, *thingar* in Old Norse, with an annual all-Iceland assembly (the Althing) at the apex. Each assembly was dominated by three or four locally based political and religious leaders, *goðar*, who were hereditary, and were certainly the most powerful and the richest local figures; each *goði* had free dependants, *thingmenn*, whom he represented at the assembly. But *thingmenn* could leave their *goði* and transfer their loyalty to a rival, thus preventing leaders from throwing their weight around too much. Later Icelandic narratives make it clear that powerful *goðar* (like Snorri *goði* in the west, Hall of Sida in the east and Guðmund 'the Powerful' in the north, leaders around 1000, the year Iceland accepted Christianity), only established temporary hegemonies based on their charisma and political skill, which would drop back on their deaths. The slowly developing Christian church came largely to fit this political pattern too.

Norway had more stable aristocratic power than this, but later laws, of the Gulathing of the western fjords and the Frostathing of the Trondheim area, show the centrality of assemblies once again, set against a hierarchy of aristocratic (and royal) patronage. It may be best to see the political hierarchy as one of patronage everywhere, in the Norwegian lands as in Iceland, with aristocratic patrons (called variously *jarlar*, *hersir*, *hauldar*, *thegnar*, *goðar*), and clients who were generally independently owning free peasants. This was not an egalitarian society, and the free peasantry had slave farm-labourers and servants as well, but royal ambition was external to it, and was resisted for a long time. It is likely, indeed, that this also explains the temporary failure of Danish royal power in the late ninth and early tenth century. Denmark did, at least, have influential local political or ritual leaders, sometimes called *goðar* in runic inscriptions, as further north. These were probably more subject to kings (and perhaps already had greater tenurial control over their dependants) than in Norway, but were probably also still capable of going it alone if they got the chance – but as patrons, not, as yet, as landowning or seigneurial lords.

Norse literature is late (thirteenth-century for the most part) but sometimes preserves earlier material: exactly how early is much discussed. The practical advice contained in the *Hávamál*, a set of verse proverbs, probably from Norway, dating quite possibly to the tenth century, conveys some of the values which run through all our sources. 'Before you walk forward, you should look at, you should spy out, all the entrances; for you can't be certain where enemies are sitting ahead in the hall.' 'The foolish man thinks that everyone is his friend who laughs with him; but then he finds when he comes to the assembly that he has few to speak on his behalf.' 'No man should step one pace away from his weapons on the open road.' 'He should get up early, the man who means to take another's life or property.' 'Such is the love of women with false minds: it's like driving a horse without spiked shoes over slippery ice (a frisky two-year-old, badly broken in), or like steering a rudderless boat in a stiff wind, or like trying to catch a reindeer on a thawing hillside when you're lame.' This careful, suspicious, macho, pragmatic, peasant culture marked Scandinavia in later centuries, and all the signs are that it did so already.

But Scandinavia also produced the Vikings; they were its best-known export in the ninth and tenth centuries, as they are, overwhelmingly so, today. It would be wrong to see them as too different from the cautious peasants of the *Hávamál* and later prose sources (such as the Icelandic family sagas); peasants will often happily grab property from the defenceless, especially if they are quick to arms, as Scandinavians generally were. It is best to see the raiding of Viking groups in the two centuries after 800 as the product of several different factors, all of them internal to Scandinavian society. One crucial element is that ship technology improved; the Danes, Norwegians and Swedes were all reliant on ships for basic communication between localities, but sails and better keels made ocean-going ships steadily more feasible. The Norwegians used this technology in the early ninth century to colonize the islands of Scotland (lightly settled, so unable to resist), and then in the late ninth and early tenth the almost uninhabited coasts of Iceland. From their Scottish base, the Norwegians then, especially from the 830s or so, raided beyond Scotland to Wales, and, above all, Ireland, where they also found relatively politically weak polities, highly susceptible to hit-and-run seaborne assaults. At roughly the same time, from the 830s, Danish pirate ships (*víkingr* simply meant 'pirate') followed the trade routes from Ribe and Hedeby down to Dorestad, London, York, and began the raids on Francia and England that we looked at in Chapters 16 and 19.

It is wrong to see merchants and pirates as too sharply distinct; any raider becomes a trader if the port is too well defended, and many traders (all necessarily armed, to hold off other pirates) will readily raid if the port, or other coastal settlement, seems weak, and then sell off the booty elsewhere. The merchant–pirate link could thus be seen as a second cause of Viking raiding, in that it could in part simply be traced to the mercantile desire for profit, set off in the case of Francia by the political difficulties of the period after 830, when the attention of Frankish armies was elsewhere. This also fits the Swedish political expansion into Russia, which was the work of trading colonies in the north Russian river systems seizing their chances, as we shall see in a moment, although this involved less raiding of a Viking type. Ships could, in addition – a third element – take away from Scandinavia (and its Scottish and Icelandic colonies) young men anxious for glory and loot before they settled down on their fathers' farms as peasants again; and also, from Denmark in particular – a fourth element – exiles, political losers in the struggles for increased royal power in the time of the Horics, keen to try their luck abroad. The existence of such exiles, essentially aristocrats or princes and their entourages, was in the ninth century specific to Denmark; they perhaps had a more violent (or 'heroic') ethos, and they contributed to the larger size of Viking armies in Francia and England (armies were never so big in Ireland), but they were only an addition to a desire for easy profit that any trader, or even peasant, could relate to. All these elements had plenty of parallels inside Frankish and Anglo-Saxon society, however; it was only ships (and thus surprise, and speedy retreat), and perhaps the absence of royal direction, that made the Vikings different. It was this which justifies Peter Sawyer's well-known description of Viking raids as 'an extension of normal Dark Age activity made possible and profitable by special circumstances'.

Viking raiding had very different effects in different areas, all the same. In Ireland, where the Scandinavians were not numerous enough for large-scale territorial conquest, their raids resulted in the formation of a network of trading towns, inserted into the fragmented hierarchies of petty kingdoms that already existed. By contrast, in Russia, where the incoherence of local political structures was even greater, relatively few Scandinavians could eventually establish themselves as a new ruling class. In Francia and England, however, raiding itself developed into a life-choice for many of the Viking leaders of the mid-ninth century, and then, above all in England, into full-blown conquest after 865. We have seen that this, too, did not require huge numbers – thousands rather than tens of thousands – but it was certainly a considerable advance in scale from the raids of previous decades.

This was where the Vikings moved away from simply being a seaborne extension of more 'normal' early medieval border relationships, and bid for power on their own behalf. It is significant that it was around then that the Danish kingdom itself failed for two generations; we do not know why in detail, but it is entirely likely that the by-now professional fighters of the river-mouth colonies of the Seine or Loire or Thames had as negative an effect on royal stability in their homeland as they did in eastern England. It is in this context, too, that we hear of our first family of Scandinavians who aimed for political power exclusively abroad, Ívar (d. 873) and his heirs (called by the Irish the Ua hImair), Ívar probably being one of the leaders of the Great Army in England in the 860s, who also ruled in Dublin, the major Norse-founded trading town in Ireland already from the 850s; his descendants held Dublin until 1036 or 1052, and also controlled York and southern Northumbria for much of the early tenth century. Ívar and his most successful emulator in the West, Rollo of Normandy after 911, were new figures, in that they broke the geopolitics of the early Middle Ages by simple force of arms, without a political base. They could also be seen as being in a way throwbacks to the fifth century, for their real counterparts as innovators were arguably Geiseric and Clovis.

This was a genuinely new contribution to the political development of this period. But, all the same, it was a restricted one. Outside the areas of mass settlement and cultural takeover in northern Scotland and Iceland, only Dublin and Normandy survived as Viking political creations, folded into the socio-political realities of Ireland and west Francia/France respectively, and soon culturally almost indistinguishable from them. Arguably, the main political legacy of the Vikings was actually developed in direct opposition to them: the invention by Alfred and Edward the Elder of the kingdom of England. The other two major Scandinavian political interventions, the temporary Danish conquest of England in the 1010s–1040s and the formation of Rus, in modern Russia and Ukraine, were not Viking operations, the former being a straightforward takeover of one kingdom by another, the latter being the crystallization of political power by merchant adventurers along Turkic models. It is true that for a time, in the tenth and eleventh centuries, Scandinavians could travel through polities governed by Norse speakers or their immediate descendants from the Arctic Circle nearly to Constantinople, and did so on occasion, as with Harald III Hardráði, 'Hard-ruler', king of Norway (1046–66), who had served with the prince of Rus and the Byzantine emperor, and who died attempting to conquer England. But this internationalism soon receded; by now Scandinavian power-politics was more normally focused only on Scandinavia, and Viking exploits became only a romantic memory.

The Slavs present more of a problem than the Scandinavians. They came to cover a vast region of central and eastern Europe, but when and how

they came there is hardly documented, either historically or archaeologically. Furthermore their origin has been an ideological football for
rival national communities, in most of the zones of the most fervent
(and most violent) nationalist disagreement in Europe across the last
century. Here, more than elsewhere, we have to make distinctions:
between the distribution of people called *Sklavēnoi/Sclaveni/Sclavi* or
variants by both Greek and Latin authors; the distribution of common
archaeological culture-elements across the zone stretching from the Elbe
in the west to the Dniepr in the east and the lower Danube in the
south; and the distribution of people speaking early versions of Slavic
languages. These three are not the same, however often they have been
intermingled. In particular, what languages people spoke in most parts
of eastern and central Europe is effectively irrecoverable before the ninth
century or so. But language, as we have seen elsewhere in this book, is
in any case no guide to identity in our period, and is the least important
of these three categories. It is best simply to see Slavic speakers as
only one section, although a substantial one, of a set of small-scale
communities of settled agriculturalists in the wide territories from the
Baltic to the Danube, and moving southwards into the Byzantine
Balkans. Nearby groups will have spoken other languages, Germanic,
Romance (in parts of Romania and elsewhere), Greek (in the southern
Balkans), Baltic (in Belarus and northwards), Finnic (in north-western
Russia), and others again, without necessarily being very different the
one from the other in material terms.

What can be said, on the other hand, is that from the sixth century a
distinct set of related archaeological characteristics can be found increasingly widely in this large region. These included villages of a few houses
each, single-roomed houses with partly sunken floors and a stone oven
or hearth, simple handmade ceramics (these however have parallels
in other small-scale early medieval societies), bow fibulae and head-
dresses for women, a tendency to cremation burials, and a relative
absence of signs of social differentiation. The lands in which these broad
common elements (with substantial local variation) are found steadily
became more extensive; in parts of the Elbe valley, for example, villages
with sunken-floored houses are first found in the late sixth or seventh
centuries, and in many places they succeed settlements with cemeteries
more similar to those in Frankish/Saxon/Aleman areas. It is likely that
the communities which lived like this had weak social and political

hierarchies; this fits the absence of strong archaeological differentiation, and also the persistent stress by east Roman/Byzantine writers of the sixth century and later on the weakness of political leadership among the *Sklavēnoi* living on the Balkan frontier of this culture-area. This doubtless means that they operated in very small political-social groups or tribes, and we know some (though only some) of their multifarious and ever-changing names. As with the *Germani* north of the Roman empire in the fourth century and earlier (see above, Chapter 2), only external observers, far from well informed, saw them as a whole; a common 'Slavic' identity did not ever exist, either in the early Middle Ages or later, and local tribal loyalties were in our period what guided them. What links them all together is simply the network of the common material culture just described. On the other hand, these small groups were not militarily or politically ineffective, as their expansion shows. In the west, they may have been moving into relatively underpopulated areas, until by the seventh century they were on the fringes of the Merovingian world; in the south, however, they took over a good part of the Balkans from the Byzantine state itself after 600, as we saw in Chapter 11.

These peoples are simply called 'Slavs' by most scholars. This, however, seems to me as problematic as calling the Germanic-speaking, or, more widely, 'barbarian', peoples of the fifth century 'Germans': these are later terms, which introduce concepts of language and identity that are anachronistic in this period. As in previous chapters, I here use the term 'Sclavenian' to cover all of the lands of the material culture discussed in the previous paragraph. This reflects the fact that both Franks and Byzantines did indeed know their neighbours collectively as *Sclaveni*, even if not all the Sclavenian communities as defined here would have necessarily been called by such a term even by the Franks and Byzantines, and even though none of the Sclavenians would have used the term themselves. Slavic languages did however spread across most – never all – of this wide culture-area in the end, of course. Already in the early ninth century Einhard claimed that the peoples on the Carolingian borders 'almost all speak a similar language', presumably Slavic; by the tenth century we can be surer that Slavic languages were a common feature of the culture-area, and for this period and later I use the term 'Slav' more freely. ('Slavic' will only be used for the language-group. Slavic languages, particularly in the south and east, are also often called 'Slavonic', but that term is used here only for the liturgy introduced by missionaries from Byzantium.)

The Sclavenians remained a large set of tiny polities into the eighth century, and often beyond. The *zoupaniai* on the Adriatic coast mentioned by Constantine VII in the mid-tenth century, some by now crystallized into Croatia though some not, had hardly more than a score of villages each, or indeed less. Tribes of this kind formed temporary alliances to make military attacks, as with the five separate named groups who besieged Thessaloniki in the 610s, much as Germanic tribes had done in the late Roman empire. Their rulers seem to have been chieftains at best, maybe only 'big men' or local leaders/patrons, like Icelandic *goðar*, subsisting on small-scale tributes. By the later eighth century, particularly in what is now eastern Germany, Poland and western Ukraine, strongholds begin to appear in the archaeology, with earth and timber ramparts, indicating more elaborate organizational hierarchies, although not necessarily larger-scale, or with permanent leaders. This fragmented political structure made Sclavenian society vulnerable once Frankish power developed in what is now central and southern Germany in the later sixth century, and even more so when Pippin III and Charlemagne revived Frankish aggression in the eighth, pushing their borders up to the edge of the Sclavenian culture-area right across Europe, from the Abodrites on the Baltic coast to the Carantani on the Adriatic. Although the Carolingian Franks never attempted permanent conquests of Sclavenian groups, they raided constantly; it was in the Carolingian period that the word *sclavus* became a new word for 'slave', and slave trading, to the Arab world in particular, became a major economic feature of the ninth century – it underpinned the prosperity of the Adriatic's new major seaport, Venice, as we shall see in Chapter 22. At the same time as this, the Byzantines re-formed their own power structures, and, from the mid-eighth century, began to make inroads on the Sclavenian communities of the central and southern Balkans. Faced with these new threats, if the Sclavenians did not organize themselves more effectively, they would be in serious trouble. They did so in two ways: by accepting external overlords, and by reorganizing themselves internally in the direction of stronger political structures, often under the influence of their Byzantine and Carolingian neighbours and enemies. Let us look at these in turn.

There had always been the possibility of wider hegemonies in the

Sclavenian world, usually established by Turkic-speaking nomadic groups coming west from central Asia into the south Russian/Ukrainian steppe lands and then, sometimes, into the Danube basin, who could be militarily very effective for short periods. As we have seen, the Huns were the first in the period of this book, at a time when Gothic tribal groups predominated in this part of Europe; in the sixth and early seventh century, it was the turn of the Avars, who had a wide domination over Sclavenian tribes in the Balkans, and who besieged Constantinople in loose alliance with the Persians in 626. This Avar power was, like that of the Huns, temporary, and already by the mid-seventh century it was restricted to the core Avar territory, the Pannonian plain, modern Hungary. In the eastern Balkans it was replaced by that of the longest lasting of these Turkic groups, the Bulgars, whose hegemony south of the Danube began in 680 and developed into a permanent state in the ninth century. As we saw in Chapters 11 and 13, the Bulgars borrowed political practices wholesale from the Byzantines; Constantinople was very close to them, so this was relatively easy, and, if they did not do so, the resurgent Byzantines would be bound to undermine their power. This did indeed happen in the end, with Basil II's conquest in 1014–18; but Bulgar survival until then (and revival two centuries later) was in great part due to direct imitation of their stronger neighbours. Their Sclavenian subjects were presumably happy for the Bulgar khagans (after c. 913, tsars) to do this; it was preferable to external attack, rapine and enslavement.

Non-Turkic hegemonies occurred as well. The first and briefest was that of Samo, the Frankish merchant who united some west Sclavenian groups roughly in the area of the modern Czech Republic for a generation in the seventh century in the face of both the Avars and Dagobert I and his heirs. Samo's power disappeared after his death, and it is not even really certain where his base was (his people are called Wends in Frankish sources, but this is almost as generic a word as *Sclavenus*); but it is clear that his hegemony was largely a reaction to Frankish danger, and it is significant that even a temporary larger-scale political structure in the west of the Sclavenian lands was the work of a foreigner, at least in this early period. The Hungarians need recognition in this respect, too, as the next major nomadic group to reach Pannonia, in the 890s, for they were Uralic-speaking, not Turkic, although in many respects they replicated Avar hegemony for a long time. They were more long-lasting as a cultural presence than the other external ruling groups discussed here, however, for when they settled down in the late tenth and eleventh centuries, and began to organize a political system along Bohemian/Polish (and thus, by extension, Frankish) lines, they continued to speak a Uralic, not a Slavic, language, and still do.

By far the most successful non-Turkic hegemony in the long run was that of the Rus. They began as Swedish merchant groups settled in the river valleys behind modern St Petersburg, and their trading settlements have been found at, above all, Staraya Ladoga in the eighth century and Gorodishche in the ninth (the latter, after the mid-tenth century, replaced by nearby Novgorod), with artisanal goods similar to those of sites like Birka. These Swedish settlers must have been the communities referred to in the *Annals of Saint-Bertin* for 839, and by Byzantine sources of the next century, as *Rhos*; the Saint-Bertin annalist also called the *Rhos* Swedes, and 'Swede' in Estonian, the nearest Finnic language, is *Root'si*. They specialized in the fur trade, taking advantage of the presence of valuable fur-bearing animals in the Russian forests, and were middlemen, along with the Bulgar merchant settlements on the Volga, for an increasingly important trade in fur and, soon, slaves along the great rivers of Russia to Iran and what is now Uzbekistan, in return for Islamic silver coins, which can be found in substantial quantities in Sweden. They had a *chacanus* in 839, that is, a khagan, a standard Turkic word for ruler, and thus some local political organization, presumably already including a hegemony over some of the local tribes (who were probably Finnic-speaking in this area). The Rus were ambitious; it is not clear when they turned their buying of furs into a tribute of furs from an increasingly large tract of forest land, but this was probably well under way when they launched an unsuccessful but extremely daring surprise attack on Constantinople itself – a long way from these northern rivers – in 860. They also extended their hegemony southwards into Slavic-speaking areas (east was blocked by the Volga Bulgars), first to Gnёzdovo (close to modern Smolensk) and then, by 900 or so, to Kiev, further south down the Dniepr on the river route to Byzantium, with which they signed very profitable trading treaties in the tenth century.

It is as rulers of Kiev that named *kagani* or *knyaz'i*, generally translated 'princes', of the Rus first begin to be reliably documented in the tenth century, in contemporary Byzantine and Frankish sources, as also in the perhaps late eleventh-century, and certainly early twelfth-, *Russian*

Primary Chronicle: Igor (d. *c*. 945), who attacked Constantinople again in 941; his widow Ol'ga, ruling for her son Svyatoslav (*c*. 945–65); Svyatoslav as an adult ruler (*c*. 965–72); and his most successful son, Vladimir (*c*. 978–1015). By then, they ruled from Novgorod to the edge of the Ukrainian steppes, and were attacking eastwards to the Bulgars on the Volga, southwards to the Khazars on the Don and into Balkan Bulgaria, and westwards to Polotsk (where Vladimir removed a rival Scandinavian, Rogvolod) and in the direction of what is now Poland. Vladimir died in control of a very large area, around the size of Ottonian East Francia, although including a far smaller population, for the area was and is mostly forest, except for settlements along the rivers. And this hegemony, unlike most others just discussed, remained stable. Vladimir's numerous heirs maintained an exclusive family dominance over this core Russian territory until the Mongol invasion of 1237–40; no matter how many principalities they created and fought over, no non-family-member ruled anywhere in the Russian lands after Rogvolod until the Mongol Batu. The dominance of Igor's family indeed went back to the earliest period they are documented, for Ol'ga's long rule as *kniagina*, only nominally associated with her son, seems to have been uncontested and effective, indicating an unchallenged dynastic stability – out of all the female rulers of different kinds in tenth-century Europe, from Marozia through Theophanu to Æthelflæd, Ol'ga may well have been the most powerful.

There cannot have been many Scandinavians in most of the territory of Rus: outside the northern trading towns, only some of the immediate entourage of the tenth-century princes had Scandinavian names, and after Igor (Ingvar) and Ol'ga (Helga) the princes themselves used East Slavic, that is, Old Russian/Ukrainian, names. All our evidence indicates that East Slavic was the dominant language in Kiev, and it steadily spread northwards; by the time of our earliest birchbark letters and documents, found by archaeologists in excavation levels starting in the eleventh century, it was dominant even in Novgorod. The Scandinavian elements in Rus probably simply consisted of the tightness and ambition of the ruling dynasty, which acted as a catalyst for a wider territorial crystallization. The core techniques of rule over that territory, by contrast, seem essentially to have been taken over from contemporary Turkic hegemonies, the Volga Bulgars and the main seventh- to tenth-century rulers over the southern steppes, the Khazars: the title khagan was borrowed from either the Bulgars or the Khazars, and the basic pattern of rule over dependent Finnic- and Slavic-speaking tribes, the extraction of tribute, was also a long-standing Turkic tradition; aristocratic or royal landownership of a type recognizable in western Europe was only a much later medieval development. The construction of an extensive network of long-distance defensive ramparts in the Kiev region under Vladimir (something which shows his control of local manpower) has Bulgarian parallels, too. The systematic foundation of large fortified towns as regional political centres from the late tenth century, which earned Rus the name of Garðaríki, the 'land of towns', in some Scandinavian texts, seems however to have had Sclavenian antecedents, as implied by the western Sclavenian fortresses already mentioned. So may have been the *druzhina* or military entourage that every rival prince had and which acted as the basic underpinning of all princely power, although such entourages were common features of all such societies, and had plenty of Germanic and Turkic parallels. But, of course, once the Rus polity developed past a simple military hegemony, it would inevitably draw more on the social structures of the main body of the population, which was increasingly clearly Sclavenian/Slav. This it did ever more steadily henceforth.

It can finally be added that, towards the end of our period, yet another political resource was added to the Kievan principality, Byzantine Christianity. The Rus, after their initial raids southwards, were more fully accepted into the Byzantine diplomatic network. As we saw in Chapter 13, it is entirely likely that Svyatoslav's attacks on Bulgaria in 967 were initially encouraged by Constantinople; Vladimir's troops were, furthermore, essential to Basil II's political success in 989. This was the setting for a religious shift as well. The Khazars had Jewish rulers; this already provided a model for taking on a new faith, but it is likely that the Rus felt they needed a different religion from the Khazars, and they were anyway close enough to the Byzantines politically for Orthodoxy to be a logical next step. Ol'ga had been personally converted in Constantinople around 955; Vladimir, for his part, formally accepted Christianity for his whole people in about 988. The conversion process was very slow to extend outside the court, but this moment of acceptance allowed the institutions of the church, and a Christian imagery of legitimate rulership, to take root in Rus and steadily to spread. The churches of Kiev were impressive, and the early eleventh-century building of

St Sophia, built by Byzantine craftsmen, still stands as the largest and most completely decorated Byzantine church of that century. Administrative and artisanal traditions were borrowed from Constantinople and developed in Kiev, too. The Rus took on these Byzantine influences without any of the dangers the Bulgars faced, as they were too far away for Constantinople to take them over, and they could thus be as creative as they liked with them. This hybrid power, Turkic, Sclavenian and Byzantine, with a dash of Scandinavian, maintained an essential stability from now on, as eastern Europe's most effective political player.

The western Sclavenian peoples did not have these external hegemonies, but in the ninth and tenth centuries they too, on the basis of internal developments, began to organize themselves into rather larger political groupings than had existed hitherto. The first of these was Moravia, the major sparring-partner of the East Franks in the ninth century, as we saw in Chapter 16; the Moravians are first referred to in the 820s, and three generations of powerful rulers, Mojmír (c. 830–46), Rastislav (846–70) and Sviatopluk or Zwentibald (870–94), extended their power widely in what is now the Czech Republic, Slovakia, Hungary and further afield still. Where their political centre was has been debated recently, with arguments proposed, on the basis of Constantine VII's ethnographic writing and the wars described in the *Annals of Fulda*, for a core Moravian principality located as far south as Sirmium, in modern northern Serbia. But the concentration of large ninth-century fortified settlements in modern Moravia (the eastern part of the Czech Republic), notably Staré Město and Mikulčice, with gold and silver finds and a more complex production of iron and pottery, is a fairly clear sign of a strong political power and of developed social hierarchies, so this traditional location for ninth-century Moravia continues to seem the most plausible. The material basis of Moravian power was a development out of the smaller-scale stronghold societies of the previous century, with autonomy made possible by now by the end of the last vestiges of Avar hegemony. All the same, the impetus for this level of political aggregation must have been the Frankish threat, which presumably legitimized more stable and ambitious political hierarchies. Frankish emulation led also to the adoption of Latin Christianity from the 830s onwards, apart from a brief flutter in 863–85 with Byzantine missionaries, Cyril and Methodios; see Chapter 13. The Moravian principality could well have developed into an organized state along Carolingian lines, however hostile it was to Carolingian political influence, just as, in the Byzantine orbit, did Bulgaria. It is increasingly clear that the same is true of the smaller Croat duchy/principality which developed in the 820s or so on the Dalmatian coast in modern south Croatia, this time under direct Carolingian patronage; ninth-century Croat material culture, notably more complex than earlier, as in Moravia, shows a strong influence of Frankish metal-working and Italian stone-carving techniques, and a handful of Latin documents from the 840s onwards show Italian influence even over concepts of landowning, as well as Carolingian-style court officials. The Hungarians destroyed Moravian power between 894 and 905, but the Croat principality continued, and Tomislav (*c*. 910–29) was even recognized as *rex*, king, by Pope John X in 925.

Bohemia, the core of the Czech lands, was closer to Francia than was Moravia, but was protected and given geographical identity by thickly forested mountains to the west, which have in fact been a political border more or less without a break from the seventh century to the present day. This region, too, shows a steady increase in hill-fort strongholds in the ninth century, implying increased social stratification, and then a move towards unification under Moravian patronage by Bořivoj I (d. *c*. 890). This early Czech polity crystallized around Prague in the early tenth century, and hesitantly (with several changes of direction) accepted Latin Christianity, especially under Václav I (921–*c*. 930, 'Good King Wenceslas') and his brother and murderer Boleslav I (*c*. 930–72). Boleslav's power extended into Moravia and modern southern Poland too, although it broke up again under his heirs, largely because of aristocratic resistance, in this case to the (temporary) benefit of the Poles. Václav was forced to accept East Frankish hegemony, which led to his death, whereas Boleslav resisted it. Either way, however, Bohemia was marked by a Latin ecclesiastical politics and by intermittent recognition of Ottonian-Salian overlordship.

To the north of Bohemia, the next polity to form was that of the Poles. The territory occupied by modern Poland had many tribes, as elsewhere in the Sclavenian (we can now say Slav) lands; the peoples of central Poland around Gniezno and Poznań were not particularly special among them. But under Mieszko I (*c*. 962–92) they rapidly achieved a dominance which extended up to the Baltic. This was a more sudden shift towards political aggregation than in Moravia or Bohemia. The abandonment of many of the ninth-century tribal strongholds of the future Polish lands in the late tenth century shows a sharp change in the structure of political power; Mieszko and his heirs, the Piast dynasty, built new ones. Mieszko was keen to ally with the Ottonians and their Saxon dukes and marquises, who were less of a threat than in Bohemia, as his power-base was set back from the areas of tenth-century Saxon conquest; he accepted Christianity in 966, with a bishop in Poznań in 968. This alliance continued in the era of the western Slav revolt against the Saxons in 983 and onwards; by then it was a cover for further Piast political expansion, and under Bolesław Chrobry, 'the Brave' (992–1025), Piast power extended into Bohemia, eastwards towards Rus, and by the 1000s was explicitly directed against the marches of Saxony. As in Moravia and Bohemia, this hegemony did not last, and the Piast polity was already in trouble by the 1030s, although Mieszko's dynasty continued until the fourteenth century, by which time Poland was a more coherent and long-lasting kingdom.

Each of these three, Moravia, Bohemia and Piast Poland, probably expanded too fast for their fairly simple political infrastructures, essentially based on tribute to the ruler and his *druzhina*, to cope. They were notably less stable than the otherwise similar Rus polity; it is likely that the Turkic models the Rus followed were more successful, but it also may be that stresses and dangers to political authority were greater in the western Sclavenian/Slav lands, given the Frankish threat there. The establishment of church hierarchies would nonetheless add eventually, after 1000, to the infrastructural resources available to these rulers, and so would more elaborate networks of political dependence, and the establishment of privately owned landed estates as the basis of aristo-cratic and royal or princely wealth, all of these developments being influenced by Frankish (we can now say German) example. It is signifi-cant that later attempts at unification in the eleventh century were more successful, both in Bohemia and (more uncertainly) in Poland. It is only then, in fact, that Bohemia and Poland can really be separated out at all; 'Poland', in particular, was invented by the Piasts out of a network of tribal groups with no natural boundaries separating them off from their neighbours.

The slow development of stable hierarchies was a common feature of the Slav world by 1000, and it extended to Hungary too, with Isztván (Stephen) I (997–1038) in the role of Mieszko and Vladimir as a Christianizer and organizer. Leaders turned into lords, chieftains into princes or kings, strongholds into towns, tribute into rent. We saw this process earlier in the western Germanic lands and in Anglo-Saxon England, and it was matched in the tenth and eleventh centuries by slower but parallel developments in Denmark and Norway too. These hierarchies and governmental systems were generally influenced, often quite heavily, by neighbours, whether Byzantine, Frankish or Turkic. They were often a direct response to Byzantine or Frankish threat, as in Moravia and Bohemia, in Bulgaria, and in part also in Denmark; we can also add here Celtic-speaking Brittany, whose mid-ninth-century independent kings, notably Salomon (857–74), clearly used Frankish techniques of government, until the kingdom went under as a result of Viking raids. But they were often also a more internal, even if often quite sudden, development, the work of ambitious political leaders riding on a tide of military success inside territories less menaced from outside, and stabilizing power using external models as a follow-on from that, as in Rus, in Poland, and, in the Germanic world, in Mercia and perhaps in Norway.

It can be added, finally, that in some places, in Bohemia and Poland, and also in Norway, this political aggregation was also resisted, at least when territorial expansion ran into difficulties: either by other leading families, or by smaller tribes reluctant to lose their own identity and traditions. In Poland, indeed, the 1030s saw a resurgence of tribal identity, and the abandonment of Christianity in some areas. This resurgence had already been presaged by the Slav revolt in the 980s, in which the Liutizi, a tribal confederation on the Baltic coast around the mouth of the Oder, threw off Saxon tribute-taking, church landowning, and all elements of Christianization. Thietmar of Merseburg indignantly recounts details of their pagan cults, and also describes their reliance on assembly politics and their avoidance of single rulers; this is significant, for by now it represented a resistance not only to Saxon rule but also to the developing hierarchies of the Slav lands themselves. Such a resistance has parallels in Iceland, as we have seen, but Iceland was safely far away in the north Atlantic; the Liutizi were under threat from both sides, from both Saxony and Poland. All the same, the Baltic coast remained a zone of relatively weak political institutions into the central Middle Ages.

The Scandinavian and Sclavenian/Slav lands were Christianized late, and our information about them derives from either Frankish/Byzantine sources or from archaeology; a survey of them has to be a rather external construct, from scattered evidence. The Celtic-speaking lands of Britain and Ireland were different from this; they were solidly Christian well before 800, when we can take up their history here, and they have their own documentation, although this is scarce for Scotland. They show parallels, all the same, to the sorts of development we have been looking at here, in particular with regard to Brittany.

In Chapter 7 we left the Welsh with four major kingdoms in 800, but with very simple politico-administrative structures, based on small-scale wars, a feasting culture linking kings to their entourages, and the taking of (probably fairly restricted) tributes from dependants and from subject territories. In the next two centuries this basic pattern continued, but with developments that went in two, opposite, directions.

The first is the evidence we have for political aggregation. The Welsh seem by now to have seen themselves as a conceptual unity, the Cymry, however politically divided. The *Great Prophecy of Britain*, *Armes Prydein Vawr*, a south Welsh text dating to around 930, prophesies the uniting of the Welsh and the expulsion of the English with great enthusiasm: 'The Cymry will prevail through battle, well equipped, unanimous, one in word and faith', and, with the help of the Irish, Scots and Dublin Vikings, will reunite Britain south of Hadrian's Wall under their rule. This sense of identity was a cultural one (it has parallels with the *Angli* of Bede and the all-English church hierarchy of Theodore of Tarsus), but it can be widely found in our sources. The Welsh probably gained definition because of the English danger, and indeed they generally saw themselves as being entitled to the whole of Britain, from most of which they had been unjustly expelled: eleventh-century Welsh prose literature, however fantastic in format, routinely centres itself around kings of 'this island', 'the island of Britain'.

Hence or otherwise, from the ninth century we find kings with rather more extensive territorial ambitions than before. Rhodri Mawr, 'the Great' (844–77), was the mould-breaker: based in Gwynedd in the north-west, long the most influential kingdom, he took over Powys in the east in 855 and Ceredigion in 872, thus coming to rule half of Wales, and raided extensively in the south. Although he was exiled to Ireland after defeat by the Vikings in 877, and was killed by the English a year later, his hegemony continued under his sons, led by Anarawd (d. 916). Anarawd's nephew Hywel Dda, 'the Good', ap Cadell (d. 950), married into the dynasty of Dyfed in the south-west and in 904 was recognized as king there; he fought his Gwynedd cousins thereafter, and in 942–50 took over their lands, thus controlling three-quarters of Wales. This hegemony was probably re-established by his grandson Maredudd ab Owain in 986–99, and certainly in 1055–63 by a later king of Gwynedd, Gruffudd ap Llywelyn, whose father had married Maredudd's daughter (Welsh genealogical legitimacy accepted female-line succession more easily than that of either England or Ireland). Gruffudd also subjected south-eastern Wales, hitherto independent of the Rhodri dynasty, in 1055, so for eight years was the first Welsh king of all Wales – and the only one ever, apart from Henry VII.

A storyline can thus be (and has been) created of steady national unification, only spoilt by the English (Harold Godwineson destroyed Gruffudd ap Llywelyn's hegemony in 1063) and, later, the Normans. This increasing royal power could be said to be reinforced by law; Welsh law, although only surviving in thirteenth-century and later texts, systematically attaches itself to Hywel Dda as a legislator, a tradition which may well be in some way authentic (though the content of the law is certainly later) – Hywel spent time in the English royal court, and could well have picked up ideas from, for instance, Æthelstan. Our church documentation, too, shows a few signs of a greater coherence of rulership by the end of the tenth century, with local military service, perhaps more systematic tribute-taking, judicial rights, from which churches such as the south-eastern bishopric of Llandaff sought to gain exemptions. The Welsh might then match the Danes, Bohemians and Bulgars as a people learning techniques of rule from the example of a much more powerful and dangerous neighbour, although one of these techniques was not, of course, the Christian church, for Wales had always been Christian.

All the same, this greater coherence had not got very far by 1000 (or 1063); and it was matched by opposite tendencies. One is that the wider hegemonies listed above were all very short; no king after Rhodri Mawr passed his conquests to his heirs, and most hegemonic rulers spent their lives fighting to maintain their power. Another is the interference of outside forces. For all the anti-Englishness of the *Armes Prydein*, kings of its writer's era were routinely subject to the king of England and paid him tribute; that was one of the reasons for the poet's anger, and also for Hywel Dda's presence in the English court. English kings from Alfred to Edgar (though not Æthelred II or Cnut) expected it. The Vikings sometimes took tribute, too; although Rhodri Mawr's fall was a chance event, Viking coastal raids were regular, and there is some evidence for a full-blown hegemony by the Norse rulers of Dublin or the Isle of Man over parts of Gwynedd in the late tenth and early eleventh century. A third development is a growing incoherence in the titles of rulers; quite unlike the trends in the Scandinavian and Slav worlds, fewer rulers are called *rex* in Latin sources after 950 or so, and a greater array of terms appear in Welsh texts from then on; the tendency of Welsh rulers to call themselves 'princes' in the twelfth and thirteenth centuries was beginning here, although the greatest rulers, like Gruffudd ap Llywelyn, could certainly still use (or be ascribed) the title of 'king'.

This shift away from royal titles is not a sign of Welsh subjection. Rather, it marks confusion: as Welsh polities became larger, they did not become markedly more stable and better organized. Kings and their retinue (*teulu*) remained at the centre of kingdoms; there were also mercenaries, but few local officials. Justice, even if more tightly organized, was still for the most part in the hands of local elders and notables, with, it would seem, more of an input from local churches than from most kings (much of our knowledge of the righting of wrongs comes from ecclesiastical narratives of churches and their saints, calling kings themselves to account for their misdeeds). Given a general lack of infrastructure, the growing claims to wide but temporary hegemonies after 850 or so were a cause, not of centralization and pacification, but of instability. In this sense Wales did not fit the Danish model; this would only come later, in strategically much more difficult times, after around 1200, when the princes of Gwynedd borrowed consistently from English practice.

Scotland had a larger core kingdom, Alba, taken over in the 840s by Cinaed mac Ailpín (Kenneth I) as we saw at the end of Chapter 7, and extending throughout most of the Scottish mainland from the Firth of Forth northwards. We know the names of its kings, all descendants of Kenneth except one (Macbeth, 1040–57), though fighting it out in Irish fashion across two or three rival lines. Its heart was the old Pictish kingdom (the name 'Alba' only appears in 900), but from the 890s or so we can see more and more signs of Irish culture and Irish church organization, and the Pictish language seems to have fallen out of use. The kings of Alba did not control the whole of modern Scotland, however. The islands and far north were all by now under Scandinavian rule, and the Orkneys and Shetlands (with Caithness) were wholly Scandinavianized; the jarls of Orkney were from the tenth century serious players, notably Sigurd 'the Stout' (d. 1014), and his son Thorfinn 'the Mighty' (d. 1065), who ruled south to the Isle of Man. South of the Forth and Clyde, there were Welsh and English polities too, the Welsh kings of Strathclyde in the Glasgow region and the south-west, and the kings of Northumbria, later lords of Bamburgh, in Lothian. These ceded ground to the Scottish kings, however; Scotland stably included Lothian after perhaps the 970s – the 1010s at the latest – and the kings of Strathclyde are not certainly heard of after 1018. By then, the mainland kingdom of Scotland was largely formed, the work of influential and long-lived kings like Constantine II (900–943), Kenneth II (971–95) and Malcolm II (1005–34).

Here, too, however, we must be cautious. We know almost nothing of the inner workings of the Scottish kingdom. Its northern third, Moray, certainly had semi-independent 'mormaers' (sometimes also called 'kings of Alba' in Irish sources) with their own dynasty – Macbeth was one of them, in fact. Mormaers appear elsewhere as local aristocrats and military leaders, too; it cannot be said how autonomous or how dynastic (or how Pictish) they were, but it would be unwise to assume full royal control over them. The early Scottish kingdom was very large by Irish (or indeed Welsh) standards, and also by and large internally stable, notwithstanding succession disputes; but it is hard not to feel that the near-total absence of documentation for it betrays a relative evanescence of royal authority. Again, more coherent political power structures belonged to a much later period, in this case the twelfth century, and were associated with a conscious policy of acceptance of English (or 'Norman') influence and even settlement: the Danish or Bohemian model again, although this time attached to a secure political system which had already achieved its basic territorial expansion.

Of these Celtic-speaking political systems, Ireland is the best documented – in fact, in many ways it is the best-documented society in this chapter – but that does not make it straightforward to read. Here, the network of tribal hierarchies, unstable, but at least unstable according to recognizable political rules in each of the five provinces of Ireland, was beginning to come apart by the eighth century, thanks to more ambitious kings (as described in Chapter 7), and here the impact of the

Vikings was to pull it further apart. Eighth-century kings were beginning to attack the major centres of wealth and power that the greater monasteries had become; over-kings were beginning to take the dependence of lesser kings for granted as a permanent part of their political base (in Latin annals, after 750 some lesser kings are beginning to be called *dux* rather than *rex*). In some areas, too, successful kingdoms were not just demanding tribute and hostages from lesser kingdoms, but appropriating their territory, as the Uí Briúin Bréifne did as they spread east and north from their base in southern Co. Leitrim into Co. Cavan in the late eighth century, or as the Déis Tuaiscirt (later called Dál Cais) did as they spread north from eastern Co. Limerick to eastern Co. Clare a generation earlier. These were both minor kingdoms, operating outside the main political networks of the Uí Néill of western Ulster and Meath and the Éoganachta of Munster, and the scale of their expansion was pretty small, but they show that the tribal kingdom map of Ireland was not written in stone.

On one level, the Vikings simply showed these processes more clearly. Initially, after 795, they just plundered coastal settlements, largely monasteries. Even when their attacks expanded in scale in the 830s, they resembled the annual inter-kingdom raiding which the Irish were very familiar with. Then, when they began to over-winter in the 840s, on Lough Neagh in Ulster, in Dublin in Meath and on Lough Ree in the centre of the island, and even more when they founded more permanent settlements, as Dublin became, followed by Cork, Waterford, Limerick, they resembled the rougher end of the small-scale ambitious kingdoms just described; indeed, the Limerick settlement largely just displaced the southern half of the Déis Tuaiscirt/Dál Cais kingdom, pushing them north into Clare. Dublin was the most powerful and dangerous of these new polities, and in the 850s it became the focus of substantial reinforcements, but the Vikings never engaged in large-scale territorial conquest in Ireland. It was too difficult, with all those tiny kingdoms, and also not hugely remunerative, as there were too few stores of movable wealth (as in eastern Europe, slaves were Ireland's most valuable exportable commodity). Dublin's main political ambitions looked westwards, to the Irish Sea and York (above, Chapter 19). By the 860s the Dublin Vikings were already integrated into Irish political alliances, and there they remained, apart from a brief period, 902–17, in which they were expelled altogether. A revival of raiding in the 910s–920s followed the same trajectory. Dublin's other, and perhaps major, role (matched on a lesser scale by the other Viking settlements) was as Ireland's first proper town, an important trading settlement, some of which has been excavated, showing intense artisanal activity in bone, leather, wood (including ship-building) and cloth: Ireland's answer to York and Hedeby.

In political terms, however, the Vikings were a catalyst in two ways. The first was that in order to defeat them, wider alliances were necessary than had been needed by province-level wars in the past, thus reinforcing the pre-existing tendency of the most ambitious kings to make their own rules of engagement. The second was that Dublin happened to be situated in one of the traditional (and also agriculturally richest) heartlands of Irish politics, Meath, the area of operation of the southern Uí Néill kingdoms. This long-term strategic weakening of the power-base of the southern Uí Néill in the end caused their eclipse, although that was not until the eleventh century. In the meantime, if the paramount dynasties of the province, notably in this period Clann Cholmáin, were to maintain their importance in insular politics, then they would have to be even more creative.

This was the background, then, for some kings to move in new directions. Let us look at three examples, to show some of the parameters now possible. The first is Feidlimid mac Crimthainn (d. 847), from the Éoganacht of Cashel, who had taken the kingship of Cashel (that is, the paramount kingship of Munster) in 820; he established unusually wide alliances in west Munster and also Leinster, and by 830–31 was attacking northwards into Connacht and Meath; by 840 he was ravaging Meath, and camped at Tara itself, locus of the Uí Néill paramount kingship, a sign of new ambition for a Munster king. Feidlimid also realized the importance of ecclesiastical politics, and attempted to form links with the major monastic centre of Armagh in northern Ireland; he became abbot of Cork in 836, and of Clonfert in Connacht in 838, and was a major patron of the ascetic Céli Dé movement. Conversely, he was ruthless with rival ecclesiastical powers, burning the monasteries of Durrow and Kildare, and, above all, Clonfert's neighbour Clonmacnois, on three or four occasions. Feidlimid was later seen as pious, and, by Irish royal standards, may well have been; but what he was doing was creating his own politico-religious structures in his own image, and was indeed, it seems, aiming at nothing less than the high-kingship of Ireland itself.

The high-kingship was a new concept; it is barely attested before this period. Exactly what it entailed was equally unclear: certainly hegemony over both Cashel and Tara, the old symbolic centres of Éoganachta and Uí Néill rule, but then what? Submission from every Irish king? Feidlimid did not securely gain even the former, still less the latter, but the idea was by now on the cards. Máel Sechnaill I mac Máele Ruanaid (d. 862) of Clann Cholmáin, king of Tara and thus hegemonic over the Uí Néill from 846, was the first king to make the claim more or less real, in the next generation. Máel Sechnaill had a powerful track record as an opponent of Vikings (unlike Feidlimid), sacking Dublin itself in 849 and fighting off their reinforcements in the 850s; he was therefore in a good position to gain submission from both Leinster and Connacht, and also, unusually, the Ulaid kingdoms of eastern Ulster, who were at risk from Viking attack. The king of Brega joined the Vikings; Máel Sechnaill executed him in 851 by the 'cruel death' of drowning, as he had done the Viking leader Turgéis (Thorgils) in 845. And he moved from the north and east into Munster, several times, taking hostages from all the province in 856, and reaching the sea in 858. It is because of all this that the *Annals of Ulster* call him 'king of all Ireland' at his death four years later: less innovative than Feidlimid, but more complete in his hegemony, he shows, like his predecessor, the new possibilities of the period.

A further step was taken by Brian Bórama – Brian Boru in common parlance – mac Cennétig, king of the Dál Cais from 976 to 1014. Leading Uí Néill kings since Máel Sechnaill I had operated as more or less major figures, more prominently than most kings of Tara in the eighth century, though less than Máel Sechnaill; Brian, however, re-created the latter's power and went beyond it, even though starting from one of the smallest autonomous kingdoms in Ireland, connected to neither of the great paramount dynasties. Brian's rise is enthusiastically and fancifully chronicled by the *War of the Gaedhil [Irish] with the Gaill [Vikings]*, written in the early twelfth century, around a century after Brian's death, for his grandson; the main lines of the narrative are confirmed by more sober (and duller) annals. He fought Vikings a lot, as is unsurprising for one of the closest kingdoms to Limerick, which he, with his brother and predecessor Mathgamain (953–76), sacked in 967. As king, he fought neighbouring Munster kings and their Norse allies, and seems already to have seized paramountcy over Munster from the Éoganachta dynasties in 978, perhaps following his brother. The Clann Cholmáin/Uí

Néill king of Tara, Máel Sechnaill II mac Domnaill (980–1022), himself one of the more powerful over-kings of the century, laid Dál Cais waste in 982 as a preventive move, but Brian moved into Connacht in the early 980s, and attacked Máel Sechnaill back. He built up his authority in Connacht and also Leinster in the next decade, an authority recognized by Máel Sechnaill himself in 1002. Finally, he moved into Ulster, gaining submission from most of their kings in 1005–8 and, last of all, the Cenél Conaill in 1011. Brian was thus, for the first time, recognized by everyone as 'king of Ireland'; indeed, in a highly ceremonial visit to Armagh in 1005 his secretary had recorded his presence there as 'emperor of the Irish'. But revolts started as soon as the following year, in Leinster this time, and in 1014 Brian, with a much reduced army (the Uí Néill kings did not support him), faced an army from Leinster and Dublin, with reinforcements from as far away as Orkney, at the Battle of Clontarf. Brian's side won, but the seventy-year-old king was killed, as were the leading king of Leinster and Jarl Sigurd of Orkney. Dál Cais hegemony collapsed instantly, and Máel Sechnaill II took back the kingship of Tara until his death.

I have recounted this career in more detail than usual (though leaving out much: Brian often fought two or three wars a year) just to show how much work was involved in establishing – really, inventing – a hegemony over Ireland, which anyway did not, could not, last. Brian is not recorded as developing any new techniques of government. He used the wealth and men of Limerick and Dublin after their subjection, but Dublin had its own political agenda, and helped to end his rule eventually. The *War of the Gaedhil with the Gaill* eagerly recounts the benefits of Brian's brief hegemony: peace, justice, much tribute; the restoration of churches, learning, roads and fortresses; and hospitality. The learning has a twelfth-century feel to it, and so do the fortresses, but even here the imagery is old; the rest is wholly traditional. Brian's remarkable career was mostly important in that it showed that skill and ruthlessness could open up an all-Ireland stage for political ambition, and could, furthermore, do so for any king. The following two centuries proved that, with Leinster and Connacht providing claimants to Irish hegemony for the first time, in rivalry with Brian's descendants and with the northern Uí Néill. But, in the absence of solid political structures, this simply replicated the instability we have already seen for Wales. Slowly, we do see more royal officials in the larger kingdoms in the eleventh century, and some interest in local territorial administration in the twelfth; more and more small kingdoms lost their autonomy and identity. Nonetheless, Ireland was still an island of many kingdoms when English invasion finally came in 1169.

'State-building' had different bases again in Christian Spain, the narrow band of polities along the northern edge of the peninsula left unconquered by the Arabs in the 710s. This northern fringe had been politically marginal already in the Visigothic period (above, Chapter 6): the only major Visigothic centre south of the Pyrenees not to be in Muslim hands in the early ninth century was Barcelona, thanks to Charlemagne's conquest of what is now northern Catalonia in 785–801. Apart from that Catalan enclave, governed by a local dynasty of counts from the late ninth century onwards, two independent kingdoms existed to the west, that of Pamplona or Navarre, and that of Asturias. The small Pyrenean kingdom of Pamplona is first documented in the early ninth century under Iñigo Arista (d. 851), a Christian relative of the neighbouring Muslim dynasty, the Banu Qasi of the upper Ebro valley; kings of Pamplona were for a century little more than a Christian version of the autonomous Muslim lords of the marches of al-Andalus (above, Chapter 14). The kingdom of Asturias started small, too, around 720, in a revolt against the Muslims in the remote northern mountains by an aristocrat called Pelagius (Pelayo in Spanish; d. 737). His second successor Alfonso I (739–57), founded a dynasty which lasted until 1037, and which was generally on rather more hostile terms with the Arab powers of the south.

The Asturian royal line started with very flexible inheritance practices. Alfonso I's son Fruela (757–68) was succeeded by his cousin, his brother-in-law, his half-brother, and another cousin, before his son Alfonso II (791–842) was allowed to take over, and father–son succession did not take root until 850. The eighth-century kings ruled from small centres in the Asturian valleys; Alfonso II, however, turned his political base, Oviedo, into a capital aimed at imitating Visigothic Toledo, with ambitious palace buildings and churches, some of which still stand, and his successor Ramiro I (842–50) built others. The kings of Asturias spent this first century of their existence extending their authority east and west across the northern mountains, from Álava in the upper Ebro and the northern core of the later county of Castile, in the east, across to Galicia in the north-west of the peninsula. They also raided south-wards over the mountains into the broad frontier-lands of al-Andalus when they could get away with it, that is, in periods of Arab political trouble; Alfonso I raided particularly systematically during the Arab civil war of the 740s. After that civil war, the Arabs no longer seem to have controlled the wide plateau-land of the Duero valley, just south of Asturias, and it remained outside anyone's visible political domination for over a century.

Ordoño I (850–66) was the first Asturian king to move south of the mountains permanently, taking León and other cities in the 850s. His son Alfonso III (866–910) pushed systematically down to the River Duero, a push which doubled the size of the kingdom; the Duero remained more or less the boundary with al-Andalus until well into the eleventh century. As the kings moved south into the rich Duero plains, they spent less and less time in Oviedo. After Alfonso III's sons overthrew their ageing father in 910, León became the main centre of the kingdom, which tends from now on to be called the kingdom of León; it soon acquired an array of buildings matching or surpassing Oviedo as well. Alfonso had been able to expand his lands because of the next round of civil wars in al-Andalus, but these ended in the 920s, and his heirs found themselves on the defensive for the rest of the century. Ramiro II (931–51), the most successful, at least held off the new caliph 'Abd al-Rahman III in 939–40, actually winning a pitched battle against him at Simancas in 939; but after an attempted coup in 959 Sancho I (956–66) owed his throne to 'Abd al-Rahman, who could regard León as his client as a result. In 981–1007 the Arabs under al-Mansur moved onto the attack, sacking León in 988 and the major cult-site of Santiago de Compostela in 997. If the caliphate had not dissolved in civil war after 1009, the survival of the kingdom might have been in doubt. Actually, it was the king of Navarre, Sancho III (1004–35), who took the initiative most quickly during that civil war, partly at the expense of the kings of León – he absorbed the county of Castile, now covering all the upper Duero valley, into his kingdom. His son Fernando I, count of Castile (1028–65), took over León itself in 1037, and his kingdom of León–Castile, enriched by large tributes from warring Muslim Taifa kingdoms, was poised for serious conquest for the first time, in the late eleventh century.

The kings of Asturias and León show us a double face. One was that of Visigothic tradition. Once the kings settled in Oviedo, they adopted all they could of the imagery and architectural display of Toledo as a capital. This does not mean that tiny Oviedo in any way resembled the latter city, even stylistically (Oviedo's churches at best represent a provincial tradition, although one with obvious late Roman roots); all the same, its surviving buildings are remarkable for such a small and agriculturally poor kingdom. Santiago, too, which had developed as a pilgrimage centre around the supposed tomb site of St James the Apostle from the early years of the ninth century, was built up, especially by Alfonso III; so was León in the next century. The new Duero territories were taken over through a network of urban foundations, on Roman sites such as Astorga, Visigothic sites such as Zamora and new sites such as Burgos, and also an array of rapidly expanding monasteries such as Cardeña, Sahagún and Celanova, who were soon the patrons of ambitious manuscript production. The kingdom regarded itself as being governed by Visigothic law, as also did Catalonia (Navarre is less clear here), and the elaborate procedures of Visigothic legal practice – more elaborate than those of either Francia or Italy – survive in both Catalan and Leonese documents, which start to be numerous in the tenth century. The kings had a palace entourage, too, which, although actually very small in size, at least nominally mirrored that of Toledo. Unlike any of the other polities described in this chapter, that of Asturias-León was also characterized by a political balance between king and aristocrats which doubtless had Visigothic antecedents, and which resembled that of the contemporary Frankish world; there were Alavese and Galician factions, and in the tenth century Castilian factions too, which kings had to contend with, and the tenth-century counts of Castile (particularly Fernán González, 931–70) were classic over-mighty subjects, willing to go it alone. As north of the Pyrenees, the politics of land played its part here, with royal cessions of property to aristocrats and monasteries prominent in our documentation, although – as indeed with the Carolingians – kings could confiscate from the disloyal too, and visibly did so. In these respects, then, Asturias-León could be seen as similar to tenth-century England, or to the principalities of southern Italy, in following lines parallel to those of Francia, although modified substantially by separate and earlier roots, in this case in the most Romanized of all the Romano-Germanic kingdoms.

But this is not the only way of seeing Asturias-León. Had it been, the kingdom would have been better discussed in Chapter 18; but the power-base of both kings and aristocrats was less certain than the preceding paragraph implies. Under the Visigoths, Asturias was remote and poor, and less Romanized or urbanized than most of the rest of the peninsula – perhaps than anywhere, with the exception of the nearby Basques, whom the Visigoths never fully conquered. Navarre was in part a Basque kingdom, although a relatively Romanized (or Visigothic) one; to its west, some Basque tribal communities remained independent into the eleventh century, and to their west some of the mountain valleys nominally subject to Asturias may have had a tribal social structure too. Even in the core areas closer to Oviedo, where Roman-style property law was certainly normal, our early (that is, ninth-century) documents show very small-scale aristocracies, and a substantial presence of a landowning peasantry.

In the new Duero lands, this was still more true in the next century. The view that the Duero valley was depopulated until a colonizing process was set in train by Ordoño and Alfonso III (the theory is above all associated with the mid-twentieth-century historian Claudio Sánchez-Albornoz) has now been abandoned, in the face of increasing archaeological and topographical demonstrations of settlement continuities. All the same, the valley had no organized political system for a long time, and when it emerges into the light of the documentation in the tenth century it is also a region of landowning peasant communities, organized through coherent village societies, sometimes with their own decision-making bodies, *concilia*. If there was a political structure that linked all these lands, it was probably organized through a network of fortified settlements, called *castros* in modern Spanish (and sometimes in the Latin of our period, too), which had at least some form of collective element to their social structure. This peasant-based, partly collective, society was given more strength the further south one went, for the southern frontier of the kingdom had to be defended. Peasants had military roles in southern León and southern Castile – as also southern Catalonia – for a long time, which reinforced their political and economic autonomy. The *fuero* (royal-granted customs) of the Castilian fortified settlement of Castrojeriz, dating probably to the early eleventh century in its present form, gave to all the male inhabitants considerable privileges (including immunities from tribute) in return for frontier defence; so did that of Cardona in Catalonia in 986, which contains the memorable line, paraphrased from the Gospel of Luke, 'if anyone wants to make himself superior [*maior*] among you, let him become inferior [*iunior*]'. It is not helpful to call the Duero societies, or even most of the Asturian societies, 'tribal', but at least they had unusually flat social structures by the standards of Francia or, by now, England, with autonomous peasantries who had more in common with those of Scandinavia or some of the Slav lands than with those of the Carolingian world.

There has been a historiographical war between historians who stress the Visigothic (or Catholic) side of the Asturian kingdom and those who stress its de-Romanized (or tribal) nature. Both views are valid, however. It is fair to see the kings, at least from Alfonso II onwards, as strikingly ambitious, given the material they had to work with. And, although the peasant basis of their kingdom was strong at the start, it weakened fast. King Aurelio (768–74) quelled a peasant revolt, somewhere in the Asturias, which must show some shift in power relations. Galicia was already a region with a relatively visible aristocracy in the ninth century, and, in the tenth, aristocrats there operated a landed politics just like that of their peers north of the Pyrenees, as with the church foundations and family manipulations of Ilduara (d. *c.* 960), an influential aristocratic widow from Lugo, who built the monastery of Celanova and put her son Bishop Rosendo (d. *c.* 980) in as its first abbot. In southern León and Castile, aristocratic power was newer; it largely derived from royal cessions of land and rights to *magnates* or *seniores* – and to monasteries – over the heads of the peasantry, including rights to local tributes which often turned into rents, as in ninth-century England; it also derived from the increased local influence of the richest and most militarized peasant stratum, which could soon turn into local dominance. Lesser aristocrats (*infanzones*), coming from the entourages of greater magnates or from families of rich peasant *milites*, or both, gained in the eleventh century a hereditary right to privilege over their non-aristocratic neighbours. The villages of the Duero had to be subjected, and sometimes resisted; they often maintained unusually coherent identities well into the central Middle Ages, for that matter. But already by the eleventh century the kingdom of León-Castile had a powerful and many-levelled aristocracy, based on rights of landownership, and also holding down roles in local government for the kings: it was ready to draw the maximum benefit possible from the weakened kingdoms of al-Andalus.

The shift to a landowning and office-holding aristocratic hierarchy, largely completed in the tenth century, thus brought the kingdom still more closely into line with the post-Carolingian world; in this respect, too, León-Castile followed, a century later, some of the developments we saw in Chapter 19 for England. But in Christian Spain the borrowings of governmental structures and political hierarchies were not from external powers, Francia or al-Andalus, as were those of the developing states of the rest of this chapter; they were largely from the Visigothic past, which had not been wholly forgotten.

The political and social systems described in this chapter covered half of Europe, and were very diverse. The Sclavenian/Slav lands were particularly extensive, and only a near-total lack of documentary or narrative detail about their affairs until very late in our period justifies treating them so summarily. Overall, however, there are common trends in all the societies described here. Kings and princes were in every region more ambitious around 1000 than they had been around 750: they often ruled wider areas, or at least were aiming at wider hegemonies, and sometimes had more elaborate structures to underpin that rule as well; they were often more relevant to local societies, too, thus ruling more deeply as well as more widely. The differences in our evidence from polity to polity sometimes stress one element in this, sometimes another. So in northern Spain there was a tendency for aristocrats to root themselves as locally powerful landowners, which has English parallels. This process was less complete in the Celtic, or Scandinavian, or Slav lands, where aristocrat–peasant relationships were more often those of patron and client, or tribute-taker and -payer, or both, until after our period ends. This was a real difference, although it may seem more acute because our documentation for landowning is far better for Spain (and England) than for elsewhere; it is quite possible, for example, that in a region like Bohemia aristocrats were already becoming landowners too in the tenth century, as not long afterwards they certainly would. We cannot tell in this case, for our sources are as yet inadequate; but we certainly have signs that this was so for Croatia, another Frankish borderland. Overall, however, the trend to wider and deeper political power seems to have been based on two sorts of developments. The first was the development of aristocratic power, and therefore of the possibility of hierarchies of political dependence extending from kings and princes down into the localities. The second was the development of techniques of rule and of control, usually (except in Spain and Ireland) borrowed from neighbour-ing powers: more specialized royal officials, a more complex and more top-down judicial system, the ability to demand military service from the population, the ability to exploit manpower to build fortifications of different types, and, in newly Christianized areas, the development of tighter official hierarchies of the church. We have seen some sign of each of these in different regions, although it would take another book to tease out the fragmentary evidence for their development as a whole.

Broadly, the more of these developments a ruler had access to, the more stable his power was, and the more ambitious he (in Rus, once, she) could be. Political aggregation was perhaps greatest in Rus, and also, in a smaller compass, Bulgaria, Denmark and Asturias-León; it was beginning, however, to crystallize in Croatia, Bohemia, Poland and maybe Norway by the end of our period as well, in a less stable and more contested way, and also (the obscurest of all) in Scotland. In Wales and Ireland, however, and also Sweden, royal ambition did not yet have an adequate infrastructural development behind it, and the expansion of kingdoms promoted instability more than solid bases for government (this was partly true of Bohemia and Poland as well); and in some places, on the Baltic coast or in Iceland (as also sometimes in Norway) such expansion was successfully resisted for some time. These represent different paths to increased political power, which was not inevitable anywhere – and also, of course, not necessarily desirable, at least if one was part of the peasant majority, for whom stronger government universally meant tighter control and more exploitation.

It is, all the same, despite these differences, striking how general the move to increased political power was across this wide swathe of Europe in the second half of our period. In 400 strong and stable political systems stopped at the Rhine–Danube border of the Roman empire. In 750, too, they hardly extended further, except in the parts of central and southern Germany under Frankish hegemony; and in the Balkans and in Britain they had actually retreated. But in 1000 recognizable polities had crystallized in most places in Europe, west of the Volga and south of the Finnic-speaking hunter-gatherer zone of the far north: weaker than the Roman empire, certainly, but with a certain staying power – half the modern European countries, indeed, and most of the larger ones, can trace themselves, however misleadingly, back to the kingdoms and principalities that existed by then. Such a widespread development must, surely, have at least some common root? One important feature of the period after 750 is that the most powerful political systems in Europe, Francia and Byzantium, regained their stability and began to expand; they were both threats to their immediate neighbours, who would have to become stronger or else succumb, and also models, for all the techniques of government just mentioned were more developed there. England used Francia as a model, and by the tenth century it was itself both a threat and a model to its Celtic neighbours; Denmark crystallized in response to Frankish pressures and influences, and by 1000 it too was both a threat and a model, inside Scandinavia. The Khazar hegemony in the Ukrainian steppes had a similar effect on Rus. The patterns of more powerful rule thus finally leapt over the Rhine–Danube line and moved steadily outwards, north, west and east. This development was not simple, and had other roots as well; it was also not continuous, as the history of (for example) Denmark shows. But it underpinned more local developments, and gave them a continent-wide coherence which would, eventually, last.

21

Aristocrats between the Carolingian and the 'Feudal' Worlds

In 967, the Saxon aristocrat Wichmann Billung was caught unawares by the Bohemian allies of his enemy Prince Mieszko of the Poles. Wichmann was fighting against his uncle Duke Hermann of Saxony at the time, on behalf of smaller Slav tribes, the Wagri and the Abodrites. Mieszko had converted to Christianity the previous year and was allied to Hermann and Otto I; Wichmann, like his father, had never forgiven Hermann for gaining the most prominence inside the family, thanks to the king/emperors, and had raised what was in effect a feud against him. Wichmann tried to flee the Slav attack but was surrounded, and fought till he was exhausted. The Slav leaders found out who he was and offered him a safe conduct. But Wichmann, 'not forgetting his former nobility and virtue' (as Widukind says, quoting Sallust), refused to 'give his hand', that is, surrender, to social inferiors, and asked them to send for Mieszko so that he could hand over his weapons to the prince himself. They agreed, but, while waiting, all continued to fight, since, of course, Wichmann had not put down his weapons; Wichmann was killed.

This insistence on social hierarchy even in such an extreme situation may well seem to us absurd, but it would have been taken for granted in the ninth and tenth centuries. Widukind himself, who rejoiced in Wichmann's death, could not avoid writing it up heroically. Aristocrats did indeed feel themselves to be totally different from the ordinary free strata of society. We can see this even in Abbot Odo of Cluny's *Life* of Gerald of Aurillac (d. 909), the first saint's life of a lay aristocrat, written around 930. Odo's Gerald was so virtuous that he broke all the rules of lay society, thus allowing Odo to picture someone as a saint who was a rich local lord, perhaps (not certainly) a count, and who never took religious orders. Some of these rules are thus implicitly laid out. Gerald never wore silk or gold; he did not take gifts from the poor before he helped them, and he allowed them to sit in his presence. He hated drunkenness and would not come drunk to judging in the law court. He would not let his men plunder the countryside when engaging in local wars, and he insisted on buying cherries from a peasant rather than taking them. When he met his fugitive dependant in another region, while journeying to Rome, and discovered that the latter was passing for a man of wealth and status, Gerald did not betray his origin – this was particularly remarkable in Odo's eyes ('who but Gerald would have done this?'). He was saved from sleeping with the daughter of one of his unfree dependants by a miracle; Odo comments at length on his chastity, thus marvellously preserved, but makes no remark about Gerald's casual command to the girl's mother to have her ready when he came, a standard lord's prerogative. Gerald's wars against his neighbours were always defensive, and therefore counted as protection of the poor (he banned not only plunder but also ambushes); he only undertook to participate in 'the right of armed force' at all because his entourage were indignant that 'a great man might suffer violence from persons of low degree who lay waste his property', and he never ever sought revenge.

These and many other parallel acts, and also plenty of miracles, made Gerald a saint, in Odo's narrative at least; and that narrative in turn had sufficient resonance with its 930s audience to contribute to a successful cult of Gerald – his own Aurillac monastery of Saint-Pierre was dedicated to him by the middle of the century, and Saint-Géraud became a pilgrimage centre, to Gerbert's great benefit, as we saw in Chapter 18. The norms of small-scale aristocratic behaviour thus become clear, as practised by men who were not saints, whether they date to the later decades of the ninth century with Gerald or to the years around 930 with Odo (who was himself from a similar lesser aristocratic background, a generation later, and, like Gerald, was a protégé of Duke William the Pious of Aquitaine). The normality of small local wars; the practical rights of the military strata to take whatever they liked from the peasantry; the assumption that aristocrats would often get angry (and drunk) and be violent to other people; the harsh and self-righteous policing of social boundaries, between unfree and free, unmilitary free and aristocratic, poor and rich: these were the aristocratic values assumed (and, to be fair, criticized) by Odo of Cluny, and they were lived by social élites throughout the Carolingian and post-Carolingian period, as also, with only minor modifications, both before and after.

Aristocratic bad behaviour was thus not born with the 'feudal revolution' of the eleventh century (see below). But nor do these almost timeless norms really clash with what else we know about aristocrats, as seen in previous chapters, such as their generalized attachment (and even loyalty) to kings and other major political figures, or their religiosity, or even their absorption of the values of Carolingian education and *correctio*. This chapter aims to look at aristocratic practices from their own standpoint, not from those of rulers and writers, in so far as that is possible given our sources, and to see what they meant to their practitioners, in the varying environments of western Europe after 750 or so. I shall start with a set of four brief case studies, to set out how different families reacted to the political changes of the period in different parts of Europe. We shall then look at three interlocking themes, the structures of local power, dependence, and then, returning to these accounts of Wichmann and Gerald, aristocratic values.

The 'Guilhelmids' were a family from Burgundy who may have been distant relations of the Pippinids; they gained importance under Charlemagne and were part of his *Reichsaristokratie*. William of Gellone (d. 812) was the first really prominent family member; he was sent south, to rule Toulouse and Septimania, in the 790s, and founded the monastery of Gellone in the latter region, near modern Montpellier, where he retired as a monk in 806. His son Bernard of Septimania (d. 844) was count of (among other places) Barcelona in the 820s before coming to Louis the Pious's court as his controversial chamberlain in 829–30 (see Chapter 16); Bernard's wife Dhuoda (d. *c.* 843), as we have also seen, wrote her *Handbook* for their son William in 841–3, the masterpiece of Carolingian lay piety, stressing regular prayer, a temperate conduct, and unequivocal loyalty to Bernard, to the Guilhelmid family as a whole, and to Charles the Bald as king. However that might be, the least one could say of the Guilhelmids was that they were equivocal; Bernard played a very ambiguous role in the civil wars of the 840s, and was executed for treason by Charles in 844; William, who was at least loyal, but to Pippin the Younger not Charles, was killed for that five years later. The family was notably unpopular in these years; Bernard's brother Gozhelm was executed and his sister Gerberga drowned as a witch by the emperor Lothar in 834.

It is hard to think of a more dramatic and even shameful political failure in this period than that of the Guilhelmids, for all Dhuoda's values. But the family did not disappear from its original Burgundian heartland. Bernard's younger son Bernard (d. 886), called 'Hairy-paws' (i.e. 'foxy') in one source, was count of Autun in Burgundy in the early 860s, and in 864, for unclear reasons, he tried to assassinate either Robert the Strong or Charles the Bald himself; he lost most of his *honores* at once, and Autun two years later. His family land still remained, all the same, and by 872 he was back in Charles's court, killing opponents but also accumulating *honores* again, probably already including the county of the Auvergne, centre of his future power, which he held until his death. In 878 he picked up many of the *honores* of the rebel Bernard of Gothia, including the March of Gothia (Septimania) again; he became the guardian of the new West Frankish king Louis III himself in 879. When he died, he ruled a string of counties from the Loire to the Pyrenees, most of which were inherited directly by his son William the Pious (d. 918), who called himself duke of Aquitaine. William behaved for thirty years as an autonomous regional power in eastern Aquitaine, running court cases in the manner of a king as much as that of a count, and seeking to detach the loyalty of royal vassals (including Gerald of Aurillac) from the king and attach it to himself. The family died out in 927 at the death of his two nephews, successive dukes of Aquitaine after him, but up to then we can see all the ingredients of the creative opportunism of an 'imperial aristocratic' family: operating by Carolingian rules until the 880s, and autonomously thereafter. It is notable that, despite the family's spectacular eclipse in the 840s, it was still a natural choice for patronage a generation later; family claims to royal interest died hard. It is also notable that Bernard Hairy-paws reconstructed his power in exactly the areas, stretching southwards from his family lands, that his father and grandfather had dealt in; this was by royal gift, but it indicates the durability of family political aspirations. Into the 920s, also, even though the Guilhelmids were by now independent players, they still operated a Carolingian-style political system, using county-based structures such as law courts, and also the control of royal abbacies (William the Pious was given the major Auvergne monastery of Brioude by King Odo in 893). The long string of their counties, 600 kilometres from north to south but seldom more than 150 east to west, also made most sense in a Carolingian political system, and William had local troubles at the end of his life; successor powers in these areas were more compact.

If we move later into the tenth century and remain in areas of powerful kingship, we continue to find families who, however ambitious, played by royal rules. In England, the families of Æthelstan 'Half-king' and Ælfhere are clear examples. In Saxony, there were many too; one was the counts of Walbeck west of Magdeburg, Bishop Thietmar of Merseburg's family, thus well documented in his *Chronicon*. Liuthar I had died fighting Slavs for Henry I in 929, but his son Liuthar II (d. 964) had been involved in a conspiracy against Otto I in 941 in the context of the early 940s civil wars and lost all his lands; he regained them the following year, having paid a hefty fine in money and land, after which he endowed a church in Walbeck to atone for the plot. His sons divided the family patrimony, Siegfried (d. 991) becoming count of Walbeck (he was succeeded by his son Henry, Thietmar's brother; both were in the entourage of the emperor Henry II). Siegfried's brother Liuthar III (d. 1003), although not always close to the Ottonian court, became marquis of the Northern March in or after 985, and thus one of the major figures in Saxony in the aftermath of the Slav revolt of 983. In this guise he was one of the king-makers of Henry II in 1002; he supported Henry not least so as to sabotage the ambitions of his rival Ekkehard of Meissen, who had broken the engagement of his daughter Liudgard to Liuthar's son Werner, and who had humiliated Werner in an assembly in 999 after Werner had abducted Liudgard (with her agreement). Werner married Liudgard after Ekkehard's death in 1002, and inherited his father's march a year later. But Werner was also an idiot; in 1009 he responded to machinations against him by Count Dedi at Henry's court by killing Dedi, and lost his march, his benefices and the king's favour. Werner instead plotted with Bolesław Chrobry of Poland in 1013, and only kept his properties by paying a large fine to Henry; in 1014 he abducted another woman, this time unwilling (Liudgard had died in 1012), and risked execution had he not died of wounds from the affray – to the huge distress of Dedi's son Dietrich, who could thus not be avenged. We see the ambition, the feuding and the general bad behaviour of major aristocrats once again, notwithstanding Thietmar's obvious partiality, but also that the whole sequence of events took place in a king-centred framework, just as the careers of Bernard Hairy-paws and his father had. Thietmar's world, it can be added, was overwhelmingly a world of counts and marquises (and bishops); no smaller lords have any impact on his narratives. A basic Carolingian political infrastructure remained in place here at least into the 1010s, and indeed much later.

Both the Guilhelmids and the counts of Walbeck had family lands as a basis on which to accumulate counties/marches and benefices. So did the Canossa in Italy, but with a slightly different result. Adalbert-Atto (d. 989) of Canossa, a castle in the Appennines above Reggio Emilia, was made count of Reggio, Modena and Mantua by Otto I in the 960s for his support against Berengar II. He used these comital positions, however, above all as a support for his further accumulation of lands, in outright property, or in lease or benefice from churches and monasteries, along the River Po in all these counties (and others), and also to a lesser extent in the Appennines. These lands were the basis of Canossan power for the next century, far more than the counties were. They were studded with castles, and the local rights which Adalbert-Atto, his son Tedald (d. *c.* 1010), and his grandson Boniface (d. 1052) held in them were as complete as any count had anywhere, whether or not the Canossa held the county they were in. This was a de-facto power that was substantially different from those of our earlier examples. Tedald added the county of Brescia to his father's collection, but, when he called himself marquis, seems to be holding a title he had claimed for himself. The Canossa did not spurn Carolingian-style public power; when they were given the march of Tuscany by the emperor Conrad II in 1027, a strong political unit, they ran it with enthusiasm in a traditional Carolingian manner until the family died out in 1115. But in their Emilian heartland they ruled in a very different way, on the basis of their extensive landholding and their informal political powers over that land, powers which historians call 'seigneurial' (see below). After their initial rise under Otto I, they also needed royal patronage rather less; they tended to be loyal to the king/emperors, and were far from unhappy to receive benefits as a result, not least in 1027, but their careers were far less focused on royal favour, even though the king/emperors remained institutionally strong in Italy. They had become regional powers with whom the kings had to deal, and in the Po valley they did not strictly need their comital offices in order to maintain their power, by 1000 at the latest.

The idea that a lay aristocrat might be powerful without being a count (or else a palatine official) was a novelty. Of course, one might not be a count at any given moment, as Bernard Hairy-paws was not for most of the first half of his career, but aristocrats systematically aspired to be one, to legitimate their status, and were thus inevitably tied into a royal patronage network. The Canossa did, of course, owe their rise to kings, and never after 962 lost comital or marchional office; they were not unrecognizable to ninth-century eyes. But their *interests* were different, all the same. They had parallels elsewhere, too. In the later tenth century, many families emerged, particularly in West Francia, who had the same focus on land, de-facto local power, and castles that the Canossa had, but operated on a far smaller scale. The lords of Uxelles were one such, in the county of Mâcon, once under the control of William the Pious but after the 920s in the hands of a local family of counts. The counts married, oddly, into the family of King Berengar II of Italy, whose male-line heirs thus controlled the Mâconnais into the eleventh century; but the first of these, Berengar II's grandson Otto-William (d. 1026), was so intent on an ambitious politics that he stirred up regional opposition and weakened his local position notably. Josseran I (d. *c.* 990) owned the *villa* of Uxelles; his descendants held the castle there, presumably from the count of Mâcon, with a set of local comital rights, over justice and tolls for example; these became hereditary in his family, and they were backed up by the solid set of family properties in the same area. Between 1000 and 1030 or so, the counts lost their power over them. By the second quarter of the eleventh century, Bernard II (d. *c.* 1050), Josseran's grandson, held a network of powers in the territory around Uxelles, based on his family land on the one hand and the privatized judicial powers associated with the castle on the other, and extending, eventually, to all sorts of military and customary dues owed by his tenants and landowning neighbours alike, which were largely invented by the Uxelles lords themselves. This was what the Canossa had in and around their own lands, and again we call it 'seigneurial'; but this time the Uxelles seigneurie was only about 100 square kilometres, by no means all of it directly controlled by the family. The tiny scale of political units of this kind (there were a dozen or so in the county of Mâcon) marked a radical change from that described up to now. This was power constructed for the most part from the bottom up, as well. The lords of Uxelles will hardly have dealt with the king, who was only an external power in this area by 1000, but from then on they also hardly needed the count either, who was little more than another seigneurial lord, with lands and powers restricted to the area just west of Mâcon. Mâcon is justly famous, for it is one of the best-documented areas of tenth- and eleventh-century Europe, thanks to the thousands of charters of the monastery of Cluny (see below), and also to Georges Duby's epoch-making regional study of 1953. But this pulverization of the structures of the county, and the takeover of all the public traditions of the state by private landholding families, has parallels across much of West Francia around 1000, and in later centuries could be found in other parts of Europe too.

These very diverse aristocratic experiences have some basic elements in common. The first, entirely predictably in the early Middle Ages, is land: nobody could be a political player before 1000, even in a tiny area, without a locally substantial property, held either in full ownership or in long-term concessions from churches or kings. A feature of the Carolingian and post-Carolingian period is that more land came to be under aristocratic control than before, and less was under the control of non-aristocrats. This change was particularly important in England, as we saw in Chapter 19, and was even more acute in Saxony, where Charlemagne's conquest resulted in a rapid takeover of land previously under peasant ownership, by the kings themselves, by churches and monasteries, by incoming Frankish lords, and (perhaps most of all) by the surviving native Saxon aristocracy. The speed of this social change provoked the largest-scale peasants' revolt in early medieval Europe, the Stellinga uprising of 841–2, during the Carolingian civil war, but this failed, and the new political powers continued to accumulate land. The newness of Saxon aristocratic power, and its close connection to royal protagonism, may well help to explain the solidity of the Ottonian political system in Saxony, as it certainly does for royal power in England. In Francia proper, and Italy too, the period 750–1000 also marks a steady increase in aristocratic wealth and power, at the expense of a surviving peasantry, thanks largely to the political opportunities for successful aristocrats under Charlemagne and his successors. As a result of this still ill-studied process, landowning peasantries are rather less visible in 1000 than in 750 throughout Francia and Italy, and in some places had disappeared altogether. We shall look at this issue again in the next chapter, but it is an essential backdrop to aristocratic affirmation at the political level; lords had more land to play with politically, and sometimes – as with the most successful monasteries, or the 'imperial aristocracy' – far more land. This was not affected by the growing regionalization of the aristocracy (outside England) after 850 or so; that process simply meant that lords increasingly used their lands as elements in a regional politics, as well as (or instead of) a kingdom-wide one.

In the case of the lay aristocracy, this land could be then added to by *honores*: royal-confirmed offices, such as counties, and benefices. These were given by kings and could, for a long time, be taken away again. Werner of the Northern March is a case in point: he lost his offices and benefices in 1009, though he kept his properties. It is not that the king/ emperor could not confiscate his properties as well; this nearly happened in 1013, indeed. But under normal circumstances (that is, anything except treason, and sometimes even then) kings would leave aristocrats with their full property even when they fell out of favour and lost the rest. We have seen in previous chapters that aristocrats always sought to preserve counties and benefices for their sons, and very often succeeded, including under Charlemagne. But until that inheritance became a right, kings kept strategic control of this large sector of aristocratic wealth and power. In most of the post-Carolingian kingdoms before 1000, and also in England, such rights to automatic succession in counties/ ealdormanries and benefices only existed on political margins, such as, in England, Northumbria, or, in Italy, parts of the march of Spoleto in the far south or Piemonte in the north-west. The major exception to this was West Francia, where such rights were in effect extended to nearly every duke and count in the decades around 900, with catastrophic effects on royal power. When this 'patrimonialization' process occurred, of course, aristocracies hugely increased their practical control over wealth and local patronage powers, for they could now add ex-royal land and local political rights to their own properties, as long as they could keep control of them in the framework of local rivalries which were no longer moderated by kings.

These collections of properties and rights in the hands of single families were heterogeneous, usually scattered (even if, as just noted, increasingly in a single region), and would be further scattered by property transfers at marriage and by partible inheritance among sons. (This was universal until past 1000, except that counties and benefices, until they were patrimonialized at least – and often later – could not be divided internally.) Families sought to give them some structure. One way was by founding a family monastery, a procedure already popular in the seventh century in Francia but steadily expanding after that; by the tenth century every aristocratic player had one, except the very smallest. Such monasteries were characteristically under full family ownership, very often with a family member as abbot (or abbess – many were nunneries in some parts of Europe, particularly Saxony); but effective family control could often be preserved through rights of patronage, even if the monastery was alienated away, as often happened, to bishops or larger (and more prestigious) monastic groupings, including if the monastery was 'reformed', as we shall see later. Ownership or patronage was characteristically shared between all family-members, a great advantage if families expanded demographically, for it represented a core of family-controlled power that was not divided; six men seem to have shared control of the Berardenghi family monastery of Fontebona in Tuscany in 1030, for example, and eleven by 1060. By then, it was the main thing keeping the family together.

Castles were another resource, by the tenth century. The origins of the widespread use of fortified sites by aristocrats is still under debate. Fortifications were already common in the sixth century in some parts of Europe (such as Italy, divided geographically as it was), but these were for the most part public structures, controlled by kings and their officials, and they often included large areas inside the walls; they were fortified villages rather than élite residences. This practice slowly extended across all Europe, not least in the context of defence against Vikings and other frontier invaders, as with the *urbes* of both the tenth-century Saxons and their Slav opponents, or the *burhs* of tenth-century England. They are very visible also in the local wars of the Seine valley chronicled in Flodoard's *Annals* in the 920s–960s, for control over them had devolved to counts and bishops, and they were much fought over. But this latter example by now poses the issue of whether aristocrats could put them up themselves. Charles the Bald certainly thought they might; in the Edict of Pîtres in 864 he banned all *castella et firmitates* built without his consent, because they were the foci for 'many depredations and hindrances for their neighbours', and he demanded that they be pulled down. Laws such as this seldom work, and Gerald of Aurillac had a castle in the late ninth century which was almost certainly private. But actually, both in archaeology and in documents, private castles were more a tenth-century phenomenon, and indeed expanded for the most part fairly slowly outside the political stratum represented by counts and bishops; for the lesser aristocracy, it was the eleventh century, not the tenth, that saw castles built widely. Major aristocrats by 950 or so nonetheless in most of continental Europe (though not England) had castles, often many in number, as points of reference for their counties and their properties. These were defences for local power (both legal and illegal), obviously; they were also centres of family cohesion, much as monasteries were. (In the eleventh century, when surnames developed, families would often come to be named after their principal castle.) Both were signs of a much less fluid political geography, for they tied aristocrats to single areas even more firmly than the steady regionalization of political interest did.

Castles came to be the typical bases for seigneurial powers. This did not have to be immediate, but such powers did increasingly crystallize in the years around 1000 or shortly after, particularly in West Francia but also in much of Italy. Both comital families and lesser lords came to be able to dispose of a wide range of rights, on their own properties and over the properties of their neighbours, by now seen as private prerogatives: the obligation to do castle-guard or to billet and feed a military detachment; dues in return for being able to travel a road, or putting in at a river port, or attending a market; dues for being able to cut wood in a common woodland; compulsory cart service on given days of the year; compulsory use of a lord's mill, with the attendant dues; or, above all, the profits of an increasingly privatized justice. This basket of rights (with different elements stressed in different places) is called the 'seigneurie banale', Georges Duby's phrase, in much modern scholarship – 'banale' because many of these rights were once royal, making up much of what Carolingian sources call the king's *bannum*. They had very diverse origins, all the same; as in the case of the lords of Uxelles, the creation of a seigneurial lordship was very often the result of a creative bricolage of old and new powers over tenants and neighbours, established both by force and by agreement. In some areas of West Francia in the twelfth century and later, seigneurial rights came to be more profitable than taking rents; but that development had not begun yet in 1000.

Castles and seigneurial rights are markers of a new attention to local dominance, beginning particularly after around 900 in the post-Carolingian lands, and steadily increasing, and becoming more localized still, after 950/1000. Aristocrats had, as we have seen in earlier chapters, previously sought identity and status above all through royal or at least ducal patronage. They needed land in order to have the wealth to play at that level, and to be able to afford the armed entourage that was equally essential for royal politics; but they did not need to be able to dominate their neighbours to have kingdom-level status, and they might anyway move around substantially in royal service. Increasingly, however, especially in the tenth century, attention to one's local power-base was essential. If one did not pay attention to it, it might break up, as we shall see in a moment. But it was also the case that lords moved around rather less by now, so might find their local power-base more of an interesting long-term commitment; and the logic of castle-guard, and the intricacies of seigneurial powers and private law courts, pointed towards quite localized political initiatives. This did not happen everywhere. Notably, it did not happen in England, where tenth-century evidence even for the lesser aristocracy shows some strikingly wide and potentially changeable areas of interest, as with the family of Bishop Oswald of Worcester, who owned from Worcestershire to the Fens, or Ælfhelm Polga, whose will of the 980s shows him holding land from Essex to Huntingdonshire, without reference to any political centre at all, even a principal place of residence. But it happened across most of post-Carolingian Continental Europe, and also in some of the crystallizing Slav and Scandinavian polities, which were themselves still fairly small-scale.

If we look at the structures of aristocratic dependence, these same processes can be seen again, from a different standpoint. Major aristocrats needed an armed entourage, of *fideles* or, to use the new terminology of the late eighth century and onwards, vassals: men who had sworn oaths of loyalty to them, and who had often, probably, gone through some form of ceremony representing dependence. As public power became weaker in many places, that ceremony became increasingly elaborate and ritualized, for personal bonds of this type became ever more clearly the key to effective political power. This was also increasingly linked to military status itself. Under Charlemagne, military service was still the theoretical obligation of all free men, but even then, in practice, warfare was carried out by professionalized soldiers, *milites*, most of them in the entourage of their sworn lords. From the ninth century onwards, military status was increasingly seen as the prerogative of an élite, and entry into it was also associated with a ceremony, increasingly often an ecclesiastical one. This network of rituals underpinned what historians after 1000 call 'knighthood', and one translation of *miles* is by now not just 'soldier', but 'knight'.

This knightly imagery really belongs to a later period than this book covers. All the same, to call oneself a *miles* was by the tenth century in some places a claim to status. Not yet in Saxony; *milites* are generally (even if not always) second-order figures in Thietmar. But, once again, in West Francia and secondarily Italy, by the later tenth century a *miles* was a significant player, and *milites* were establishing themselves as the lowest rung of the aristocracy, rather closer to counts than they were to the upper strata of the peasantry. This time, England goes in part with West Francia, for *miles* there, although still often representing quite humble soldiers, was also one of the standard Latin translations of *thegn*, the basic stratum of the late Anglo-Saxon aristocracy, and fairly comfortably off (every thegn was supposed to hold five hides of land, roughly 2 square kilometres, not a small amount of full landholding; Ælfhelm Polga, a rather more substantial landowner, seems to have been a king's thegn). The lords of Uxelles, who were rather richer than this, were *milites* (and also, significantly, *nobiles*) around 1000; in Italy, a famous law of 1037 of Conrad II conceded to all *milites* the right to inherit benefices, given not only by kings but also by counts and bishops; although they could still lose them if they committed certain offences, the gap between full property and benefices was receding at the level of legislation too. In many parts of Italy, indeed, *milites* themselves came in two levels, *capitanei* and *valvassores*; even the latter could be socially prominent, and would form the ruling class of twelfth-century cities, but the former were certainly, by 1000 at the latest, political leaders by contemporary Italian standards.

What these processes mean is that, in practice, more people could by now be counted as what we call 'the aristocracy'. By the Carolingian period, the word *nobilis* can effectively be translated 'aristocrat', its bearers marked out by wealth and lifestyle. It was by no means a legally defined category, but it denoted a rather restricted and special group, those with a great deal of property, those with *Königsnähe*, those who might expect counties. This was changing by the later tenth century, and *milites* who had rather localized lands, like the lords of Uxelles, by now could be called *nobilis*, could behave like richer aristocrats, and, increasingly, could be treated as near-equals by counts. This stratum of the lesser aristocracy was all the same closer to the peasantry, of course, simply because it was less rich than the great 'imperial aristocratic' families. 'Military' families might be the lesser branches of great aristocratic clans, or the descendants of vassals of Carolingian counts and bishops, but they might well also be descended from the medium landowners of the eighth century, locally prominent families with close connections to their peasant neighbours, who had stayed in the professional military arena. *Milites* were therefore also much more likely to be interested in local domination, for the local level was the one they were closest to. Many of the more detailed aspects of the seigneurie banale were pioneered by *milites*. This was reinforced by the emergence of a sharp division between the aristocratic/military class and the peasant majority, theorized already by King Alfred in the late ninth century, and extended considerably in early eleventh-century political writings in West Francia, as the difference between 'those who fight' and 'those who work'. That sharp division marks the defining of an aristocratic stratum fundamentally distinct from the peasantry, which legitimated the local dominance of even quite small castle-holding lords. But all this also means that the local, castle-holding, seigneurie-building lords of the Mâconnais and other parts of West Francia and Italy in 1000, however aristocratic they by now saw themselves as being – and were seen by others as being – would have been regarded as of no account at all by a Merovingian *vir inluster* or a Carolingian 'imperial aristocrat'. Not only membership of 'the aristocracy', but also the right to an independent political protagonism, was now extended to far more people, even if, still, only to a small proportion of the population at large.

Carolingian lords, just as in the period before 750, rewarded their military clienteles in different ways: by outright gifts of land, by hereditary leases, by revocable benefices. The difference between these latter was not always huge; unlike at the high aristocratic level, small-scale *fideles* and vassals might not be able to make their outrage felt if even their full property was confiscated by a count or bishop or abbot. As lay aristocrats, and also bishops and abbots, increased their land, they increased their entourages – their armies – by granting out more of it. In the tenth century, they would put their most prominent *milites* in charge of their castles and the local political powers associated with castle-holding. This would have been safe in the ninth century, because no *miles* could go it alone without facing ruin. In the later tenth century, however, when in some parts of Europe the 'military' stratum was gaining aristocratic identity and a sense of political protagonism, it was more risky. If counts could go it alone with respect to kings, castellans could also go it alone with respect to counts, as with the lords of Uxelles in relation to the counts of Mâcon. If a count or bishop lost control of his castellans, the whole framework of his power could unravel, and often did. Here, the 'politics of land' led firmly to political fragmentation of a most extreme kind – seldom before 1000, but often by 1050. The whole shape of politics could potentially change; the public world of the Carolingians might vanish, with nothing remaining in some areas except tiny private lordships.

This process has been called the 'feudal revolution' (or 'mutation') by many historians in recent years, and the issue has been sharply debated. Indeed, the 'feudal revolution' has become for some historians (particularly in France) shorthand for epochal change, the end of the ancient world itself in the most extreme formulations of the idea. The debate cannot be reprised here (it mostly has an eleventh-century focus), but some points can be made about it. One is that the catastrophist tone of many historians is out of place; the new 'feudal' world of the eleventh century may have been marked by more violence, for example, than its predecessor, but the difference was only in degree, not kind, as any reader of Flodoard's *Annals* or Odo's *Life* of Gerald (or, for that matter, the *Annals of Saint-Bertin*) will realize; military aristocrats of all types are always violent, and this did not change now that lesser *milites* were counted in. Another is, however, that there were real changes in some places, some of them very fast, as the Carolingian order was replaced by seigneuries; public assemblies finally vanished, relations of dependence became more prominent, power became more personal, even when it was in the hands of the same people. Comital power in a tenth-century autonomous county tended to have a very Carolingian format; but attempts to see a local seigneurie banale as simply the Carolingian political system writ small have not succeeded. As argued earlier, these shifts make the eleventh-century political world structurally different from the tenth, at least in the parts of Europe where they occurred.

Conversely, this was not the case everywhere. Such shifts certainly did not occur in 'outer Europe', where no aristocrats were as yet sufficiently powerful, except in León-Castile. There is no sign that they were about to occur in 1000 in Anglo-Saxon England and Ottonian East Francia, and indeed, in the former, they never did (seigneurial-type powers in England were in the next centuries only held inside a lord's own lands, and over unfree dependants). In most of what one can now call Germany, analogous processes were hardly beginning before 1100, and never had the form they took in what one can now call France. Even in Italy, where seigneurial fragmentation was often extreme, the continuing centrality of cities in most of the peninsula meant that there was always an alternative locus of political order, however informal, to that of the local lordship. In cities such as Milan or Lucca, the 'military' strata largely remained city-dwelling, even when, in the eleventh century, their rural lands acquired castles and seigneurial territories; this thus perpetuated a political community covering the whole city territory. We are left with France as the fulcrum of these 'revolutionary' changes. And not everywhere in France either, for, as we shall see in a moment, in Flanders, Normandy, Anjou and Toulouse, counts kept control of their castellans and of substantial elements of the Carolingian political pattern, into the twelfth century and beyond. The 'feudal revolution', particularly in its most dramatic form, as in the Mâconnais or, as authoritatively argued, in Catalonia, cannot be extended as a model to more than a minority of Europe, and not to large parts even of France.

The 'politics of land' is, it must be stressed, hard for kings and other lords to keep on top of. There is a potential zero-sum game, in which the more a king or lord grants out, the less he has to give, and the less attractive his patronage seems. Marc Bloch in 1940 called this 'the fragmentation of powers', and his phrase still works as an image. There is an underlying tendency to the break-up of larger political systems in favour of smaller ones, at least at the edges of the systems, and in extreme cases (as with tenth-century West Francia) even in the centre. But an underlying tendency is not an inescapable one. Merovingian and Carolingian – and Lombard, Visigothic and post-750 Anglo-Saxon – royal courts were unavoidable points of reference for all political power. Those who failed to get there or did not try were failures, those who went it alone without them seldom survived. Similarly, some counts in tenth-century West Francia could ride the tiger of fragmentation into smaller units still, by avoiding civil war, by policing their castellans tightly, by fighting successfully on frontiers and thus having booty and sometimes extra land to give to their *milites*, by keeping control of justice, by tying their military dependants to them with as ceremonious a set of ties as possible, and (perhaps above all) by using force as violently and as ruthlessly as they could against anyone who tried to defy them. At the very end of the tenth century, Fulk Nerra managed this in Anjou, Richard II in Normandy, Baldwin IV in Flanders; they successfully kept the balance of power firmly on the comital side, even as some of their neighbours failed to do the same. The Ottonians and the West Saxon kings found the same task rather easier. There was nothing inevitable about the 'feudal revolution'.

Aristocratic status derived from a variety of elements: high birth, land, office, royal favour, lifestyle, the respect of one's peers. No one theorized the relative importance of these elements; people 'just knew' how they balanced out, and different people had different views about their importance, or their applicability to individuals. When Thegan denounced Ebbo, archbishop of Reims, saying that Louis the Pious 'made you free, not noble, which is impossible' (cf. above, Chapter 17), he invoked an absolute criterion that was seldom put so sharply in this period. Ebbo may have been of servile origin; but other political players criticized for their 'low birth', like Hagano, Charles the Simple's counsellor, in Richer's words, or Willigis archbishop of Mainz (975–1011), Otto I's former chancellor, in those of Thietmar, seem to have come from lesser aristocratic families, who may well have seen themselves as *nobiles*. There was not a noble 'caste', marked out by unbreakable rules of blood-line, as emerged in some parts of later medieval Europe; there was a grey area of negotiation, marked out by the snobbery of social superiors at every level. It was inside this grey area that *milites* in some parts of Europe began to take on aristocratic trappings, and to make claims to a status hitherto unavailable to them, which many by 1000 were prepared to grant them. But in order to do so they had to behave like their richer and better-established peers.

Aristocratic behaviour had in many respects not changed greatly from the period before 750, discussed in Chapter 8. Silk clothes with gold and silver decoration, military expertise, hunting, remained basic aristocratic markers, as did a ready use of violence – the markers that were implicit in Odo of Cluny's characterization of Gerald of Aurillac. Odo refers to Gerald's education in 'the worldly exercises customary for noble boys' – hunting, archery, falconry – but only enough literacy to read the Psalter (though an extreme bout of acne persuaded his parents in Gerald's case to give him a fuller literary education, in case they had to make him a priest). The Carolingian educational programme seems to have already become rather weaker, if this story relates to Gerald's youth in the 860s rather than to Odo's own day, although Gerald was at best on the fringes of the Carolingian aristocracy, and also living in a remote area. All the same, Gerald's Psalter reminds us that the aristocratic sense of innate virtue – a feature of this period, as earlier – was not just expressed through military valour and the like, but also through an (at least imagined) sense of a special religious charisma and commitment, as we shall see in a moment. Aristocrats were also supposed to be welcoming and generous, at least to their equals; Henry I before he became king of East Francia invited his neighbours to a wedding feast in Merseburg, according to Thietmar, and 'treated them with such familiarity that they loved him as a friend and honoured him as a lord'. Whether the *hilaritas*, 'jolliness', praised in some narrative sources, was the same emotion as the drunken overbearingness to social inferiors criticized in the *Life* of Gerald is not clear, though it is likely often enough to have been the case. One of the key elements in the lifestyle of the aristocracy was indeed the potential violence to social inferiors that our sources constantly stress. This was taken for granted when one was dealing with the highest aristocrats; if it often seems that the increasing local power of the military strata in West Francia is associated with more complaints of violence than had been the case for the Carolingian 'imperial aristocracy', it is likely that this is not just because *milites* were establishing seigneuries by a liberal use of force, but also because they were not yet (particularly by vocal ecclesiastical victims) regarded as having a legitimate claim to the violent behaviour of more 'noble' figures. If so, however, they soon would.

We saw in Chapter 18 that a sense of a more dynastic family identity was stronger in the tenth-century aristocracy than formerly. This should not be pushed too far. Growing family rights to offices, and the consequential more prominent role of women as intermediaries between generations, are visible in the tenth century, at least in the highest aristocratic strata. But families were still fairly flexible entities; kinship ties of all kinds had gained in strength by now. Men and women were not tied to a single male-line lineage for their identity; surnames rarely existed yet. Thietmar pays almost as much attention to his mother's kin, the counts of Stade, as to the counts of Walbeck on his father's side. Furthermore, if maternal ancestors had a higher status than paternal, or more political purchase, they were often stressed more by their descendants, as when around 1012 Constantine, biographer of Bishop Adalbero II of Metz (d. 1005), stressed his descent from Henry I of East Francia, his mother's mother's father, above all; his father, Duke Frederick of Upper Lotharingia, by contrast does not have his ancestors listed, presumably because they were less distinguished. All the same, paternal kin, other things being equal, already mattered most; it was from them that most land would be inherited, and with them that it would be – sometimes acrimoniously – divided. This would simply be accentuated as office-holding became less vital an element of aristocratic identity and land became more important.

Families continued to feud with each other, too. The imagery of *faida*, 'feud', or, more generally, *bellum*, 'war', frequently appears in narratives, as in the 'Babenberger'-'Conradine' *bellum* of the 900s in the Middle Rhine, in which the Babenberger Henry was killed in 902, then his brother Adalbert killed Conrad, father of the future king Conrad I, before King Louis the Child was able to intervene, executing Adalbert in 906. All the same, not all these feuds reinforced patrilineal families: the murder of the leading Lotharingian count Megingaud in 892 was avenged on his killer Alberic in 896 by his widow's second husband's uncle. These were regional alliances fighting for supremacy, more than kin-groups expressing identity through honour-killings, even if the imagery of revenge was there, and was powerful. At the highest level, indeed, political rivalry could break families up; we saw at the start of this chapter how Ottonian patronage had split the Billungs. On a smaller scale, Thietmar himself found his paternal uncle Marquis Liuthar extremely unwilling to let him take over the family church of Walbeck in 1002, until Thietmar gave Liuthar a large pay-off (and also paid off his predecessor, whom Liuthar had put in), though this may simply be the product of tensions implicit in all inheritance divisions, which have indeed broken up many tight lineages in history, and certainly did so in the ninth and tenth centuries. Which is to say: we must not overstate family solidarity. Families could break up, and be redefined; family links were in any case only one available social bond, alongside personal dependence on kings and other lords, and political/factional alliances of other kinds. All the same, the imagery of kinship was important to aristocrats and widely used; it was kin who could choose whether to accept compensation for killings or continue the *faida* (as we see, for example, in Charlemagne's capitularies; he sought to make compensation compulsory); family and kin bonds underlie all inheritance, much political strategy, and an increasing proportion of aristocratic identity.

Aristocratic 'virtue' was also, as we have seen, religious. The family monastery channelled that religious superiority, as well as helping to keep the kin-group together. So did the extensive land-giving to churches of all kinds that marks the late eighth century in Carolingian Europe, and, after a break, the tenth and eleventh centuries too. Aristocratic control of monasteries has often been seen as in opposition to monastic 'reform', which removed family control and set up (or, sometimes, reinstated) rigorous and autonomous religious communities who chose their own abbots and were beholden to no one. This opposition does exist in some reforming texts, which stress lay resistance to reforming activity, and (especially in the eleventh century) often see lay control as a pollution of monastic spirituality. This is not, however, how aristocrats themselves saw it, or indeed most monks. Bishop Adalbero I of Metz, Adalbero II's uncle, reformed the great Lotharingian house of Gorze in 933–4, with plenty of rhetoric, overstated, about the monastery's previous irreligiosity, and later accepted a famous ascetic, John of Gorze (d. 976), as abbot; but the process can also be seen as Adalbero's family gaining control of Gorze from a rival (the 'Matfridings', counts of Metz). In other cases, families themselves reformed monasteries, instituted monastic elections of abbots according to the *Rule of St Benedict*, but still maintained patronage of the reformed house. In cases such as these they could themselves benefit substantially from the new monastic spirituality, for monastic prayers for the family would be more efficacious; and, not least, as already in the eighth century, the generosity of others to the monastic house would frequently increase if its spiritual reputation was higher, thus boosting the wealth of a church which still maintained its original family links. At a royal level, this sort of religious/political concern is also seen in the monastic reforms of late tenth-century England, very much organized for the spiritual and political benefit of the king, queen and leading ealdormen; this was equally true, for that matter, of the ninth-century Carolingians, who were keen to impose the *Rule* universally in their domains, but nonetheless disposed of monastic land and appointed abbots with considerable detachment.

The classic instance of a reformed monastery at the end of our period is Cluny, in the county of Mâcon: it was founded in 909–10 by William the Pious, but put, not under his own family patronage, but under that of the pope, to keep it separate from any direct lay domination. Nor did that occur; Mâcon was on the edge of Guilhelmid power, and the family anyway died out in 927; successive abbots were of aristocratic background, for sure, but their families had no authority over them. (Nor did the pope, of course, a marginal figure in most aspects of tenth-century politics, as we have seen.) Cluny was very unusual in its formal separation from lay authority, and its abbots had to be – and were – unusually able so as to maintain it. But its growing reputation as a centre for organized spiritual activity made it the most successful recipient of lay landed generosity anywhere in contemporary Europe, with a thousand charters of gift from the tenth century alone. These did not come with domination, but with relationships, with both aristocrats and smaller neighbours (village élites and peasant cultivators alike – all gave Cluny land), who wanted to see their gifts used to their own spiritual advantage as expertly and authoritatively as possible. Cluny turned into a lordship on a par with the others in the Mâconnais, and far richer than most. It did so not by threatening aristocratic spiritual attitudes, but by drawing on them and validating them. It was its second abbot, Odo (927–42), who wrote the *Life* of Gerald, after all, the founding text for a lay aristocratic version of spirituality. Odo became an expert in monastic reform, called in across West Francia, and even by Alberic, prince of Rome. Cluny was the very opposite of a critique of tenth-century society: it was in many respects the most perfect product of the aristocratic values, including religious ones, discussed in this chapter.

22

The Caging of the Peasantry, 800–1000

859. The Danes ravaged the places beyond the Scheldt. Some of the common people [*vulgus*] living between the Seine and the Loire formed a sworn association [*coniuratio*] amongst themselves, and fought bravely against the Danes on the Seine. But because their association had been made without due consideration [*incaute*], they were easily slain by our more powerful people.

So the *Annals of Saint-Bertin* recount the fate of the only popular resistance to the Vikings in the Carolingian period. This brief narrative leaves much unexplained, of course. What does *incaute* really mean? Does it mean that a sworn association was in itself seen as a seditious act? Charlemagne had banned *coniurationes*, after all, because their oaths were potentially in rivalry with oaths to the king (above, Chapter 16). But whether this was the principal problem or not, the fighting peasants of 859 were acting autonomously of the Carolingian political hierarchy, and were thus at best suspect, at worst actively dangerous. Not just the local aristocracy who destroyed them, but the whole political class, would have perceived this danger; and it would have seemed that much more serious because of the way Frankish society had developed in the last half century. Free peasants had traditionally been able to serve in royal armies; as late as Charlemagne's reign we can find laws about such army service, and this military capacity, however rarely exercised, was one of the marks of freedom, along with the right to participate in public assemblies, especially law courts. By the 850s, however, despite the military danger which the Vikings represented, armies were more and more aristocratic, and military service was slowly becoming seen as an aristocratic privilege, as we saw in the last chapter. The peasants of the Seine–Loire region may have thought that they were following in the footsteps of their grandfathers, assembling for military defence at a time when they were seriously needed. Charles the Bald's aristocrats by now saw such military readiness as inappropriate for peasants, however. This only made worse the fact that the peasants had done this autonomously, without any formal call-up. So they died. But if free peasants did not do military service any more, what did their freedom consist of? They were that much less useful to kings, and kings would be that much less worried if there were other threats to their freedom. This was a general development of the ninth and tenth centuries in the West: peasants were slowly and steadily excluded from the public sphere, and, in more general terms, ever more clearly subjected to aristocrats and churches, the great private landowners.

The way this happened, and the extent to which it happened, varied from place to place in western Europe. As many as five separate socio-economic changes can be invoked here. First, in some non-Carolingian regions, the ninth and tenth centuries were the period in which landowning itself developed, and a really wealthy aristocracy emerged for the first time. Secondly, in Carolingian Europe, aristocrats and churches gained property, by force or otherwise, from their landowning peasant neighbours, thus reducing the numbers of independent peasants. Thirdly, dependent peasants, tenants, faced increasing rents and greater control exercised over their labour. Fourthly, peasants were increasingly excluded from the public world of the army and assembly, and thus from the purview and interest of kings. Fifthly, in some parts of Europe (notably France, but also much of Italy), this exclusion was, already by 1000, coming to mean the direct subjection of peasant communities to the judicial control of local lords, in the framework of the seigneurie banale. These were largely separate developments, but they nonetheless all pointed in the same direction. Overall, the relatively autonomous early medieval peasantry, discussed in Chapter 9, lost more and more of its autonomy in the last two centuries of our period. I have called this process the 'caging' of the peasantry: more and more, the huge peasant majority of the population of western Europe became divided up into localized units, controlled more and more by local lords. The word is a rough translation of Robert Fossier's term *encellulement*, literally the division of society into a cellular pattern, which he sees as the key element in the shift from the early to the central Middle Ages. The force of this latter image is most closely tied to that of the 'feudal revolution', which in a strict sense is only the fifth (and the most localized) of my five developments. But, overall, the peasantry was everywhere systematically more restricted, more caged, as a result of all five processes. We shall look at them in turn here, and then step back, and look at their broader economic contexts and consequences too.

We saw in Chapter 20 that rulers became slowly more powerful in most of non-Carolingian Europe after 800. The flip-side of this development was a general increase in aristocratic power. Aristocrats were in the eighth century or so political patrons of their free peasant neighbours, as in Scandinavia, Ireland or Brittany, or takers of tribute from otherwise autonomous dependants, as in England and, soon, Rus, rather than full-scale landowners taking rents from non-landowning tenants. In much of England, the ninth century seems to have been the cusp moment in which landownership took shape. In northern Spain, there may have been various moments for the same process between the late eighth and the tenth. In Croatia, the key moment seems to have been the ninth. In Denmark, it may have been the late tenth and eleventh; as usual, we cannot be sure, for our documents only begin in the late eleventh, but full aristocratic landownership (together with a substantial surviving peasant landowning stratum) certainly existed by then. In other parts of 'outer Europe', equivalent changes occurred later, out of our period, although they would in the end occur everywhere. These shifts towards aristocratic landowning on a large scale are in every case ill-documented, and their context (and their immediate effect on the peasantry) will remain obscure. But the result was in each case clear: the emergence of a powerful élite group, which had for the first time the right to coerce those sections of the peasant majority who were their immediate dependants. These rights were no greater than those of aristocrats in Merovingian Francia and Lombard Italy who were already landlords in the sixth century; it took until 900 for lords in England, and until 1000–1050 for lords in Denmark, to gain the powers that were considered normal in the Romano-Germanic kingdoms. But peasants were losing ground all the same, and in England, as we saw earlier, where almost no landowning peasants survived by the eleventh century, they lost ground more fully than anywhere else in Europe.

Only slightly better documented is the expansion of aristocratic and ecclesiastical landowning inside Carolingian Europe. One aspect of this is, it is true, very clear in our material, for when peasants gave land to churches, the charters recording their donations were systematically kept. In eighth- and early ninth-century northern and central Italy, and central and southern Germany, we have a large number of texts of this type; so do we in tenth-century Burgundy, Catalonia and León. Many such documents were the work of aristocrats or near-aristocrats, men and women with enough landed wealth to be able to give generously for the good of their souls without threatening their well-being and political power; but in numerous cases it is evident that peasant cultivators were the donors – either of single fields or of their entire holdings. What were peasants intending when they gave such gifts? To get closer to heaven because of their generosity, certainly (the relationship is explicit in most such texts, which generally say that they are gifts 'for the soul', or for prayers by clerical professionals, and in Italy sometimes invoke a 'hundred-fold counter-gift in heaven'). But the socio-political context for this was more varied. Sometimes such gifts were to what might be called a 'neutral' institution, to a newly founded local church, which simply represented a convenient nearby location for a priest capable of prayers of intercession, or to a monastery with a reputation for spirituality, whose prayers might be more efficacious for that reason (Cluny was one such in the early tenth century). Peasants might give small portions of their lands, or a childless couple might give all or most of their property, for purely spiritual reasons under these circumstances. But the institution might be locally powerful as well, either because it was associated with a major aristocratic family or a bishop, or simply because it was gaining wealth and thus power from the gifts of the faithful, as was increasingly the case for Cluny across the tenth century; under these circumstances, to be associated with it through one's generosity might bring political benefits too, patronage in this world as well as in the next. Finally, the richest and most powerful institutions could become major players, seigneurial lords over their neighbours, and then any gifts to them by the weak would be decidedly double-edged, and might well contain a substantial element of coercion.

Not all rising churches and monasteries got this far. There is a visible tendency in many European villages for pious gifts to dry up when religious institutions became locally powerful and therefore less 'neutral'; we can see this in many places in Germany and Italy in the ninth century, after the first great wave of gift-giving, for example. But communities could also miscalculate, and carry on giving long enough to tilt the local balance of power too firmly towards a major local monastery. The local dominance of Fulda and Lorsch in central Germany and Farfa in central Italy by 850, Redon in eastern Brittany by 900, and by 1000 Cluny as well, had just such roots. Such monasteries henceforth operated as major political players, often at the expense of the heirs of the pious donors who were the origin of their power.

Both churches and lay aristocrats also increased their lands by more direct methods, that is to say by force. This was unlikely to be recorded in legal documents, of course, but we do occasionally have signs of it in court records. In Milan in 900 eleven peasants from nearby Cusago sought to prove their full freedom in court against the count of Milan, their landlord for some of their land; he was claiming that they were *aldii*, half-free, but they counter-argued that they owned their own property as well. Property-ownership was restricted to the free, so, if this was accepted, it would prove their case; conversely, however, they would lose their land as well as their freedom to the count if they failed. In this case, very unusually, the peasants won; but other parallel cases where they lost show at least that peasants were often sure of the justice of their cause. They may also have done so because they hoped for royal support. Both Charlemagne and Louis the Pious legislated against the expropriation of the poor, in fact; in 811 the former noted that the poor were telling him that bishops, abbots and counts were despoiling them of their property, and, if the powerful could not get that property, they were seeking excuses to undermine its owners, including by sending them endlessly on military expeditions (a sign of freedom, but often an expensive one) until they gave in and sold up. But, of course, however sympathetic a king/emperor might be, his local judicial representatives were the same bishops and counts, who were rarely going to let peasants raise successful pleas against themselves.

Overall, as noted in the previous chapter, the Carolingian period was one in which great lords became steadily wealthier, and peasant landowners are less and less visible in our sources. This process continued into the tenth century as well, by which time there is also no longer any sign that kings were worried about such matters. In 800, in most parts of Europe for which there are documents, we can find active societies of owner-cultivators. By 1000 these were notably fewer, particularly north of Burgundy and of the Alps. In southern France and Italy, too, such networks, even though they survived, were by now weaker. Legally or illegally, independent peasantries were on the retreat.

Peasants did sometimes resist by force. This was a losing strategy, for aristocratic armies were so much more powerful; that they tried it at all is a sign of their desperation. Such resistance tended to be commonest in mountain areas, further from centres of political power, and in areas where collective exploitation of woodland and pasture led to stronger peasant communities: we have examples from the Alps, the Appennines and the Pyrenees. The best instance is that of the peasants of the Valle Trita, in the highest part of the central Appennines, who resisted attempts by the monastery of S. Vincenzo al Volturno to claim their lands and to declare them unfree, during a whole century, 779–873, and across nine separate court hearings; it may have been another century before they finally lost. The only large-scale peasants' revolt in this period was that of the Stellinga in Saxony in 841–2; this seems to have extended across all or most of Saxony. But that was an extreme situation, for Carolingian conquest had displaced an entire peasant society and economy, more similar to contemporary Denmark than to contemporary Francia, and Frankish-style aristocratic power had imposed itself in little more than a generation. The Saxon peasantry thus faced a new totalizing subjection, and this explains why such a large group took to arms. They lost, too, however. Royal rhetoric aside, the Carolingian century was a bad time for peasant autonomy, the time in which, in Francia and Italy, the momentum towards generalized aristocratic dominance first became inescapable.

The situation for dependent peasants, that is to say tenants, became harsher in the same period. The century after 750 saw the steady extension, particularly in northern Francia and southern Germany, but also in northern Italy, of new estate structures, which we call 'bipartite estates' or 'manors'. These were estates divided into two parts, a 'demesne' (*dominicum* and variants in Latin), all of whose produce went directly to the lord, and the tenant holdings of the peasantry. Some of the produce from the tenant holdings was paid in rent; the rest was kept by the tenant workforce, male and female (for rent was sometimes in cloth, which was almost always woven by women), for their own subsistence. This was not new; the novelty was the demesne, for this was above all farmed by the forced labour of the tenant population, who owed labour service, up to three days a week in some cases, as part of their rent. Such demesnes varied greatly in size; some of the major north Frankish monasteries had substantial ones, and high labour service; east of the Rhine they were smaller, and in much of Italy they were both small and fragmented, with labour obligations correspondingly low, maybe only two to three weeks a year. But in nearly all cases they marked an intensification of labour, for such patterns are hardly documented in the Frankish lands before the 740s. This change, too, was sufficiently visible to come to the attention of kings; in 800, when Charlemagne was in the territory of Le Mans, the peasants of both royal and ecclesiastical lands sought a ruling from him on how much labour service they should owe, as it was so variable in the area, extending in some cases to a whole week. He enacted that a tenant family on a quarter-*factus* (a local word for holding) with its own animals should do no more than a day's service a week (though two if it had no animals), and less if it had less land. This sounds generous, although we do not know how much a 'quarter-*factus*' actually was (peasant families might have routinely held two or more, for example), but the need for such equalization points at the novelty of the obligation.

Demesne farming was special, because it was entirely controlled by the lord. Such a care for estate management and for the intensification of labour points to the sale of produce. It used to be argued that manorial economies were 'closed', autarkic units which produced just enough for the needs of landlords and also all their own needs, thus making buying and selling unnecessary. The growing evidence for exchange after 750–800 in particular, as we shall see later in the chapter, makes such an argument problematic; but anyway Carolingian estate documentation makes frequent reference to the transport of produce, sometimes over substantial distances, not only to monastic centres, but also to markets or ports. In general, the manorial system was tied up with the expansion of exchange. But it also represented a greater weight of exploitation for the population of manorial estates, and this showed that tenants, too, not just peasant landowners, were feeling the effects of the power of landed élites.

We know an unusually large amount about manorial estates, particularly of monasteries, in the Carolingian period, far more than about the inner workings of European estates in any other period before the twelfth century. This is because the ninth century is the great period for estate surveys, known as polyptychs, which were often very detailed indeed. One of the first polyptychs we have, for the suburban Paris monastery of Saint-Germain-des-Prés, from the 820s or slightly earlier, lists every member of each tenant family (with a slight under-recording of daughters), the legal status of both husband and wife, the size of their *mansus* (tenant holding), with grain-fields, vineyards and meadows counted separately, and all the rents and services they owed, which could be very complex, including weaving, cart-service, wood-cutting, basket-making, building and iron-working. More than two dozen similar texts survive across the next century (the last major ones were for Prüm near Trier in 893 and for S. Giulia in Brescia in the years around 900). The sort of information we have for Saint-Germain was typical of such surveys; we may not always have the names of peasant children, but we sometimes have ages (Marseille cathedral, 813–14), or the rations given to demesne workers (S. Giulia), or information hinting at grain yields (Annappes, c. 800; S. Tommaso in Reggio, after 900), or the types of grain crop grown (S. Giulia; Saint-Remi in Reims, c. 850). Statistical work can be done on texts like this, to show a rise in population (Marseille; Saint-Germain), or the tendency for legally unfree men to marry free women, thus ensuring the freedom of their children (Saint-Germain among others), or the relative regularity of rents and labour service – which could be great, indicating strong central direction, or much more variegated, indicating ad-hoc negotiation or the persistence of local customs. The attraction of this sort of detail for a long time stood in the way of a realization by historians that such estates were not typical, in either their size or their degree of organization (see also above, Chapter 9). Not only were they restricted geographically, but they were also, probably, a sign above all of ecclesiastical landowning, and perhaps some royal landowning too; lay lords can be seen to have developed demesnes, but it is unlikely that they were as tightly organized as this, not least because lay estates were divided between heirs, and changed hands rather more often. All the same, the world of the polyptychs was *one* ninth-century reality, at least, and probably the most productive one. Monasteries did not only write estate surveys, either; we have a guide to estate management from Abbot Adalard of Corbie, Charlemagne's cousin, from 822, and even a map of an ideal monastery, with all the workshops marked, from St. Gallen, drawn around 825–30.

The appearance of such a range of estate documents from the early years of the ninth century onwards might already make them seem to be part of the Carolingian political programme, and indeed they were:

the first one of all, the *Brevium Exempla* of *c.* 800, includes surveys of five royal demesnes including Annappes, listing all the utensils, grain and animals found there, and also of a village of the monastery of Wissembourg, with comments such as 'and you should list others of such things in the same way, and then list the livestock'. These were models, coming from royal government; and the early ninth-century manuscript of the *Brevium Exempla* has as its next text the *Capitulare de Villis*, a capitulary also dating to about 800, which is in effect another estate manual, less detailed but more complete than Adalard's, this time constructed by a royal official. The highly moralized royal political practice of the early ninth century (cf. above, Chapter 17) extended even to estate management, that is to say. The *Capitulare de Villis* urges proper record-keeping (in more detail than the average polyptych managed, in fact), to ensure that royal estates should 'serve our needs entirely, and not those of other men', and also urges estate managers (*iudices*) to do justice, and to ensure that 'our workforce [*familia*] works well at its affairs, and does not go wasting time at markets'. The concern for a moral way of life that permeates all Carolingian legislation thus melds with a concern for adequate profit. This concern spread from the king to the great Carolingian monasteries, and lasted as long as the Carolingians themselves did. Charlemagne's court did not, of course, invent demesne farming, only its recording; manors were developing for quite different reasons. But the Carolingian programme provided a further impulse towards systematization and control.

In the tenth century polyptychs ceased to be written, but manors by no means went away. In some areas, they extended geographically; demesne farming had spread to England by 900, as the Hurstborne Priors survey indicates (above, Chapter 19), showing that both landlordship and the tight control of estates had taken root there. In Italy, the manorial system did lose ground after 900; references to labour services drop sharply across the tenth century, and there was a general trend to rents in money, rather earlier than in northern Europe, with demesnes increasingly divided into tenures. This however still showed an estate management directed towards exchange; it is just that the buying and selling of agricultural produce would be done by the tenants, not by the lords; this was an easier process in Italy than further north, for cities were larger, and thus demand for grain and wine was higher. In France, Germany and England, demesne agriculture and labour service remained a normal part of lord–tenant relationships into the twelfth century (in England, the fourteenth). By then, it had often become routinized, as an instrument of control rather than of the intensification of agrarian profit; but it could always be turned into the latter if there was opportunity, as in thirteenth-century England.

Tenants on great estates were, as before 800, socially very diverse. On every estate there were both free and unfree dependants, and sometimes the half-free as well, with an intermediate set of rights. In regions of Europe with a written vernacular tradition, such as England and Germany, we find even more social strata, each with a separate vernacular name, owing slightly different arrays of services. All or most strata owed labour service, but heavy labour service on demesnes broadly went with unfreedom; legal status was thus tied up with economic subjection. All the same, the tendency was for legal status to become less important. On the village-sized estates of Saint-Germain, where everyone was a tenant, intermarriage between free and unfree was common, as we have just seen, and it became possible to imagine that unfreedom would die out. On one level, unfreedom was no longer necessary to lords, as most peasants were already tenants; the next developments we will discuss, the exclusion of the free from the public world and the development of the seigneurie banale, also lessened the privileges of freedom, making it easier for lords to allow the unfree to gain it. Very slowly, the traditional concept of unfreedom lost its purchase in western Europe. This happened first in Italy, where unfree tenants were already rare in the eleventh century (though domestic servants remained unfree for much longer); it happened next in France, though somewhat later in Germany and England, and later still in Scandinavia. Tenurial subjection remained, and the central medieval concept of 'serfdom', of being tied to the land and subject to the justice of the lord, was not very different in practice from the legal unfreedom of the early Middle Ages – indeed, it used the same word as the classical Roman word for 'slave', *servus*. By now, however, the degree of tenurial, economic, subjection to a lord was much more important than the traditional free–unfree division.

The other two trends which reduced the autonomy of the peasantry of Europe in the period 800–1000 have already been discussed (in Chapters 18 and 21) and need less detail here. Peasants were increasingly excluded from the army in Carolingian Europe, as we have seen.

This was not complete; it did not happen in England, nor in Saxony, where all hands were needed for the Slav wars in the tenth century. Elsewhere, however, aristocratic status itself was by 1000, and indeed earlier, associated with being a *miles*, and aristocratic clienteles became the only fighting forces. Public assemblies, too, lost their importance in parts of tenth-century Europe, particularly in West Francia; they continued into the late eleventh century in Italy, but abruptly ended there too. It was above all in England that earlier traditions of public assemblies with judicial powers, extending to all free men, continued without a break. This was a major reason why the free–unfree divide remained strong in England, too; indeed, a rather larger proportion of the population was legally unfree there by 1200 or so than in any of the post-Carolingian lands. Elsewhere, though, the world of the public was increasingly barred to the peasantry, who were as a result more and more subject to lords.

This then developed into the seigneurie banale in parts of West Francia/France and Italy, in areas where the state lost almost all force and private lordships took over almost everything. Seigneurial lords claimed legal rights even over their free landowning neighbours, if they lived in the lord's seigneurial territory, especially if they were peasants, as in the case of the lordship of Uxelles in the Mâconnais discussed in the last chapter. It should be evident that the seigneurie banale was only an extreme development of the general tendency for the free peasantry, of all social and economic conditions, to be excluded from the public world, a process already beginning in the Carolingian period. The sort of control that lords could have even without formal seigneurial rights is well shown by the *incastellamento* process of central Italy, the lands around Rome in particular. In this process, in the tenth and eleventh centuries lords moved their free dependants, often by force, from their previous settlements to hill-top villages, sometimes on new sites, reorganizing their tenures and their rents as they did so. This was harder in northern Italy, where the land of lords was more fragmented; *incastellamento* there just meant the foundation of castles as signs of political power and status, alongside or above pre-existing villages and hamlets, as in northern Europe. In the centre of the peninsula, however, lords often had larger blocks of land, and were more powerful as a result. Peasants inside the new castles were already that much further from the world of the public, although the seigneurie banale did not fully develop in these regions until well into the eleventh century. But with the new seigneuries of the decades around and after 1000, the trap snapped shut on the peasantry, who were from then on legally subjected to lords, with varying degrees of severity, for all their affairs. This would continue until seigneurial powers were picked at from both sides, in the twelfth century and onwards, by peasants who established agreed sets of rights with their lords, called franchises ('freedoms') in Romance-speaking countries; and by rulers, kings or counts in France, cities in Italy, who were keen to expand the remit of public justice again. But by then it was a very different political world.

These trends had separate roots, but they interacted with each other, and this interaction meant that the effects of each were greater; the exclusion of peasants from the public world was all the more serious because such peasants were also losing their lands, or, as tenants, were becoming more subjected to the demands of landlords, and vice versa. It is in this context that we can talk of a caging process, as peasant societies were steadily separated from each other, each more subject to a local lord, even without the imposition of the seigneurie banale, although still more fully if that form of lordship developed. That local lords in some cases were rising, militarized, families from the same community, former village-level medium owners or even former rich peasants (above, Chapter 21), did not make things any better; such families had a local knowledge that made domination easier, and also often had capillary hierarchical links with their neighbours or former neighbours, in the form of patron and client as well as landlord and tenant. Villages, and local communities in general, became more shot through with vertical social bonds. As we saw in Chapter 9, villages themselves became more carefully structured: they were often larger, often more nucleated. After 800 or so, they increasingly often had a church (the priest was another focus of patronage relations), and by 1000 they might sometimes already have a castle. If we look at the archaeological record for villages, we also frequently see from the ninth century the slow development of signs of distinction and power, such as estate centres, maybe walled, as at Montarrenti in Tuscany (above, Chapter 10); these were sometimes the lineal ancestors of the fortifications of the tenth and the eleventh centuries. But what castles, towers and the like meant was a much more formalized hierarchy. These hierarchies and new structurings added to the caging process for the peasantry, for they took away the flexibility that can be seen in our evidence from the earliest Middle Ages. Peasants 'knew their place' more from now on; they had less negotiating power.

These are very wide generalizations, and there were all sorts of regional nuances. By and large, regions (or villages) where a peasant landowning stratum survived could maintain a certain independence of action, at the local level at least, for many centuries to come; we can see examples in twelfth- or thirteenth-century northern Italy, for example, even in areas where private seigneuries were strong. But, overall, village society became more hierarchical, with a different pacing in each locality.

Let us look at some concrete examples of this. We saw in Chapter 9 that the villages around Redon in eastern Brittany were very autonomous in the early ninth century, with an active public sphere, and a peasantry capable of independent actions of all kinds, from land transactions to local policing. Chance collections of documents surviving from the Carolingian period give us a number of parallels to this pattern. The Rhineland villages around Mainz were sites of a large amount of aristocratic (including monastic and royal) landowning, for the area was one of the main 'royal landscapes' of the Carolingian world, but there were plenty of peasant owners as well, organized into groups of public witnesses, who largely kept out of aristocratic networks. The smaller villages around Milan or Lucca in Italy in the ninth century show more patronage links, between peasants and larger owners (both lay and ecclesiastical), but also a considerable flexibility of action for village-level dealers: they might all or mostly have patrons in the city, but there was a good deal of choice, for all powerful people had a city base. In the mountains, further from cities, peasants could develop a variety of different strategies. One example of this is the area around Rankweil in the upper Rhine valley, in the Alps above Lake Constance, whose inhabitants can be seen in a document collection of the 820s cautiously developing a land-based patronage relationship with the *scultaizus* Folcwin, a local official. Folcwin was probably brought in from outside as part of the extension of Carolingian public authority into the Alps, but he seems to be being absorbed into a local society rather than changing it from without. Another example comes from the Adriatic side of the central Italian Appennines, the land around the monastery of Casauria, founded (not far from the Valle Trita) by Emperor Louis II in 873. The documents from one village, Vico Teatino, surviving from the period 840–80, show among others a prosperous medium owner called Karol son of Liutprand (d. c. 870), who, with his family, engaged in a dense set of property transactions aimed at developing local social networks, and, above all, at setting his children up with attractive marriage-portions. Karol dealt with officials and greater landowners too, and doubtless had patronage relations with them – he was indeed climbing socially by marrying his children to them – but he moved with a great fluidity inside his own society. These were the years just before Casauria abruptly arrived, with royal patronage, on the political scene of this microregion; Casauria changed local politics profoundly, just as Redon did for the villages around it (hence, as usual, the survival of Karol's documents, in the monastic archive), but up until then the flexible social world persisted.

This 'Carolingian' world, of villages structured by public power and large landowners but not necessarily dominated by them, became weaker in the next century. The Cluny documents, which illuminate a number of villages around the monastery in considerable detail, do show us villagers in some places, into the late tenth century, operating strategies of the sort we have just seen, with only occasional gifts to the monastery; but in others, a more hierarchical structure was beginning to appear. The family of Arleus son of Ingelelm (d. after 1002) was a similar family of medium owners to that of Karol, based in a set of villages just north of the monastery; in the last half of the tenth century they gave most of their land in one of these, Flagy, to the monastery, so as to develop a patronage relationship with Cluny, while keeping that in other villages such as Merzé. But Arleus also had more formal relationships; Josseran of Uxelles was his *senior*, lord. The seigneurie banale was coming in, and it would, besides restricting the legal rights of those subject to it, bring personal relations of lordship, too. Arleus' heirs would escape this, and ended up as *milites* and petty lords in Merzé, on the aristocratic side of the dividing-line. His neighbours, however, many of whom he and his family also transacted with or witnessed for, did not.

The documents for Farfa in central Italy show analogous patterns. Farfa had founded the nearby castle (that is, fortified village) of Salisano between 953 and 961 as part of the *incastellamento* process, and the bulk of the local inhabitants seem already to have been living there in the late tenth century. Most of the land of Salisano was already the monastery's, since the ninth century. In the late tenth, documents show it accumulating the rest, mostly in gift, from the surviving landowning peasant population (they sometimes resisted, but lost in court); the donors then got the land back in lease, and their heirs became monastic tenants. Once again, however, some of the inhabitants swam to the surface; Azo son of Andrea, a local owner, leased the castle itself in 961, and his rivals (or maybe heirs), the Gualafossa family, ended up across the next century as petty castle lords, dependent on the monastery and active in its clientele, with military status, and also controlling a subsidiary castle which Farfa did not fully get its hands on until 1093. The seigneurie banale did not begin here until the 1010s, but we already see an increasingly firm local hierarchy, with a military edge, a generation or more earlier.

These last two examples are from areas close to powerful monasteries, and therefore on one level it might not seem surprising that the imagery of lordship should come through strongly. But so were the Carolingian examples, for the most part, and lordship was less strong all the same. Furthermore, as already stressed, the parts of Europe where non-aristocratic landowning still existed were by now rather fewer. If the Parisian villages subject to Saint-Germain-des-Prés were atypical in their subjection in 820, they certainly were not so a hundred and fifty years later. Flagy, Merzé and Salisano show the caging process for the land-owning peasantry beginning to operate; but in villages entirely owned by lords it was already more totalizing, and, as seigneurial rights came in, would become still more so.

These were not the only socio-economic changes of the ninth and tenth centuries in western Europe. This was a period of steady economic expansion in the widest sense: in population, in agricultural production, in artisanal activity, in exchange. It can be argued that the driving force for all of this was the process of peasant subjection we have just looked at; but it led to a much greater complexity of the economy at all levels. Let us look at each in turn.

Between the early Middle Ages and the beginning of the fourteenth century, the population of Europe grew consistently, perhaps tripling in size. Figures are hypothetical in most areas, post-Conquest England being the major exception; but both villages and towns increased in both size and number, with obvious cumulative effects, and the average size of peasant holdings dropped substantially, with quarter-*mansi* becoming normal holdings by the twelfth century in many places. The roots of that growth seem to have lain in the Carolingian period, for many of the villages recorded in, for example, the polyptych of Saint-Germain were already large, and lists of children, here and in other polyptychs, allow us to calculate that they were already – slowly – getting larger. *Mansi* in polyptychs and other documents were already increasingly often divided, at least into two, which is, here as later, a rough indicator of population growth as well. Why this growth began, and exactly when, is not yet fully clear, but slow demographic expansion, probably increasing in speed after 950 or so, underpins the last two centuries covered by this book.

One consequence of a demographic rise was, of course, that there had to be enough food for an increasing population. Early medieval populations were low; the approximately two million people calculated for *Domesday Book* England (compared with sixty million today) could be fed fairly easily, even with the farming methods then available, and so could at least part of the increased population after that, simply by using all available agricultural space, as intensively as was possible. The pressures for intensive cultivation were even then not always irresistible; only at the very end of our period did northern Europeans begin widely to adopt a three-course rotation of crops, with only one year in three left fallow rather than one in two, which had been common earlier (and which remained common in the Mediterranean); three-year cycles were already known about in 800 (they appear in some polyptychs), but they only became generally used when population pressures increased.

The same is true for land clearance. We saw in Chapter 9 that most land in the early medieval West should not be thought of as being trackless wild forest. Some of Germany was, and so was much of the Slav lands and Scandinavia, but to the west of the Rhine and south of the Alps, and still more in England, woodland, however extensive, was for the most part more divided up, and, if not managed for timber and coppice, was at least regarded as a resource, for peasant subsistence and aristocratic or royal hunting. Woods were often part of peasant holdings, indeed, and their use (for grazing, the gathering of woodland fruits, and of course firewood) formed part of standard peasant economic strategies. If population pressure built up, it would be these woods that would go first, cut down and replaced with grain-fields, which would produce more calories, although also a less varied diet. This small-scale land clearance, known as 'assarting', is more extensively documented in the ninth century than earlier; this may just be because our evidence is better, but it does fit the signs of demographic growth in the Carolingian period. All the same, the take-off of land clearance, the move to clear woodland and also marshland on a large scale, does not begin anywhere before 950 or so, and it often happened later. Population pressure was only really building up at the very end of our period, from slow Carolingian beginnings. The great clearance period, which changed the face of central-eastern Europe in particular, post-dates the end of this book.

It is worth adding that, once peasants did commit themselves to land clearance, they could clear faster than their numbers rose, at least for a time, and this could add to their resources, at least in grain. This was particularly true on agricultural margins, in mountain areas or on the edge of the great woodland zones of Germany, where there was more to clear – landlords frequently offered lower rents in return for a commitment to clearance. Here, at least, was one area where peasants could gain, not lose, from the socio-economic changes in the last century or so of our period. An anecdotal example of this is the archaeological site of Charavines, on a small lake in the Dauphiné, on the edge of the French Alps, where a small settlement was found in an area of land clearance. The handful of houses there was found in waterlogged conditions, which means that wood survived: the houses can be dated by tree rings to the period 1003–40. Charavines did not last long, but it was notably prosperous for a few decades. The houses had extensive finds, wooden tools and bowls (and musical instruments), cloth, shoes, imported ceramics, and an unusual amount of metalwork, including weapons and coins, the imported goods perhaps paid for by the sale of pigs, which dominated animal bones on the site. We cannot generalize from this (though people have done so), but we should recognize that this is a much richer set of finds than one would expect on most rural sites in previous centuries; one of the buildings may have been aristocratic, but the others were not. We may be seeing here the sort of prosperity that agrarian expansion could bring at the close of our period, temporarily at least, until population rises caught up again, or until lords increased rents and seigneurial dues.

Artisanal production and exchange was developing elsewhere, too, and had been since the Carolingian period. We saw in Chapter 9 that before 800 exchange was localized in most places. This was least true in northern Francia, where there was a measurable movement of goods along the great river valleys like the Rhine and the Seine, matching in the eighth century a set of North Sea ports. Most Italian exchange hardly extended outside single city territories, however, and, in England, very little exchange at all existed beyond the level of the village. This was even more true of Scandinavia, and the Slav and Celtic lands, except for luxury items, which travelled to their élite buyers across the North Sea and Baltic, and along the Russian rivers, as easily as they did in Francia and Italy. All these patterns became more elaborate after 800.

Francia between the Loire and the Rhine was the most economically complex part of the West, after as before 800. We find increasing urban activity in the archaeology, with Mainz joining Dorestad, Cologne and Paris as major artisanal and mercantile centres, and by the tenth century urban populations appear as political actors, with the inhabitants of Metz and Cambrai rising up against their bishops in 924 and 958 respectively, among others. In the tenth century we also find more evidence than earlier for active Jewish commercial populations in the Rhineland cities. A set of smaller new urban centres developed as well, as with the *burgus* that grew up around Saint-Denis just outside Paris, and the first activity in the network of Flemish towns such as Bruges, Ghent and Saint-Omer, which seem to have begun to expand in the late ninth century. When Dorestad failed in the same period, new Rhine-mouth centres emerged to replace it, notably Tiel, where excavations show substantial tenth-century development. Written evidence for markets across the whole of northern Francia increases as well, and in the tenth century they extended far across East Francia too, as numerous grants of market rights by the Ottonians show. Iron production is increasingly visible in the archaeology. And ceramic production, always the clearest indicator of the scale of economic systems, continued to develop, with the Badorf and Pingsdorf kilns near Cologne joined by major and widely distributed products from, for example, Andenne in the Meuse valley and Beauvais north of Paris. Badorf/Pingsdorf products are also found in the trading centres of Scandinavia such as Ribe and Hedeby (where, however, they may have been seen as luxuries). We can even plot land trade routes by now, linking the great river basins, studded with *vici* and *burgi* acting as markets; these routes can be tracked by coin distributions, the wine of Burgundy and the Paris region probably exchanged for wool from the Rhine delta, the future Flanders. The sales from the great monastic estates, which we have seen documented in the polyptychs, fed into this network. Even in Francia, most exchange was always relatively local; some 80 per cent of coins are found inside a 100-kilometre radius of their mints. But there was enough of an interregional traffic in bulk goods to give us an impression of considerable activity. This continued without a break from now on, with the cloth production of the Flemish towns taking off after 1000, and the great Champagne fairs developing in the next century; these marked a new stage in the complexity of exchange, but they had firm ninth- and tenth-century roots.

These signs of activity were matched elsewhere, but on a smaller scale. In England, large-scale production and internal exchange began in the tenth century, and was matched by some urban development, particularly in York. In southern Germany, Regensburg on the Danube was clearly an active urban and mercantile centre by the tenth century, expanding beyond its Roman walls, with merchants rich enough to buy land. A document from about 905 listing tolls owed at Raffelstetten on the Danube near Linz shows that Moravians, Bohemians and maybe even the Rus were using the river to trade with the Bavarians. Here, however, the goods listed were dominated by salt, which had been sold from the Salzburg region since the Iron Age and before; slaves and horses took second place. There is no reference to artisanal products, a major sign of bulk trade. The Danube did not yet match the Rhine, Meuse or Seine as a trade route.

This has some parallels in Italy, too. As Italy was the closest part of the Latin West to the important exchange networks of the Muslim southern and eastern Mediterranean, there were increasingly active long-distance sea-routes around the peninsula, with Venice developing rapidly as an entrepôt after the late eighth century, particularly for the slave trade to the Arabs fuelled by the Carolingian-Sclavenian wars; in 829 its duke Justinian in his will refers to his 'working *solidi*' invested in ships due to return, the first reference in medieval history to mercantile capital. Venice by the tenth century was an autonomous maritime power, making trade treaties not only with kings in Italy but even, in 992, with the emperor Basil II, Venice's nominal sovereign. In the tenth century Venice was also matched in southern Italy, the richest part of the peninsula, by the trading activity of Amalfi, Salerno, Gaeta, and (the largest of them) Naples. They, even more than Venice, looked to the Arab world. All the same, this international exchange did not fully reflect the more somnolent activity of Italy's internal economy. The inland Italian cities were very large by western standards; they all had active markets, and they were expanding in the tenth century in particular, as rising figures for house prices show for Milan. Some of them were points of reference for wider exchange, notably Pavia and Cremona. But the others were exchange-centres above all for their immediate territories. The north Italian cities as yet had little connection with Venice (less than southern Italian cities had with Amalfi and Naples); the complex and vibrant production and exchange of the Po plain and northern Tuscany in the twelfth century is hardly visible before 1000, or 950 at the earliest. The most we can say is that the Italian urban network was poised on the edge of that economic take-off, a hundred to a hundred and fifty years later than in Francia.

Venice and Amalfi were already anticipated in the eighth century by the ports of the North Sea, Dorestad, Quentovic, London, Ipswich, Southampton, York, Ribe, extending up the Baltic to Birka, with Hedeby founded around 800. It was down the trade routes with Scandinavia that the Vikings came, and Viking raids on Dorestad and other Frankish coastal towns, and also many inland centres in West Francia, did considerable damage in the late ninth century. But, as we saw in Chapter 20, Viking activity had close links to merchant activity; often enough, indeed, raiders took goods simply to sell elsewhere. In the tenth century, North Sea exchange picked up quickly (if indeed it had ever lessened, taken as a whole), and the presence of Scandinavian communities all across the north, Dublin, York and Rouen to the west, and Staraya Ladoga, Novgorod and Kiev to the east, greatly extended the scope of that exchange.

We must not overstate North Sea economic activity. This exchange was similar to that of the new northern Mediterranean ports, above all in luxuries, or near luxuries such as slaves. All the same, the existence of the North Sea (and Irish Sea, and Baltic, and Russian river) long-distance exchange network was important for the future. When, in the eleventh and twelfth centuries, the internal economies of the major north European regions became sufficiently complex to begin to specialize in their production, the North Sea network was ready for bulk exchange, sending English wool to be made into Flemish cloth, and sending French and Rhenish wine, Norwegian and German timber, north Norwegian dried fish, to anywhere that needed them. But already by 1000 this sort of bulk exchange was a feature of the Islamic Mediterranean; closer and more organic links between the Muslim regions, al-Andalus, Tunisia, Sicily, Egypt, the Levant, had already begun in the tenth century (see above, Chapter 15). The Mediterranean indeed had more potential for growth in interregional bulk exchange in 1000 than the North Sea had, and in the next century it would expand further, as Italy entered it more fully, and other regions too. In the North Sea region, by contrast, this trading world was a feature of the central Middle Ages, not earlier, and was hardly visible in 1000, except perhaps in Flanders. But the North Sea would match the Mediterranean in the end; and its roots lie in the luxury exchange network of the early Middle Ages. The sea-lanes and roads of the twelfth century were not so very different from those of the eighth, ninth and tenth.

In these pages, I am stressing the increasing exchange activity of the period 800–1000, but we must not exaggerate its significance. In particular, we must not overemphasize the importance of long-distance routes. Venetians and Swedes and Rhinelanders can all be found in Constantinople in the tenth century, but this does not mark any systemic links between Italy, Sweden/Rus and Germany on the one hand and Byzantium on the other. It marks only the luxury network, bringing wealth to a handful of lucky merchants, one major city (Venice), and few others. One might look at the long-distance trading of tenth-century Scandinavians, from Dublin to Rus, and suppose that this meant that economic activity was as great in Scandinavia as in Francia, or as in Egypt, whose merchants were only beginning to move outside the Nile valley in the same period. This would be false, however. The Egyptian economy was far more complex than any other; in Europe, the Frankish economy was vastly more complex than that of Scandinavia, whose major entrepôts had almost no link with their hinterlands at all. As in the Mediterranean, it is the internal economies of Europe that mattered most; most goods were transported, bought and sold inside, not outside, economic regions (this is still true today, never mind a thousand years ago), and economic complexity, 'development', depended above all on that. If we concentrate on the internal economic activity of the major west European regions before 1000, only northern Francia and the

Rhineland are really looking dynamic, even though a more complex internal exchange was steadily extending more widely, as Otto I's market grants in East Francia, East Anglian wheel-thrown pottery, or the long-term fight between the citizens of Cremona and their bishop over river tolls on the Po all show (the latter went on for at least two hundred years, c. 850–1050). Internal exchange would need to become properly rooted in other regions than the Loire–Rhine area, however, for it to be possible to have a *bulk* trade between these regions, not just a luxury trade. This was only on the edge of taking place in western Europe in 1000.

There was thus some exchange vitality in western Europe at the end of our period, but not exchange take-off. This also fits the steady but not yet rapid rise in population and in land clearance; the eleventh century and the twelfth show so much more activity that one risks seeing none before 1000, which would be as misleading an interpretation as an upbeat one focused on international routes. What explains the exchange activity that one *can* see in the ninth and tenth centuries, however? I argued in Chapter 9 that the motor of exchange before 800 was, broadly, aristocratic wealth and buying-power; the richer élites were, the more they were able to sustain large-scale networks of production and distribution. After 800, and even more after 950 or so, one could add to that the increased economic complexity that a rising population would bring on its own; furthermore, even peasants could benefit from the economic expansion brought by clearing land, at least sometimes, and lords, who had rents from more people and places, certainly did. But the main motor was still aristocratic. And in this context the caging of the peasantry was a vital element. All the trends towards the greater subjection of the peasantry described in the first half of this chapter had as an important result the concentration of peasant surplus in the hands of lords, through rents and seigneurial dues. The proportion of global production that ended up in the hands of lords steadily (sometimes, as in England, rapidly) increased. Aristocratic buying-power thus increased too. It was this that fed the expansion of exchange in the ninth and tenth centuries, and would do so for some centuries to come, for it was not until much later in the Middle Ages that capillary exchange anywhere became sufficiently relied on by peasants for it to become self-sustaining. The loss of autonomy of the peasantry and the increase in the complexity of exchange were thus two sides of the same coin. Historians tend to like exchange complexity, and they use value-laden words like prosperity, development, and (as I have done) dynamism to describe it. But complexity has costs, and the cost in this period was a decisive move to restrict the autonomy (and sometimes, indeed, the prosperity) of between 80 and 90 per cent of the population.

23
Conclusion: Trends in European History, 400–1000

This book has argued that not only the early Middle Ages as a whole, but every large- and small-scale society which existed during it, needs to be analysed in its own terms, and without hindsight. Such a concern makes a conclusion almost unnecessary; for I have tried consistently to stress the difference of local experience. I have compared rather than generalized, throughout the book, in order to respect those differences, and to make sense of them.

This hostility to hindsight, which too often brings a moralizing condemnation of the early Middle Ages, does not mean, however, that one should feel a need to see the people of the period as 'just like us', or, worse still, to infuse the period with any kind of nostalgia. For, of course, the early Middle Ages was very unlike twenty-first-century western Europe, in which I am writing. Current values, such as liberalism, secularism, toleration, a sense of irony, an interest in the viewpoints of others, however skin-deep in our own society, were simply absent then, or at best only vestigially present, as indeed they have been absent from most of the societies of the past. Early medieval people did have a sense of humour, needless to say, but what was funny to them (largely mockery and dreadful puns) by no means makes them seem closer to us; they used irony, but it was usually pretty savage and sarcastic. Nearly all writers of the period, even religious rigorists committed to the egalitarianism of New Testament or Qur'anic theology, took for granted the irreducible nature of social hierarchy, and the innate moral virtue of the aristocratic social strata they mostly themselves came from. Servility to social superiors and the self-righteous coercion of social inferiors were normal and even virtuous; so was the universal (as far as we can see) assumption that men were intrinsically superior to women. The only absentee from our modern litany of awful behaviour was essentialist racism, but a generalized chauvinistic belief that foreigners were inferior and stupid certainly filled the gap here. I have amused myself while writing this book by trying to identify which, if any, late antique or early medieval writers (that is, those whose personality we can recapture, at any rate in part, with least mediation) I could imagine meeting with any real pleasure. It comes down to remarkably few: Theodoret of Cyrrhus, Gregory the Great, Einhard, maybe Braulio of Zaragoza – and, with less enthusiasm, Augustine, for his remarkable intelligence and self-awareness however, not for his tolerance. But, for all its distance from us, and in large part because of it, the early Middle Ages – the many different early medieval realities – are *interesting*. It is its interest I have tried most to bring out and make apparent in this book, not an overarching structural patterning for the period, a metahistorical narrative, most of the current examples of which, for the reasons outlined at the start of Chapter 1, are inventions.

All the same, there were indeed trends in the history of early medieval Europe. The task of this final chapter is to bring them out, and make them explicit, although all of them have been alluded to in the course of the book. There seem to me to have been six major shifts (or breaks) in the course of the six centuries covered in this book, three in the West, two in the East, one in the North, which I will characterize in chronological order; and I would also wish to stress a set of underlying structures, underpinning all of the political and social systems of the period, which will be discussed at the end.

The first break, and the most momentous, remains the break-up of the western Roman empire. As we have seen, reactions to the old moralistic reading of the 'end of ancient civilization' have often in recent decades sought to stress continuities across the fifth century, particularly in cultural and religious practices, and partly in political aspiration too; these continuities were real. The old image of the sweeping away of Roman culture by vital Germanic barbarism (succeeded by Roman-German 'fusion' under the aegis of Catholic churchmen) is irretrievably outdated as a result. But this does not mean that the fifth century in the West was not a major period of change (see above all Chapter 4). The fiscal basis of the Roman state, the land tax, was steadily removed from centrality in the post-Roman kingdoms, if not in the fifth century, then in the sixth. None of the post-Roman kingdoms except possibly Ostrogothic Italy even attempted to reproduce the Roman state on a smaller scale, as post-'Abbasid states did in the Islamic world (see Chapter 14); local realities in the West favoured simpler political systems, and practices steadily diverged, with the exception of a militarization of political culture, which was generalized across Latin Europe (see Chapters 5 and 6). The economic unity of the western Mediterranean was broken, too; aristocracies became more localized and usually poorer, and material culture in most places became much simpler (see Chapter 9). The bricolage that marks much early medieval political and cultural (and, even more, architectural) practice was a natural result of the fragmentation of Roman models and resources (see for example Chapters 8 and 10), even though the fragments remained operative for a long time; hence my concern in Chapters 2 and 3 to explain how late Rome worked, as an essential foundation to what followed. That bricolage was both very creative, and necessary because of Roman fragmentation. It was an integral part of early medieval political and social activity for many centuries.

The eastern parallel to the fifth-century break, and indeed the major moment of change in the East, was the high point of Arab conquest in 636–51 (see Chapters 11 and 12). This threw the east Roman/Byzantine world into two centuries of crisis, and indeed permanently pushed Byzantium into a different political trajectory, more centralized and more militarized. The Arab caliphate was of course entirely new, even though its structural roots were arguably quite as Roman as were those of the Byzantines. The wealth of the caliphate and the weakness of the seventh-century Byzantine state (not to speak of the western kingdoms) pushed the epicentres of politics further eastwards than they had been for nearly a millennium, first to Syria and then, after 750, to Iraq. When medium-distance commerce began to revive in the Mediterranean after 800 or so, its focus was an Egypt which (unlike in the Roman empire) looked quite as much to the east as to the north and west (see Chapter 15). The continuities in state structures in the seventh-century East, and later, make the changes of the 640s less total than were those of the fifth century in the West; but they were more dramatic, indeed more terrifying (for victors and defeated alike), than any others in this book. Caliphs 'Umar I and 'Uthman have no real rivals in our period as architects of huge, unreversed, political and (eventually) cultural shifts; even Charlemagne does not match them there, and fifth-century conquerors like Geiseric and Clovis do not run them close.

The second major shift in the West was cultural: it was the development of an explicitly moralized political practice, above all in the century 780–880. There was a tradition of moralized Christian politics going back to late Rome, of course (see Chapter 3), but it did not have a direct relationship to secular political programmes. Visigothic Spain (see Chapter 6) was arguably the first polity to develop this, but it was Charlemagne and his successors (see Chapters 16 and 17) who first created, in an integrated way, a political programme aimed at bringing a whole people, over a large segment of Europe, closer to salvation. The Carolingians linked the state and a semi-autonomous church together in a tight partnership, which became the norm in the Latin West for over two centuries, until popes from Gregory VII (1073–85) onwards sought to separate them again, which they only managed in part – and even this was reversed again in northern Europe in the Reformation of the sixteenth century. Perhaps more important, the Carolingians created the presumption that kings and their acts could and should be policed by churchmen for their morality, which created problems for rulers such as Louis the Pious and Lothar II already in the ninth century, and would continue to cause problems for many of their successors in Europe (including, from the tenth century, England: see Chapter 19) for a long time to come. This package of changes was a genuine Carolingian innovation, with only ad-hoc precedents before, and marked out western political practice as different from then on. The Byzantine empire and the caliphate certainly matched the Carolingians in their religious confidence, but, as explored at the end of Chapter 17, neither of the great eastern empires matched the urgency of the Carolingian programme. Salvationist movements marked Muslim politics throughout the seventh century, and again in 747–50 and (in North Africa) in the tenth century, but they were focused on who was to be caliph, more than on precise programmes. This was a specifically western shift.

The third western break was the end of the Carolingian world: not so much the failure of the unity of the Frankish political system in the mid- to late ninth century, which no one even at the time expected to last, but rather the failure of the structures of public power themselves in some parts of that system, notably West Francia and (to an extent) Italy, in and around the year 1000 (see Chapters 18, 21, 22). That failure marks the end of this book, and made the eleventh century in much of Europe a very different period in its basic paradigms. I will come back to some of the implications of that in a moment; for this, like the fifth-century break, is a change that has been both overstated by moralizers and other catastrophists, and over-contested by continuitists. One has to recognize the reality of the change, without becoming overwhelmed by it.

The second eastern change was, similarly, the break-up of the caliphate in the early tenth century (see Chapter 14). As already noted, most of the post-'Abbasid polities did indeed preserve the state structures of the caliphate, which could more easily be reproduced on the regional level than those of the western Roman empire. The Arab world was thus less dramatically altered by disunity than one might have expected. All the same, it ceased to be politically dominant, for it was of course too divided. This allowed a newly stable Byzantine empire to come into its century of military glory in the mid-tenth century, and to dominate its neighbours (see Chapter 13); once al-Andalus disintegrated in civil war after 1009, Basil II was by far the strongest ruler in Europe, and probably outmatched the Fatimids in the southern Mediterranean too. Only new Muslim conquerors from the east, the Seljuk Turks, would undermine that power in the late eleventh century. And Muslim unity in the Mediterranean lands would have to wait until the Ottoman conquests of the sixteenth century to be re-established. The Ottomans indeed, in a sense, restored the empire of Justinian, with a Mediterranean newly centred on Constantinople/Istanbul, and made it last rather longer, too. But the thousand-year gap between the two makes that re-creation no more than an interesting historical parallel; the genealogical links between the two were of far less importance than the huge structural differences, which had begun with the seventh century and were pushed along in the tenth.

The major change in the North came above all in the tenth century: it was the steady extension of stable political and social hierarchies across the whole wide area between the Frankish and Byzantine empires in the South and the hunter-gatherers of the far northern forests. First to make use of their opportunities here were Anglo-Saxon kings in the eighth century (see Chapters 7 and 19); in the tenth they were followed by many more, Danes, Poles, Bohemians, Hungarians and Rus, although more falteringly as yet in the rest of Scandinavia, or in Wales and Ireland (see Chapter 20). I attributed this to the stability and expansionism of the Franks and Byzantines (and, by extension, the English, and, later, the Danes), which made them both models to emulate, and threats if the northern polities could not reorganize to oppose them. The crystallization of kingship and hierarchy in the North was in most places permanent; this fact in itself demonstrates the solidity of the political systems created by Charles Martel, Pippin III and Charlemagne to the west, the Iconoclast and Macedonian emperors to the east, in the second half of our period. In the West, this solidity outlasted even the Carolingian eclipse, for the Ottonians and their successors in East Francia had as much hegemony in the Slav and Scandinavian lands as Charlemagne, if not more. Francia and Byzantium together bestrode early medieval Europe after about 750 as much as the Roman empire itself had, three hundred years earlier. They were not as powerful, and they faced a far more powerful rival to the south-east, the 'Abbasid caliphate (for a century the strongest power in the world), but they had more impact on their northern neighbours than the Romans ever did.

The political patterns of Europe and the Mediterranean across the period 400 to 1000 thus resolve themselves into three blocks, roughly separable chronologically. In the first, the Roman empire dominated western and southern Europe and the Mediterranean, without rivals to the north at all. This ended in the fifth century in the West, of course, although Justinian partly reversed that in the western Mediterranean; it continued until the early seventh in the East. The second period was one of polycentric power; by 700 the major western polities were three – Merovingian Francia, Visigothic Spain and Lombard Italy – fairly evenly matched and each more powerful than any other neighbour, set against the expanding Umayyad caliphate and a Byzantine empire hanging on by its teeth. The third period was one of three major powers, the Franks, the Byzantines and the 'Abbasids, which by 950 was reduced to the first two of these, the Franks weakening, the Byzantines strengthening; these two were hegemonic in Europe by the late eighth century, and helped the polities of the North to develop as well, by 1000 or shortly after. I have earlier compared the striking self-confidence of all three of the powers in this third block of time; they all knew they were stronger than their immediate predecessors, and than everywhere else west of China, and they each regarded this as a proof of their moral superiority and a justification for further expansion. The notably self-aware protagonism of not just the Carolingians, but, in different ways, their Byzantine and Arab contemporaries as well, is a direct consequence of this; and all three left traces long into the future. But it would be an error to allow this to eclipse the smaller-scale innovations which were made in the second block of time, too, such as the establishment by the Merovingians of the Paris–Rhine region as a political epicentre (an innovation which has lasted ever since), or the episcopal politics of seventh-century Spain, or Byzantine Iconoclasm, or, above all, the Umayyad political settlement. No one can study any one of these, never mind all of them, and conclude that the early Middle Ages lay outside the narratives of 'real' history; and, by now, no one does.

Underpinning the political systems and political changes just discussed was a network of structures common to all the societies of this book. They were not specific to the early Middle Ages – indeed, they arguably characterized most of the pre-capitalist world – but they need to be recognized if the period is to be understood. I shall here separate them into three: the accumulation of wealth, the institutionalization of politics, and the culture of the public, and each will be characterized briefly.

Wealth and power in our period were overwhelmingly based on the land. The more one could take from the land, that is, from its peasant cultivators, either in rents or in taxes, the richer one was, the more resources one could manipulate, the more armed men one could support, the more power one had. Taxation was the surest means of exploiting the land and the peasantry, for in theory everyone had to pay it, not just the tenants of one's own properties – hence the relative prominence of Byzantium and the caliphate, which were tax-raising states, unlike those of the post-Roman West. But, even in the West, Frankish kings in particular could get rich just by taking rents from extensive royal lands, even in times, like the late seventh century, when they were not taking wealth from their neighbours too. The same logic worked for the aristocracies of each political system. A rich aristocracy generally aided rulers, for in early medieval political conditions most aristocracies were closely involved with royal/imperial power. The stronger kings were, the more they could give to, and thus attract, their élite supporters; the accumulation of wealth thus doubly reinforced political cohesion. The only major exception to this was the caliphate, where local aristocracies had relatively little to do with political power. For a long time, caliphs were so rich that this did not matter, but it was in the end a contributing factor to the break-up of 'Abbasid unity.

The link between wealth and power meant that a strong state essentially depended on peasant exploitation. We cannot easily say which peasants would have preferred: the security most powerful rulers could give them (a security which was only relative: the reigns of Justinian, Charlemagne and Basil II have all left clear evidence of local violence and oppression); or the autonomy, and lower rents and tributes, which most peasants had in the small and weak polities of Britain or the Slav and Scandinavian worlds before the tenth century, an autonomy which was risky if stronger invaders came through on raiding and slaving expeditions. We simply do not have the information that would allow us to tell, and nor indeed did most early medieval peasants themselves; which seems preferable will thus largely depend on one's own presuppositions (I think they would have preferred autonomy). But the wealth and power of the rich did go with the exploitation of the poor, and with restrictions on the fluidity of peasant life. As just implied, peasants were for a long time less restricted in the North. They were also, in parts of the post-Roman western provinces, and maybe also in parts of the Byzantine empire, more autonomous in the sixth to eighth centuries (in Byzantium, the seventh to ninth) than before or after; states and aristocracies were generally weaker in the earliest Middle Ages than under the Carolingians or the Macedonian emperors. With the arrival of stronger powers, local controls on the peasantry increased again, and in the West these controls continued to increase even when Carolingian power broke up, spreading northwards across the European continent too.

With wealth also came exchange. Rich aristocracies (and churches, and kings) had more disposable wealth to buy artisanal goods, which could thus be produced in larger quantities, and sold more widely – even to peasants, in some cases. Poorer aristocracies and more autonomous peasantries generated less specialized productions. There was more complex production and exchange in the Roman empire than in the western successor states, or than in eighth-century Byzantium; later, at a lower level, there was more complex production and exchange (by far) in the Merovingian heartland of northern Francia than in its English or north German/Scandinavian neighbours; with the Carolingians exchange expanded in Francia again, although not matching Roman levels or those of the active economies of the Muslim world. This tight linkage between aristocratic wealth and peasant exploitation on the one hand and economic complexity on the other would last for a long time into the Middle Ages; it only began to weaken when large-scale production became so general and the sale of its products so capillary that it could begin to rely on peasant, not aristocratic, demand. With the possible exception of Egypt (where, however, the work has not yet been done which could tell us either way), this would not begin to be the case in Europe and the Mediterranean until after 1200 at the earliest, and often much later. In our period, the concentration of wealth, exploitation, exchange and political power went hand in hand, and (with due caution) one can be used as a guide to the others – which, given the scattered nature of our evidence, is often useful.

The second element to be stressed here is the degree to which power was based on permanent political patterns. It was all very well for a king to have landed resources, but if his power was simply based on the personal loyalty of his armed men – a loyalty which never came free – then, unless he was permanently expanding the area he controlled, he would risk running out of land, having given too much of it away, and his power would go as well. This was seen by Marc Bloch as a permanent tendency of feudal society in the West after 900, and we have seen the problems of the 'politics of land' on a number of occasions in this book, most recently in the context of the collapse of royal authority in West Francia in the tenth century (Chapters 18 and 21), which is indeed the classic example of the pattern. How did rulers cope? For, outside the highly personalized and small-scale political systems of (for example) post-Roman Britain and Ireland, early medieval rulers did indeed often manage to maintain large and effective states for long periods of time, even though they were constantly granting their resources away.

This was relatively easy for tax-raising states, the Roman and Byzantine empires and most of the Islamic polities. There, the state had a major resource-base which could pay for a salaried army, largely independent of aristocratic support, and also reward the loyal on a very large scale; only in extreme crisis circumstances (as with the fifth-century West, or the break-up of al-Andalus in the 1010s) could aristocrats contemplate going it alone, and normally they associated themselves as closely with rulers as the latter would let them. Tax-raising states also needed a complex bureaucratic hierarchy just to collect the taxes, which, together with the military hierarchy, created a career-structure for the ambitious based on a set of stable – even if often inchoate – institutions. This institutionalization of political practice was a direct inheritance from the Roman (and also Sassanian) empire, to Byzantium and the caliphate. It was in each sufficiently complex to sustain two separate élites, one civilian, the other military. Under Rome, the civilian élite had the highest status, and attracted the landed aristocracy most firmly into it; under all their successors the military hierarchy was dominant. But either way the state was, in its basic structures, pretty solid, as the survival of the Byzantine empire after the Arab conquests shows.

In the post-Roman West, most of the bureaucratic hierarchy dissolved together with the tax system, and the army became a set of aristocratic military followings; the institutions of the Roman state were much reduced. They did not go away, however; there were counts and dukes and palace officials still in Francia, Italy, Visigothic Spain, and these positions were highly remunerative (they had lands attached) and competed for. The Carolingians extended this with their temporary concessions of *honores*, which could involve office, royal land, or control over monasteries. Almost every political player had to have an office of some kind, or else be very close to the king on a personal level, as Einhard was. Again, going it alone was for long inconceivable, except on political margins, such as the mountains of northern Spain in the sixth century or the eastern Alps around Chur in the sixth to eighth. The political community was also regularly united in public assemblies, in church councils, in the army-muster, and in the king's court, as we shall see in a moment; those who failed to attend risked losing their lands, at least those conferred by kings. These meetings were sufficiently regular for them to be in large and ramshackle polities like Francia and Spain, as important an institutional underpinning as office-holding was. As we saw in Chapters 5 and 16, political players in Francia, even those who lived a long way from court, needed to know where the king was; patronage, faction-fighting, sometimes even a sense of public responsibility, all depended on royal direction. This centrality for kings – or for their courts when kings were minors, or marginalized, as in Francia in the late seventh century – was reinforced by the knowledge that the disloyal would face a retribution which was fairly certain to come in the end, even if it did not come immediately. Fear reinforced self-interest in the political calculations of the aristocracy, and both helped the cohesion of the major post-Roman states. By the tenth century at the latest, and in some respects already in the eighth, this political logic also extended to England.

Linked to this is the final element in early medieval political systems which I want to stress here, the culture of the public, the strongest inheritance of Rome. The Roman empire had a strong sense of the difference between the public, the arena of the state and the community, and the private sphere; the boundary was not drawn in exactly the same place as it is today, and there was no neat opposition between 'public' and 'private', but the uses of the word *publicus* were analogous to those we are used to. This difference was easy to maintain in a tax-raising state, for the taxes emanated from and supported the public sphere. The Byzantines continued the concept without change, and the Muslim polities, though using different terminology, invested such 'public' functions as law and collective worship with the same sort of importance. But the post-Roman western polities maintained the idea of the public arena too; it was a very important image in Visigothic, Lombard, Merovingian and Carolingian practice. Royal property, law courts, royal officials, and assemblies both great and small were regularly described as *publicus* in early medieval Latin texts.

The clear sense that we get from our western sources that the world of royal power was also the public world of the collectivity (of free males) as a whole is the best justification I can offer for consistently using, in this book as elsewhere, the word 'state' to describe these western political systems. Although one essential resource for this public sphere, taxation, was already vestigial by the seventh century, the assembly, an import into political practice from the Germanic North, was a further reinforcement. In Scandinavia, and for a long time in England, the assembly was the only collective element in a political power-structure that otherwise relied entirely on the personal bonds between kings (or lords) and their closest retainers. In Francia and the other Romano-Germanic kingdoms, by contrast, it came to form a crucial part of the imagery of a public sphere which was otherwise Roman in its origin, and indeed it extended it further, in that the assembly, at least in theory, linked the king directly to all the free male population. That real politics was also based on a manipulation of constantly shifting factions and personal relationships does not take away from this conception of the public sphere; indeed, in the high Carolingian period the whole moral project of the king and his kingdom, the *correctio* of the faithful, could be described as a (or the) *res publica*. It is not, on this level, surprising that Roman law could be explicitly drawn on in the legislation of Charles the Bald; its presuppositions about the nature of the political system continued to be entirely apposite. This of course further strengthened the relevance of royal politics for the ambitious; *privatus* did not denote any sort of 'private' political activity, but, when used in this context, came simply to mean 'powerless'. Public power was all there was, even if the resources of the Roman public world were no longer available.

It is the public world in this sense that weakened in the tenth century and, in particular, the eleventh in the West, above all in the west Frankish lands. The parameters of politics changed, as we saw in the last chapters of the book. In a seigneurie banale, the old public rights now taken over by local lords were seen as part of their property, and could be divided between heirs or alienated away. Lordship could be claimed by people who had never met a king; the title of count could be assumed in some areas by anyone who was powerful enough, and passed on to his heirs. Kings in France or cities in Italy in the twelfth century used the terminology of *publicus*, but they had to construct it from the ground upwards, in a bricolage of links of personal dependence and collective reaffirmation which by now had very little to do with the Roman past. This more 'private' world was not worse than that of the Carolingians and their predecessors; aristocrats behaved badly in both, to their peers and to their (and other people's) peasantries. But it was different: the dialectic between the public sphere and (what we call) private interest had gone. The local powers that castle lords managed to enforce over the villages around were no longer illegal or quasi-legal, as opposed to the public law of kings, but instead became a new legality: in France, in particular, for a century in some regions, this is all there was.

The years around 1000 are a better end-point for some regions of Europe than for others. They do not work for Byzantium at all; at the other end of Europe, they work very well for al-Andalus (and also for the 'Abbasid caliphate, though 950 would there have been better). The late tenth century also denotes a break in much of Slav and Scandinavian history, as it marks the beginnings of durable state-formation there. In East Francia/Germany and in England, in both of which Carolingian political parameters easily survived past 1000 (in England, indeed, they never went away), the millennium is not such a good divide; it comes a little early for Italy (1080 would have been better as a date for the end of the public sphere there: the judicial assembly, in particular, survived until then without much difficulty), though it works well for West Francia/France. Which is to say: no date is perfect. I chose 1000 simply because I wanted to explore the divergencies of the Carolingian successor states and of post-Alfredian England, and the years of Byzantine success, in the tenth century, and did not want to add in the Seljuk Turks, or the problems of 'Gregorian reform' and the start of the grand narrative of moral progress which I lamented in Chapter 1, in the eleventh. But ending with a fundamental shift in the concepts of political power, even if only in a few parts of Europe, does not seem unreasonable. The inheritance of Rome, in those regions at least, lasted right up to around 1000; but after that its shadow faded away.

Notes and Bibliographic Guides

Abbreviations

Bede, *HE*   Bede, *Ecclesiastical History of the English People*, ed. and trans. B. Colgrave and R. A. B. Mynors (2nd edn., Oxford, 1991)

CAH   *The Cambridge Ancient History*

Cap.   MGH, *Capitularia*, ed. A. Boretius and V. Krause, 2 vols. (Hanover, 1883–97); NS (Hanover, 1996–), one vol. to date

CDL   *Codice diplomatico longobardo*, ed. L. Schiaparelli *et al.*, 5 vols. (Rome, 1929–2003)

ChLA   *Chartae Latinae Antiquiores*, ed. A. Bruckner and R. Marichal (Olten-Zürich, 1954–98)

CJ   *Codex Iustinianus*, ed. P. Krueger (Berlin, 1929)

CTh   *The Theodosian Code*, trans. C. Pharr (Princeton, 1952)

EHB   *The Economic History of Byzantium*, ed. A. E. Laiou (Washington, 2002)

EHD   *English Historical Documents*, ed. D. Whitelock, 2nd edn. (London, 1979)

EME   *Early Medieval Europe*

MGH   *Monumenta Germaniae Historica*

NCMH   *The New Cambridge Medieval History*

ODB   *The Oxford Dictionary of Byzantium*, ed. A. Kazhdan, 3 vols. (Oxford, 1991)

PLRE   *The Prosopography of the Later Roman Empire*, ed. J. R. Martindale *et al.*, 3 vols. (Cambridge, 1971–92)

SRM   *Scriptores rerum Merovingicarum* (*MGH*)

Chapter 1

Authors of basic current approaches in English to the whole period are cited in the body of the text of this chapter. For initial introductions to documentary source material, and also basic syntheses, century by century, five large Cambridge collective histories are an essential point of reference, *CAH*, vols. 13 and 14, and *NCMH*, vols. 1–3. All were published after 1995. There is no equivalent for archaeology. These volumes also leave out the Arab world, although a revised *Cambridge History of Islam*, vol. 1, is nearing publication. The major journal in English for the period is *EME*, which began in 1992. The largest set of source material in translation is the invaluable and steadily expanding web collection, http://www.fordham.edu/halsall/sbook.html; the translations there are generally old, but it is an excellent starting point.

p. 4. National identities: an excellent comparative analysis of Britain and Ireland is by T. M. Charles-Edwards, in R. Evans (ed.), *Lordship and Learning* (Woodbridge, 2004), pp. 11–37.

p. 7. The Transformation of the Roman World series was published in 12 volumes by Brill of Leiden. They are, as a group, notably more innovative in their methodology than the Cambridge histories. They focus on the West up to 800.

p. 9. Riposte to continuity: B. Ward-Perkins, *The Fall of Rome and the End of Civilization* (Oxford, 2005); see further A. Giardina, 'Esplosione di tardoantico', *Studi storici*, 40 (1999), pp. 157–80, and cf. for an overview C. Wickham in *South African Journal of Medieval and Renaissance Studies*, 14 (2004), pp. 1–22.

p. 10. Overviews: R. Collins, *Early Medieval Europe, 300–1000* (Basingstoke, 1991; revised edition 1999); J. M. H. Smith, *Europe after Rome* (Oxford, 2005), with a remarkable annotated bibliography; for archaeological approaches, R. Hodges and D. Whitehouse, *Mohammed, Charlemagne and the Origins of Europe* (London, 1983), even though it was written so early, remains the only significant overview. Social history is dominated by surveys in French: P. Depreux, *Les Sociétés occidentales du milieu du VIᵉ à la fin du IXᵉ siècle* (Rennes, 2002); R. Le Jan, *La Société du haut Moyen Âge* (Paris, 2003); J.-P. Devroey, *Économie rurale et société dans l'Europe franque (VIᵉ–IXᵉ siècles)* (Paris, 2003); idem, *Puissants et misérables* (Brussels, 2006).

p. 13. Critical recent approaches to Gregory include W. Goffart, *The Narrators of Barbarian History (A.D. 550–800)* (Princeton, 1988); M. Heinzelmann, *Gregory of Tours* (Cambridge, 2001); I. Wood, *Gregory of Tours* (Oxford, 1994), and in *Revue belge de philologie et d'histoire*, 71 (1993), pp. 253–70; K. Mitchell and I. Wood (eds.), *The World of Gregory of Tours* (Leiden, 2002).

Chapter 2

The best brief introductions to the later Roman empire are by Peter Brown, *The World of Late Antiquity* (London, 1971), and by Averil Cameron, *The Later Roman Empire* (London, 1993) and *The Mediterranean World in Late Antiquity AD 395–600* (London, 1993). The essential detailed surveys in English are A. H. M. Jones, *The Later Roman Empire 284–602* (Oxford, 1964) and *CAH*, vols. 13 and 14. S. Mitchell, *A History of the Later Roman Empire, AD 284–641* (Oxford, 2007) is another useful introductory account. The sixth century in the East is filled out further by M. Maas (ed.), *The Cambridge Companion to the Age of Justinian* (Cambridge, 2005). For further bibliographies on all the topics in this chapter, see these works. Some issues in this chapter are discussed in greater detail in my *Framing the Early Middle Ages* (Oxford, 2005). Other important recent late Roman surveys include G. Bowersock *et al.* (eds.), *Late Antiquity* (Cambridge, Mass., 1999); A. Giardina (ed.), *Società romana e impero tardoantico*, 4 vols. (Bari, 1986); A. Carandini *et al.* (eds.), *Storia di Roma*, vol. 3 (2 vols.) (Turin, 1992); and A. Demandt, *Die Spätantike* (Munich, 1989).

p. 21. Primer: A. C. Dionisotti, 'From Ausonius' Schooldays?', *Journal of Roman Studies*, 72 (1982), pp. 83–125; for torture, see J. Harries, *Law and Empire in Late Antiquity* (Cambridge, 1999), pp. 122–34. For wider issues of violence, see H. A. Drake (ed.), *Violence in Late Antiquity* (Aldershot, 2006).

p. 21. Games: Augustine, *Confessions*, trans. H. Chadwick (Oxford, 1991), 6.8. Banning by Constantine: Jones, *Later Roman Empire*, p. 977; A. Cameron, *Circus Factions* (Oxford, 1976), pp. 216 ff.

p. 22. Show trials for magic: see the account in J. F. Matthews, *The Roman Empire of Ammianus Marcellinus* (London, 1989), pp. 209–17.

p. 22. Andronikos: Synesios of Cyrene, *Correspondance*, ed. and trans. A. Garzya and D. Roques (Paris, 2000), nn. 41–2, 72, 79, 90; cf. D. Roques, *Synésios de Cyrène et la Cyrénaïque du Bas-Empire* (Paris, 1987), pp. 195–206, 366–70.

p. 23. Capital cities and their feeding: J. Durliat, *De la ville antique à la ville byzantine* (Rome, 1990); E. Lo Cascio, in W. V. Harris (ed.), *The Transformations of Urbs Roma in Late Antiquity* (Portsmouth, RI, 1999), pp. 163–82; A. E. Müller, 'Getreide für Konstantinopel', *Jahrbuch der österreichischen Byzantinistik*, 43 (1993), pp. 1–20.

p. 23. Cost of games: R. Lim, in Harris, *Transformations*, pp. 265–81, at pp. 271–5.

p. 24. *Order of Noble Cities*: Ausonius, *Works*, vol. 1, ed. and trans. H. G. E. White (Cambridge, Mass., 1919), pp. 269–85.

p. 24. End of *curiae* and informal élites: J. H. W. G. Liebeschuetz, *The Decline of the Ancient City* (Oxford, 2001); A. Laniado, *Recherches sur les notables municipaux dans l'empire protobyzantin* (Paris, 2002); C. Rapp, *Holy Bishops in Late Antiquity* (Berkeley, 2005), pp. 274–89.

p. 25. Sidonius: J. Harries, *Sidonius Apollinaris and the Fall of Rome* (Oxford, 1994).

p. 26. 30,000 officials: Jones, *Later Roman Empire*, p. 1057; see further for Roman bureaucracy, C. Kelly, *Ruling the Roman Empire* (Cambridge, Mass., 2004), the best analysis of late Roman bureaucratic culture, and C. Kelly and P. Heather, in *CAH*, vol. 13, pp. 138–210.

p. 26. Travel: figures from M. McCormick, *Origins of the European Economy* (Cambridge, 2001), pp. 474–81; his evidence is Carolingian and onwards, but it is unlikely to have been very different for fast horse-borne messengers under late Rome; further timings and bibliography in Kelly, *Ruling*, pp. 115–17.

p. 27. John Lydos, *On Powers*, ed. and trans. A. C. Bandy (Philadelphia, 1983) (1.14 for Romulus, 2.20–21, 3.57–72 for John the Cappadocian; see M. Maas, *John Lydus and the Roman Past* (London, 1992); Kelly, *Ruling*, pp. 11–104.

p. 27. Petronius Maximus: see refs. in *PLRE*, vol. 2, pp. 749–51; Sidonius Apollinaris, *Letters*, ed. and trans. W. B. Anderson, *Poems and Letters* (Cambridge, Mass., 1962–5), 2.13.

p. 28. *Otium*: see J. R. Matthews, *Western Aristocracies and Imperial Court AD 364–425* (Oxford, 1975), pp. 1–12.

p. 29. Symmachus: *Epistulae*, 1.52, ed. O. Seeck, *MGH*, *Auctores Antiquissimi*, 6.1 (Berlin, 1883).

p. 29. Paeonius: Sidonius, *Letters*, 1.11.5.

p. 29. Petronius Probus: Ammianus Marcellinus, *Res Gestae*, ed. and trans. J. C. Rolfe, 3 vols. (Cambridge, Mass., 1935–9), 27.11.1.

p. 29. Melania: *The Life of Melania the Younger*, trans. E. A. Clark (Lewiston, NY, 1982), c. 15.

p. 30. Juvenal: Ammianus, *Res Gestae*, 28.4.14. For élite culture, see A. Cameron in *CAH*, vol. 13, pp. 665–707.

p. 30. Libanios and magic: P. Brown, *Religion and Society in the Age of Saint Augustine* (London, 1972), pp. 127–34.

p. 30. Julian: see for example the critical comments in the otherwise sympathetic Ammianus, *Res Gestae*, 22.10.7, 25.4.20; cf. D. Hunt in *CAH*, vol. 13, p. 67.

p. 30. Reading Augustine's work: Sidonius, *Letters*, 2.9.4.

p. 30. Estate management: Palladius, *Opus Agriculturae*, ed. R. H. Rodgers (Leipzig, 1975).

p. 31. Law: good recent surveys are Harries, *Law and Empire*; P. Garnsey and C. Humfress, *The Evolution of the Late Antique World* (Cambridge, 2001), pp. 52–82; D. Liebs in *CAH*, vol. 14, pp. 238–59; C. Humfress, *Orthodoxy and the Courts in Late Antiquity* (Oxford, 2007).

p. 31. Alypius in Rome: Augustine, *Confessions*, 6.8–10.

p. 32. Egypt: T. Gagos and P. van Minnen, *Settling a Dispute* (Ann Arbor, 1994), pp. 30–46.

p. 32. Eustochius: Augustine, *Letters*, trans. W. Parsons and R. B. Eno, 6 vols. (Washington, 1951–89), letter 24*.

p. 32. Salvius: C. Lepelley, in *Antiquités africaines*, 25 (1989), pp. 235–62, at pp. 240–51.

p. 33. Amphorae: O. Karagiorgou, in S. Kingsley and M. Decker (eds.), *Economy and Exchange in the Eastern Mediterranean during Late Antiquity* (Oxford, 2001), pp. 129–66.

p. 33. Factories: Jones, *Later Roman Empire*, pp. 834–6.

p. 33. Weight and regional incidence of tax: this follows Wickham, *Framing*, pp. 62–80.

p. 33. Tied occupations: A. H. M. Jones, *The Roman Economy* (Oxford, 1974), pp. 396–418.

p. 35. Apions: *The Oxyrhynchus Papyri*, ed. and trans. B. P. Grenfell, A. S. Hunt *et al.*, 65 vols. to date (Oxford, 1898–), vol. 16, nn. 1906–8, vol. 62, 4350–51.

p. 36. Slavery: D. Vera, 'Le forme del lavoro rurale', *Settimane di studio*, 45 (1998), pp. 293–342.

p. 36. Egyptian towns: R. S. Bagnall and B. W. Freer, *The Demography of Roman Egypt* (Cambridge, 1994), pp. 53–7.

p. 36. *Coloni* laws: see the articles collected in E. Lo Cascio (ed.), *Terre, proprietari e contadini dell'impero romano* (Rome, 1997), for recent debate.

p. 37. Estate profit: Palladius, *Opus Agriculturae*; P. Sarris, *Economy and Society in the Age of Justinian* (Cambridge, 2006).

p. 37. Syrian villages: G. Tate, *Les Campagnes de la Syrie du Nord du IIe au VIIe siècle*, vol. 1 (Paris, 1992).

p. 37. Thagaste: *Vita Melaniae Latina*, ed. M. Rampolla del Tindaro, *Santa Melania Giuniore* (Rome, 1905), pp. 3–40, c. 21.

p. 37. Justinian: *CJ*, 11.48.21.

p. 37. Egyptian tenure: R. Bagnall, *Egypt in Late Antiquity* (Princeton, 1993), pp. 110–23, 148–53; J. Gascou and L. MacCoull, in *Travaux et mémoires*, 10 (1987), pp. 103–51; compare for Italy, *Vita Melaniae Latina*, c. 18.

p. 38. Dioskoros: L. S. B. MacCoull, *Dioscorus of Aphrodito* (Berkeley, 1988); J.-L. Fournet, *Hellénisme dans l'Égypte du VIe siècle* (Cairo, 1999); for Aphrodito in an Egyptian context, see J. G. Keenan, in *CAH*, vol. 14, pp. 612–37; for the murder, P. J. Sijpesteijn (ed.), *The Aphrodite Papyri in the University of Michigan Papyrus Collection (P. Mich. XIII)* (Zutphen, 1977), nn. 660–61.

p. 39. Fussala: Augustine, *Letters*, 209 and 20*; see further S. Lancel, in C. Lepelley (ed.), *Les Lettres de saint Augustin découvertes par Johannes Divjak* (Paris, 1983), pp. 267–85.

p. 40. Pottery: the best overview is still C. Panella, 'Merci e scambi nel Mediterraneo in età tardo antica', in Carandini *et al.*, *Storia di Roma*, vol. 3.2, pp. 613–97; for cloth see Jones, *Later Roman Empire*, pp. 848–50, and S. Lauffer (ed.), *Diokletians Preisedikt* (Berlin, 1971), cc. 19–28.

p. 41. Egyptian wine: D. M. Bailey, *Excavations at el-Ashmunein*, vol. 5 (London, 1998), pp. 118–38; *Life of St John the Almsgiver*, trans. E. Dawes and N. H. Baynes, *Three Byzantine Saints* (London, 1948), pp. 199–262, c. 10.

p. 42. Egypt: see esp. Bagnall, *Egypt*, pp. 32, 45–67.

p. 42. Theodora: J. Maspero (ed.), *Papyrus grecs d'époque byzantine*, vol. 3 (Cairo, 1916), n. 67283.

p. 42. Patronage: A. Wallace-Hadrill (ed.), *Patronage in Ancient Society* (London, 1989); P. Brown, *Power and Persuasion in Late Antiquity* (Madison, 1992); Kelly, *Ruling*, esp. pp. 138–85; J.-U. Krause, *Spätantike Patronatsformen im Westen des römischen Reiches* (Munich, 1987).

p. 42. Zotikos: John Lydos, *On Powers*, 3.26–7.

p. 42. Abinnaios: H. I. Bell *et al.* (eds.), *The Abinnaios Archive* (Oxford, 1962), esp. papyri nn. 7, 10, 12, 15, 19, 21, 26–8, 32–4, 44–57.

p. 43. Libanios: Libanius, *Selected Works*, vol. 2, ed. and trans. A. F. Norman (Cambridge, Mass., 1977), *Oration* 47.

p. 43. Persia: there is no good recent detailed account. See in general E. Yarshater (ed.), *The Cambridge History of Iran*, vol. 3 (Cambridge, 1983), and for article-length overviews the differing positions of Z. Rubin, in *CAH*, vol. 14, pp. 638–61, and (more convincing to me) J. Howard-Johnston, in A. Cameron (ed.), *The Byzantine and Early Islamic Near East*, vol. 3 (Princeton, 1995), pp. 157–226.

p. 44. Berbers: Synesios, *Correspondance*, nn. 122, 130, 132; D. J. Mattingly, *Tripolitania* (London, 1995), pp. 173–80; Y. Modéran, *Les Maures et l'Afrique romaine (IVe–VIIe siècle)* (Rome, 2003).

p. 45. Quadi: Ammianus, *Res Gestae*, 29.6.2ff., 30.6.

p. 45. Alemans: Ammianus, *Res Gestae*, 16.12.1, 23, 26; cf. J. F. Drinkwater, *The Alamanni and Rome 213–496* (Oxford, 2007), pp. 117–26, 236–44.

p. 45. Gothic sources: P. Heather and J. Matthews, *The Goths in the Fourth Century* (Liverpool, 1991), pp. 102–10, 124–85.

p. 46. Archaeology and ethnicity: this is highly contested. My views fit with, among others, G. Halsall, in J. F. Drinkwater and H. Elton (eds.), *Fifth-century Gaul* (Cambridge, 1992), pp. 196–207; B. Effros, *Merovingian Mortuary Archaeology and the Making of the Middle Ages* (Berkeley, 2003), pp. 100–110.

p. 46. Denmark: L. Hedeager, *Iron-Age Societies* (Oxford, 1992), pp. 45–51.

p. 46. Frontier societies: here I follow C. R. Whittaker, *Frontiers of the Roman Empire* (Baltimore, 1994). Against the old idea that the late imperial army was more 'barbarized' than before: H. Elton, *Warfare in Roman Europe, AD 350–425* (Oxford, 1996), pp. 134–54.

p. 47. Silvanus: Ammianus, *Res Gestae*, 15.5; for Firmus, 29.5.39.

p. 48. Huns: Ammianus, *Res Gestae*, 31.2; for Gothic entry, 31 *passim* – cf. P. J. Heather, *Goths and Romans 332–489* (Oxford, 1991), pp. 122ff., and H. Wolfram, *History of the Goths* (Berkeley, 1988), pp. 117ff.

Chapter 3

For introductions, most of the books cited in Chapter 2 are equally important. P. Garnsey and C. Humfress, *The Evolution of the Late Antique World* (Cambridge, 2001), pp. 132–215, and P. Brown, *Power and Persuasion in Late Antiquity* (Madison, 1992), are original rereadings of the evidence. On Christianity, A. Cameron, *Christianity and the Rhetoric of Empire* (Berkeley, 1991); P. Brown, *The Rise of Western Christendom* (2nd edn., Oxford, 1997); and R. Markus, *The End of Ancient Christianity* (Cambridge, 1990), are key points of reference.

p. 50. Sidonius: *Letters*, ed. and trans. W. B. Anderson, *Poems and Letters* (Cambridge, Mass., 1962–5), 4.25 (Chalon), 7.5, 8, 9 (Bourges); cf. J. Harries, *Sidonius Apollinaris and the Fall of Rome* (Oxford, 1994), pp. 179–86. For a context, R. Van Dam, *Leadership and Community in Late Antique Gaul* (Berkeley, 1985) is basic. For the complexity of the roles and authority of bishops, see above all C. Rapp, *Holy Bishops in Late Antiquity* (Berkeley, 2005).

p. 51. Synesios: *Correspondance*, ed. and trans. A. Garzya and D. Roques (Paris, 2000) nn. 105 (open letter), 10, 15, 16, 46, 81, 124, 154 (to Hypatia); for Theophilos and Cyril, C. Haas, *Alexandria in Late Antiquity* (Baltimore, 1997), pp. 159–69, 295–316; see in general D. Roques, *Synésios de Cyrène et la Cyrénaïque du Bas-Empire* (Paris, 2000), pp. 301–16.

p. 51. 'Pagan': this is an unsatisfactory word. Traditional Graeco-Roman religion had no word for its practitioners; *paganus*, originally meaning 'rustic', is used already to mean 'not Christian (or Jewish)' in the early third century, however, and became common by the late fourth (e.g. *CTh*, 16.2.18, for the year 370). 'Hellene' is another late Roman word which came to be used for 'pagan'. Some modern authors prefer 'polytheist', but not all 'pagans' were polytheistic.

p. 52. Late paganism: see G. W. Bowersock, *Hellenism in Late Antiquity* (Cambridge, 1990); F. R. Trombley, *Hellenic Religion and Christianization c.370–529*, 2 vols. (Leiden, 1993–4); G. Fowden, in *CAH*, vol. 13, pp. 538–60; Garnsey and Humfress, *Evolution of the Late Antique World*, pp. 152–60; John of Ephesos, *Ecclesiastical History*, ed. and trans. E. W. Brooks (Louvain, 1935–6), 2.44, 3.36.

p. 52. Jews: see S. T. Katz (ed.), *The Cambridge History of Judaism*, vol. 4 (Cambridge, 2006), pp. 67–82, 404–56, 492–518.

p. 52. Laws: *CTh*, 16.10.10–12 (391–2), *CJ*, 1.11.10 (Justinian). Edessa: John of Ephesos, *Ecclesiastical History*, 3.27–8.

p. 53. First of January: Markus, *End of Ancient Christianity*, pp. 103–6, and in general for festivals, pp. 97–135.

p. 54. Sunday: Gregory of Tours, *The Miracles of the Bishop St Martin*, trans. in R. Van Dam, *Saints and their Miracles in Late Antique Gaul* (Princeton, 1993), pp. 199–303, e.g. 2.24, 3.29, 4.45.

p. 54. Augustine: *Letters*, trans. W. Parsons and R. B. Eno, 6 vols. (Washington, 1951–89), *letter 29*.

p. 54. Brioude: Van Dam, *Saints and their Miracles*, pp. 41–8. Drinking at martyrs' tombs: Augustine, *Letters*, 22; Augustine, *Confessions*, trans. H. Chadwick (Oxford, 1991), 6.2.2. Gregory the Great: Bede, *HE*, 1.30. For a general discussion of religious space and its contexts in the Mediterranean, see P. Horden and N. Purcell, *The Corrupting Sea* (Oxford, 2000), pp. 403–60.

p. 55. Christian topography: see e.g. N. Gauthier, 'La Topographie chrétienne entre idéologie et pragmatisme', in G. P. Brogiolo and B. Ward-Perkins (eds.), *The Idea and Ideal of the Town between Late Antiquity and the Early Middle Ages* (Leiden, 1999), pp. 195–209.

p. 55. Rome: R. Krautheimer, *Rome: Profile of a City, 312–1308* (Princeton, 1980), pp. 71, 75.

p. 55. Intramural burials: see, for an analysis of developments in Italy, N. Christie, *From Constantine to Charlemagne* (Aldershot, 2006), pp. 252–9. For dead saints, see P. Brown, *The Cult of the Saints* (Chicago, 1981).

p. 56. Demons: see B. Caseau, in G. Bowersock *et al.* (eds.), *Late Antiquity* (Cambridge, Mass., 1999), pp. 406–7.

p. 56. Theodore of Sykeon: *Vie de Théodore de Sykéôn*, ed. and trans. A. J. Festugière (Brussels, 1970), cc. 37, 43, 91–4, 103, 114–16, 162, etc.

p. 57. Foucault: e.g. M. Foucault, *Discipline and Punish* (London, 1977). For the patterns of everyday Christianity, see esp. P. Brown, in *CAH*, vol. 13, pp. 632–64.

p. 57. Gregory of Nyssa: Garnsey and Humfress, *Evolution of the Late Antique World*, pp. 207–10.

p. 57. Jerome: *Select Letters of St Jerome*, ed. and trans. F. A. Wright (Cambridge, Mass., 1963), *letter 22*, is a good example.

p. 57. Divorce: see A. Arjava, *Women and Law in Late Antiquity* (Oxford, 1996), pp. 177–92; G. Clark, *Women in Late Antiquity* (Oxford, 1993), pp. 21–7; A. Giardina, in *CAH*, vol. 14, pp. 392–8.

p. 58. Jewish patriarch: D. Goodblatt, in Katz, *Cambridge History of Judaism*, vol. 4, pp. 416–23.

p. 59. Church as a career structure: see e.g. Rapp, *Holy Bishops*, pp. 172–207.

p. 60. Donatists: see W. H. C. Frend, *The Donatist Church* (Oxford, 1952), p. 167 for the bishops; P. Brown, *Religion and Society in the Age of Saint Augustine* (London, 1972), pp. 237–331.

p. 60. Pelagians: Brown, *Religion and Society*, pp. 183–226; B. R. Rees, *Pelagius*, 2nd edn. (London, 1998).

p. 61. Clerical celibacy: R. Gryson, *Les Origines du célibat ecclésiastique du premier au septième siècle* (Gembloux, 1970).

p. 61. Eastern Christological debates: H. Chadwick, in *CAH*, vol. 13, pp. 561–600, and P. Allen, in *CAH*, vol. 14, pp. 811–34, give useful narratives. The historiography is huge; I have found particularly useful the crisp and incisive theological introductions in F. M. Young, *From Nicaea to Chalcedon* (London, 1983). For 'Arianism', see most recently D. M. Gwynn, *The Eusebians* (Oxford, 2007).

p. 62. 'Arianism' in Constantinople: see J. H. W. G. Liebeschuetz, *Barbarians and Bishops* (Oxford, 1990), pp. 157–89.

p. 63. Monophysite episcopal hierarchy: D. D. Bundy, 'Jacob Baradaeus', *Le Muséon*, 91 (1978), pp. 45–86; L. Van Rompay, in M. Maas (ed.), *The Cambridge Companion to the Age of Justinian* (Cambridge, 2005), pp. 239–66.

p. 64. Mobs: Haas, *Alexandria*, pp. 258–330; Frend, *Donatist Church*, pp. 172–7 (but who exactly Circumcellions were is much debated: see B. D. Shaw, in A. H. Merrills (ed.), *Vandals, Romans and Berbers* (Aldershot, 2004), pp. 227–58); T. E. Gregory, *Vox Populi* (Columbus, Ohio, 1979).

p. 64. Patriarch Juvenal: Evagrios, *The Ecclesiastical History of Evagrius Scholasticus*, trans. M. Whitby (Liverpool, 2000), 2.5; Cyril of Scythopolis, *Life of Euthymios*, in *Lives of the Monks of Palestine*, trans. R. M. Price (Kalamazoo, Mich., 1991), pp. 1–83, cc. 27–30.

p. 65. Ascetics: the seminal article is P. Brown, *Society and the Holy in Late Antiquity*, (London, 1982), pp. 103–52, updated in *CAH*, vol. 14, pp. 780–810; the very substantial recent bibliography on ascetics and saints is summed up in two conferences, published as J. Howard-Johnston and P. Hayward (eds.), *The Cult of Saints in Late Antiquity and the Early Middle Ages* (Oxford, 1999), and *Journal of Early Christian Studies*, 6 (1998), pp. 343–671.

p. 65. Stylites: *Life of Daniel the Stylite*, trans. E. Dawes and N. H. Baynes, *Three Byzantine Saints* (London, 1948), pp. 7–71, c. 62; Theodoret of Cyrrhus, *A History of the Monks of Syria*, trans. R. M. Price (Kalamazoo, Mich., 1985), 26.22. See for Theodoret, T. Urbainczyk, *Theodoret of Cyrrhus* (Ann Arbor, 2002), esp. pp. 115–47.

p. 65. Gaza advice: Barsanouphios and John, *Correspondance*, ed. and trans. F. Neyt *et al.*, 3 vols. (Paris, 1997–2002), nn. 636, 671, 777, 775, 776, 669, 841.

p. 66. Brown quote: *CAH*, vol. 14, p. 806.

p. 66. Paula: Jerome, *Letters*, 45.

p. 66. Monasticism: see in general D. J. Chitty, *The Desert a City* (Oxford, 1966); P. Rousseau, *Ascetics, Authority and the Church in the Age of Jerome and Cassian* (Oxford, 1978); C. Leyser, *Authority and Asceticism from Augustine to Gregory the Great* (Oxford, 2000).

p. 66. Benedict: *The Rule of St Benedict*, ed. and trans. J. McCann (London, 1952). So there!

p. 67. Infill in cities: H. Kennedy, 'From *polis* to *madina*', *Past and Present*, 106 (1985), pp. 3–27.

p. 67. *Adventus* and victory: Ammianus Marcellinus, *Res Gestae*, ed. and trans. J. C. Rolfe, 3 vols. (Cambridge, Mass., 1935–9), 16.10.4–13; S. G. MacCormack, *Art and Ceremony in Late Antiquity* (Berkeley, 1981), pp. 33–61; M. McCormick, *Eternal Victory* (Cambridge, 1986), pp. 189–230 for Constantine VII and other later accounts.

p. 68. Clermont: Gregory of Tours, *Life of the Fathers*, trans. E. James (Liverpool, 1985), 4.2; siege of Constantinople: see below, Chapter 11.

p. 68. Pilgrimages: see e.g. Van Dam, *Saints and their Miracles*, pp. 116–49.

p. 68. Games, factions: A. Cameron, *Circus Factions* (Oxford, 1976), pp. 225–96.

p. 69. Edessa: *The Chronicle of Pseudo-Joshua the Stylite*, trans. F. R. Trombley and J. W. Watt (Liverpool, 2000), c. 31.

p. 69. Sidonius: *Letters*, 2.13.4 (quote), 1.11 (Majorian).

p. 69. Persians: Ammianus, *Res Gestae*, 23.6.80.

p. 69. Petitions: J. Harries, *Law and Empire in Late Antiquity* (Cambridge, 1999), pp. 82–4, 184–7.

p. 69. Basiliscus: *Life of Daniel the Stylite*, cc. 70–84.

p. 69. Attila: Priskos, fragment 11.2, ed. and trans. in R. C. Blockley, *The Fragmentary Classicizing Historians of the Later Roman Empire*, vol. 2 (Liverpool, 1983), pp. 247–9, 257.

p. 70. Housing: S. Ellis, *Roman Housing* (London, 2000), esp. pp. 166–83; B. Polci, in L. Lavan and W. Bowden (eds.), *Theory and Practice in Late Antique Archaeology* (Leiden, 2003), pp. 79–89; K. Cooper, 'Closely Watched Households', *Past and Present*, 197 (2007), pp. 3–33.

p. 70. Augustine: *Confessions*, 9.9; *Letters*, 262 (to Ecdicia); see esp. B. Shaw, 'The Family in Late Antiquity', *Past and Present*, 115 (1987), pp. 3–51. See also G. Nathan, *The Family in Late Antiquity* (London, 2000). For eastern attitudes to family violence, see L. Dossey, 'Wife-beating in Late Antiquity', *Past and Present*, 199 (2008), pp.3–40.

p. 70. Egyptian divorce and marriage papyri: J. Beaucamp, *Le Statut de la femme à Byzance (4ᵉ–7ᵉ siècle)*, 2 vols. (Paris, 1990–92), vol. 2, pp. 139–58, 127–9.

p. 71. Domestic slaves: Augustine, *Confessions*, 9.9; *Querolus*, ed. and trans. C. Jacquemard-le Saos (Paris, 1994), c. 67.

p. 71. Augustine's dislike for his father: *Confessions*, 2.3, 5.8.

p. 71. Paulina: *Corpus Inscriptionum Latinarum*, 6.1 (Berlin, 1876), n. 1779, with partial trans. and comment in K. Cooper, *The Virgin and the Bride* (Cambridge, Mass., 1996), pp. 97–103.

p. 71. Women and law: Arjava, *Women and Law*; Beaucamp, *Le Statut*, vol. 1.

p. 71. Monica: Augustine, *Confessions*, 3.4.

p. 71. Patrikia: *Greek Papyri in the British Museum*, ed. F. G. Kenyon and H. I. Bell, 5 vols. (London, 1893–1917), vol. 5, n. 1660.

p. 71. Hypatia: M. Dzielska, *Hypatia of Alexandria* (Cambridge, Mass., 1995).

p. 72. Economic activities in Egypt: Beaucamp, *Le Statut*, vol. 2, pp. 227–47; R. Bagnall, *Egypt in Late Antiquity* (Princeton, 1993), pp. 92–9, 130–33.

p. 72. Actresses: Beaucamp, *Le Statut*, vol. 1, pp. 206–8; V. Neri, *I marginali nell'Occidente tardoantico* (Bari, 1998), pp. 233–50. Theodora: our problem here is that our sole source for her career as an actress is Prokopios, *Secret History*, ed. and trans. H. B. Dewing (Cambridge, Mass., 1935), c. 9, which is a free-standing rhetorical denunciation: see L. Brubaker, 'Sex, Lies and Textuality', in eadem and J. M. H. Smith (eds.), *Gender in the Early Medieval World* (Cambridge, 2004), pp. 83–101. It would be unsafe to assume that it even had a grain of truth.

p. 72. Female ascesis: see E. A. Clark, *Ascetic Piety and Women's Faith* (Lewiston, NY, 1986), esp. pp. 175–208.

p. 73. Contrast with early medieval West: see J. M. H. Smith, 'Did Women have a Transformation of the Roman World?', *Gender and History*, 12.3 (2000), pp. 22–41.

p. 73. Female weakness: see e.g. Clark, *Women*, pp. 56–62, 119–26.

p. 73. Decorum and anger: Brown, *Power and Persuasion*, pp. 35–61.

p. 73. Faustus: see R. Mathisen, *Roman Aristocrats in Barbarian Gaul* (Austin, Tex., 1993), pp. 50–51.

p. 73. Valentinian: Ammianus, *Res Gestae*, 30.8; Sidonius: *Letters*, 1.11, esp. 11.12.

Chapter 4

The fullest overall narrative of this period is still E. Stein, *Histoire du Bas-Empire*, 2 vols. (Paris, 1949–59); up-to-date (and very different) analytical narratives for the West are now P. Heather, *The Fall of the Roman Empire* (London, 2005), and G. Halsall, *Barbarian Migrations and the Roman West, 376–568* (Cambridge, 2007), which pays attention to material culture. *CAH*, vol. 14, M. Maas (ed.), *The Cambridge Companion to the Age of Justinian* (Cambridge 2005), and A. Cameron, *The Mediterranean World in Late Antiquity AD 365–600* (London, 1993), are state-of-the-art introductions, as is H. Wolfram, *The Roman Empire and its Germanic Peoples* (Berkeley, 1997). For the integration of the 'barbarians' into the Roman world, the Transformation of the Roman World series, published by Brill, is now an essential starting point, including W. Pohl (ed.), *Kingdoms of the Empire* (Leiden, 1997), and H.-W. Goetz et al. (eds.), *Regna and Gentes* (Leiden, 2003). B. Ward-Perkins, *The Fall of Rome and the End of Civilization* (Oxford, 2005) is a powerful counterblast against excessive continuitism. Scholars disagree, often fiercely, about the issues discussed in this chapter, and are likely to go on doing so for some time.

p. 76. Huneric: Victor of Vita, *History of the Vandal Persecution*, trans. J. Moorhead (Liverpool, 1992), 2.38–40, 3.2–14 (quotes from 3.3.3, 7); for 411, *Actes de la Conférence de Carthage en 411*, ed. S. Lancel, 3 vols. (Paris, 1972–5), and *CTh*, 16.5.52, for 412, Huneric's model.

p. 77. Vandals: see in general C. Courtois, *Les Vandales et l'Afrique* (Paris, 1955), and the wide-ranging conference published as *L'Antiquité tardive*, vols. 10 and 11 (2002–3); Possidius, *Life of Augustine*, trans. R. J. Deferrari, in *Early Christian Biographies* (Washington, 1952), pp. 73–131, cc. 28–30; Prokopios, *Wars*, ed. and trans. H. B. Dewing (Cambridge, Mass., 1914–28), 4.6.5–9. For Africa in the period, see A. H. Merrills (ed.), *Vandals, Romans and Berbers* (Aldershot, 2004).

p. 78. Population of Rome: J. Durliat, *De la ville antique à la ville byzantine* (Rome, 1990), pp. 92–123.

p. 79. Marcellinus: B. Croke, 'A.D. 476: The Manufacture of a Turning Point', *Chiron*, 13 (1983), pp. 81–119.

p. 79. 400–425 in the West: see J. R. Matthews, *Western Aristocracies and Imperial Court AD 364–425* (Oxford, 1975); H. Wolfram, *History of the Goths* (Berkeley, 1988), pp. 139–75; P. J. Heather, *Goths and Romans 332–489* (Oxford, 1991), pp. 193–224.

p. 81. Gainas, Eudoxia: see J. H. W. G. Liebeschuetz, *Barbarians and Bishops* (Oxford, 1990). Eudoxia, Pulcheria: K. G. Holum, *Theodosian Empresses* (Berkeley, 1982); L. James, *Empresses and Power in Early Byzantium* (Leicester, 2001), pp. 59–82. For Theodosius II's reign as a whole, see F. Millar, *A Greek Roman Empire* (Berkeley, 2006).

p. 82. Suevi, etc.: for fifth-century Spain, J. Arce, *Bárbaros y romanos en Hispania, 400–507 A.D.* (Madrid, 2005), is basic.

p. 82. Bagaudae: the best overview of a contested subject is J. C. Sánchez León, *Los Bagaudae* (Jaén, 1996).

p. 82. Orosius: *Seven Books of History against the Pagans*, trans. R. J. Deferrari (Washington, 1964), 7.41; Augustine: see R. A. Markus, *Saeculum* (Cambridge, 1970), pp. 45–71, 147–53.

p. 83. *Theodosian Code*: see J. Matthews, in J. Harries and I. Wood (eds.), *The Theodosian Code* (London, 1993), pp. 19–44.

p. 83. Aetius: J. M. O'Flynn, *Generalissimos of the Western Roman Empire* (Edmonton, 1983), pp. 74–103; more critical is J. R. Moss, in *Historia*, 22 (1973), pp. 711–31.

p. 83. Western legislation in the 440s: see esp. *Novels of Valentinian*, n. 15, in *CTh*, pp. 529–30.

p. 84. Salvian: *On the Governance of God*, trans. J. F. O'Sullivan, in *The Writings of Salvian, the Presbyter* (Washington, 1947), pp. 25–232; cf. Priskos, fragment 11.2, in Blockley, pp. 267–73; compare also Orosius, *History*, 7.41.7.

p. 84. Huns: basic on them (and on fifth-century politics in general) is P. Heather, 'The Huns and the End of the Roman Empire in Western Europe', *English Historical Review*, 110 (1995), pp. 4–41.

p. 85. Avitus and Theoderic: Sidonius Apollinaris, *Poems and Letters*, ed. and trans. W. B. Anderson (Cambridge, Mass., 1962–5), *poem* 7, lines 392–602.

p. 85. For 456–75, see e.g. P. MacGeorge, *Late Roman Warlords* (Oxford, 2002).

p. 86. Odovacer as king: J.-O. Tjäder, *Die nichtliterarischen lateinischen Papyri Italiens aus der Zeit 445–700* (Lund, 1955–82), nn. 10–11 (for 489).

p. 86. 476: talked down by many historians, of which the classic is A. Momigliano, 'La caduta senza rumore di un impero nel 476 D.C.', *Annali della Scuola Normale Superiore di Pisa*, 3rd ser., 3.2 (1973), pp. 397–418.

p. 86. Euric: Wolfram, *History of the Goths*, pp. 181–222.

p. 86. Auvergne: J. Harries, *Sidonius Apollinaris and the Fall of Rome* (Oxford, 1994), pp. 222–38; quote: Sidonius, *Letters*, 8.2.2.

p. 87. Changes in Gaul: see J. F. Drinkwater and H. Elton (eds.), *Fifth-century Gaul* (Cambridge, 1992); MacGeorge, *Warlords*, pp. 71–164; E. James, *The Franks* (Oxford, 1988), pp. 58–91.

p. 87. Northern Gaul: P. Van Ossel and P. Ouzoulias, in *Journal of Roman Archaeology*, 13 (2000), pp. 133–60; Sidonius, *Letters*, 4.17; *Vita Genovefae*, ed. B. Krusch, *MGH*, *SRM*, vol. 3 (Hanover, 1896), pp. 215–38, cc. 35–8.

p. 87. Noricum: Eugippius, *Life of Severinus*, trans. L. Bieler (Washington, 1965).

NOTES TO CHAPTER 4

p. 89. Zeno and Anastasius: A. D. Lee, in *CAH*, vol. 14, pp. 49–62; for the Theoderics, Heather, *Goths and Romans*, pp. 240–308.

p. 90. Theoderic after 489: J. Moorhead, *Theoderic in Italy* (Oxford, 1992); P. Heather, in *EME*, 4 (1995), pp. 145–73; for the 500 visit, see the *Anonymus Valesianus*, ed. and trans. in Ammianus, *Res Gestae*, vol. 3, pp. 548–57; Cassiodorus, *Variae*, are partially trans. S. J. B. Barnish (Liverpool, 1992), and summarized as a whole in T. Hodgkin, *The Letters of Cassiodorus* (London, 1886).

p. 90. Orosius: *History*, 7.43.2–8.

p. 91. Sidonius and his contemporaries: J. Harries, in Drinkwater and Elton, *Fifth-century Gaul*, pp. 298–308; *PLRE*, vol. 2, pp. 157–8, 995–6, 1162–3, 1168; R. Mathisen, *Roman Aristocrats in Barbarian Gaul* (Austin, Tex., 1993).

p. 91. Hydatius: *The Chronicle of Hydatius and the Consularia Constantinopolitana*, ed. and trans. R. W. Burgess (Oxford, 1993), pp. 70–122; in Victor of Vita, *History of the Vandal Persecution*, 1.37 and 3.62 are the only references to Romans.

p. 91. Jerome: J. N. D. Kelly, *Jerome* (London, 1975).

p. 92. Justinian: perhaps the best, and certainly the crispest, of the many overviews is A. Cameron, in *CAH*, vol. 14, pp. 65–85; for the change in atmosphere of the period, eadem, *Christianity and the Rhetoric of Empire* (Berkeley, 1991), pp. 190–221. For the world of Justinian (though not too much on the emperor himself), see Maas, *Age of Justinian*.

p. 93. Prokopios: *On Buildings*, ed. and trans. H. B. Dewing (Cambridge, Mass., 1940). For redatings, see e.g. G. Brands, *Resafa VI* (Mainz, 2002), pp. 224–35.

p. 94. *Secret History*: see A. Cameron, *Procopius and the Sixth Century* (Berkeley, 1985), pp. 49–83; L. Brubaker, 'Sex, Lies and Textuality', in eadem and J. M. H. Smith (eds.), *Gender in the Early Medieval World* (Cambridge, 2004), pp. 83–101.

p. 94. Maurice: M. Whitby, *The Emperor Maurice and his Historian* (Oxford, 1988), esp. pp. 3–27; M. Whittow, *The Making of Orthodox Byzantium, 600–1025* (Basingstoke, 1996), pp. 38–68, is effectively upbeat.

p. 95. 'Roman civilization . . .': A. Piganiol, *L'Empire chrétien (325–395)* (Paris, 1947), p. 422.

p. 96. Basiliscus: S. Krautschick, 'Zwei Aspekte des Jahres 476', *Historia*, 35 (1986), pp. 344–71, at pp. 344–55; the link with Odovacer, which is a major reinterpretation of the period, hangs however on the placing of a single comma and an 'and' in a text, and it is not clear that this is better than the traditional reading (in R. C. Blockley, *The Fragmentary Classicizing Historians of the Later Roman Empire*, vol. 2 (Liverpool, 1983), pp. 372–3).

p. 96. Balkan melting pot: P. Amory, *People and Identity in Ostrogothic Italy, 489–554* (Cambridge, 1997), pp. 277–91.

p. 96. Intermarriage: A. Demandt, in E. K. Chrysos and A. Schwarcz (eds.), *Das Reich und die Barbaren* (Vienna, 1985), pp. 75–86.

p. 97. Empresses: see James, *Empresses and Power*.

p. 97. Anicia Juliana: L. Brubaker, 'Memories of Helena', in L. James (ed.), *Women, Men and Eunuchs* (London, 1997), pp. 52–75; *PLRE*, vol. 2, pp. 635–6; R. Harrison, *A Temple for Byzantium* (Austin, Tex., 1989).

p. 98. Ethnicity in Italy: see in general the critique in Amory, *People*, which I have not entirely followed. See *PLRE*, vol. 2, pp. 791–3 for Odovacer's career.

p. 99. Ethnogenesis: for guides, see e.g. H. Wolfram and W. Pohl (eds.), *Typen der Ethnogenese*, 2 vols. (Vienna, 1990); P. J. Geary, 'Ethnic Identity as a Situational Construct in the Early Middle Ages', *Mitteilungen des anthropologischen Gesellschaft in Wien*, 113 (1983), pp. 15–26; W. Pohl, in A. Gillett (ed.), *On Barbarian Identity* (Turnhout, 2002), pp. 221–39, for bibliography, rethinking, and a taste of the sharpness of polemic on the issue; and, most recently, Halsall, *Barbarian Migrations*. T. F. X. Noble (ed.), *From Roman Provinces to Medieval Kingdoms* (London, 2006), republishes many of the other key articles.

p. 99. Frankish origin-stories: Fredegar, *Chronica*, ed. B. Krusch, *MGH*, *SRM*, vol. 2 (Hanover, 1888), pp. 18–168, 2.4–6, 3.9: see A. C. Murray, in idem (ed.), *After Rome's Fall* (Toronto, 1998), pp. 121–52.

NOTES TO CHAPTER 5

p. 100. Communication: Amory, *People*, pp. 102–8, 247–56, for Gothic; M. Banniard, *Viva voce* (Paris, 1992), pp. 253–86 for Francia (though he is mostly concerned with Latin versus proto-Romance).

p. 100. Anthimus: see B. Effros, *Creating Community with Food and Drink in Merovingian Gaul* (Basingstoke, 2002), pp. 61–7.

p. 100. Assemblies: see in general P. S. Barnwell and M. Mostert (eds.), *Political Assemblies in the Earlier Middle Ages* (Turnhout, 2003); for *placita*, see W. Davies and P. Fouracre (eds.), *The Settlement of Disputes in Early Medieval Europe* (Cambridge, 1986).

p. 101. Theoderic II: Sidonius, *Letters*, 1.2.

p. 102. Shift to land, and tax changes: C. Wickham, *Framing the Early Middle Ages* (Oxford, 2005), pp. 80–93 for an overview of the debate; see more recently W. Goffart, *Barbarian Tides* (Philadelphia, 2006), pp. 119–56, and M. Innes, in *Transactions of the Royal Historical Society*, 6th ser., 16 (2006), pp. 39–74.

p. 103. Mercenaries: G. Halsall, *Warfare and Society in the Barbarian West, 450–900* (London, 2003), pp. 111–15.

p. 103. Economic simplification: Wickham, *Framing*, pp. 720–59, 794–805; Halsall, *Barbarian Migrations*, pp. 320–70.

p. 105. Avitus: Sidonius, *Poems*, 7, lines 251–94; Apollinaris and Arcadius: Gregory of Tours, *Histories*, trans. L. Thorpe as *The History of the Franks* (Harmondsworth, 1974), 2.37, 3.9, 12, 18; Cyprian: Cassiodorus, *Variae*, 8.21–2.

p. 106. Episcopal career structure: Mathisen, *Roman Aristocrats*, pp. 89–104; R. Van Dam, *Leadership and Community in Late Antique Gaul* (Berkeley, 1985), pp. 157–229; M. Heinzelmann, *Gregory of Tours* (Cambridge, 2001), pp. 7–28 for Gregory's family.

p. 106. Clothing: W. Pohl, 'Telling the Difference', in idem and H. Reimitz (eds.), *Strategies of Distinction* (Leiden, 1998), pp. 17–69, at pp. 40–51; M. Harlow, 'Clothes Maketh the Man', in Brubaker and Smith, *Gender*, pp. 44–69.

p. 107. Memory of Rome: see e.g. J. M. H. Smith, *Europe after Rome* (Oxford, 2005), pp. 253–92.

p. 108. Shifts for local élites: see e.g. Heather, 'Huns', pp. 37–9.

Chapter 5

The best survey of the Merovingian period in any language is Ian Wood's *The Merovingian Kingdoms 450–751* (Harlow, 1994). Good shorter introductions are S. Lebecq, *Les Origines franques Vᵉ–IXᵉ siècle* (Paris, 1990), and P. Geary, *Before France and Germany* (Oxford, 1988); E. James, *The Franks* (Oxford, 1988), which includes more archaeology, stops around 600, although his *The Origins of France* (London, 1982) continues to 1000. I. Wood (ed.), *Franks and Alamanni in the Merovingian Period* (Woodbridge, 1998) contains stimulating articles. J. M. Wallace-Hadrill, *The Long-haired Kings* (London, 1962) is the basic earlier point of reference. Important for social history are G. Halsall, *Settlement and Social Organization* (Cambridge, 1995) and R. Le Jan, *Famille et pouvoir dans le monde franc (VIIᵉ–Xᵉ siècle)* (Paris, 1995). R. Van Dam and P. Fouracre, in *NCMH*, vol. 1, pp. 193–231, 371–96 are brisk syntheses.

p. 111. Rauching: Gregory of Tours, *Histories*, trans. L. Thorpe as *The History of the Franks* (Harmondsworth, 1974), 6.4, 9.9, 12, cf. 5.3.

p. 111. Appointment of Gregory: Venantius Fortunatus, *Poems*, 5.3, ed. F. Leo, *MGH, Auctores Antiquissimi*, vol. 4.1 (Berlin, 1881), partial trans. (not including this poem), J. George, *Venantius Fortunatus: Personal and Political Poems* (Liverpool, 1995). For Gregory's literary structure, see the notes to p. 13.

p. 112. Private fortifications: R. Samson, 'The Merovingian Nobleman's Home: Castle or Villa?', *Journal of Medieval History*, 13 (1987), pp. 287–315.

p. 112. Clovis's Arianism: Avitus of Vienne, *Letters and Selected Prose*, trans. D. Shanzer and I. Wood (Liverpool, 2002), *Letters*, 46, with commentary, pp. 362–9.

p. 113. Royal palaces: J. Barbier, 'Le Système palatial franc', *Bibliothèque de l'École des Chartes*, 148 (1990), pp. 245–99.

p. 113. Merovingian name: see A. C. Murray, in idem (ed.), *After Rome's Fall* (Toronto, 1998), pp. 136–7.

p. 114. Theudebert: see R. Collins, 'Theodebert I, "rex magnus Francorum" ', in P. Wormald (ed.), *Ideal and Reality in Frankish and Anglo-Saxon Society* (Oxford, 1983), pp. 7–33; Agathias: *The Histories*, trans. J. D. Frendo (Berlin, 1975), 1.4; Gregory of Tours, *Histories*, 3.25, 34, 36.

p. 114. Admonitory letters: for some episcopal letters translated, A. C. Murray, *From Roman to Merovingian Gaul* (Peterborough, Ont., 2000), pp. 260–68; for Venantius Fortunatus, *Poems, passim*.

p. 115. Gregory's meetings with Guntram and Chilperic: Gregory of Tours, *Histories*, 5.18, 44, 8.2–6, 9.20; cf. 6.46 for Chilperic's obituary.

p. 116. Queens: see above all J. L. Nelson, *Politics and Ritual in Early Medieval Europe* (London, 1986), pp. 1–48; for resentment, see e.g. Gregory of Tours, *Histories*, 10.27.

p. 117. Flaochad: Fredegar, *Chronica*, 4.89; Fredegar's fourth book and continuations are ed. and trans. in J. M. Wallace-Hadrill, *The Fourth Book of the Chronicle of Fredegar* (London, 1960).

p. 117. Saints' lives as sources: see the important analysis of the genre by P. Fouracre, 'Merovingian History and Merovingian Hagiography', *Past and Present*, 127 (1990), pp. 3–38.

p. 117. Pippinids: I. Wood, in L. Brubaker and J. M. H. Smith (eds), *Gender in the Early Medieval World* (Cambridge, 2004), pp. 234–56, shows that their (female-line) Pippinid ancestry was more important to this family after 687 than their male ancestors.

p. 117. Childeric and Childebert: see Wood, *Merovingian Kingdoms*, pp. 227–38, 262–6; P. Fouracre, *The Age of Charles Martel* (Harlow, 2000), pp. 48–54; countered by T. Kölzer, in M. Becher and J. Jarnut (eds.), *Der Dynastiewechsel von 751* (Münster, 2004), pp. 33–60.

p. 118. Godin: Fredegar, *Chronica*, 4.54; Grimoald and Bodilo: *Liber Historiae Francorum*, partially trans. in P. Fouracre and R. Gerberding, *Late Merovingian France* (Manchester, 1996), pp. 87–96, cc. 43, 45.

p. 118. Childebert as Sigebert's adopted son: of the competing modern analyses, I largely follow R. Gerberding, *The Rise of the Carolingians and the Liber Historiae Francorum* (Oxford, 1987), pp. 47–66; but see also M. Becher, in J. Jarnut *et al.* (eds.), *Karl Martell in seiner Zeit* (Sigmaringen, 1994), pp. 119–47.

p. 118. Ebroin's king: *Passio Prima Leudegarii*, trans. in Fouracre and Gerberding, *Late Merovingian France*, pp. 215–53, c. 19.

p. 119. Samo: Fredegar, *Chronica*, 4.48, 68–77; Radulf: 4.87; Aquitaine: see M. Rouche, *L'Aquitaine des Wisigoths aux Arabes, 418–781* (Paris, 1979), pp. 90–129.

p. 119. Charles Martel: see Fouracre, *Charles Martel*.

p. 120. Taxation: see W. Goffart, *Rome's Fall and After* (London, 1989), pp. 213–31; C. Wickham, *Framing the Early Middle Ages* (Oxford, 2005), pp. 102–15.

p. 120. Gold content: see M. F. Hendy, 'From Public to Private', *Viator*, 19 (1988), pp. 29–78, at pp. 62–8.

p. 121. *Thesaurus*: e.g. Fredegar, *Chronica*, 4.38, 42, 60, 67, 75, 85; *Liber Historiae Francorum*, cc. 45, 48, 52–3.

p. 121. Writing: see I. Wood, in R. McKitterick (ed.), *The Uses of Literacy in Early Medieval Europe* (Cambridge, 1990), pp. 63–81; tax accounts: *ChLA*, vol. 18, n. 659, vol. 47, nn. 1404–5.

p. 121. Royal acts: *Marculfi Formulae*, ed. K. Zeumer, *MGH, Formulae Merovingici et Karolini Aevi* (Hanover, 1886), pp. 36–106, 1.6–8, 11, 12, 20, 26–9, 40; *ChLA*, vol. 13, nn. 550, 565; J. Havet, 'Questions mérovingiennes, V', *Bibliothèque de l'École des Chartes*, 51 (1890), pp. 5–62, at pp. 47–50; Desiderius of Cahors, *Letters*, ed. W. Arndt, *MGH, Epistolae*, vol. 3 (Berlin, 1892), pp. 193–214, *letter* 2.17.

p. 122. *Referendaril* and other officials: see P. S. Barnwell, *Kings, Courtiers and Imperium* (London, 1997), pp. 23–40.

p. 122. Bishop Praejectus: *Passio Praeiecti*, trans. in Fouracre and Gerberding, *Late Merovingian France*, pp. 271–300, cc. 23–7.

p. 122. Assemblies: see P. S. Barnwell, in idem and M. Mostert (eds.), *Political Assemblies in the Earlier Middle Ages* (Turnhout, 2003), pp. 11–28; Saxons: Gregory of Tours, *Histories*, 4.14; sixth-century participation: ibid., 3.14, cf. H. Grahn-Hoek, *Die fränkische Oberschicht im 6. Jahrhundert* (Sigmaringen, 1976); Ebroin: *Passio Prima Leudegarii*, c. 5.

p. 123. Legal assemblies: see P. Fouracre, in W. Davies and P. Fouracre (eds.), *The Settlement of Disputes in Early Medieval Europe* (Cambridge, 1986), pp. 23–43.

p. 123. Salic law: see *The Laws of the Salian Franks*, trans. K. F. Drew (Philadelphia, 1991), prologue, 57; H. Nehlsen, in P. Classen (ed.), *Recht und Schrift im Mittelalter* (Sigmaringen, 1977), pp. 449–502, at pp. 461–83; later law: *Cap.*, vol. 1, pp. 1–23.

p. 124. Royal justice: Gregory of Tours, *Histories*, 6.73; Fredegar, *Chronica*, 4.58. For Chlotar and councils, see M. de Jong, in S. Airlie *et al.* (eds.), *Staat im frühen Mittelalter* (Vienna, 2006), pp. 125–7.

p. 124. Aristocratic wealth: see Wickham, *Framing*, pp. 168–203.

p. 124. Abbo: see P. Geary, *Aristocracy in Provence* (Stuttgart, 1985); for aristocratic identity, see F. Irsigler, in T. Reuter (ed.), *The Medieval Nobility* (Amsterdam, 1978), pp. 105–36.

p. 124. Agilolfings: see Le Jan, *Famille et pouvoir*, pp. 387–92.

p. 124. Administrators as having obligations to fight: see e.g. Venantius Fortunatus, *Poems*, 7.16; *Vita Eligii*, trans. J. A. McNamara, http://www.fordham.edu/halsall/basis/eligius.html, 1.10–11.

p. 125. Counts and bishops of low-born origin: Gregory of Tours, *Histories*, 5.48; *Vita Eligii*, 1.1; *Passio Praeiecti*, c. 1. See, in general, P. Fouracre, in *Bulletin of the Institute of Historical Research*, 57 (1984), pp. 1–14, and, for bishops in the army, F. Prinz, *Klerus und Krieg im früheren Mittelalter* (Stuttgart, 1971), pp. 46–72.

p. 125. Founding monasteries: see e.g. Wood, *Merovingian Kingdoms*, pp. 181–202; Balthild: *Vita Balthildis*, trans. in Fouracre and Gerberding, *Late Merovingian France*, pp. 118–32, c. 9.

p. 126. 'Episcopal republics': E. Ewig, *Spätantikes und fränkisches Gallien* (Munich, 1976–9), vol. 2, pp. 211–19.

p. 127. Clermont: I. Wood, in Wormald (ed.), *Ideal and Reality*, pp. 34–57; Gregory: *Histories*, 5.49.

p. 127. Arnulf of Metz: *Vita Arnulfi*, ed. B. Krusch, *MGH, SRM*, vol. 2 (Hanover, 1888), pp. 432–46, c. 16; Leudegar: *Passio Prima Leudegarii*, cc. 21–4.

p. 127. Desiderius: *Letters*, 1.5, 9–11 (nostalgia), 1.2, 6, 8, 2.9 (patronage), 2.12, 15 (royal movements), 1.13, 15, 2.5, 21 (local politics); see further B. Rosenwein, *Emotional Communities in the Early Middle Ages* (Ithaca, NY, 2006), pp. 130–55; *Vita Desiderii*, ed. B. Krusch, *MGH, SRM*, vol. 4 (Hanover, 1902), pp. 563–602, cc. 1–8, 12–13 (career), 16, 17, 31 (building), 29, 30, 34 (huge wealth). Eligius: J. Lafaurie, 'Eligius Monetarius', *Revue numismatique*, 6th ser., 19 (1977), pp. 111–51; M. F. Hendy, 'From Public to Private', pp. 65–8.

Chapter 6

The most detailed account of Visigothic Spain in English, E. A. Thompson, *The Goths in Spain* (Oxford, 1969), is outdated in methodology and approach; L. A. García Moreno, *Historia de España visigoda* (Madrid, 1989) is also flawed. Much better are D. Claude, *Adel, Kirche und Königtum im Westgotenreich* (Sigmaringen, 1971), and R. Collins, *Early Medieval Spain* (London, 1983); the latter, which goes up to 1000, is now comprehensively updated and filled out in idem, *Visigothic Spain 409–711* (Oxford, 2004), which is now the best place to start. A short and up-to-date synthesis is G. Ripoll and I. Velázquez, *La Hispania visigoda* (Madrid, 1995).

For Italy, see C. Wickham, *Early Medieval Italy* (London, 1981), P. Cammarosano, *Nobili e re* (Bari, 1998), C. La Rocca (ed.), *Italy in the Early Middle Ages* (Oxford, 2002), all of which go up to 1000, and G. Tabacco, *The Struggle for Power in Medieval Italy* (Cambridge, 1989), which goes up to 1350. N. Christie, *The Lombards* (Oxford, 1995), and P. Delogu, 'Il regno longobardo', in G. Galasso (ed.), *Storia d'Italia*, vol. 1 (Turin, 1980), pp. 3–216, cover Lombard areas; important rethinkings are found in P. Cammarosano and S. Gasparri (eds.), *Langobardia* (Udine, 1990), W. Pohl and P. Erhart (eds.), *Die Langobarden* (Vienna, 2005), and P. Delogu (ed.), *The Langobards* (Woodbridge, 2009). T. S. Brown, *Gentlemen and Officers* (Rome, 1984) is a brilliant survey of Byzantine Italy, now to be supplemented by E. Zanini, *Le Italie bizantine* (Bari, 1998), for the archaeology. The basic archaeology-based survey of Italy is N. Christie, *From Constantine to Charlemagne* (Aldershot, 2006). For Rome, see among many J. Richards, *The Popes and the Papacy in the Early Middle Ages* (London, 1979) and T. F. X. Noble, *The Republic of St Peter* (Philadelphia, 1984).

p. 130. Councils of Toledo: see J. Vives (ed.), *Concilios visigóticos e hispano-romanos* (Barcelona, 1963), XII Toledo cc. 1, 2, cf. VI Toledo c. 17, IV Toledo c. 75; for unction, Julian of Toledo, *Historia Wambae*, ed. W. Levison, *MGH, SRM*, vol. 5 (Hanover, 1910), pp. 500–535, cc. 2–4, trans. J. M. Pizarro, *The Story of Wamba* (Washington, 2005), pp. 179–84.

p. 132. Ceramic production: L. C. Juan Tovar and J. F. Blanco García, 'Cerámica comun tardorromana', *Archivo español de arqueología*, 70 (1997), pp. 171–219; for a survey in English, see P. Reynolds, in K. Bowes and M. Kulikowski (eds.), *Hispania in Late Antiquity* (Leiden, 2005), pp. 403–10; the whole book is now the essential account of late Roman Spain.

p. 132. Semi-autonomous communities: John of Biclar, *Chronicle*, trans. K. B. Wolf, *Conquerors and Chroniclers of Early Medieval Spain* (Liverpool, 1990), pp. 61–80, cc. 36, 27, 61, 32, 20, with Braulio, *Life of Aemilian*, trans. A. T. Fear, *Lives of the Visigothic Fathers* (Liverpool, 1997), pp. 15–43, cc. 18, 22, 24, 33. For Spain up to 600, see M. Kulikowski, *Late Roman Spain and its Cities* (Baltimore, 2004), pp. 151–309.

p. 132. Mérida: *Lives of the Fathers of Mérida*, trans. Fear, *Lives*, pp. 45–105, 4.2.15–18, 5.3; for churches, P. Mateos Cruz, 'Augusta Emerita', in G. Ripoll and J. M. Gurt (eds.), *Sedes regiae (ann. 400–800)* (Barcelona, 2000), pp. 491–520, at pp. 506–16.

p. 133. Northern collectivities: for a survey, see S. Castellanos and I. Martín Viso, in *EME*, 13 (2005), pp. 1–42.

p. 133. Taxation: Cassidorus, *Variae*, ed. T. Mommsen, *MGH, Auctores Antiquissimi*, 12 (Berlin, 1894), 5. 39; Vives, *Concilios*, p. 54.

p. 133. Leovigild and Mérida: R. Collins, 'Merida and Toledo: 550–585', in E. James (ed.), *Visigothic Spain* (Oxford, 1980), pp. 189–219.

p. 133. Toledo: I. Velázquez and G. Ripoll, in Ripoll and Gurt, *Sedes regiae*, pp. 521–78.

p. 134. Fredegar, *Chronica*, ed. and trans. J.-M. Wallace-Hadrill, *The Fourth Book of the Chronicle of Fredegar* (London 1960), 4.82.

p. 135. Councils of bishops: see R. Stocking, *Bishops, Councils and Consensus in the Visigothic Kingdom, 589–633* (Ann Arbor, 2000).

p. 135. Chindasuinth: Fredegar, *Chronica*, 4.82; *Leges Visigothorum*, ed. K. Zeumer, *MGH, Leges*, vol. 1 (Hanover, 1902), 2.1.8; XIII Toledo c. 1; and Claude, *Adel*, pp. 115–33. For Eugenius, *MGH, Auctores Antiquissimi*, vol. 14, ed. F. Vollmer (Berlin, 1905), pp. 250–51.

p. 135. Ervig and Egica: *Leges Visigothorum*, 6.5.12–14, 9.2.8–9; XV Toledo. Laws: see P. D. King, *Law and Society in the Visigothic Kingdom* (Cambridge, 1972); on territoriality I follow I. Velázquez, in P. Heather (ed.), *The Visigoths* (Woodbridge, 1999), pp. 225–59, and Collins, *Early Medieval Spain*, pp. 27–30, 123–5.

p. 136. Byzantine models and victory ceremonies: see M. McCormick, *Eternal Victory* (Cambridge, 1986), pp. 297–327; J. Herrin, *The Formation of Christendom* (Princeton, 1987), pp. 227–49, brings out the ambiguities in Visigothic attitudes to the East.

p. 136. Jews: see King, *Law and Society*, pp. 130–45.

p. 137. *Officium palatinum*: see P. C. Díaz, in Heather, *The Visigoths*, pp. 321–56, at pp. 335–48; A. Isla Frez, 'El "officium palatinum" visigodo', *Hispania*, 62 (2002), pp. 823–47; Claude, *Adel*, pp. 198–210.

p. 137. Ervig and Egica: XII Toledo, *Tomus*, in Vives, *Concilios; Leges Visigothorum*, 9.1.21.

p. 137. Archaeology: C. Wickham, *Framing the Early Middle Ages* (Oxford, 2005), pp. 656–65, 741–58.

p. 138. Slates: I. Velázquez Soriano (ed.), *Documentos de época visigoda escritos en pizarra (siglos VI–VIII)* (Turnhout, 2000); n. 75 for Toledo.

p. 138. Army: D. Pérez Sánchez, *El ejército en la sociedad visigoda* (Salamanca, 1989), pp. 146–74.

p. 138. Church and oaths: A. Barbero and M. Vigil, *La formación del feudalismo en la Península Ibérica* (Barcelona, 1978), pp. 53–104, 126 ff.; a very important book.

p. 138. Isidore: see above all J. Fontaine, *Isidore de Séville et la culture classique dans l'Espagne wisigothique*, 2nd edn. (Paris, 1983); a neat cultural survey is in Collins, *Early Medieval Spain*, pp. 59–87. Braulio's letters are trans. C. W. Barlow, *Iberian Fathers*, vol. 2 (Washington, 1969), pp. 15–112.

p. 139. Strong Visigothic state: I follow R. Collins, *The Arab Conquest of Spain, 710–97* (Oxford, 1989), pp. 7–22; Claude, *Adel*, pp. 204–10.

p. 139. Break-up of Spain: E. Manzano Moreno, *Conquistadores, emires y califas* (Barcelona, 2006), pp. 34–53.

p. 140. Structural separation: F. Marazzi, in R. Hodges and W. Bowden (eds.), *The Sixth Century* (Leiden, 1998), pp. 119–59, at pp. 152–9.

p. 141. Byzantine militarization: Brown, *Gentlemen*, pp. 39–108.

p. 141. Queens: P. Skinner, *Women in Medieval Italian Society 500–1200* (London, 2001), pp. 56–8.

p. 142. Agilulf: see Paul the Deacon, *History of the Langobards*, trans. W. D. Foulke (Philadelphia, 1907), 4.1–40; cf. McCormick, *Eternal Victory*, pp. 287–96. For the seventh century as a whole, see P. Delogu, in idem, *The Langobards*.

p. 142. Arianism: S. Fanning, 'Lombard Arianism Reconsidered', *Speculum*, 56 (1981), pp. 241–58.

p. 142. *Edict* of Rothari: trans. K. F. Drew, *The Lombard Laws* (Philadelphia, 1973), pp. 39–130; for Lombard views of the past, see W. Pohl, in Y. Hen and M. Innes (eds.), *The Uses of the Past in the Early Middle Ages* (Cambridge, 2000), pp. 9–28.

p. 143. Liutprand's laws: trans. Drew, *The Lombard Laws*, pp. 144–214; cited are cc. 136, 135, 6. For eighth-century politics and the state, see P. Delogu, in *NCMH*, vol. 2, pp. 290–303.

p. 144. Military culture: S. Gasparri, in *Rivista storica italiana*, 98 (1986), pp. 664–726; pp. 681–3 for wills.

p. 144. Judgements: *CDL*, vol. 2, n. 255, vol. 3, nn. 6, 12, 13, vol. 1, nn. 19, 20; see S. Gasparri, in Cammarosano and Gasparri, *Langobardia*, pp. 237–305, at pp. 241–54.

p. 145. Legislation and governmental writing: N. Everett, *Literacy in Lombard Italy, c. 568–774* (Cambridge, 2003), pp. 163–96, with *CDL*, vol. 4.2, nn. 39, 45 for Benevento.

p. 145. Cities: Paul, *History*, 5.36–41; see in general, D. Harrison, *The Early State and the Towns* (Lund, 1993).

p. 146. Aristocratic wealth and identity: C. Wickham, in A. C. Murray (ed.), *After Rome's Fall* (Toronto, 1998), pp. 153–70; Cammarosano, *Nobili*, pp. 74–83; G. Tabacco, 'La connessione fra potere e possesso nel regno franco e nel regno longobardo', *Settimane di studio*, 20 (1972), pp. 133–68.

p. 146. Taxation: W. Pohl, in idem (ed.), *Kingdoms of the Empire* (Leiden, 1997), pp. 75–133, at pp. 112–31.

p. 146. Cities in Italy: Wickham, *Framing*, pp. 644–56; Christie, *From Constantine to Charlemagne*, pp. 183–280, currently the fullest account in English; R. Meneghini and

R. Santangeli Valenzani, *Roma nell'alto medioevo* (Rome, 2004), the basic archaeological survey of the largest Italian city.

p. 146. Naples: P. Arthur, *Naples* (London, 2002), pp. 16–20; Venice: M. Pavan and G. Arnaldi, in L. C. Ruggini *et al.* (eds.), *Storia di Venezia*, vol. 1 (Rome, 1992), pp. 432–51; Istria: C. Manaresi (ed.), *I placiti del regnum Italiae*, vol. 1 (Rome, 1955), n. 17.

p. 147. Sergius I: *The Book of Pontiffs*, trans. R. Davis (Liverpool, 1989), p. 85.

p. 147. Roman hierarchies: Noble, *Republic*, pp. 212–55; P. Toubert, '*Scrinium* et *palatium*', *Settimane di studio*, 48 (2001), pp. 57–117.

Chapter 7

The historiography in English on the topics covered in this chapter is, for obvious reasons, very extensive. On Wales, the least fully studied area, W. Davies, *Wales in the Early Middle Ages* (Leicester, 1982) is basic. On England, F. M. Stenton, *Anglo-Saxon England*, 3rd edn. (Oxford, 1971) and J. Campbell (ed.), *The Anglo-Saxons* (Oxford, 1982) are respectively the classic and the best (relatively) recent overview. On early Anglo-Saxon kingdoms, equally basic are S. Bassett (ed.), *The Origins of Anglo-Saxon Kingdoms* (Leicester, 1989) and B. Yorke, *Kings and Kingdoms of Early Anglo-Saxon England* (London, 1990). For early Anglo-Saxon archaeology, see C. J. Arnold, *An Archaeology of the Early Anglo-Saxon Kingdoms*, 2nd edn. (London, 1997).

On Ireland, F. J. Byrne, *Irish Kings and High-kings* (London, 1973), N. Edwards, *The Archaeology of Early Medieval Ireland* (London, 1999), and T. M. Charles-Edwards, *Early Christian Ireland* (Cambridge, 2000) are the key points of reference; shorter overviews are G. Mac Niocaill, *Ireland before the Vikings* (Dublin, 1972) and D. Ó Cróinín, *Early Medieval Ireland, 400–1200* (London, 1995). D. Ó Cróinín (ed.), *A New History of Ireland*, vol. 1 (Dublin, 2005), awaited for decades, contains valuable essays and has extensive bibliographies, but is sketchier on political structure. For the church, apart from Charles-Edwards, see K. Hughes, *The Church in Early Irish Society* (London, 1966) and L. Bitel, *Isle of the Saints* (Ithaca, NY, 1990).

On Scotland, M. O. Anderson, *Kings and Kingship in Early Scotland*, 2nd edn. (Edinburgh, 1980) is the basic account; A. A. M. Duncan, *Scotland: The Making of the Kingdom* (Edinburgh, 1975) goes up to 1286; A. P. Smyth, *Warlords and Holy Men* (London, 1984) is a well-argued alternative view. The historiographies of Ireland and Scotland in this period remain in flux, with sharply divergent basic interpretations. T. M. Charles-Edwards (ed.), *After Rome* (Oxford, 2003) is the only attempt to link four historiographies together; W. Davies, 'Celtic Kingships in the Early Middle Ages', in A. J. Duggan (ed.), *Kings and Kingship in Medieval Europe* (London, 1993), pp. 101–24, and in *NCMH*, vol. 1, pp. 232–62, links three of them.

p. 150. Samson: R. Fawtier (ed.), *La Vie de Saint Samson* (Paris, 1912), pp. 92–155.

p. 151. Economic meltdown: A. S. Esmonde-Cleary, *The Ending of Roman Britain* (London, 1989); for Hadrian's Wall and the countryside, P. Dark, *The Environment of Britain in the First Millennium AD* (London, 2000), pp. 140–56.

p. 151. Post-Roman polities: D. Dumville, in G. Ausenda (ed.), *After Empire* (Woodbridge, 1995), pp. 177–216, and C. A. Snyder, *An Age of Tyrants* (Stroud, 1998) are the best of many competing accounts. Gildas is trans. in M. Winterbottom, *Gildas: The Ruin of Britain and Other Documents* (Chichester, 1978).

p. 151. Arthur: see T. M. Charles-Edwards and P. Sims-Williams, in R. Bromwich *et al.* (eds.), *Arthur of the Welsh* (Cardiff, 1991), pp. 15–71.

p. 152. Ergyng, etc.: see W. Davies, *An Early Welsh Microcosm* (London, 1978), pp. 65–107; eadem, 'Land and Power in Early Medieval Wales', *Past and Present*, 81 (1978), pp. 3–23.

p. 153. Hill-fort sites: E. Campbell, in K. R. Dark (ed.), *External Contacts and the Economy* *of Late Roman and Post-Roman Britain* (Woodbridge, 1996), pp. 83–96; J. Wooding, *Communication and Commerce along the Western Sealanes*, AD 400–800 (Oxford, 1996), pp. 41–54.

p. 153. Cadwallon: Bede, *HE*, 2.20, 3.1.

p. 154. Poems: *Marwnad Cynddylan*, trans. and commentary in J. Rowland, *Early Welsh Saga Poetry* (Cambridge, 1990), pp. 120–41, 174–8 (see also Davies, *Wales*, pp. 99–102); *Y Gododdin*, trans. K. Jackson, *The Gododdin* (Edinburgh, 1969), pp. 141–2 and 118 for quotes.

p. 155. Picts: see I. Henderson, *The Picts* (London, 1967), and Anderson, *Kings*, pp. 119–31, 165–204, for the standard view, contested in various ways by Smyth, *Warlords*, pp. 57–83; D. Broun, 'Pictish Kings 761–839', in S. M. Foster (ed.), *The St Andrews Sarcophagus* (Dublin, 1998), pp. 71–83; B. T. Hudson, *The Kings of Celtic Scotland* (Westport, Conn., 1994), pp. 8–33, not all of whom I follow. Even Pictish matriliny is contested; see the overview in A. Woolf, 'Pictish Matriliny Reconsidered', *Innes Review*, 49 (1998), pp. 147–67; see also idem, in *Scottish Historical Review*, 85 (2006), pp. 182–201, for the location of Fortriu.

p. 156. *Regiones*, etc.: see S. Bassett, in idem, *The Origins*, pp. 3–27; C. Scull, in *Anglo-Saxon Studies in Archaeology and History*, 6 (1993), pp. 65–82; J. Blair, *Anglo-Saxon Oxfordshire* (Stroud, 1994), pp. 29–32; H. Hamerow, in *NCMH*, vol. 1, pp. 263–88. For the Fens, W. Davies and H. Vierck, 'The Contexts of Tribal Hidage', *Frühmittelalterliche Studien*, 8 (1974), pp. 223–93. The date of the *Tribal Hidage* is disputed.

p. 157. Archaeology: Arnold, *An Archaeology*, esp. pp. 33–100; H. Hamerow, *Early Medieval Settlements* (Oxford, 2002), pp. 46–51, 93–9; C. Hills, *Origins of the English* (London, 2003).

p. 158. Yeavering: B. Hope-Taylor, *Yeavering* (London, 1977).

p. 159. Mercia: N. P. Brooks, in Bassett, *The Origins*, pp. 159–70; S. Bassett, in *Anglo-Saxon Studies in Archaeology and History*, 11 (2000), pp. 107–18.

p. 159. Texts: *Beowulf* has many translations; S. Heaney, *Beowulf* (London, 1999) is a poetic classic; but I have used that in S. A. J. Bradley, *Anglo-Saxon Poetry* (London, 1982), pp. 408–94. Felix, *Life of St Guthlac*, ed. and trans. B. Colgrave, *Felix's Life of Saint Guthlac* (Cambridge, 1956), here cc. 16–18. The *Anglo-Saxon Chronicle* has a convenient trans. in *EHD*, vol. 1, 2nd edn. (London, 1979), pp. 146–261, here at pp. 175–6, 180; see S. D. White, in *Viator*, 20 (1989), pp. 1–18, by far the best analysis of 786 in Wessex.

p. 160. Bede on land: *Letter to Ecgbert*, trans. *EHD*, vol. 1, pp. 799–810.

p. 160. Ports: the best recent surveys are C. Scull, in J. Hines (ed.), *The Anglo-Saxons* (Woodbridge, 1997), pp. 269–310; D. Hill and R. Cowie (eds.), *Wics* (Sheffield, 2001). The classic is R. Hodges, *Dark Age Economics* (London, 1982).

p. 161. Exiles: e.g. *The Wanderer*, trans. *EHD*, vol. 1, pp. 870–71; Felix, *Life of St Guthlac*, cc. 40, 42.

p. 161. Land units becoming estates: R. Faith, *The English Peasantry and the Growth of Lordship* (Leicester, 1997).

p. 161. Conversion: see B. Yorke, *The Conversion of Britain, 600–800* (Harlow, 2006); J. Blair, *The Church in Anglo-Saxon Society* (Oxford, 2005), pp. 8–181; H. Mayr-Harting, *The Coming of Christianity to Anglo-Saxon England*, 3rd edn. (London, 1991); J. Campbell, *Essays in Anglo-Saxon History* (London, 1986), pp. 1–84; P. Wormald, 'Bede, "Beowulf" and the Conversion of the Anglo-Saxon Aristocracy', in R. T. Farrell (ed.), *Bede and Anglo-Saxon England* (Oxford, 1978), pp. 32–95.

p. 162. Church organization: C. Cubitt, *Anglo-Saxon Church Councils, c.650–c.850* (Leicester, 1995). Bede's imagery: P. Wormald, in idem (ed.), *Ideal and Reality in Frankish and Anglo-Saxon Society* (Oxford, 1983), pp. 99–129; N. Brooks, *Bede and the English* (Jarrow, 1999).

p. 163. Law: P. Wormald, *Legal Culture in the Early Medieval West* (London, 1999), pp. 179–99.

p. 163. The end of autonomous kingdoms: Yorke, *Kings*, pp. 31–2, 51; H. P. R. Finberg, *The Early Charters of the West Midlands*, 2nd edn. (Leicester, 1972), pp. 177–80.

p. 163. Common burdens: N. Brooks, *Communities and Warfare, 700–1400* (London, 2000), pp. 32–47.

p. 163. Offa's Dyke: P. Squatriti, in *Past and Present*, 176 (2002), pp. 11–65.

p. 163. Coins: P. Grierson and M. Blackburn, *Medieval European Coinage*, vol. 1 (Cambridge, 1986), pp. 158, 277–82; J. Story, *Carolingian Connections* (Aldershot, 2003), pp. 190–5. Councils: Cubitt, *Church Councils.*

p. 164. Canterbury: N. P. Brooks, *The Early History of the Church of Canterbury* (Leicester, 1984), pp. 111–27.

p. 164. Civil wars in Wessex, Mercia and Northumbria: P. Wormald, in Campbell, *The Anglo-Saxons*, pp. 114–16.

p. 164. Offa and Charlemagne: J. M. Wallace-Hadrill, *Early Germanic Kingship in England and on the Continent* (Oxford, 1971), pp. 98–123; Story, *Carolingian Connections*, pp. 169–211.

p. 165. Clientship in Ireland: see F. Kelly, *A Guide to Early Irish Law* (Dublin, 1988), pp. 29–33 (the whole book is the best survey of the law tracts); T. M. Charles-Edwards, *Early Irish and Welsh Kinship* (Oxford, 1993), pp. 337–63; idem, '*Críth Gablach* and the Law of Status', *Peritia*, 5 (1986), pp. 53–73; N. Patterson, *Cattle-lords and Clansmen*, 2nd edn. (Notre Dame, Ind., 1994), pp. 150–78.

p. 166. Expansion of kingdoms: D. Ó Corráin, 'Nationality and Kingship in Pre-Norman Ireland', in T. W. Moody (ed.), *Nationality and the Pursuit of National Independence* (Belfast, 1978), pp. 1–35, esp. pp. 9–10.

p. 166. *Críth Gablach*: trans. E. O. MacNeill, in *Proceedings of the Royal Irish Academy*, 36 C (1921–4), pp. 281–306; here p. 304, translation modified.

p. 166. Gessa: Byrne, *Irish Kings*, p. 23 (and in general pp. 15–35 for rituals).

p. 166. Fifth century: see esp. Charles-Edwards, *Early Christian Ireland*, pp. 441–68.

p. 167. Diarmait and Báetán: Byrne, *Irish Kings*, pp. 87–114.

p. 167. Cathal, Donnchad, Feidlimid: Byrne, *Irish Kings*, pp. 202–29; Charles-Edwards, *Early Christian Ireland*, pp. 594–8.

p. 168. Bishops and monasteries: see Charles-Edwards, *Early Christian Ireland*, pp. 241–81, 416–29; M. Herbert, *Iona, Kells and Derry* (Oxford, 1988), esp. pp. 53–6. Columba is the subject of the Irish world's emblematic saint's life, trans. most recently in R. Sharpe, *Adomnán of Iona: Life of St Columba* (Harmondsworth, 1995). The classic here is Hughes, *Church in Early Irish Society.*

p. 169. Picts: for debates, see notes to p. 155; for Dál Riata see J. Bannerman, *Studies in the History of Dalriada* (Edinburgh, 1974); Anderson, *Kings*, pp. 145–65, 179 ff.; R. Sharpe, 'The Thriving of Dalriada', in S. Taylor (ed.), *Kings, Clerics and Chronicles in Scotland, 500–1297* (Dublin, 2000), pp. 47–61.

p. 169. Kenneth, etc.: see Anderson, *Kings*, pp. 196–200; Hudson, *Kings*, pp. 36–47; P. Wormald, in B. Crawford (ed.), *Scotland in Dark Age Britain* (St Andrews, 1996), pp. 131–60.

Chapter 8

The key overviews which cover this chapter as a whole are P. Brown, *The Rise of Western Christendom* (2nd edn., Oxford 1997), and J. M. H. Smith, *Europe after Rome* (Oxford, 2005), which is the best current synthesis of cultural history. See further B. Rosenwein, *Emotional Communities in the Early Middle Ages* (Ithaca, NY, 2006). For the interface between Christianity and traditional cultures, V. I. J. Flint, *The Rise of Magic in Early Medieval Europe* (Oxford, 1993) is essential; for East and West, so is J. Herrin, *The Formation of Christendom* (Princeton, 1987). J. M. Wallace-Hadrill, *The Frankish Church* (Oxford, 1983) is a valuable overview. R. McKitterick (ed.), *The Early Middle Ages* (Oxford, 2001), covers social and cultural history. For social history as a whole, the best surveys are in

French, P. Depreux, *Les Sociétés occidentales du milieu du VIe à la fin du IXe siècle* (Rennes, 2002) and R. Le Jan, *La Société du haut Moyen Âge* (Paris, 2003). All these books cover the Carolingian period as well. For gender, see the notes to p. 195.

p. 170. Valerius: ed. and trans. C. M. Aherne, *Valerio of Bierzo* (Washington, 1949).

p. 170. Martin of Braga: *De Correctione Rusticorum* is trans. C. W. Barlow, *Iberian fathers*, vol. 1 (Washington, 1969), pp. 71–85. Slate text: I. Velázquez Soriano (ed.), *Documentos de época visigoda escritos en pizarra (siglos VI–VIII)* (Turnhout, 2000), n. 104.

p. 171. Weather magic: Flint, *Rise of Magic*, pp. 110–15, 187–90. Gregory: *The Miracles of the Bishop St Martin*, trans. R. Van Dam, *Saints and their Miracles in Late Antique Gaul* (Princeton, 1993), pp. 200–303, 1.34 (cf. 1.11 and Gregory of Tours, *Histories*, trans. L. Thorpe as *The History of the Franks* (Harmondsworth 1974), 5.37 for Martin of Braga). Note that manuscripts of *De Correctione* were available in Gaul by the start of the seventh century, and thus perhaps in Gregory's lifetime: see Y. Hen, in E. Cohen and M. B. de Jong (eds.), *Medieval Transformations* (Leiden, 2001), pp. 35–49.

p. 171. Gregory's letters: see R. A. Markus, *Gregory the Great and his World* (Cambridge, 1997), pp. 206–9, and more generally pp. 163–87.

p. 172. Gregories: Gregory the Great, *Letters*, 1.41, trans. J. R. C. Martyn, *The Letters of Gregory the Great* (Toronto, 2004); Gregory of Tours, *Histories*, 9.15 for Toledo, 5.43, 6.40 for dinner-time polemics.

p. 172. Priscillianists: I Braga, c. 8, in J. Vives (ed.), *Concilios visigóticos e hispano-romanos* (Barcelona, 1963).

p. 173. Literacy: see in general R. McKitterick (ed.), *The Uses of Literacy in Early Medieval Europe* (Cambridge, 1990).

p. 173. Gregory of Tours: see M. Bonnet, *Le Latin de Grégoire de Tours* (Paris, 1890), pp. 48–76.

p. 173. Bede's library: Bede, *Lives of the Abbots of Wearmouth and Jarrow*, trans. J. F. Webb, *The Age of Bede* (Harmondsworth, 1983), pp. 185–208, cc. 4, 6, 9; for polemics, Bede, *Letter to Plegwin*, in idem, *The Reckoning of Time*, trans. F. Wallis (Liverpool, 1999), pp. 405–15.

p. 174. Gregory's unpopularity: see P. Llewellyn, in *Journal of Ecclesiastical History*, 25 (1974), pp. 363–80.

p. 174. Columbanus: *Sancti Columbani Opera*, ed. and trans. G. S. M. Walker (Dublin, 1957), *letter 5*.

p. 174. 'Micro-Christendoms': Brown, *Rise of Western Christendom*, ch. 13.

p. 175. Prostitutes: Boniface, *The Letters of Saint Boniface*, trans. E. Emerton (New York, 1940), *letter 72*; passports: Ratchis, law 13, trans. K. F. Drew, *The Lombard Laws* (Philadelphia, 1973), p. 224, cf. W. Pohl, in idem *et al.* (eds.), *The Transformation of Frontiers* (Leiden, 2001), pp. 117–41.

p. 176. Irminsul: *Royal Frankish Annals*, trans. B. W. Scholz, *Carolingian Chronicles* (Ann Arbor, 1970), pp. 48–9. See in general for the issue of paganism J. Palmer, in *EME*, 15 (2007), pp. 402–25.

p. 176. Eostre: Bede, *The Reckoning of Time*, pp. 53–4.

p. 176. Eligius: *Vita Eligii*, trans. J. A. McNamara, http://www.fordham.edu/halsall/basis/eligius.html, 2.16, 20. Boniface on Rome: *Letters*, 40–41.

p. 177. Gregory: *Histories*, 6.6, 8.15–16 (ascetics), 9.6, cf. 10.25 for further south (unauthorized miracle-workers), 5.21, 8.34 (Winnoch), with *Life of the Fathers*, trans. E. James (Liverpool, 1985), 2.2 (dead saints). For bishops and cults, see R. Van Dam, *Leadership and Community in Late Antique Gaul* (Berkeley, 1985), pp. 179–201, 230–76; idem, *Saints and their Miracles*, pp. 50–81.

p. 178. Gregory the Great: Markus, *Gregory the Great*, pp. 17–31. Gregory on ascetics: see his *Dialogues*, trans. O. J. Zimmerman (Washington, 1959).

p. 178. Muirchu: *Life of St Patrick*, trans. A. B. E. Hood, *St Patrick* (Chichester, 1978), pp. 81–98, cc. 17, 18, 24, 26, 29.

p. 178. Cuthbert: see *Two Lives of Saint Cuthbert*, ed. and trans. B. Colgrave (Cambridge, 1940).

p. 178. Aldebert: Boniface, *Letters*, 47.

p. 179. 'Rustic': Bede, *Life of Cuthbert* (in *Two Lives*, pp. 143–307), c. 3; cf. P. Brown, *The Cult of the Saints* (Chicago, 1981), pp. 119–27.

p. 179. Martin: Van Dam, *Saints and their Miracles*.

p. 179. Six cult sites: *Vita Balthildis*, trans. in P. Fouracre and R. Gerberding, *Late Merovingian France* (Manchester, 1996), pp. 118–32, c. 9; cf. Fredegar, *Chronica*, ed. and trans. J. M. Wallace-Hadrill, *The Fourth Book of the Chronicle of Fredegar* (London, 1960), 4.54, and Van Dam, *Saints and their Miracles*, pp. 22–7.

p. 180. Martin's body: Gregory, *Histories*, 1.48.

p. 180. Wonder-workers: see Flint, *Rise of Magic*, a remarkable analysis. Laws: Rothari 376, Liutprand 84–5, trans. Drew, *The Lombard Laws: Laws of the Salian Franks*, trans. K. F. Drew (Philadelphia, 1991), c. 19.

p. 180. Gregory: Van Dam, *Saints and their Miracles*, pp. 191–2 (plague); Gregory of Tours, *Histories*, 7.44, 5.14; for the *sortes*, Flint, *Rise of Magic*, pp. 220–6, 273–86.

p. 181. Anglo-Saxon medicine: texts are ed. and trans. O. Cockayne, *Leechdoms, Wortcunning and Starcraft of Early England*, 3 vols. (London 1864–6); see K. L. Jolly, *Popular Religion in Late Saxon England* (Chapel Hill, NC, 1996).

p. 182. Doctors: Gregory of Tours, *Histories*, 5.6 (but cf. 5.35); *Miracles of the Bishop St Martin*, 2.1; Flint, *Rise of Magic*, p. 150 for Caesarius; *Lives of the Fathers of Mérida*, trans. A. T. Fear, *Lives of the Visigothic Fathers* (Liverpool, 1997), 4.1–2.

p. 182. Parishes: for Lucca, M. Giusti and P. Guidi (eds.), *Rationes decimarum Italiae nei secoli XIII e XIV. Tuscia*, vol. 2 (Rome, 1942), pp. 255–85; for Francia, Le Jan, *La Société*, pp. 61–3; for England, J. Blair, *The Church in Anglo-Saxon Society* (Oxford, 2005), pp. 79–134, 368–504; for a comparative discussion of rural churches in the West, S. Wood, *The Proprietary Church in the Medieval West* (Oxford, 2006), pp. 33–108.

p. 183. Daniel: Boniface, *Letters*, 51, 92.

p. 183. Ravenna: Agnellus, *The Book of Pontiffs of the Church of Ravenna*, trans. D. Mauskopf Deliyannis (Washington, 2004), pp. 248–53.

p. 183. Prisoner miracles: e.g. Venantius Fortunatus, *Vita Germani*, MGH, SRM, vol. 7 (Hanover, 1920), pp. 372–418, cc. 10, 30–1, 61, 66–7; *Vita Eligii*, MGH, SRM, vol. 4 (Hanover, 1902), pp. 663–741, 1.31, 2.15, 66, 80 (also available from the website cited in n. to p 176); *Vita Amandi*, MGH, SRM, vol. 5 (Hanover, 1920) pp. 428–49, c. 14; Arbeo, *Vita Corbiniani*, MGH, SRM, vol. 6 (Hanover, 1913), pp. 560–93, cc. 10–13, all ed. by B. Krusch and W. Levison.

p. 183. Ransoming: in general, see W. Klingshirn, in *Journal of Roman Studies*, 77 (1985), pp. 183–203.

p. 183. Fidelis, Masona: *Lives of the Fathers of Mérida*, 4.7–9, 5.8.19, cf. Sisebut, *Life of Desiderius*, trans. Fear, *Lives*, pp. 1–14, c. 11. (The Mérida text partially copies Sisebut's *Life*, hence similarities in phrasing.)

p. 184. Praeiectus of Clermont: *Passio Praeiecti*, trans. in Fouracre and Gerberding, *Late Merovingian France*, cc. 24, 29–31; *Vita Boniti*, ed. Krusch, MGH, SRM, vol. 6, pp. 119–39.

p. 184. War: F. Prinz, *Klerus und Krieg im früheren Mittelalter* (Stuttgart, 1971), pp. 46–72. Savaric and Hainmar: P. Fouracre, *The Age of Charles Martel* (Harlow, 2000), pp. 90, 92. Trier: E. Ewig, *Trier im Merowingerreich* (Trier, 1954), pp. 133–43. Walprand: *CDL*, vol. 1, n. 114.

p. 185. Columba, etc.: M. Herbert, *Iona, Kells and Derry* (Oxford, 1988), pp. 36–67; Bede, *HE*, 4.23; *Vita Geretrudis*, trans. in Fouracre and Gerberding, *Late Merovingian France*, pp. 319–29, c. 1. For monastic expansion in general, see M. Dunn, *The Emergence of Monasticism* (Oxford, 2000), pp. 107–208; for the associated hagiography, see A.-M. Helvétius, *Le Saint et le moine* (Paris, in press). For an important comparative analysis of the complexity of control over monasteries across Europe, see Wood, *Proprietary Church*, pp. 109–244. Note that 'monasteries', here and later, include nunneries, and also the double monasteries, with monks and nuns, headed by an abbess, which were common in this period.

p. 186. False monasteries: Bede, *Letter to Ecgbert*, trans. *EHD*, vol. 1, pp. 799–810, cc. 11–14 (cf. P. Sims-Williams, *Religion and Literature in Western England, 600–800* (Cambridge, 1990), pp. 126–9, and Blair, *Church*, pp. 100–108); *Regula Monastica Communis*, trans. C .W. Barlow, *Iberian Fathers*, vol. 2 (Washington, 1969), pp. 176–206, cc. 1, 2.

p. 186. Land: D. Herlihy, 'Church Property on the European Continent, 701–1200', *Speculum*, 36 (1961), pp. 81–105; for gift exchange, e.g. M. de Jong, *In Samuel's Image* (Leiden, 1996), pp. 267–77. The basic international starting point for gifts to churches is F. Bougard *et al.* (eds.), *Sauver son âme et se perpétuer* (Rome, 2005).

p. 187. Burial, etc.: see C. La Rocca, in L. Paroli (ed.), *L'Italia centro-settentrionale in età longobarda* (Florence, 1997), pp. 31–54; for paganism and competition, G. Halsall, *Early Medieval Cemeteries* (Glasgow, 1995), pp. 61–8, gives a succinct survey.

p. 187. Balthild: *Vita Balthildis*, c. 12.

p. 188. Sigeberht, Heremod: Bede, *HE*, 3.18; *Beowulf*, trans. S. A. J. Bradley, *Anglo-Saxon Poetry* (London, 1982), pp. 408–94, lines 1707–23.

p. 189. Hunting: see J. Jarnut, *Herrschaft und Ethnogenese im Frühmittelalter* (Münster, 2002), pp. 375–408; *Cap.*, vol. 1, nn. 23 c.17, 49 c.1, 140 c.7, 141 c.22.

p. 189. Eligius: *Vita Eligii*, 1. 11–12.

p. 189. Halls: Depreux, *Les Sociétés occidentales*, pp. 124–5. Drink: Y. Hen, *Culture and Religion in Merovingian Gaul, AD 481–751* (Leiden, 1995), pp. 234–49; for Salic law, G. A. Beckmann, 'Aus den letzten Jahrzehnten des Vulgärlateins in Frankreich', *Zeitschrift für romanische Philologie*, 79 (1963), pp. 305–34; *The Tale of Macc Da Thó's Pig* is trans. J. Gantz, *Early Irish Myths and Sagas* (Harmondsworth, 1981), pp. 179–87.

p. 190. Dining or not: Sulpicius Severus, *Vita Martini*, trans. in T. F. X. Noble and T. Head (eds.), *Soldiers of Christ* (State College, Pa., 1995), pp. 3–29, c. 20; *Vita Eucherii*, ed. Levison, *MGH, SRM*, vol. 7, pp. 46–53, c. 8.

p. 190. Wilfrid, etc.: Stephanus, *Vita Wilfridi*, ed. and trans. B. Colgrave, *The Life of Bishop Wilfrid by Eddius Stephanus* (Cambridge, 1927), c. 2; *Beowulf*, line 358; Bede, *HE*, 3.5.

p. 190. Wealhtheow: *Beowulf*, lines 607–41; see M. J. Enright, *Lady with the Mead Cup* (Dublin, 1996), pp. 2–37 and *passim*; cf. Theodelinda in Paul the Deacon, *History of the Langobards*, trans. W. D. Foulke (Philadelphia, 1907), 3.30.

p. 191. Argait: Paul the Deacon, *History*, 6.24; for military tactics, G. Halsall, *Warfare and Society in the Barbarian West, 450–900* (London, 2003), pp. 194–204.

p. 192. *Precariae*: for the politics see e.g. I. Wood, in W. Davies and P. Fouracre (eds.), *Property and Power in the Early Middle Ages* (Cambridge, 1995), pp. 31–52.

p. 192. Kin: see esp. R. Le Jan, *Famille et pouvoir dans le monde franc VIIe – Xe siècle* (Paris, 1995), pp. 159–262, 381–427; Smith, *Europe after Rome*, pp. 83–114.

p. 192. Ireland: see T. M. Charles-Edwards, *Early Irish and Welsh Kinship* (Oxford, 1993), pp. 49–61, 422 ff.; Italy: Liutprand 13, trans. Drew, *The Lombard Laws*.

p. 193. Feud: Liutprand 199; Gregory of Tours, *Histories*, 10.27, 7.47, 9.19. For an important critique of the idea of feud in this period see G. Halsall, in idem (ed.), *Violence and Society in the Early Medieval West* (Woodbridge, 1998), pp. 1–45; though I use a different definition of 'feud' from him, I have followed his analyses. For Frankish feud, see J. M. Wallace-Hadrill, *The Long-haired Kings* (London, 1962), pp. 121–47; P. Fouracre, in Halsall (ed.), *Violence*, pp. 60–75; P. Depreux, in D. Barthélemy *et al.* (eds.), *La Vengeance, 400–1200* (Rome, 2006), pp. 65–85.

p. 194. Landibert: *Vita Landiberti*, ed. Krusch, *MGH, SRM*, vol. 6, pp. 353–84, cc.11–17.

p. 194. Aristocratic status markers: Depreux, *Les Sociétés occidentales*, pp. 149–84; Le Jan, *La Société*, pp. 133–55; Bede, *HE*, 4.22.

p. 195. Women's roles: for gender in general, largely but not only seen through the optic of women's history, see S. F. Wemple, *Women in Frankish Society* (Philadelphia, 1981);

P. Skinner, *Women in Medieval Italian Society 500–1200* (London, 2001); L. M. Bitel, *Women in Early Medieval Europe 400–1100* (Cambridge, 2002); L. Brubaker and J. M. H. Smith (eds.), *Gender in the Early Medieval World* (Cambridge, 2004); Smith, *Europe after Rome*, pp. 115–47; J. L. Nelson, *The Frankish World, 750–900* (London, 1996), pp. 183–221 (brief and crucial insights); Le Jan, *La Société*, pp. 211–32; H.-W. Goetz, *Frauen im frühen Mittelalter* (Cologne, 1995); S. Lebecq *et al.* (eds.), *Femmes et pouvoirs des femmes à Byzance et en Occident* (Lille, 1999). For queens, P. Stafford, *Queens, Concubines and Dowagers* (London, 1983); J. L. Nelson, *Politics and Ritual in Early Medieval Europe* (London, 1986), pp. 1–48 for Merovingians; Gregory, *Histories*, 5.18, 39, 6.4.

p. 196. Erminethrudis and Burgundofara: ChLA, vol. 14, n. 592; J. Guérout, 'Le Testament de Sainte Fare', *Revue d'histoire ecclésiastique*, 60 (1965), pp. 761–821.

p. 196. Female monastic founders: see R. Le Jan, in M. de Jong and F. Theuws (eds.), *Topographies of Power in the Early Middle Ages* (Leiden, 2001), pp. 243–69. On women and double monasteries, see S. Foot, *Veiled Women*, vol. 1 (Aldershot, 2000), pp. 49–56.

p. 196. Plectrude: see Fouracre, *Charles Martel*, pp. 43–65; I. Wood, in Brubaker and Smith, *Gender*, pp. 234–56.

p. 197. Anglo-Saxons: see e.g. H. Leyser, *Medieval Women* (London, 1995), pp. 19–39.

p. 197. Visigoths and Lombards: John of Biclar, *Chronicle*, trans. K. B. Wolf, *Conquerors and Chroniclers of Early Medieval Spain* (Liverpool, 1990), cc. 55, 90; Paul the Deacon, *History*, 2.28–9, 3.30–4.41; CDL, vol. 4.2, nn. 39–42 (Scauniperga); Gregory the Great, *Letters*, 1.11, 3.1–2, 9.85, 10.6–7 (Clementina); Skinner, *Women*, pp. 54–9.

p. 199. Rottruda, Taneldis: CDL, vol. 2, n. 163, vol. 5, n. 50. On Taneldis, see C. La Rocca, in *Mélanges de l'École française de Rome: Moyen âge*, 111 (1999), pp. 933–50; on widows in general, J. L. Nelson, in Davies and Fouracre, *Property and Power*, pp. 82–113.

p. 199. Morning-gifts: L. Feller, *Les Abruzzes médiévales* (Rome, 1998), pp. 468–82. In general on dowries see F. Bougard *et al.* (eds.), *Dots et douaires dans le haut Moyen Âge* (Rome, 2002).

p. 199. Protection: Liutprand 120, 141, trans. Drew, *The Lombard Laws*; see Skinner, *Women*, pp. 35 ff; R. Balzaretti in Halsall, *Violence*, pp. 175–92, and, more generally, in W. Pohl and P. Erhart (eds.), *Die Langobarden* (Vienna, 2005), pp. 361–82.

p. 200. Britons: see e.g. T. M. Charles-Edwards, in R. Evans (ed.), *Lordship and Learning* (Woodbridge, 2004), pp. 11–37, at pp. 24–9. On ethnicity in general, see e.g. Smith, *Europe after Rome*, pp. 257–67 and *passim*.

p. 200. Memory: see Y. Hen and M. Innes, *The Uses of the Past in the Early Middle Ages* (Cambridge, 2000).

p. 201. Isidore: trans. Wolf, *Conquerors*, pp. 82–3.

p. 201. Guidebooks: see esp. the *Einsiedeln Itinerary*, ed. in R. Valentini and G. Zucchetti, *Codice topografico della città di Roma*, vol. 2 (Rome, 1942), pp. 176–207.

p. 201. Ireland: Smith, *Europe after Rome*, p. 285.

p. 201. Carolingians: M. Innes, in Hen and Innes, *Uses of the Past*, pp. 227–49; R. McKitterick, *History and Memory in the Carolingian World* (Cambridge, 2004), pp. 196–210; and eadem, *Perceptions of the Past in the Early Middle Ages* (Notre Dame, Ind., 2006), pp. 35–61, for a nuanced account of Carolingian attitudes to Rome and its buildings.

Chapter 9

For peasant society in this period, see P. Depreux, *Les Sociétés occidentales du milieu du VIe à la fin du IXe siècle* (Rennes, 2002); R. Le Jan, *La Société du haut Moyen Âge* (Paris, 2003); J.-P. Devroey, *Puissants et misérables* (Brussels, 2006); and the old classic, A. Dopsch, *Economic and Social Foundations of European Civilization* (London, 1937). For the economy, see J.-P. Devroey, *Économie rurale et société dans l'Europe franque (VIe–IXe siècles)* (Paris, 2003); M. McCormick, *Origins of the European Economy* (Cambridge, 2001); S.

Loseby and S. Lebecq, in *NCMH*, vol. 1, pp. 605–59; R. Hodges and D. Whitehouse, *Mohammed, Charlemagne and the Origins of Europe* (London, 1983); R. Hodges and W. Bowden (eds.), *The Sixth Century* (Leiden, 1998); I. L. Hansen and C. Wickham (eds.), *The Long Eighth Century* (Leiden, 2000). The classic here is G. Duby, *The Early Growth of the European Economy* (London, 1974). This chapter, more than others, reflects the arguments of my *Framing the Early Middle Ages* (Oxford, 2005) very closely; wider bibliographies will be found there. I have, however, as far as possible chosen different examples to illustrate the argument here.

p. 203. Anstruda and Campione: the documents are now all assembled, and both the text and Campione society are commented on from a variety of standpoints, in S. Gasparri and C. La Rocca (eds.), *Carte di famiglia* (Rome, 2005). Anstruda's text is document n. 1; the others cited are, respectively, nn. 3, 4, 2. (It does not seem to me likely that Anstruda was half-free to start with, as hypothesized by L. Feller, ibid., p. 203.) Anstruda on one level did not get such a good deal, for formula-books and other evidence from Francia show that free women who married unfree men could have all their children recognized as free: see A. Rio, in *Past and Present*, 193 (2006), pp. 16–23; Italy may have been more restrictive here.

p. 204. Aristocratic wealth: see Wickham, *Framing*, pp. 168–232, 314–64; for Bavaria, K. L. R. Pearson, *Conflicting Loyalties in Early Medieval Bavaria* (Aldershot, 1999), pp. 84–100.

p. 205. Rhineland: M. Innes, *State and Society in the Early Middle Ages* (Cambridge, 2000), pp. 51–68.

p. 206. Palaiseau: *Das Polyptichon von St.-Germain-des-Prés*, ed. D. Hägermann (Cologne, 1993), Section 2. For the society of the polyptychs, see E. Power, *Medieval People*, 10th edn. (London, 1963), pp. 18–38.

p. 207. Gœrsdorf: *Traditiones Wizenburgenses*, ed. K. Glöckner and A. Doll (Darmstadt, 1979), nn. 6, 7, 12, 15, 38, 43, 46, 78, 81, 92, 104, 114, 124, 128, 132, 142, 145, 150, 186; for Sigibald and the dukes, see H. J. Hummer, *Politics and Power in Early Medieval Europe* (Cambridge, 2005), pp. 46–63, 111–13; for Rhineland village societies in general, see F. Schwind, in H. Jankuhn *et al.* (eds.), *Das Dorf der Eisenzeit und des frühen Mittelalters* (Göttingen, 1977), pp. 444–93; for general issues of peasant society, see Wickham, *Framing*, pp. 383–588.

p. 208. Redon: see W. Davies, *Small Worlds* (London, 1988); pp. 153–4, 196 for Anau.

p. 211. Villages: see E. Zadora-Rio, in E. Mornet (ed.), *Campagnes médiévales* (Paris, 1993), pp. 145–53. An alternative view is in J. Chapelot and R. Fossier, *The Village and House in the Middle Ages* (London, 1985), pp. 71, 129; C. Lewis *et al.*, *Village, Hamlet and Field* (Macclesfield, 1997), pp. 191, 198–201.

p. 212. Policing of free–unfree line: P. Bonnassie, *From Slavery to Feudalism in South-western Europe* (Cambridge, 1991), pp. 19–25; mixed marriages in Palaiseau, etc.: H.-W. Goetz, *Frauen im frühen Mittelalter* (Cologne, 1995), pp. 263–7. On unfreedom, see in general W. Davies, in M. L. Bush (ed.), *Serfdom and Slavery* (Harlow, 1996), pp. 225–46.

p. 213. Weaving as 'womenly work': D. Herlihy, *Opera Muliebria* (New York, 1990).

p. 213. Peasant women: see in general Goetz, *Frauen*; P. Skinner, *Women in Medieval Italian Society 500–1200* (London, 2001), pp. 44–9.

p. 214. Army size: see in general G. Halsall, *Warfare and Society in the Barbarian West, 450–900* (London, 2003), esp. pp. 119–33, and p. 93 for Charlemagne; for England, R. P. Abels, *Lordship and Military Obligation in Anglo-Saxon England* (Berkeley, 1988), pp. 35–6.

p. 215. Leudast: Gregory of Tours, *Histories*, trans. L. Thorpe as *The History of the Franks* (Harmondsworth, 1974), 5.48.

p. 216. Woods and forests: C. Wickham, *Land and Power* (London, 1994), pp. 155–99.

p. 216. Villages: H. Hamerow, *Early Medieval Settlements* (Oxford, 2002), for northern Europe; for southern Europe, the best current overview is G. P. Brogiolo and A. Chavarría

NOTES TO CHAPTER 9

Arnau, *Aristocrazie e campagne nell'Occidente da Costantino a Carlo Magno* (Florence, 2005).

p. 216. Collective groups of villagers: L. Feller, *Les Abruzzes médiévales* (Rome, 1998), pp. 540–46; J. Jarrett, in *EME*, 12 (2003), pp. 241–8.

p. 217. Fall in settlement density: see e.g. T. Williamson, *The Origins of Norfolk* (Manchester, 1993), pp. 57–8.

p. 217. Plague: see above all the articles collected in L. K. Little (ed.), *Plague and the End of Antiquity* (Cambridge, 2007), authoritative but in my view too sure of the plague's serious effect, and the divergent view of J. Durliat in *Hommes et richesses dans l'empire byzantin*, vol. 1 (Paris, 1989), pp. 107–19.

p. 218. Exchange: see for all this section Wickham, *Framing*, pp. 693–759, 794–824.

p. 218. Cloth and metal-working in England: C. J. Arnold, *An Archaeology of the Early Anglo-Saxon Kingdoms*, 2nd edn. (London, 1997), pp. 92–3, 135–46.

p. 219. Imports into Wales and Ireland: J. Wooding, *Communication and Commerce across the Western Sealanes, AD 400–800* (Oxford, 1996).

p. 219. Andalucía and Rome: G. Ripoll López, *Toréutica de la Bética (siglos VI y VII d.c.)* (Barcelona, 1998); M. Ricci, in L. Paroli (ed.), *L'Italia centro-settentrionale in età longobarda* (Florence, 1997), pp. 239–73.

p. 220. Rome's size: see e.g. L. Saguì, in *Archeologia medievale*, 29 (2002), pp. 7–42.

p. 220. Marseille: S. T. Loseby, in Hansen and Wickham, *The Long Eighth Century*, pp. 167–93.

p. 220. Reims, Gregory, etc.: *MGH, Epistolae*, vol. 3, pp. 129 (Reims), 214 (Cahors); Gregory of Tours, *Histories*, 3.34 (Verdun); *ChLA*, vol. 14, n. 586 (Saint-Denis). For all this, see D. Claude, in K. Düwel *et al.* (eds.), *Untersuchungen zu Handel und Verkehr der vor- und frühgeschichtlichen Zeit in Mittel- und Nordeuropa* (Göttingen, 1985), vol. 3, pp. 9–99.

p. 221. Paris and Cologne: Gregory, *Histories*, 6.32; H. Hellenkemper *et al.*, in *Kölner Jahrbuch*, 34 (2001), pp. 621–944; cf. Wickham, *Framing*, pp. 677–81.

p. 223. Pirenne: (London, 1939). See the critique by A. Riising, in *Classica et Medievalia*, 13 (1952), pp. 87–130; the archaeological updating in Hodges and Whitehouse, *Mohammed*; and the rewriting of the history of western Mediterranean trade (based on documents) by D. Claude, in Düwel, *Untersuchungen*, vol. 2.

p. 224. Spice accessibility: McCormick, *Origins*, pp. 708–16.

p. 224. Merchants: Gregory the Great, *Letters*, 4.43; Gregory of Tours, *Histories*, 6.5, 17, 10.26; Fredegar, *Chronica*, ed. and trans. J. M. Wallace-Hadrill, *The Fourth Book of the Chronicle of Fredegar* (London, 1960), 4.48, 68, 74–5 (Samo); *Lives of the Fathers of Mérida*, trans. A. T. Fear, *Lives of the Visigothic Fathers* (Liverpool, 1997), 4.3; G. Dagron and V. Déroche, in *Travaux et mémoires*, 11 (1991), pp. 17–273; *MGH, Diplomata Karolinorum*, vol. 1, ed. E. Mühlbacher (Berlin, 1906), n. 46. See in general Claude, in Düwel, *Untersuchungen*, vol. 3, pp. 62–83; S. Lebecq, in Hansen and Wickham, *The Long Eighth Century*, pp. 121–48.

p. 225. Wandalbert: *Miracula S. Goaris*, ed. O. Holder-Egger, in *MGH, Scriptores*, vol. 15.1 (Hanover, 1887), pp. 363–72, cc. 20, 26, cf. 28; see e.g. McCormick, *Origins*, pp. 657–60.

p. 225. Routes and Willibald: McCormick, *Origins*, pp. 129–34, 502–8.

p. 226. Comacchio: R. Balzaretti, in N. Christie and S. Loseby (eds.), *Towns in Transition* (Aldershot, 1996), pp. 213–34; but see below, note to p. 230.

p. 226. Money: see the basic survey, P. Grierson and M. Blackburn, *The Early Middle Ages* (Cambridge, 1986), updated by M. Blackburn in *NCMH*, vol. 1, pp. 660–74 and vol. 2, pp. 538–59; for a structural context see M. F. Hendy, 'From Public to Private', *Viator*, 19 (1988), pp. 29–78; for Italy, A. Rovelli, in Hansen and Wickham, *The Long Eighth Century*, pp. 193–223.

p. 227. Synod of Frankfurt: *Cap.*, vol. 1, p. 74, trans. P. D. King, *Charlemagne* (Kendal, 1987), p. 225.

588

p. 227. Distribution maps: D. M. Metcalf, *Thrymsas and Sceattas in the Ashmolean Museum Oxford*, vol. 3 (London, 1994).

p. 228. Embassies: Cassiodorus, *Variae*, trans. S. J. B. Barnish (Liverpool, 1992), 1.45, pp. 20–23; *Royal Frankish Annals*, trans. B. W. Scholz, *Carolingian Chronicles* (Ann Arbor, 1970), s.a. 757, among others.

p. 228. Gift exchange: P. Grierson, *Dark Age Numismatics* (London, 1979), study II; Duby, *Early Growth*, pp. 48–57. See further Le Jan, *La Société*, pp. 258–67; Devroey, *Économie rurale*, pp. 175–93. For a critical updating, see F. Curta, in *Speculum*, 81 (2006), pp. 671–99. For Byzantine objects in the West, see A. Harris, *Byzantium, Britain and the West* (Stroud, 2003).

p. 228. Praetextatus: Gregory of Tours, *Histories*, 5.18.

p. 229. Suspicion of merchants: Ine, law 25, trans. *EHD*, vol. 1, p. 401; Liutprand 79, trans. Drew, *The Lombard Laws*.

p. 229. Agricultural production: Wickham, *Framing*, pp. 280–301.

p. 230. *Emporia*: R. Hodges, *Dark Age Economics* (London, 1982); U. Näsman, in Hansen and Wickham, *The Long Eighth Century*, pp. 35–68; and above, note to p. 160.

p. 230. Charlemagne letter: trans. *EHD*, vol. 1, pp. 848–9.

p. 230. Comacchio and the Adriatic: see S. Gelichi *et al.*, in *Archeologia medievale*, 33 (2006), pp. 19–48.

Chapter 10

This chapter owes much to the advice and ideas of Leslie Brubaker, as expressed in particular in her forthcoming *Looking at Byzantium*, which I have seen in early draft. Valuable guides to the political effect of architectural display can be found in M. de Jong and F. Theuws (eds.), *Topographies of Power in the Early Middle Ages* (Leiden, 2001). The architecture of the period is surveyed competently in three classic manuals published by Penguin, R. Krautheimer and S. Ćurčić, *Early Christian and Byzantine Architecture*, 4th edn. (Harmondsworth, 1986); R. Ettinghausen and O. Grabar, *The Art and Architecture of Islam, 650–1250* (Harmondsworth, 1987); K. J. Conant, *Carolingian and Romanesque Architecture*, 2nd edn. (Harmondsworth, 1966). More up-to-date surveys are needed. There are of course a host of more localized accounts, including of single buildings, some of which are cited below.

p. 232. Hagia Sophia: see esp. R. J. Mainstone, *Hagia Sophia* (New York, 1988). For contemporary descriptions, Prokopios, *On Buildings*, ed. and trans. H. B. Dewing (Cambridge, Mass., 1940), 1.1; Paul the Silentiary, *Description of the Holy Wisdom*, partially trans. in C. Mango, *The Art of the Byzantine Empire, 312–1453* (Englewood Cliffs, NJ, 1972), pp. 80–96. There is a full trans. of the latter into Italian in M. L. Fobelli, *Un tempio per Giustiniano* (Rome, 2005).

p. 235. Great Mosque: see above all F. B. Flood, *The Great Mosque of Damascus* (Leiden, 2001); for context, O. Grabar, *The Formation of Islamic Art* (New Haven, 1973), esp. pp. 104–38; Ettinghausen and Grabar, *Art and Architecture*, pp. 37–45.

p. 237. City plans: see H. Kennedy, *Past and Present*, 106 (1985), pp. 3–27.

p. 238. Yeavering: B. Hope-Taylor, *Yeavering* (London, 1977); C. Scull, in *Medieval Archaeology*, 35 (1991), pp. 51–63; J. Blair, *The Church in Anglo-Saxon Society* (Oxford, 2005), pp. 54–7.

p. 239. *The Ruin*: trans. S. A. J. Bradley, *Anglo-Saxon Poetry* (London, 1982), p. 402.

p. 240. S. Prassede: see C. J. Goodson, 'Revival and Reality', *Acta ad Archaeologiam et Artium Historiam Pertinentia*, 15 (2005), pp. 61–92, reacting against a 1942 article by R. Krautheimer, published in *Studies in Early Christian, Medieval and Renaissance Art* (New York, 1969), pp. 203–56 (a still important article); J. J. Emerick, in *Mededelingen van het Nederlands Instituut te Rome*, 59 (2000), pp. 129–59; C. J. Goodson, *Pope Paschal I and the Churches of Rome* (Cambridge, in press). A full analysis of the mosaics is R. Wisskirchen, *Das Mosaikprogramm von S. Prassede in Rom* (Münster, 1990). For ninth-century Rome, see further T. F. X. Noble, *The Republic of St Peter* (Philadelphia, 1984), pp. 299–324, and the classic, R. Krautheimer, *Rome: Profile of a City, 312–1308* (Princeton, 1980), with the topographical critiques of R. Coates-Stephens, in *Papers of the British School at Rome*, 54 (1996), pp. 239–59, and 55 (1997), pp. 177–232. Noble convincingly argues in 'Topography, Celebration and Power', in de Jong and Theuws (eds.), *Topographies of Power*, pp. 45–91, that the papal building of the century after 750 made Rome a visibly 'papal city' for the first time.

p. 240. *Liber Pontificalis*: trans. R. Davis, *The Lives of the Ninth-century Popes* (Liverpool, 1995), pp. 1–30 (Paschal), 9–13 (S. Prassede).

p. 241. Germigny-des-Prés: see A. Freeman, in *Speculum*, 32 (1957), pp. 699–701, and 40 (1965), pp. 280–82; eadem and P. Meyvaert, in *Gesta*, 40 (2001), pp. 125–39; L. Brubaker, in *Dumbarton Oaks Papers*, 58 (2004), pp. 177–82.

p. 243. Frankish palace excavations: see the materials for France in A. Renoux (ed.), *Palais royaux et princiers du Moyen Âge* (Le Mans, 1996). A quick survey in English of those in modern Germany is G. P. Fehring, *The Archaeology of Medieval Germany* (London, 1991), pp. 126–35. There are useful sets of plans in C. Stiegemann and M. Wemhoff (eds.), *799: Kunst und Kultur der Karolingerzeit* (Mainz, 1999), pp. 130–96. See also, for critical comment, R. Samson, in M. Locock (ed.), *Meaningful Architecture* (Aldershot, 1994), pp. 99–131.

p. 243. Heroic literature: *Beowulf*, trans. Bradley, *Anglo-Saxon Poetry*, lines 69, 331–98; *Marwnad Cynddylan*, trans. J. Rowland, *Early Welsh Poetry* (Cambridge, 1990), pp. 484–5; *Culhwch and Olwen*, trans. G. and T. Jones, *The Mabinogion* (London, 1949), pp. 95–136.

p. 243. Priskos: R. C. Blockley, *The Fragmentary Classicising Historians of the Later Roman Empire* (Liverpool, 1983), vol. 2, pp. 265–93 (quotes from pp. 265 and 285); cf. W. Pohl, in de Jong and Theuws (eds.), *Topographies of Power*, pp. 439–66.

p. 243. Ingelheim: C. Rauch, *Die Ausgrabungen in der Königspfalz Ingelheim 1909–1914*, ed. H. J. Jacobi (Mainz, 1976); W. Sage, in *Francia*, 4 (1976), pp. 141–60. For the paintings etc., see Ermold, *In Honorem Hludovici Pii*, partially trans. P. Godman, *Poetry of the Carolingian Renaissance* (London, 1985), pp. 251–5.

p. 244. Notker: trans. L. Thorpe, *Two Lives of Charlemagne* (London, 1969), 2.6 (Byzantines), 1.30 (windows); cf. S. Airlie, 'The Palace of Memory', in S. Rees Jones *et al.* (eds.), *Courts and Regions in Medieval Europe* (York, 2000), pp. 1–19, at p. 5.

p. 244. Liutprand: *Antapodosis*, 6.5, in *The Complete Works of Liudprand of Cremona*, trans. P. Squatriti (Washington, 2007), pp. 197–8.

p. 245. Villages: before 800, see in general C. Wickham, *Framing the Early Middle Ages* (Oxford, 2005), pp. 442–518. Limestone Massif and Serjilla: H. C. Butler, *Syria*, vol. 2B (Leiden, 1920), pp. 113–33; G. Tchalenko, *Villages antiques de la Syrie du Nord*, 3 vols. (Paris, 1953–8); G. Tate, *Les Campagnes de la Syrie du Nord du IIe au VIIe siècle*, vol. 1 (Paris, 1992); G. Charpentier, 'Les Bains de Sergilla', *Syria*, 71 (1994), pp. 113–42.

p. 246. Western villages: see esp. H. Hamerow, *Early Medieval Settlements* (Oxford, 2002); É. Peytremann, *Archéologie de l'habitat rural dans le nord de la France du IVe au XIIe siècle* (Saint-Germain-en-Laye, 2003).

p. 247. Vorbasse: for a brief overview in English, see S. Hvass, in K. Randsborg (ed.), *The Birth of Europe* (Rome, 1989), pp. 91–9.

p. 247. Lauchheim: in English, see F. Damminger, in I. Wood (ed.), *Franks and Alamanni in the Merovingian Period* (Woodbridge, 1998), pp. 60–64.

p. 248. Churches: for England, see Blair, *Church*, esp. pp. 383–425.

p. 249. Montarrenti: see F. Cantini, *Il castello di Montarrenti* (Florence, 2003), with the generalizations to the rest of Tuscany in M. Valenti, *L'insediamento altomedievale nelle campagne toscane* (Florence, 2004), and to the rest of Italy in R. Francovich and R. Hodges, *Villa to Village* (London, 2003). For a general context for internal village spatial hierarchization, see L. Feller, *Paysans et seigneurs au Moyen Âge, VIIIe–XVe siècles* (Paris, 2007), pp. 76–81.

Chapter 11

There are many histories of Byzantium in English. The best one-volume starting point is M. Whittow, *The Making of Orthodox Byzantium, 600–1025* (Basingstoke, 1996); the best monographic surveys of this period are J. F. Haldon, *Byzantium in the Seventh Century*, 2nd edn. (Cambridge, 1997) and L. Brubaker and J. F. Haldon, *Byzantium in the Iconoclast Era (ca.680–ca.850)* (Cambridge, 2009); I am grateful to the authors for letting me see the typescript. C. Mango, *Byzantium: The Empire of New Rome* (London, 1980), A. Cameron, *The Byzantines* (Oxford, 2006) and J. Herrin, *Byzantium* (Princeton, 2008), are insightful. J. Herrin, *The Formation of Christendom* (Princeton, 1987) is important for the church. *ODB* is an invaluable reference book.

p. 255. *Parastaseis*: A. Cameron and J. Herrin (eds.), *Constantinople in the Early Eighth Century* (Leiden, 1984). Cited in order are cc. 61, 28, 61, 65, 75.

p. 257. Maurice: see esp. M. Whitby, *The Emperor Maurice and his Historian* (Oxford, 1988).

p. 257. Avars: W. Pohl, *Die Awaren* (Munich, 1988).

p. 257. Coups: W. E. Kaegi, *Byzantine Military Unrest 471–843* (Amsterdam, 1981); for army ideology, J. F. Haldon, in *Klio*, 68 (1986), pp. 139–90. For hereditary succession and legitimacy, G. Dagron, *Emperor and Priest* (Cambridge, 2003), pp. 13–45, 54–83.

p. 258. Phocas: see D. M. Olster, *The Politics of Usurpation in the Seventh Century* (Amsterdam, 1993), a very up-beat account.

p. 258. Heraclius: see W. E. Kaegi, *Heraclius* (Cambridge, 2003), another up-beat account.

p. 259. George of Pisidia: Giorgio di Pisidia, *Poemi*, vol. 1, ed. and trans. A. Pertusi (Ettal, 1959), p. 109.

p. 259. Michael Hendy: M. F. Hendy, *Studies in the Byzantine Monetary Economy, c.300–1450* (Cambridge, 1985), pp. 619–67 (quote from p. 620).

p. 260. Byzantine navy: H. Ahrweiler, *Byzance et la mer* (Paris, 1966), pp. 17–92.

p. 260. Apocalyptic writing: see e.g. G. Dagron and V. Déroche, 'Juifs et Chrétiens dans l'Orient du VIIe siècle', *Travaux et mémoires*, 11 (1991), pp. 17–273, esp. pp. 38–43; R. G. Hoyland, *Seeing Islam as Others Saw It* (Princeton, 1997), pp. 257–316; an important example, pseudo-Methodios, is partially trans. by S. P. Brock, in A. Palmer, *The Seventh Century in the West-Syrian Chronicles* (Liverpool, 1993), pp. 230–42. For the highly religious nature of the writings of this period, see A. Cameron, J. Haldon, G. J. Reinink, in A. Cameron and L. I. Conrad (eds.), *The Byzantine and Early Islamic Near East*, vol. 1 (Princeton, 1992), pp. 81–187.

p. 261. Army: see Haldon, *Byzantium in the Seventh Century*, pp. 208–32; idem, in *Dumbarton Oaks Papers*, 47 (1993), pp. 1–67, idem, *Warfare, State and Society in the Byzantine world 565–1204* (London, 1999), pp. 71–123.

p. 262. Aristocracies: C. Wickham, *Framing the Early Middle Ages* (Oxford, 2005), pp. 233–9 gives a brief survey with bibliography.

p. 263. St Artemios: *The Miracles of St Artemios*, ed. and trans. V. S. Crisafulli and J. W. Nesbitt (Leiden, 1997), esp. cc. 7, 10, 17, 18, 26, 27, 29, 32, 44, and pp. 19–21.

p. 263. Platon: *ODB*, vol. 3, p. 1684.

p. 263. Bureaucracy: Haldon, *Byzantium in the Seventh Century*, pp. 180–207; W. Brandes, *Finanzverwaltung in Krisenzeiten* (Frankfurt, 2002), pp. 116–238.

p. 264. Public space: M. McCormick, *Eternal Victory* (Cambridge, 1986), pp. 131–230; L. Brubaker, in M. de Jong and F. Theuws (eds.), *Topographies of Power in the Early Middle Ages* (Leiden, 2001), pp. 31–43; Dagron, *Emperor and Priest*, pp. 103–14. For 765, *The Chronicle of Theophanes*, trans. C. Mango and R. Scott (Oxford, 1997), p. 605.

p. 264. Roman form to the city: P. Magdalino, *Constantinople médiévale* (Paris, 1996), pp. 48–50.

p. 265. Leo III: Dagron, *Emperor and Priest*, pp. 158–91.

p. 266. Army and councils: Brubaker and Haldon, *Byzantium in the Iconoclast Era*, ch. 1; for the 681 events, *Chronicle of Theophanes*, pp. 491–2 (misdated to 669).

p. 267. *Ekloga: A Manual of Roman Law*, trans. E. H. Freshfield (Cambridge, 1926); quote from p. 67.

p. 268. Constantine V reforms: *Chronicle of Theophanes*, pp. 608, 611; J. F. Haldon, *Byzantine Praetorians* (Bonn, 1984), pp. 228–56.

p. 268. Iconoclasm: see in general Brubaker and Haldon, *Byzantium in the Iconoclast Era* (see ch. 1 for before 720); and also iidem, *Byzantium in the Iconoclast era (ca.680–850): The Sources* (Aldershot, 2001). For early icons, I follow L. Brubaker, 'Icons before Iconoclasm?', *Settimane di studio*, 45 (1998), pp. 1215–54, against the classic E. Kitzinger, 'The Cult of Images in the Age before Iconoclasm', *Dumbarton Oaks Papers*, 8 (1954), pp. 85–150. For 626, see B. V. Pentcheva, in *Byzantine and Modern Greek Studies*, 26 (2002), pp. 2–41. For other contributions, see the bibliographies in these works; but A. Bryer and J. Herrin (eds.), *Iconoclasm* (Birmingham, 1977) is a valuable survey of the then state of knowledge, and P. Brown, 'A Dark-age Crisis', *English Historical Review*, 88 (1973), pp. 1–34 is a brilliant reinterpretation. The Gregory the Great quote is cited and contextualized by H. L. Kessler, in *Studies in the History of Art*, 16 (1985), pp. 75–91.

p. 269. Constantine V and Nikephoros: Nikephoros, *Antirrhēsis*, trans. M.-J. Mondzain-Baudinet, Nicéphore, *Discours contre les Iconoclastes* (Paris, 1989); p. 325 has a list of the Constantine citations.

p. 269. 'Unlawful art': D. J. Sahas, *Icon and Logos* (Toronto, 1986), a translation of the acts of Second Nicaea, p. 75.

p. 269. Stephen the Younger: *La Vie d'Étienne le Jeune par Étienne le diacre*, ed. and trans. M.-F. Auzépy (Aldershot, 1997), cc. 69 (death), 28 (flight).

p. 270. Eirene: see, in addition to the general surveys, L. James, *Empresses and Power in Early Byzantium* (Leicester, 2001), esp. pp. 54–6, 68–72, 89–92, 112–14, 125–7; a detailed account of her reign, as of her successors, not fully critical of the primary sources, is W. Treadgold, *The Byzantine Revival 780–842* (Stanford, Calif., 1988).

p. 271. Nikephoros I: Treadgold, *Byzantine Revival*, pp. 127–95; *Chronicle of Theophanes*, pp. 655 (802), 667–9 (vexations).

p. 272. The Balkans: J. V. A. Fine, *The Early Medieval Balkans* (Ann Arbor, 1983), pp. 66–105, and F. Curta, *Southeastern Europe in the Middle Ages, 500–1250* (Cambridge, 2006), pp. 70–110, 147–65, give recent narrative accounts; the classic, D. Obolensky, *The Byzantine Commonwealth* (London, 1971) is less detailed on this period. For casual references to Slavic languages in the tenth century, Constantine Porphyrogenitus, *De Administrando Imperio*, ed. and trans. G. Moravcsik and R. J. H. Jenkins (Washington, 1967), cc. 31, 32, 34, 36.

p. 273. Constantine V's memory: *Chronicle of Theophanes*, pp. 679–80, 684–5.

p. 274. Alexander and Caesar: Nikephoros, *Antirrhēsis*, 3.73 (Nicéphore, *Discours*, pp. 281–3).

p. 274. Bishops as mainly Iconoclast: see M. Kaplan, in idem (ed.), *Monastères, images, pouvoirs et société à Byzance* (Paris, 2006), pp. 183–205.

p. 274. *Graptoi*: Treadgold, *Byzantine Revival*, pp. 311, 447; several sources recount the event.

p. 274. Great Fence: see P. Squatriti, in *Past and Present*, 176 (2002), pp. 11–65.

p. 275. Eirene's body: J. Herrin, *Women in Purple* (London, 2001), p. 213.

p. 275. Nikephoros: Nikephoros, *Antirrhēsis*, 1.20, 30, 43, 2.18 (Nicéphore, *Discours*, pp. 87, 110, 135, 178). Ignatios: *The Correspondence of Ignatios the Deacon*, ed. and trans. C. Mango (Washington, 1997), *letter* 21 for Pythagoras; pp. 239–41 for non-biblical citations. For all these figures, see above all P. Lemerle, *Byzantine Humanism* (Canberra, 1986), pp. 137–204. For Ignatios' career, see *Correspondence of Ignatios*, pp. 3–24; letters cited are 30 (Nikephoros), 46 (location of exile), 39 (poverty), 38 (straying).

p. 277. Theophilos and building: Brubaker and Haldon, *Byzantium in the Iconoclast Era*, ch. 5.

p. 277. Peter Brown: 'A Dark-age Crisis'; p. 8 for quote.

p. 278. Palestinian Christians: Brubaker and Haldon, *Byzantium in the Iconoclast Era: The Sources*, pp. 30–36; R. Schick, *The Christian Communities of Palestine from Byzantine to Islamic Rule* (Princeton, 1995), pp. 180–219.

Chapter 12

A general framing for some of the problems of Arab history is R. S. Humphreys, *Islamic History*, revised edn. (Princeton, 1991). For narratives to 750, see H. Kennedy, *The Prophet and the Age of the Caliphates* (London, 1986); G. R. Hawting, *The First Dynasty of Islam* (Carbondale, Ill., 1987); P. Crone, *Slaves on Horses* (Cambridge, 1980), very crisp and succinct, but requiring prior knowledge; M. A. Shaban, *Islamic History: A New Interpretation*, vol. 1 (Cambridge, 1971), older and more problematic; and the old classic, J. Wellhausen, *The Arab Kingdom and its Fall* (Calcutta, 1927). An essential research tool is the *Encyclopaedia of Islam*, 2nd edn. (Leiden, 1954–2001).

p. 279. Murder of 'Uthman: texts include *The Armenian History Attributed to Sebeos*, trans. R. W. Thomson *et al.* (Liverpool, 1999), vol. 1, p. 154; *The History of al-Tabari*, trans. E. Yar-Shater *et al.*, 39 vols. (Albany, NY, 1985–2000), vol. 15, pp. 145–252. For reconstructions of the events and their problems, see R. S. Humphreys, in F. M. Clover and R. S. Humphreys (eds.), *Tradition and Innovation in Late Antiquity* (Madison, 1989), pp. 271–90 (the more critical); M. Hinds, *Studies in Early Islamic History* (Princeton, 1996), pp. 29–55. For some context, Humphreys, *Islamic History*, pp. 98–103; E. L. Petersen, *'Ali and Mu'āwiya in Early Arabic Tradition* (Copenhagen, 1964); P. Crone, *Medieval Islamic Political Thought* (Edinburgh, 2004), pp. 17–32. For Sayf, E. Landau-Tasseron, in *Der Islam*, 67 (1990), pp. 6–26; P. Crone, in *Journal of the Royal Asiatic Society*, 3 ser., 6 (1996), pp. 237–40.

p. 281. Narrative sources: see C. F. Robinson, *Islamic Historiography* (Cambridge, 2003); A. Noth, *The Early Arabic Historical Tradition*, ed. L. I. Conrad (Princeton, 1994); F. M. Donner, *Narratives of Islamic Origins* (Princeton, 1998). All these engage with the most critical recent historiography from different positions, and show what Arab sources look like. Important examples of that historiography include Crone, *Slaves on Horses*, pp. 3–17; L. I. Conrad, 'The Conquest of Arwād', in A. Cameron and L. I. Conrad (eds.), *The Byzantine and Early Islamic Near East*, vol. 1 (Princeton, 1992), pp. 317–401. Non-Muslim sources are discussed in R. G. Hoyland, *Seeing Islam as Others Saw It* (Princeton, 1997).

p. 282. Muhammad: a good short introduction is M. A. Cook, *Muhammad* (Oxford, 1983).

p. 282. *Constitution of Medina*: Ibn Ishaq, *The Life of Muhammad*, trans. A. Guillaume (London, 1955), pp. 231–3; see Humphreys, *Islamic History*, pp. 92–8.

p. 282. Qur'an: trans. A. J. Arberry, *The Koran Interpreted* (London, 1955), among many. For dates, J. Wansbrough, *Quranic Studies* (Oxford, 1977), pp. 43–52; P. Crone, in *Jerusalem Studies in Arabic and Islam*, 18 (1994), pp. 1–37; Donner, *Narratives*, pp. 35–63. For the Dome of the Rock texts, Hoyland, *Seeing Islam*, pp. 696–9 (cf. 545–59, 591–8).

p. 283. 643 text: A. Grohmann, *From the World of Arabic Papyri* (Cairo, 1952), pp. 113–15.

p. 283. *Khalīfa*: see P. Crone and M. Hinds, *God's Caliph* (Cambridge, 1986), pp. 4–23 (the first contemporary references are for 'Abd al-Malik).

p. 283. Conquests: see F. M. Donner, *The Early Islamic Conquests* (Princeton, 1981), more trusting of the sources than his later *Narratives*; the basic Arabic text is al-Baladhuri, *The Origins of the Islamic State*, trans. P. K. Hitti and F. C. Murgotten (New York, 1916–24).

p. 285. *Dīwān*: see esp. H. Kennedy, *The Armies of the Caliphs* (London, 2001), pp. 59–78.

p. 285. Arab landowning: see among others Donner, *Conquests*, pp. 239–50; Kennedy, *Armies*, pp. 81–5; K. Morimoto, 'Land Tenure in Egypt during the Early Islamic Period', *Orient*, 11 (1975), pp. 109–53. The numerous individual examples of land cessions do not undermine the main point.

p. 285. Tax: see in general, among many, J. B. Simonsen, *Studies in the Genesis and Early Development of the Caliphal Taxation System* (Copenhagen, 1988).

p. 285. Mansur family: see M. F. Auzépy, in *Travaux et mémoires*, 12 (1994), pp. 194–203. The 700 date comes from al-Baladhuri, *Origins*, vol. 1, p. 301.

p. 286. *Mawālī*: there is a huge debate over their role. I follow P. Crone in talking down their political importance, as, for example, in *Slaves on Horses*, pp. 49–57.

p. 286. Conversion: see esp. R. W. Bulliet, *Conversion to Islam in the Medieval Period* (Cambridge, Mass., 1979).

p. 286. Egypt: see e.g. C. Wickham, *Framing the Early Middle Ages* (Oxford, 2005), pp. 133–44, 251–5, 419–28; for early Arabization, see esp. now P. M. Sijpesteijn, *Shaping a Muslim State* (Oxford, in press); eadem in *Proceedings of the British Academy*, 136 (2007), pp. 183–200 for administrative continuities.

p. 287. Syria: see several articles in P. Canivet and J. P. Rey-Cocquais (eds.), *La Syrie de Byzance à l'Islam, VIIe–VIIIe siècles* (Damascus, 1992); J. B. Segal, *Edessa* (Oxford, 1970), pp. 202–3. For papyri, C. J. Kraemer (ed.), *Excavations at Nessana*, vol. 3 (Princeton, 1958), nn. 55–88, 92–3 (the *dīwān* text); A. Grohmann (ed.), *Arabic Papyri from Hirbet el-Mird* (Louvain, 1963). For archaeological continuities and the occasional change, A. Walmsley, *Early Islamic Syria* (London, 2007); J. Magness, *The Archaeology of the Early Islamic Settlement in Palestine* (Winona Lake, Ind., 2003). For the Arabs in the Jazira and Iraq, not discussed here, the key books are C. F. Robinson, *Empire and Élites after the Muslim Conquest* (Cambridge, 2000), and M. G. Morony, *Iraq after the Muslim Conquest* (Princeton, 1984); there is no good book on Iran.

p. 288. Samuel: Kraemer (ed.), *Excavations at Nessana*, vol. 3, n. 75.

p. 288. Egyptian tax revolts: K. Morimoto, *The Fiscal Administration of Egypt in the Early Islamic Period* (Dohosha, 1981), pp. 145–72.

p. 288. Incomplete cultural separation: T. Sizgorich, in *Past and Present*, 85 (2004), pp. 9–42; for Rusafa, E. K. Fowden, *The Barbarian Plain* (Berkeley, 1999), esp. pp. 60–100, 130–91. Bahira discussed by Christians: Hoyland, *Seeing Islam*, esp. pp. 270–76. Sinai: Kraemer (ed.), *Excavations at Nessana*, vol. 3, nn. 72–3; R. Schick, *The Christian Communities of Palestine from Byzantine to Islamic Rule* (Princeton, 1995), pp. 410–12.

p. 289. Mu'awiya: see R. S. Humphreys, *Mu'awiya ibn Abi Sufyan* (Oxford, 2006).

p. 289. Second Civil War: see the narrative surveys cited in the introduction, and also C. F. Robinson, *'Abd al-Malik* (Oxford, 2005), a basic account of that ruler.

p. 290. Africa: see M. Brett, in *The Cambridge History of Africa*, vol. 2 (Cambridge, 1978), pp. 490–555.

p. 291. Kalb/Yaman vs. Qays: see above all P. Crone, 'Were the Qays and Yemen of the Umayyad Period Political Parties?', *Der Islam*, 71 (1994), pp. 1–57.

p. 291. 'Abd al-Hamid: see W. al-Qāḍī in Cameron and Conrad, *Byzantine and Early Islamic Near East*, vol. 1, pp. 215–75. For 'Abd al-Malik and Islamization, see F. M. Donner, 'The Formation of the Islamic State', *Journal of the American Oriental Society*, 106 (1986), pp. 283–96; Robinson, *'Abd al Malik*; Crone and Hinds, *God's Caliph*, pp. 24–57.

p. 292. Buildings: R. Ettinghausen and O. Grabar, *The Art and Architecture of Islam: 650–1250* (Harmondsworth, 1987), pp. 28–71.

p. 292. Representation of humans: Qur'an, esp. 5.92, 6.74; cf. O. Grabar, *The Formation of Islamic Art* (New Haven, 1973), pp. 75–103.

p. 293. Al-Walid II and Yazid III on their religious roles: see texts trans. in Crone and Hinds, *God's Caliph*, pp. 115–28 (pp. 124, 123 for quotes).

p. 293. Qusayr 'Amra: G. Fowden, *Empire to Commonwealth* (Princeton, 1993), pp. 143–9, developed in idem, *Qusayr 'Amra* (Berkeley, 2004).

p. 294. Sa'id: S. Bashear, *Arabs and Others in Early Islam* (Princeton, 1997), p. 36; the whole book explores Arab ethnic attitudes. For the non-tribal nature of factions, see Crone, 'Were the Qays'; earlier, Donner, *Conquests*, pp. 251–63.

p. 294. Al-Farazdaq: *Divan de Férazdak*, trans. R. Boucher (Paris, 1870), quotes from n. 21,

p. 94 and n. 8, p. 32; see in general *Encyclopaedia of Islam*, vol. 2, pp. 788–9; S. K. Jayyusi, in A. F. L. Beeston *et al.* (eds.), *Arabic Literature to the End of the Umayyad Period* (Cambridge, 1983), pp. 401–12; Crone and Hinds, *God's Caliph*, pp. 30–40.

p. 295. Hisham: see the political narrative in K. Y. Blankinship, *The End of the Jihād State* (Albany, NY, 1994), a far too apocalyptic account. For Hisham as short of money, cf. Kennedy, *Armies*, pp. 74–6.

p. 295. Yazid III and tax: Crone, 'Were the Qays', p. 41.

p. 295. 'Abbasid 'revolution': the enormous historiography includes Wellhausen, *Arab Kingdom*, pp. 456–566; M. A. Shaban, *The 'Abbāsid Revolution* (Cambridge, 1970); M. Sharon, *Black Banners from the East* (Jerusalem, 1983); J. Lassner, in Clover and Humphreys, *Tradition and Innovation*, pp. 247–70. See the sensible literature survey in Humphreys, *Islamic History*, pp. 104–27.

Chapter 13

The late ninth and tenth centuries do not have a monographic account. M. Whittow, *The Making of Orthodox Byzantium, 600–1025* (Basingstoke, 1996), remains a good survey; so do the articles by J. Shepard in *NCMH*, vol. 3, pp. 553–604; some more general Byzantine overviews also give useful attention to the period, including J. F. Haldon, *Byzantium: A History* (Stroud, 2000); P. Magdalino, 'The Medieval Empire (780–1204)', in C. A. Mango (ed.), *The Oxford History of Byzantium* (Oxford, 2002), pp. 169–208; and the old (and sometimes outdated) classic, G. Ostrogorsky, *History of the Byzantine State* (Oxford, 1956). Some emperors (Leo VI, Nikephoros II, Basil II) have good recent analyses in English: see below. But we do not have anything in any language that confronts the period as a whole on its own terms. For Bulgaria, see the note to p. 305.

p. 298. *Book of Ceremonies*: Constantin VII Porphyrogénète, *Le Livre des cérémonies*, ed. and trans. A. Vogt, 2 vols. (Paris, 1967; only half the book was edited in this modern edition), esp. 1.1. 9, 46; quotes from the preface, pp. 1–2. I accept the restricted list of works that can be plausibly ascribed to Constantine in I. Ševčenko's arch but convincing article, in J. Shepard and S. Franklin (eds.), *Byzantine Diplomacy* (Aldershot, 1992), pp. 167–95.

p. 299. Ceremonial: see A. Cameron, in D. Cannadine and S. Price (eds.), *Rituals of Royalty* (London, 1987), pp. 106–36; M. McCormick, in *Jahrbuch der österreichischen Byzantinistik*, 35 (1985), pp. 1–20; idem, *Eternal Victory* (Cambridge, 1986), pp. 150–230; G. Dagron, *Emperor and Priest* (Cambridge, 2003), pp. 204–19; R. Morris, in C. Cubitt (ed.), *Court Culture in the Early Middle Ages* (Turnhout, 2003), pp. 235–54. Liutprand: *The Complete Works of Liudprand of Cremona*, trans. P. Squatriti (Washington, 2007), pp. 244–7, *Embassy*, cc. 9–13.

p. 300. Photios and Arethas: P. Lemerle, *Byzantine Humanism* (Canberra, 1986), pp. 205–308 (pp. 234–5 for rigorist critiques of Photios); N. G. Wilson, *Scholars of Byzantium* (London, 1983), pp. 89–135. For the *Bibliothēkē*, N. G. Wilson, *Photius: The Bibliotheca* (London, 1994), is a partial translation.

p. 300. Some imperial books: Constantine Porphyrogenitus, *De Administrando Imperio*, ed. and trans. G. Moravcsik and R. J. H. Jenkins (Washington, 1967); *Le Traité sur la guérilla de l'empereur Nicéphore Phocas (963–969)*, ed. and trans. G. Dagron and H. Mihăescu (Paris, 1986); E. McGeer, *Sowing the Dragon's Teeth* (Washington, 1995), pp. 12–59.

p. 301. Leo Choirosphaktes: P. Magdalino, 'In Search of the Byzantine Courtier', in H. Maguire (ed.), *Byzantine Court Culture from 829 to 1204* (Washington, 1997), pp. 141–65; idem, *L'Orthodoxie des astrologues* (Paris, 2006), pp. 70–82; G. Kolias, *Léon Choerosphaktès* (Athens, 1939), pp. 76–90, cf. 35–40.

p. 301. Nicholas I: *Letters*, ed. and trans. R. J. H. Jenkins and L. G. Westerink (Washington, 1973), *letters* 5–11, 14–31; Théodore Daphnopatès: *Correspondance*, ed. and trans.

J. Darrouzès and L. G. Westerink (Paris, 1978), *letters* 5–7 (to Symeon), 14 (to Romanos); Leo of Synnada: *The Correspondence of Leo, Metropolitan of Synada and Syncellus*, ed. and trans. M. P. Vinson (Washington, 1985), *letter* 31 (will).

p. 302. Constantine VII on Romanos I: *De Administrando*, c. 13.

p. 302. Law: see e.g. M. T. Fögen, in L. Brubaker (ed.), *Byzantium in the Ninth Century: Dead or Alive?* (Aldershot, 1998), pp. 11–22. For the revival of Roman-ness, see P. Magdalino, 'The Distance of the Past in Early Medieval Byzantium (VII–X centuries)', *Settimane di studio*, 46 (1999), pp. 115–46.

p. 303. Banning from Hagia Sophia: see e.g. Dagron, *Emperor and Priest*, pp. 106–9.

p. 304. Bali: C. Geertz, *Negara* (Princeton, 1980).

p. 304. Liutprand: Liutprand, *Antapodosis*, 6.5, 10, in *Complete Works*, pp. 197–202.

p. 304. Orthodoxy procession: Constantin, *Livre des cérémonies*, 1.37.

p. 305. Bulgaria: see in general J. Shepard, in *NCMH*, vol. 3, pp. 567–85; D. Obolensky, *The Byzantine Commonwealth* (London, 1971), pp. 114–204; J. V. A. Fine, *The Early Medieval Balkans* (Ann Arbor, 1983), pp. 94–201; P. Stephenson, *Byzantium's Balkan Frontier* (Cambridge, 2000), pp. 18–79; F. Curta, *Southeastern Europe in the Middle Ages, 500–1250* (Cambridge, 2006), pp. 119–24, 147–79, 213–47.

p. 306. Rome and Constantinople: F. Dvornik, *The Photian Schism* (Cambridge, 1948), with caution.

p. 307. Symeon in 924: Théodore Daphnopatès, *Correspondance, letter* 5.

p. 307. Bogomils: *Le Traité contre les Bogomiles de Cosmas le Prêtre*, trans. H.-C. Puech and A. Vaillant (Paris, 1945); p. 86 for social attitudes.

p. 307. Military handbooks: see the list in A. Dain, 'Les Stratégistes byzantins', *Travaux et mémoires*, 2 (1967), pp. 317–92. See, on Leo in general, S. Tougher, *The Reign of Leo VI (886–912)* (Leiden, 1997).

p. 308. Romanos and Constantine: Théodore Daphnopatès, *Correspondance, letter* 6; Constantine, *De Administrando*, c. 50.

p. 308. John Kourkouas, Bardas, Nikephoros: see e.g. Whittow, *The Making*, pp. 317–53.

p. 308. Nikephoros Phokas: see R. Morris, in *Byzantine and Modern Greek Studies*, 12 (1988), pp. 83–115; and in P. Magdalino (ed.), *New Constantines* (Aldershot, 1994), pp. 199–214, for the repercussions of his death.

p. 310. Nikephoros' sense of being constrained by ceremonial: Liutprand, *Embassy*, c. 55, in *Complete Works*, p. 273.

p. 310. Nikephoros Ouranos: *ODB*, vol. 3, pp. 1544–5; C. Holmes, *Basil II and the Governance of Empire (976–1025)* (Oxford, 2005), pp. 349–52, 384, 409–11, 523–4. Argyroi: J. F. Vannier, *Familles byzantines: les Argyroi* (Paris, 1975), pp. 36–42; for Romanos' culture, Michael Psellos, *Chronographia*, trans. E. R. A. Sewter as *Fourteen Byzantine Rulers* (London, 1966), pp. 63–4.

p. 310. Basil Lekapenos: see esp. W. G. Brokkaar, 'Basil Lacapenos', in W. F. Bakker *et al.* (eds.), *Studia Byzantina et Neohellenica Neerlandica* (Leiden, 1972), pp. 199–234.

p. 311. Basil II: see esp. Holmes, *Basil II*. See also some of the articles in P. Magdalino (ed.), *Byzantium in the Year 1000* (Leiden, 2003). The quote, and also the tunnels rumour, are from Psellos, *Chronographia*, trans. Sewter, pp. 45–6.

p. 312. Army structure: see esp. J. F. Haldon, *Warfare, State and Society in the Byzantine World 565–1204* (London 1999), pp. 84–5, 123–32, 217–23.

p. 313. Family origins: see *ODB*, vol. 1, pp. 165, 655, vol. 2, pp. 1156, 1203, vol. 3, pp. 1666, 1911, for quick guides and bibliography. For the crystallization of the aristocracy, see E. Patlagean and A. P. Kazhdan, in M. Angold (ed.), *The Byzantine Aristocracy, IX to XIII Centuries* (Oxford, 1984), pp. 23–57; M. Kaplan, *Les Hommes et la terre à Byzance du VIᵉ au XIᵉ siècle* (Paris, 1992), pp. 328 ff; J.-C. Cheynet, *The Byzantine Aristocracy and its Military Function* (Aldershot, 2006), studies I–V.

p. 313. Leo VI and Basil I: *Taktika*, 2.22–5, in *Patrologia Graeca*, vol. 107, ed. J.-P. Migne (Paris, 1863), col. 688; E. McGeer, *The Land Legislation of the Macedonian Emperors* (Toronto, 2000), Novel O, Prologue 3, 4.

p. 313. Locations of lands: M. F. Hendy, *Studies in the Byzantine Monetary Economy, c. 300–1450* (Cambridge, 1985), pp. 100–108; J.-C. Cheynet, *Pouvoir et contestations à Byzance (963–1210)* (Paris, 1990), pp. 207–48; *Digenis Akritis*, ed. and trans. E. Jeffreys (Cambridge, 1998).

p. 313. Phokades: J.-C. Cheynet, 'Les Phocas', in Dagron and Mihăescu, *Le Traité sur la guérilla*, pp. 289–315.

p. 314. Need for office-holding: Holmes, *Basil II*, pp. 463–8 (p. 466 n. for the lions quote); for 1022, ibid., pp. 515–22, and Cheynet, *Pouvoir et contestations*, pp. 36–7.

p. 315. Danelis: Kaplan, *Les Hommes*, pp. 333–4.

p. 315. Laws: McGeer, *Land Legislation*, translates them all; cited laws are Novels C, 1.2 (2.1 for the famine); E, 3.3; O, Prologue 4, 7.1–2. For definitions of *dynatoi*, Novels B, 2.2; C, 1.2; D, 3.1. Out of the huge bibliography on these texts, R. Morris, 'The Powerful and the Poor in Tenth-century Byzantium', *Past and Present*, 73 (1976), pp. 3–27 and Kaplan, *Les Hommes*, pp. 406–44, stand out.

p. 316. Nikephoros in 966/7: McGeer, *Land Legislation*, Novel K, 1.1.

p. 316. Aristocratic and peasant landowning: see in general A. Harvey, *Economic Expansion in the Byzantine Empire, 900–1200* (Cambridge, 1989), pp. 67–79. For the Thebes Cadaster, see N. Svoronos, in *Bulletin de correspondance hellénique*, 83 (1959), pp. 1–145 (pp. 11–19 for the text). Athos: *Archives de l'Athos*, vol. 5, *Actes de Lavra, I*, ed. P. Lemerle *et al.* (Paris, 1970), n. 6; vol. 6, *Actes du Prôtaton*, ed. D. Papachryssanthou (Paris, 1975), nn. 1, 4–6; vol. 14, *Actes d'Iviron, I*, ed. J. Lefort *et al.* (Paris, 1985), nn. 1, 4–5, 9 (cf. the laws of Nikephoros and Basil in McGeer, *Land Legislation*, Novels J and O, 3). Hierissos had a bishop but also a stratum of peasant proprietors (Kaplan, *Les Hommes*, pp. 226–9); it could be called an 'agro-town'. For monastic expansion in this period, patronized not least by Nikephoros II despite his own legislation, see R. Morris, *Monks and Laymen in Byzantium, 843–1118* (Cambridge, 1995), pp. 166–99. For southern Italy, see J.-M. Martin, *La Pouille du VIᵉ au XIIᵉ siècle* (Rome, 1993), pp. 293–301. I am grateful here to discussions with Mark Whittow.

p. 316. Peasant society: Kaplan, *Les Hommes*, is the best guide. (I ascribe less dominance to 'the powerful' than he does.)

p. 317. Justice: R. Morris, in W. Davies and P. Fouracre (eds.), *The Settlement of Disputes in Early Medieval Europe* (Cambridge 1986), pp. 125–47; documentary examples, beside those cited in the note to p. 316, are *Actes du Prôtaton*, nn. 2, 7; *Archives de l'Athos*, vol. 2: *Actes de Vatopédi, I*, ed. J. Bompaire *et al.* (Paris, 2001), nn. 1, 2, mostly for trouble between monasteries.

Chapter 14

For 'Abbasid and post-'Abbasid history, the best overall guide in English is H. Kennedy, *The Prophet and the Age of the Caliphates* (London, 1986), which devotes its strongest sections to this period. For the tenth century, his is indeed the only overview, apart from the more problematic M. A. Shaban, *Islamic History: A New Interpretation*, vol. 2 (Cambridge, 1976). (See notes to pp. 335–8 for more localized studies.) For the period before 908, three other books by Kennedy also need citation, *The Early Abbasid Caliphate* (London, 1981), *The Armies of the Caliphs* (London, 2001), and *The Court of the Caliphs* (London, 2004), an attractive popular history based heavily on 'Abbasid narratives, which is arguably the best place to start. The most wide-ranging synthesis of the 'Abbasids as a whole is D. Sourdel, *L'État impérial des califes abbassides* (Paris, 1999). For the culture of the period, the classic survey is G. E. von Grunebaum, *Medieval Islam*, 2nd edn. (Chicago, 1953); M. J. L. Young *et al.* (eds.), *Religion, Learning and Science in the 'Abbasid Period* (Cambridge, 1990) and J. Ashtiany *et al.* (eds.), *'Abbasid belles-lettres* (Cambridge, 1990), together cover every literary genre in detail. P. Crone, *Medieval Islamic Political Thought* (Edinburgh, 2004) and C. F. Robinson, *Islamic Historiography* (Cambridge, 2003) both have a wide remit. The basic primary source, *The History of al-Tabari*, is translated in 39 vols., ed. E. Yar-Shater

(Albany, NY, 1985–2000); vols. 27 onward cover the period 750–915. The tendency to accept almost everything al-Tabari and other authors say, which is present in most writers on the period, including some cited above, is effectively critiqued in T. El-Hibri's important *Reinterpreting Islamic Historiography* (Cambridge, 1999).

p. 318. Palermo in Ibn Hawqal: Ibn Hauqal, *Configuration de la terre*, vol.1, trans. J. H. Kramers and G. Wiet (Beirut and Paris, 1964), pp. 117–30, quotes from pp. 123, 127.

p. 319. Ibn Hawqal's comparisons: *Configuration*, vol. 1, pp. 144, 111, 178, 97–8.

p. 320. Baghdad's size: for a range of estimates, all based on bad data, see F. Micheau, in J.-C. Garcin (ed.), *Grandes villes méditerranéennes du monde musulman médiéval* (Rome, 2000), pp. 92–3; see also P. Guichard, ibid., p. 269; I go for a higher estimate than many, bearing in mind the half-million inhabitants of late imperial Rome and Constantinople and the 250,000 fairly plausibly argued for eleventh-century Fustat/Cairo (A. Raymond, *Cairo* (Cambridge, Mass., 2000), p. 62; cf. the cautious remarks of Garcin, *Grandes villes*, p. 207).

p. 321. Vizirs: see above all D. Sourdel, *Le Vizirat 'abbāside de 749 à 936*, vol. 1 (Damascus, 1959); pp. 78–90 for Abu Ayyub.

p. 322. Barmakid government: Sourdel, *Le Vizirat*, pp. 127–81; H. Kennedy, in C. Melville (ed.), *Persian and Islamic Studies in Honour of P. W. Avery*, vol. 1 (Cambridge, 1990), pp. 89–98.

p. 322. Arab historians on 803: El-Hibri, *Reinterpreting Islamic Historiography*, pp. 31–53.

p. 322. Khurasani tension: Kennedy, *Early Abbasid Caliphate*, pp. 125–7.

p. 323. Al-Rida: al-Tabari, *History*, vol. 32, pp. 60–62; cf. Crone, *Medieval Islamic Political Thought*, pp. 89–94.

p. 323. Egypt: K. Morimoto, *The Fiscal Administration of Egypt in the Early Islamic Period* (Dohosha, 1981), pp. 156–72.

p. 324. Al-Ma'mun's armies: Kennedy, *Armies*, pp. 108–11.

p. 324. Books: *The Fihrist of al-Nadīm*, trans. B. Dodge, 2 vols. (New York, 1970); vol. 1, p. 214 for al-Waqidi. See Robinson, *Islamic Historiography*, pp. 3–8.

p. 325. *'Ulamā'* and biographical dictionaries: see M. J. L. Young, in idem, *Religion, Learning and Science*, pp. 169–77; R. S. Humphreys, *Islamic History*, revised edn. (Princeton, 1991), pp. 187–99; R. P. Mottahadeh, *Loyalty and Leadership in an Early Islamic Society* (Princeton, 1980), pp. 135–50.

p. 325. Law schools: J. Schacht, *An Introduction to Islamic Law* (Oxford, 1964), pp. 28–75.

p. 326. *Adab*: see the introductions in von Grunebaum, *Medieval Islam*, pp. 250–57; R. Allen, *An Introduction to Arabic Literature* (Cambridge, 2000), pp. 139–57; Ashtiany, *'Abbasid belles-lettres*, pp. 16–30, 89–95.

p. 326. 'Curiosities': *The Latā'if al-ma'ārif of Tha'ālibī*, trans. C. E. Bosworth (Edinburgh, 1968), pp. 45, 48, 73, 82, 86, 113.

p. 327. Al-Tanukhi: *The Table-talk of a Mesopotamian Judge*, trans. D. S. Margoliouth, vol. 1 (London, 1921); vols. 8 and 2 (Hyderabad, 1929–32).

p. 327. Al-Fadl: al-Tanukhi, *Table-talk*, 8.12–15, with al-Tabari, *History*, vol. 33, pp. 28–35 (cf. Sourdel, *Le Vizirat*, pp. 246–53); peculation: al-Tanukhi, 8.6,11, etc.; the retired clerk: ibid., 8.12.

p. 328. Ibn al-Zayyat: al-Tanukhi, *Table-talk*, 8.4; al-Tabari, *History*, vol. 34, pp. 65–72 (cf. Sourdel, *Le Vizirat*, pp. 254–69).

p. 328. Khayzuran and Zubayda: N. Abbott, *Two Queens of Baghdad* (Chicago, 1946); Kennedy, *The Court*, pp. 163–89; for source-critical analyses, El-Hibri, *Reinterpreting Islamic Historiography*, pp. 42–4, and in general J. Bray, in L. Brubaker and J. M. H. Smith (eds.), *Gender in the Early Medieval World* (Cambridge, 2004), pp. 121–46.

p. 329. Shaghab: Bray, in Brubaker and Smith, *Gender*, pp. 143–6; N. M. El Cheikh, ibid., pp. 147–61.

p. 329. Image of al-Ma'mun: al-Tabari, *History*, vol. 32, pp. 232–57; El-Hibri, *Reinterpreting Islamic Historiography*, pp. 108–11; M. Cooperson, *Classical Arabic Biography*

(Cambridge, 2000), pp. 24–69. Science, caliphal authority and the *miḥna*: D. Gutas, *Greek Thought, Arabic Culture* (London, 1998), esp. pp. 75–104 (who makes it clear that al-Mam'un was not the originator of the translation movement); more generally, Sourdel, *L'État impérial*, pp. 100–12; Crone, *Medieval Islamic Political Thought*, pp. 130–33; P. Crone and M. Hinds, *God's Caliph* (Cambridge, 1986), pp. 80–99; cf. *Ibn al-Muqaffaʿ, 'conseilleur' du caliphe*, trans. C. Pellat (Paris, 1976), esp. cc. 8, 10, 13–17, 36, 55.

p. 330. Samarra: see C. F. Robinson (ed.), *A Medieval Islamic City Reconsidered* (Oxford, 2001); M. S. Gordon, *The Breaking of a Thousand Swords* (Albany, NY, 2001) and Kennedy, *Armies*, pp. 118–47, for the Turkish army.

p. 331. Al-Afshin's fall: al-Tabari, *History*, vol. 33, pp. 180–200.

p. 331. Ishaq and al-Muʿtasim: al-Tabari, *History*, vol. 33, pp. 214–15. For Turkish dangers, Kennedy, *Armies*, pp. 196–8, less catastrophist than P. Crone, *Slaves on Horses* (Cambridge, 1980), pp. 74–85.

p. 332. Crisis of 860s: Gordon, *The Breaking*, pp. 89–140; D. Waines, 'The Third Century Internal Crisis of the 'Abbasids', *Journal of the Economic and Social History of the Orient*, 25 (1977), pp. 282–306, seems to me too apocalyptic.

p. 332. 870–908 and after: Kennedy, *The Prophet*, pp. 175–99, gives a good account. For the Zanj, see A. Popovic, *The Revolt of African Slaves in Iraq in the 3rd/9th Century* (Princeton, 1999).

p. 334. Tenth-century politics: Kennedy, *The Prophet*, pp. 200–308 (250–66 and 285–308 for Kurds and bedouins); Crone, *Slaves on Horses*, pp. 82–9; Mottahadeh, *Loyalty and Leadership*, pp. 40–116, 175–90.

p. 335. Local societies in Iran: Mottahadeh, *Loyalty and Leadership*, pp. 120–32, 150–57; R. P. Mottahadeh and R. W. Bulliet, in D. S. Richards (ed.), *Islamic Civilization 950–1150* (Oxford, 1973), pp. 33–45, 71–91; W. Madelung, in R. N. Frye (ed.), *The Cambridge History of Iran*, vol. 4 (Cambridge, 1975), pp. 198–239; cf. for a brief structural overview, C. Wickham, *Land and Power* (London, 1994), pp. 56–62. For the general issue of governors and local élites, see for an earlier period H. Kennedy, in *Bulletin of the School of Oriental and African Studies*, 44 (1981), pp. 26–38. For 'Alid chic, Crone, *Slaves on Horses*, p. 86; and see further now T. Bernheimer, 'A Social History of the 'Alid Family from the Eighth to the Eleventh Century', University of Oxford, D.Phil. thesis, 2006, esp. pp. 136–66.

p. 336. Mosul in 989: Mottahadeh, *Loyalty and Leadership*, p. 124; Kennedy, *The Prophet*, pp. 274–5.

p. 336. Fatimids: Kennedy, *The Prophet*, pp. 313–45; C. F. Petry (ed.), *The Cambridge History of Egypt*, vol. 1 (Cambridge, 1998), pp. 111–74; P. E. Walker, *Exploring an Islamic Empire* (London, 2002), especially for sources; Y. Lev, *State and Society in Fatimid Egypt* (Leiden, 1991); Crone, *Medieval Islamic Political Thought*, pp. 197–218, for Isma'ilism; but the fundamental guide for the early period is now M. Brett, *The Rise of the Fatimids* (Leiden, 2001).

p. 338. Fatimid governmental procedures: see the documents in G. Khan (ed.), *Arabic Legal and Administrative Documents in the Cambridge Genizah Collections* (Cambridge, 1993), esp. nn. 104–5, 115, 132, 137, 140–59.

p. 338. Umayyad al-Andalus: the new basic structural analysis is E. Manzano Moreno, *Conquistadores, emires y califas* (Barcelona, 2006), with full historical and archaeological bibliography. In English, brief up-to-date surveys are H. Kennedy, *Muslim Spain and Portugal* (London, 1996), focusing on political history, T. F. Glick, *Islamic and Christian Spain in the Early Middle Ages* (Princeton, 1979), for social history, and idem, *From Muslim Fortress to Christian Castle* (Manchester, 1995), for archaeology. The eighth century is further covered in P. Chalmeta, *Invasión e islamización* (Madrid, 1994); the wide frontier regions in E. Manzano Moreno, *La frontera de al-Andalus en época de los Omeyas* (Madrid, 1991). The old classic is E. Lévi-Provençal, *Histoire de l'Espagne musulmane*, 3 vols. (Leiden and Paris, 1950–53), which contains by far the most detailed political narrative. A selection of significant recent articles in Spanish is translated in M. Marín (ed.), *The Formation of al-Andalus*, vol. 1 (Aldershot, 1998); vol. 2, ed. M. I. Fierro and J. Samsó (Aldershot, 1998), focuses on intellectual history.

p. 339. The eighth-century economy of Spain: C. Wickham, *Framing the Early Middle Ages* (Oxford, 2005), pp. 656–65, 741–59; for cities, see further S. Gutiérrez Lloret, in Marín, *Formation*, vol. 1, pp. 217–47.

p. 340. Syrian settlement in Spain: Manzano, *Conquistadores*, pp. 93–113; an English translation of an earlier version is in Marín, *Formation*, vol. 1, pp. 85–114.

p. 340. *Chronicle of 754* on tax: published in *Conquerors and Chroniclers of Early Medieval Spain*, trans. K. B. Wolf (Liverpool, 1990), pp. 111–58, cc. 59, 62, 82, 91.

p. 340. *Thugūr*: Manzano, *La frontera*.

p. 340. Tribal groups: P. Guichard, *Structures sociales 'orientales' et 'occidentales' dans l'Espagne musulmane* (Paris, 1977) is the classic analysis.

p. 341. 'Abd al-Rahman II: see Lévi-Provençal, *Histoire*, vol. 1, pp. 193–278.

p. 341. Murcia: see A. Carmona González, in Marín, *Formation*, vol. 1, pp. 205–16.

p. 341. Ziryab: Manzano, *Conquistadores*, pp. 307–8.

p. 342. Christians: R. W. Bulliet, *Conversion to Islam in the Medieval Period* (Cambridge, Mass., 1979), pp. 114–27; his figures have been revised both up and down, but are still a significant point of reference. The most nuanced survey is A. Christys, *Christians in al-Andalus (711–1000)* (Richmond, 2002); pp. 52–79 for the relative unimportance of the 'martyrs of Córdoba'; see further K. B. Wolf, *Christian Martyrs in Muslim Spain* (Cambridge, 1988) and J. A. Coope, *The Martyrs of Cordoba* (Lincoln, Nebr., 1995).

p. 342. The *fitna*: see the debate between M. Acién Almansa, in *Entre el feudalismo y el Islam*, 2nd edn. (Jaén, 1997) and M. I. Fierro, in Marín, *Formation*, vol. 1, pp. 291–328; Manzano, *Conquistadores*, pp. 341–59; and V. Salvatierra Cuenca, *La crisis del emirato omeya en el alto Guadalquivir* (Jaén, 2001).

p. 343. 'Abd al-Rahman III and the caliphate: see M. Fierro, '*Abd al-Rahman III* (Oxford, 2005); Lévi-Provençal, *Histoire*, vols. 2 and 3, remains basic.

p. 344. Madinat al-Zahra': A. Vallejo Triano, *Madinat al-Zahra* (Seville, 2004); for ceremonial, *Vita Iohannis Gorzensis*, in *MGH, Scriptores*, vol. 4 (Hanover, 1841), pp. 337–77, cc. 118–36; M. Barceló, in Marín, *Formation*, vol. 1, pp. 425–55. For a detailed description of Córdoba, see Ibn Hauqal, *Configuration*, vol. 1, pp. 110–12.

p. 344. Ceramics: see Manzano, *Conquistadores*, pp. 448–51; for *al-mulk*, M. Barceló, in A. Malpica Cuello (ed.), *La cerámica altomedieval en el sur de al-Andalus* (Granada, 1993), pp. 293–9.

p. 345. Ibn al-Qutiya: for a Spanish translation, see J. Ribera, *Colección de obras arábigas de historia y geografía, que pública la Real Academia de Historia*, vol. 2 (Madrid, 1926), pp. 1–101; for commentary and sizeable quotes in English, Christys, *Christians*, pp. 158–83; see further M. I. Fierro, in *Al-Qantara*, 10 (1989), pp. 485–512.

p. 346. Second *fitna* and Taifas: Kennedy, *Muslim Spain*, pp. 122–44, gives a brisk and nuanced analysis; see further P. C. Scales, *The Fall of the Caliphate of Córdoba* (Leiden, 1994) and D. Wasserstein, *The Rise and Fall of the Party-kings* (Princeton, 1985).

p. 347. Governorships: Lévi-Provençal, *Histoire*, vol. 3, pp. 47–53; Manzano, *Conquistadores*, pp. 425–44.

Chapter 15

The Byzantine economy as a whole is covered in the collective three-volume *EHB*; the best overviews of the period as a whole are the editor, A. E. Laiou's own synthetic article, 'Exchange and Trade, Seventh–Twelfth Centuries', *EHB*, vol. 2, pp. 697–770, and the first half of Laiou and C. Morrisson, *The Byzantine Economy* (Cambridge, 2007). For the early period, see J. F. Haldon, *Byzantium in the Seventh Century*, 2nd edn. (Cambridge, 1997), pp. 92–172, and L. Brubaker and J. F. Haldon, *Byzantium in the Iconoclast Era ca.680–ca.850* (Cambridge, 2008), ch. 7; for the later period, see A. Harvey, *Economic Expansion in the Byzantine Empire, 900–1200* (Cambridge, 1989). For the economic dimension of the fiscal system, M. F. Hendy, *Studies in the Byzantine Monetary Economy, c.300–1450* (Cambridge 1985) is essential; so, for rural society, is M. Kaplan, *Les Hommes et la terre à Byzance du VIᵉ au XIᵉ siècle* (Paris, 1992).

The economy of the Islamic world does not have anything approaching the quality of these overviews. E. Ashtor, *A Social and Economic History of the Near East in the Middle Ages* (London, 1976), the only competitor, and an essential text, is outdated, moralistic and contains some unconvincing structural assumptions. For the period to 800, I refer to my own *Framing the Early Middle Ages* (Oxford, 2005), which contains a bibliography of monographic work; from then onward, local studies (some of them very important) will be referred to as we proceed.

p. 348. City regulations: an English translation of the *Book of the Eparch* by E. H. Freshfield (1938), is in *To eparchikon biblion, the Book of the Eparch, le livre du préfet* (London, 1970), pp. 223–70; cf. Laiou, 'Exchange', pp. 718–36, G. Dagron, in *EHB*, vol. 2, pp. 405–61, and Hendy, *Studies*, pp. 561–9.

p. 349. Constantinople size: the figure is a guess, but fits with the detailed analyses in P. Magdalino, *Constantinople médiévale* (Paris, 1996).

p. 349. Liutprand: *The Complete Works of Liutprand of Cremona*, trans. P. Squatriti (Washington, 2007), pp. 271–3, *Embassy*, cc. 53–5.

p. 349. State control in al-Andalus: O. R. Constable, *Trade and Traders in Muslim Spain* (Cambridge, 1994), pp. 112–37.

p. 350. State and economy in Egypt: S. D. Goitein, *A Mediterranean Society*, 6 vols. (Berkeley, 1967–93), vol. 1, pp. 217–21, 267–72; for grain, Y. Lev, *State and Society in Fatimid Egypt* (Leiden, 1991), pp. 162–78.

p. 351. Jeme: T. Wilfong, *Women of Jeme* (Ann Arbor, 2002); Wickham, *Framing*, pp. 419–28.

p. 351. *Genīza*: for an introduction, Goitein, *Mediterranean Society* (the classic *genīza* study), vol. 1, pp. 1–23.

p. 352. Byzantium: see for what follows the overviews mentioned earlier, with Wickham, *Framing*, pp. 124–9, 460–64, 626–35, 780–94.

p. 352. Theodore and *Farmer's Law*: *Vie de Théodore de Sykéôn*, ed. and trans. A.-J. Festugière (Brussels, 1970); W. Ashburner (ed. and trans.), 'The Farmer's Law', *Journal of Hellenic Studies*, 30 (1910), pp. 85–108; 32 (1912), pp. 68–95.

p. 353. Post-550 urban dip: see most recently, for a critique, M. Whittow, in L. Lavan (ed.), *Recent Research in Late-antique Urbanism* (Portsmouth, RI, 2001), pp. 137–53.

p. 353. Sardis, Ankara, Gortyn: J. S. Crawford, *The Byzantine Shops at Sardis* (Cambridge, Mass., 1990); C. Foss, 'Late Antique and Byzantine Ankara', *Dumbarton Oaks Papers*, 31 (1977), pp. 29–87; E. Zanini and E. Giorgi, in *Annuario della Scuola archeologica italiana di Atene*, 80 (2002), pp. 212–32.

p. 353. Corinth: G. D. R. Sanders, in *EHB*, vol. 2, pp. 647–54.

p. 354. Post-850/900 urban expansion: Harvey, *Economic Expansion*, pp. 207–24, C. Foss, *Byzantine and Turkish Sardis* (Cambridge, Mass., 1980), pp. 66–76; P. Arthur, 'Hierapolis tra Bisanzio e i Turchi', in D. De Bernardi Ferrero, *Saggi in onore di Paolo Verzone* (Rome, 2002), pp. 219–20.

p. 355. Naval law: *Nomos rodiōn nautikos: The Rhodian Sea-law*, ed. and trans. W. Ashburner (Oxford, 1909).

p. 356. Corinth coins: Sanders, in *EHB*, vol. 2, p. 649.

p. 356. Ceramics after 800: J. Čimbuleva, in *Nessèbre*, vol. 2 (Sofia, 1980), pp. 202–15; P. Armstrong, in W. Cavanagh *et al.*, *The Laconia Survey*, vol. 1 (London, 2002), pp. 353–5; eadem, 'Byzantine Thebes', *Annual of the British School at Athens*, 88 (1993), pp. 304–6; T. Totev, 'L'Atelier de céramique peinte du monastère royal de Preslav', *Cahiers archéologiques*, 35 (1987), pp. 65–80; C. H. Morgan, *Excavations at Corinth XI* (Cambridge, Mass., 1942), pp. 14, 36–53, 72–5; N. Günsenin, in *Eupsychia*, vol. 1 (Paris,

1998), pp. 281–7; F. M. Hocker, in S. Kingsley (ed.), *Barbarian Seas: Late Rome to Islam* (London, 2004), pp. 61–3, for the wreck.

p. 356. Linen and glass: *Book of the Eparch*, c. 9; Laiou, 'Exchange', p. 726; Laiou and Morrisson, *The Byzantine Economy*, p. 77, and see pp. 70–89 for an overview of this economic revival.

p. 356. Danelis: Kaplan, *Les Hommes*, pp. 333–4; Basil: E. McGeer, *The Land Legislation of the Macedonian Emperors* (Toronto, 2000), Novel O, 7.

p. 357. Byzantines in Egypt: Goitein, *Mediterranean Society*, vol. 1, pp. 44–6; D. Jacoby, in *Thesaurismata*, 30 (2000), pp. 25–77.

p. 357. Eleventh-century agricultural specializations: Harvey, *Economic Expansion*, *passim*; Laiou and Morrisson, *The Byzantine Economy*, pp. 90–115.

p. 357. Syria: see, before 800, A. Walmsley, *Early Islamic Syria* (London, 2007).

p. 358. Madaba: M. Piccirillo, *The Mosaics of Jordan* ('Amman, 1992), pp. 49–256; see in general for rural settlement, J. Magness, *The Archaeology of the Early Islamic Settlement in Palestine* (Winona Lake, Ind., 2003).

p. 358. Bet She'an: Y. Tsafrir and G. Foerster, in *Dumbarton Oaks Papers*, 51 (1997), pp. 85–146.

p. 358. Athanasios: *The Seventh Century in the West-Syrian Chronicles*, trans. A. Palmer (Liverpool, 1993), pp. 202–4.

p. 359. Changing forms of cities: the classic is H. Kennedy, 'From *polis* to *madina*', *Past and Present*, 106 (1985), pp. 3–27. For Iran, see R. W. Bulliet, *The Patricians of Nishapur* (Cambridge, Mass., 1972).

p. 360. Syro-Palestinian exchange under the early 'Abbasids: A. Walmsley in I. L. Hansen and C. Wickham (eds.), *The Long Eighth Century* (Leiden, 2000), pp. 265–343; A. Northedge and A. Walmsley, in E. Villeneuve and P. Watson (eds.), *La Céramique byzantine et proto-islamique en Syrie-Jordanie* (Beirut, 2001), pp. 207–14, 305–13.

p. 361. Nahrawan canal: R. McC. Adams, *Land behind Baghdad* (Chicago, 1965), esp. pp. 69–106, 115 (and 97–8 for dating); for a critique, M. Morony, in G. R. D. King and A. Cameron (eds.), *The Byzantine and Early Islamic Near East*, vol. 2 (Princeton, 1994), pp. 221–9.

p. 361. Raqqa: K. Bartl, *Frühislamische Besiedlung im Balīh-tal/Nordsyrien* (Berlin, 1994).

p. 361. Sharecropping, etc.: M. 'Abdul Jabbār, in M. G. Morony (ed.), *Manufacturing and Labour* (Aldershot, 2003), pp. 235–51; cf. Ashtor, *Social and Economic History*, pp. 87–90, 97–9, 109–14, 143–58 for the economic networks focused on Baghdad; and for Arab-period agricultural diversification in general, A. M. Watson, *Agricultural Innovation in the Early Islamic World* (Cambridge, 1983).

p. 362. Siraf and the Indian Ocean: R. Hodges and D. Whitehouse, *Mohammed, Charlemagne and the Origins of Europe* (London, 1983), pp. 133–49; M. Tampoe, *Maritime Trade between China and the West* (Oxford, 1989); K. M. Chaudhuri, *Trade and Civilization in the Indian Ocean* (Cambridge, 1985); Buzurg, *The Book of the Wonders of India, Mainland, Sea and Islands*, trans. G. S. P. Freeman-Grenville (London, 1981).

p. 362. Egypt to 800: Wickham, *Framing*, pp. 133–44, 609–12, 759–69. For the urban-dwelling percentage in Roman Egypt, see R. S. Bagnall and B. W. Freer, *The Demography of Roman Egypt* (Cambridge, 1994), pp. 53–6.

p. 363. Rise of large landowning: K. Morimoto, in *Orient*, 11 (1975), pp. 109–53; G. Frantz-Murphy, *Arabic Agricultural Leases and Tax Receipts from Egypt 148–427 A. H./765–1035 AD.* (Vienna, 2001) – crucial on tax-farming; cf. Goitein, *Mediterranean Society*, vol. 1, pp. 117–18 for *day'a* in the eleventh century.

p. 364. Fayyum papyri: Y. Rāġib, *Marchands d'étoffes du Fayyoum au IIIe/IXe siècle*, 4 vols. so far (Cairo, 1982–96); for Qus, 1.3, 8, 10, 2.14; for Alexandria and Tinnis, 3.33.

p. 365. Linen: Y. Lev, 'Tinnīs', in M. Barrucand (ed.), *L'Égypte fatimide, son art et son histoire* (Paris, 1999), pp. 83–96; G. Frantz-Murphy, in *Journal of the Economic and Social History of the Orient*, 24 (1981), pp. 274–97; Ibn Hauqal, *Configuration de la terre*, vol. 1, trans. J. H. Kramers and G. Wiet (Beirut and Paris, 1964) p. 150, for sale to Iraq.

p. 365. Exports: Goitein, *Mediterranean Society*, vol. 1, pp. 153–6, 209–17, and *passim*.

p. 365. Ibn 'Awkal: N. A. Stillman, in *Journal of the Economic and Social History of the Orient*, 16 (1973), pp. 15–88 (his sons were adults in 1008 – cf. p. 17 – so he was probably around forty by then); M. Gil, ibid., 46 (2003), pp. 273–319; Goitein, *Mediterranean Society*, vol. 6, p. 56, indexes the numerous references to him there; S. D. Goitein, *Letters of Medieval Jewish Traders* (Princeton, 1973), nn. 1 (Samhun), 13, 14, 70.

p. 368. Exports from al-Andalus: Constable, *Trade and Traders*, pp. 169–208; cf. 79–92 for merchants.

p. 368. Rome-Constantinople route: M. McCormick, *Origins of the European Economy* (Cambridge, 2001), pp. 502–8. Small-scale network of boats: P. Horden and N. Purcell, *The Corrupting Sea* (Oxford, 2000), pp. 123–72.

p. 369. Venice: McCormick, *Origins*, pp. 238–40 (St Mark), 523–31, 733–77.

p. 369. Amalfi: McCormick, *Origins*, pp. 511–15, 627–30; B. M. Kreutz, *Before the Normans* (Philadelphia, 1991), pp. 75–93.

p. 369. Olive oil in 880, Arab wrecks off France: McCormick, *Origins*, pp. 955–6, 599 (cf. 674–8).

p. 369. Byzantine exports: Laiou, 'Exchange', pp. 725–8; D. Jacoby, in *Thesaurismata*, 30 (2000), pp. 25–77; Goitein, *Mediterranean Society*, vol. 1, p. 46.

p. 370. Almería: Constable, *Trade and Traders*, pp. 18–19; Goitein, *Mediterranean Society*, vol. 1, pp. 61, 64, 210, etc.

p. 370. Tunisian ceramics: G. Berti and L. Tongiorgi, *I bacini ceramici medievali delle chiese di Pisa* (Rome, 1981), pp. 162–75; for Tunisian prosperity, see in general G. Vanacker, in *Annales ESC*, 28 (1973), pp. 659–80.

p. 371. Egypt as hub: see J. L. Abu-Lughod, *Before European Hegemony* (New York, 1989), pp. 213–47, and *passim* for the medieval trade cycle as a whole.

Chapter 16

There are many books on the Carolingians, more than on any topic in our period after the end of the western empire. The best single-author survey remains R. McKitterick, *The Frankish Kingdoms under the Carolingians, 751–987* (Harlow, 1983); crucial article collections, also aiming for completeness, are *NCMH*, vol. 2, and R. Le Jan (ed.), *La Royauté et les élites dans l'Europe carolingienne* (Lille, 1998), much of which is in English. As one would expect, French and particularly German historiography are also very strong; these books and others cite it at length. Charlemagne has many personalized accounts, of which the most recent (and best) are J. Story (ed.), *Charlemagne* (Manchester, 2005), and R. McKitterick, *Charlemagne* (Cambridge 2008); Louis the Pious has fewer, but see P. Godman and R. Collins (eds.), *Charlemagne's Heir* (Oxford, 1990), a rather severe set of articles; for his son Charles, see above all J. L. Nelson, *Charles the Bald* (Harlow, 1992). For Carolingian culture, see the next chapter. Other key points of reference are J. L. Nelson's article collections, *Politics and Ritual in Early Medieval Europe* (London, 1986), *The Frankish World, 750–900* (London, 1996), and *Courts, Elites and the Workings of Power in the Early Medieval World* (Aldershot, 2007); M. Innes, *State and Society in the Early Middle Ages* (Cambridge, 2000); and an innovative rereading of Carolingian political rhetoric, P. E. Dutton, *The Politics of Dreaming in the Carolingian Empire* (Lincoln, Nebr., 1994). Many primary sources are in translation, in particular in P. D. King, *Charlemagne* (Kendal, 1987) and P. E. Dutton, *Carolingian Civilization* (Peterborough, Ont., 1993). This outpouring of recent work largely replaces its English-language predecessors, but see, still, H. Fichtenau, *The Carolingian Empire* (Oxford, 1963), F. L. Ganshof, *Frankish Institutions under Charlemagne* (Providence, RI, 1968), and D. Bullough, *The Age of Charlemagne* (London, 1965).

p. 375. Fastrada letter: trans. King, *Charlemagne*, pp. 309–10.

p. 375. Charlemagne's age: M. Becher, 'Neue Überlieferungen zum Geburtsdatum Karls des Grossen', *Francia*, 19 (1992), pp. 37–60.

p. 376. Charlemagne's tastes: Einhard, *Life of Charlemagne*, trans. P. E. Dutton, *Charlemagne's Courtier* (Peterborough, Ont., 1998), cc. 18, 22–4, 29.

p. 376. Charles Martel: P. Fouracre, *The Age of Charles Martel* (Harlow, 2000).

p. 376. Coup: *Royal Frankish Annals*, trans. B. W. Scholz, *Carolingian Chronicles* (Ann Arbor, 1970), s.a. 751 (with modifications); R. McKitterick, *History and Memory in the Carolingian World* (Cambridge, 2004), pp. 133–55; P. E. Dutton, *Charlemagne's Mustache* (New York, 2004), pp. 3–42 for hairstyles.

p. 377. Church councils: M. A. Claussen, *The Reform of the Frankish Church* (Cambridge, 2004), pp. 24–57; J. M. Wallace-Hadrill, *The Frankish Church* (Oxford, 1983), pp. 162–80; for tithes, *Cap.*, vol. 1, n. 17.

p. 379. Duke Tassilo: see S. Airlie, in *Transactions of the Royal Historical Society*, 6 ser, 9 (1999), pp. 93–119; for death/imprisonment, J. Busch, in *Historische Zeitschrift*, 263 (1996), pp. 561–88; for blinding, G. Bührer-Thierry, in B. H. Rosenwein (ed.), *Anger's Past* (Ithaca, NY, 1998), pp. 75–91.

p. 380. Bavarian aristocracies: see K. L. R. Pearson, *Conflicting Loyalties in Early Medieval Bavaria* (Aldershot, 1999); W. Brown, *Unjust Seizure* (Ithaca, NY, 2001).

p. 380. Einhard on the Avars: *Life of Charlemagne*, c. 13.

p. 380. End of expansion: T. Reuter, *Medieval Polities and Modern Mentalities*, ed. J. L. Nelson (Cambridge, 2006), pp. 251–67.

p. 381. Carolingian control of monasteries: S. Wood, *The Proprietary Church in the Medieval West* (Oxford, 2006), pp. 247–69.

p. 381. Chosen people: M. Garrison, 'The Franks as the New Israel?', in Y. Hen and M. Innes (eds.), *The Uses of the Past in the Early Middle Ages* (Cambridge, 2000), pp. 114–61, nuancing earlier views. Jews: see B. S. Bachrach, *Early Medieval Jewish Policy in Western Europe* (Minneapolis, 1977), pp. 66–131.

p. 381. Einhard in Greek: *Life of Charlemagne*, c. 16.

p. 382. Aachen: J. L. Nelson, in M. de Jong and F. Theuws (eds.), *Topographies of Power in the Early Middle Ages* (Leiden, 2001), pp. 217–41.

p. 382. *Correctio*, etc.: this, and wider 'reform' terminology, is preferable to the common phrase 'Carolingian Renaissance', for nothing was 'reborn' in this period, least of all classical Antiquity, with which the Carolingians saw hardly broken links. The *General Admonition* and the letter of education (*Cap.*, vol. 1, nn. 22, 29) are trans. King, *Charlemagne*, pp. 209–20, 232–3.

p. 383. Alcuin: see D. A. Bullough, *Alcuin* (Leiden, 2004).

p. 383. Dhuoda: *Handbook for William*, trans. C. Neel (Lincoln, Nebr., 1999).

p. 384. Louis's smile: Thegan, *Life of Louis*, c. 19, trans. Dutton, *Carolingian Civilization*, pp. 141–55; cf. M. Innes, in G. Halsall (ed.), *Humour, History and Politics in Late Antiquity and the Early Middle Ages* (Cambridge, 2002), pp. 131–56.

p. 384. Legislation: P. Fouracre, 'Carolingian Justice', *Settimane di studio*, 42 (1995), pp. 771–803; R. Le Jan, 'Justice royale et pratiques sociales dans le royaume franc au IXᵉ siècle', *Settimane di studio*, 44 (1997), pp. 47–85; for law books, R. McKitterick, *The Carolingians and the Written Word* (Cambridge, 1989), pp. 23–75; P. Wormald, *The Making of English Law*, vol. 1 (Oxford, 1999), pp. 30–70.

p. 385. Ansegis, 803 capitulary: *Cap.*, vol. 1, nn. 183, 39; Ansegis is re-edited in G. Schmitz, *Collectio Capitularium Ansegisi*, MGH, *Cap.*, NS vol. 1; for manuscripts of 803, see also H. Mordek, *Bibliotheca Capitularium Regum Francorum Manuscripta* (Munich, 1995), pp. 1083–4.

p. 386. Assemblies: Hincmar, *On the Organization of the Palace*, trans. Dutton, *Carolingian Civilization*, pp. 485–99; Nithard, *Histories*, 2.9, trans. Scholz, *Carolingian Chronicles*. For Nithard, see Nelson, *Politics and Ritual*, pp. 195–237. For how assembly etiquette and the ritual of public communication worked, see C. Pössel, 'Symbolic Communication and the Negotiation of Power at Carolingian Regnal Assemblies, 814–840', University of Cambridge, Ph.D. thesis, 2003.

p. 386. *Scabini*: Ganshof, *Frankish Institutions*, pp. 77–83; F. Bougard, *La Justice dans le royaume d'Italie* (Rome, 1995), pp. 140–58.

p. 386. Oaths: *Cap.*, vol. 1, n. 23, c. 18; n. 25; n. 33, c. 2; banned oaths: n. 20, c. 16; n. 44, cc. 9, 10 (trans. King, *Charlemagne*, pp. 221, 223 in part, 234, 204, 249). See M. Becher, *Eid und Herrschaft* (Sigmaringen, 1993), esp. pp. 78–87, though I tend to prefer a 792–3 dating for *Cap.* n. 25. For the 785–6 revolts, see R. McKitterick, *Perceptions of the Past in the Early Middle Ages* (Notre Dame, Ind., 2006), pp. 63–89.

p. 387. Control of the empire: see in general on government K. F. Werner, 'Missus-marchio-comes', in W. Paravicini and K. F. Werner (eds.), *Histoire comparée de l'administration (IVᵉ–XVIIIᵉ siècles)* (Munich, 1980), pp. 191–239; J. L. Nelson, in *NCMH*, vol. 2, pp. 383–430; eadem, in R. McKitterick (ed.), *Carolingian Culture* (Cambridge, 1994), pp. 52–87; eadem, *Frankish World*, pp. 1–36; M. Innes, in Story, *Charlemagne*, pp. 71–89. For courts, see e.g. S. Airlie, 'The Palace of Memory', in S. Rees Jones *et al.* (eds.), *Courts and Regions in Medieval Europe* (York, 2000), pp. 1–19.

p. 387. Gifts: see Reuter, *Medieval Polities*, pp. 239–43; for provisions, and the link to gifts, see esp. *Cap.*, vol. 1, n. 75 (trans. King, *Charlemagne*, p. 260).

p. 388. *Reichsaristokratie*: G. Tellenbach, *Königtum und Stamme in der Werdezeit des Deutschen Reiches* (Weimar, 1939), pp. 42–55; developed by e.g. K. F. Werner, 'Important Noble Families in the Kingdom of Charlemagne', in T. Reuter (ed.), *The Medieval Nobility* (Amsterdam, 1978), pp. 137–202. See S. Airlie, in *NCMH*, vol. 2, pp. 431–50, and in Story, *Charlemagne*, pp. 90–102, for the basic accounts in English, and R. Le Jan, *Famille et pouvoir dans le monde franc (VIIᵉ–Xᵉ siècle)* (Paris, 1995), esp. pp. 401–13. For the aristocratic commitment to the state, see further S. Airlie, in idem *et al.* (eds.), *Staat im frühen Mittelalter* (Vienna, 2006), pp. 93–111.

p. 388. Widonids: E. Hlawitschka, 'Waren die Kaiser Wido und Lambert Nachkommen Karls des Grossen?', *Quellen und Forschungen*, 49 (1969), pp. 366–86; Innes, *State and Society*, pp. 125, 211–15, 235–6; Le Jan, *Famille et pouvoir*, pp. 95–6, 250–51, 422, 441; Nithard, *Histories*, 1.5.

p. 389. Vassals: Werner, 'Missus-marchio', pp. 228–30; S. Reynolds, *Fiefs and Vassals* (Oxford, 1994), pp. 84–105.

p. 389. *Missi*: Werner, 'Missus-marchio'; written reports: Nelson, *Frankish World*, pp. 14–34; Rižana: C. Manaresi (ed.), *I placiti del 'Regnum Italiae'*, vol. 1 (Rome, 1955), n. 17.

p. 390. Written instructions, etc.: *MGH*, *Epistolae*, vol. 5, ed. K. Hampe and E. Dümmler (Berlin, 1899), pp. 277–8; Einhard, *Letters* (trans. and renumbered, Dutton, *Charlemagne's Courtier*, pp. 131–65), nn. 20–21; *The Letters of Lupus of Ferrières*, trans. G. W. Regenos (The Hague, 1966), *letter* 41; *Cap.*, vol. 2, n. 261; cf. Hincmar, *On the Organization*, c. 36.

p. 390. Looking for the king: see e.g. Lupus of Ferrières, *Letters*, 17, 118, 123 (and compare Ch. 5 for Desiderius of Cahors).

p. 390. Aristocratic literacy: McKitterick, *Carolingians and the Written Word*, pp. 211–70.

p. 391. Abuses: Theodulf, *Contra Iudices*, partially trans. P. Godman, *Poetry of the Carolingian Renaissance* (London, 1985), pp. 162–5; Manaresi, *I placiti*, vol. 1, n. 25; Paschasius Radbert, *Epitaph of Arsenius*, 1.26, trans. in A. Cabaniss, *Charlemagne's Cousins* (Syracuse, NY, 1967) – but the Wala story is a moral tale with no pretension to accuracy; for Agobard, *MGH*, *Epistolae*, vol. 5, p. 202; see P. Depreux, 'Le Comte Matfrid d'Orléans', *Bibliothèque de l'École des Chartes*, 152 (1994), pp. 331–74.

p. 391. Hincmar: Wallace-Hadrill, *Frankish Church*, p. 299.

p. 392. Peasants in court: C. Wickham, *Framing the Early Middle Ages* (Oxford, 2005), pp. 578–83.

p. 392. State and local societies: see above all Innes, *State and Society*, pp. 180–225, for a heartland region, however.

p. 392. Charlemagne's daughters: Nelson, *Frankish World*, pp. 237–42.

p. 393. Louis's administration: K. F. Werner, in Godman and Collins, *Charlemagne's Heir*, pp. 3–123; and above all P. Depreux, *Prosopographie de l'entourage de Louis le Pieux (781–840)* (Sigmaringen, 1997).

p. 393. Attigny: M. de Jong, 'Power and Humility in Carolingian Society', *EME*, 1 (1992), pp. 29–52; for Theodosius, Astronomer, *Life of Louis*, c. 35, trans. A. Cabaniss, *Son of Charlemagne* (Syracuse, NY, 1961).

p. 394. Einhard: see his *Letters*, nn. 34, 40–45, 52–4, 26–8; cf. Dutton, *Charlemagne's Courtier*, p. 8, for Walahfrid.

p. 395. Nithard: *Histories*, 1.3 for 829, 4.6 for Fontenoy scaring the magnates. For Lothar's perspective, see E. Screen, in *EME*, 12 (2003), pp. 25–51.

p. 396. Post-Carolingian Francia: C. R. Brühl, *Deutschland-Frankreich* (Cologne, 1990), esp. pp. 287–302.

p. 396. Louis the German: see above all E. J. Goldberg, *Struggle for Empire* (Cambridge, 2006), with T. Reuter, *Germany in the Early Middle Ages c. 800–1056* (Harlow, 1991), pp. 70–111; for Saxony, *Annals of Fulda*, trans. T. Reuter (Manchester, 1992), s.a. 852.

p. 397. Louis II: P. Delogu, in *Bullettino dell'Istituto storico italiano per il medio evo*, 80 (1968), pp. 137–89; F. Bougard, in Le Jan, *La Royauté et les élites*, pp. 249–67.

p. 398. Frisia: S. Coupland, 'From Poachers to Gamekeepers', *EME*, 7 (1998), pp. 85–114.

p. 399. General tax: E. Joranson, *The Danegeld in France* (Rock Island, Ill., 1924).

p. 399. 858 and 875–7: Nelson, *Charles the Bald*, pp. 170–96, 239–52.

p. 400. Charles and magnates: Nelson, *Charles the Bald*, pp. 166–7, 183, 209–10, 221–2, 231–4, 240–43; for Odo and Charles, *Annals of Saint-Bertin*, trans. J. L. Nelson (Manchester, 1991), s.aa. 866, 868; for Bernard of Gothia, ibid., s.a. 878. For Boso, see C. B. Bouchard, *'Those of my Blood'* (Philadelphia, 2001), pp. 74–97.

p. 400. Compiègne: Airlie, 'Palace of Memory', pp. 13–16. Ponthion: *Annals of Saint-Bertin*, s.a. 876 (see Ch. 17 below). Pîtres: *Cap.*, vol. 2, 11, n. 273, cf. Nelson, *Politics and Ritual*, pp. 91–116; eadem, *Frankish World*, pp. 93–8.

p. 401. *Reguli*: *Annals of Fulda*, s.a. 888. Boso: apart from Bouchard, as at note to p. 400 above; see S. MacLean, in *EME*, 10 (2001), pp. 21–48; Airlie and Staab, in Le Jan, *La Royauté et les élites*, pp. 138–43, 365–82.

p. 401. Pippin of Beauvais (or perhaps Senlis): see K. F. Werner, in *Die Welt als Geschichte*, 20 (1960), pp. 87–119, at p. 93.

p. 402. Charles the Fat: S. MacLean, *Kingship and Politics in the Late Ninth Century* (Cambridge, 2003).

p. 402. Royal power and regionalization: e.g. Reuter, *Germany*, pp. 75–7. Nithard: *Histories*, 2.2–4, 7, 9, 3.2, 4.4. Matfrid: Thegan, *Life of Louis*, c. 55. 861: *Annals of Fulda*, s.a. 861. Note also that both Charlemagne and Louis the Pious already envisioned that, after their empire was divided between their sons, benefices (though not properties) would already be regionalized: *Cap.*, vol. 1, n. 45, c. 9; n. 136, c. 9 (trans. King, *Charlemagne*, p. 253, and Dutton, *Carolingian Civilization*, p. 178).

p. 403. Everard and Gisela: see C. La Rocca and L. Provero, 'The Dead and their Gifts', in F. Theuws and J. L. Nelson (eds.), *Rituals of Power* (Leiden, 2000), pp. 225–80.

p. 403. Welfs: *Annals of Fulda*, s.a. 858; E. Krüger, *Der Ursprung des Welfenhauses und seine Verzweigung in Süddeutschland* (Wolfenbüttel, 1899), pp. 68–129, with a bit of care.

p. 404. Paris: see Le Jan, *Famille et pouvoir*, pp. 255–6, 442.

p. 404. Bavaria: *Annals of Fulda*, s.a. 884; see C. R. Bowlus, *Franks, Moravians and Magyars* (Philadelphia, 1995), pp. 208–16.

Chapter 17

For general surveys of these themes, see Chapter 16, especially *NCMH*, vol. 2; see further R. McKitterick (ed.), *Carolingian Culture* (Cambridge, 1994), and P. Wormald (ed.), *Lay Intellectuals in the Carolingian World* (Cambridge, 2007). McKitterick's monographs, especially *The Carolingians and the Written Word* (Cambridge, 1989) and *History and Memory in the Carolingian World* (Cambridge, 2004), and J. M. Wallace-Hadrill, *The Frankish Church* (Oxford, 1983), are also important starting points, with, of an older literature, W. Ullmann, *The Carolingian Renaissance and the Idea of Kingship* (London, 1969).

p. 405. For all this see Einhard, *Translation and Miracles of Saints Marcellinus and Peter*, trans. P. E. Dutton, *Charlemagne's Courtier* (Peterborough, Ont., 1998), pp. 69–130, esp. books 1 and 2 (2.1 for Einhard and Hilduin, 4.7 for Gerward). For the role of the arch-chaplain, see Hincmar, *On the Organization of the Palace*, trans. P. E. Dutton, *Carolingian Civilization* (Peterborough, Ont., 1993), cc. 19–20. Window: Notker, *Deeds of Charlemagne*, trans. L. Thorpe, *Two Lives of Charlemagne* (London, 1969), pp. 93–172, 1.30. For relic thefts, see P. J. Geary, *Furta Sacra* (Princeton, 1978), pp. 40–59. The best recent discussion in English of this whole sequence is J. M. H. Smith, in K. Mills and A. Grafton (eds.), *Conversion in Late Antiquity and the Early Middle Ages* (Rochester, NY, 2003), pp. 189–223.

p. 406. Palace: Hincmar, *On the Organization*, cc. 12–28; for noise, see Paschasius Radbert, *Life of Adalard*, trans. A. Cabaniss, *Charlemagne's Cousins* (Syracuse, NY, 1967), c. 27.

p. 407. Notker: *Deeds of Charlemagne*, 1.11 (etiquette), 1.34 (never at court). Cf. for etiquette, J. L. Nelson and M. Innes, in C. Cubitt (ed.), *Court Culture in the Early Middle Ages* (Turnhout, 2003), pp. 39–76.

p. 407. Patronage: Hincmar, *On the Organization*, c. 18; Notker, *Deeds of Charlemagne*, 1.4; Einhard, *Letters*, trans. Dutton, *Charlemagne's Courtier*, e.g. nn. 9, 32, 49, appendix B, and see also above, Chapter 16.

p. 407. Moral centre: see e.g. M. de Jong, 'Sacrum palatium et ecclesia', *Annales HSS*, 58 (2003), pp. 1243–69. Priest and king: Astronomer, *Life of Louis*, trans. A. Cabaniss, *Son of Charlemagne* (Syracuse, NY, 1961), c. 19 (with c. 37 for 823 portents). Famine of 805: *Cap.*, vol 1, n. 124 (trans. P. D. King, *Charlemagne* (Kendal, 1987), pp. 245–7).

p. 407. Just and unjust kings: see J. M. Wallace-Hadrill, *Early Medieval History* (Oxford, 1975), pp. 181–200 for treatises, and R. Meens, *EME*, 7 (1998), pp. 345–57.

p. 408. Einhard and Imma: *The Letters of Lupus of Ferrières*, trans. G. W. Regenos (The Hague, 1966), letter 3.

p. 408. Accusations against queens: see esp. G. Bührer-Thierry, 'La Reine adultère', *Cahiers de civilisation médiévale*, 35 (1992), pp. 299–312; for Judith, see E. Ward, in W. J. Sheils and D. Woods (eds.), *Women in the Church* (Oxford, 1990), pp. 15–25, and Paschasius Radbert, *Epitaph of Arsenius*, trans. Cabaniss, *Charlemagne's Cousins*, 2.7–9; for Uota, T. Reuter, *Medieval Polities and Modern Mentalities*, ed. J. L. Nelson (Cambridge, 2006), pp. 217–30.

p. 409. Einhard: *Translation*, 1.13, 14, 2.3, 4, 6 (hunting), 11.

p. 409. Hunting: *Annals of Saint-Bertin*, trans. J. L. Nelson (Manchester, 1991), s.a. 835; Astronomer, *Life of Louis*, cc. 46, 52; see J. Jarnut, 'Die frühmittelalterliche Jagd', *Settimane di studio*, 31 (1985), pp. 765–98, and J. L. Nelson, *The Frankish World 750–90* (London, 1996), pp. 120–24.

p. 409. Penaces in 822 and 833: Paschasius, *Life of Adalard*, c. 51; *Cap.*, vol. 2, n. 197, c. 1; M. de Jong, 'What was *Public* about Public Penance?', *Settimane di studio*, 44 (1997), pp. 863–902 (esp. pp. 887–93).

p. 410. Ritual and political claims: see above all P. Buc, *The Dangers of Ritual* (Princeton, 2001), pp. 51–87 and *passim*.

p. 410. Ponthion synod: *Annals of Saint-Bertin*, s.a. 876; compare *Annals of Fulda*, trans. T. Reuter (Manchester, 1992), s.a. 876.

p. 411. Aristocrats sneering at the low-born: Thegan, *Life of Louis*, trans. Dutton, *Carolingian Civilization*, pp. 141–55, cc. 20, 44, 50, 56; *Annals of Fulda*, s.a. 887 (I).

p. 411. Education: see e.g. J. J. Contreni, in *NCMH*, vol 2, pp. 709–47; P. Riché, *Écoles et enseignement dans le haut Moyen Âge* (Paris, 1989), esp. pp. 49–118.

p. 412. Books: Lupus of Ferrières, *Letters*, 124; for Everard, McKitterick, *Carolingians and the Written Word*, pp. 245–8.

p. 412. Texts of 828–9: see esp. *Cap.*, vol. 2, n. 185; *MGH, Concilia*, vol. 2, ed. A. Werminghoff (Hanover, 1906), n. 50; Paschasius, *Epitaph of Arsenius*, 2.1.2–3; Einhard, *Translation*, 3.13 (*capitula* of Gabriel), 14 (Wiggo). See, for the whole sequence, P. E. Dutton, *The Politics of Dreaming in the Carolingian Empire* (Lincoln, Nebr., 1994), pp. 92–101, M. de Jong, in S. Airlie *et al.* (eds.), *Staat im frühen Mittelalter* (Vienna, 2006), pp. 129–31, and D. Ganz, in P. Godman and R. Collins (eds.), *Charlemagne's Heir* (Oxford, 1990), pp. 545–6.

p. 413. Events of 833–4: Paschasius, *Epitaph of Arsenius*, 2.18; *Cap.*, vol. 2, nn. 197–8; *Annals of Saint-Bertin*, s.a. 835; Dutton, *The Politics of Dreaming*, p. 103; and see C. Pössel, 'Symbolic Communication and the Negotiation of Power at Carolingian Regnal Assemblies, 814–840', University of Cambridge, Ph.D. thesis, 2003, pp. 129–232, for rival narratives of 830–34.

p. 413. Bilingualism: Einhard, *Life of Charlemagne*, c. 25; Thegan, *Life of Louis*, c. 19 (both also supposedly had a – rare – passive knowledge of spoken Greek); Paschasius, *Epitaph of Arsenius*, 1.1.2.

p. 413. Latin as separated from Romance by Alcuin: R. Wright, *Late Latin and Early Romance in Spain and Carolingian France* (Liverpool, 1992), pp. 103–35; for an aristocracy unaffected by Latin, see M. Richter, *The Formation of the Medieval West* (Dublin, 1994), esp. pp. 69–77.

p. 414. Lupus, Dhuoda: Lupus of Ferrières, *Letters*, 7; Dhuoda, *Handbook for William*, trans. C. Neel (Lincoln, Nebr., 1999) (on Dhuoda see most recently J. L. Nelson, 'Dhuoda', in Wormald, *Lay Intellectuals*); and see in general McKitterick, *Carolingians and the Written Word*, pp. 211–70.

p. 414. Preaching: see R. McKitterick, *The Frankish Church and the Carolingian Reforms, 789–895* (London, 1977), pp. 80–114. For the Bible, see C. Edwards, 'German Vernacular Literature', in McKitterick, *Carolingian Culture*, pp. 141–70; and H. J. Hummer, *Politics and Power in Early Medieval Europe* (Cambridge, 2005), pp. 130–54, who makes clear the complexity of the project.

p. 414. Weather, dust: Agobard of Lyon, *On Hail and Thunder*, partially trans. Dutton, *Carolingian Civilization*, pp. 189–91 (c. 16 for dust), cf. Paschasius, *Epitaph of Arsenius*, 2.1.4, and perhaps also *Cap.*, vol. 1, n. 54, c. 4.

p. 415. Italian documents: see A. Petrucci and C. Romeo, *'Scriptores in urbibus'* (Bologna, 1992), esp. pp. 57–76, 109–26; note that in Italy the lay professional strata (notaries, merchants, etc.) were already literate as well.

p. 415. Priests: McKitterick, *Frankish Church*, pp. 45–79; C. van Rhijn, *Shepherds of the Lord* (Turnhout, 2007), pp. 82–112, 171–212; cf. S. Wood, *The Proprietary Church in the Medieval West* (Oxford, 2006), pp. 519–34, 659–62.

p. 415. Hraban Maur: M. de Jong, in Y. Hen and M. Innes (eds.), *The Uses of the Past in the Early Middle Ages* (Cambridge, 2000), pp. 191–226.

p. 415. Book-copying: D. Ganz, in *NCMH*, vol. 2, pp. 786–808; Lupus of Ferrières, *Letters*, 1, 5, 8, 21, 53, 69, 87, 95, 100 (quote), 101, 108; B. Bischoff, *Latin Palaeography* (Cambridge, 1990), pp. 106–18.

p. 416. Adoptionism and Iconoclasm: D. Ganz, in *NCMH*, vol. 2, pp. 762–6, 773–7; A. Freeman, 'Carolingian Orthodoxy and the Fate of the Libri Carolini', *Viator*, 16 (1985), pp. 65–108; see Dutton, *Carolingian Civilization*, pp. 247–51 for extracts from Claudius of Turin.

p. 417. Bodo: *Annals of Saint-Bertin*, s.a. 839; see F. Riess, 'From Aachen to Al-Andalus', *EME*, 13 (2005), pp. 131–57.

p. 417. Amalarius: see A. Cabaniss, *Amalarius of Metz* (Amsterdam, 1954); Wallace-Hadrill, *Frankish Church*, pp. 326–9.

p. 417. Gottschalk, etc.: see Wallace-Hadrill, *Frankish Church*, pp. 362–9, and D. Ganz,

'The Debate on predestination', in M. Gibson and J. Nelson (eds.), *Charles the Bald* (Oxford, 1981), pp. 353–73.

p. 419. Paschal I: *Royal Frankish Annals*, trans. B. W. Scholz, *Carolingian Chronicles* (Ann Arbor, 1970), s.a. 823. For Roman politics, see in general T. F. X. Noble, *The Republic of St Peter* (Philadelphia, 1984), for the period up to 825; R. Davis, *The Lives of the Ninth-century Popes* (Liverpool, 1995); T. F. X. Noble, in *NCMH*, vol. 2, pp. 563–86.

p. 420. Nicholas I: see Davis, *The Lives*, pp. 189–203, for the best recent account in English.

p. 420. Lothar and Theutberga: the best account is now S. Airlie, 'Private Bodies and the Body Politic in the Divorce Case of Lothar II', *Past and Present*, 161 (1998), pp. 3–38.

p. 422. Gunther and Hincmar: *Annals of Saint-Bertin*, s.aa. 864 (quote), 865.

p. 422. Hadrian II: *Annals of Saint-Bertin*, s.a. 869; J. L. Nelson, *Charles the Bald* (Harlow, 1992), pp. 229, 235–8.

Chapter 18

The huge historiography on the Carolingians largely dries up in the tenth century, except in German. The only up-to-date survey of the post-Carolingian world as a whole (without a political narrative) is J. Fried, *Die Formierung Europas 840–1046* (Munich, 1991). *NCMH*, vol. 3 provides the best collective overview in English of political and religious-intellectual history; *Settimane di studio*, 38 (1991) also focuses on tenth-century surveys. Basic accounts of the history of individual successor-states in English are the relevant chapters in T. Reuter, *Germany in the Early Middle Ages c. 800–1056* (Harlow, 1991), with his *Medieval Polities and Modern Mentalities*, ed. J. L. Nelson (Cambridge, 2006), for some crucial articles; C. Wickham, *Early Medieval Italy* (London, 1981); G. Tabacco, *The Struggle for Power in Medieval Italy* (Cambridge, 1989); J. Dunbabin, *France in the Making, 843–1180* (Oxford, 1985). Similar accounts in other languages will be cited later. H. Fichtenau, *Living in the Tenth Century* (Chicago, 1991) is the best introduction to the political culture of the period as a whole; G. Althoff, *Family, Friends and Followers* (Cambridge, 2004) is an important guide to socio-political structures.

p. 427. Gerbert: see in general P. Riché, *Gerbert d'Aurillac* (Paris, 1987), a somewhat heightened account. For his career to 983, Richer of Reims, *Historiae*, 3.43–65, ed. and trans. R. Latouche, *Richer: histoire de France (888–995)* (Paris, 1930–37); his *Letters* are trans. H. P. Lattin, *The Letters of Gerbert with his Papal Privileges as Sylvester II* (New York, 1961), but for dating see the standard *MGH* edition, *Die Briefsammlung Gerberts von Reims*, ed. F. Weigle (Berlin, 1966) – the two use different numbering, but each cites the other numeration.

p. 428. Gerbert and books: *Letters*, 14–16, 32–3, 47, 50, 92, 98, 132, 138, 142, 156, 175, trans. Lattin.

p. 428. Gerbert and Otto: *Letters*, 230–31, trans. Lattin. Thietmar's *Chronicon* is trans. D. A. Warner, *Ottonian Germany* (Manchester, 2001); 6.100 for Gerbert.

p. 429. Otto and Charlemagne: Thietmar, *Chronicon*, 2.45.

p. 429. Historians: apart from those cited already, for Flodoard, see *The Annals of Flodoard of Reims 919–966*, trans. S. Fanning and B. S. Bachrach (Peterborough, Ont., 2004); for Liutprand, see *The Complete Works of Liudprand of Cremona*, trans. P. Squatriti (Washington, 2007); Widukind, *Res Gestae*, untranslated into English, is in *Widukindi Monachi Corbeiensis: Rerum Gestarum Saxonicarum Libri Tres*, ed. P. Hirsch and H.-E. Lohmann, *MGH* (Hanover, 1935).

p. 429. 'France' and 'Germany': for a frontal attack on the idea that they yet existed, see C. R. Brühl, *Deutschland-Frankreich* (Cologne, 1990), esp. pp. 83–153, 205–33 for tenth-century terminology; for citations, see Flodoard, *Annals*, s.aa. 920, 921, etc.; Widukind, *Res Gestae*, 1.27, etc.; 3.17; Thietmar, *Chronicon*, 1.19.

p. 430. East Francia: essential works include *NCMH*, vol. 3; Reuter, *Germany*; and three books by K. Leyser: *Rule and Conflict in an Early Medieval Society* (London, 1979), *Medieval Germany and its Neighbours 900–1250* (London, 1982), and *Communications and Power in Medieval Europe: The Carolingian and Ottonian Centuries* (London, 1994), the last two being article collections. Of the large German historiography, important recent surveys include H. Keller and G. Althoff, *Die Zeit der späten Karolinger und die Ottonen, 888–1024* (Stuttgart, 2008); and J. Fried, *Die Ursprünge Deutschlands bis 1024* (Berlin, 1994).

p. 431. The slow crystallization of Saxony: see M. Becher, *Rex, Dux und Gens* (Husum, 1996), pp. 25–194. Most of the duchies have good individual articles in *NCMH*, vol. 3, pp. 267–327.

p. 431. Election of 919: see J. Fried, in M. Borgolte (ed.), *Mittelalterforschung nach der Wende 1989* (Munich, 1995), pp. 267–318; P. Buc, 'Noch einmal 918–919' (in English), in G. Althoff (ed.), *Zeichen-Rituale-Werke* (Münster, 2004), pp. 151–78.

p. 431. 'Friendship': G. Althoff, *Amicitiae und Pacta* (Hanover, 1992), pp. 21–36.

p. 432. Election of 936 : Widukind, *Res Gestae*, 2.1–2.

p. 432. Synod of Ingelheim: Flodoard, *Annals*, s.a. 948.

p. 433. Election of 1002: Thietmar, *Chronicon*, 4.50–54, 5.3.

p. 433. Ida: Widukind, *Res Gestae*, 3.6.

p. 433. Ottonian government: see in general K. Leyser, 'Ottonian Government', in his *Medieval Germany*, pp. 69–101. For kings and aristocrats on the ground, see Leyser, *Rule and Conflict*, pp. 9–47; M. Innes, *State and Society in the Early Middle Ages* (Cambridge, 2000), pp. 225–41.

p. 434. Silver: see I. Blanchard, *Mining, Metallurgy and Minting in the Middle Ages*, vol. 1 (Stuttgart, 2001), pp. 529–38.

p. 434. Slav wars: see G. Althoff in *NCMH*, vol. 3, pp. 278–88; Leyser, *Medieval Germany*, pp. 14–42.

p. 434. *Indiculus Loricatorum*: *MGH*, *Constitutiones*, vol. 1, ed. L. Weiland (Hanover, 1893), n. 436.

p. 435. Kingdom of Italy: essential works include G. Sergi, in *NCMH*, vol. 3, pp. 346–71; Wickham, *Early Medieval Italy* (which dates the break-up of the Italian kingdom too early); Tabacco, *Struggle*; F. Bougard, *La Justice dans le royaume d'Italie* (Rome, 1995); L. Provero, *L'Italia dei poteri locali* (Rome, 1998); G. Sergi, *I confini del potere* (Turin, 1995); P. Cammarosano, *Nobili e re* (Bari, 1998), pp. 218–321. Sergi and Provero cite the more local studies which are at the centre of Italian historiography.

p. 435. Aldobrandeschi: S. Collavini, *'Honorabilis domus et spetiosissimus comitatus'* (Pisa, 1998), pp. 21–108.

p. 436. Berengar I: basic are P. Delogu, 'Vescovi, conti e sovrani nella crisi del regno italico', *Annali della Scuola speciale per archivisti e bibliotecari*, 8 (1968), pp. 3–72; B. Rosenwein, 'The Family Politics of Berengar I, King of Italy (888–924)', *Speculum*, 71 (1996), pp. 247–89. The panegyric is *Gesta Berengarii Imperatoris*, ed. P. von Winterfeld, *MGH, Poetae*, vol. 4.1 (Berlin, 1899), pp. 354–401; it does stress Berengar's imperial coronation of 915.

p. 437. Liutprand: see P. Buc, *The Dangers of Ritual* (Princeton, 2001), pp. 15–50.

p. 438. Otto III: see G. Althoff, *Otto III* (State College, Pa, 2003).

p. 438. Southern Italy: see G. A. Loud, in *NCMH*, vol. 3, pp. 624–45; P. Skinner, *Family Power in Southern Italy* (Cambridge, 1995); B. M. Kreutz, *Before the Normans* (Philadelphia, 1991); J.-M. Martin, in *Structures féodales et féodalisme dans l'Occident méditerranéen (Xᵉ–XIIIᵉ siècles)* (Rome, 1980), pp. 553–86; H. Taviani-Carozzi, *La Principauté lombarde de Salerne (IXᵉ–XIᵉ siècle)* (Rome, 1991).

p. 439. Rome: see above all P. Toubert, *Les Structures du Latium médiéval* (Rome, 1973), pp. 960–1024.

p. 439. Burgundy: see C. B. Bouchard in *NCMH*, vol. 3, pp. 328–45. Note that the duchy of Burgundy was different from the kingdom, and was further north, in West Francia.

p. 440. West Francia: essential works include *NCMH*, vol. 3; Dunbabin, *France*; J.-P. Poly and É. Bournazel, *The Feudal Transformation, 900–1200* (New York, 1991); K. F. Werner, *Les Origines avant l'an Mil* (Paris, 1984), pp. 487–561; the elegant defence of the period in G. Koziol, 'Is Robert I in Hell?', *EME*, 14 (2006), pp. 233–67; and the old classic, J. Dhondt, *Études sur la naissance des principautés territoriales en France (IXᵉ–Xᵉ siècle)* (Bruges, 1948).

p. 440. Flodoard: *Annals*, s.a. 920.

p. 441. Rudolf 'summoned': Flodoard, *Annals*, s.aa. 923, 925.

p. 441. Louis vs Hugh: Flodoard, *Annals*, s.aa. 945, 946, 948, 950. Otto I and Brun: ibid., s.aa. 954, 958–60, 962; cf. Brühl, *Deutschland-Frankreich*, pp. 479–92. Lothar: see G. Koziol, *Begging Pardon and Favor* (Ithaca, NY, 1992), pp. 113–21.

p. 442. Election of 987 and Hugh: among many, Y. Sassier, *Hugues Capet* (Paris, 1987); C. Carozzi, in *Le Moyen Âge*, 82 (1976), pp. 453–76. Gerbert quote: *Letters*, 55, trans. Lattin.

p. 443. 'Principalities': see Dhondt, *Naissance*; D. Bates and M. Zimmermann, in *NCMH*, vol. 3, pp. 398–455, with extensive bibliographies of regional monographs. For Normandy, an important one in English is D. Bates, *Normandy before 1066* (London, 1982); see also E. Searle, *Predatory Kinship and the Creation of Norman Power, 840–1066* (Berkeley, 1988); particularly thoughtful is, for Maine, R. E. Barton, *Lordship in the County of Maine, c. 890–1160* (Woodbridge, 2004).

p. 443. William V: see T. Head and R. Landes (eds.), *The Peace of God* (Ithaca, NY, 1992), esp. the articles by A. Debord and R. Landes, pp. 135–64, 184–218; J. Martindale, *Status, Authority and Regional Power* (Aldershot, 1997), studies VI (peace councils), VII–VIII (Hugh of Lusignan); B. S. Bachrach, in *Journal of Medieval History*, 5 (1979), pp. 11–21.

p. 444. Abbo: M. Mostert, *The Political Theology of Abbo of Fleury* (Hilversum, 1987), e.g. p. 137.

p. 445. Literary activity: see C. Leonardi, in *NCMH*, vol. 3, pp. 186–211 for a survey. For Hrotsvitha, see P. Dronke, *Women Writers of the Middle Ages* (Cambridge, 1984), pp. 55–83.

p. 445. Translators: Liutprand, *Concerning King Otto*, c. 11, in *Complete Works*, pp. 228–9. Cf. Flodoard, *Annals*, s.a. 948 and Richer, *Historiae*, 3.85, both also dealing with translations of ceremonial or diplomatic Latin.

p. 445. *Gesta Ottonis*: trans. in B. H. Hill, *Medieval Monarchy in Action* (London, 1972), pp. 118–37.

p. 445. Hugh to Theophanu: Gerbert, *Letters*, 146, trans. Lattin.

p. 446. Organization: Liutprand, *Antapodosis*, 5.33, in *Complete Works*, p. 194; Thietmar, *Chronicon*, 4.38 for the Arneburg, discussed with Meissen in Leyser, 'Ottonian Government', p. 84.

p. 446. Assemblies: see the overview by T. Reuter, in P. Linehan and J. L. Nelson (eds.), *The Medieval World* (London, 2001), pp. 432–50; Richer, *Historiae*, 4.11; Widukind, *Res Gestae*, 2.10, 3.16, 32, 41, 70. For French judicial assemblies, see G. Duby, *Hommes et structures du moyen âge* (Paris, 1973), pp. 7–60 for the classic model; the recent debate on French justice (see esp. W. C. Brown and P. Górecki, eds., *Conflict in Medieval Europe*, Aldershot, 2003) does not affect these points.

p. 446. *Spielregeln*: see G. Althoff, *Spielregeln der Politik im Mittelalter* (Darmstadt, 1997), esp. pp. 21–56, 157–84, 229–57. Althoff, *Family, Friends and Followers*, pp. 136–59, sets out the model briefly in English. See further Leyser, *Communications*, pp. 189–213; Fichtenau, *Living*, esp. pp. 30–77, 403–16.

p. 447. Meetings: Flodoard, *Annals*, s.a. 948; *MGH*, *Constitutiones*, vol. 1, n. 1; Flodoard, *Annals*, s.a. 924; Rodulf Glaber, *Historiae*, ed. and trans. J. France (Oxford, 1989), 1.5. For all this and what follows see Koziol, *Begging Pardon and Favor*, the basic analysis.

p. 447. *Adventus*: Liutprand, *Antapodosis*, 3.41, in *Complete Works*, p. 131; Richer, *Historiae*, 2.4.

p. 447. Dogs: Widukind, *Res Gestae*, 2.6. Cf., for Louis II, *Cap.*, vol. 2, n. 218, c. 9.

p. 447. Subversion: Dudo, *History of the Normans*, trans. E. Christiansen (Woodbridge, 1998), 2.29; Thietmar, *Chronicon*, 2.28, 5.3–7. For the general issue of literary presentation, see Buc, *Dangers of Ritual*.

p. 448. Peace of God: see in general Head and Landes, *Peace of God*.

p. 448. Silvester and Agapitus: Gerbert, *Letters*, 244, trans. Lattin; Flodoard, *Annals*, s.aa. 947–9. See the sensible brief survey in G. Tellenbach, *The Church in Western Europe from the Tenth to the Early Twelfth Century* (Cambridge, 1993), pp. 65–74.

p. 449. Queen-mothers, etc.: P. Stafford, *Queens, Concubines and Dowagers* (London, 1983), pp. 149–52 and *passim*; R. Le Jan, *Famille et pouvoir dans le monde franc (VIIᵉ–Xᵉ siècle)* (Paris, 1995), pp. 372–9, who also stresses the increased importance of the nuclear family group as a reason for the power of widows. For Matilda, see Thietmar, *Chronicon*, 4.41. For Liutprand, see P. Buc, 'Italian Hussies and German Matrons', *Frühmittelalterliche Studien*, 29 (1995), pp. 207–25.

p. 452. Forgetting the tenth century: P. J. Geary, *Phantoms of Remembrance* (Princeton, 1994), esp. pp. 134–57; C. Wickham, *Land and Power* (London, 1994), pp. 275–93; Rodulf Glaber, *Historiae*, 1.5, 7, 9.

p. 452. Remembering Charlemagne, etc.: A. G. Remensnyder, *Remembering Kings Past* (Ithaca, NY, 1995), pp. 116–211; see in general also T. N. Bisson, in *Speculum*, 65 (1990), pp. 281–308.

Chapter 19

The best overviews of England in the ninth and tenth centuries are P. Wormald and E. John in J. Campbell (ed.), *The Anglo-Saxons* (Oxford, 1982), pp. 132–206; S. Keynes in *NCMH*, vol. 2, pp. 37–42, and vol. 3, pp. 456–84; and (the key text for the period after 900) P. Stafford, *Unification and Conquest* (London, 1989). P. Stafford, 'King and Kin, Lord and Community', in eadem, *Gender, Family and the Legitimation of Power* (Aldershot, 2006), study VIII, is an important analysis of English society in the period, close to the arguments in this chapter. The old classic remains F. M. Stenton, *Anglo-Saxon England*, 3rd edn. (Oxford, 1971). The fundamental bibliographical guide is S. Keynes, *Anglo-Saxon History: A Select Bibliography* (Cambridge, regularly updated and reissued); a slightly earlier version than the current one can be found at <http//www.trin.cam.uk/sdk13/asindex>. For government, the most recent survey is A. Williams, *Kingship and Government in Pre-Conquest England, c.500–1066* (Basingstoke, 1999); for the church, the new classic is J. Blair, *The Church in Anglo-Saxon Society* (Oxford, 2005).

p. 453. Wynflæd–Leofwine: the text is ed. and trans. A. J. Robertson, *Anglo-Saxon Charters* (Cambridge, 1939), n. 66; the fullest commentary is in P. Wormald, 'Giving God and King their Due', *Settimane di studio*, 44 (1997), pp. 549–90. The laws are 3 Edgar, cc. 2, 5.2, trans. *EHD*, vol. 1, pp. 432–3. Basic for court cases is P. Wormald, in W. Davies and P. Fouracre (eds.), *The Settlement of Disputes in Early Medieval Europe* (Cambridge, 1986), pp. 149–68.

p. 455. Kent: S. Keynes, in *EME*, 2 (1993), pp. 111–31. Mercia: idem in M. A. S. Blackburn and D. N. Dumville (eds.), *Kings, Currency and Alliances* (Woodbridge, 1998), pp. 1–45. The other ninth-century kingdoms are treated best in the overviews above.

p. 455. Vikings: basic on their impact and scale is N. P. Brooks, 'England in the Ninth Century: The Crucible of Defeat', now in his *Communities and Warfare, 700–1400* (London, 2000), pp. 48–68; for the Scandinavian context, see P. Wormald, in R. T. Farrell (ed.), *The Vikings* (Chichester, 1982), pp. 128–53; see also the notes to p. 465.

p. 456. Alfred: see S. Keynes and M. Lapidge, *Alfred the Great* (Harmondsworth, 1983), which includes translations of most Alfredian texts; R. Abels, *Alfred the Great* (London, 1998), the best biography; T. Reuter (ed.), *Alfred the Great* (Aldershot, 2003); P. Wormald, 'Alfred (848/9–899)', in *Oxford Dictionary of National Biography* (Oxford, 2004), accessible online at <http://www.oxforddnb.com/view/article/183>.

p. 457. Titles used for Alfred: see Asser, c. 87, and the *Anglo-Saxon Chronicle*, s.a. 900, trans. in Keynes and Lapidge, *Alfred*, pp. 99, 120.

p. 457. Edward the Elder: see above all S. Keynes, in N. J. Higham and D. H. Hill (eds.), *Edward the Elder 899–924* (London, 2001), pp. 40–66.

p. 458. Æthelstan: M. Wood, *In Search of the Dark Ages* (London, 1981), pp. 126–50; D. N. Dumville, *Wessex and England from Alfred to Edgar* (Woodbridge, 1992), pp. 141–71. For his titles, see W. de G. Birch (ed.), *Cartularium Saxonicum* (London, 1885–93), e.g. nn. 677, 730, 746.

p. 458. Queens: see P. Stafford, *Queens, Concubines and Dowagers* (London, 1983), pp. 124–34, 148–51. Aristocrats: important analyses include C. R. Hart, *The Danelaw* (London, 1992), pp. 569–604; A. Williams, 'Princeps Merciorum Gentis', *Anglo-Saxon England*, 10 (1982), pp. 143–72; B. Yorke, in eadem (ed.), *Bishop Æthelwold* (Woodbridge, 1988), pp. 65–88; Stafford, *Unification*, pp. 150–79; R. Fleming, *Kings and Lords in Conquest England* (Cambridge, 1991), pp. 22–39; Stafford, 'King and Kin', pp. 1–12, who stresses regional tensions and the difficulties of aristocratic decision-making.

p. 459. Dunstan, Æthelwold, Oswald: each of these figures has a recent conference, N. Ramsey (ed.), *St Dunstan* (Woodbridge, 1992); Yorke, *Bishop Æthelwold*; N. P. Brooks and C. R. E. Cubitt (eds.), *St Oswald of Worcester* (London, 1996); these volumes are synthesized by C. R. E. Cubitt in 'The Tenth-century Benedictine Reform in England', *EME*, 6 (1997), pp. 77–94, the best overview of its subject.

p. 459. Æthelred II: S. Keynes, *The Diplomas of King Æthelred 'the Unready', 978–1016* (Cambridge, 1980), pp. 154–231; A. Williams, *Æthelred the Unready* (London, 2003).

p. 460. Political spin: see R. H. C. Davis, 'Alfred the Great: Propaganda and Truth', *History*, 66 (1971), pp. 169–82. Fulk, and Asser on illness: trans. in Keynes and Lapidge, *Alfred*, pp. 182–6, 88–90, 101 (Asser, cc. 74, 91); see further P. Kershaw, in *EME*, 10 (2001), pp. 201–24; J. Campbell, *The Anglo-Saxon State* (London, 2000), pp. 129–55. For political ideas, see for example J. M. Wallace-Hadrill, *Early Germanic Kingship in England and on the Continent* (Oxford, 1971), pp. 140–51; Abels, *Alfred*, pp. 246–57; J. L. Nelson, in A. J. Duggan (ed.), *Kings and Kingship in Medieval Europe* (London, 1993), pp. 125–58; Wormald, 'Alfred'.

p. 461. Boethius, cc. 17, 27.3, trans. in Keynes and Lapidge, *Alfred*, pp. 132–4. Moses: see P. Wormald, *The Making of English Law*, vol. 1 (Oxford, 1999), pp. 417–27.

p. 461. Oaths: Alfred, *Laws*, 1, cf. Intro. 49.9, trans. in Keynes and Lapidge, *Alfred*, pp. 164–5; J. Campbell, *Essays in Anglo-Saxon History* (London, 1986), p. 162; P. Wormald, in Campbell, *The Anglo-Saxons*, p. 155.

p. 461. Alfred's government: see esp. N. P. Brooks, in Reuter, *Alfred*, pp. 153–73.

p. 462. Shires, hundreds, assemblies: Campbell, *Essays*, pp. 155–70, developed also in idem, *Anglo-Saxon State*, pp. 1–30. These two books argue forcefully for the strength of the tenth-century English state. For pre-tenth-century Mercian fortifications, see S. Bassett, in *EME*, 15 (2007), pp. 53–85.

p. 462. Law: see Wormald, *Making*, vol. 1, pp. 277–330; for 7 Æthelred, the 1009 code, see *EHD*, vol. 1, pp. 447–8.

p. 462. Æthelstan and Francia: *The Annals of Flodoard of Reims, 919–966*, trans. S. Fanning and B. S. Bachrach (Peterborough, Ont., 2004), s.aa. 936, 939. 887–8: Keynes and Lapidge, *Alfred*, p. 98 (Asser, c. 85); *EHD*, vol. 1, p. 199.

p. 463. Æthelwold and the Continent: see P. Wormald, in Yorke, *Bishop Æthelwold*, pp. 13–42. Wulfstan: see M. Townend (ed.), *Wulfstan, Archbishop of York* (Turnhout, 2004); Wormald, *Making*, vol. 1, pp. 330–66.

p. 463. Ansegis: Wormald, *Making*, vol. 1, p. 344, cf. 425–6. Self-confidence: ibid., pp. 444–5.

p. 464. Writing: S. Keynes, 'Royal Government and the Written Word in Late Anglo-Saxon England', in R. McKitterick (ed.), *The Uses of Literacy in Early Medieval Europe* (Cambridge, 1990), pp. 226–57.

p. 464. Ravaging: *Anglo-Saxon Chronicle*, s.aa. 969, 986, 1041 (*EHD*, vol. 1, pp. 227–33, 260, cf. 284).

p. 464. Taxation: see M. K. Lawson, in *English Historical Review*, 99 (1984), pp. 721–38, and the subsequent debate with J. Gillingham, in 104 (1989), pp. 373–406, and 105 (1990), pp. 939–61.

p. 465. Viking impact: this issue has aroused a long debate since P. Sawyer, *The Age of the Vikings* (London, 1962) first sought to minimize it. His talking down of the size of Viking armies is no longer accepted (Brooks, 'England in the Ninth Century'; G. Halsall, *Warfare and Society in the Barbarian West, 450–900* (London, 2003), pp. 120, 123); but more nuanced recent work by both historians and archaeologists tends to support a relatively minimalist approach: D. M. Hadley, *The Northern Danelaw* (Leicester, 2000), pp. 298–341; eadem, *The Vikings in England* (Manchester, 2006); J. D. Richards, *Viking Age England* (Stroud, 2000), pp. 49–77. These last two books are a new starting point for Anglo-Scandinavian studies.

p. 466. Maldon: see D. G. Scragg (ed.), *The Battle of Maldon, A.D. 991* (Oxford, 1991), with a text of the poem, and J. Cooper (ed.), *The Battle of Maldon* (London, 1993). Compare *Anglo-Saxon Chronicle*, s.a. 1010 (*EHD*, vol. 1, p. 243). For Byrhtnoth, see also Hart, *Danelaw*, pp. 131–5.

p. 466. *Domesday Book* spread: D. Hill, *An Atlas of Anglo-Saxon England* (Oxford, 1981), pp. 101–4 (the whole book has very valuable maps); P. A. Clarke, *The English Nobility under Edward the Confessor* (Oxford, 1994), pp. 13–60, 147–50.

p. 467. Hurstborne: Robertson, *Anglo-Saxon Charters*, n. 110. For this and the pages following see especially R. Faith, *The English Peasantry and the Growth of Lordship* (Leicester, 1997), pp. 1–177; and in addition J. Blair, *Anglo-Saxon Oxfordshire* (Stroud, 1994), pp. 77–9; Hadley, *Northern Danelaw*; C. Wickham, *Framing the Early Middle Ages* (Oxford, 2005), pp. 314–26, 347–51. The classic is F. W. Maitland, *Domesday Book and Beyond* (Cambridge, 1897). For the *Rectitudines*, trans. in *EHD*, vol. 2, pp. 875–9, see P. D. A. Harvey, in *English Historical Review*, 108 (1993), pp. 1–22.

p. 468. Worcester thegns: see A. Wareham and V. King, in Brooks and Cubitt, *Oswald*, pp. 46–63, 100–116.

p. 468. Villages: C. Lewis *et al.*, *Village, Hamlet and Field* (Macclesfield, 1997).

p. 468. Urban and productive network: Richards, *Viking Age England*, pp. 78–108, 139–77, gives a good overview. See in addition the document-based discussion of wool, etc. in P. H. Sawyer, 'The Wealth of England in the Eleventh Century', *Transactions of the Royal Historical Society*, 5 ser., 15 (1965), pp. 145–64, at pp. 161–3.

p. 469. Raunds: G. E. Cadman, 'Raunds 1977–1983', *Medieval Archaeology*, 27 (1983), pp. 107–22. Goltho: G. Beresford, *Goltho* (London, 1987). Churches: Blair, *Church*, pp. 368–425.

p. 469. Danelaw sokemen and fragmentation: Hadley, *Northern Danelaw*, pp. 165–211; Faith, *English Peasantry*, pp. 121–5.

p. 470. Displacement of families: Fleming, *Kings and Lords*. For royal strategic control of land into the eleventh century, when many land-grants were attached to office and revocable, see S. Baxter and J. Blair, in *Anglo-Norman Studies*, 28 (2006), pp. 19–46.

p. 471. Military participation: R. P. Abels, *Lordship and Military Obligation in Anglo-Saxon England* (Berkeley, 1988). Hundred assembly: see '1 Edgar', from the 940s or 950s, trans. in *EHD*, vol. 1, p. 430.

Chapter 20

No overviews cover all the societies in this chapter, and each broad culture-area will have its more general and more detailed bibliography presented separately.

Basic introductions to the history of Scandinavia up to 1000 in English are in K. Helle (ed.), *The Cambridge History of Scandinavia*, vol. 1 (Cambridge, 2003), and B. and P. Sawyer, *Medieval Scandinavia* (Minneapolis, 1993); both go to 1500. See also P. Sawyer,

Kings and Vikings (London, 1982). There are some valuable articles in J. Jesch (ed.), *The Scandinavians from the Vendel Period to the Tenth Century* (Woodbridge, 2002).

On the Vikings, English-language bibliography explodes uncontrollably, and only key surveys can be cited. G. Jones, *A History of the Vikings* (Oxford, 1968) is a traditional literature-based survey; P. Sawyer, *The Age of the Vikings* (London, 1962) is the classic problem-focused analysis, to which all later work reacts; recent collective works include J. Graham-Campbell (ed.), *Cultural Atlas of the Viking World* (Abingdon, 1994) and P. Sawyer (ed.), *The Oxford Illustrated History of the Vikings* (Oxford, 1997).

p. 472. Rimbert: the *Life* of Anskar, trans. C. H. Robinson, is available on <http://www.fordham.edu/halsall/basis/anscar.html>; cc. 26–8 for the Swedes (quote, my trans., from c. 26); see I. Wood, *The Missionary Life* (London, 2001), pp. 123–41.

p. 472. Håkon: Snorri Sturlason, *Heimskringla*, trans. S. Laing and P. Foote (London, 1961), 4.32.

p. 474. Gudme: see above all P. O. Nielsen *et al.* (eds.), *The Archaeology of Gudme and Lundeborg* (Copenhagen, 1994). For Denmark before 700, see also L. Hedeager, *Iron-age Societies* (Oxford, 1992); several articles in *Anglo-Saxon Studies in Archaeology and History*, 10 (1999); and U. Näsman, in R. Hodges and W. Bowden (eds.), *The Sixth Century* (Leiden, 1998), pp. 255–78.

p. 474. Godofrid and Horic's Denmark: see K. Randsborg, *The Viking Age in Denmark* (London, 1980); E. Roesdahl, *Viking Age Denmark* (London, 1982); U. Näsman, in I. L. Hansen and C. Wickham (eds.), *The Long Eighth Century* (Leiden, 2000), pp. 35–68; P. Sawyer, 'Kings and Royal Power', in P. Mortensen and B. Rasmussen (eds.), *Fra stamme til stat i Danmark*, vol. 2 (Højbjerg, 1991), pp. 282–8. After 900, see the general works cited above.

p. 476. Norway before Harald: see e.g. B. Myhre, 'Chieftains' Graves and Chiefdom Territories in South Norway in the Migration Period', *Studien zur Sachsenforschung*, 6 (1987), pp. 169–87; for after Harald, see the general works cited above.

p. 476. Iceland: J. Byock, *Viking Age Iceland* (London, 2001), esp. pp. 63–141. For assembly politics, see Sawyer and Sawyer, *Medieval Scandinavia*, pp. 80–99. For Norwegian law, see L. M. Larson, *The Earliest Norwegian Laws* (New York, 1935).

p. 477. Slaves: R. M. Karras, *Slavery and Society in Medieval Scandinavia* (New Haven, 1988).

p. 477. *Hávamál*: trans. C. Larrington, *The Poetic Edda* (Oxford, 1996), pp. 14–38; quotes from stanzas 1, 25, 38, 58, 90.

p. 479. Political losers: see P. Wormald, in R. T. Farrell (ed.), *The Vikings* (Chichester, 1982), pp. 141–8; S. Coupland, *EME*, 7 (1998), pp. 85–114.

p. 479. Sawyer quote: *Age of the Vikings*, p. 194.

p. 480. Ívar: see esp. A. B. Smyth, *Scandinavian Kings in the British Isles, 850–880* (Oxford, 1977).

p. 480. Harald: Snorri, *Heimskringla*, 10.2–6, 79–92.

The early Sclavenians or Slavs are increasingly well covered by English-language surveys based on the extensive archaeology of eastern Europe. The best are now F. Curta, *Southeastern Europe in the Middle Ages, 500–1250* (Cambridge, 2006), developing his *The Making of the Slavs* (Cambridge, 2001), focused on south-eastern Europe; and, more generally, P. M. Barford, *The Early Slavs* (London, 2001). Early Rus is analysed brilliantly by S. Franklin and J. Shepard, *The Emergence of Rus 750–1200* (London, 1996). I have relied extensively on these four. Shorter accounts by Czech and Polish scholars are M. Gojda, *The Ancient Slavs* (Edinburgh, 1991) and P. Urbańczyk (ed.), *Origins of Central Europe* (Warsaw, 1997); there are also important insights in F. Curta (ed.), *East Central and Eastern Europe in the Early Middle Ages* (Ann Arbor, 2005), which contains a huge bibliography of English-language works. Every wing of the ethnogenesis debate about the Germanic peoples (see above, Chapter 4) is represented in these works too. The tenth century is well analysed by

T. S. Noonan, J. Strzelczyk, K. Bakay (for Hungary) and J. Shepard, in *NCMH*, vol. 3, pp. 487–552, 567–85; for this period see also the older, more traditional but still interesting, non-archaeological survey by F. Dvornik, *The Making of Central and Eastern Europe* (London, 1949). L. Leciejewicz, *Gli Slavi occidentali* (Spoleto, 1991) is an important synthetic overview of the western lands.

p. 481. Making distinctions: here I am closest to Curta, *The Making*.

p. 481. Settlements and eighth-century strongholds: see esp. Barford, *The Early Slavs*, pp. 47–88, 113–23, 131–3; Curta, *The Making*, pp. 247–310; Gojda, *The Ancient Slavs*, pp. 16–43, 78–94; Z. Kobyliński, in Urbańczyk, *Origins*, pp. 97–114; Barford, in Curta, *East Central and Eastern Europe*, pp. 66–70.

p. 482. Einhard: *Life of Charlemagne*, trans. P. E. Dutton, *Charlemagne's Courtier* (Peterborough, Ont., 1998), pp. 15–39, c. 15.

p. 483. *Zoupaniai*: Constantine Porphyrogenitus, *De Administrando Imperio*, ed. and trans. G. Moravcsik and R. J. H. Jenkins (Washington, 1967), c. 30 (cf. cc. 29, 32, 34 for *zoupanoi*).

p. 483. Thessaloniki: *Les Plus Anciens Recueils des miracles de Saint Démétrius*, vol. 1, ed. and trans. P. Lemerle (Paris, 1979), pp. 169–74.

p. 483. Slave trade: M. McCormick, *Origins of the European Economy* (Cambridge, 2001), pp. 733–77 (pp. 737–8 for *sclavus* and slave).

p. 484. Avars: see above all W. Pohl, *Die Awaren* (Munich, 1988).

p. 484. Hungarians: see K. Bakay, in *NCMH*, vol. 3, pp. 536–52; A. Bartha, *Hungarian Society in the Ninth and Tenth Centuries* (Budapest, 1975).

p. 485. Rus: Franklin and Shepard, *The Emergence*, pp. 3–180; T. S. Noonan, in *NCMH*, vol. 3, pp. 487–513; Barford, *The Early Slavs*, pp. 232–49. I follow Franklin and Shepard on the dating of the Rus occupation of Kiev.

p. 486. Rogvolod, Ol'ga: *The Russian Primary Chronicle: Laurentian Text*, trans. S. H. Cross and O. P. Sherbowitz-Wetzor (Cambridge, Mass., 1973), pp. 91, 78–87. The text dates essentially to the 1110s, although earlier material may begin in the 1060s: see A. Rukavishnikov, *EME*, 12 (2003), pp. 53–74.

p. 486. East Slavic: see esp. S. Franklin, *Writing, Society and Culture in Early Rus, c. 950–1300* (Cambridge, 2002), pp. 36–40, 83–100, 110–15 (on Old Norse survivals), 123–4.

p. 487. Ramparts and towns: Franklin and Shepard, *The Emergence*, pp. 170–80; Barford, *The Early Slavs*, pp. 246–7; compare P. Squatriti, in *Past and Present*, 176 (2002), pp. 11–65.

p. 488. Moravia: see e.g. Barford, *The Early Slavs*, pp. 108–11; F. Graus *et al.*, *Das grossmährische Reich* (Prague, 1966), in German and French; Curta, *Southeastern Europe*, pp. 124–34; J. Poulík, 'Mikulčice', in R. Bruce-Mitford (ed.), *Recent Archaeological Excavations in Europe* (London 1975), pp. 1–31.

p. 488. Sirmium theory: see I. Bóba, *Moravia's History Reconsidered* (The Hague, 1971); C. R. Bowlus, *Franks, Moravians and Magyars* (Philadelphia, 1995), esp. pp. 5–18.

p. 489. Croatia: see in English Curta, *Southeastern Europe*, pp. 134–47, 191–201; N. Budak, in *Hortus Artium Medievalium*, 3 (1997), pp. 15–22; and the articles by M. Ančić and N. Jakšić, in G. P. Brogiolo and P. Delogu (eds.), *L'Adriatico dalla tarda Antichità all'età carolingia* (Florence, 2005), pp. 213–43, with citations of other work in Italian and Croat.

p. 489. Bohemia and Poland: see J. Strzelczyk, in *NCMH*, vol. 3, pp. 516–35; Barford, *The Early Slavs*, pp. 251–67; P. Manteuffel, *The Formation of the Polish State* (Detroit, 1982); and P. Barford, P. Urbańczyk and A. Buko, in Curta, *East Central and Eastern Europe*, pp. 77–84, 139–51, 162–78.

p. 491. Brittany: J. M. H. Smith, *Province and Empire* (Cambridge, 1992).

p. 491. Liutizi: Thietmar, *Chronicon*, trans. D. A. Warner, *Ottonian Germany*, (Manchester, 2001), 3.17–19, 4.13, 6.22–5 (25 for assemblies), 7.64.

Wales is discussed most fully by Wendy Davies in two books, *Wales in the Early Middle Ages* (Leicester, 1982) and *Patterns of Power in Early Wales* (Oxford, 1990); also relevant are Rees Davies's important synthesis of the period after 1063, *Conquest, Coexistence and Change* (Oxford, 1987), and K. L. Maund, *Ireland, Wales, and England in the Eleventh Century* (Woodbridge, 1991). For Scotland, see A. A. M. Duncan, *Scotland: The Making of the Kingdom* (Edinburgh, 1975) and A. P. Smyth, *Warlords and Holy Men* (London, 1984); for Scandinavian areas, B. E. Crawford, *Scandinavian Scotland* (Leicester, 1987); for an alternative view, see B. T. Hudson, *The Kings of Celtic Scotland* (Westport, Conn., 1994). Here, a new synthesis of the period is implicit in recent detailed work, but is currently most clearly expressed in relatively brief surveys, notably those of T. O. Clancy and B. E. Crawford, in R. A. Houston and W. W. J. Knox (eds.), *The New Penguin History of Scotland* (London, 2001), pp. 56–81; S. M. Foster, *Picts, Gaels and Scots* (London, 2004), pp. 104–14; K. Forsyth, in J. Wormald (ed.), *Scotland: A History* (Oxford, 2005), pp. 21–34; and D. Broun, *Scottish Independence and the Idea of Britain* (Edinburgh, 2007), pp. 71–97. See now also A. Woolf, *From Pictland to Alba, 789–1070* (Edinburgh, 2007). Ireland is the least satisfactorily synthesized of these three; the books cited in Chapter 7 either end in 800–850 or else have weak ninth- and tenth-century sections. The latter is particularly true of D. Ó Cróinín (ed.), *A New History of Ireland*, vol. 1 (Dublin, 2005), which manages to omit Brian Boru! D. Ó Corráin, *Ireland before the Normans* (Dublin, 1972), despite its short compass, is easily the best guide. See also N. Patterson, *Cattle-lords and Clansmen* (Notre Dame, Ind., 1994).

p. 492. *Great Prophecy*: see *Armes Prydein*, ed. and trans. I. Williams and R. Bromwich (Dublin, 1972); quote from lines 125–6.

p. 493. Maredudd: see D. E. Thornton, in *Welsh History Review*, 18 (1996–7), pp. 567–91.

p. 493. Increasing coherence of rulership: e.g. W. Davies, 'Adding Insult to Injury', in eadem and P. Fouracre (eds.), *Property and Power in the Early Middle Ages* (Cambridge, 1995), pp. 137–64, at pp. 161–2.

p. 494. Viking hegemony: Davies, *Patterns of Power*, pp. 56–60.

p. 496. *Dux* and *rex*: D. Ó Corráin, 'Nationality and Kingship in Pre-Norman Ireland', in T. W. Moody (ed.), *Nationality and the Pursuit of National Independence* (Belfast, 1978), pp. 1–35, at pp. 9–11.

p. 496. Territorial expansion: see e.g. F. J. Byrne, *Irish Kings and High-kings* (London, 1973), pp. 180–81; Ó Corráin, *Ireland*, pp. 10, 30–31.

p. 497. Dublin excavations: see S. Duffy (ed.), *Medieval Dublin*, vol. 1 (Dublin, 2000), and P. F. Wallace, in Ó Cróinín, *New History*, vol. 1, pp. 815–41.

p. 497. Feidlimid: see Byrne, *Irish Kings*, pp. 211–29.

p. 498. Máel Sechnaill I: see Byrne, *Irish Kings*, pp. 256–66. For the Viking impact, see further B. Jaski, in *Peritia*, 9 (1995), pp. 310–51. Quotes: *The Annals of Ulster*, ed. and trans. S. Mac Airt and G. Mac Niocaill, vol. 1 (Dublin, 1983), s. aa. 845, 851 and 862.

p. 498. Brian Boru: see J. V. Kelleher, in E. Rynne (ed.), *North Munster Studies* (Limerick, 1967), pp. 230–41 for early Dál Cais; Ó Corráin, *Ireland*, pp. 120–31; and now above all M. Ní Mhaonaigh, *Brian Boru* (Stroud, 2007).

p. 499. Wealth of Limerick and Dublin: *Cogadh Gaedhel re Gallaibh: The War of the Gaedhil with the Gaill*, ed. and trans. J. H. Todd (London, 1867), pp. 79–81, 113–15; Brian's rule: ibid., pp. 137–41.

By far the best overview of Christian Spain, 711–1000, is A. Isla Frez, *La alta edad media* (Madrid, 2002). An important recent synthesis of social development is J. A. García de Cortázar, 'La formación de la sociedad feudal en el cuadrante noroccidental de la Península Ibérica en los siglos VIII a XIII', *Initium*, 4 (1999), pp. 57–121. In English, the basic short guide is R. Collins, in his *Early Medieval Spain* (London, 1983), pp. 225–68, updated in *NCMH*, vol. 2, pp. 272–89 and vol. 3, pp. 670–91, and in his *The Arab Conquest of Spain* (Oxford, 1989); these concentrate on political history. P. Linehan, *History and the Historians of Medieval Spain* (Oxford, 1993), pp. 73–171, is a stimulating discussion of the changing imagery of legitimization in Asturias–León. W. Davies, *Acts of Giving* (Oxford, 2007) is basic on the rural society of the tenth-century. For an English version of the active Spanish-language social history of the period, see S. Castellanos and I. Martín Viso, 'The Local Articulation of Central Power in the North of the Iberian Peninsula (500–1000)', *EME*, 13 (2005), pp. 1–42. These works cite wider bibliography, almost all in Spanish or Catalan.

p. 500. Oviedo artistic tradition: J. D. Dodds, *Architecture and Ideology in Early Medieval Spain* (State College, Pa., 1990), pp. 27–46. For Asturian–Leonese royal ideology in general, and its strong attachment to the Visigothic past, see T. Deswarte, *De la destruction à la restauration* (Turnhout, 2003).

p. 502. Court cases: R. Collins, in W. Davies and P. Fouracre, *The Settlement of Disputes in Early Medieval Europe* (Cambridge, 1986), pp. 85–104.

p. 502. Palace entourage: see e.g. Isla, *La alta edad media*, pp. 143–51; for counts of Castile, I. Álvarez Borge, *Poder y relaciones sociales en la Castilla de la edad media* (Valladolid, 1996), pp. 73–108, with earlier bibliography.

p. 503. Navarre: see J. J. Larrea, *La Navarre du IVᵉ au XIIᵉ siècle* (Brussels, 1998), pp. 213–26, cf. pp. 111–60.

p. 503. Depopulation theory: C. Sánchez–Albornoz, *Despoblación y repoblación del valle del Duero* (Buenos Aires, 1966).

p. 503. *Castros*, etc: Castellanos and Martín, 'Local Articulation'; I. Martín Viso, *Poblamiento y estructuras sociales en el Norte de la Península Ibérica (siglos VI–XIII)* (Salamanca, 2000); J. Escalona Monge, *Sociedad y territorio en la alta edad media castellana* (Oxford, 2002). The core work at the back of the interpretation of these latter writers is A. Barbero and M. Vigil, *La formación del feudalismo en la Península Ibérica* (Barcelona, 1978).

p. 503. Castrojeriz (dated to 974, but interpolated) and Cardona: G. Martínez Díez, *Fueros locales en el territorio de la provincia de Burgos* (Burgos, 1982), n. 1; J. M. Font Rius, *Cartas de población* (Barcelona, 1969), n. 9 (cf. Luke 22: 26).

p. 504. Ilduara: M. del C. Pallares Méndez, *Ilduara, una aristócrata del siglo X* (A Coruña, 1998).

p. 504. Peasant resistance: see esp. R. Pastor, *Resistencias y luchas campesinas en la época de crecimiento y consolidación de la formación feudal* (Madrid, 1980). Compare for Catalonia the sharp move from peasant autonomy to aristocratic and seigneurial power in the eleventh century (esp. *c.* 1030–60) in a context of civil crisis; this is one of the clearest examples of the 'feudal revolution' in the west Frankish lands, but it is significant that it took place south of the Pyrenees. See in English P. Bonnassie, *From Slavery to Feudalism in South–western Europe* (Cambridge, 1991), pp. 104–31, 149–69, 243–58.

p. 505. English parallel: this is best developed in I. Álvarez Borge, *Comunidades locales y transformaciones sociales en la Alta Edad Media* (Logroño, 1999).

Chapter 21

The best single-volume analysis of the aristocracy in this period is R Le Jan, *Famille et pouvoir dans le monde franc (VIIᵉ–Xᵉ siècle)* (Paris, 1995), focused on Francia. In English, the translated collection of articles ed. T. Reuter, *The Medieval Nobility* (Amsterdam, 1978) remains essential, together with G. Duby, *The Chivalrous Society* (London, 1977), and C. B. Bouchard, *'Those of my Blood'* (Philadelphia, 2001), also article collections. Before 900, start with S. Airlie, in *NCMH* vol. 2, pp. 431–50; after 900, H. Fichtenau, *Living in the Tenth Century* (Chicago, 1991), pp. 30–156, and G. Althoff, *Family, Friends and Followers* (Cambridge, 2004). For the society and culture of the period, see J. M. H. Smith, *Europe after Rome* (Oxford, 2005); and, stopping closer to 900, P. Depreux, *Les Sociétés occidentales du milieu du VIᵉ à la fin du IXᵉ siecle* (Rennes, 2002), and R. Le Jan, *La Société du haut Moyen Âge* (Paris, 2003). For the very end of our period, see P. Bonnassie and P. Toubert (eds.),

Hommes et sociétés dans l'Europe de l'An Mil (Toulouse, 2004), an important collection of survey articles.

p. 508. Wichmann: Widukind, *Res Gestae*, in *Widukindi Monachi Corbeiensis: Rerum Gestarum Saxonicarum Libri Tres*, ed. P. Hirsch and H.-E. Lohmann, *MGH* (Hanover, 1935), 3.69; see the commentary in K. Leyser, *Communications and Power in Medieval Europe: The Carolingian and Ottonian Centuries* (London, 1994), pp. 191–2.

p. 508. Gerald: Odo of Cluny, *Vita Geraldi*, trans. in G. Sitwell, *St Odo of Cluny* (London, 1958), pp. 89–180; citations here from 1.7–9, 11, 13–14, 16–20, 22–3, 30, 33. See S. Airlie, in *Journal of Ecclesiastical history*, 43 (1992), pp. 372–95.

p. 510. Guilhelmids: J. Dhondt, *Études sur la naissance des principautés territoriales en France (IXᵉ–Xᵉ siècle* (Bruges, 1948), pp. 177–217; C. Bouchard, 'Those of my Blood', pp. 59–73, 181–91; C. Lauranson-Rosaz, in R. Le Jan (ed.), *La Royauté et les élites dans l'Europe carolingienne* (Lille, 1998), pp. 417–36; J. L. Nelson, *Charles the Bald* (Harlow, 1992), pp. 139–40, 211–12, 232–3, 255, all give partial accounts.

p. 512. Counts of Walbeck: Thietmar, *Chronicon*, trans. D. A. Warner, *Ottonian Germany* (Manchester, 2001), 1.10, 2.21, 4.17, 39–42, 52, 6.15, 43–4, 48–50, 84–6, 90, 7.4–7. Commentary: Warner's introduction, pp. 49–52, and K. Leyser, *Rule and Conflict in an Early Medieval Society* (London, 1979), pp. 32–45.

p. 513. Canossa: out of a very extensive bibliography in Italian, see V. Fumagalli, *Le origini di una grande dinastia feudale* (Tübingen, 1971); G. Sergi, *I confini del potere* (Turin, 1995), pp. 230–41; R. Rinaldi, *Tra le carte di famiglia* (Bologna, 2003); *Studi matildici*, 4 vols. (Modena, 1964–97).

p. 514. Uxelles: G. Duby, *La Société aux XIᵉ et XIIᵉ siècles dans la région mâconnaise*, 2nd edn. (Paris, 1971), pp. 127, 137–45, 336–9; C. B. Bouchard, *Sword, Miter and Cloister* (Ithaca, NY, 1987), pp. 160–68, 300–307.

p. 515. Landed base: G. Tabacco, 'L'allodialità del potere nel medioevo', *Studi medievali*, 11 (1970), pp. 565–615.

p. 515. Stellinga: see E. J. Goldberg, in *Speculum*, 70 (1995), pp. 467–501.

p. 516. Carolingian aristocratic wealth: the best current introduction is J.-P. Devroey, *Économie rurale et société dans l'Europe franque (VIᵉ–IXᵉ siècles)* (Paris, 2003), pp. 267–96.

p. 516. Family monasteries: S. Wood, *The Proprietary Church in the Medieval West* (Oxford, 2006), pp. 339–412, 601–27; for Fontebona, P. Cammarosano, *La famiglia dei Berard-enghi* (Spoleto, 1974), pp. 71–84.

p. 517. Castles: G. Fournier, *Le Château dans la France médiévale* (Paris, 1978), pp. 35–79, 100–114; G. P. Fehring, *The Archaeology of Medieval Germany* (London, 1991), pp. 95–118; R. Francovich, 'Changing Structures of Settlements', in C. La Rocca (ed.), *Italy in the Early Middle Ages* (Oxford, 2002), pp. 150–67; A. A. Settia, *Castelli e villaggi nell'Italia padana* (Naples, 1984), pp. 41–246. For Pîtres, *Cap.*, vol. 2, n. 273, appendix, c. 1; for Gerald, Odo, *Vita Geraldi*, 1.36, 38–9, 2.5, 3.1, 4.10.

p. 518. 'Seigneurie banale': e.g. J. P. Poly and E. Bournazel, *The Feudal Transformation, 900–1200* (New York, 1991), pp. 25–39; C. Wickham, *The Mountains and the City* (Oxford, 1988), pp. xx–xxiii, 105–8, 307–35; C. Violante and G. Dilcher (eds.), *Strutture e trasformazioni della signoria rurale nei secoli X–XIII* (Bologna, 1996).

p. 519. Oswald and Ælfhelm: A. Wareham, in N. P. Brooks and C. R. E. Cubitt (eds.), *St Oswald of Worcester* (London, 1996), pp. 46–63; D. Whitelock (ed.), *Anglo-Saxon Wills* (Cambridge, 1930), n. 13.

p. 519. Vassals: see S. Reynolds, *Fiefs and Vassals* (Oxford, 1994), pp. 17–34, 84–105, 124–33, for a convincing minimalist view.

p. 520. *Milites* and 'knighthood': see, before 1000, J. L. Nelson, *The Frankish World 750–900* (London, 1996), pp. 75–87; D. Barthélemy, *La Mutation de l'an mil a-t-elle eu lieu?* (Paris, 1997), pp. 174–296; Duby, *Chivalrous Society*, pp. 162–8.

p. 520. Thegns: H. Loyn, in *English Historical Review*, 70 (1955), pp. 529–49; N. P.

Brooks, *Communities and Warfare, 700–1400* (London, 2000), pp. 138–61; for five hides, *EHD*, vol. 1, n. 51a.

p. 520. Conrad II: Reynolds, *Fiefs and Vassals*, pp. 199–207.

p. 520. *Capitanei* and *valvassores*: H. E. J. Cowdrey, *Popes, Monks and Crusaders* (London, 1984), study IV.

p. 520. *Nobilis*: Le Jan, *Famille et pouvoir*, pp. 32–4, 59–76, 99–153, etc.; H.-W. Goetz, *Vorstellungsgeschichte* (Bochum, 2007), pp. 173–205; J. Martindale, in *Past and Present*, 75 (1977), pp. 5–45.

p. 521. Alfred, etc.: G. Duby, *The Three Orders* (Chicago, 1980), pp. 13–119; for the military/non-military boundary, see e.g. H. Keller, *Adelsherrschaft und städtische Gesellschaft in Oberitalien (9.–12. Jahrhundert)* (Tübingen, 1979), pp. 342–79; Wickham, *Mountains*, pp. 285–92.

p. 522. The 'feudal revolution' debate: see, in English (referring to French bibliography), T. N. Bisson, D. Barthélemy, S. D. White, T. Reuter and C. Wickham, in *Past and Present*, 142 (1994), pp. 6–42; 152 (1996), pp. 196–223; 155 (1997), pp. 177–225. R. E. Barton, *Lordship in the County of Maine, c. 890–1160* (Woodbridge, 2004), an excellent local study, also now contains the most sustained critique of 'feudal revolution' theory in English (see esp. pp. 112–45); his arguments still leave space for considerable shifts in the parameters of politics and political legitimacy in the early eleventh century.

p. 523. Milan and Lucca: Keller, *Adelsherrschaft*, pp. 251–302; C. Wickham, in A. Spicciani and C. Violante (eds.), *Sant' Anselmo vescovo di Lucca (1073–1086)* (Rome, 1992), pp. 391–422.

p. 523. 'Fragmentation of powers': M. Bloch, *Feudal Society* (London, 1961), p. 446 (translation slightly modified).

p. 524. Anjou, etc.: a good guide is J. Dunbabin, *France in the Making, 843–1180* (Oxford, 1985), pp. 184–90, 199–213.

p. 524. Thegan and Ebbo: Thegan, *Life of Louis*, trans. P. E. Dutton, *Carolingian Civilization* (Peterborough, Ont., 1993), pp. 141–55, c. 44; Thietmar, *Chronicon*, 3.5; Richer, *Historiae*, ed. and trans. R. Latouche, *Richer: Histoire de France (888–995)* (Paris, 1930–37), 1.15.

p. 524. Gerald: Odo, *Vita Geraldi*, 1.4.

p. 525. Values, generosity: Fichtenau, *Living*, pp. 50–64; Thietmar, *Chronicon*, 1.5.

p. 525. Family structures and consciousness: see in general Le Jan, *Famille et pouvoir* (pp. 44–5 for Constantine), and the other books cited at the start of the notes to this chapter.

p. 526. Babenberger: Regino of Prüm, *Chronicon*, ed. F. Kurze, *MGH* (Hanover, 1890), s.aa. 902, 903, 906; Widukind, *Res Gestae*, 1.22; Liutprand, *Antapodosis*, 2.6, in *The Complete Works of Liudprand of Cremona*, trans. P. Squatriti (Washington, 2007), pp. 77–9. Megingaud: Regino, *Chronicon*, s.aa. 892, 896; cf. M. Innes, *State and Society in the Early Middle Ages* (Cambridge, 2000), pp. 225–8.

p. 526. Walbeck: Thietmar, *Chronicon*, 6.43–4.

p. 527. Charlemagne: *Cap.*, vol. 1, n. 20, c. 22, n. 33, c. 32, trans. P. D. King, *Charlemagne* (Kendal, 1987), pp. 205, 240–41.

p. 527. Gorze: J. Nightingale, *Monasteries and Patrons in the Gorze Reform* (Oxford, 2001), pp. 15–16, 59–105; patronage: Wood, *Proprietary Church*, pp. 812–50.

p. 528. Cluny: B. Rosenwein, *Rhinoceros Bound* (Philadelphia, 1982); eadem, *To Be the Neighbor of St Peter* (Ithaca, NY, 1989); G. Tellenbach, *The Church in Western Europe from the Tenth to the Early Twelfth Century* (Cambridge, 1993), pp. 111–21; J. Wollasch, in *NCMH*, vol. 3, pp. 174–80; G. Constable, in *Settimane di studio*, 38 (1991), pp. 391–448.

Chapter 22

No single book covers the themes of this chapter. G. Duby's two classic surveys, *The Early Growth of the European Economy* (London, 1974) and *Rural Economy and Country Life in the Medieval West* (London, 1968) are the closest to a general overview in English. For the ninth century, A. Verhulst, *The Carolingian Economy* (Cambridge, 2002) is basic. There are also some guides in the socio-economic chapters of *NCMH*, vols. 2 and 3. In French, J.-P. Devroey's two recent books, *Économie rurale et société dans l'Europe franque (VIe–IXe siècles)* (Paris, 2003) with *Puissants et misérables* (Brussels, 2006), and R. Fossier, *Enfance de l'Europe, X^e–XIIe siècles* (Paris, 1982), together offer an important regionally nuanced account, though they differ very substantially (where they differ, I am with Devroey); Fossier reprised some of his arguments in English in *NCMH*, vol. 3, pp. 27–63. M. McCormick, *Origins of the European Economy* (Cambridge, 2001) is a rich analysis of exchange and communications, with many wider implications.

p. 529. Quote: *Annals of Saint-Bertin*, trans. J. L. Nelson (Manchester, 1991), s.a. 859; see J. L. Nelson, *Charles the Bald* (Harlow, 1992), p. 194, and S. Epperlein, *Herrschaft und Volk im Karolingischen Imperium* (Berlin, 1969), pp. 42–50.

p. 530. *Encellulement*: Fossier, *Enfance*, p. 288 and following. A good overview of the peasantry is R. Le Jan, *La Société du haut Moyen Âge* (Paris, 2003), pp. 186–206.

p. 531. Denmark: e.g. B. P. McGuire, 'Property and Politics at Esrum Abbey', *Medieval Scandinavia*, 6 (1973), pp. 122–50.

p. 532. Peasant gift-giving and its pacing: see e.g. C. Wickham, *The Mountains and the City* (Oxford, 1988), pp. 54–5, 190–97, 210–15, 266–8. For motivations, B. Rosenwein, *To Be the Neighbor of St Peter* (Ithaca, NY, 1989), *passim*.

p. 533. Cusago: *I placiti del 'Regnum Italiae'*, ed. C. Manaresi (Rome, 1955–60), vol. 1, nn. 110, 112; see further some of the cases discussed by J. L. Nelson, in W. Davies and P. Fouracre (eds.), *The Settlement of Disputes in Early Medieval Europe* (Cambridge, 1986), pp. 45–64.

p. 533. Legislation: *Cap.*, vol. 1, n. 44, c. 15, n. 73, cc. 2–3 (quote), etc. (trans. P. King, *Charlemagne* (Kendal, 1987), pp. 250, 264) – see E. Müller-Mertens, *Karl der Grosse, Ludwig der Fromme und die Freien* (Berlin, 1963), pp. 100–101 for a list.

p. 534. Peasant resistance: see in general C. Wickham, *Framing the Early Middle Ages* (Oxford, 2005), pp. 570–88 (p. 583 for Trita).

p. 534. Manors: Duby, Verhulst and Devroey, cited above, all discuss manors and give (a very extensive) bibliography. For intensification, see also Wickham, *Framing*, pp. 287–301. Le Mans: *Cap.*, vol. 1, n. 31.

p. 535. Manors and exchange: see further P. Toubert, *L'Europe dans sa première croissance* (Paris, 2004), pp. 27–115, 145–217; J.-P. Devroey, *Études sur le grand domaine carolingien* (Aldershot, 1993), esp. study XIV.

p. 535. Saint-Germain: *Das Polyptichon von St-Germain-des-Prés*, ed. D. Hägermann (Cologne, 1993) is the most recent edition.

p. 536. Adalard: L. Levillain, 'Les Statuts d'Adalhard', *Le Moyen âge*, 4 (1900), pp. 333–86; St. Gallen: W. Horn and E. Born, *The Plan of St Gall* (Berkeley, 1979).

p. 537. *Brevium Exempla* and *Capitulare de Villis*: *Cap.*, vol. 1, nn. 128, 32 (quotes from cc. 1, 54; trans. H. R. Loyn and J. Percival, *The Reign of Charlemagne* (London, 1975), pp. 98–105, 64–73, slightly modified).

p. 537. Manorial decline in Italy: Toubert, *L'Europe*, pp. 170–78; B. Andreolli and M. Montanari, *L'azienda curtense in Italia* (Bologna, 1983), pp. 201–13. Non-decline elsewhere: see e.g. Duby, *Rural Economy*, pp. 197–212.

p. 538. Free and unfree: see e.g. Duby, *Rural Economy*, pp. 186–96; W. Davies, in M. L. Bush (ed.), *Serfdom and Slavery* (Harlow, 1996), pp. 225–46; for Italy, F. Panero, *Servi e rustici* (Vercelli, 1990), pp. 37–55. For the complexities of serfdom in France after 1000, see P. Fouracre, in *Transactions of the Royal Historical Society*, 6th ser., 15 (2005), pp. 29–49.

p. 539. *Incastellamento*: P. Toubert, *Les Structures du Latium médiéval* (Rome, 1973), pp. 315–68, 450–93; for the north, A. A. Settia, *Castelli e villaggi nell'Italia padana* (Naples, 1984); one important conference among several on this enormously debated subject is published as *Archeologia medievale*, 16 (1989).

p. 540. Church and castle: J. Chapelot and R. Fossier, *The Village and House in the Middle Ages* (London, 1985), pp. 129–50.

p. 541. Rhineland, Italy: C. Wickham, in *NCMH*, vol. 2, pp. 510–37; M. Innes, *State and Society in the Early Middle Ages* (Cambridge, 2000), chh. 4, 5. Rankweil: K. Bullimore, 'Folcwin of Rankweil', *EME*, 13 (2005), pp. 43–77. Karol: L. Feller *et al.*, *La Fortune de Karol* (Rome, 2005).

p. 542. Arleus: Rosenwein, *To Be the Neighbor*, pp. 69–74, 226–8; S. E. Halton, 'The Church and Communities: Cluny and its Local Patrons', University of Birmingham Ph.D. thesis, 2005, pp. 238–61.

p. 542. Salisano: C. Wickham, *Il problema dell'incastellamento nell'Italia centrale* (Florence, 1985), pp. 62–4, developed and corrected in A. Sennis, 'Cenni storici', *Archeologia medievale*, 19 (1992), pp. 456–61.

p. 543. Population rise: M. Zerner-Chardavoine, 'Enfants et jeunes au IXe siècle', *Provence historique*, 31 (1981), pp. 355–81, for Marseille; more generally, Devroey, *Économie rurale*, pp. 65–75; Fossier, *Enfance*, pp. 88–107.

p. 544. Agricultural expansion: Verhulst, *Carolingian Economy*, pp. 61–4, Duby, *Rural Economy*, pp. 88–122, Devroey, *Économie rurale*, pp. 108–29, Fossier, *Enfance*, pp. 152–87, 654–6. Duby and Fossier are more downbeat about the Carolingian economy than later writers; more recent historiography substantially revises upwards, among others, Carolingian grain yields, the availability of iron, and the density of mills.

p. 545. Charavines: M. Colardelle and E. Verdel, *Les Habitats du lac de Paladru (Isère) et leur environnement* (Paris, 1993).

p. 546. Exchange: see above all O. Bruand, *Voyageurs et marchandises aux temps carolingiens* (Brussels, 2002). For towns, P. Johanek, in *NCMH*, vol. 3, pp. 64–94, A. Verhulst, *The Rise of Cities in North-west Europe* (Cambridge, 1999), pp. 44–100, and H. Sarfatij, 'Tiel in Succession to Dorestad', in idem *et al.* (eds.), *In Discussion with the Past* (Zwolle, 1999), pp. 267–78.

p. 547. Raffelstetten: *Cap.*, vol. 2, n. 253 (note McCormick, *Origins*, p. 556 n. for caution about the Rus).

p. 547. Venice: McCormick, *Origins*, pp. 254–60, 523–31, 761–77; the will of 829 is partially trans. in R. S. Lopez and I. W. Raymond, *Medieval Trade in the Mediterranean World* (New York, 1955), pp. 39–41.

p. 547. Amalfi, etc.: B. Kreutz, *Before the Normans* (Philadelphia, 1991), esp. pp. 75–93; P. Skinner, *Family Power in Southern Italy* (Cambridge, 1995), pp. 247–81.

p. 548. North Sea: see e.g. H. Clarke and B. Ambrosiani, *Towns in the Viking Age*, 2nd edn. (Leicester, 1995).

p. 550. Cremona: see G. Tabacco, *The Struggle for Power in Medieval Italy* (Cambridge, 1989), pp. 323–31 for a brief survey.

Chapter 23

p. 552. Humour: see G. Halsall (ed.), *Humour, History and Politics in Late Antiquity and the Early Middle Ages* (Cambridge, 2002).

p. 553. Fifth-century break: I explored the consequences of this in *Framing the Early Middle Ages* (Oxford, 2005), esp. pp. 825–31.

p. 560. Politics of land: see in general M. Bloch, *Feudal Society* (London, 1961).

p. 561. Chur: R. Kaiser, *Churrätien im frühen Mittelalter* (Basel, 1998).

p. 562. Muslim sense of the public sphere: see e.g. P. Crone, *Medieval Islamic Political Thought* (Edinburgh, 2004), pp. 286–314, 393–8. My use of the term 'public sphere' is borrowed from Jürgen Habermas, at least as translated into English, but he used it in a very different way.

p. 562. Carolingian *res publica*, etc.: see e.g. M. de Jong, in *Settimane di studio*, 44 (1997), pp. 893–902, and M. Innes, *State and Society in the Early Middle Ages* (Cambridge, 2000), pp. 254–63, although Innes, in particular, draws diverging conclusions from me.

Index of Names and Places

All place-names are ascribed to modern, not medieval, countries. *al-* in Arab names is ignored for the purpose of alphabetizing. Place-names beginning St, Saint, San, Santa, Santi are all listed under Saint, alphabetized by saint's name.

Ælfric, ealdorman of Mercia, 459

Ælfthryth, mother of Æthelred II, 453, 458–9

Ælfwyn, daughter of Æthelflæd, Lady of the Mercians, 457

Æthelbald, king of Mercia, 163

Æthelberht, king of Kent, 158, 163

Æthelflæd, Lady of the Mercians, 457–8, 486

Æthelfrith, king of Bernicia, 158, 169

Æthelred I, king of Wessex, 456

Æthelred II of Mercia, 456–7

Æthelred II, king of England, 10, 453, 458–60, 462–4, 470, 494

Æthelstan Half-king, ealdorman of East Anglia, 458–9, 466, 470, 512

Æthelstan, king of England, 458, 462–4, 493

Æthelwine, ealdorman of East Anglia, 459

Æthelwold, bishop of Winchester, 459, 463

Æthelwulf, king of Wessex, 455–6

Aetius, general, 11, 83, 105, 256

Afghanistan, 43, 284

Africa, 21, 23, 29, 32, 34, 37, 39–41, 43, 52, 59–60, 76–80, 83, 85, 88, 91, 93, 103–5, 108, 134, 137, 139, 218–19, 258–9, 266, 285, 290, 295, 319–20, 323, 337, 339, 341, 366, 555

al-Afshin, Iranian prince, 331

Agapitus II, pope, 449

Agathias, historian, 114

Aghlabid dynasty, 333, 337

Agila, Visigothic king, 131

Agilolfing family, 114, 124, 141, 196

Agilulf, Lombard king, 140–42, 149

Agnellus, historian, 183

Agobard, archbishop of Lyon, 180, 381, 391, 413–14, 417–18

Ahmad ibn Buya, see Mu'izz al-Dawla

Ahmad ibn Tulun, ruler of Egypt, 332, 365

Aidan, bishop of Lindisfarne, 190

Aistulf, Lombard king, 143–4

Akhmim, Egypt, 363

Alahis, duke of Trento, 145

Alans, 76, 83

Alaric I, Visigothic king, 79–80, 90, 114

Alaric II, Visigothic king, 90, 92

Álava, Spain, 500

Alba, 169, 494–5; see also Scotland

Albania, 273

Alberic, prince of Rome, 439, 526, 528

Albi, France, 126

Alboin, Lombard king, 140, 197

Alcuin, 383–4, 411, 413–14, 416, 424, 463

Aldebert, bishop, 178

Aldfrith, king of Northumbria, 162

Aldobrandeschi family, 435

Alemans, Alemannia, Germany, 44–7, 112, 119–20, 174, 200, 216, 247–8, 376, 379, 388, 395–6, 403, 429, 430; see also Swabia

Aleppo, Syria, 333, 335, 337, 360

Alexander the Great, 274, 284

Alexander, patriarch of Alexandria, 61

Alexandria, Egypt, 38, 51–2, 58, 61–2, 64, 71, 73, 174, 260, 363–4, 366, 369, 370–71

Alfonso I, Asturian king, 500–501

Alfonso II, Asturian king, 500–504

Alfred, king of Wessex/England, 134, 162, 164, 456–7, 460–61, 463, 466–7, 469, 471, 480, 493, 521

Algeria, 23, 39, 290, 336

'Ali ibn Musa, 323

'Ali, caliph, 279–83, 289, 295, 336

'Alids, 296, 323, 329, 335–6

Allah, 280

Almería, Spain, 344, 370–71

Alps, 4, 80, 90, 121, 175, 189, 199, 203, 246, 377, 394, 405, 420, 436–8, 533–4, 541, 544, 561

Alsace, France, 126, 206–8, 376, 394

Althing, all-Iceland assembly, 476

Althoff, Gerd, 446

Alvar, 342

al-Waqidi, historian, 279, 324

al-Wathiq, caliph, 324, 328, 330, 346

Alypius, bishop of Carthage, 21–2, 31, 60

Amalaric, Visigothic king, 92, 131

Amalarius of Metz, 417–18, 421, 463

Amalfi, Italy, 369, 438, 547–8

Amandus of Maastricht, 175

Amandus, bishop of Sorrento, 198

Ambrosius Aurelianus, 151

al-Amin, caliph, 322–3, 328

'Amman, Jordan, 292, 294

Ammianus Marcellinus, historian, 29–30, 33, 45–8, 67

Castile, Spain, 500–502, 503–5, 522
Castrojeriz, Spain, 503
Catalonia, Spain, 392, 427, 451, 500–504, 523, 532
Cathal mac Finguine, king of Éoganacht Glendamnach, 167
Cathars, 307
Catholics, 40, 57, 76–7, 90, 112, 134, 142–3, 197, 553
Catterick, Enghand, 154
Caucasus, 258
Cavan, Ireland, 496
Ceawlin, king of Wessex, 158
Celanova, Spain, 502, 504
Céli Dé movement, 497
Cenél Conaill, Ireland, 165, 499
Cenél nÉogain, Ireland, 167
Cenwulf, king of Mercia, 163–4, 454–5
Ceolwulf II, king of Mercia, 456
Ceredigion, Wales, 492
Chalcedon, Turkey, 418
  ecumenical council at (451), 62, 64, 83
Chalcedonians, 63, 259, 264
Chalon-sur-Saône, France, 50
Champagne, France, 401, 443, 547
Charavines, France, 545
Charibert II, king of the Franks, 119
Charlemagne, king/emperor, 6, 8–10, 12, 120, 144, 148, 163–4, 174–6, 189, 201, 215, 226, 230, 244–5, 250, 273, 293, 375–6, 378–9, 381–3, 385–8, 392, 395–7, 400, 403, 405–7, 410, 413, 415–17, 419, 421–2, 429, 432, 437–8, 444, 452, 454, 460–62, 464, 470, 475, 483, 500, 510, 515–16, 519, 527, 529, 533, 535–7, 554–5, 557, 559
Charles Martel, *maior* of the Franks, 119, 121, 126, 129, 133, 143, 148, 184, 190, 197, 244, 376–7, 380, 382, 396, 404, 557
Charles the Bald, king/emperor, 386, 390–91, 395–6, 398–401, 410–11, 413, 418, 421–2, 425, 455, 461, 463–4, 510–11, 517, 530, 563
Charles the Fat, king/emperor, 402–4, 408, 425, 430, 436, 441
Charles the Simple, king of the West Franks, 401, 431, 440–41, 447–8, 452, 462, 524

Charles, duke of Lower Lotharingia, 427–8, 442
Chelles, France, 117, 187
Chester, England, 158, 469
Cheviot hills, England/Scotland, 238
Childebert I, king of the Franks, 105, 150
Childebert II, king of the Franks, 111–12, 115–16, 173, 244
Childebert III, king of the Franks, 117
Childebert 'the adopted', king of the Franks, 118
Childeric I, king of the Franks, 112
Childeric II, king of the Franks, 117–18, 122–3, 128, 280
Childeric III, king of the Franks, 376–7, 379
Chilperic I, king of the Franks, 115, 124–5, 181, 224, 228
Chiltern hills, England, 157–8
Chimnechild, queen of the Franks, 195, 122
China, 29, 63, 292, 333, 362
Chindasuinth, Visigothic king, 11, 135, 137, 188
Chlotar I, king of the Franks, 114, 123
Chlotar II, king of the Franks, 114–21, 124, 127
Chnodomar, king of the Alemans, 45
Chramnesind, 194
Christ, 52, 62, 179, 240, 268, 308, 416, 418
Christians, 4, 21, 30–31, 35, 40–41, 44–5, 52–60, 64–5, 68–9, 71–2, 74, 76–7, 82–4, 90, 139, 152–3, 155, 161, 165, 168, 171, 175–7, 180, 187–8, 236, 238–9, 242, 244, 259–60, 264, 268, 270–71, 278, 280, 282, 286, 288–9, 294, 300, 304–6, 308, 323, 334, 338, 340, 342–5, 347, 358–60, 363, 382, 414, 423, 461, 465, 472, 475–93, 500, 505–6, 508, 555
Christopher, saint, 171
Chrodegang, bishop of Metz, 377
Chur, Switzerland, 561
Cilicia, Turkey, 305, 309
Cinead mac Ailpín, king of the Picts and Dál Riata, 169, 494
Circumcellions, 64
Circus Maximus, Rome, 68, 234
Clann Cholmáin, Ireland, 167, 497–8

popes, 39, 42, 55, 58, 60, 62–3, 141,
143–4, 147–8, 161, 171–2, 174, 176,
178–9, 197–8, 224, 240–42, 250–51,
265, 267–8, 270, 306, 376–8, 398,
411, 415, 419–22, 427–8, 439,
448–9, 489, 555.
Portugal, 131
Possidius, hagiographer, 77
Powys, Wales, 15–3, 492
Poznań, Poland, 489–90
Praejectus, bishop of Clermont, 122, 125,
184
Praetextatus, bishop of Rouen, 228
Praetextatus, Roman aristocrat, 71
Prague, Czech Republic, 489
Praxedis, saint, 240–41
Preslav, Bulgaria, 305, 307, 309, 356
Priscillianists, 172–3
Priscus of Paris, 224
Priskos, historian, 84, 243–4
Prittlewell, Essex, 158
Prokopios, historian, 72, 77, 93–4, 102,
233, 235, 303
Protestants, 57
Provence, France, 86–7, 119, 122, 126–7,
172, 220, 376, 380, 387, 396, 401
Prudentius of Troyes, 173, 418
Prüm, Germany, 536
Ptolemais, Libya, 22, 51
Ptolemy, 329
Puglia, Italy, 140
Pulcheria, empress, 62, 81, 83, 89, 97,
271–2
Pyrenees, France/Spain, 211, 216, 500,
502, 504, 511, 534
Pythagoras, 275

Qa'lat Sim'an, Syria, 250
Qadisiyya, Iraq, 283
Qaramita dynasty, 333
Qays, Arab tribe, 290–91, 295, 339
Quadi, 45–6
Quedlinburg, Germany, 433, 445
Quentovic, France, 230, 548
Quierzy, France, 417–18
Qur'an, 251, 277, 282–3, 292, 325, 327,
329–30, 552
Quraysh, Arab tribe, 283, 295
Qurra ibn Sharik, governor of Egypt, 286,
291

Qus, Egypt, 364–5
Qusayr 'Amra, Jordan, 292–3

Radagaisus, 80
Radulf, duke of Thuringia, 119
Raffelstetten, Austria, 547
Ramiro I, Asturian king, 500
Ramiro II, king of León, 501
Ramla, Israel, 360
Ramsey, England, 187, 459
Rankweil, Switzerland, 541
Raqqa, Syria, 330, 361
al-Rashid, caliph, 320–23, 327–8, 330, 336
Rastislav, ruler of the Moravians, 306,
397, 488
Ratchis, Lombard king, 143–4
Rather, bishop of Verona, 445
Ratleig, notary, 405
Ratramn of Corbie, 418
Rauching, duke, 111, 115, 124, 244
Raunds, England, 469
Ravenna, Italy, 23, 81, 88–9, 91, 140–44,
146–7, 171–2, 183, 267, 428
Rayy, see Teheran
Reccared, Visigothic king, 134, 197
Reccesuinth, Visigothic king, 135–6, 138
Recópolis, Spain, 133
Red sea, 359–60
Redon, France, 208–11, 214, 533, 541–2
Regensburg, Germany, 547
Reggio Emilia, Italy, 513, 536
Reichenau, Germany, 391, 395
Reims, France, 111, 113, 128, 220, 390,
427–8, 440–41, 443–4, 536
Rheged, Scotland, 152
Rhine, river, 32–3, 44, 46–7, 80, 82,
112–13, 119, 186, 218, 220–21,
225–6, 229–30, 388, 397–8, 429–30,
447, 506–7, 535, 541, 544, 546–7,
550, 558
Rhineland, 4, 34, 114, 123–4, 128, 205–7,
209, 404, 541, 549
Rhodri Mawr, Welsh king, 492, 494
Rhône, river, 83, 86–7, 220, 226, 401,
404, 439
Rhos, see Rus
Ribe, Denmark, 230, 474, 478, 546, 548
Richard II, count of Normandy, 524
Richard the Justiciar, duke of Burgundy,
441